'By which strategies will we reclaim "our" cons[...] of global capitalist markets and turn them int[o] freedom they were meant to serve: the freedo[m...] A masterfully orchestrated plethora of arg[uments...] philosophical depth and practical legal de[sign...] theory at its best.'

    Bert van Roermund, Professor (Emeritus), Tilburg Law School

'This is the most profound critical theory of constitutionality I know of. The enormous range of social and political theories Christodoulidis is engaging with is breathtaking. He discusses them in depth, not from the cool distant standpoint of neutral scholarship but from the perspective of a political constitutionalism that seeks to synthesise Karl Marx's heritage with Niklas Luhmann's ultra-modern systems theory. His devastating critique of emerging transnational constitutions has one main target – the imperialism of total market thinking. However, what makes his analyses even more fascinating, is that Christodoulidis does not restrict himself to the usual exercises in critical theory, which suffer from their lack of credible alternatives. He develops strategies for a renewed constitutionality which break the monopoly of nation-state constitutions and search for a political constitutionalisation of society, particularly continuing the tradition of "autogestionnaire" labour constitutionalism. He follows a double strategy. While the reformist strategy of "militant formalisms" seeks to protect the integrity of law against the intrusions of economic rationality, the strategy of "rupture" and the strategy of "immanent critique" follow a more radical agenda.'

    Gunther Teubner, Professor of Private Law and Legal Sociology,
                   Goethe Universität Frankfurt

'No-one has captured the distinction between market constitutionalism and political constitutionalism more vividly or more insightfully than Christodoulidis. And no-one has framed the choice between them more profoundly. This is a book that captures contemporary law's critical condition, but also its continuing critical contribution, with great subtlety and imagination.'

Neil Walker, Regius Professor of Public Law and the Law of Nature and
          Nations, University of Edinburgh Law School

'Since Aristotle, jurists and philosophers have studied how human societies are constituted. In a fascinating and poetic fresco, Emilios Christodoulidis also shows how they are today dislocated by market constitutionalism. In a thoughtful dialogue with an impressive variety of authors, he also sheds light on the resources that the law offers to escape the grip of the "total market".'

         Alain Supiot, Professor of Law, Collège de France

THE REDRESS OF LAW

From a legal-philosophical point of view, *The Redress of Law* presents a critical analysis of a number of related doctrinal fields: constitutional, labour and EU Law. Focusing on the organisation and protection of work, this book asks what it means to protect work as an essential aspect of human (individual and collective) flourishing. This is an ambitious and highly sophisticated intervention in contemporary academic and political debates around a set of critically important questions connected to processes of globalisation and market integration. The author redefines the nature of legal and political thought in an age in which market rationality has exceeded its classic domain and has come to pervade the organization of social and political life. This restatement of critical legal theory is intended to defend the concept of constitutionalism and suggest new ways to deploy the law strategically.

EMILIOS CHRISTODOULIDIS holds the Chair of Jurisprudence at the University of Glasgow. He is the author of the award-winning *Law and Reflexive Politics* (1996), edits the book series Critical Studies in Jurisprudence, and serves as managing editor of *Law & Critique*.

GLOBAL LAW SERIES

The series provides unique perspectives on the way globalization is radically altering the study, discipline and practice of law. Featuring innovative books in this growing field, the series explores those bodies of law which are becoming global in their application, and the newly emerging interdependency and interaction of different legal systems. It covers all major branches of the law and includes work on legal theory, history, and the methodology of legal practice and jurisprudence under conditions of globalization. Offering a major platform on global law, these books provide essential reading for students and scholars of comparative, international, and transnational law.

Series Editors
M. E. A. Goodwin
Tilburg University
Randall Lesaffer
Tilburg University
David Nelken
King's College London
Han Somsen
Tilburg University

Books in the Series

Intimations of Global Law Neil Walker

Legalized Families in the Era of Bordered Globalization Daphna Hacker

Transnational Sustainability Laws Phillip Paiement

The Sociology of Law and the Global Transformation of Democracy Chris Thornhill

Authority and the Globalisation of Inclusion and Exclusion Hans Lindahl

The Law of the List: UN Counterterrorism Sanctions and the Politics of Global Security Law Gavin Sullivan

Democratic Crisis and Global Constitutional Law Christopher Thornhill

THE REDRESS OF LAW

Globalisation, Constitutionalism and Market Capture

EMILIOS CHRISTODOULIDIS
University of Glasgow

CAMBRIDGE
UNIVERSITY PRESS

University Printing House, Cambridge CB2 8BS, United Kingdom

One Liberty Plaza, 20th Floor, New York, NY 10006, USA

477 Williamstown Road, Port Melbourne, VIC 3207, Australia

314–321, 3rd Floor, Plot 3, Splendor Forum, Jasola District Centre, New Delhi – 110025, India

79 Anson Road, #06–04/06, Singapore 079906

Cambridge University Press is part of the University of Cambridge.

It furthers the University's mission by disseminating knowledge in the pursuit of education, learning, and research at the highest international levels of excellence.

www.cambridge.org
Information on this title: www.cambridge.org/9781108487030
DOI: 10.1017/9781108765329

© Emilios Christodoulidis 2021

This publication is in copyright. Subject to statutory exception and to the provisions of relevant collective licensing agreements, no reproduction of any part may take place without the written permission of Cambridge University Press.

First published 2021

A catalogue record for this publication is available from the British Library.

ISBN 978-1-108-48703-0 Hardback
ISBN 978-1-108-73210-9 Paperback

Cambridge University Press has no responsibility for the persistence or accuracy of URLs for external or third-party internet websites referred to in this publication and does not guarantee that any content on such websites is, or will remain, accurate or appropriate.

what then (whites?)

① Communication (Habermas)
② parity of participation (Fraser)
③ thin normative foundations (Jaeggi)
④ thick contextual foundations (Cooke)

To Jane

criticism
- internal coherence

① metaphysical foundations
② functionalist (Jaeggi)
③ context-transcending — Habermas
④ recognitions
nihilistic

~Jaeggi's forms of life~

- regress infinitely

[box: is normative foundations normative]

immanent — problem insolvable
- always begs the question
- cannot be justified by appeal to any standards
- needs to justify itself
- fallacy — trapped b/w 2 poles
- questioning basic assumptions of foundations
  — there is nothing new but impossible to justify

* account for the reasons why the world isn't as it should be

* we have to reflexively look for grounds — critical theory

categorical imperative is normative

Why is universal morality wrong?

I disagree

I defence of human good?

Adorno

Lamour Scanlon

meta-ethics

constructivists can overcome regress

[Jaeggi's]

justifications don't bottom

— Grounds which support conclusions

CONTENTS

Acknowledgements xii

Introduction 1

PART I Political Phenomenology 15

1.1 Hannah Arendt and the Theory of the Bourgeois Public Sphere 17
The Phenomenology of the Political 17
Arendt's Arrested 'Worldliness' 29
   'World-Making' in the 'Material' Dimension 30
   'World-Making' in the 'Temporal' Dimension 33
   'World-Making' in the 'Social' Dimension 35
The Spectre of Antagonism 40

1.2 Simone Weil: Necessity and Courage 43
Weil's Materialism 43
Weil's Hellenism 51
   The Poem of Force 51
   Tragedy, Necessity, Rationality Undone 55
Weil's Wager 63

1.3 The Phenomenology of Work 72
The Promise of Social Labour 72
   The Hegelian-Marxian Heritage 72
   Post-Fordist Mutations 78
The Forgetting of Labour 86
   The Ethical Deficit: Unnecessary Suffering 86
   The Political Deficit: Unworldly Labour 93
   The Philosophical Deficit: Phenomenological Blockage 102
Semantics and Structures I: The Movement of Concepts and Structures 111

x   CONTENTS

1.4 **Towards a Critical Phenomenology**   119
Improbable Disclosures   119
The Phenomenological Method   129
Elements of a Critical Phenomenology   138

PART II   **Political Constitutionalism**   149

2.1 **Constituent Power and the Constitutional Distinction**   151
The Constitutional Distinction   151
Theorising 'Constituent Power': A Short History in Four Chapters   158
    Rousseau's Radical Proposition   158
    The Jacobin Constituent Moment   163
    Hegel and the French Revolution   168
    Marx on Constituent Power   171
Theorising 'Constituted Power': Eclipsing the Constituent   180

2.2 **Constitutionality**   193
Prolegomena   193
Self-Reference   200
The Dimensions of Constitutional Meaning   209
    The Material Dimension   211
    The Social Dimension   216
    The Temporal Dimension   224

2.3 **Labour, Solidarity and the Social Constitution**   229
Constitutional Value and the Dogmatic Question   229
Homo Juridicus, Laborans   242
Social Rights Constitutionalism   247
    The Radical Marshall   247
Semantics and Structures II   255

2.4 **Constitutionalism Adrift**   259
Constitutionalisation and Pluralism   259
Semantics and Structures III   277

PART III   **Market Constitutionalism**   295

3.1 **Market Trajectories**   297
From Differentiation to Fragmentation   297
The Generalisation of Economic Reason: Hayek's Legacy   308

3.2 **Total Market Thinking**   327
The New Worlds of Governance   329
The Democratic Co-Option   335

CONTENTS

    The Epistemological Co-option   343
        The Logic of Equivalence: Substitution and Unaddressability   343
        The Hidden Normativity of Indicators   348
    The Eclipse of the Political Constitution   354

3.3 **Europe's 'Social Market' and the Disembedding of Labour Protection**   365
    Europe's Social Constitution: 'Moments' and Milestones   367
    The Ordoliberal Synthesis   377
    New European Governance and the Social Constitution   384

3.4 **The Deep Commodification of Labour**   395
    Laval/Viking Jurisprudence   395
    The New Functionalism   403
    Proportionality as Market Exposure   407
    Market Access as Social Dumping   419

PART IV   Strategies of Redress   431

4.1 **The Constitutional Situation**   433
    Taking Stock   433
    Communicative and Strategic Constitutional Action   443
    Strategy, Critique, Redress: Opportunities and Limitations   455

4.2 **Militant Formalisms**   461
    Formalism as Strategy   461
    'Societal Constitutionalism': Meta-Level Deployments   467

4.3 **Constitution, Autogestion, Rupture**   480
    The Scandal of Democracy   480
        Poland's Short Summer of Anarchy   480
        Democracy as Enactment: The Legacy of Athens   487
    The Mass Strike: Luxemburg, Sorel, Benjamin   494
    The Meaning of Negation   507

4.4 **Constitutionalising Contradiction: Towards an Open Constitutional Dialectic**   524
    Materialism and the 'Adventure' of the Dialectic   524
    Phenomenology, Contradiction and the Open Dialectic   532
    Semantics and Structures IV: The Constitutional 'Dispositif'   541

Epilogue   556

References   558
Index   584

ACKNOWLEDGEMENTS

I have had the good fortune to write this book at the Law School of the University of Glasgow, at both an institution and a city still graced with a democratic sense and a humanist sensibility. I am fortunate to have worked here with exceptional scholars, and many will see clear evidence of their influence in the book. My most profound gratitude goes to my closest colleagues of the Glasgow Legal Theory research group, George Pavlakos, Lilian Moncrieff, Lindsay Farmer, Marco Goldoni and Ruth Dukes, with Anna Chadwick and Toni Marzal having joined it more recently. I thank them for their inspiration and friendship, ongoing collaborations, co-teaching and co-authorship, marked by a sense of intellectual generosity and camaraderie which I hold dear. I owe a profound debt also to five close friends and collaborators, for conversations over many years, in which many of the ideas here developed: Scott Veitch, Johan van der Walt, Chris Thornhill, Andrew Patrizio and Hans Lindahl. During my career in Edinburgh and Glasgow I have had some wonderful doctoral students, many now colleagues, who have opened new vistas for me and challenged my stubborn views. And of course also to those who were my teachers, David Garland, Gunther Teubner, Zenon Bankowski and the late Neil MacCormick. To them all my heartfelt thanks.

I have some other important institutional debts to acknowledge: the manuscript began while I was a fellow at the Institute of Advanced Studies in Nantes (IEA) at an Institution that embodied openness and genuine interdisciplinarity in the tradition of Enlightenment thinking. Under the direction of Alain Supiot it was a rare site of inspiring intellectual exchange. I am grateful for that, as I am to Alain for lending his voice so generously to support the attempt in my own country, Greece, to stem the barbarity visited on its people during the darker years of austerity. I am thankful to him, as I am to Muriel Fabre-Magnan and Samuel Jubé for their friendship and scholarship.

ACKNOWLEDGEMENTS

I owe a debt to Valerie Kerruish and Uwe Petersen and the Altona Stiftung (ASFPG). In setting up this forum, Valerie and Uwe gave me and others a wonderful opportunity to come together over the years in intense, critical, sometimes passionate engagement with ideas; for their exceptional generosity, thank you to them both, as well as to Scott Veitch, Stewart Motha and Tarik Kochi for so many discussions under its auspices.

Thank you to my friends at Birkbeck Law School, an institution that has been a second home to me, and especially my closest colleagues and friends Fiona MacMillan and Costas Douzinas with whom I co-edit *Law & Critique*.

Many individuals have contributed in diverse ways to the ideas in the book, a manuscript that has taken nearly ten years to complete, and I am grateful to them all, teachers, colleagues, students and friends: Andy Schaap, Agustin Menendez, Anel Boshoff, Awol Allo, Basak Ertur, Bert van Roermund, Carlo Pinnetti, Carrol Clarkson, Christian Joerges, Christian Tams, Claudio Michelon, Dan Matthews, Daniel Augenstein, Donald Buglass, Emmanuel Melissaris, Fernando Atria, Gregor Clunie, Hanna Lukkari, Illan Wall, Jarna Petman, John Charney, Kaarlo Tuori, Karin van Marle, Katrin Becker, Kerry Rittich, Kevin Walton, Kyle McGee, Luciana Grassano Melo, Marcelo Neves, Marco Dani, Marija Bartl, Martin Krygier, Maurice Glasman, Michelle Everson, Mike Wilkinson, Monica Judith Sanchez-Flores, Neil Walker, Pablo Marshall, Panu Minkkinen, Poul Kjaer, Robert Salais, Samuli Hurri, Stacy Douglas, Stephanie Jones, Stephen Bogle, Su Bian, Thorsten Fuchsbuber, Victor Tadros, Vikki Bell and Yiannis Tassopoulos. My brother Nick Christodoulidis' sobering reading helped to rein in some of the book's more extravagant moments. My gratitude to you all.

Morag Goodwin has been a fantastic series editor. I am grateful to her and to Finola O'Sullivan at Cambridge University Press for endorsing the project, and Marianne Nield has been hugely helpful and patient about my many delays.

I conclude with some personal debts to my family. To Jane, to whom this is dedicated, for her unwavering support, her openness to the world and her wonderful attention to what is fragile in it. To our children, Theo, Annie and Andreas, who as young adults are making their own way in the world now, with a profound trust in its humanity and the insistent demand that it will not be diminished. To my father whose commitment to the university taught me – by example not by word – that the university is something greater than our own career choices, alliances and personal objectives; like Alasdair MacIntyre's idea of *practice*, it

xiv ACKNOWLEDGEMENTS

holds up its own internal standards of excellence and offers its teachers a privilege and a debt that can never be fully discharged. And finally to my mother, who passed away at the time that I began writing this book, for her gentleness and deep kindness, her faith that everything would be alright in the end, even if she was wrong in that, with the promise that *nothing is lost*, that *all is un-forgotten*.

Introduction

The title's reference to *redress* is tribute to Seamus Heaney's *The Redress of Poetry*. Heaney quotes from Simone Weil's *Gravity and Grace* where she announces with 'typical extremity and succinctness':

> When we know in what way society is unbalanced, we must do what we can to add weight to the lighter scale ... We must be ever ready to change sides like justice, that fugitive from the camp of conquerors.

'And so far as poetry', adds Heaney, 'is an extension and refinement of the mind's extreme recognitions, and of language's most unexpected apprehensions, it too manifests the workings of Weil's law.'
What is this 'law'? Heaney says:

> Her whole book is informed by the idea of counterweighting, of balancing out of the forces, of *redress* – tilting the scales of reality towards some transcendent equilibrium. ... [It involves the activity of] placing a counter-reality on the scales – a reality which may be only imagined but which nevertheless has weight because it is imagined within the gravitational pull of the actual and can therefore hold its own and balance out against the historical situation. The redressing effect comes from its being a glimpsed alternative, a revelation of potential that is denied or constantly threatened. (Heaney, 1995: 3–4)

To take 'redress' as the tilting that forces appearance – of 'a reality which can only be imagined' – is the insight that underpins the analysis of constitutionalism that this book offers. My argument will be that such redress has become highly improbable under conditions of a significant shift from a political to a market conception of constitutionalism. Redress aims to capture, and where unavailable to force, law's countervailing gesture. Since it is increasingly forged in a context that resists that gesture it calls for strategic thinking. The key *phenomenological* question is 'under what conditions might something *emerge* as a problem?' This is where *political rationality*, the possibility to think the given otherwise, meets *a critical phenomenology*, the *forcing* to appear. Redress is not to be understood as the compensatory gesture that would commit to the already defeated site of a skewed equilibrium. Instead, as per Weil, redress asks of us to 'do what we can' to imagine alternatives and equip them with a 'gravitational pull' such that the weight of necessity does not submerge them. That at least is the aspiration that links the phenomenological account of the first part of the book with the strategic account of the final part. It is with the help of phenomenology that we explore the shaping of the constitutional imaginary of the age; with systems theory, oriented to the 'appearance of difference', that we explore what is selected and what suppressed as its expression in constitutional reason; and with critical theory in the tradition of 'immanent critique' that we explore strategic deployments. While a phenomenology that navigates its way between Marxism and systems theory is going to be selective in its debts, there is scope, I argue, to extract significant dividends from the way in which appearance is thematised in both, allowing the traditions of phenomenology and Marxism to converge in a restatement of praxis philosophy: as a restatement, in the words of the phenomenologist Bernhard Waldenfels, of *a vision that transforms the seen*.

The 'redress *of* law' plays on the ambivalence of the connective *of*: law becomes both the means of redress and itself the object of redress. In the former sense the emphasis lies in its strategic deployment; in the latter sense it captures the move that is performed throughout the analysis, of turning the law upon itself in a gesture of *self*-reflection.

- ★ -

The subtitle of the book – *Globalisation, Constitutionalism and Market Capture* – carries three referents. *Globalisation*, at the most basic level, refers to the operation of the economy at the supranational level, an operation poised to ensure that the global flows of capital maximise its rates of return by circumventing welfare states and the loci of labour and social protection. At the level of the political and legal systems, globalisation has forced a comprehensive shift, and the main part of the book, presented in the mirror-image Parts II and III, describes the two competing paradigms of *constitutionalism*. It tracks the *paradigmatic* shift of constitutional thought from the first to the second, from a political to a market register. '*Market capture*' is a term that signifies the comprehensive intrusion of market thinking into the constitutional imaginary. More specifically it marks neo-liberalism's highly successful venture to replace, I will argue, political constitutionalism's guiding distinction between the constituent and the constituted with asymmetries for which the market is both the site of production and regulation. Once uploaded to the transnational level constitutional processes are laid open to market capture through operations that appear to be beyond the purview of political control. The search for functional equivalents to the constitution at the global level misses a crucial fact: that to the extent that globalisation *consists in* the competitive alignment of national systems of labour protection, the search for functional equivalence (of labour protection) at the global level is a misnomer. This is the position critical theory finds itself in today, wrong-footed by the compelling ideological manoeuvre of the advocates of the free market to co-opt its founding commitments to justice and democracy and to subsume without remainder political rationality to market thinking.

The book is a defence of political constitutionalism, where the predication 'political' imports a particular reflexivity, which critical phenomenology is deployed to sustain: to sustain the integrity of constitutional rationality from folding into market thinking. At the level of what appears, of what appears otherwise than given, and at the level of how to act on it, critical phenomenology and strategy give meaning to redress.

- ★ -

The writing of this book is characterised by an attention to (what belatedly came close to an obsession with) symmetry. Each of the four parts of the book has four chapters. The third chapter of each part, like a current running through each of the parts, is about *work*. The two middle parts of the book are mirror images of the two paradigms of constitutionalism whose shift the book attempts to track. Of the two 'bookend' parts, I and IV, the first part sets out the methodology to ask the *phenomenological* question: under what conditions does something appear, and under what conditions might it be *forced to appear as a problem*? The final chapter attempts an answer to the question 'what can be done?' under conditions of market capture of constitutionalism, and invites us to think about law, beyond the communicative paradigm, as *strategy*. They too, however, mirror each other. The reason for such an attachment to symmetry is that the book's breadth would make it unmanageable, and each part could be a book in its own right. This also explains why the writing is pulled taut at times. The argument of the book is in the linkages. For example, *contradiction* is *first* linked in 1.4 to the tapping of a critical phenomenology, *then* in its constitutional expression in 2.1, *subsequently* in the way it subtends the promise of social rights constitutionalism in 2.3, finally as political strategy in 4.4. Linkages proliferated, and the process of writing the book became a difficult balance between paring back the spread of any one argument to hold on to the symmetry, while allowing space for the manifold connections to emerge. I cannot anticipate them all in this introduction, partly because I cannot frontload adequate complexity to do it, and also because the pleasure of writing it consisted largely in allowing them to unfold in their own time and pace.

The argument spans an unlikely range as it moves from thoughts about the role of necessity in tragedy and the Homeric epic, to unemployment statistics and the use of indicators. What has preoccupied me throughout and serves to gather it together, is what is at the heart of *critical theory*: the distribution of contingency and the meaning of necessity, with all the ambivalence that such a formulation carries. Concerns that underlie the whole analysis are the emphasis on making meaningful, the interposition of distance from what impacts as compulsion, the putting to question, the imagination of alternatives, in other words the claiming of the space for contingency with which to counter the supposed necessity of the factual, of the '*fait accompli*', of the unavailability of options. Reclaiming contingency becomes integral to political rationality, a rationality that at a deeper level cannot be divorced from ethics, and which informs the capacity of society to act on the distinction between necessary and unnecessary suffering.[1]

I have tried to reset the parameters on which the discussion of necessity and politics can be undertaken as a question about the *constitution*. The book, as a treatise in critical constitutional theory, centres the discussion on phenomenality (appearance), critique and strategy. It has involved a selective excavation of the concepts that frame and distribute givens and opportunities on the constitutional terrain, a *genealogical* excavation to ensure that established path-dependencies do not always repeat the givens of the past. Against what comes to install itself as the apparent objectivity of the present, the genealogical method re-orients our reading of the past to the history of blocked opportunities, interruptions, discontinuities and 'false starts'. As ever the subjugation of those histories and opportunities is coincident with the emergence of current

---

[1] A point insightfully made by Maurice Glasman in *Unnecessary Suffering* (1996).

certitudes about the 'rational' scope of opportunity. We ask whether institutional forms of solidarity were not too speedily sacrificed in the process, whether democratic institutions and the tradition of virtue, which had force within the economy, were not too readily abandoned to the *a priori* truths of 'rational action' thinking. We ask why starts were deemed 'false', what options were blocked, under what pretension were sanction and representativeness withdrawn from collective procedures, what harnessed the distribution of rationality and irrationality to competition and accumulation.

- ★ -

A concern with what appears, under what circumstances and at the cost of what exclusions, is why the methodology of this book is defined as a *critical* phenomenology; it overlaps with the critique of ideology in the Marxist sense. Part I of the book argues within the tradition of phenomenology *against* Hannah Arendt and *with* Simone Weil. It asks why such a profound a phenomenological exercise such as Arendt's, perhaps the most influential phenomenology within political theory today, yields so anaemic an understanding of the public sphere. It argues that it is because her phenomenology sustains the meaning of the public sphere by forever renewing and re-embedding the constitutive distinction between what is 'political' and what merely 'social'. The result is disempowering: the pivot on the distinction as formative of the political perspective as such becomes impossible to redress from that perspective. Against Arendt, for Weil the rationality of work is not to be consigned to a vacuous instrumentality but should be understood as an intelligence to be collaborated with. It is not the blind working of necessity (labour) or the means-ends instrumentality (work) that *The Human Condition* set at the antipode of communication, the latter for Arendt and, later, Habermas offered as the supposed meaningful alternative to meaningless labour, immured behind categorical distinctions and conceptual boundaries. In contrast, Weil invites us to hold on to the notion of *attention* towards lives lived under conditions of necessity. We owe to Weil that she turns her phenomenology towards lives that are denied worldliness, a *redress* in the full sense that Heaney gives the term. And we owe thanks to Jacques Rancière for the careful ethnography of workers' lives in *Nights of Labour, a recuperation certainly*, but not one premised on usurping the worker's speaking position. Instead, he offers us a painstaking recollection and reassembly of those voices, the diary entries and the short stories that dignified lives lost to 'the forces of servitude'.² This is an 'attention' indexed not just to proximity but to humility: no grand reconstructions of historical regularities for Rancière, no Marxist 'overdetermination' or 'stageism', but instead the staging of resistance of what breaks incongruently with the crushing regularities of days expended. To the extent that the analysis in this book is undertaken as a critical phenomenology it aspires to do something similar, certainly not in terms of the ethnographic exactitude of Rancière's writing, but in the *form-giving* impetus that fashions something as a problem and as worthy of attention. It is Aristotle who argues that 'equality or inequality comes down to *aporia* and political philosophy'.³ Rancière adds that philosophy becomes 'political' when it embraces aporia as its proper quandary. The third chapter of this first part (1.3) turns this problematic frontally to 'the forgetting of labour', to re-think it in terms of democracy, solidarity and dignity, *aporetic* to the measure that those registers are ordinarily denied it. The final chapter of this part (1.4) provides a statement of the phenomenological method as critical thought.

- ★ -

The shift from political to market constitutionalism is the subject of the central parts of the book. The discussion here engages diverse interlocutors: while Arendt, Weil and Husserl move to the background, Marx and Luhmann remain on centre stage, joined now by Polanyi, Foucault, Hayek and Gorz amongst others. All have in various ways contributed their profound insights to forging an understanding of the constitutional paradigm shift that faces us, and some to tracking what we might *immanently* identify as redress. Let me say something more at the outset about what I take to be the paradigm shift from 'political' to 'market' constitutionalism.

The meaning of *political constitutionalism*, developed in Part II of the book, draws constitutively on the distinction between constituent and constituted power. The meaning of the 'constituent' finds its root in the revolutionary tradition, and imports into constitutionalism – understood

---

[2] 'What [these workers] found intolerable was not exactly poverty and low wages, or the ever-present spectre of hunger. It was something more basic: the anguish of time [expended] every day working up wood or iron, sewing clothes, or stitching footwear, for no other reason than to maintain indefinitely the forces of servitude with those of domination; the humiliating absurdity of having to go out begging, day after day, for this labour in which one's life was lost.' (Rancière, 1989, vii.)

[3] In *Politics* III 1282 b. 21, trans. T. A. Sinclair (1992), p. 207.

as the *form* of the distinction that holds the two poles together – the irreducible measure of *potentiality* at the 'constituent' pole. The other pole routes that potentiality back to the pathways of the 'constituted'. As a dynamic relationship the antinomic articulation between 'constituent' and 'constituted' captures what is particular about constitutional 'reflexivity'. The first chapter (2.1) contains an analysis of the concept of *constituent power*; the second chapter (2.2) contains an account of Luhmann's constitutional theory, and in particular his difficult and oft-misunderstood account of the reflexivity of recursively closed ('autopoietic') systems. 'Constituent' is the term that carries the animus of democracy into the distinction. (I take it, relatively uncontroversially, that *democracy* is the organising principle of the political and that any concept of the political that does not incorporate democracy as constitutive of its meaning falls short definitionally, not merely normatively.) The other pole of the distinction, the 'constituted', captures the moment of institutionalisation. It is clearly conceded here that the *pure* constituent moment attains to no *self*-reflection, and finds no *unmediated* expression in political constitutionalism. Instead, what is provided in these two chapters taken together is a definition of political constitutionalism as an evolutionary achievement that keeps the two terms alive and 'co-original'. The relationship of mutual implication that defines political constitutionalism means that the solutions in each case are measured against the other pole, the former (constituent) as reservoir of constitutional 'energies', the latter (constituted) as defining the reach of constitutional reflexivity, its measure and limit. The chapters contain an analysis of the notion of reflexivity in its institutional specificity across the three dimensions of its meaning:[4] in the *social* dimension the question is over the subject that the constitution names; in the *temporal* dimension the question is over the constitution's ability to recruit the past in its expectation-binding operation for the future; in the *material* dimension the question is over the threshold of *unity* that would gather it (the legal system) as a meaningful whole. These are threshold requirements for ascribing constitutional meaning, and it is in that function that they underpin and organise all expressions of *constitutional reflexivity*.

Where the second chapter looks at the *formal* dimension of the constitution, the third chapter (2.3) concerns the *substantive* dimension, with an emphasis on the *social* constitution. It looks at *social rights* and

---

[4] On the three dimensions of meaning, see Luhmann, 1992, and Chapter 1.1 below.

specifically the protection of work. Drawing on the 'dogmatic' resource of *solidarity*, and with specific references to the democratic thinking of industrial relations, this chapter looks at how the tradition of labour constitutionalism has drawn constitutively on the legal-dogmatic resources of solidarity and dignity. To understand solidarity as the foundation of the social state and the founding commitment to mutualise the risks of existence through the provision of social protection, is to understand societal valorisation as irreducibly collective. Solidarity and dignity, then, in this tradition of thought, are what the *ratio juris* upholds by virtue of its very deployment. They sustain what Ernst Bloch famously called 'the *orthopedia* of upright carriage' that for him 'pointed far beyond the tradition of the bourgeois world' (Bloch, 1986: 174). In all cases, the withdrawal and contraction of the constitutional values of solidarity and dignity is a sign of profound pathology of constitutional thought.

The fourth, and final, chapter of this part (2.4) tracks this pathology by looking at the process of the *undoing* of the constitutional form under the pressure of *total market thinking*. Two developments mark this transition. The first is the rise of celebratory 'pluralisms' of 'cosmopolitan' and other 'radical' varieties that herald the rediscovery of constitutionalism at the global level. At the same time, and this is the second development, constitutionalism has come undone from any antecedent framing function and has been reconceived in a new temporal modality as *ongoing constitutionalisation*. At this double juncture of 'constitutional pluralism' and 'constitutionalisation', the released energies of the constitutional imagination are running amok: constitutional actors proliferate, values multiply, any differentiation of levels of lawmaking disappears and the orchestration of the complex hierarchy of emphasis that was constitutional ordering collapses. The liberation of constitutional energies lays the field bare except for the markers that allow the new circulation: these are the new markers of 'market constitutionalism'. And with this, the impasse is turned productive, the paradox of the crippling justice deficit of the European and the global 'constitution' is unfolded in what is becoming the *evolutionary achievement* of a global constitutionalism, with pluralism substituting for democracy and constitutionalisation substituting for constitutionality.

- ★ -

Where the logic of the undoing is described in the last chapter of Part II, the rise and rise of market constitutionalism is the subject of Part III.

Constitutional function initially shrinks to what Hayek calls 'catallaxy' – the protection of property title and the stability of expectations. But this particular function is subsequently part-generalised and part-displaced under the pressure of globalisation, and as the differentiation it promises gives way to fragmentation. We look at processes whereby constitutional actors and values are variably flattened, re-grouped, re-named, dispersed, re-configured more generally and in relation to the labour constitution and with special emphasis on Europe. The main argument here is that under conditions of a comprehensive *market turn* in constitutional thinking, the opportunity to fashion a political register as proper to public and constitutional law thinking is undercut by a *comprehensive substitution*. The 'market turn' informs and underwrites a different constitutional imaginary, on a terrain it re-configures so as to make any meaningful sense of 'the constituent' disappear. Gone is the notion of the common good, unpinned from any 'natural' constituency for it, and then pluralised, the two moments jointly generating a dislocation so severe that it undercuts society as a field of association. Lost are the histories of practices and the forms of collectivity that made societies meaningful to people in terms of the mutuality of action and the recognition of dependency. The space vacated is stormed by new pluralisms that aggregate utilities through indicators, management-speak and the aspiration of optimisation, *whatever* the object and *however* it is understood in *the new worlds of governance* imbued, as they are, by the new spirit of 'democratic experimentalism'. This widely celebrated 'plasticity' comes constitutively tied to the rigidities of price-setting markets in labour, land and money (Polanyi) that install and accelerate both commodification and circulation. Under the pressure of globalisation and the incessant search to increase the rates of return for capital, the ferocity of the market re-launches the 'common good' on the global scale, severed off from tradition, mutuality and association, and reconfigured through competition as what the optimal function of the market envisions. As a question about the constitution, the devastating consequence that we can only project at this stage, is that the absorption of the constituent into the constituted is the high mark of a market constitutionalism whose forever renewed, forever inclusive gesture allows every contestation to find its place in the mobilisation of those adaptive devices through which the constituent 'excess' is incorporated as productive to total market thinking.

By drawing on legal theory we revisit and insist on the difference between what public law and private law promise and allow, and confront the pervasive move that no longer pits them against each other but in an inclusionary way underwrites them both: where the market principle – previously understood as the principle subtending the transactional nature of private law as distinct from public law – gradually becomes the arbiter of the separation itself and guarantor of the circulation ('balancing' in the preferred idiom) of public goods. The substitution it effects is played out on the legal plane under the sign of *governance*. The new worlds of governance come with the panoply of 'democratic experimentalism', and institutional plasticity on which to perform it. The result is that we suffer a loss of language as we move from level to meta-level. As framing the debate, the market principle receives the immunity that all framing conditions enjoy: they cannot be simultaneously deployed and queried. The 'critique of economic reason' attempted in this part of the book takes the form of challenging the self-propelling of market thinking to economic, democratic and epistemological levels.

The third and fourth chapters (3.3 and 3.4) look at Europe's 'social market' and the hollow promises of 'capability' and 'proportionality' to give labour protection its due weight in it, and to restore it to its dignity. The analysis here places special emphasis on 'social' Europe where the logic of *debt* raises the matter of the 'social' to the first intensity. One cannot talk about politics today without taking account of how debt is experienced, how it furnishes the horizon of action in terms of modalities, opportunities, undertakings, but also of subject-positions as the latter are determined through lines of addressivity of the 'indebted man'.[5] And of how it informs our capacity today to re-imagine the European citizen at the difficult juncture of market fanaticism, indebtedness, the various 'exits', and the xenophobic contraction of public space – the space that affords appearance to political subjects. In other words, in a Europe where the pursuit of market utopia[6] is forcing the shrinkage of the idea of collective subjecthood back to the depleted and largely abhorrent identifications with a defensive nationalism, the European challenge to think of the many sites of subjecthood and the variety of subject-positions becomes both more urgent and more improbable during the twilight of European constitutionalism.[7]

- ★ -

[5] The reference is to Lazzarato, 2012.
[6] For 'market utopia' see Polanyi, 1944.
[7] The reference is to Dobner and Loughlin, 2010.

The last part of the book returns to the question of redress as a question of praxis, and as a question of constitutional opportunity. If collective *self*-determination appears improbable on a constitutional register today, it is because market constitutionalism invokes and invites it in terms that connect it to *economic* imperatives. Against the collapse of the political dimension, and against the short-circuiting to the market, self-determination can only mean this: that the constitution gives a people – as *their* Constitution – the possibility to *act* and, where they find themselves other-determined, to *act back*. Part IV of the book involves thinking strategically about, and with, the constitution. It resists the invitation to subsume constitutional argument to the comprehensive framework of 'communicative reason'. The reasons why this is disarming of critique are explored (in 4.1). Thereafter, three directions are outlined for constitutional strategy. The first involves the strategic use of formalism (4.2: 'militant formalisms') and draws on the critical resources of systems theory; the second strategy (4.3) deploys the logic of rupture to follow in the traditions of 'autogestionnaire' labour constitutionalism; the final chapter (4.4) provides an analysis of constitutional strategy in the tradition of 'immanent critique'.

A thread on 'semantics and structures' is a key organising theme of the book and is delivered in four instalments. The question it tracks is what it might mean, and what it might take, to hold on to a constitutional semantics that holds against structural drift, against the way, that is, that it is usually assumed that semantic developments will always adapt to new structural givens. We ask: what would it mean to hold on to the semantic resources that the constitution offers to resist the slippage from normative to cognitive expectations, to return constitutional reason to its dogmatic resources, to hold the line against delivering constitutional value over to market determination?

- ★ -

I close this introduction with some points about methodology. The first concerns the controversial linkage of critique with systems theory. Even if the two do combine (as I will explain) in the field of phenomenology, it will be asked *what* does it mean to insist, against Luhmann's unambiguous rejection, on the *critical potential* of systems theory? I borrow from systems theory the following theoretical suggestions: that processes of meaning-creation are tied to differentiated systems; that forms of closure accompany the processes of meaning-creation; that these moments of closure remain unaddressable, as blind spots, from the point of view of the systems themselves; and that the inter-traffic of cross-cutting and under-cutting identifications marks the history of democratic struggle, as struggle over and against political ascriptions and given semantics. I deploy systems theory as critical theory to take issue with the problem, as I see it, that 'the political' in its various 're-entries' into sub-systems, and as aligned to sub-systemic rationalities, abandons in the process something fundamental about its organising principle (democracy) and horizon (equality). My focus and interest throughout the book is in the relationship between the differentiated systems of law, politics and economics. If the political system is constitutively oriented to democracy and equality, the economic system under conditions of functional differentiation and sub-systemic autonomy, has effectively removed the processes of the organisation of production from its field of reference. The economically rational is now measured in terms of how scarce means are allocated to competing ends against the background or in the context of 'substitutable choices'. Against the generalisation of economic reason, where the logic of the political system is submitted to the logic of the economic system, my suggestion is that constitutional reflexivity, understood by systems theory as involving the coupling of systems at the meta-level, can be called upon as a *blocking device*. My suggestion, in other words, is to recruit constitutional reflexivity in a political role of *guiding the selective withdrawal of certain areas of social action from the logic of price*.

The second point on method concerns the meaning of critique, and it relates to the analysis of the logic of 'rupture' and of 'immanent critique'. As Michel Foucault puts it:

> Critique doesn't have to be the premise of a deduction that concludes, "this, then, is what needs to be done." It should be an instrument for those who fight, those who resist and refuse what is. Its use should be in the process of conflict and confrontation, essays in refusal. It doesn't have to lay down the law for the law. It isn't a stage in programming. It is a challenge directed to what is.
>
> (Foucault, 1991: 236)

Redress fastens onto the crisis-points of articulation, of expressibility and of intelligibility of our political experience, and at the points of the emergence of contradiction. Contradictions, for Marx, point to a shortfall of the categories available to us to make sense of the processes of value production and social reproduction, the mismatch between the categories of thought and the modes of social being. 'Redress' borrows from Weil the idea of *counterweighting*, of a balancing out of forces applied to those points of tension. To focus thus on 'contradiction' and 'counterweighting' is to pick up from Hegel, with Marx, not the drive to culmination and synthesis, but the self-undermining moment of contradiction, of thought hitting upon its limit *given* the categories available to it. What is significant in the glimpsed alternative is that it asserts itself against meaninglessness, provides some hermeneutic traction in particular experiential contexts and thus carries potential energies.

Strategy involves harnessing those energies to act on the question *'What remains, today, really heterogeneous to what capital demands?'* as a question of constitutional imagination and of the deployment of law. The strategic is the counter-point of the communicative (as associated with the work of Habermas in discourse theory). Against a 'communicative' or 'deliberative' distribution of speaking positions, against the aspirational dimension of the communicative model as a *self-correcting public sphere*, legal strategy aims to re-negotiate institutional opportunity against the model's limitations as well as its blind spot regarding those limitations. In this, last, case, the strategic model submits legal communication to a critical-instrumental treatment with a view to identifying a spectrum of possible political interventions *in relation to* law, rather than *under its auspices*, a decision, in other words, about whether to play the system or to confront it. The key notion here involves a 'strategy of rupture'. And the critical task is to disrupt the semblance that law harbours the open processes of communication or that it instantiates the pure form of communicative rationality, and to call instead for militant attention to the points of tension upon which the management of consensus depends.

- ★ -

It was Lucio Magri, that veteran of the Italian new left of the 1960s and 70s and founder of *Il Manifesto*, who said that writing was a 'waste of intelligence' when 'no longer an instrument of political struggle but a surrogate for it'. In the end, theory as political intervention measures itself on its political relevance, not, of course, on any assumed or projected *impact* of its success, but on the *courage* of its undertaking: Simone Weil here, as in so much else, showed that courage, showed what was staked on it, and its price.

Since I began writing this book, my own country, Greece, lived its own *'kurze Sommer der Anarchie'*[8] in the six months between the 2015 January

---

[8] The reference is to Hans Magnus Enzensberger's book from 1972.

election of the Syriza party into power and the referendum in June overwhelmingly rejecting the EU conditions for the 'bail-out'. Between these two events, Greeks witnessed a period of enhancement of the political. If the EU succeeded in both crushing and co-opting the resistance with implacable brutality, the moment of intense politicisation, the way in which its message permeated Greek society and the force with which something extra-ordinary was expressed, are defeated constitutional moments whose defeat does not erase them from the constitutional imaginary of this generation. It remains *a project with unspent claims on the future*. The unspent claim for what, borrowing again from Magri, we might set as the task of critical theory, calling it to 'a politics of at once radical and realistic ambition'.

PART I

Political Phenomenology

1.1

Hannah Arendt and the Theory of the Bourgeois Public Sphere

> *And when I should remember the paragons of Hellas*
> *I think instead*
> *Of the crooks, the adventurers, the opportunists,*
> *The careless athletes and the fancy boys,*
> *The hair splitters, the pedants, the hard-boiled sceptics*
> *And the Agora and the noise*
> *Of the demagogues and the quacks; and the women pouring*
> *Libations over graves*
> *And the trimmers in Delphi and the dummies at Sparta and lastly*
> *I think of the slaves*
> *These dead are dead*
> *And how one can imagine oneself among them*
> *I do not know*
>
> (Louis MacNeice)

The Phenomenology of the Political

In the largely hagiographical literature that surrounds Hannah Arendt's work, the 'social weightlessness' of her account of the political is customarily singled out as at least potentially problematic, the distinction she stubbornly draws between the 'political and the social' sometimes taken to be 'untenable'.[1] Such qualifying moves misread Arendt. The

---

[1] Having been introduced and systematically developed in *On Revolution* (1963), at least 'since the Toronto Conference of 1972 it has become customary in the academic literature to claim that Arendt makes an untenable distinction between the political and the social' (Volk, 2015: 54). Reference to 'social weightlessness' is from Lois McNay (2014). For Pitkin the separation is 'profoundly incoherent', 'extraordinarily confusing and confused' (1998: 219, 225); also Bernstein (1986), Parekh (1981) Frank (2010) are amongst those who have criticised her on the 'social question'. Castoriades talks of Arendt's 'enormous blunder' of not recognising the social question as a political question in 'Does the idea of revolution still make sense' (1990: 125). Hauke Brunkhorst, to my mind one of the most acute of her readers and critics, warns that we 'should be somewhat sceptical about certain elements of [her] critique (Arendt's entirely negative view of politics as the quest for social

distinction is *all too tenable* and it subtends Arendt's construction of the public sphere; the 'social question' of meeting social needs is introduced by her as a key *counter*point to the conceptualisation of what is properly political. Related, relentless, if less criticised, are the sets of distinctions that organise her account of social praxis, the stark partitions between labour and work on the one hand, and of action as distinguished from both on the other. Importantly, for much of this secondary literature, the first problem can be *excised* from the body of her thought and set aside without compromising it; in the second case conceptual analysis may be *tempered* as to the starkness of the dichotomies it deploys. But neither of these qualifications to Arendt's line of argument take her position seriously. Both gestures are intrinsic to her phenomenological method as constitutive of how Arendt gives meaning to the political. As framing conditions, both 'moments' run through the political to the root.

Given that both are constitutive *limitations*, why, then, begin with Arendt? It is because, with Antonio Negri, we must recognise the profound phenomenological insight that sustains her account of the political as pure *constituent*. 'Arendt well understood this truth about constituent power', says Negri with admiration for her 'fierce phenomenological exercise' (Negri, 1999a: 16): 'Constituent power insofar as it constitutes the political from nothingness is an expansive principle.' Indeed the definition of the constituent that she introduces is grounded on nothing but its own beginning and takes effect through nothing but its own expression. Its radical quality is absolute. But, as Negri goes on to add, the radicality of this vision of the eruption on the scene of the political terrifies Arendt, so that at 'the very moment when she illuminates the nature of constituent power, Arendt renders it indifferent in its ideality ... Each of the characteristics attributed to constituent power loses its intensity, becomes pale and reveals its opposite' (1999a: 16). The disclosive power of the political is blinding; exactly at this point, writes Negri, 'Arendt's thought runs into an insurmountable roadblock',[2] and Arendt will spend the most part of her significant oeuvre reining it in, in order to ground it in the institutions of bourgeois legality and render it

---

justice, for example) even as we utilize her profounder insights about the nature of politics and freedom' (Brunkhorst, 2000). See also Jonas on the 'astonishing superficiality' of her historical analysis of the social question, cited in Volk (2015: 54).

[2] '... when she discovers that nothing resembles constituent power so much as the most radical and deep, most desperate and fierce, negation' (Negri, 1999a: 21).

perfectly compatible with the basic organising tenets and structures of democratic capitalism.

The aim of this chapter is to explore that ambivalence of Arendt's phenomenological move, of managing the selective opening to the principle of a constituent politics while rendering that very principle innocuous regarding its constituent force. Ambivalence is perhaps too loose a term for her strategy of selectively releasing and withholding, which set, in her account, the structural conditions of the emergence of the public sphere in its distinctively bourgeois instantiation. To appreciate the dynamic fully we will probe further, in subsequent chapters, into the phenomenological method, of which Arendt's is undoubtedly a principal instantiation. There the 'ambivalence' takes on the more decisive form of a directive 'bracketing'; and what is crucial is the relationship of what is suspended to what is disclosed in that gesture.

So let us then at the outset, against the caveats, qualifications and selective excisions, assume that Arendt is a coherent thinker who meant to write what she wrote, and give her credit for her profound phenomenological insight; which means *not* treating the severing between the social and the political that she so eloquently performs as *incidental* to her phenomenological vision, but as intrinsic to it. If Alasdair MacIntyre famously warned that moral philosophy, and *a fortiori* one could add political theory, 'always presupposes a sociology' (MacIntyre, 1981: 36), Arendt's emphatic statement is that the political *should not* become so fettered by its embeddedness in social conditions. Nowhere is this clearer than in her analysis of the revolutionary tradition. She says: 'Crucial then to any understanding of revolutions in the modern age is that the idea of freedom and the experience of new beginning should coincide' (1963: 21–2) an insight carried in the American revolution, that 'transcended the social ... by instituting a public space of freedom', but lost in the French Revolution, the Jacobin obsession to direct power to the needs of the wretched masses allowing the 'social question' to spin emptily out of control. What leads Arendt to revile the French Revolution is the Jacobin dimension of political thought and action and indirectly Rousseau's understanding of the general will, that 'monstrous' expression of the will of the people as a singular, undivided and unreflective entity. Instead it is *plurality* that founds the political. The 'startling unexpectedness of beginnings' that in one way or another she celebrates throughout her oeuvre, *the event of world-disclosure* occurs on condition that it sheds off its social encumbrance. The shedding off becomes no less than the condition of appearing. The *emergence* of the political, thus, draws its leverage, constitutively, from the negation of both the 'social question' (as a matter of the proper *domain* of the political) and the 'Jacobin solution' (as a matter of the proper *subject* and proper *time* of the political). For Arendt, the meaning of the political emerges out of praxis in terms of a negation of, and in contradistinction to, the 'social' question of need and the 'Jacobin' assumption of a collective subject position. This double negation props up and sustains Arendt's phenomenologically grounded conception of the public sphere. To the extent that the double negation furnishes Arendt's phenomenology it cannot be stepped behind or redressed; in effect, in her thought the political appears *as coincident with its bourgeois instantiation*. The task we face is to *reclaim* the phenomenology of the political for the *critical* tradition.

Arendt's phenomenology of the public sphere is the subject of this first chapter of the book, with the emphasis on the distinctions, and attendant exclusions, that sustain it, and the rejection of the dialectic that might have reconciled them. This first section takes issue specifically with the 'social question', or the constitutive distinction between the 'social' and the 'political', and with her rebuttal of the dialectic. Both arguments are best understood, I will argue, as an inversion of Marx's thought. Following that, we will explore how the exclusion of social need from politics, of a politics that could never dialectically reach into the sphere of need, sustains her phenomenology of the political in its material, social and temporal dimensions.

An important note about methodology: The notion that *meaning* can be analysed along these three dimensions - *material, social and temporal* - is borrowed from Niklas Luhmann, and will emerge in the course of the argument of this book as a key methodology in the analysis of meaning-construction. This is our first encounter with it. 'We must clarify', says Luhmann, 'the decomposition of the *abstractum* "meaning". This can be done with the help of the concept "meaning dimensions". . . . We view factual references as merely one of several meaning dimensions. These factual references are not set against the subject but if meaning is complex enough, they must adapt themselves to complicated interdependencies with temporal and social meaning references' (Luhmann, 1995a: 74). In the course of the analysis of Arendt's theory of the political, the three dimensions of meaning will lend a useful analytic to her thought, and at the same time will be given content that showcases how useful a heuristic they provide in terms of what is actualised as meaning and what is potentialised alongside it. Alongside the dimensions of meaning, the term 'guiding distinctions', again borrowed from

Luhmann, refers to those distinctions that organise the semantic field. We will explore much of what Arendt builds on and makes dependent on the stark binarisms of her own 'guiding distinctions' that operate in her theory as blind spots. In Luhmann's phenomenological method the starting question involves a distinction on the basis of which an indication is made always in the mirror of the other, the non-indicated, side. We will ask how the *distinctions* operate in Arendt's method and what *indications* are suggested. Hers are stubborn demarcations that once indicated no longer yield to any dialectical movement. Action is contrasted to work and to labour; the political is contrasted to the social and the personal; political 'presence' to representation; compassion to pity; freedom to necessity. *These are Arendt's guiding distinctions; this is the field of meaning that they map; this is the world-disclosure they offer.*

Her guiding distinction between the social and the political is accompanied by a further contradistinction of *labour* to *work*, and then of both to *action*. The partitions combine in the following way. The analysis of 'action' as separate from 'labour' and 'work' aims to conceptualise *action* as that which is distinct from processes of social reproduction and instrumental rationality respectively. *Labour*, for Arendt, is caught in the 'cyclical movement of the body's life process', with neither beginning nor end, whereas work may have 'a definite beginning and a definite end' but that commits it to culminate in an empty intentionality. Only action can properly foreground plurality and the 'making' of world. The contrast to the 'social question' answers the question of what the political is *about* (the material dimension of its meaning) and Arendt will answer that it is emphatically *not about need*. In terms of the *time* of appearance (and therefore the temporal dimension of its meaning), Arendt is keen to resist any sense in which the political may appear in terms of the pure performative act (the dreaded 'Jacobin' expression of the pure constituent) and will further insist that the (phenomenological) achievement of *remaining apparent* is achieved in terms of *institutional* duration. The temporality of the political, in other words, must come in the modality of the *renewal* of institutions, *not in advance* of them. Which also answers why the *social* dimension of the political can under no circumstances be answered in terms of presence, but only of representation. Representational structures must pre-exist the expression of the will; any move from representation to presence and with it to the constituent, and democracy immediately shades into totalitarianism.

Next we will turn to track the various moves of Arendt's phenomenological exercise in more detail. With her help, key concepts will be introduced along the three dimensions of meaning: social, material and temporal. If opening the book with the focus on Arendt, however, is poignant, it is neither to follow her lead, nor to identify methodological shortcomings per se. It is rather because her profound phenomenological endeavour provides a counterpoint to the *critical* phenomenology developed in this work. Arendt's phenomenological reductions operate as points of disclosure and foreclosure, immune to negotiation, critical objection or dialectical movement. They install and police the scope of contingency, of politics and 'world-making' within definite and particular limits: a meta-political move that severely curtails the scope of the reflexivity of the political at the same time as it so eloquently celebrates it.

*

'The concern with appearance', as Johan van der Walt puts it in an important paper, 'the fundamental concern of the tradition of European philosophical inquiry that came to be called *phenomenology*, runs like a constant thread through Arendt's work' (van der Walt, 2012: 63). And famously, for Arendt, the political breaks into the world as irreducibly plural. In one of the most quoted passages in political theory, Arendt links *plurality* to *action* as constitutive of the political because condition of its appearance:

> Action, the only activity that goes on directly between men without the intermediary of things or matter, corresponds to the human condition of plurality, to the fact that men, not Man, live on the earth and inhabit the world. While all aspects of the human condition are somehow related to politics, this plurality is specifically *the* condition – not only the *conditio sine qua non*, but the *conditio per quam* – of all political life.
>
> (Arendt, 1958: 7)

A mutually reinforcing relation amongst the key terms installs plurality as nothing short of the *conditio humana*: *action* and *plurality*, a conjunction out of which the political is hoisted as initiatory or as Arendt puts it well, the performance of the 'infinitely improbable'. 'The fact that man is capable of action means that the unexpected can be expected from him' (Arendt, 1958: 158). In all this, the political is conceived of as the sole guarantor of its own performance, a profound re-statement of constituent power that Arendt offers us, and then spends the rest of her oeuvre retracting.

The power of these insights goes some way to explaining Arendt's sweeping influence on political theory today. Praxis, natality, world-disclosive activity, acting-out the infinitely improbable are celebrated as terms that carry the radical potential for re-launching political thought. It is at this point, *and in the name of plurality,* that Arendt contrasts political-communicative action to instrumental action. Action to be free, she says, 'must be free from motives and intentions on the one hand and aims and consequences on the other' (Arendt, 1958: 205). Action is vested with a rationality that is properly political, and as such contrasted to the means-ends rationality of work. It is the same instrumentality that attaches to strategic thinking, this too needing to be contrasted to communicative processes that elevate political interaction as *their own end* and justification. Communicative actions, or simply action, converge on a world of common meanings, and for that convergence to reflect commonality it must *not* be harnessed to the achievement of aims formed in advance of the encounter that founds intersubjectivity. Action must be understood only as performance within a context of *intersubjective deliberation*. A great deal hangs on this: the institution of public space pivots on the '*inter*' of the intersubjective, and the in-between is both the site of performance and its effect. The difference for Arendt is between expressing spontaneity and enacting a plan. The distinction between spontaneity and planning clearly correlates to the distinction between the communicative and the instrumental, whose conceptualisation as mutually denying leads directly to the rejection of strategic thinking in politics.

The emphasis on frailty is matched by the emphasis on contingency. 'Contingent', which in Luhmann's diction carries the productive ambivalence of both 'dependent on' and 'possible otherwise', loses the dimension of dependency to denote only *release* from necessity in order that it harbour the unpredictable. 'History is a story of events and not of forces or ideas with predictable courses' (Arendt, 1958: 252). But it is not just *temporality* that centres Arendt's project on contingency. Contingency is key to how Arendt re-launches the political across all axes of its meaning, over its proper modality and proper *content*, as well as over its conceptualisation as *plurality* and the resistance to the givenness of social role and identity. Together these constitute the framework in terms of which the appearance of the political is made possible. In terms of phenomenological *method*, where what appears is contingent on what is bracketed, the emphasis in what follows is less on the splendour of what appears and more on the withdrawal of what is bracketed in order to enable that appearance. Not so much on the exalted tones of their pure expression but in the profound ambivalence that marks their deployment by Arendt, as keen to *announce* the constituent moment as she is to *withdraw* from it its radicality.

A rough attempt to draw together the threads of her critique of Marx as found scattered in her work, and to re-construct something of an elementary dialogue, yields four key themes. First, her defence of 'plurality' as pitted against '*mass society*', which reduces individuals to the same undifferentiated and generic content (1951: 466ff), is increasingly re-directed against collective subjecthood and class identity. Arendt attacks Marx's 'preference for collective subjects – like the proletariat or mankind – which act in accordance with supposed class or species interests' (Villa, 2000: 7). Heidegger's thinking of authenticity blends here with her own critique of mass society and the production of subjects incapable of spontaneity. Marx's reliance on class-*collective* subject-positions undercuts the very thing that Arendt identifies as quintessential to politics: diversity amongst equals, and with it the constitutive plurality of the political.³ Secondly, as she develops it at length in the last chapter of *Origins*, totalitarianism, in both its national-socialist and soviet varieties, attempts to '*still*' action through terror in order to pursue the law of History, whose laws of movement replace the spontaneous action of free men. '*Process thinking*' removes the initiatory gesture from political actors and entrusts it to History. With it 'terror', the 'essence of totalitarian domination', is deployed to 'stabilize men', 'to liberate the forces of nature or history' in the name of the 'fabrication of mankind', 'eliminating individuals for the sake of the species, sacrificing the 'parts' for the sake of the 'whole' (Arendt, 1951/1973: 465). What in *Origins* is clearly pitted against Nazism gradually spills over to Marxism. Where for Arendt it is action, as opposed to work and to labour, that sustains the political, Marx's productivist bias insists on social labour, and in the way the latter is elevated to the expression of species-being, it imports it as constitutive of human association. Thirdly, Marx's overarching orientation to the satisfaction of needs elevates the '*social question*' to eclipse the 'political'. The political hubris of totalitarianism, which Arendt defines as

---

³ Compare Mary Dietz: 'Arendt's condition of plurality itself provides the *ethical* dimension that a truly emancipatory politics requires' (Dietz, 1994: 882, my emphasis).

HANNAH ARENDT AND THE BOURGEOIS PUBLIC SPHERE

a 'climactic pathology' of modern European history, stands at the counterpoint of what it means to preserve and share a 'world'. A 'world' for Arendt involves the institutions and structures that mediate man's relation to nature, mark civilised life, and constitute man's medium of freedom. Totalitarianism collapses that space and subsumes the political to the state's direct administration, including the management of needs.[4] And with this comes another approximation no longer to the state, but to economics. Arendt likens the two pathologies and brings them both under the sign of the 'a-political' or 'improperly political', in that both constitute instances of decisive absolution of civic responsibility. In the case of totalitarianism the absolution is to powerful government, in the case of economics it is to policy-makers and the administrative apparatus of the State. For Arendt, that the political sphere came to be identified with the 'national household' involved a category mistake that collapsed political thinking into administration; instead it is their contradistinction that upholds the autonomy of the political. Fourthly, the Jacobin principle of *speaking for* the dispossessed masses removes the experiential (and existential) element of authentic politics, an injunction that attaches also to Marx and the authority assumed by the vanguard or the Party to speak on behalf of those whom necessity or ideology condemn to silence.

This last injunction of Arendt's is particularly revealing. When Robespierre declared that everything which is necessary to maintain life must be common good and only the surplus can be recognised as private property, for Arendt he was subjecting the welfare of the people, 'to the most irrefragable of all titles, necessity'. For her it was necessity, the urgent needs of the people, that unleashed the terror and sent the Revolution to its doom. She cites Jefferson approvingly, when he declared that a people 'so loaded with misery would [not] be able to achieve what had been achieved in America' (1963: 68).[5] Best to have left it till the time was ripe: it was Robespierre's impatience and relentless insistence on the social question that forced him to miss the 'historical moment' to 'found freedom'. This somewhat absurd injunction is then projected forward to Marx. 'It took more than half a century before the transformation of the

---

[4] 'Everything which can really be figured out, in the sphere that Engels called the administration of things – these are social things in general. That they should be subject to debate seems to me phony and a plague.' (Quoted in Hill, 1979: 317.)

[5] And about John Adams' 'conviction' that a free republican government 'was as unnatural ... as it would be over elephants, lions, wolves [etc] in the royal menagerie at Versailles', she proclaims, rather disturbingly despite the softening qualifier, that 'years later, events to an extent proved him right ...' (Arendt, 1963: 68).

Rights of Man into the Rights of the Sans-Culottes, the abdication of freedom before the dictate of necessity, had found its theorist in Marx' (1963: 60-1). What a strange formulation this is, couched in a vocabulary of abdication, and thus of a certain refusal of a different route. What, one might pause to ask, does 'abdication of freedom' mean for the sans-culottes? What possibility of freedom did the Parisian mob forego in bringing the 'needs of the body' into the streets? Return to Arendt: Marx's genius and ultimately his theoretical error, she says, is that he *read the social question in political terms*. That means that he read the question of *poverty* as a question of the suppression of *freedom*, and the way he achieved this was through the theory of *exploitation*, which is what facilitated the mediation between the two. Arendt is vehement on this point:

> Marx's transformation of the social question into a political force is contained in the term 'exploitation', that is in the notion that poverty is the result of exploitation through a 'ruling class' which is in the possession of the means of violence ... His most explosive and indeed most original contribution ... was that he interpreted the compelling needs of mass poverty in political terms as an uprising, not for the sake of bread or wealth, but for the sake of freedom as well. ... [His achievement was] to conjure up a spirit of rebelliousness that can spring only from being violated, not from being under the sway of necessity; ... and to 'persuade' them that poverty itself is a political not a natural phenomenon, the result of violence and violation rather than scarcity.
>
> (1963: 62)

This is of course staggeringly shallow in ignoring the Marxian analysis of the socially wasteful effects of the class ownership of the means of production, the extraction of surplus value from labour, the violent and ideological processes that underlie the domination of capital, sustain it and exonerate it.[6] It cannot be that Arendt has missed all this. So why does she set out to prove Marx wrong to have interpreted the 'predicament of poverty in categories of oppression and exploitation' (Arendt, 1963: 63) by *simply restating* the embeddedness of her own founding distinction, the foundational character of the disconnect between social and political that is, after all, *precisely Marx's focus of critique*? Methodologically it has to be because she begins with a fundamental counterdistinction between social and political that cannot be thematised

---

[6] As Hanna Pitkin comments, Arendt's 'detailed formulations [of the interpretation of Marx] are almost always mistaken, sometimes blatantly so' (1998: 115).

from within the perspective it fashions. At a second level, it is because Arendt withdraws that structuring distinction from history and any reflexive re-configuration that might have been forged as a result of the strain placed on the theoretical categories by the material processes of social reproduction. What she had to distance herself from, at any price, was Marx's suggestion of the 'real movement that abolishes the present state of things' (*The German Ideology*, 56–7) that aims at realising the 'self-activity' of workers. For Arendt, the recovery of the ability to act cannot emerge where it does not already exist. The logic of 'emancipation' as tied to history would involve a problematic *becoming-political*, the politicisation of processes that are not already that. The stakes are too high, which explains why Arendt's objection becomes so shrill here against Marx's attachment to Hegel, the philosopher par excellence of 'becoming', and his dialectic method in which 'freedom would directly rise out of necessity', a dialectic and a coincidence that Arendt with unusual vehemence characterises as 'perhaps the most terrible and, humanly speaking, least bearable paradox in the body of modern thought' (Arendt, 1963: 57). If the denunciation takes such a desperately urgent tone here, it is because Arendt sees in dialectical thought the overcoming of the conditions she has assumed constitutive of the political, its startling unexpectedness that cannot and should not be underwritten by historical processes. It is this profoundly anti-dialectical impulse that explains the unflinching insistence that the two spheres – political and social – are not and cannot be tied dialectically in what Arendt calls 'process thinking', and why necessity never gets a foothold in a dialectic of action, nor of any sort for that matter.

If for Adorno dialectical thought was an attempt to break through the coercion of logic by its own means, for Arendt dialectical thought involves the opposite: the steamrollering over the uniqueness and unpredictability of events in order to call them into line and order them in sequence as the unfurling of a world-historical logic. Arendt's fairly cursory rebuttal of Marx as a 'process-thinker'[7] ties with another which brings us back to the 'social question'. She accuses Marx of

---

[7] What does 'process thinking' involve for Arendt? It involves 'that of making something … whose laws of motion can be determined (for instance as dialectical movement) and whose innermost content can be discovered (for instance as class struggle)' (1961: 79). Politics is then reduced to a super-structural manifestation of the struggle between classes. As she puts it in the essay 'the ex-communists', 'Marxism could be developed into a totalitarian ideology because of its perversion, or misunderstanding, of political action as the making of history' (Arendt, 2011).

'strengthen[ing] more than anybody else the politically most pernicious doctrine of the modern age, namely that life is the highest good and that the life process of society is the very centre of human endeavour'. With this new emphasis 'the role of revolution is no longer to liberate men from the oppression of their fellow men, let alone to found freedom, but to liberate the life process of society itself from the fetters of scarcity so that it would swell into a stream of abundance. Not freedom but abundance became the new aim of revolution' (Arendt, 1963: 64), involving a displacement of the very aspiration of political action, a falling-short that turns out to be a radical undercutting of its logic. More important than this throw-away rejection is what Arendt cannot accept is staked on the political in its 'Jacobin' instantiation: first, the expression of the political will *outwith* the institutions and structures of representation *as* instead *enacted* and *claimed on behalf of* the masses; and, secondly, the connection of the political with the question of decisions over distribution and responsiveness to need (the 'social question'). And Arendt famously returns to the flowering of democracy in the *Athenian polis* to retrieve above all the purity of the public/private dichotomy in order to support and defend the unencumbered public sphere.[8] The simultaneous constitution of the spheres of political and civil society as separate, which Marx attacked in *On the Jewish Question*, is what Arendt endorses as lever of the political. Interestingly, some years later so will Luhmann, though it is unlikely that Arendt would have picked him as a fellow-traveller. Both celebrate the political system's unburdening itself of functions that are not political. For Luhmann this was the achievement of the evolutionary decomposition of society into discrete functionally determined spheres (economy, law, science, etc.) where the political dividends came from society's *immunisation* from 'saturation with political contest'. For Arendt the achievement lies in the protection of the political system from the 'social question' and any demands that may originate in the sphere of production and social labour. For her, too, the public sphere is *immunised* through this move of displacement and obfuscation.

'*Do not say that social movement excludes political movement. There is never a political movement that is not at the same time social*', wrote Marx in the *Poverty of Philosophy*. In reconstructing Arendt's critique of Marx on this point and on the dialectical method, the aim was not to rescue

---

[8] Arendt looks to the experience of the Greek polis because 'a freedom experienced in the process of acting and nothing else – though, of course, mankind never lost this experience altogether – has never again been articulated with the same classical clarity' (1961: 165).

Marx from her objections, but something altogether more significant for critical theory. It is to ask the question: why so profound a phenomenological endeavour such as Arendt's produced so stunted a phenomenality of the political? It is, I suggest, because of her insistence on holding on to the distinctions that sustained her phenomenology of the political, and a refusal to discern any dialectical movement between the realms of necessity and freedom. Until the bitter end she will defend her hostility to the dialectic and her proud 'anti-hegelianism'. Here she is in an exchange with Albrecht Wellmer of the Frankfurt School: 'I would say that by these fancy methods you have eliminated distinction and have already done this Hegelian trick in which one concept, all of its own, begins to develop into its own negative. *No it doesn't!*'[9] And it is because of the fierce polemic against the dialectical overcoming of her founding disjunction in the direction of a political reading of social necessity, that Arendt's thought capitulates before the authority of the status quo, the givenness of the situation (the distributions and dependencies of exchange-based capitalist societies) that her phenomenology leaves not merely unaddressed but unaddressable.

Arendt's Arrested 'Worldliness'

As we move deeper into Arendt's phenomenology, we appreciate how the conditions that enable and sustain the appearance of the political become simultaneously what harness it constitutively to the reproduction of the deep structural logic of bourgeois democracy. The sections that follow track the phenomenology that makes this possible. For that which is politically disclosed, for what is initiated, we ask 'with the help of what distinctions'? Speaking from the phenomenological point of view, disclosure has to be based on a reduction that can be operationalised *because* it cannot be queried. Any defence of Arendtian politics must remain clear about the stakes of the unquestionability of the guiding distinctions.

Much has been said already about the 'what?', the 'who' and the 'when?' of politics: its content and modality in the first case, its protagonists in the second, the logic of its emergence in the third case. We will now undertake a more systematic analysis of the three dimensions of the meaning of the political, tracking along each of them Arendt's

---

[9] Quoted in Holman (2011: 340); Holman argues that her concern with preserving distinctions was a consequence of the lack of Hegelian elements in her thought.

prescription of how the political is disclosed. Along each of the dimensions there occurs simultaneously a celebration of the political in the manifold of its expression, while at the same time the hidden displacement conditions, the structural absences, operate to rein it in and subject it to the immunity conditions of a bourgeois politics. Ultimately any form of radical critique that does not already take its place innocuously on the plane of her *agonistic* politics, but presents itself as *antagonistic* to that frame, is defined away and the damage sealed over as a matter of meaning construction.

'World-Making' in the *'Material'* Dimension

On 24 April 1793 Robespierre attempted and failed to persuade the Convention to amend Condorcet's *Declaration* in the direction of what he described as an 'arrangement required by the interest of humanity': to establish a progressive basis of taxation. Is there 'any principle more obviously derived from the nature of things and from eternal justice,' he asks, 'than one that obliges the citizens to contribute to public expenditure progressively, in accordance with the advantages they draw from society?' The main aim is the alleviation of poverty: 'The committee has also forgotten to quote the duties of fraternity which unite all men ... and their rights to mutual assistance' (Robespierre, 2007: 68).

Not for Arendt this preoccupation with poverty and mutual assistance, though her response is not quite Malthus', who famously, in the first edition of the *Essay on the Principle of Population* in 1798, denounced the ideas of the French Revolution as the 'fermentation of disgusting passions', and took issue in particular with the right to subsistence as a 'delusive argument'. If for Malthus the right to subsistence was 'delusive' in displacing the only true principle of politics, which for him was the principle of hunger, for Arendt, if it can be called 'delusive', it is because hunger is not a proper question for politics. The demand to have the needs of existence met is not 'delusive' because it contravenes the principle of politics but because it mis-directs it to the social question of redistribution through taxation and the relief of hunger.

For Arendt the content of political speech and action cannot be social and economic policies; the *content* of properly political action is politics itself. And if politics is defined by this reflexivity its content *cannot* be the *salus populi*, the alleviation of suffering, the meeting of need. Her critique of Marx, and of Jacobinism which found its belated champion in him, was that by turning it to need, it placed the final goal of politics beyond politics. Against the subsumption of politics to economics, against the penetration of 'national household' concerns into the realm of the properly political, against interpretations derived from the realm of production, she offers us instead a clear statement of the principle of the constituent, in which politicisation is cast as its own principle and the political inaugurates its own conditions and field of reference.[10] Her phenomenology of the political finds truth in itself, that is, in its own possibilities, as it returns reflexively to subvert the *givenness* of appearance.[11] What is shed in the process are the kind of collective identities that people may have assumed in the workplace, family, neighbourhoods, movements, from histories and traditions of association; shed, that is, as 'points of entry' into the public sphere and as constitutive of political participation. Instead, Arendt will proclaim that the hallmarks of the political – *isonomia*, political equality, political life as the *vita activa* – establish in an *initiatory*, performative way what it means to share; it does not and cannot rely on inherited, *already* shared, and therefore *pre-political* forms.

What has the account of meaning-construction along this first, material, dimension shown us? In Arendt's phenomenology, the constitutive severing from the social has propped up the political as autonomous from the vagaries of social encumberment, and *therefore as constituent*. We have looked at the gesture whereby she closes politics reflexively around its own principle and safeguards its own conditions. Key to this safeguarding was the purity and rigidity of the framing distinctions between action/work/labour, that subtend the modality of the political, and that between the political and the social that informs its content. In the process of their submission to these distinctions, a process that has selectively opened up and foreclosed the space of political appearance, the social demands for recognition and distribution are no longer conceived as political demands. The tortured distinction between action and labour, the question-begging disempowering gesture par excellence, places material practice below the threshold of political redress. Maybe

---

[10] At least as developed in *The Human Condition*. By the time we encounter the distinction again in *On Revolution* its novelty has shrivelled into an alarmed injunction at the prospect of anything like a claim to meet social needs, appended on a metapolitical argument.

[11] In a not uncharacteristic eulogy, Michael Marder invites us to read in the *Human Condition* 'the last instantiation of phenomenology as consonant with the political principle of a self-disrupting multiplicity, the condition of human plurality and natality, and the *locus essendi* of critical political phenomenology' (Marder, 2014: 94).

this sounds too Marxist to worry the Arendtians too much. But a phenomenology exalting 'world-making' splendour needs to answer also for lives that fall below the level where they may be dignified with 'worldliness', the lives of the sans-culottes, lives in the ghettos and the slums, lives exhaustively consumed in the domain of need and blind necessity. The reflexive reach of Arendt's politics is set by condition of its orientation *away* from concern with material deprivation, and from any instrumental deployment in the direction of its redress. The result is that it can no longer be reflexive *about* the conditions, or re-configure its reach in view of those conditions. The denial of the claims of the dispossessed are then doubly forgotten, when the very purity of the constituent demands that its statement in political terms proper – as expression of freedom *– is its unburdening from the social dimension.* This unburdening founds the bourgeois public sphere as cleansed of the social demand that needs be met. A bourgeois sphere that makes nonsense of a claim to recognition other than the attribution of the status of *equal* citizen, *politically* impossible *as a demand* because either already granted or deprived a register,[12] and that furnishes a claim to equality that severs it from the political economy, and expels it as a *democratic* demand from the sphere of production. Thereafter the demands of the social only come through as noise, at one level at least of the innocuous kind that Arendt's worldliness celebrates.[13] Hers is a bourgeois philosophy whose function, in the most basic terms of ideological analysis, aims to depoliticise the consequences of capitalist distributions by circumventing the language of exploitation and, by a move at the meta-political level, leaving them *politically unaddressable*. Out of the severing from the social processes of value production Arendt hoists the constituent event, eloquently, radically, gloriously *vacuous*.

[12] Arendt finds her theory confronted with this dilemma, and discusses it with reference to the figure of the refugee (1951). Her conundrum over 'the right to have rights' has since informed a multitude of theorisations.

[13] On a lighter note, and as Seyla Benhabib relates the story, an exasperated Mary McCarthy put it thus to her friend during a frank exchange at the University of Toronto: "'speeches can't be just speeches. They have to be speeches about something." ... At one point or another Arendt had excluded poverty, welfare and housing provisions, procreation, nourishment, family life and even education from the realm of the public, as social or pre-political by nature' (Benhabib, 1996: 155); or as Pitkin puts it: 'What is it that they talked about together in that endless palaver in the agora?' (Pitkin, 1981: 327).

HANNAH ARENDT AND THE BOURGEOIS PUBLIC SPHERE

'World-Making' in the 'Temporal' Dimension

The event of politics is the capacity to begin anew. Of course, even where the emphasis is on the temporal dimension, the *when* of action brings forth both its content (the *what*) and its subject (the *who* of politics): a beginning best conceived 'not [as] the beginning of something out of something but of somebody, who is a beginner itself' (1958: 177). And yet there is something significant to separate off and track exclusively along this dimension of time that characterises what in *The Life of the Mind* she calls the 'highly self-destructive' practice of phenomenology: that it is subject to its own principle of *interruption*.

Arendt's theory of the *time of the political* encompasses two constitutive features that express two key moments of constituent power: first, nothing pre-determines or over-determines emergence; secondly, the unfolding of any given sequence is always potentially subject to interruption. Regarding the first feature: *politicisation* assumes in the temporal dimension the form of *inaugurating* its own conditions. This is what so attracted Negri to Arendt's theorisation of the constituent: that it carries a critique of origin and foundation. But this critique of political foundationalism, now also spills over into a critique of the arrangements that may have had radical beginnings but *policed* their continuation and the suppression of the new, as in the case of the French Revolution happened with the reign of terror. That is why interruption matters. Self-inauguration and interruption are the two key aspects and signs of the constituent in the temporal dimension, and together they inform the meaning of 'natality'.

This is an improbable synthesis, and 'natality' must balance within its unlikely temporality both novelty and the function of ordering the relations amongst men,[14] navigating between stasis – or the mere repetition of what already exists – and the randomness of the permanently revolutionary. Arendt finds its purest expression in the American Revolution, which expressed everything that Arendtian phenomenology celebrates: it aspired to a world inhabited by 'men in the plural', which must be a 'joint' endeavour; the American founders enacted a 'new order for the ages' beyond all possible anticipation, while leaving the property regime in place largely untouched; intersubjectivity invoked and called on 'others for help'; the founding found expression in a speech act – 'we hold …' – that simultaneously broke new ground and found its authorisation in

---

[14] For her discussion of 'natality', see in particular Arendt, 1958: 178–80, 189.

mutuality; a mutuality that as 'action in concert' generated the bonds that would underwrite it, etc. Institutions such as 'forgiving' and 'promising' played the key role. The openness of politics requires a constant renegotiation along both temporal axes of present/past and present/future – in other words, the performance of politics in the present requires the double orientation to both past and future, and that double orientation or double openness takes the form of *forgiving* when it comes to the past and of *promising* in what concerns the future. For action to sustain itself in the present both the potentialities of forgiving the past and promising the future must remain simultaneously alive.

Here is Arendt on the notion of the revolutionary beginning:

> *Every act*, seen from the perspective not of the agent but of the *process* in whose framework it occurs and whose automatism it *interrupts*, is a '*miracle*' – that is, something which could not be expected.... It is in the very nature of every new beginning that it breaks into the world as an 'infinite improbability,' and yet it is precisely this infinitely improbable which actually constitutes the very texture of everything that we call real.
>
> (1961: 169–70, my emphases)

'Interrupts' is important here. Interruptions arise in *media res* and acquire their character as 'breaks' retrospectively. Once they have occurred and transform the situation they find themselves in, they work back to reconfigure themselves as initiatory. Arendt will argue that the opposition between founding and renewing is largely false, as is unfounded the opposition between the 'concern with stability and the spirit of the new'. *Re*-negotiation of the founding moment is an ongoing, plural affair. Importantly, it can be accommodated *institutionally*. It is this logic of retroaction, re-signification and institution, that has stood as a source of inspiration for US constitutional scholarship. New beginnings and the undertaking of action-in-concert are accommodated in more expansive constitutional forms and semantics. Of course these forms are re-negotiated in the process of such undertakings, heightened moments of participation and the forcing open of new fields of constitutional disclosure. Agonism is thus integral to the constitutional imaginary that calls forth new patterns and variations of inscription. In other words, the boundlessness of the expression of the constituent, catalyses in the institution. 'Natality' is thereby harboured in the institutional form, that offers expression to authenticity, genuine plurality and an unexpectedness that breaks with regular or fated continuities. The challenge for Arendt, and for the tradition that draws inspiration from Arendt, is to navigate the difficulty that duration is at odds with novelty, in the direction of a constitutionalism that is both 'revolutionary' and durable. The effort, in other words, is to sustain a constitutional agonism that gives expression to the constituent event without suffocating 'natality', while at the same time securing its containment in institutional form.[15]

At the juncture of its ordinary rhythms and extraordinary accelerations, Arendt has offered to link the political and the legal institution in a constitutionalism that harbours, over and above mere reconciliation, a sense of mutual enablement. In it we witness the double gesture that underlies Arendt's political phenomenology, the selective release and withdrawal of the political, imbued with interruption and natality but crucially in a way that links back to the logic of institution. Let us simply note that Arendt's 'constituent' temporality expends its claim to renewal in an *agonism* that polices path-dependency and installs itself as the horizon of every possible inauguration and every possible 'interruption'.

'World-Making' in the 'Social' Dimension

Arendt's discussion of the constituent in the social dimension centres on an argument about open plurality as a communicative relation. The modality of that appearance – we will see why – dissolves the paradox that the political self needs to be conceptualised as both constituted (as collective 'self') and as constituent ('novel'). Received subject-positions – the proletariat, the ethnic group, mankind – acting in accordance with class, racial or species interests, involve, for Arendt, 'pre-political' identifications. They are pre-political because they frame speaking positions that come already defined through what is shared – as interest, as identity, as vocation – outside politics. They thus stand opposed to the worldly in-between space wherein men are mutually related. In the communicatively staged encounter plurality is negotiated and thematised across lines of difference that *are crossed*. Before the crossing there is no *political* meaning to the encounter. In that foundational sense (as 'grammar', remember) plurality makes the political possible.

Political speech ties constitutively the 'what' of politics to the social dimension of the 'who': political is the bridging that in the modality of a communicative offer suspends the social dimension across the political

---

[15] At this juncture Arendt's suggestion involves a combination of two understandings of law, *nomos* and *lex*, whose radically different modalities combine to accommodate newness *and* durability. (See Arendt, 1958.)

space of *intersubjectivity*, the space between subjects. Speech is the condition of appearance: phenomena appear in being spoken about, and *logos* holds together many beginnings in the form of communicative offers across the space between subjects. Therefore the modality of the political, as speech, enjoins actors in plurality and is played out *institutionally* in terms of promises or commitments that are voluntarily assumed. There are speech acts that do not meet the high threshold: instrumentality and, *a fortiori*, strategy harness communication to aims beyond persuasion, and violence marks the breaking-off point of the political as denial and denying of speech. And while 'deliberation' is perhaps too colourless a world for what Arendt has in mind as the *'agon'* of politics, her influence on theories of discursive rationality is staggering. If Arendt, and later Habermas, see the interdependency that plurality introduces through the medium of speech as *radical*, it is because nothing underwrites it except its very performance.

There is not much to disagree with in this benign formulation, until we are confronted with what it is designed to debunk. Rousseau is Arendt's key adversary both in terms of his theorisation of the *general will* and of *solidarity*. Regarding the former, says Arendt, Rousseau's *volonté générale* could only express the will of the people as a singular, undivided and unreflective entity. In that it is akin to a Leviathan, analogous to a unity that collects and embodies political experience and intention. 'Rousseau's thoughts were so extraordinarily convenient because with his help a number of people could be formed into a many-headed monster ... that moves as one body ... possessed by one will' (1963: 72). This denies the essential premise of politics, its predication on irreducible human plurality, irreducible precisely because it cannot be collected in the unifying and homogenising concepts of the general will. In her posthumously published *Denktagebuch* she will go as far as to say that 'Rousseau's "volonté générale" is perhaps the most murderous solution to the squaring of the circle, namely the fundamental problem of all Western political philosophy, how to make a singularity out of plurality – in Rousseau's words: "réunir une multitude en un corps".'[16]

To appreciate the strength of this denunciation of Rousseau we need to remember that, for Arendt, action is the moment of disclosure of the subject achieved in contexts of plurality, and if its opportunity is marked by frailty it is because the emergence of a 'we' presupposes that political

---

[16] Arendt, *Denktagebuch*, quoted in Volk (2015: 67).

actors are, as she puts it, *'neither for nor against but only "with" others'*. Otherwise 'human togetherness is lost' (1958: 180). The either/or of this formulation sets limits on both sides of the 'with others'. The limit to the boundlessness of action on the one side is set by the dimension of the antagonistic. Where action acquires antagonistic form (*'against others'*), instrumentality and strategy prevail, the frail world is broken and the possibility of appearance is undercut. More problematic is the second limit set by the terms *'for others'*. To be clear about how the social bond is to be understood politically, if *solidarity* is going to capture something of the political dimension of plurality, it must be first clearly distinguished from what it means to act 'for others': 'togetherness' cannot be based on compassion. With Marx Arendt expelled 'antagonism' and 'exploitation' from the political; with Rousseau she is now poised to expel 'compassion'. In *On Revolution* her critique of Rousseau is driven by its political application at the hands of the Jacobins. Echoing Heinrich Heine's belief that Rousseau's words had turned into Robespierre's murderous crimes, she argued that if Rousseau had introduced compassion into political theory, Robespierre had carried it over into revolutionary practice 'with the vehemence of his great revolutionary oratory' (1963: 76).

The very definition of the term 'le peuple' that designates those who were spoken for and on behalf of, is 'born out of compassion' and the 'term became equivalent for misfortune'. Those who find themselves thus withdrawn from the vita activa, incapable of voice let alone of forgiveness or promising, must rely on the 'compassionate zeal' of those who were prepared to raise it to 'the rank of the supreme political passion and highest political virtue' (1963: 75). But the grave threat to authentic politics, it appears now, comes from the profoundly misguided attempt to act from intense moral distress. *'Le peuple, les malheureux m'applaudissent'*, claimed Robespierre, and when Marat was portrayed as the sans-culotte Jesus, the implications for acting could not be clearer.[17] This speaking *on behalf of* came to supplant 'all processes of exchange of opinions and an eventual agreement between them' (1963: 76). In the absence of political mediation, the 'representatives' of the people *could only express the 'will' of the people through an act of substitution* for it and

---

[17] Brunkhorst notes the Christian imagery through which the work of the Jacobins was sometimes expressed. The constitution was presented as the 'catechism of the human race', as 'sacred as the gospel'; Marat was presented as the 'sans-culotte Jesus'. Brunkhorst comments that the revolutionary appropriation of Christian imagery entailed a 'complete re-orientation of worldview from God to Humanity' (2000: 62).

the cue they took from Rousseau was that the general will was what bound the many into one: '*Il faut une volonté une*' insisted Robespierre, and thus it had to be, one or not at all. In the zeal and impetus of this supplanting, the will is uprooted from the worldly institutions which alone underwrote what they had in common, and thus cancelled it out.

It is on these grounds that Arendt will condemn the colonisation of public space by the ideals of compassion and virtue that substitute for solidarity. 'Robespierre's, instead, was a "terror of virtue", and key to understanding it is the role compassion had come to play in the minds and hearts of those who acted in the course of the French Revolution' (1963: 79). Compassion, with its gaze on concreteness and particularity, is inappropriate institutionally and destructive when it informs the acts of the 'virtuous' because it collapses the space in-between that commonality demands as constitutive of what it means to share a world.

> Because compassion abolishes the distance, the worldly space between men where political matters, the whole realm of human affairs, are located, it remains, politically speaking, irrelevant and without consequence ... As a rule it is not compassion which sets out to change worldly conditions in order to ease human suffering, but if it does, it will shun the drawn-out wearisome processes of persuasion, negotiation and compromise, which are the processes of law and politics, and lend its voice to the suffering itself, which must claim for swift and direct action, that is, for action with the means of violence.
>
> (1963: 86–7)

By the time we reach the later sections of the relevant chapter, 'les malheureux' have respectively given way to 'les faibles' and 'compassion' has given way to 'pity'.[18] Pity has a 'vested interest in the existence of the unhappy' (1963: 89) and, she explains, has also 'proved to possess a greater capacity for cruelty than cruelty itself'. *Proved* is an odd word here in the midst of the conceptual analysis, but Arendt has become impatient. All too quickly in *speaking for* others, what begins as compassion turns into pity, substitutes for decision making to become the 'cardinal virtue of the political' with the Jacobins, with the consequence

---

[18] And Rancière speaks of her 'assumption that modern democracy had been wasted from the very beginning by the "pity" of the revolutionaries for the poor people, by the confusion of two freedoms: political freedom opposed to domination, and social freedom opposed to necessity. In her view the rights of Man were not an ideal fantasy of revolutionary dreamers, as Burke had put it. They were the paradoxical rights of the private, poor, unpoliticized individual' (2004c: 298).

that *hypocrisy and mistrust* come to reign. This quasi-historiography that substitutes for political analysis continues: since the revolution had opened the gates of the political realm to the poor, this realm had indeed become 'social'. 'It was overwhelmed by the cares and worries which actually belonged in the sphere of the household and which, even if they were permitted to enter the public realm, could not be solved by political means, since they were matters of administration, to be put into the hands of experts, rather than issues which could be settled by the twofold process of decision and persuasion' (1963: 91). And further: 'Their [the revolutionaries'] need was violent, and as it were, pre-political; it seemed that only violence could be strong and swift enough to help them.' *Help them*? This dire section of *On Revolution* finds its disturbing culmination in the concluding paragraph where Arendt asserts: 'Nothing we might say today, could be more obsolete than to attempt to liberate mankind from poverty by political means; nothing could be more futile and more dangerous' (1963: 114). What began as an extraordinary analysis of the phenomenology of the revolutionary event, of the constituent and of the novelty of the concept of beginning, winds up as unabated bourgeois alarmism. And just as Arendt's was a disquieting refusal to turn politics toward questions of (material) distribution, it is also a disquieting refusal to accommodate demands of (social) recognition. As ever, any notion of solidarity must be measured against 'the grandeur of man' or the 'honor of the human race', and outwith such elevation it can mean nothing but the destruction of authentic politics at the hands of powerful moral passions and the derivative sentiments. This leaves *the malheureux* unworthy of solidarity, irredeemably lacking in both dignity and redress. For them, it seems, politically there is nothing that can be done.

What does Arendt leave us with as available interpretation of the French Revolution? Was it, then, merely a force of destruction, a demand for bread against existing distributions of wealth, weirdly indistinguishable from other *actions-against*? Would these include the violence in the South African townships, the Palestinian uprisings, the occupations of land and factories in South America? How disturbing it sounds to collect together these *acts of the 'mob'* across space and time, on the grounds that in all such cases the action is not undertaken toward sharing a world but claiming one, in other words because this action – although Arendt wouldn't dignify forms of random striking-out as action – is antagonistic rather than agonistic. Mob politics is not the politics of citizenship, and the political action of the French enragés, the unemployed and unemployable youths of Saint-Denis, of the Gaza strip, the dispossessed of Soweto and of Kayelitsa is denied the dignity of 'action' because it is the striking-out of the wretched. Any argument for *distribution* falls into the gap that opens up irredeemably between the social (poverty) and the political (formal equality). Because if we take the latter to find complete expression in the equal distribution of political rights amongst citizens to participate in the political transactions available to them constitutionally, then its fulfilment as constitutive *political* condition pits it against the aspiration of *social* equality. The distinction as harnessed to the logic of the bourgeois public sphere (what Lenin famously called 'the ideal political shell for capitalism') celebrates political empowerment on the back of an indifference to social conditions of engagement, and collapses any notion of equality as adequate to the promotion of dignity. Equality, split down the middle, ceases to do the gathering, rationalising work that would make it the genuine aspiration of the political. Any argument for *recognition* that might have carried the mob over to political subjecthood is cut at the root.[19] The will to overcome poverty by mass violence is viewed by Arendt as a 'negation of the negation', and no Hegelian negativity can do any work in the Arendtian world where recognition is either always-already or impossible as a *political* claim.

The Spectre of Antagonism

Arendt offers a critical phenomenology that promises to turn it reflexive, but what it delivers is a hollow phenomenology of the bourgeois public sphere. The 'failure' is instructive. We have followed her through the twists and turns of the argument. We will now pause to gather the elements so far: the analytical schema of the three dimensions of meaning; the phenomenology of the political; a first elaboration of the constituent as emergent and spontaneist; the way the spontaneity is circuited back to the institution forcing the constituent to *mutate* into the constituted; the idea of agonism, antagonism and critique.

The appearance of the political in Arendt combines it constitutively with contingency and 'frailty'. Along the three dimensions of its meaning, material, temporal and social, she offers us contingency, natality, and plurality respectively. These concepts mark the entry points into the political because they are moments of the pure constituent: these moments are underwritten by nothing but their own performance.

[19] Cf J.-P. Deranty and E. Renault (2009: 43).

She raises the stakes considerably by inviting us, repeatedly, to ask the foundational question: *what is the political and what are the conditions of thinking it?* If the stake is the appearance of the people on the scene of politics, it is with the help of those concepts and the distinctions they depend on, that political opportunity breaks into the world. That is Arendt's promise. And it is the radicality of these insights that attracted Negri to her 'fierce phenomenological exercise' before he became uneasy about a move that 'at the very moment when she illuminates the nature of constituent power Arendt renders it indifferent in its ideality or equivocal in its historical exemplification' (1999a: 17). Negri's criticism concerns the logic of a certain substitution that sustains the 'ideality' of constitutional practice against the *materiality* of the reproduction of social life. Negri's objection is correct, but it tells only part of the story. To cast it wider we must focus on how the logic of substitution gradually takes sway in Arendtian phenomenology (as it does in the massive oeuvre of 'radical' democratic theory that has been produced in its wake) which is constitutively tied to the denial of antagonism. Her painstaking drawing of distinctions forecloses the space for the appearance of the *antagonistic event*.

Her political phenomenology is instead launched on a platform that as agonistic (always-already) denies antagonistic speaking positions. Plurality means that conflict-dependent collective identifications and any historical density of constituent action must be denied *in the name of politics*; that speech must deny any instrumentality (Habermas, too, will later contrast communicative to strategic action); that political action *must* shed off social concerns and distance itself from work or labour; that representation *must* stand in for presence. Note that what is captured by this series of *imperatives* are the requirements of correct theory. Like all meta-level conditions they install conditions of legibility. The purity of the constitutional question demands that its statement in political terms proper is *its unburdening from the antagonistic dimension;* and the act of *claiming* falls outside the triad of 'forgiving', 'promising' and 'persuading' that jointly exhaust the modalities of political action. As a result *praxis philosophy* is domesticated in its *agonistic* form, in an introversion that cancels it out. As in ideology's most pervasive move, the enabling move displaces alternatives that are simultaneously subordinated and forgotten. If freedom cannot be dialectically tied to necessity it was because to address necessity was to fold or collapse the space for the appearance of freedom. There is no political space in which the social question can find political expression because political expression – the realm of the in-between, etc. – is what necessity *denies*. And so on. In each case we encounter the systematic withdrawal of that space of appearance; in each case the effacement is at the level of context, at the level of what opens up meaningfully to perception. The loss or disappearance of the antagonistic impacts constitutively on the theory of the political, each case a case of *impossible redress*.

In one of her rare engagements with what Marx *actually* said, Arendt said this of the *11th thesis on Feuerbach*:

> When Marx declared he no longer wanted to interpret the world but to change it, he stood, so to speak, on the threshold of a new concept of Being and world, by which Being and world were no longer givens but possible products of man.
>
> (2011: 171)

Her insight here reveals a rare moment of doubt as it lingers between the world as *made* and the world as *given*. She is leaning toward world-*making* but her world is *given* in terms of the intransigence her own framing conditions of what world-making entails, her stubborn opposition to any dialectic movement, her fixating on the separateness of spheres (political, social, personal) and on the principles proper to them: equality for the political, discrimination for the social, uniqueness for the personal. These principles of differentiation operate as conditions of appearance, and therefore as fundamental and constitutive of the possibilities of critique. If a tension appears in her thought between world-making and what is non-negotiable in that undertaking, it becomes resolved in the direction of a conservative endorsement of bourgeois constitutionality: the political is understood as incremental renewal of institutional givens, as divorced from the social question of need and against any collective speaking-position. These are framing conditions for the political, for what might appear on the scene of politics, and thus overdetermine political potentiality. Because they are operationalised to give visibility to the political, they cannot be observed and thematised *politically* themselves.

So as Arendt confronts in the eleventh thesis the critical injunction to which her philosophy most fervently attaches and which it most radically undercuts, we are left with this question: If our concern is about the social processes of de-politicisation and degradation, what to make of the endlessly renewed recourse of the political thinking of our time to the analytical categories Arendt insists on, that in a grotesque reversal of the eleventh thesis *describe* society in a way that guarantees that *it cannot be changed*?

1.2

Simone Weil: Necessity and Courage

> *Sophocle et tous les autres,*
> *Redites-nous la tragèdie et l'infamie de nos oublis*
> (Pierre Legendre)

Weil's Materialism

'C'est par le travail', writes Simone Weil, 'que le raison saisit le monde et s'empare de l'imagination folle.'[1] Work was for Weil, as Alain Supiot puts it, the 'site of our inscription in the natural order of the world; work puts our imagination to the test of reality' (Supiot, 2010b: 3). It is the medium of our engagement and the site where our creativity comes up against the materiality of practice, for Weil quite literally, with her preoccupation with work 'being brought up before matter devoid of lenience'.[2] Her philosophy of work, says Supiot, 'embeds itself and takes root [s'enracine] in the world of the factory' (2010b: 2). And what cost this embedding had for Weil, who suffered years of ill-health and depression in her insistence that the workers would not be *spoken for*, that only her own partaking in the practice would authorise her speaking position, one that this eternal outsider never properly managed to claim for herself.

Weil writes explicitly about what it means to 'seize the world' in a short treatise on Descartes (1996) that first introduces her thinking about action in the context of the *materiality* of practices. From her teacher Alain she had adopted the idea that 'the will does not exist except in action'. In the treatise she breaks decisively with Cartesianism in claiming that 'the self knows itself only in the action that it exercises on the exterior world',[3] and she will link the Cartesian motto constitutively to

---

[1] It is through work that reason ceases the world and partakes in its foolhardy imagination (Weil, 1987: 59).
[2] She describes it as 'matière sans indulgence' (Weil, 1955: 83).
[3] As per Jules Lagneu, quoted in Blum and Seidler (1989: 86).

the material practices of work. 'The pilot who in the tempest directs the tiller, the peasant who swings his scythe, knows himself and knows the world in the way expressed by the saying: "I think therefore I am"; and the whole cortege of ideas that goes with it.' (Weil, 1987: 59.)

'Enracinement', 'inscription', 'saisir', 's'emparer': words that connote immanence and engagement. And yet Weil remains forever a failed 'engagée' in a way that raises philosophically and politically pertinent questions. The first is about what it means to claim a speaking position, let alone to seize a world and take hold of its imaginary potential, under conditions of submission to necessity. This first question immediately raises a second one, about the power to initiate resistance: if one finds oneself always-already under conditions of submission which, for Weil, significantly entail a severing off of thought from action, from where does one *begin* to conceptualise resistance and redress? With these two questions of work-as-submission to necessity and the problem of inaugurating resistance, we are already on the terrain of ideology in the Marxist sense. From Althusser we could borrow the devastating sense of how the materiality of capitalist practices of extraction of surplus value exact allegiance, and of how, in their relentlessness (and Weil returns to this again and again), they *sever* thought from productive action. Althusser draws from Pascal to denote the brutal, unthinking insertion of the individual into material practices, where any spontaneous resistance to the inhumanity of such a 'calling' is countered with a gesture that is typical of all totalitarianisms: '*kneel and you shall believe*'.

Weil's was very much a response to her times, to the hopes fostered by the Russian Revolution, the horror of European fascism and the threat of the world war, and the political terrain on which she operated combined the tradition of French syndicalism and the communism of the second and third Internationals. French syndicalism, in particular its anarcho-syndicalist variant, deeply influenced Weil's political thinking.[4] Weil was particularly attracted to its *autogestionnaire* dimension, its opposition to organised interests, political parties and the state. What anarchism had brought to syndicalism at the turn of the century had been an emphasis on direct action, a vision of small-scale, decentralised economic organisation, and crucially the notion of *autogestion* that we shall consider at length later (4.3). In the early work, much of it written when she was in

---

[4] Alain Supiot speaks of 'le caractère sauvage et foisonnant de cette oeuvre qui ne se laisse ni enfermer dans une théorie achevée, ni réduire aux prismes disciplinaires' (2010b: 3).

her mid-twenties, Weil never strayed far from the idea that the working class can be the agent of the radical transformation of society. She writes: 'for power really to pass into the hands of the workers they would have to unite, not through the imaginary ties created by the community of opinion but through the real ties created by the community of their productive function'.[5] It is this emphasis on the community of work and material practice that attracts Weil to Marxism as a live tradition. Her relationship to Marxism is far from unambiguous,[6] and while she endorses Marx's affirmation of the dignity of labour and his analysis of how capitalism degrades the worker, she remains deeply critical of the theory of history, and departs radically from Marx when it came to the understanding of the moral foundations of political action. She also famously maintained a strong opposition to Leninism. For Weil it is nothing short of scandalous that Lenin, committed to retaining the methods of maximising productivity, and never challenged the form of the 'Taylorist' rationalisation of work. For Weil the extraction surplus value from labour is only part of the attack on workers' dignity, and that is why she chooses oppression rather than exploitation as the word that names the human damage.

Her urgent injunction to both the dominant traditions of political thought of her time is that they both miss the humiliations and indignities of factory work: liberalism by relying on the fictions of free contract, Marxism-Leninism by advancing a general theory of subordination with no attention to the micro-dynamics of oppression, the brutality of the organisation of work under Taylorism and Fordism. Ambivalence sets in at that point, as what attracts her to Marx – the theory of social labour in its emancipatory potential – is what she condemns in the unblinking pursuit of increased productivity, on whose altar (both in the West and in the Soviet Union) so many lives had been diminished. She admired Rosa Luxemburg's injunction to Lenin, regarding his proclamation of the 'factory as a school for discipline', that 'it is nothing but an incorrect use of the word when at one time one

---

[5] Quoted in Pétrement (1988: 76–7).
[6] Such ambivalence invoked a hostile response from a number of Marxists, though perhaps the most notable is that of Trotsky. When Weil published *Prospects* it provoked an uncharitable response by Trotsky: 'Despairing over the unfortunate experience of the "dictatorship of the proletariat" Simone Weil has found consolation in a new mission: to defend her personality against society. A formula of the old liberalism, refurbished by a cheaply bought anarchist exaltation.'

designates as discipline two so opposed concepts as the absence of thought and will in the mass ..., and the voluntary coordination of conscious political acts by a social stratum' (Luxemburg, 1904/1971: 291). For Weil productivity must be contained and limited by the value of dignity in work. She finds it in 'that which has been almost forgotten' by Marxism-Leninism, 'the glorification of productive labor, considered as man's greatest activity; the assertion that only a society wherein the act of work brought all of man's faculties into play, wherein the man who works occupied the front rack, would realize human greatness to the full' (1955: 154). If in the works of Marx, of Proudhon and of the revolutionary syndicalists there survived a tradition which put the dignity of productive labour at the centre of all social questions, there is also something profound here to be extracted from the link drawn between social labour and political action. Marx, as we will discuss at some length in the next chapter, connected the two, arguing that social labour harboured political potential and would release collective learning processes to be harnessed in revolutionary political action. While she shared with Luxemburg the premise that the vanguard party would stifle the spontaneous *autogestion* of the workers' movement to be expressed in its most radical form in the 'mass strike', she did not share Luxemburg's revolutionary optimism. For Weil 'progress' came with no historical guarantees; it could only 'ever play a moral rather than a historical role in political action' (Blum and Seidler, 1989: 45). The assertion of moral categories in political thinking is crucial to her, and that is why the attempt to separate affective from dispassionate (theoretical) thinking is one that Weil, more than most political thinkers, finds impossible to perform. Her reflection is emotion, her writing always about giving voice to those silenced, political engagement involving the urgency 'to bring everything into question again' (1955: 37). Not for Weil the world-historical mission of the working class, the liberation of the forces of production, or the assurance that the revolution is carried on the tide of history. If there is some connectedness to Marxism it is that her painstaking attentiveness to moral motivation, the attempt to recover the submerged and fractured vocabularies to redress the undercutting of symbolic, semiotic and moral economies, aims at the articulation of a *moral-democratic vocabulary of production*. It is her insistence on the intrinsically *collective* nature of labour that brings Weil closest to Marx, though there is little evidence that she had read the 1844 *Manuscripts*.

*

This brings us to Weil's argument about necessity. It is articulated in the context of the materiality of work, and against suffering that brings mute incomprehensibility.

There is no easy separation between the necessary and the contingent in Weil. At no point does she invite the question of how necessity *as such* may be shaken off. The materialist premise, foundational and irreducible, comes in the shape of necessity as embedded in practices of production. This is a premise that attaches to the human condition: the burden of necessity is always with man, but this accompaniment does not mean he is unfree so long as it can be thought about and acted on. Its demand on him is, in fact, *ennobling*.

Weil says:

> The source of any kind of virtue lies in the shock produced by the human intelligence being brought up against a matter devoid of lenience and of falsity. It is not possible to conceive of a nobler destiny for man than that which brings him directly to grips with naked necessity. Without his being able to expect anything except through his own exertion, and such that his life is a continual creation of himself by himself.
>
> (1955: 60)

Weil turns this into an argument for the intelligence and intelligibility of grappling with 'matter devoid of lenience'. Where Arendt struggles to safeguard the purity of reflection and praxis from their contamination by means-ends rationality, and contrasts it relentlessly with labour and work, Weil offers us something of a 'liberatory' instrumentality,[7] a rehabilitation of a thick notion of instrumental reason, such that might harbour meaningful social labour. In the direct contact with the material world, as André Gorz puts it, a 'manual intelligence which was impossible to formalize affirmed itself' (Gorz, 1989: 56). Against the kind of reductive understanding that sees 'the need of the master for assistants ... as the only company that grows out of workmanship' (Arendt, 1958: 161), Weil suggests an understanding of association that engages solidarity as constitutive. If the material dimension – *sachlich* we might call it more appositely in this context – of practice, and the *social*

---

[7] Borrowed from Mary Dietz: 'Weil's theory of action embraces a liberatory instrumentality' (873); Dietz goes on to suggest that 'Weil's notion of work is potentially compatible with Arendt's notion of interaction' (1994: 874). But if 'teamwork is only ever [conceived as] the routinised performance of motions that prohibits deliberation', Arendt stands unable to distinguish between 'instrumental action as utilitarian objectification and instrumental action as purposeful performance' (Dietz, 1994: 878).

dimension of solidarity, are at the root of the thinking of work, it is in the *temporal* dimension that Weil makes an important point about natural fit and proper measure. Her *Reflections* include an illuminating description of her experiences with the Newfoundland fishermen in which she notes that in primitive forms of production – hunting, fishing, gathering – 'action seems to receive its form from nature itself' (1955: 62). There is the all important reference to the *rhythm* which ties to the activity of work, which Weil will contrast to the monotonous uniformity of time that defines factory work. As Supiot puts it: 'Le temps du travail industriel n'est plus rythmé par l'effort, mais cadencé par le machine' (2010b: 10). There is nothing objectifying about the thicker notion of instrumentality that defines work. The freedom to bring the mind to grips with necessity defines labour in terms of what is 'wrought out of inert matter by human effort' and places it in a continuum with action and freedom. It is thus in necessity, understood now as the material embeddedness of action at the sites where labour is expended, that the thought-action continuum needs to be re-claimed. If this appeal to what is 'zweckrational' neither cancels out plurality nor diminishes freedom it is because, first, its aim ('zweck') involves a combination variously and jointly of human grappling with necessity; and, secondly, because the 'rational' component is oriented to accomplishing the aim in a way that restores the connection of thought to action. Weil here returns us to a materialist understanding of social labour where dignity and empowerment do not involve a flight from necessity but the free collective organisation of human intelligence and capacity in order to grapple with it.

'Thought is certainly man's supreme dignity' (1955: 105). It is a minimum threshold of dignified work that the worker is given a task the point of which he understands. She denounces management's monopoly on the understanding of the processes of work:

> The efforts of the modern worker are imposed on him by a constraint as brutal, as pitiless and which holds him in as tight a grip as hunger does the primitive ... [And yet] however tied and bound a primitive man was to routine and blind gropings [tâtonnements aveugles], he could at least try to think things out, to combine and innovate at his own risk, a liberty which is absolutely denied to a worker engaged in a production line.
>
> (1955: 77).

Dignified work, then, is about restoring a proper relation between thought and action, and the loss of connection between them devastates.

And she will characterise as 'tragic' the fact that 'although the work is too mechanical to engage the mind it nevertheless prevents one from thinking of anything else'. For Weil, '[t]he problem is therefore quite clear: it is a question of knowing whether it is possible to conceive of an organization of production which, though powerless to remove the necessities imposed by nature and the social constraint arising therefrom, would enable these at any rate to be exercised without grinding down souls and bodies under oppression' (Weil, 1955: 56). And for politics, the problem 'comes to this: to find, in conditions as they are [necessity], a form of society which would conform to the demands of reason and which at the same time would take into account necessities ... A method as materialist as this is absolutely necessary if good intentions are to be changed into actions' (Weil, 1978: 130). That is why the marked tendency to gather Weil's critique under the narrower sense of reification-as-machine-like work at the expense of her critique of reification on a broader plane that engages commodification at the level of recognition, misreads her political argument. It is the continuity between rationalisation and oppression that underpins her critique of Capitalism's great deformation of the relations of production, in the way it impacts on the worker's sense of self, value and speaking position. What comes undone (the severing of thought from action) generates compulsion and sustains oppression along all these dimensions.

It is in this way that Weil draws a separation within the realm of necessity which as materiality underpins human action, between a reality that allows dignity, cooperation and creativity to be realised, and one that collapses the space between thought and action. Much of Weil's courageous, often self-denying and self-destructive *agon* has to do with a heroic effort to reverse that collapse. It is heroic because the reversal is integrally linked to the logic of systemic reproduction, 'systemic' in a sense that Weil too would understand. What she sought was a reconnection of thought to action, but sought it in conditions that made the crossing back at least improbable, because systemic reproduction also undercuts the intellectual opportunity to take cognisance of it and resist it. We are here in the realm of ideology at its most pervasive: the imposition of a logic to work that makes action unthinking, and a rhythm that makes sustaining thought impossible other than as reflex. What recognition, then, of a speaking position under a flattening of experience that eliminates distance from the object of attention and radically undercuts initiatory action? Action in the face of this eclipse must first claim its stage.

But if methodical-instrumental thinking applied to work 'forms the human act *par excellence*', Weil's devastating account is of the inhumanity of the organisation of industrial work under capitalist conditions. I want to emphasise capitalist conditions because her staggered argument culminates in the combination of different elements: the submission to the machine and the smothering of methodical thinking; the managerial suffocation of the workplace; the withdrawal of recognition. In their combination the forms of disempowerment combine in the complex term *exploitation*. And in this, her indictment carries beyond the indignities of subjection to *industrial* discipline, to the indignities visited on workers today under the new management of under-employment.

First, regarding the smothering of autonomous thought. 'The spectacle of men over machines is nearly always one of wretched haste destitute of all grace and dignity' (1987: 61). Note the insistence on dignity and its compromise in man's submission to the machine, and thought-controlling motion. Her desperate insistence is to rescue out of this rhythm of necessity the possibility of *attention*, of the ability of thought to find a worthy object to attach to, that does not fragment into meaninglessness. We will return to this concept of hers, as well as to the *rhythms* that withdraw it. At each step, the connection between thought and action that emplaces us in the world is severed, and with it we have an absorption into a blind world of necessity.

Second, the emphasis on the removal of initiative from the workers is complex, and we must resist the temptation to reduce Weil's injunction against the submission to the machine to a critique of *automation*, in the way that, for example, Arendt does. Weil's indictment is a critique of exploitation. In the context of the latter she denounces management's monopoly on the understanding of the processes of work and her discussion of *human dignity* is central to this argument. For Weil, '[i]t matters little whether the actions in themselves are easy or painful: … pain and failure can make a man unhappy but cannot humiliate him as long as it is he himself who disposes of his own capacity for action' (1955: 58). Dignified work then is about restoring a proper relation between thought and action. The problem is the disruption of the relation between thought and its proper object that, given the centrality of work in Weil, withdraws familiarity and lifeworld, in her words the capacity '*to know one's way around the world.*'

The refusal to concede the separation of thought and action, the injunction against the indignities, culminate, in Weil's indictment, in an argument about *recognition*. How one preserves self-respect while locked into this submission becomes for Weil the main preoccupation, that emerges most poignantly during the time of her subjection to the 'discipline' of factory life. Her experience of how that submission leads to a feeling of 'counting for nothing' is pitted against learning, and the assumption of political capacity pitted, therefore, against the denial of recognition.

Weil's Hellenism

The Poem of Force

Weil's recourse to the Greeks concerns both the epic and the tragic genres. I will say less about the epic[8] because the spectrum of what the Greeks called tragic casts a longer shadow over Weil's 'agonism'. Like Arendt's hellenism, Weil's too exemplifies the phenomenology of the political, but not in Arendt's celebratory idiom of worldliness, but in the elusive world-disclosure that emerges under the weight of necessity, of its sweeping effacements and the reduction of the world to pure facticity. It is above all this preoccupation with necessity that draws Weil to the *Iliad*, the 'poem of force' of the age of Heroes. In the epic Weil gives us the most complete and uncompromising account of what it means to act with *courage* against the blinding exercise of force, in a way that discloses and makes appear humanity in its vulnerability. In tragedy the disclosure of humanity finds a more complex expression in the yieldings and 'blind gropings' of a thwarted agonism. In Arendt, and the literature that she has inspired, the ancient Greek notion of *agonism* has become paradigmatic in the thinking of the 'political'. The recourse to Weil at this juncture aims to put this political imaginary to question for its rather facile appropriation of a tradition that is a great deal more ambivalent about what constitutes and what withdraws the élan vital of politics than that which informs current agonisms.

Written in 1940, after the outbreak of the war, Weil's essay on the *Iliad* is a phenomenological exercise of rare insight. Weil begins it with a statement about force that reduces to object: 'The true hero, the true subject, the centre of the *Iliad* is force. Force wielded by man, force that subjects man, force before which man's flesh retracts . . . Force that turns

---

[8] For a longer treatment, see Christodoulidis (2020).

whomever is subjected to her to a thing.'⁹ The *Iliad* reflects force in its rawness, the sweep of sheer momentum, '*des forces aveugles qui ne sont qu'elan*' (27), as Weil beautifully puts it, on a register that 'no fiction intervenes to soften' (4). The mirror of another world, quotidian, ordinary, only serves to accentuate the violence and compulsion of the one lived in and toiled in. And on that continuum, in striking resemblance to the argument she had made earlier about the meaninglessness that ensues from repetition under the burden of necessity for industrial workers, she returns again to *time that endures*. Like workers toiling under meaning-shattering compulsion, the burden of necessity again undercuts reflexivity, undoes the constitutive connection between thought and action:

> The spirit is held at a pitch that it can withstand for only so long; but each new dawn brings the same necessity; day on day add up to years. The soul suffers violence every day. Every morning the soul mutilates itself of all aspiration, because thought cannot traverse [project itself across] time without encountering death. In this way war effaces all sense of purpose, including the sense of the aims of war. To be outwith the situation so violent makes it incomprehensible; to be in it makes its purpose unthinkable.
>
> (1940: 23)

There is something very interesting in this formulation, that I have rather loosely rendered as 'the spirit is held at a pitch that it can withstand for only so long',¹⁰ also in terms of our earlier discussion of the dehumanising rhythm of the machine, the darker recesses of necessity. And yet, if necessity shadows this world it is not in order to illustrate *that* that Weil writes the essay. Weil's text weaves itself through and around the epic to bring out a tension that alone *discloses a world*. What the *Iliad* achieves has to do with the fact that the disclosure is effected in and against the overwhelming context of force: the submission to necessity and an extraordinary attachment to life work *in tandem*. The epic itself delivers the tension irreducibly. I would suggest that this is a *tension that suspends the poem in grace*.

---

⁹ (All translations are mine unless otherwise indicated.) 'Le vrai héros, le vrai sujet, le centre de L'Iliade, c'est la force. La force qui est maniée par les hommes, la force qui soumet les hommes, la force devant quoi la chair des hommes se rétracte ... La force, c'est ce qui fait de quiconque lui est soumis une chose.' (1940: 3)

¹⁰ In the original: 'L'esprit est alors tendu comme il ne peut souffrir de l'être que peu de temps'.

The epic is strung between two poles. The first is, as we saw, necessity. The other is what Weil identifies as 'cette influence indéfinissable de la presence humaine' (1940: 8) – an indefinable influence of human presence, in contexts of an improbable reciprocity. Because with no outside leverage or warrant, no institutional dimension or framework of solidarity, no 'proper distance' or public space, this is reciprocity that is lifted out of the contexts of necessity only through *attention*. Here we come to Weil's precious contribution. Attention inserts the distance between that which is understood as 'pure momentum', impacts as fact, and is lived as compulsion, and a reflexivity that endows life with grace. In *Gravity and Grace* she had relied on the language of *mystery* to invoke that which is attentive to otherness, to reciprocity, to the 'ethical constitution of the self' which is co-original with attention. It would be a misreading of Weil to see this constitutive moment as preceding, underlying dialectically, or otherwise linked to that of necessity. For if there is grace there is also the gravity of the world. Force inscribes itself in the world in a way that allows neither distance nor overcoming. *It is lived as contradiction.* Weil says: 'That a human being can be a thing, there is in this, from the logical point of view, contradiction: but when the impossible becomes reality, the contradiction comes to tear the soul' (1940: 8).[11]

But if *attention* interrupted necessity in its tracks, the bewildering distribution of chance in the *Iliad* confronts necessity with contingency: the epic is shot through by an overwhelming sense of the randomness in the distributions of fortune, accentuated by the ceaseless capricious acts of the Gods, their petty changing of sides, their gut reactions, likenesses and fancies, their authorised and unauthorised (by convention or command) interventions in the fates of the warriors. And of course fates that change so radically over the course of *the Iliad* will change again. The audience knows well how short-lived even the glory of Troy's conquest was, how the Greek kings, looters of Troy, in turn faced the loss of their worlds as the age of the heroes came to a close: Achilles slain on the battlefield by the arrow of Apollo, Agamemnon slain on his return to Mycenae, Ajax's descent into madness, Odysseus's tortured journey back and the loss of his comrades to a man.

---

[11] 'Qu'un être humain soit une chose, il y a là, du point de vue logique, contradiction; mais quand l'impossible est devenu une réalité, la contradiction devient dans l'âme déchirement' (1940: 8).

Let us pause on this random distribution of fortunes, this geometry of luck ('géometrie de hasard'). For Weil it is planned, balanced, distributed by the Gods. From the *Iliad:*

> Then Zeus the father took his golden scales / In them he put the two fates of death that cuts down all men / One for the Trojans, tamers of horses, one for the blonde-haired Greeks / he seized the scales by the middle/ it was the fatal day for Greece that sank.

Why does Weil talk of an 'extraordinary sense of equity' as traversing the *Iliad*? This is her in one of the essay's most important passages:

> Since other people do not impose on their movements this interval of pause from which alone proceeds our regard – our attentiveness – to our brethren, they conclude that fate has given all license to them, and none to their inferiors. Beyond this point they exceed the measure of force at their disposal ... The penalty of a geometrical rigour, operating to punish automatically the abuse of force was the main subject of Greek thought. It constitutes the soul of the epic. Under the name of Nemesis it is the main source of the tragedies of Aeschylus.
>
> (1940: 16)

This is a tradition that has been lost to the world, Weil explains. 'We are only geometricians before matter; the Greeks were, first of all geometricians in their apprenticeship to virtue.' (1940: 16)

This passage provides a bridge to Greek tragedy. While 'apprenticeship in virtue' recalls an Aristotelian vocabulary that is not, emphatically not, the vocabulary of the tragic poets, Weil's thought here captures what was quintessential to the Greek concept of tragedy, with all the complexity and nuance that attends this notion in the trajectory of tragic theatre during the 'short' century of its development in Athens. That all tragedy is about excess and force – in the way that Weil describes it as the 'inevitable loss of measure' – is expressed famously in tragedy as *hubris*. Tragedy is about *aporia*, and in each case what assumes the form of hubris is the hero's blindness to there being no solution afforded them. But, if with the tragic poets, force is bereft of the comprehension of its exercise, which is only reserved for the Gods, then the geometry of 'virtue' is undone in tragedy, because there is no possible correlation to its measured deployment in the world of mortals. And yet a certain geometry of rigour remains, impenetrable, impossibly demanding and tragically devastating. As we will see in the next section, in its last phase, with Euripides' radicalisation of the genre of tragedy during its twilight phase, the disconnect between the two geometries pushes against the limits of its form.

Tragedy, Necessity, Rationality Undone

> Attic tragedy, at least that of Aeschylus and Sophocles, is the true continuation of the epic. The thinking of justice enlightens it without ever intervening in it; here force appears in its coldness and harshness, always attended by consequences whose fatality cannot be evaded by neither those who deploy it nor those who suffer it. The humiliation of the soul under its grip is neither disguised nor enveloped in facile pity nor held up to scorn; more than a being hurt or degraded by misfortune it is held up to admiration.
>
> (Weil, 1940: 35)

There is no space here for a comprehensive discussion of tragedy, and we must therefore follow a selective route. And the cue we take is from the omission of the third great tragic poet from Weil's list of those who 'continue the epic'. It is a perplexing omission not least because Euripides was the poet most explicitly insistent on 'necessity'. It is Euripides that reminds us in *Alcestis*, that *'Ananke [Necessity], mother of the fates,* and of Nemesis, has neither altars nor statues in the Greek World'. As Roberto Calasso notes, Euripides 'also offers a comment that "nothing more powerful" can be encountered. She pays no heed to sacrifices' (1994: 72).

It is not clear whether Weil had read Nietzsche's *Birth of Tragedy* but Nietzsche, in that work of his youth, similarly singles out Euripides and then showers him with scorn for sacrificing what is at the very heart of tragedy, the *mythical.*

> Even though you, you presumptuous Euripides ... hunted out all the passions from their beds and charmed them into your circle, even though you sharpened and filed a really sophisticated dialectic for the speeches of your heroes – nevertheless your heroes have only fake, masked passions and speak only a fake, masked dialogue. And because you abandoned Dionysus, you were then abandoned also by Apollo.[12]

Nietzsche is referring here to the holding together *in sublime tension* of the Apollonian and Dionysian moments – the *'Kunsttriebe'* ('artistic impulses') – that he famously argued constituted the great achievement of tragedy. The Dionysian moment enters tragedy from the music and

---

[12] Nietzsche continues: 'What did you want when you sought to force the dying man [a metaphor here for "myth"] once more into your cheerful service? He died under your powerful hands ... And as myth died with you, so with you died the genius of music as well ...'. Nietzsche, *The Birth of Tragedy*, 1872, section X. I have used the translation by Ian Johnston (Vancouver: Richer Resources Publications, 2009).

the dances of the τραγωδοι (those who 'sang in goatskins') where echoed the single utterance, more cry than signifier, with which for centuries Dionysus was to be evoked: ευοι. The Apollonian moment is the achievement of logos. Tragedy is the vehicle for the *expression* of this incongruence, where the Dionysian excess grafts itself, improbably, on the unfamiliar register of the word, vests itself as logos in order to emerge onto the plane of the rational with the opportunity for the first time to bring to expression the deeper recesses of the mythical. The Homeric 'naivety' (the term is Schiller's) is the predominance of the Apollonian 'illusion' that gave form to those ideals of beauty, courage, etc., that allowed the Greeks, however briefly, to transcend the compulsion of necessity and affliction with the 'aesthetic offer' of the Olympians.[13]

It is with the great exponents of the genre, Aeschylus and Sophocles, that this is achieved. And for Nietzsche it is Euripides who spectacularly collapses it, spectacularly because of the *beautiful* shallowness of his verse. The failure of Euripides was to submerge the Dionysian moment, 'charming' it in 'sophisticated dialectic' and in his extraordinary, 'luminous', verse, that Nietzsche identifies as a 'rationalisation'. And Euripides gradually morphs into Socrates in Nietzsche's narrative, and at times he talks of them interchangeably. Nietzsche of course had no time for the wordsmith Socrates and he reserves for Euripides a similar contempt for having traded in the sublime fusion of the Apollonian and Dionysian moments for the 'dialectic' of Socrates' rationalism, which leads, for Nietzsche, to the collapse of what in its great moments (in Aeschylus and Sophocles) the tragic holds in tension and in mutual enablement.

*

We can locate the shift that troubles Nietzsche and that he dismisses so passionately, already in Euripides' *Iphigenia in Aulis*. There is indeed something that bears out Nietzsche's insight here and it inheres in the play's radical re-conceptualisation of the meaning of *sacrifice*; the sacrifice that is the focus of the tragedy involves a *secularisation* and with it an altogether different register and economy of exchange, that chimes well with what Nietzsche condemns as Euripides' unacceptable *ekfylismos* (debasement) of the tragic genre. In the play Iphigenia is led to the altar

---

[13] With the transition from the terror of the *theogony* of the Titans (amongst whom *Anange* (Necessity)), to that of the Olympian Gods, a people so attuned to affliction began to reflect in the image of those gods the image of beauty and joy. See Vernant (1962).

on the irresistible promise of a marriage to Achilles. What she does not know is that it has been mandated that only her sacrifice will appease the Gods and allow the Greek fleet, desperately marooned in windless Aulis, to depart for Troy. Odysseus has concocted the plan to lure Agamemnon's daughter to Aulis on this false promise, and she is led in her bridal dress to the altar by Agamemnon himself. When her fate is revealed, when she realises Agamemnon will not yield to her imploring, when she realises the inevitability of the 'wicked spilling of blood by a wicked father', what she comes to recognise as justification extraordinarily refers *not* to cosmology or the dictates of the Gods *but* to a human order and economy of sacrifice: it is because her death will allow 'the Greeks to rule over the barbarians rather than the barbarians over the Greeks' that she is willing to die, because 'the barbarians stand for slavery and the Greeks for freedom'. 'When a speech like this', writes Roberto Calasso, 'pours rapidly, confidently, from the mouth of the virgin of Mycenae, it's clear that any cosmic vision of sacrifice has already foundered. Sacrifice here no longer has to do with the equilibrium between gods and men but between men and other men, between the "kings of men" and the dangerous multitude milling around the tents' (Calasso, 1994: 108).

This first *pro patria mori* marks Euripides' extraordinary departure from the cosmic architecture of tragedy that is structured across the relationship between gods and men, the deciphering of the will, the overstepping of the limit, the learning through suffering. He brings to it a moment of secularisation (of sacrifice) that collapses the 'cosmic scaffolding that had stood between gods and men', and with the collapse, says Calasso, 'life seemed to be more buoyant and resplendent but lonely too' (Calasso, 1994). For my part, I do not think that it is splendour or liberation that comes with the collapse of the 'scaffolding' in Euripides, but something altogether more desperate that undoubtedly clutches at life; Iphigenia says in the same speech: 'To look into the light is the sweetest thing for a mortal; what lies beneath the earth is nothingness.' (Euripides, *Iphigenia in Aulis*, 1318, 1378, 1250-1.)

Note all that withdraws here, with Euripides, away from the 'theological' idiom of Aeschylus and in the direction of the human condition. But one can add more. For a genre that pivots on *hubris*, in a world replete with it, Euripides reserves a more limited role for it because the human adventure has cut adrift from the divine 'geometry of virtue' – remember Weil – that underlay the tragedies of Aeschylus and Sophocles. Take the *Medea*. If there is hubris here it is Jason's unwavering defence of the principles and institutions of the polis (that sanction and support his parental power and role). The conflict in that tragedy is one of registers: Medea enters the Hellenic world directly from a world of myth and through the sacrifice of her brother; she exits that world again by a similar act of killing her own. These are acts that can be neither assimilated nor comprehended by the world that Jason inhabits, for whom relations are governed by a whole different economy. It is perhaps the genius of Euripides that at some level redeems this storming of the world that Jason represents, and that his audience inhabit, by a mythical force – Medea's. What role hubris plays in all this, and who stands to learn, is something that the play fundamentally unsettles. But it is worthy of note that in this collision of worlds, a distribution of rationality and irrationality that *still* bears the hallmarks of the genre, of the refracted will of the gods, of hubris, and of tragic choice, is present, if now precariously.

But then we come to *Helen*, Euripides' penultimate tragedy. This, in a nutshell, is the plot of the play. Drawing on an unfamiliar version of the myth associated with the poet Stesichoros, Euripides opens the play with Helen on the banks of the Nile in Egypt.[14] In fact she was never in Troy; it was a double, a phantom (an '*eidolon*') that Paris had taken with him to Troy.[15] She resides in the palace of the king, Proteus, and is keen to avoid marriage to his son Theoklymenos. Teucer, brother of Ajax and celebrated archer, lands in Egypt on the way back from Troy, to consult the priestess Theonoe, all-knowing daughter of Proteus. He is on his way to Cyprus to found the *new* Salamis. His father had exiled him from Salamis, never having forgiven him for not preventing his brother's descent into madness. He sees the 'hated' Helen on the banks of the Nile and tells her of the looting of Troy and of the presumed death of her

---

[14] This is Stesichoros' *Palinode* addressed to Helen of Troy (fragm 192, *Poete melici Graeci*):

> No, there is no truth in that story,
> No, you didn't ride in the well-rowed ships,
> No, you never came to the towers of Troy.

The *Palinode* is referred to in Plato's dialogue *Phaedrus* (243a) where Socrates suggests that Stesichoros 'who was a philosopher and knew the reason why' he had found himself blinded for 'reviling the lovely Helen', unlike Homer 'who never had the wit to discover why he was blind', at once sat down to compose the *Palinode* – (the counter-ode) – to absolve Helen of all blame for the Trojan War. 'He recognised the cause and purged himself. And the purgation was a recantation ... Immediately his sight returned to him.'

[15] Also echoed in Christa Wolf's beautiful *Cassandra* (2000: 102–3): '"Father," [Cassandra] said urgently, "No one can win a war waged for a phantom."'

husband Menelaos, shipwrecked in the Aegean. Helen decides to ask Theonoe about the truth of Teucer's words and finds out that her husband is still alive. In the next scene Menelaos makes his ship-wrecked appearance, is understandably disbelieving having been accompanied from Troy by the phantom-Helen, and there follows a scene of eventual mutual recognition and a giving of reasons and promises, not before a messenger comes to tell him that his phantom-wife has (conveniently) disappeared. They plan to escape together or die, and Theonoe is persuaded to keep silent after hearing the couple's pleas. The remainder of the play is about tricking Theoklymenos into entrusting Helen with a ship and crew (under the pretext of disposing of her dead husband's ashes), an escape that is attempted, and finally guaranteed, by the appearance of the celestial twins Castor and Pollux, brothers of Helen.

I want to argue that in this farce we encounter the most *philosophical* of Euripides' plays. There will be objections. *Helen* is no *Medea*, it is long-winded, chatty, the long-awaited reunion of Helen and Menelaos unworthy of either of them. It is also not *quite* a tragedy, a discussion that has carried on forever.[16] It has, of all things, a happy ending! There is no obvious hubris, nor overstepping, no learning to be had through suffering because the suffering is relieved, not introduced, in the play. Everything appears a matter of luck, with no obvious link back to responsibility. The chorus is forever going off on tangents, and who can blame it? Some of the choric odes are only tenuously linked to the action, and the final one, the culmination, *not at all*! The *deus ex machina*, Euripides' hallmark device, solves nothing even at the level of appearance: it is comforting to know that Helen's brothers have come to the rescue but the couple were already on their way. And surprisingly: why is Theonoe, the all-knowing priestess who is close at hand throughout the 17 years of Helen's sojourn on the Nile, never been asked about what happened in Troy or the whereabouts of Menelaos? (Helen learns about all this from Teucer, in the first act, and then Teucer disappears from the play without trace.) I would suggest that these problems, variously criticised, are all facets of the kind of radicalisation that Euripides is now introducing to the tragic genre.

We must remember that Euripides writes *Helen* in one of his darkest moments, in terms of both his personal life and the history of Athens. The writing of the play is dated back to 412 BC, at which time, facing

---

[16] Indicatively, Lattimore (1957) on why it is, Webster on 'not taking it too seriously' (1967) and Segal on why the distinction is 'irrelevant' (1971).

charges of impeachment in Athens, he has abandoned his beloved city to take refuge in the Court of the Macedonian King. Athens has just suffered the greatest military defeat of its history. The 'Sicilian expedition' that marked the end of the second phase of the Peloponnesian War, had gone disastrously wrong. Athens' ill-conceived attempt to extract wealth from Sicily, marked by the same colonial brutality that had characterised the sacking of Melos a year earlier, had collapsed, and with it Athens had lost, it is estimated, a quarter of its adult male population. So why has Euripides allowed the war that precipitates the end of Athens to be reflected in that other great war, the Trojan war that wiped out a whole race of heroes, and be told as a farce, a futile expedition over a phantom?

Tragedy was never intended as a critique of institutions or policy choices and I am not suggesting that *Helen* should be read at that level; this is not Euripides making a political point. What is at stake is something a great deal more profound that only the unity of the work of Euripides can allow us to comprehend. Let us return to Teucer for that. He has encountered Helen on the banks of the Nile. He is dumbfounded. What to make of this appearance in Egypt of the woman over whom occurred the extraordinary carnage at Troy? In a verse sometimes attributed to him, sometimes to the messenger, he says:

$$Τι \; φης; \; / \; νεφελης \; αρ \; αλλως \; ειχομεν \; πονους \; περι; \; (706/7)^{17}$$

and later, the chorus will ask:

$$ο \; τι \; θεος \; η \; μη \; θεος \; η \; το \; μεσον; \; (1137).^{18}$$

These are extraordinary lines, lines that celebrate and re-define what is most profound about Greek poetry. The question that has preoccupied the Greeks, that will preoccupy them for centuries to come, the problem of right action, of '*orthōs prattein*', here reaches an impasse that confronts the hero with the limits of the rational. With the tragic poets before this, with Aeschylus and Sophocles, the answer to '*orthōs prattein*' comes with a 'learning obtained through suffering' (*pathonta gnōnai*). There is of course the irreducible role of luck in human lives, there are no secure answers and the good is multifaceted. Nevertheless, against this play of contingency, the *will of the gods* is there to be interpreted through the signs, and the tragic hero, who is compelled to do what is his

---

[17] [What are you saying? All this suffering for a cloud [phantom]?]
[18] [What is god, what not god, and what separates the two?]

undoing, is admonished for hubris, for failing to respond appropriately and hence, also, to have squandered the possibility of learning.[19]

If we go deeper into the architecture of tragedy we will see that it comes with certain givens. The first is that there is a divine Will and a divine justice. And that Zeus, or the gods (plural), represents the unity of reference. That Will has been refracted into ungatherable parts, and access to it, if access is the right word, can only be effected through the particular, the fragment of the whole. In committing *hubris* the tragic hero is guilty of a substitution. The hero has generalised the partial, taken the fragment for the whole,[20] and thus claimed to know what the gods willed on the basis of that generalised partiality. Men occupy positions across the spectrum of the refracted will and what has been refracted cannot be traced back to its underlying unity. Throughout each of the tragedies Zeus remains silent. In his silence is assumed the balance of the contradictory elements of reality, and the holding together of the practical, the ethical and the aesthetic, the separation of the unity of which will herald the birth of modern man (Axelos, 1962). But in the ancient world these contradictory facets of what is constitutive of action – of *prattein orthos* – are held together in what perhaps Weil tried to capture with the term 'geometry of virtue'. The point that the tragic poets made over and over again was that this geometry was unknown and unknowable to mortals, because the will can only be represented at the level of its unity, not recollected through its fragments; and yet that geometry held the key to what could be aspired to. That is why the names reserved for Zeus are '*deinos*' (awe-inspiring) and '*anoikios*' (inhospitable); because his will cannot be known *as such*.

This is the picture that Euripides' tragedies dent, breach and now, with *Helen* (and finally with the *Bacchae*), shatter. First, the unity of the myth is broken, with his catastrophic variation of the story of the Trojan War (Stesichoros' precedent was never more than a playful tease). If 'learning through suffering' is what is at stake, Teucer's despairing question: 'all this suffering for a phantom?' puts the stake to question. Again and again the question of the relation between reality and appearance is

---

[19] To choose just one example, Oedipus in *Oedipus Tyrannus* was 'unable to recognise any dimension of his life's meaning other than the one he already knew'. In this sense 'he denied the possibility of tragedy until he was overwhelmed by it' (Lear, 1998: 50).

[20] Agamemnon attaches the rightness of action to kingship not fatherhood, Creon to ruleship not family ties, Antigone to family duty not citizenship, Prometheus to his love for man not duty to the gods, etc.

posed – scholars tell us it is repeated nearly 30 times in 1,700 lines. And where in tragedy previously, the gods entered a dialogue-of-sorts with the tragic heroes, even where the latter were bound to mis-read the signs, now in *Helen* the possibility of *any* reading collapses. Where is the reference in this to any divine will, reason of justice, what oblique unity is one meant to glimpse behind the multi-faceted? *Everything equivocates.* Helen was both in Troy and in Egypt. Paris has both possessed her and not. Menelaos possesses both the adulterous Helen-eidolon that Paris possessed and the Helen on the Nile that, she keeps assuring him, no other man possessed (the deeply conservative, brilliant mythologist Johann Bachofen comments in 1861 that 'Helen is not decked out with all the charms of Pandora in order to give herself to the exclusive possession of *one*').[21] If *spectral* is the speech-act that involves a dislocated speaking position, this accumulation of dislocations creates a play of mirrors. Even Helen's saviours appear in double, in this other play of the spectral, Helen having been a twin to her twin brothers. Theonoe has only 'the shrine in her heart' to guide her out of this double-play. It is for this that the chorus concludes, devastatingly:

> 'what is God, what not God, and what separates the two?'

In this world that allows no passage except random striking-out even the *deus ex machina* retreats to a meaningless formality, a moment of uninterpretable *decision*, leaving no space to 'learn through suffering', leaving merely suffering, nothing but the random distribution of fates, a Beckettian farce.[22]

But this has led afar, and it is time to pull some of it back to our discussion of necessity for the Greeks in these years of Athenian democracy fraught with calamity and the beginning of the end of its extraordinary brilliance. I have argued that the rationalisation of tragedy, that Nietzsche does not forgive Euripides for, is in fact a radicalisation that pushes the genre to the limit, and in that sense one that in fact reflects a deeper continuity with the other tragic poets. It also closes the cycle of tragedy in the most profound and irrevocable way. Euripides does this with the *Bacchae*, with which the Apollonian moment of 'logos',

---

[21] Quoted in Bloch (1986: 106).
[22] As in Hölderlin, *Stumm ist der Delphische Gott / ... / Ohne göttliches unser Geschlecht / Und immer und immer unfruchtbar / Wie die Furien, bleibt die Mühe der Armen* (Mute is the Delphic God/ ... / our kind is without the Godly/ and always, always sterile/ like the furies / stays the toil of the poor).

which in *Helen* has come undone, is overflown by the 'last force of the old nature' and disappears into the recesses of the Dionysian return to the ecstatic, to paroxysm (*'paralerema'*) and the irrational [the α-λογον]. One might pause to ask this: what other tradition in the history of art has come to an end *irrevocably* on a sublime note? The *Bacchae* is the very final tragedy that the extraordinary century of Athens produced; it closed that cycle because it left nothing else to say in the tragic genre. A different answer had to be found to chance writ large, to contingency running amok, where the possibility of appropriate response had become a nonsense. That answer was provided a decade later by Plato in the form of the excision of contingency altogether, *the banning of the poets from the republic,* that marks the endeavour to seal off rationality from chance, and to make lives immune to luck.

Weil's Wager

Let us now tentatively retrace this discussion of immunity and luck, of necessity and tragedy, back to Simone Weil. Not that there is ever a moment of hubris in Weil, her intense commitment tempered by a humility before human need and weakness. But *unyielding* is her engaged and nuanced attention to how necessity frames the human condition and what it dictates to it. If her un-worldliness, the extraordinary 'forgetfulness of self' – that those who encountered her so often found remarkable[23] – is important here it is not a moment of (tragic) unyielding, but something else. In her essay on the *Iliad*, as we saw, she wrote of how the Greeks exhibited a 'geometrical' sense of proportion which she correlated to a geometry of virtue. In a letter to her brother she returns to that thought: 'If by the sense of *disproportion between thought and the world* you mean the sense of being an exile in the world, then I agree: the Greeks experienced intensely that the soul is in exile.' And returning to necessity: 'But such a feeling does not involve anguish however, but only bitterness ... More than any other people the Greeks possessed a feeling of necessity. It is a bitter feeling, but it precludes anguish' (in McLellan, 1989: 159). Embeddedness was what she craved, exile what she faced. And her final book, *l'Enracinement,* was all about rootedness

---

[23] From a student's impressions of her: 'everything about her emanated a feeling of total frankness and forgetfulness of self, revealing a nobility of soul that was certainly at the root of the emotions she inspired in us, but that at first we were not aware of', quoted in McLellan (1989: 4).

(a term that signifies *accomplishment* rather than *lack* as suggested by the English translation *The Need for Roots*). And we might ask whether at the time of writing the letter, her courage too wasn't waning. A certain futility of the *agon* is reflected in her essay on the poem of force, her counter-positioning of rigour and virtue, the submission of lives to necessity, the advent of disproportion, the severing of action from thought.

If rootedness is so cherished a property for Weil, it is because her own world was so painfully adrift. The *mediating* institutions to which she dedicated her short life never really allowed it properly to embed in the contexts of reciprocity that she desired to belong: the workplace, the union, the schools for the workers, the Durruti column in the Spanish civil war, the organisation of the Free French in London. These were all attempts to *forge* reciprocity, solidarity and community. And her *L'Enracinement* (1949/2002) is a personal testimony of how these mainstays of the *human condition* – to reclaim the term from Arendt's *deracinated* worldliness – cannot be hoisted out of *any* set of givens *whatsoever*, that their recall already presupposes a certain 'thickness' on the ground. On no ground does Weil's passion for justice find a home, forever resistant, forever strange, her contradictions real, experienced with no promise of redemption or overcoming. Hers is a liberty asserted against necessity and as acted upon and acted out *truer* for that,[24] on the register that we identified as *tragic*.

For now let us remain with the aspiration of 'rootedness' (*enracinement*), of the initiation and partaking of action that is in *media res*, and thus undertaken in the 'thick of' practices that, to a variable extent, are framed by necessity. It is because action has to be reflective that it must gain distance from what installs itself in the life of men as necessary. That is why the stakes for initiatory political action are so demanding. It is against necessity that its task will be undertaken and measured. And have we not come full circle to where we began, with the need to make rational the suffering experienced by those subjected to necessity, and to draw clearly that line between the necessary and the unnecessary forms of suffering that is the site and sign of political reflexivity? There is a certain tragic dimension to this agonism of Weil's, an existential dialectic that never comes close to synthesis. More than anyone else, for Weil *the wager of political action* demands courage; for her it involved a

---

[24] The allusion here is to Blum and Seidler's book of 1989 *A Truer Liberty*.

commitment to truths she refused to forsake in the teeth of the bitter experience of failure and disappointment at so many turns. This is what she writes in *Oppression and Liberty*:

> The only question that arises is whether we should or should not continue the struggle; if the former then we shall struggle with as much enthusiasm as if victory were assured. There is no difficulty whatever, once one has decided to act, in maintaining intact, on the level of action, those very hopes which a critical examination has shown to be well-nigh unfounded; in that lies the very essence of courage.
>
> (1955: 22)

It is a courage that she maintains unwavering along the whole trajectory of the unfolding of necessity, through the political writings, her defence of work, the subsequent turn to the Greeks and to Christianity and the account of the 'gravity of the world'. In *Gravity and Grace*, as if a note on tragedy, she will write: 'All true good carries with it conditions which are contradictory and as a consequence is impossible. He who keeps his attention really fixed on this impossibility and acts will do what is good.' In that context Weil's heroic effort carries the commitment, pursued within the sphere of immanence, on the factory floor and in the classes she ran for workers, that a different understanding and organisation of work might be counter-posed to the world of brutality and compulsion. What to make of the urgency to act out this counter-factual – and to do so courageously – in full knowledge that *the wager* will be 'shown to be well nigh unfounded' and that there is no telling whether *history is on one's side or not?* Nevertheless she will be clear about the task at hand: to 'work toward a clear comprehension of the object of our efforts, so that, if we cannot accomplish that which we will, we may at least have willed it' (1955: 23).

She died in August 1943 in Kent at the age of 34. According to the coroner's report, the cause of death was 'cardinal failure due to myocardial degeneration of the heart muscles due to starvation and pulmonary tuberculosis'. She had stopped eating. John Berger quotes her in his 'A Girl like Antigone': 'There is a natural alliance between truth and affliction because both of them are mute supplicants, eternally condemned to stand speechless in our presence' (Berger, 1996: 122).

*

It would be too easy to *contrast* this 'difficult worldliness' and the thwarted promise of work that fully enjoys its product, to a certain reading of Marxism where the shaking off of compulsion is carried in the teleology of history. But there is a dissident Marxism closer to Weil, that takes leave of these certainties; that places centre stage not the telos but the wager of history; where the redemption waged seems to accrue increasingly long odds against it; and where the immanence of action unfolds 'an existential dialectic ... that never attains ultimate synthesis' (Cohen, 1994: 277). This is Lucien Goldmann's 'tragic Marxism' where, like the Zeus of Greek tragedy, the redeeming God remains a *Dieu Caché* (Goldmann, 1955).[25]

A brilliant student of Lukács', Goldmann is part of the French wave of Marxism of the 1960s, but remains at odds with both its dominant trends of the time, rejecting the 'corresponding and complementary' positions of Althusser's structuralist and Sartre's existentialist Marxism. Against the Cartesian ego he sets Pascal's 'sentence that is perhaps outrageous though practically a manifesto: "*Le moi est haïssable*"'[26] – too hateful to sustain a political subject-position proper. Pascal's idea is that man is not a self-sufficient monad but a partial element in a whole which transcends him. Following Pascal, Goldmann's suggestion, rendered in the rather cumbersome terminology of 'trans-individualism', sustains 'as foundation of history' the dialectic of political subjectivity, 'the relation between man with other men, the fact that the individual "I" exists only against the background of community'. The individual *Verstand* (Hegel's term for the shallow non-dialectical understanding) is dialectically transcended into the trans-individual *Vernunft* (Hegel's term for Reason).[27] And this (trans-individual) action-in-concert, while inescapably immanent and class-inflected, if oriented toward universality, that is 'not toward a particular sector of the global social organisation but toward this global organisation as such' (Lowy, 1997: 29) will allow the passage to a real 'comprehension of social realities'. And while Goldmann never takes the dialectic as far as his teacher Lukács did, the early work carries something of that optimism and, in combining it with Heidegger, also the

---

[25] Goldmann's very particular take on Marxism is developed in his major work of 1955 *The Hidden God*. With its publication something truly novel breaks onto the scene. It carries the subtitle: *A Study of Tragic Vision in the Pensées of Pascal and the Tragedies of Racine*. What attracts Goldmann to Pascal's seventeenth-century Jansenism is that its 'tragic and non-revolutionary character' 'allowed it to avoid some of the illusions of progressivist rationalism' (Goldmann, 1955, quoted in Lowy, 1997: 33).

[26] Trans: 'the "I" is hateful'. In Goldmann, 1955/2016: 24.

[27] For this key Hegelian distinction, see Chapter 1.4.

promise of authenticity of human community.[28] Goldmann is adamant that a coherent ethics can only be articulated in connection to community and, like Weil, refuses to attribute either teleology or determinism to processes in which individuals are *active* in shaping the meaning of history and of collective action. Any situation harnessed to the activity of those involved cannot follow laws of motion. The opposition to Althusser and Sartre confined him to the periphery of Marxist thought, and in the last decade of his life he became drawn to the dissident Marxism of André Gorz.

If we return to Goldmann's fascinating work it is not only because for him dialectical thought is heir to the anxieties of the tragic vision of the world. It is above all because Pascal's notion of the *wager* runs like a golden thread through *The Hidden God*, to reconceptualise the meaning of Marxism as a revolutionary wager. The wager is placed on the working class as agent of a revolution to bring about an authentic human community. The wager of action is unavoidable *not* because the revolution might fail. The wager transfers one step back, one level up. It is a wager on an 'immanent signification', on a self-understanding that, *if* achieved, *will have carried* the revolution and positioned the proletariat as its agent, whose subject position is *not yet* in place at the time of committing to action. Goldmann is indebted to Lukács for this point,[29] except that in his version we find the suggestion that the wager will deliver this future-anterior, that the current, irrational, depleted terrain of social reproduction is in some sense the vacant site of *another* process that will bring about the authentic human community, granting rationality *ex post* to the process that delivered it. What changes with Goldmann is that the wager is explicitly placed on *faith*, and Pascal's imprint could not be clearer. If Goldmann gives Lukács a tragic turn, it is because *nothing guarantees* that the praxis will deliver its conditions in the undertaking itself. There is nothing of the exalted tones of *History and Class Consciousness* in Goldmann; neither Lukács suggestion of an opening for an act to intervene in a situation (the *Augenblick)*; nor a privileged subject position of the proletariat in the

---

[28] See Goldmann (1977).

[29] Lukács' praxis philosophy is precisely about such as realisation of the conditions of action in its very undertaking. And Gorz is implicitly reflecting Lukács when he speaks in *The Critique of Economic Reason* of the process whereby 'workers who take reflexive possession of themselves in order to become the subjects of what they are' (94).

role of 'meta-theoriser' of the revolutionary undertaking.[30] There are simply no guarantees. And yet, and this is the second profound debt to Pascal, to the question *'should* one make a wager?' Pascal answers that man is *'always already embarked'*. And for Goldmann, this idea becomes henceforth 'the central idea of any philosophical system which recognises that man is not a self-sufficient and isolated monad but a partial element inside a whole to which he is linked by his aspirations, his actions and his faith ... A trans-individual source of succour on whose existence he must wager, for he can live and act only in the hope of a final success which he must have *faith in'* (1955/2016: 90). Significant about the wager and its connection to faith are, first, that action is not waged on the risk of failure (the engaged political subject cannot step back from risk); and, second, that the wager is not subject to proof because it carries its truth and calls forth 'a total attitude'[31] to judge it: transcendent are 'the comprehension of social reality, the value that judges it and the action that transforms it' (ibid.).

How revealing this connection for the insight it brings to the reading of collective action. What is waged on *the immanent signification* is the possibility of the historical manifestation of an authentic human community. For this humanism-in-action, signification is immanent; it furnishes an outlook that is historically poised, class-inflected, partial and incomplete. 'The whole movement of history', says Goldmann, will have been meaningful even though it is currently observed from abstracted and refracted parts. His 'hypothesis' (1955: 95) is that as we discern the relationship between the 'parts and the whole, the series of events and the wider context' we 'improve our understanding' of both; but the dialectic remains open, because nothing guarantees that the synthesis will be fortuitous and that the collective comprehension will be adequate to receive it. It is a wager staked on the success of achieving this adequacy. That is the task set before a *critical* phenomenology.

There are points of affinity that can be extracted between Goldmann and Weil, elective but significant, also for the deeper, deeply humanist, cadences, around the notions of the wager and the tragic. In the words of Mitchell Cohen, 'Goldmann, the dialectician by accepting the possibility of a historical dialectic unfulfilled opened the possibility of a tragic Marxism. This brings him to an existential dialectic, that is, to one that never attains ultimate synthesis' (1994: 277). If the wager for Goldmann

---

[30] See Thornhill (2001).
[31] Michael Lowy will call it (1997: 31).

has the potential to integrate theory and practice (1955/2016, 90) it is not because the class subject would somehow slip into that space, and materialise in historical practice, to come into its own and realise its historical role. For Goldmann political space is increasingly contracting: 'The central problem of tragic thought, the only problem that dialectical thought can resolve on a moral plane ... is to know whether in this rational space there is still a way, some hope of reintegrating transindividual moral values; whether man can still find God or what for us is synonymous and less ideological: the community and the universe' (1955: 35). None of which makes any less urgent the wager on the triumph of the authentically human option 'in the alternative facing humanity of a choice between socialism and barbarity', he borrows the formulation first used by Rosa Luxemburg in her 'Junius' pamphlet of 1915. Daniel Bensaïd puts it beautifully in his 1997 *Le Pari mélancholique*. 'Lucien Goldmann', he comments, 'saw this wage as a key turning point in modern thought: the transition from individualist philosophies to tragic thought.' Few knew better than Bensaïd how political commitment was bound up with the uncertainties of action: 'as [action] strains against the manifold of necessity in human affairs, it remains irreducibly a kind of wager. In the religion of the hidden God *as in the politics of the improbable event* this obligation of the wager defines the tragic condition of the modern man.'[32]

On her part, Weil never retracts from the commitment to action. It is this that makes her essay on the *Iliad* an exercise of extraordinary dignity, because the disclosure of a *human* world it gifts us is offered from an existential position increasingly ill at home in the world. My suggestion has been that what attracted Weil to the Greek epic was that such *disclosure was asserted* there *on a register of necessity*, only exceptionally with success. Weil's appeal to 'courage' becomes nearly untenable across the polarisation between the two, necessity and worldliness. That is what drew her to the *Iliad*: in her reading of the epic poem Weil gives us the most complete and uncompromising account of what it means to act with courage in the face of necessity in a way that yields, *and makes appear*, humanity in its vulnerability.

*

It is time to take stock of the two contrasting political phenomenologies of Arendt and Weil. Arendt's was a liberal phenomenology, a celebration

---

[32] Bensaïd (1997); see also Lowy (1997: xxiv).

of the *res publica*, a defence of the political in terms of shielding it behind distinctions that had to be defended against dilution, conflation and certainly any dialectical crossing. Arendt's was an expansive, celebratory phenomenology of world disclosure, pivoting on plurality and natality, an agonism of splendour and purity. Weil's 'agonism', so radically apart, measures itself against necessity. From within the materiality of lives lived labouring under the grip of necessity, Weil suggests to us something of an improbable phenomenology of the political, forced out of a situation of compulsion, in the way perhaps some decades later Alain Badiou described as 'fidelity to the event'. But not for Weil the vindicated lives of other French intellectuals; for the 'utopian pessimist' that she was it was only the 'as if' of courage that dignified action, notwithstanding that history was not on one's side. If we dwelled unusually long on tragedy earlier, it was because it is in the genre of tragedy that disclosure finds its most human expression, in the yieldings and 'blind gropings' of a thwarted agonism. Tragedy is the site of the arrested dialectic between fragments and totality, of a world known only in its fragments, and of the 'Dieu caché'. Arendt too is a reader of tragedy, but her own return to the Greeks was to seek 'a freedom experienced in the process of acting ... [that] has never again been articulated with the same classical clarity' (1961: 165). J. Peter Euben argues in this context that Arendt 'sides with a notion of redemption that retains tragedy as institution and sensibility' (2000: 158). This, too, was the site of Weil's difficult, improbable, worldliness, *but it did not afford redemption*.

The first axis of divergence between Arendt and Weil is the concept of *necessity*. For Arendt worldliness is pitted against necessity which marks the cut-off point of the political; the political is sphere and principle of disclosure where anything is possible, against the sphere of necessity where all is given. But if necessity marks the cut-off point of the political, for Arendt, where that limit is placed is not itself a political question but a meta-political one. The distinction between contingency and necessity is not an object or stake of political rationality but its condition; politics activated on the one side of the distinction as against the field of givenness which remains immune to it. There is nothing to be *claimed* or *waged* at this juncture. Against this, it is precisely the notion of an irreducible *claim and wager* that informs Weil's *critical* phenomenology. Critique is what unsettles boundaries, what measures itself against the immunities which they deliver. A critical phenomenology is what forces appearance. And the wager, one that she could not for a moment step back from, was that however courageous, the engagement would be blunted, the claim suffused; that 'truth and affliction' – remember both of them 'mute supplicants eternally condemned to stand speechless in our presence' – would remain that. Truth would be waged on 'attention' for suffering to be addressed.

But the thing that most starkly divides the two phenomenologies is *work*. Arendt's dogged insistence not to surrender the political either to instrumentality or to the materiality of labour contrasts with Weil for whom coping in the world offered it up to us as a field of practical significance and site of labour. And have we not come full circle to where we began, with the need to make appear the suffering experienced by those subjected to necessity, and to draw clearly that reflexive line between the necessary and the unnecessary forms? Against *a responsibility that could not but be assumed,* Weil's courage is in the 'and yets' and in the 'despites' of this responsibility she could neither see through nor forsake, and from which she could not get a distance except by giving the lie to what she *thought,* and for someone whose reflection *was* emotion and commitment, also therefore to who she *was.*

1.3

The Phenomenology of Work

> Labour is the living, form-giving fire;
> it is the transitoriness of things, their temporality,
> as their formation by living time.
>
> [Marx, *Grundrisse*]

The Promise of Social Labour

The Hegelian-Marxian Heritage

What in Hegel's philosophy is the original breach in which Spirit is severed from itself and thereby sets the dialectic of History in motion, finds materialist expression in Marx as class conflict. Where in the *Phenomenology* Spirit grasps contradiction as two aspects of an unfolding process and collects the brokenness of the contradictory elements of reality in the movement that synthesises them, in Marx *that brokenness is played out on the terrain of social labour,* in the activity, as he puts it, of producing the world. The history of all hitherto societies, famously in Marx, is the history of class conflict, in other words, the succession of states of brokenness. What drives forward the dialectic of history, the supersession of the successive states of breach, is the development of the forces of production that carries with it the unfolding of class conflict, changing as it develops the nature of both class relations and needs: both are caught up in the historical dynamic of redefinition. Conflict – *material, embodied, waged, suffered* – is, in Marx's materialisation of Hegel's breach, the very condition of history: it pushes it forward, because history cannot be reconciled with any of the contradictory states through which it passes. It founds the promise of its eventual consummation in the authentic human community that the working class as *universal* class will have brought about 'for itself'. If history, then, *will have been* the eventual recollection as a unity of the mutilated fragments, the *current* historical conjuncture, absent the guarantee of retrospection, comprehends reality in the partial and revisable ways in which theory may reflect the current fragmented experience of the class-conflictual situation. 'Fragmented' captures what it means to come face-to-face with forms of suffering that offer no handle to their comprehension, let alone redemption.

Verstand is Hegel's term for that fractured logic, for undialectical thought. He offers the distinction between the terms *understanding* (*Verstand*) and *reason* (*Vernunft*) to capture the shortfall. The activity of 'bringing to reason' involves an ambitiously synthetic activity that contrasts to the more superficial, commonsensical, perception of the *givenness* of phenomena as discrete and separate entities. *Reason* recollects the fragments on the basis of criteria of salience. Herbert Marcuse puts it well when he writes: 'As the given world [is] bound up with rational thought and, indeed, ontologically dependent on it, all that contradicts reason or is not rational is posited as something that has to be overcome. Reason [is thereby] established as *a critical tribunal.*' (Marcuse, 1989: 148, emphasis added.) Applied to social labour, the task, I will argue, that faces a critical phenomenology of work, is to sustain what connection it can to the value of *solidarity* that is constitutive of the exercise of labour as a social, collective undertaking and which underpins its rationality (*Vernunft*) *against* what is parcelled out as economic *givens,* the relentless econometrics of labour (*Verstand*). We will return to this. For now let us hold Marx to the promise of a critical philosophical thinking of social labour. Which, at least for Hegelian Marxism, means this: If the true meaning of what appears to actors is only recoverable in the light of an *eventual* synthesis of current states of breach, and is *currently* expressed in historical contradictions, then the theoretical reckoning of the state of the social, *now,* carries the limitations of historically poised, partial, class-inflected, perpetually incomplete reason. That is why a certain *humility* attaches to theoretical reflection in Marxism, a self-consciousness of limitation. On the one hand reflexivity is introduced deep into the workings of history; on the other its possibilities and its limits are determined *and* limited to any current conjuncture. Our discussion of 'reification', of the 'fetish phenomenon' in this chapter, and the relation between 'semantics and structures' that runs through the book all refer to this problématique.

That work is a means of self-actualisation is of course an insight that Marx owes to Hegel. In the *Phenomenology* Hegel analyses how work catalyses self-consciousness in the world; self-consciousness is objectified in the products of work and this objectification retroactively impacts on the worker because it provides him with the means of *recognition*. Marx introduces a double 'advance' to Hegel's philosophical analysis of the meaning of labour. The first is that he ties this process of self-actualisation through work to a critique of the *political economy*, the production of social value by labour. This combines with a second 'advance' in which Marx adopts the notion of 'species-being', as developed by Ludwig Feuerbach. This debt allows Marx to draw from Hegel's account of work as self-realisation a re-interpretation now portraying work as the 'self-generative act of the *species*',[1] and, in the *Paris Manuscripts*, to suggest a rehabilitation of the anthropological concept of non-alienated labour as a *constitutively co-operative endeavour*. The meaning of labour is in this constitutively tied to the process of *collective* self-realisation. Together these advances carry the political meaning of work in a phenomenological vein, by way of what appears to workers as self-generative practice and as site of intersubjective recognition.

Both advances have been the object of fierce controversy, the latter, the anthropological conception of *praxis,* often fiercest when emanating from Marxist circles of the 'scientific' or structuralist varieties. In the gentler rebuttal of Habermas, neither structuralist nor Marxist, 'when Marx borrowed from Romanticism (through Hegel) the expressivist ideal of self-formation, transferred aesthetic productivity to the practical working life of the species, conceived social labour as the collective self-realisation of the producers ... he found himself faced with a series of difficulties.' 'The romantically transfigured concept called upon by Marx is hardly adequate', Habermas is quick to point out, and in a way that neatly foregrounds his own departure from Marxism, he queries 'whether this paradigmatic mode of activity [labour] is as universal as purposive activity and communication' (Habermas, 1982: 224–5).

The idea of *alienation*, principally associated with the early *Paris Manuscripts*, gives us a key to Marx's Hegelian synthesis as it inscribes itself *negatively* on both registers, of the political economy as the reduction of living labour to dead labour, and on the anthropological register as negation of human potentiality. And although the term is abandoned by Marx after *The German Ideology*, it finds its way obliquely into the famous passage that provides the climax to volume 1 of *Capital* on the general law of capitalist accumulation:

---

[1] In Habermas' formulation (1968/1987: 53).

> [W]ithin the capitalist system all methods for raising the social productiveness of labour are brought about at the cost of the individual labourer; all means for the development of production transform themselves into means of domination over, and exploitation of, the producers; they mutilate the labourer into a fragment of a man, degrade him to the level of an appendage of a machine, destroy every remnant of charm in his work and turn it into a hated toil; they estrange from him the intellectual potentialities of the labour-process ... [2]

The key difficulty Marx faces is how the negative, expressed as alienation, might be transcended; how, in practice, the degradation of social labour – the very abstraction that turns living labour to dead labour in the circuits of the capitalist political economy – might nevertheless translate into political capacity. The difficulty is captured in Hans-Jürgen Krahl's important question, 'whether Marx has succeeded in presenting the dialectic of work not only as a misfortune in the utilisation of capital but also as an anti-capitalist productive, emancipatory force – that is whether Marx has proven that the forces of production as such can also be the forces of liberation?' (Krahl, 1971: 387). The negative finds expression in the meaning-shattering, crushing effects of factory work as well as in the many ways that capital annexes the world of labour to its needs. Marx's response is well known: it is that very experiential deficit that will mobilise resistance. Where proletarianisation becomes extreme alienation, degradation becomes the point of dialectical reversal.[3] In the early, Hegelian, works Marx argues that the processes of social labour release learning potential and an emergent awareness of (suppressed) subject positions such that might be harnessed to overturn the means of domination. The acceleration of the capacity of production brings the proletariat onto the world stage and creates a universal class of labourers caught in the contradiction between forces and relations of production by a division of labour that traps them into submission to capital. The contradiction, as experienced and suffered in the form of submission, will *forge* in the repressed class the capability to take over the mode of

---

[2] Marx continues: '... they distort the conditions under which he works, subject him during the labour-process to a despotism more hateful for its meanness; they transform his lifetime into working time; and drag his wife and child beneath the wheels of the juggernaut of capital ... Accumulation of wealth at one pole is, therefore, at the same time accumulation of misery, agony of toil, slavery, ignorance, brutality, mental degradation, at the opposite pole, i.e., on the side of the class that produces its own product in the form of capital.' (Karl Marx, *Capital*, vol. 1, Moscow: Progress Publishers, undated, p. 604.)
[3] See E. Bloch, 1986/2008: 21.

production that brought that class into being. The historical process that imposes those constraints is also therefore the process that will lead to their supersession. It is vital for Marx that social labour harbour this double movement and that the dialectic not be undone under the staggering force that turns living labour dead. Marxism understood as critical phenomenology (more on this later) both depends and must overcome the conditions that make appear subject positions and modalities of action. Praxis philosophy locates itself at the site of the overcoming of the conditions that occasioned it. This phenomenology[4] of praxis finds its most profound theoretical expression in Georg Lukács' work of 1923 *History and Class Consciousness,* with its fascinating suggestion – fascinating for *any* phenomenology – of the *Augenblick*: of what might be *glimpsed* against the coordinates that make visible.[5] To counter the *givenness* of phenomena, subject positions and structures, remains the challenge before which the traditions of critical theory and of praxis philosophy are set.

Whatever the conceptual difficulties that attach to this pairing of labour and emancipation, it is incontestable, and fascinating, that Marx draws the constitutive tie at their juncture, and locates there the site of praxis, as the only proper foundation of democratic practice. From Marx we inherit the notion that praxis is constituent power as it inheres in social labour. The wielder of this power, its subject-to-be, is the labour movement. But its condition is opaque to it in the historical circumstances under which it labours. The challenge becomes how to give due credence to that opacity while at the same time giving theoretical expression to the undertaking of self-conscious revolutionary action. Labour under capitalist conditions is conceived as both the expression of alienation and the site of recognition and emancipation. Marx talks in *The Holy Family* of 'an indignation necessarily aroused in the class by the

---

[4] For reference to the 'phenomenological strain of Marxism', see Habermas (1968/1987: 28). If social practice does not only accumulate the successes of instrumental action but also, through class antagonism, produces and reflects on objective illusion, then, as part of this process, the analysis of history is possible only in a phenomenologically mediated mode of thought.' The connection will be drawn out more fully in the next chapter.

[5] As Chris Thornhill explains Lukács' idea, 'as soon as consciousness has acquired unitary knowledge of itself and of the objective conditions of its formation, it must express this knowledge in a single revolutionary moment.' For Thornhill's highly critical text, Lukács' 'is the most far-reaching attempt to envisage a political condition ... in which human cognitive/ethical and active/practical life were unified in a social order that integrated human life in its totality' (2010b: 37).

contradiction between its nature and its life situation'.⁶ That first move, links to a second, where the two moments, the two advances, combine, to make the 'economic' concept of labour the source of self-formative (emancipatory) action.

The *phenomenological breakthrough* in Marxism is the move whereby the class-in-itself becomes the class-for-itself, transparent to and cognisant of itself, the emancipatory moment of recognition par excellence. The phenomenological breakthrough is not 'carried' in, or warranted by, history, as Marx has sometimes been taken to suggest in the 'science of history' interpretations. And yet there is in the phenomenological strain of Marxism – and Marxism is nothing if not a critical phenomenology – a profound 'historical sense' in the way Victor Serge, that extraordinary figure of the European revolutionary tradition, spoke of *'le sens de l'histoire'*:

> With Hegel and Marx the vision of *history suddenly acquires a kind of plenitude*; with Marx it is buttressed by a desire for dynamic, objective, impassioned action, and we might wonder whether the enormous spiritual magnetism of Marx's work cannot be explained to a considerable measure by this revelation of a *historical sense*.⁷

What we retain from this analysis of early Marx is how in his thinking about work, as the co-operative – in the full ethical sense that solidarity gives the term – expression, the systematic critique of capital links with praxis philosophy. Social production and praxis converge in the concept of social labour. Of course the range of needs is not static; the human species gains awareness of its needs in the same process (of social labour) that reproduces its existence. The dynamism built into the process is expressed twofold: in the emergence of new needs and new capabilities but also in the growing awareness that this emergence is frustrated by the structures in place. The latter is where emancipation acquires purchase in the very structures that reproduce domination. That is why for Marx social labour harbours the emergence of emancipatory conflict potential.

It is in the light of its promise that we will look at what it means for labour to be 'forgotten'.⁸ We will track the successive steps of a certain disarticulation where the 'forgetting' of labour is a result of what will be described as an ethical, then a political and finally a philosophical deficit.

---

[6] I borrow the quote from Bloch, 1986: 156.
[7] Serge, 1985: 53. Diary entry: 5 January 1944.
[8] In the *Dialectic of Enlightenment*, Adorno and Horkheimer write that 'all reification is forgetting' (Adorno and Horkheimer, 1944/2002: 191).

We will analyse how the promise of an adequate 'phenomenality' of social labour on which are staked both recognition and emancipation is undercut, in turn, by an ethical deficit where suffering is rendered meaningless, a political deficit where the supposed demarcation of politics proper eclipses work, and a philosophical deficit centred on the cipher of the commodity. On the ethical register we will see how the pervasive 'reification' of labour, and its 're-feudalisation' under the new exigencies and dependencies of post-Fordist work relations, withdraw meaning and recognition from work and normalise suffering. On the political register the emancipatory promise of social labour has been partly lost to critical thought. In the tradition of the Frankfurt School, Habermas' highly influential move was to sever the emancipatory project from labour and to route it to communication instead. For Habermas no social class (even under the assumption of its elevation to universal class) can claim *its* interest as the emancipatory interest *tout court*. But this comprehensive re-orientation away from the 'promise of social labour' surrenders too readily the materiality of practice to the ideality of communication. We will look at how historical, and therefore contingent, outcomes become entrenched in theoretical thinking as categorical departures: labour is contra-distinguished to action, work to communication, instrumental to deliberative reason. The political deficit follows from this theoretical construction, not simply unaddressed but as a result of its categorical immunisation, also un-addressable, a 'critical' tradition that renews the theoretical blindspot of Arendt and Habermas to reverse Marx's insight of the rootedness of praxis in labour, and instead conceptualise 'praxis' in contradistinction to it. Finally, on the philosophical register we will look at the generalisation of the logic of the commodity form. It is the phenomenology of work that is at stake throughout in all its normative import.

But first, and in order to ground it, the theoretical analysis of the 'forgetting' needs to be undertaken against an updated picture of the state of labour relations. The following section attempts such an update, of necessity in relatively broad strokes. Where I am able to, I will reference some of the wealth of the literature in the field.

Post-Fordist Mutations

When Michel Foucault spoke of *biopower* as the 'indispensable element in the development of capitalism', and defined it as the 'controlled insertion of bodies into the machinery of production' (1990: 140), he had predominantly in mind what Frederick Taylor had extolled as 'scientific workplace management' in 1911. Taylor's *Principles of Scientific Management* combined large-scale production, which Henry Ford implemented in the 'assembly line', with the 'scientific' rationalisation of the work process. *Rationalisation* for Taylor meant the progressive elimination of all that was celebrated in the 'romantic' allusion to work as self-realisation, crucially the elimination of human and individual attributes of workers in favour of abstract, specialised operations. Taylor's scientific model involved precise managerial control over every aspect of the process of production. In order to enhance the intensity of the movement of individual workers so as optimally to accelerate the rhythm of work (what he called 'the code of motion'), it introduced control mechanisms along the assembly line and the re-configuration of space-time coordinates of work: the acceleration of the time of production involved the spatial containment of workers at their work station and the mechanisation of carriage instead. With this fragmentation comes quite clearly a *dissociation* of conception from execution, of the planning work from the process of carrying out work. Everything that Marx had denounced in 'alienation' found in Taylor its apocalyptic affirmation.

For Marx of the *Grundrisse*, while labour is still in the hands of labourers it 'undergoes a merely formal modification' by the fact that it turns into fixed capital. 'But once adopted into the production process of capital ... and the automatic system of machinery ... the workers are cast as its conscious linkages ... and the worker's activity, reduced to a mere abstraction of activity, is determined and regulated on all sides by the movement of the machinery ... Scattered [it becomes] subsumed under the total process of the machinery itself' (Marx, 1857/2005: vi). The 'Hegelian moment' of *recognition* of the worker in the form in which his creativity was externalised is thus effaced. 'Effaced' is the word Marx uses in his critique of automation of industrial production: 'Through the subordination of man to the machine the situation arises in which men are effaced by their labour. Therefore we should not say that one man's hour is worth another man's hour but rather that one man during an hour is worth just as much as another man during an hour. Time is everything, man is nothing; he is at the most an incarnation of time.'[9] Work is collapsed into expenditure of energy over time, labour reduced

---

[9] K. Marx, *The Poverty of Philosophy*, 58 (quoted in Lukács, 1923/1971: 89).

to time spent on the factory floor, expended on the mechanical repetition of a minutely regulated and minimal set of actions.

If Taylorism had accelerated the flow production through assembly-line organisation and the subdivision and fragmentation of tasks, the rigidity of such organisation came increasingly to weigh down competitiveness. With the advance of capitalism and with the organisation of production progressively going global, competitiveness was re-aligned to the opportunities of mobility and fluidity, and largely shifted toward rapidity in the design, production and circulation of new products. Continual improvisation came to displace the advantages of the Fordist/Taylorist model of organisation of mass production of standardised products. As André Gorz explains the changes in *Reclaiming Work*, 'the end of Fordist growth left companies with two ways of attempting to escape stagnation. They could either win additional market share or renew their product range at a faster rate and increase its built-in obsolescence.' As regards the first option, firms had to try and gain a foothold in emerging countries. As for accelerated obsolescence, this 'required not only intense, sustained efforts in terms of innovation, but also the capacity to produce in ever shorter product runs at lower and lower unit costs. Both options necessarily entailed breaking with the Fordist mode of production' (Gorz, 1999: 27).

Whatever innovations are ushered in by *new management* thinking there remain deeper-level continuities at the level of the capitalist control of production. Of course there were reversals, sometimes significant, in the forms of management and the organisation of control. The Taylorist workshop had involved the intensification of flows through the standardisation of action, and its 'scientific' management ran alongside technological repression, geared to eliminating workers' initiative. The *new management* techniques proclaimed to expand worker initiative. Francis Fukuyama's *Trust* caused a storm in management thinking. Toyota's early implementation of the 'Ohno' system rapidly led to Western adaptations, heralding in the new 'philosophy' of management in which the ingenuity and creativity of workers were propounded as sources of innovation and growth.[10] Workers would be involved in the piecemeal but continuous adjustment of the manufacturing process to the changing environment (Coriat, 1994). Flexible productive cooperation is what

---

[10] Boltanski and Chiapello (1999/2005) provide perhaps the most systematic account of the re-organisation of capitalism since the 1960s and its re-orientation to network-based forms of organisation.

merged productivity, adaptability and continuity. The formal, hierarchical organisation gave way to 'the network of interconnected flows, co-ordinated at their nodes by self-organised collectives, none of which occupies a central position' (Gorz, 1999: 31). This combined a limited form of highly controlled workers initiative concentrated amongst elite layers of the work force, balanced carefully against the need for automation, and the exportation of Taylorist practices to other branches of industry, typically to subcontractors and to the periphery.

Capital accrued staggering dividends from the autonomy, involvement and identification of the elite workforce with the company on the one hand, and the maintenance of the multi-tier system on the other, as it did from the control of the boundary between upper and lower tiers. In fact the new, dual regime is at the basis of the new cartography that possesses a number of key features: (1) the multi-tier system of workforce organisation; (2) the undercutting of trade unionism; (3) the large-scale introduction of 'flexibility' in employment; (4) the expansion of automation; and (5) the control of migration as key aspect of the organisation of production. These developments will be variably chartered and discussed in subsequent chapters. At this point we will confine ourselves to a few general points under each heading.

(1) The professed key move of *post-Fordist* management thinking, at least in its 'Toyotist' form, was the creative involvement of workers.[11] The point now became to 'get the workers to think about the work'. A significant caveat needs to be inserted here. The post-Fordist inclusion of workers has been effected in a *layered* way. The separation between the elite of 'involved' participants and the heavily Taylorised subcontractors means that skill levels and wages drop dramatically the further down the pyramid one moves – at the lower, near-sweatshop end of the economy the difference is staggering.[12] The 'fragmented workplace' in the developed economies has not actually eclipsed the increasingly Taylorised forms deployed by subcontractors where the work is outsourced. The level of dependency between the parent company and the subcontractors allows the

---

[11] See Gorz, 1999: ch. 2, also Breen (2007). One of the best-known examples, involved Volvo's Uddevalla factory.
[12] Even Toyota itself, the originator of the Ohno system employs 10–15% of the labour force involved in manufacturing its product. The remainder (85–90%) is absorbed in a total of 45,000 subcontracting companies where, the closer one moves to the base, the more 'Taylorised' they are.

former to pass onto the latter a large part of the fluctuations in demand.

(2) Corporate identification replaces any other form of, typically, class or group identification (assisted by the fact that the recruitment procedure involves pre-selection to filter out past, current or prospective syndicalists). Corporate behaviour is enhanced and rewarded; corporate loyalty outstrips other allegiances and identifications. André Gorz identifies this move as a regression to pre-modern forms of dependence. For Paolo Virno the result is 'universally subservient labour, total subjection: it is the whole person, the ability to think and act – in short, each person's species being' – which is subjugated.'[13] In *Homo Juridicus,* Supiot (2007) accounts for the changes as a new form of the feudal bond, with its intricate net of allegiances and dependencies, and obligations of loyalty. He describes the new 'empowerment' as a form of directed freedom subject to goals agreed, and in *Governance by Numbers* (2017) speaks of the 're-feudalisation' of society. This is the first level where the contradiction of social labour is lifted. Taylorism had allowed, if not inadvertently fostered, the development of class identity and solidarity on the shop floor. The rigidity of the organisation of Fordist mass production was also the source of its vulnerability because it enhanced the 'negative power' of organised labour, their potential for slow-downs and for the many forms of disruption of assembly line production. The vulnerability in turn made employers keen to set terms through processes of collective bargaining which became the main form of regulation of industrial relations. The model was based on fixity, of the terms agreed, of work schedules, etc. What flexibilisation was introduced in this set was mainly through the use of overtime. And 'working time' was a major focus of battles fought and often won, over the reduction of the working week and the placing of limits on employers' hold over the worker's life. Now, under the new disposition, the stable core of capital's elite workers join the strata of management in terms of sharing a stake in the availability of work. But if this co-option has proven functional for capital, the question of whether the contradiction is pushed onto different terrain becomes key to the interpretation of the new dynamics.[14] The very

---

[13] P. Virno, *Mondanità*, 1994, quoted in Gorz, 1999: 38.

[14] For Gorz the contradiction that emerges under post-Fordist conditions as relates to the co-option of the workforce is this: 'the more they identify with work and with their

(3) One way to appreciate the sea-change that came with the end of Fordism, approximately in the wake of the 1973 crisis, was the radical change in the time horizon of the employment relationship. 'Homogeneous time', stresses the 'Supiot Report' published at the end of the millenium,[15] 'is no longer the central reference for regulating time.' Now what dominates is the 'fragmentation of working time'. Limited flexibility gave way to flexibilisation writ large under the banner of *flexicurity*, and an unprecedented level of employers' control over labour time. Alongside it, the standard employment relationship gave way to a proliferation of informal models, the coordination of the variety of which comes *in tandem* with the proliferation of product and service diversity. This is not to say of course that developments across economies are identical: the southern European countries, at least prior to the crisis, maintained relatively stable skilled workforces, and in the case of Germany a highly skilled workforce.[16] But the move away from stable patterns of employment to the much flaunted 'flexicurity' has involved a radical shift towards instability and ephemerality in the employees' experience of working time. Notable in this context is both the shading of working time into what used to be leisure time, but also *the acceleration and fragmentation of working time*. That globalisation is tied to acceleration is a standard reference. Less of a standard reference is perhaps what these accelerations achieve and externalise in the way that they harness the organisation of work to inhumanly quickening rhythms. The horizon of *the short term* that organises the production of work, and of corporate thinking in the age of globalisation,

---

company's successes, the more they contribute to producing and reproducing the conditions of their subjection, to intensifying the competition between firms and hence to making the battle for productivity more lethal, the threat to everyone's employment – including their own – more menacing' (Gorz, 1999: 45).

[15] See Supiot et al. (2001: 64). The 'Supiot Report', commissioned by the European Commission and submitted to it in 1999, looked in a critical comparative vein at the changing nature of work across European countries over a period of twenty years. A collaboration of lawyers, economists and political scientists, it provided a comparative study of labour law, and focused on a number of key themes, such as the competitive pressures on firms, the delivery of public services, the changing role of women in the workplace, as well as the legal framework and the structures and organizations which represent the interests of workers and employers.

[16] See Boltanski and Chiapello (1999/2005).

transfers extraordinary demands on workers of the type that for Weil devastated the experience of work.

(4) When John Maynard Keynes spoke of 'technological unemployment' in 1931 (in *Economic Possibilities for our Grandchildren*) it was to describe the 'unemployment due to our discovery of means of economising the use of labour outrunning the pace at which we can find new uses for labour'. Since the publication of that essay there has emerged significant literature around the so-called 'end of work thesis'. While the debate continues over whether the diagnosis is not premature,[17] the role of technology in industrial relations today poses the double, combined, threat, where under the sway of increasing robotisation of work the amount of necessary work is decreasing, a decrease now combining with a new complex relationship between technological innovation and capitalist discipline.[18] It is not the first time, of course, that capitalism has turned to technological forms of repression.[19] What *is* novel, however, is that the question over technology, and the decision over when and what to switch to automation, now amounts to the control of the boundary between necessary and superfluous workforce. What is too often lost in this debate is that the way that technology re-distributes capacity, the balance between labour-intensive and capital-intensive forms of production, are all *political* matters, and that automation can and should be controlled democratically at the level of political decision-making.

As we move to looking at the 'ethical' side of the 'forgetting of labour' we encounter unprecedented levels of existential precarity that the loss of jobs to automation, and the way that automation

---

[17] On the dystopian literature of the 'post-workists', see indicatively Srnicek and Alex Williams (2015) and Srnicek (2017) as well as Hunnicutt (1988). For a not altogether convincing 'sobering' rebuttal, see Susskind (2020).

[18] One amongst numerous examples borrowed from Rogers (2017): 'Trucking companies today monitor drivers closely through "telematics" devices that gather and analyze data on their location, driving speed, and delivery efficiency ... Some long-haul trucking companies use telematics to push drivers to drive for all the hours permitted per day under federal law, at times waking them up or even overriding drivers' own judgments about whether it is safe to drive. UPS has used the technologies to reduce its stock of drivers, and many have noted the stress that "metrics-based harassment" puts on workers.'

[19] Though many of André Gorz's practical recommendations appear dated today, the most important ones remain central, even prophetic; not least his critique of 'scientific management' of work and its 'robotisation' (Gorz, 1982: 87).

combines with capitalist discipline, have instilled in the workplace. Heike Geissler's *Seasonal Associate* documents the 'sheer endurance' required to work at an Amazon distribution warehouse. 'The employees', she writes, 'were nothing but a placeholder for machines that have already been invented ... though it doesn't yet make sense to replace you and your workmates who are very low cost.'[20] A number of devastating accounts of precarious, deadening labour have been published in recent years about the lived experience of work as provisional.

(5) 'At about the same time that Tronti and others were rediscovering Marx in the hidden abodes of Fordist production, Andre Gunder Frank launched the metaphor of the 'development of underdevelopment' to describe the huge divergence generated by global capitalist expansion between wealth in its core locations and underdevelopment everywhere else' (Arrighi, 2007: 21). According to Giovanni Arrighi and Immanuel Wallerstein's 'world-systems analysis', the expansion of capitalism comprised two interrelated processes: the formation of an economic world-system and the formation of an inter-state world-system (Arrighi, 1994; Wallerstein, 2004). In the case of the former, 'core' regions of capital-intensive production came to subordinate the economies of 'peripheral' regions. The case of the emergence of the inter-state system was premised on opening up new spaces to exploitation. This world-system produced a number of crucial antagonisms and anti-systemic movements – between landed and landless in predominantly agrarian, peripheral societies and between capital and wage-labour in predominantly industrial, core societies (Arrighi, Hopkins and Wallerstein, 2012). This new cartography of exploitation, describing the geographies and ecologies captured under the capitalist processes of real subsumption, connects with the control of the relationship between actual and potential labour (and all gradations in between). It allows capital to manipulate the threshold of inclusion and extract surplus value out

---

[20] Geissler (2018). See also Brishen Rogers (2017): '"Amazon needs only a minute of human labor to ship your next package," read a CNN headline last October. The company has revolutionized its warehouse operations using an army of 45,000 robots and other technologies. Previously workers known as "pickers" would walk among shelves to find goods. Now robots bring the shelves to them; pickers select goods, scan them, and put them into bins; after robots whisk the shelves away. A network of automated conveyer belts then sends the bins to "packers," who spend just fifteen seconds on each, sealing boxes with tape that is automatically dispensed at the perfect length.'

of this move. Nowhere is the control more evident than in the uses of migration, whether it is the use of national borders as mechanisms for creating worldwide labour reserves for global capital (Sassen, 1990), or whether it is the internal (to the nation state) manipulation of borders to extract surplus value out of internal migration. But the use of the 'border' as a means of extracting surplus value from labour is not confined to geographical borders. (See Mezzadra, 2013) And while the spatial border between the actual participants in the production process and the potential and peripheral participants remains crucial, the same logic of extraction extends to the boundary-use between the employed and the unemployed in the various forms of underemployment, between the regular worker and the casualised other, the self-employed outworker, the freelancer or zero-employee.

The Forgetting of Labour

The Ethical Deficit: Unnecessary Suffering[21]

When Marx described the *odyssey* of human suffering[22] in 1844 in the *Manuscripts,* he could not have foretold the advances of the scientific management of factory production brought about by Taylorism, but by 1923 Lukács was able to describe them in *History and Class Consciousness*. Lukács spoke of the 'rational mechanisation' introduced with Taylorism as extending 'right into the worker's soul'. Taylorism is a key focus of the early part of the book as a description of the processes of destruction of the meaning of work. Lukács is famous for introducing the term *reification* into the vocabulary of critical theory, a term that carries a potentially catastrophic implication for the emancipatory promise of social labour. It is the implication that given a set of structural conditions it finds itself in, the collective subject of history can only perform its task largely unaware of its historical role. Reification is the word for a certain forgetting that installs itself at the point of recovery of the meaning of social labour as collective emancipatory action. The recovery of the revolutionary subject's sense of identity and the recognition of itself in the very process of the revolutionary undertaking are, for Lukács, the constitutive elements of praxis.[23]

---

[21] I borrow the terms 'unnecessary suffering' from Maurice Glasman (1996).
[22] The formulation is Agnes Heller's (1982).
[23] The reception of Lukács has been typically contested over whether this privileged position should be afforded to any view, let alone why its monopoly should be granted to a class.

Taking the cue from Marx's analysis of the expansion and intensification of the processes of commodity-exchange, Lukács describes by *reification* the process whereby the commodity form takes over the relation of producers to their product, to each other, as well as to the very activity that externalises their humanity in the world: labour. All are colonised by, and given expression in, the 'commodity-structure'. Reification involves a generalisation that spreads the commodity form beyond the realm of strictly economic action and across the totality of facets and practices of social life. 'The problem of commodities must not be considered in isolation or even regarded as the central problem in economics, but as the central, structural problem of capitalist society in all its aspects.' 'The commodity form can only be understood in its undistorted essence when it becomes the universal category of society as a whole.' (Lukács, 1923: 83, 86.) Reification names the comprehensive displacement of the social onto the '*sachlich*' (thing-like). In its 'undistorted' form it is 'crucial for the subjugation of men's consciousness to it', to become, per Lukács, 'second nature', coincident therefore with man's proper nature or, better, collapsing the distance between true and false appearance that might have brought 'mis-identification', skewed intent, mis-conduct, or any kind of moral terminology into play.[24]

More important perhaps than the idea of *expansion* is the dimension of *intensification* that reification introduces to subjective and intersubjective agency. Lukács talks of how the commodity structure tips over into a structural role and comes to mediate the constitutive facets of engagement in the world in a way that interposes an experiential distance, a sense in which action in the world is at a remove. Commodity thinking sustains that gap (that Marx in the 1844 *Manuscripts* referred to as 'alienation') in which the (reciprocal) calculation of benefits and costs of interaction substitutes for the meaning of association, and where one's individual abilities, talents and work first receive their value in the terms that they may be cashed out. Detachment becomes part of what 'second nature' means here. And it is perhaps the depth of the colonisation of human action *by an order of calculation* that Louis Althusser misses when he famously sneers at the quaint humanism of Lukács' 'reification' as 'depending on a projection of the theory of alienation onto the theory of fetishism [of Capital] ... An ideology of reification that sees "things"

Such is Axel Honneth's position for example, though the revival of interest in Lukács concept of reification is largely due to Honneth's important book (2008).

[24] For an elaboration of this point, see Honneth, 2008, esp. 25–6.

everywhere in human relations confuses in this category "thing" (a category more foreign to Marx cannot be imagined) every human relation' (Althusser, 1962/1990). Because at a deeper level this is precisely the logic of mediation that Marx's analysis of value in *Capital* brings to the fore. Lukács writes this:

> Just as the capitalist system continuously produces and reproduces itself economically on higher and higher levels, the structure of reification progressively sinks more deeply, more *fatefully* and more definitively into the consciousness of man.
>
> (1923, 93)

*

Few have written so forcefully and so hauntingly about this *fateful* internalisation than Simone Weil; fateful because, as she witnessed in the period of factory work, it could not be reconciled with life. The year she spent working in factories in Paris left her, as she recollects later, 'in pieces, body and soul'. 'There I received the mark of slavery', she wrote in her diary. And in *Reflexions*, with reference to the rhythm of work and the sense of measure:[25] 'We are living in a world in which nothing is made to man's measure: everything is disequilibrium' ('tout est déséquilibre') (1955: 81).

When Weil applied to work in the factory in 1935 it was with the explicit intention to *comprehend* from a position that situated her directly in the field of manual labour. But if what drove Weil was always the humility not to assume to speak on behalf of others who suffered, it is seriously to be doubted whether *understanding* was accomplished through her experience on the factory floor. She worked as an unskilled novice, and was subjected to rhythms she found impossible to cope with. Naturally clumsy and with abnormally slow reflexes, Weil filled her

---

[25] If the disequilibrium is the disruption of the continuity of the creative process through the Taylorist operationalisation of a temporal modality that undercuts the human measure, what it results in, devastatingly, is the severing of thought from its object. For someone who wrote so probingly about attention, this severing is devastating. Here are extracts from her 'Seventy letters': '[t]he tragedy is that although the work is too mechanical to engage the mind it nevertheless prevents one from thinking of anything else'; '[o]ne's attention has nothing worthy to engage it, but is constrained to fix itself second by second, upon the same trivial problem'; one is left only with sadness – and the great temptation to lapse into semi-somnolence outside working hours.' 'One *cannot* be conscious.' And: 'Nothing is more difficult to know than the nature of unhappiness; a residue of mystery will always cling to it. For following the Greek proverb, it is dumb.' (All extracts from 'Factory work', in Weil (1987).)

diaries with copious calculations intended to prepare her to meet the targets expected of her: at the stamping press she operated at Alsthom; then at Carnaud where again she operated a press stamping out metal pieces. These are documents that record her anxiety in broken sequences of snippets of ratios to be achieved,[26] records of docked wages for failure to meet targets, accounts of recurring migraines, of freezing washrooms, of abuse, of the ever-present threat of instant dismissal, and of her despair at witnessing injuries suffered by workers around her. 'The modern factory reaches perhaps the limit of horror', she wrote later, in her essay 'On Human Personality'. 'What man needs is silence and warmth: what he is given is an icy pandemonium' (in McLellan, 1989: 278).

In his biography *Utopian Pessimist,* David McLellan has carefully recollected fragments from Weil's diaries. They form a testament to increasing levels of anxiety and to severe health problems she suffered during that long year of factory work. Many of her writings turn on a recurring preoccupation with *'cadence',* the rhythm of work she found crushing. In later writings that are usually associated with the critique of 'automation' she will be able to recollect the way that time is operationalised in factory work as a means of instilling powerlessness in the workers because, she says, it contravenes the natural rhythm of human life and the unfolding of human creativity. 'The machine is not modelled on human nature but on the nature of coal and compressed air, and its movements follow a *rhythm* profoundly alien to the rhythm of life's movements, violently bending the human body to its service.' And from her 'factory diary': 'Time and rhythm constitute the most important factor of the whole problem of work ... Rhythm implies moments of pause, however short, as when the peasant swings the scythe. But the spectacle of men over machines is nearly always one of wretched haste destitute of all grace and dignity' (1987: 61). It is notable that Weil here locates dignity at the level of motion, of thought-controlling motion. And she continues on an important note about the role of measure: 'It comes natural to man, and it befits him, to pause on having finished something, if only for an instant. In order to contemplate his handiwork ... Those lightening moments of thought, of immobility and equilibrium, one has to learn to eliminate utterly in a working-day at the factory.' (1987: 61)

---

[26] A typical entry in her diary runs: 'afternoon: stamping press; pieces very difficult to position at .56 per hundred (600 from 2:30 to 5:15); half an hour to reset the machine...' (Quoted in McLellan, 1989: 95–6.)

As Weil describes it, the submission experienced by workers wastes the potential for learning and action. Her experience, as she put it in a letter to her factory boss Bernard, 'taught [her] two lessons. The first, the bitterest and most unexpected, is that oppression, beyond a certain degree of intensity, does not engender revolt but on the contrary, an almost irresistible tendency to the most complete submission ... the second lesson is that humanity is divided into two categories – the people who count for something and those who count for nothing. When one is in the second category one comes to find it quite natural to count for nothing.'[27]

*

Weil's indictment remains pertinent to the workplace today, in terms of how the *systematic* form of insecurity and existential precariousness (the 'counting for nothing') are instilled through contemporary forms of the organisation of work. What concerns the current analysis, of the 'forgetting of labour' as an ethical deficit, is the way in which the new patterns affect workers in their experience of work, and the distribution of what is necessary, contingent, meaningful, or nonsensical within it. And of how capitalism has made functional the mass immiseration it produces. For this we need to turn to the connection between work and suffering. We saw it already haunting Weil's 'factory life'; it is renewed in the post-Taylorist, post-Fordist constellation.

In terms *of the suffocation of the workplace by managerial prerogative*, we witness the systematically organised competition in the workplace, the pressure to achieve ever increasing productivity targets, the pressure to cope with rapid and constant change, the exploitation of discontinuous time ('on call'), and with it the unprecedented level of control over workers' lives. The *withdrawal of recognition* occurs in the transferral over to the worker of the responsibility over his or her availability and preparedness, over the acquisition of the information to perform it adequately, and in the perception of working time as a currently unremunerated 'investment'. Where it *is made to appear* that there is no other rational way to organise the workplace than through the maximisation of individual utility, the withdrawal of recognition appears in the assumption of *individual* responsibility for one's occupational degradation, the necessary surrender to the dictates of management.

[27] In *Seventy letters*, quoted in Blum and Seidler (1989: 155).

The meaninglessness is felt as the privatisation of discontent and sense of occupational failure.

In his important book *The Disposable American*, Louis Uchitelle provides a devastating account of lay-offs and their consequences in the United States. The inevitability of lay-offs, he argues, is presented as the price for keeping the economy from stagnation or collapse under the realities of competition and the necessity of adaptation. The economic violence exacted on workers in terms of their imminent disposability makes lay-offs a structural part of the *experience* of work, one that is presented as a necessary side-effect of the economic realities of the labour market. As of 2004, Uchitelle calculates, 7 or 8 per cent of American full-time workers had been laid off on average biennially. A significant aspect of Uchitelle's analysis concerns the deep internalisation of corporate identity, the disciplinary effect of corporate identification not just in the extraction of sacrifice in the day-to-day working of the company but even in the limit case of losing one's job. Uchitelle writes:

> More than two decades have passed since the modern layoff first appeared as a mass phenomenon in American life. Until that happened, companies tried to avoid layoffs. They were a sign of corporate failure. Over the years however the separation of people from their jobs gradually became standard management practice, and in the 1990s we finally acquiesced.
>
> (2006: ix)

Uchitelle identifies a number of 'myths' as offering reasons why lay-offs were seen as necessary in the United States, amongst which is also that those laid off somehow deserved it. The political antagonism between the workers and the representatives of capital whose decision the lay-off is, is turned into a moral case of the undeserving employee. This is the limit development of strategies of responsibilisation where employees take responsibility themselves for economic consequences and conditions over which they have no leverage.

*

Christophe Dejours popularised the term 'banalisation of suffering' in his important book *Souffrance en France : La banalisation de l'injustice sociale* to capture the normalisation that suffering receives under conditions of the post-Fordist settlement. Suffering is in fact the anchor of Dejours' work. As a clinical psychologist he had the opportunity to conduct a number of studies in workplaces across France. His diagnosis of the individual and collective pathologies, dysfunctions and break-downs he studied attributed them to increased anxiety and 'precariousness', understood on a broad spectrum; subjective phenomena of 'drift' and 'disaffiliation' connected to structural changes of the post-Fordist organisation of work. Notable above all for its unremarkability, suffering is caught up in a vicious cycle in which it can no longer attach to the notion of *security*. With the demise of the work collectives and supportive networks, security becomes a nonsense in the face of market exigencies, precariousness becomes a given, 'fear is factored in in the new social contract' (Deranty, 2008: 461) and the invocation of work security as a political claim becomes a sign of naivety. At the collective level are lost the minimal conditions of cooperation that make work meaningful and undercut society's commitment to upholding forms of association and its investment in solidarity. For Dejours, contrary to the picture of post-Fordist work as involving an increase in responsibility, autonomy and creativity, contrary, then, to the strategies disseminating this *'mensonge institué'*[28] (to borrow the title of one of the chapters in *Souffrance*) promoted by economists, administrators and all those 'whose interest it is to be lied to', Dejours diagnoses a massive intensification of suffering centring largely on the spread of *fear*; fear that originates in the unprecedented sense of precariousness of one's employment. Factors that aggravate the anxiety for the worker is the fear of a lay-off but also, under flexibilised employment, the fears that come with the various forms in which work becomes unavailable for freelancers, part-timers and zero-contract employees; the systematically organised competition in the workplace; the pressure to achieve ever increasing productivity targets; the pressure to cope with rapid and constant change, or as Alain Supiot puts it, updating Weil, the inhuman 'cadence' of the *rhythme informatique*. The relentless re-skilling for high-tech opportunity, the aspired-to 'knowledge worker' of the new economy frequently is all about hiding de-skilling, and job losses.[29]

Sociologists of work have long alerted us to the psychological effects of the changing nature of work. Richard Sennett has analysed the

---

[28] 'Obstacles to the revelation of truth (about the reality of work) have always been present in the organisation of work but the manipulation of the threat to silence contradictory opinions and to confer to the "official" description of work a real power over the minds of all is incomparably more extended than twenty years ago.' (Dejours, 1998: 75.)

[29] This argument, in relation to the US is made by Wypijewski in her exceptional article (2006). In the five years between 2001 and 2006, for example, the decline in the information sector workforce in the US was 17.4%, while in computer design and related work it was 8.5% (2006: 145).

asymmetry between the radical flexibilisation of work with the imposition of irregular, fragmented and condensed working times against the need for stable timeframes to accommodate social life, personal ties, school and family schedules (Sennett, 2006). Robert Castel has written eloquently about the dismantling of the networks and mechanisms of social protection (Castel, 2003). And Emmanuel Renault, whose work is inspired by Honneth and with particular focus on the question of recognition, calls for a 'philosophie sociale' which might redress the deficit of non-recognition for those at work more generally (Renault, 2007). He shows that with the widespread use of performance indicators, 'the recognition of the reality of work is challenged' and the feeling of injustice increases.[30] What Dejours adds to the important oeuvre of sociologists of work here is the dimension of psychological damage and the insight that given the centrality of work to the notion of self-worth: 'It is not so much the extent of mental or psychic constraints in work that lets suffering appear ... , but rather the impossibility of its lessening. The certainty that the level of dissatisfaction can no longer diminish, marks the entrance into suffering' (Dejours, 2000: 79). For Dejours the invisibility, the absence or denial of recognition, of suffering is a form of *damage*, in the way that Lyotard used the term to draw our attention to what could find no redress because it was doubly denied recognition. Pathologies arise and their experiencing is insulated, internalised and suffered alone: removed from shared contexts of contestation, and forgotten. For a phenomenology of work much is staked on this withdrawal of the vocabularies and shared contexts of contestation.

The Political Deficit: Unworldly Labour

Axel Honneth puts it well in his diagnosis that 'the revolutionary notion that an intellectual and strategic socialization of the proletariat is possible within the framework of capitalist industrial work has foundered on *the reality of massive disqualification*' (1982: 37). We explored the 'disqualification' first in terms of Weil's devastating breach between thought and action, then of the generalisation and normalisation of insecurity and its devastating unexceptionality. But there is another side to the massive

---

[30] 'La reconnaissance de la difficulté du travail qui n'est jamais prise en compte correctement par les indicateurs de performance, la reconnaissance des conditions effectives du travail qu'un management centré sur les indicateurs de gestion ne peut jamais parvenir a appréhender adéquatement' (Renault, 2007: 74).

disqualification that has a clear *political* dimension, and concerns the weakening of the fabric of association and the collective ties of labour. This effects a significant breach in the dialectic between exploitation and resistance. The contradiction that held the promise that work would, eventually, provide the plane for emancipatory action, comes undone before the decomposition of labour processes increasingly difficult to recollect meaningfully, let alone normatively, as horizon of emancipatory self-development and the renewal of the critical project.

For Jürgen Habermas the 'reality of the disqualification' signals the need to re-route the renewal of the critical project away from labour and to re-conceptualise it on the plane of communication. For Habermas it is not to be lamented that the critical-emancipatory project of Modernity lost what Marxism had identified as its historical addressee. 'The destruction of the historico-philosophical certainty that the industrial working class and the European labour movement were ... bearers of a politically pursued revolutionary transformation is not, in my view, entirely a disadvantage' (Habermas, 1982: 222). Especially since changes in the global organisation and division of labour have meant that the accumulation of 'conflict potentials' that, for a time, appeared to be going global by spreading to the periphery, through anti-colonial and anti-imperial struggle have now largely *dissipated*. From the fact that capital has met with unanticipated success in fashioning a working class according to its needs, fragile, decomposed, anxious, large sways of it reduced to quasi-redundancy, Habermas surmises that the 'historical development of industrial labour is cutting the ground from under the philosophy of praxis'.

There is something profoundly disquieting about Habermas' point in terms of theory-construction. The diagnosis, he insists, must be supplemented by 'clear analytical thinking'. Is the 'economic concept of labour', he asks, as *universal* as purposive activity and communication? If not, it appears that *whatever* Marx's aspirations, the whole tradition of praxis theory as it developed through Lukács, Sartre, Goldmann, the Yugoslav and Budapest groups, the Frankfurt School and his own teacher Marcuse, must face up to the historical-theoretical error of having universalized the particular – social labour – which could not carry the project of emancipation. A breathtaking indictment this, that requires further elaboration.

Habermas is not the first to recoil in the face of a crisis that beset Marxist thinking. The crisis stems from the uncomfortable realisation that while the internal contradictions of capitalism have grown and erupted catastrophically on the global scene, they have neither been centred on, nor expressed in terms of, *the contradiction* between the development of the forces of production and the class antagonism they harbour. In the crisis-ridden context in which we currently attempt to measure the destruction that capitalist crises have wrought on societies, it remains uncontested and incontestable that capitalism has been extraordinarily successful in externalising the devastations it has caused, managing its dysfunctions and even turning them productive as catastrophe is re-entered into the cycle of profit. Writing in 1980, an exasperated André Gorz lamented 'the present state of affairs'. 'Capitalism', he wrote, 'has called into being a working class (or more loosely a mass of wage earners) whose interests, capacities and skills are functional to the existing productive forces, which themselves are functional solely to the rationality of capital' (Gorz, 1982: 15).

But what Gorz laments as a fatal co-option, Habermas takes as opportunity to reclaim the emancipatory project not merely away from work but from the form of rationality that underlies and sustains it: *instrumental rationality*. In Habermas' typology, instrumental and strategic reason are contrasted to *communicative* reason. The effect of this 'turn' is that Habermas abandons social labour as a political project: he turns away from addressing the indignities of work and the alienation of the worker as an undercutting of political capacity. Instead he opts for severing off labour and its attendant 'instrumentality' from communicative reason that, for him, now alone sustains the critical project.

What is the 'clear analytical thinking' behind the theoretical trajectory that *cleanses* labour of its emancipatory significance and political leverage? If it is the normative dimension of work that in Marx sustains the very possibility of praxis, Habermas is clear that he has no time for this 'philosophically dramatised concept of labour' (1982: 225). Such impatience finds its foundation, explicitly, in the writings of Arendt. Her concept of 'action' informs that of 'interaction' in Habermas in order to sever praxis from labour and to link it to rationality as constitutively opposed to both instrumentality and teleology. The break from labour, conceptualised by both theorists in the state of fragmentation and decomposition that define it under the *historical* conditions of Taylorism and subsequent mutations, becomes the move that founds praxis – now on a *conceptual* level – as the opposite of labour. This is a founding that, in both theories, remains unreflective as far as the categorial function it performs is concerned.

But what to make of this disquieting deployment of conceptual categories in 'clear analytical thinking'? Habermas falls into step here with Arendt, who in *The Human Condition* drew the analytical separation of the *vita activa* into labour, work and action. This allowed her to develop her own version of the Aristotelian conception of the public sphere. From Aristotle she borrowed the distinction between *poiesis* and *praxis*. *Praxis* is action that is meaningful *in itself* whereas *poiesis*, that is as production, action is overdetermined by the instrumentality of harnessing it to goals *external* to it. In the forms of *poiesis* action is lost to itself, externalised no longer as praxis but merely as labour or work. In this three-fold partition, man's active life (the *vita activa* as opposed to the *vita contemplativa*) is divided into action that expresses man's freedom in its world-disclosive political dimension and action that facilitates, *but does not express*, that life. The sphere of action that merely contributes to, rather than expresses, human excellence is itself divided between labour and work. Labour is, like work, committed to instrumentality, except that it ends up losing that orientation because under the conditions of mass production and automation it submits to necessity and to the horrors of blind, cyclical regeneration, 'follow[ing] closely the metabolic process of biological life' (1958: 307) without intelligence or imagination. Work, on the other hand, refers back to the tradition of craftsmanship.[31] If work, too, is not graced with any kind of emancipatory or world-disclosive function, it is because it remains rooted within the domain of instrumental rationality. A few years after the publication of *The Human Condition* where the partition is introduced, she writes the following in *Between Past and Future*: 'Whenever men pursue their purposes, tilling the effortless earth, forcing the free-flowing wind into their sails, crossing the ever-rolling waves, they cut across a movement which is purposeless and turning within itself' (1961: 42). It is interesting to note that these very activities are those recalled both by Creon and the chorus in the *Antigone* as celebrating the greatness of man; by the chorus in its famous 'ode to man', by Creon where he extols the virtues of statesmanship

---

[31] 'The work of our hands as distinguished from the labor of our bodies – *homo faber* who makes and literally "works upon" as distinguished from the *animal laborans* which labours and "mixes with" – fabricates the sheer unending variety of things whose sum total constitutes the human artifice' (1958: 136). The trichotomy between labour, work and action that distinguishes between the former two terms but pits them *together* against the third has been much discussed and often contested by scholars of Arendt. I leave these objections to those who think that internal criticism of this kind may cleanse the Arendtian project from its impurities.

(captaining the ship of the polis in a storm (670ff)) and of marriage ('furrow for [Haemon's] plough' (569)). I do not know whether Arendt's allusion to Creon's reference to these precise activities is intentional, or intentionally subversive. But there is something interesting going on in these rhetorical flourishes of Arendt's: 'the purposeless movement' that is 'cut across' is man's purposeful intervention in nature.[32] This certainly alludes to Marx and his faith in labour as the motor of progress in the mastery of nature and as the human activity par excellence, and Arendt's aim in all this is certainly to release man from Marx's productivist bias. Having now set him up – Marx's, Creon's – protagonist as *homo faber* (remember, this is no longer the degenerative version of the Taylorist *homo laborans* but the champion of *poiesis* himself), she levels the blow against 'his instrumentalisation of the world, his confidence in tools and in the productivity of the maker of artificial projects; his trust in the all-comprehensive range of the means-ends category; his conviction that every issue can be solved and every human motivation reduced to the principle of utility; his sovereignty, which regards everything as material and thinks of the whole of nature as an immense fabric from which we can cut out whatever we want ...' (1958: 305–6).

Arendt's guiding distinctions find a route into Habermas' conceptual scheme and correlate with his own framing distinction between means-ends instrumentality on the one hand and the expressly non-instrumental, linguistically mediated forms of communicative reason on the other, to which *alone* emancipation may attach. Arendt's logic is carried quite straightforwardly into this conceptualisation, the 'labour/work' duality on the side of instrumental and strategic reason, 'action' on that of communicative reason for much the same reasons that Arendt's repertoire dictates. And the reason that this is of interest to a discussion of the phenomenology of work is that it maps onto Habermas' contra-distinction between work and interaction. In *Knowledge and Human Interests*, Habermas writes:

> Emancipation from the compulsion succeeds to the degree that institutions based on force are replaced by an organisation of social relations that is bound only to communication free from domination. This does not occur directly through productive activity, but rather through the revolutionary activity of struggling classes (including the critical activity

---

[32] She will add, 'that "does it violence"' (1961: 43). Earlier in (1958), *homo faber* was a 'destroyer of nature' who rips and cuts his materials 'out of the womb of the earth', as quoted by Dietz (1994: 877).

of reflective sciences). Taken together, both categories of social practice make possible what Marx, interpreting Hegel, calls the self-generative act of the species.

(1968/1987: 53)

In 1968, the 'self-generative act of the species' while uploaded from productive activity to 'communication free of domination', still retained its revolutionary credentials during the transferral, and was located, immanently, in the 'struggle' of the classes. As Habermas gradually abandons the Marxism of his youth, the moral insight that will lead from domination to mutual understanding (undistorted communicative exchange) will henceforth be carried in a logic of action that is not only distinct from social labour but, as *interaction*, in fact defines itself in contradistinction to it.[33] Habermas' sovereign move is thus to re-route the project of emancipation away from production and toward communication. The gesture of this re-routing that is represented by the 'intersubjective turn' (*intersubjektive Wende*) in critical social theory, involves the disembedding of *intersubjectivity* from social labour as the cooperative activity of producers, and its reconfiguration as communicative exchange. And the rationality proper to communication becomes that which aims to *persuade* rather than to *succeed*. The rationality of action is structured across this divide of communicative *versus* goal-oriented. The first pole holds firm the communicative rationality of the equality of speakers, the filtering out of structures of authority and domination from communication, the openness of perspectives. And it holds firm against the latter in the various forms in which the latter splits: goal-oriented as both instrumental and strategic, strategic into openly or covertly so, covertly as either systematically distorted or directly manipulated, etc. But the splintering of the success-oriented pole does not taint the integrity of that steadfast value-rationality of communicative exchange, dignified progressively with no less than the Kantian imperative of treating others as ends.

---

[33] Habermas is not alone amongst 'second generation' Frankfurt scholars to criticise Marx's elevation of labour over interaction. The rift is replicated with the Frankfurt School across the two 'generations': Albrecht Wellmer too has criticised Adorno for adopting a conception of spirit as labour which generalises Marx's critique of capitalism into a monolithic philosophy of history that *reduces all action to labour* (Wellmer, 1974) Habermas, in *Between Naturalism and Religion* characterises as an 'astoundingly oversimplified understanding of modern reason, all set against a metaphysical assumption of the primacy of a non-reified nature' (2008: 200). Axel Honneth's *Critique of Power* of 1991 speaks of an outdated subject-centred philosophy of consciousness, a monolithic and totalised critique of action as labour inherited from Marx (1991: xvi).

It is not clear what comes first, but then, perhaps, it does not matter. Does the Taylorist collapse of work into expended energy on the factory floor make the category of labour, for Habermas like it was for Arendt, unworthy of recognition? Or is it that the conceptual exercise of differentiation between work and action, instrumental and communicative, proceeds irrespective? By taking on board as given the decomposition of the processes of work and the fragmented nature of interpersonal workplace relationships, any notion of the teleology of work, of the realisation of cooperation and association in the workplace has been collapsed as pertaining to the shallower domain of instrumentality and orientation to success. It is difficult under the circumstances to make sense of Axel Honneth's claim, in his otherwise astute analysis, that 'at the more highly developed theoretical level at which Habermas is working, the concept of instrumental action obviously preserves the economic and anthropological dimension of meaning which Marx invested in his concept of work' (Honneth, 1982: 51). What exactly is 'obvious' here, let alone 'more highly developed'? Is it not instead that the historical fragmentation of the integral act of work, the fissured workplace[34] as subjected to the old and new management techniques, the usurpation of any form of democratic control of the workplace and work process, *all* fall on this side of the instrumental/communicative divide and as such remain incapable of addressing the historical deformation of work by aligning it to 'the economic and anthropological dimension of the meaning' that Marx attached to social labour? It seems easy to surmise that '[t]he concept of labour has been purged of all normative content in industrial sociology and has been discharged from the role of an emancipatory driving force in social philosophy' or that 'the historical development of industrial labour is cutting the ground from under the philosophy of praxis' (Habermas, 1982: 225). But what a strange response to the evacuation of the concept of labour it is to merely switch praxis across to communication. And why does the 'purging of all normative content' from work become the unquestioned starting point and limit point of critical redress? This is not an unfair question for Habermas, whose organising concern with *systemic* distortions of *interactional* contexts was at the heart of his defence of the *lifeworld*, and of his whole critical endeavour of the 'theory of communicative

---

[34] The reference is to David Weil (2014). The term 'fissured' work has been used widely to describe relationships such as that of Uber's with its drivers, or McDonald's with its franchisees' workers.

action'. Because there is something strikingly parallel to the way in which work and communication are distorted under conditions of the 'colonisation of the lifeworld',[35] and to immure the former – work – but not the latter – communication – behind conceptual demarcations that take the distortion for granted is a bewildering way to understand the role of critical theory. Why does the 'philosophy of praxis' migrate from material to discursive practices, undercutting the possibility of restoring work to goal-rational action against what demeans it, reduces it, distorts it, while allowing manipulative managerial practices and the deformation of work to receive immunity from democratic correction? The loss of concepts as far as the field of labour is concerned is a result of the withdrawal of 'mutual understanding' from it as a matter of improper ascription, and supposedly as category mistake.

A certain self-sufficiency seals over communicative reason at this point, a certain kind of self-immunisation. We should perhaps pause to ask whether something else fundamental isn't lost to Habermas with this re-orientation of the emancipatory project from social labour to communication. Similarly to Marx, for Habermas the project of emancipation is seen as immanent in social life. And there is at least a parallel in the way that Marx describes how the class-in-itself raises itself through realising the emancipatory action into the universal class-for-itself, and the way that for Habermas intersubjectivity hoists itself out of the contexts of systematically distorted and interest-driven communication toward more accomplished realisations through the pragmatics of discourse. But here is the catch. For Marx the emancipatory project, human progress, was intrinsically tied to suffering. The class-in-itself was a class subjected to suffering, *and suffering moves people to react*. Of course, as we have seen with Weil, and then with Dejours, there is a point beyond which it is experienced as pure compulsion, incomprehensible and numbing, exacted with a force that flattens world disclosure. But to the extent that the injunction 'this is unjust' might be articulated (more on this in the next chapter), suffering *can* drive resistance, and if resistance can be directed strategically against the points of foreclosure that underwrite the reproduction of the order of capital, then the emancipatory project is underway, *immanently*. Famously, the deficit that mobilises the dialectic of History receives its experiential dimension as

---

[35] Agnes Heller certainly has a point when she writes: 'Undistorted goal-rationality has been no less and no more present in human history than undistorted communication; but I would add that every instance of human work is a claim to goal-rational creativity. Accomplished human freedom means socialisation of our inner nature without repression, both in communication and creation' (1982: 35).

the suffering of the proletariat. But Habermas can rely on no such experiential deficit to mobilise the emancipatory undertaking. If the latter is indeed immanent in social life in the forms of communicative action, a reason that is external[36] to them is required to set them in motion. And reason alone does not move people to act. Those who commit wrong by withdrawing in indifference, or who commit wrong by addressing the destitute with the speech act 'your suffering does not interest me' will not be *forced* to retract because communicative rationality somehow demands it. [Let us interject to ask: Does it demand it? Can the speech act *'your suffering does not interest me'* not be offered as an act oriented toward mutual understanding, an attempt to explain, sincere and truthful to the pragmatics of its utterance, freely offered in contexts of uncoerced communication?] But let us assume for the sake of argument that such communicative 'offers' of indifference do not stand up to communicative rationality. How will the project of emancipation get off the ground at all against such institutionalised indifference if not by an *added* reason, therefore not immanently?[37] Marx captures this 'immanence' well in *The Holy Family* when he talks about the illusion of freedom:

> The possessing class and the proletarian class represent one and the same human self-alienation. But the former feels satisfied and affirmed in this self-alienation, experiences the alienation as a sign of its own power, and possesses in it the appearance of human existence. The latter however feels destroyed in this alienation, seeing in it its own impotence and the reality of *inhuman* existence.

And here is the crux:

> This [proletarian] class is, *within depravity, an indignation against this depravity*, an indignation *necessarily* aroused in this class by the contradiction between its human nature and its life situation which is a blatant, outright and all-embracing denial of that very nature.

At this point let us draw this argument about the *political* 'forgetting of labour' to a close. In the discussion of Habermas and Arendt we turned our attention to the slippage they perform between what is historically contingent and what categorially given, in their refusal to grant any

---

[36] On external and internal reasons, see Bernard Williams (1979).
[37] A reason added for reasons of compassion, as per Weil, or by a secular form of 'charity' as per Robert Owen, who put it so well: 'Without charity, pure practical charity, for all mankind, there can be no real virtue of rationality in the mind and conduct of men.' (Owen, 1849: 87).

thicker sense of goal- or associative rationality to *work* other than that which can be read off its *deformed state*, no longer capable, as we were told, of 'grounding the philosophy of praxis'. But why start from *that* as the form-giving moment? Then deformation becomes un-addressable since it is definitional of form. Compare this to Weil, who held on to a concept of the dignity of work and the worker as formative, in the face of the most extreme counter-factuality. Her *Reflections* measured oppression against a standard of dignified work, of work embodying liberty, where understanding, Habermas' central category, was central for her too. And yet their *meta-political* disagreement is irreconcilable: for Weil, the *criterion* for assessing political action is the mitigation of oppression and the promotion of a humane and dignified form of work organisation; for Habermas the criterion of emancipatory action operates at a level above the instrumental logic of work, the realm of what Arendt pejoratively calls the 'in order to'. The turn to communicative reason in both Arendt and Habermas is built around this disempowering gesture, a refusal to elevate the activities that fall under 'labour' to the dignity granted the agonistic and the political. Political rationality as harnessed instead to interaction, natality, worldliness and communicative reason is stripped of its embeddedness in the processes of social labour and the satisfaction of needs. Given this clearing exercise at the definitional level of the political, we might ask the Arendtians, including Habermas of course, what *redress* might be envisaged for the lives that fall below the level of recognition where they may be collected as agonistic narratives and imbued with political meaning? Below the level, that is, where they may be dignified with 'worldliness'? The answer has to be that world-disclosure bifurcates. As *already* carried in the performance of political/communicative action, association unproblematically taps the cosmopolitan aspiration; as reproduced in the base processes of the reproduction of material life, association is offered up to the logic of accumulation *without* political redress.

The Philosophical Deficit: Phenomenological Blockage

Labour is value-producing activity. The value produced must be returned to those who laboured. So arrestingly simple is Marx's fundamental injunction, an injunction against the class appropriation of the surplus value of labour. Whatever complexity attaches to the analysis of value, it aims to restore that fundamental condition of justice.

If complexity attaches from the very start to the simple injunction to return social value to its producers, it is because its resolution has to be thought from within – and therefore also as over-determined by – the capitalist economic conditions that organise the extraction of value. *Value production is only ever recognised at the site where it is already appropriated.* And the class of labourers bursts onto the world scene 'elevated' by capitalism to *universal* class under condition of its submission to capital. The value of labour enters the circuits of value production *always-already* as the value of its exchange, and expressed in its price. Commodification and the fetish phenomenon – *the forgetting of living labour* – are located here, inextricably bound to its very expression. It is this that amounts to phenomenological blockage.

Here is Marx's famous analysis of commodification in the first chapter of *Capital*:

> Since the producers do not come into social contact with each other until they exchange their products, the specific social character of each producer's labour does not show itself except in the act of exchange. In other words, the labour of the individual asserts itself as a part of the labour of society only by means of the relations which the act of exchange establishes directly between the products, and indirectly, through them, between the producers. . . . It is only by being exchanged that the products of labour acquire, as values, one uniform social status, distinct from their varied forms of existence as objects of utility. *This division of a product into a useful thing and a value becomes practically important, only when exchange has acquired such an extension that useful articles are produced for the purpose of being exchanged,* . . . From this moment the private labours of the producers actually acquire *a twofold social character.* On the one hand they must as definite useful labours satisfy a definite social need, and thus prove themselves as members of the total labour, of the naturally grown system of the social division of labour. On the other hand, they can satisfy the manifold needs of the individual producers themselves only in so far as every particular useful private labour can be exchanged with every other kind of useful private labour, i.e. counts as *equal* to it.
>
> Equality of completely different labours can only consist in an abstraction from their real inequality, in the reduction to the common characteristic which they have as an expenditure of human labour power, human labour in the abstract.

Let us begin to unpack the complexity of Marx's analysis from the temporal side. In this analytic of value *time* plays an important role. It is captured in the notion of the 'division of a product into a useful thing and a value *becoming* practically important', or in labours '*acquiring* the twofold character'. In both expressions something is already *underway*. From the point of view of the temporal unfolding of the practice of work, of how work is undertaken, experienced and intended, labourers are already *thrown* into its processes, because human labour power is not expended in the abstract. As Valerie Kerruish explains it in *The Wrong of Law*, an analysis of the double form of the commodity turns on both what it *is* and of what it *does*: 'These transformations and the double character of the commodity and of the labour embodied in it will now be re-traversed, re-covered, from the perspective of its "activity": the perspective of practice, based for Marx on what people do [and] how they perceive the products of that doing.' And remaining with the dimension of time: the actual processes in time of *deepening* and intensification of commodity exchange describe a process of substitution *taking hold* of the imaginary in the context of the materiality of practice. But crucially it involves a hold on the future too in terms of anticipatory states: exchange value expresses the anticipation that the work will be realised as value. Capitalism turns on anticipation because capital is process, not a thing: capital is the *anticipated* return on current investment.[38] In the dimension of time, Marx's 'fetish' phenomenon names the transition from living labour to dead labour in the totalising gesture that, decades later as we saw, Lukács captured by the term 'reification'.[39] The temporal dimension – of process and of *becoming*, of the *taking hold* of the value expression that hollows out and diminishes labour – is vital to understanding both how the value reversal comes about and how the reversal is 'naturalised'. Naturalisation marks the moment of 'forgetting' that centres this analysis.

But this is moving too quickly and we need to step back from the temporal dimension and ask what differentiates – now in the *material* dimension – the forms of value. In the text quoted above, Marx is describing the regress back to the point of putting-into-relation (the 'reduction to a common characteristic', he says) on the back of which 'commonality' can be established. But this commonality can only *be imported* in the form of commensuration; 'imported' because abstract labour is an abstraction *away* from the particularity of individual labours. As condition of its exchange, individual labour creates value but, Marx says, 'is not itself value'. But how are we to understand the standing back from commensuration to address this '*itself*' of labour, since it enters the sphere of value in and through an equation of individual labours in

---

[38] See John Commons (1924) for a more elaborate formulation. Also in Chapter 4.1.
[39] Lukács controversially does not draw a distinction between reification and the fetish phenomenon, but treats them interchangeably.

exchange? At the point of entry value is *always-already* comprehended from the point of view of how it is 'socialised' as a relation between commodities. In this, value is constitutively caught up in commensuration, it is coincident with the process of abstracting labour in the *form* of the commodity as aligned to the universal equivalent (the money-form). At this point Marx, as reaction perhaps to the impasse that confronts him designates the appearance of the 'value form' as a *'mystery'*.

> A commodity is therefore a *mysterious* thing, simply because in it the social character of men's labour appears to them as an objective character stamped upon the product of that labour; because the relation of the producers to the sum total of their own labour is presented to them as a social relation, existing not between themselves, but between the products of their labour. Through this substitution *(quid pro quo)* the products of labour become commodities, social things whose qualities are at the same time perceptible and imperceptible by the senses. The commodity form thus assumes that definite social relations between humans themselves assume for them the *phantasmagorisch* (bizzare, fantastic) form of a relation between things.
>
> (Marx, *Capital*, vol. 1, emphases added)

The problem is how to understand the *quid pro quo* of the substitution. Now, it is well known that Marx introduces the distinction between use-value and exchange-value in order to allow a conceptualisation of value *across* that difference. Then, at one level, the *quid pro quo* can be understood as the substitution of exchange-value for use-value. Jacques Derrida explains: 'It is just the abstraction from their use value that *evidently* characterises the exchange relation of commodities' (127). But how convincing is this? Let us be clear that 'mystification' cannot be understood as naming a simple supervenience of one layer of signification *over* another, of exchange value *over* use-value, of form *over* content.[40] Instead the substitution (if we can still call it that) runs deep enough to be constitutive of what is being mystified. Because as we saw the alienation of the commodity – the sale of abstract labour – concerns an activity that, Marx insists, is not itself already a value but whose insertion into commodity exchange realises *as* value. It is *its capacity to be alienated from the labourer that is inscribed in the system as its value*.

---

[40] Such suggested simplifications misread Marx. It is a simplification to assume that Marx is talking about the imposition of form over a basic unproblematic content of quasi-naturalistic existence, so that the release of the latter from the former would simply uncover it.

Labour 'realises' itself in the market by alienating itself into the general equivalent, by acquiring, in other words, an exchange-value.[41] Before its alienation it does not carry value. It is difficult to conceptualise how one might bracket these two steps of constitution – labour as value and value as price – in order to comprehend the substitution (the 'quid pro quo'), let alone to appreciate what is lost in it. Because on what terrain is the 'step back' to find its footing, to recover (use) value from its collapse into market valorisation? The forgetting of labour becomes structural in the comprehensive substitution that leaves no mystery as such – it is all out there evident in its materiality and fully given! – except for Marx's enigmatic formulation of the *quid pro quo*. There is no discernible moment of substitution in all this, and any loss is only discernible working backward, from the realisation of value in exchange back to a projection of value that inheres in use. What makes the process 'enigmatic' is that there is no autonomous appearance of either pole in the substitution, there is a complicity *ab origine*, and therefore no substitution, no *quid pro quo* properly understood.

It is for this reason that it becomes so difficult to find a register to express, *as we must*, the indictment against commodification, that Derrida expresses in the beautiful opening line of the final chapter of *Spectres of Marx*: 'An articulation assures the movement of this relentless indictment' (1994: 125). *Why movement?* I ask this, because is it not the case that the rendering of use-value and exchange-value as an 'articulation' already overstates it? How will the *play* between the values *carve out a space for itself* if use value can only ever be extrapolated from exchange? Derrida's nod to the dialectic is in the term 'assures' and in the 'giving of some play' which forever ('relentlessly') rises to indict the reproduction of injustice. He will seek leverage in Marx's description of the substitution as *'phantasmagorisch'* to develop the 'articulation' as the play between the spirit (Geist) and the spectre (Gespenst) and avoid having to explain how the 'articulation' might gain *real* traction. And the term 'assures' marks, perhaps, Derrida's faith that this improbability, this *aporia*, will remain active and that deconstruction will always disrupt the sealing over of the value of 'use' into the register of exchange.

---

[41] Marx is perfectly able to formulate this alienation as it operates within the system: not only does the commodity-economy entail the capacity of the commodity to be alienated, the capacity ideally inscribed in the commodity *as* its value (and expressed in its price) – it also entails that the commodity actually alienates itself into the general equivalent, that it 'realises' itself on the market (Mocnik, 1999: 118).

We will not follow him there, but remain with his profound question and what it might mean for the dialectic to acquire purchase *at all* in the sphere of the givenness of market exchange where the fetish phenomenon lends structure and content to the field of appearance. At stake here, says Derrida, is the 'apparition of the inapparent', an apparition, he will add, that requires nothing less than a 'phenomenological "conjuring trick"' (1994: 125) in order to appear. What is the 'trick'? I understand Derrida to be saying that the 'trick' aims to release the phenomenon from its givenness and to give it back to the play of history, to articulation, and to the promise of justice. In speaking of 'the phenomenological fold', Derrida in fact attributes to Marx 'that difference, both decisive and insubstantial at the same time, that separates being from appearing. The appearing of being, as such, as phenomenality of its phenomenon, is and is not the being that appears' (1994: 145). In this equivocation, the 'is and is not' of the 'being that appears' Derrida reads in Marx the insertion of a certain spilt between phenomenon and essence and therefore a certain *restlessness* that suggests that structures will not overwhelm and ideology overdetermine. Is that not the meaning of the 'articulation [that] assures the movement of [the] relentless indictment'? There is something profound, if disconcerting, in this playful phenomenology of figurations, counter-figurations and conjuring tricks, of spectral 'hauntologies' and the spectral play, as if nothing except the most outlandish efforts are capable of returning the language of value to the meaning of labour. Most problematically it leaves decentred the agent of the praxis, their speaking position doubled in the 'spectral', and as we know by now 'spectral' is an utterance with a *dislocated* position of uttering. Derrida reminds us: 'The [speaking] position from which a [critique] of ideology can possibly be uttered undermines the very possibility of its utterance' (1994: 113).

For those of us still struggling with articulations and improbabilities of a *structural* variety, and the opportunities of *political redress*, let us not dispense readily with Marx's theoretical difficulty. Instead with Marx and along trajectories taken or envisaged, we must explore how the conditions of a critical phenomenology may still be situated in social labour. If with Marx we insist on staking political praxis on social labour, we confront a series of challenges to the possibility of recovering the meaning of labour as emancipatory activity. Let us then ask again: Why does Marx call the importation of the exchange value of labour a 'mystery': *what exactly is substituted for what in the 'quid pro quo'?* What exactly is lost in the substitution? Any discussion of labour, the distinction between it and work, the 'fictitious' commodity-form of labour, the disappearing that the fiction effects, the question of compulsion and necessity, and therefore also of redress, all must begin from his question over the 'mystery of the commodity form'. It is, remember, a *quid pro quo*:

> [The objectification] reflects the social relation of the producers to the sum total of labour as a social relation between objects, a relation that exists apart from and outside the producers. Through this substitution [*quid pro quo*] the products of labour become commodities, sensuous things which are at the same time supersensible or social ... It is nothing but the definite social relation between men themselves which assumes here, for them, the fantastic [*phantasmagorische*] form of a relation between things.
>
> (*Capital*, 164–5)

It is a disturbing fact that in all this *there is no mystery* in this 'social relation between objects'! For a critical phenomenology the problem becomes how to get behind the 'objectification', to prise open the coincidence and insert distance between the poles of *quid* and *quo* in a way that might allow the observation of difference, 'uncover' the substitution, *force it to appear* in order that the givenness might be put to question. But how to step back from the pathological state? *What will give purchase to that question* if the meaning of value is already given in the exchange relation? Questions proliferate at this juncture. How is the fetish *phenomenon* to be set apart and scrutinised if it subtends phenomenality as such? What 'conjuring trick' is a critical phenomenology to rely on to circumvent the phenomenological blockage and put the fetish to question, if the fetish, in the form of the commodity, is what underlies and constitutes appearance? The commodity, Karel Kosik reminds us, is 'an absolute reality' for the capitalist society.[42] How is the point of view to situate itself in a space that is not already foreclosed by the coincidence of value with its quantification in exchange? As far as the activity of *subjects* is concerned we might ask: if we indeed take this as a problem for phenomenology, of how the 'true' meaning of their work *appears* to the workers who perform it, how are we to find a way back from the problem that Marx so poignantly struggles with, of how to think value immanently from the point of view of its transmutation? If exchange value, in other words,

---

[42] Kosik states: 'it is the unity of all determinations, the germ of all contradictions, in Hegelian terms the unity of being and not-being, of identity and non-identity' (1967: 76). For Rubin's important work (1973) 'the theory of fetishism is per se the basis of Marx's entire economic system of value.'

installs itself at the point of recovery of the meaning that their activity has for labourers as a *social* activity – the *socius* that binds men to each other – if, in other words, it is constitutively implicated in the phenomenality of value, how is the meaningfulness of use-value to be recovered in its stead? It is difficult to see how the *categorical framework* of the three terms *value, use-value and exchange-value* might restore a meaningful political (emancipatory) dimension to labour in place of the alienation that faces workers who do not recognise in exchange value the social character of their own labour, its expenditure experienced as necessary. At the point at which this 'objectivity' takes hold, market forces are released as precisely that, as *forces*. The objectification marks the *social* activity as *ab initio* sustained in the medium of exchange, and the double character of the commodity operates to naturalise capitalist relations. In 'revealing' the origin of the universal form of value – that as such must be expressed as an objectivity – in the historical, accidental form it takes under capitalist conditions, the substitution undercuts the possibility of any other understanding of value except in the form of commensuration as market exchange. Critique, the imagination of alternatives, reflexivity itself, are all denied traction in this totalising substitution.

If social labour and emancipation appear to be tied in contradiction at this juncture, we return to where we started, with Krahl's question, earlier, over the emancipatory promise of social labour. The most obvious answer to the tie, is to sever the project of emancipation from labour. For this line of theory, it is the *productivist bias* of Marxism that unnecessarily short-circuits the question of emancipation to the question of the recovery of the political promise of labour. The answer in Jean Baudrillard's quite brilliant polemic is to shatter the *Mirror of Production* and to recover a meaning of human potentiality beyond the confines of Marx's organising hypothesis and blind spot, the elevation of production as the site of truth. For Habermas' critical theory, we saw that the severing involved an Aristotelian/Arendtian argument that contradistinguished political action and labour. A third solution derives from within the structuralist Marxist camp: where dialectical articulations have long disappeared into the 'always-already' of commodification, the tendency is to remain with the fetish character of the commodity as an actual social phenomenon of commodity producing societies where capitalist production is dominant, and to argue that it shall disappear with the disappearance of capitalist social relations. The easier way out of the aporia, that is, is to argue that for Marx history is realised by historical agents who are *unaware* that they are performing the labour of history. History is here working behind their backs, as it were, and through their practice, the emancipatory significance of which the proletariat cannot see through as its subject except *a posteriori*. But from the point of view of critical theory this easy teleology misses Marx's most important insight, contained in the eleventh thesis, with philosophy harnessed to the project of emancipation, conscious all the time that any philosophical undertaking in this vein cannot but be dedicated 'reflexively to incorporate its own historical conditions of possibility' (Rastko, 1999: 110), which attaches to it both a humility and a demand to remain adequate to the task. There have been other interesting ways to carve up the field with reference to the connection between labour and emancipation, and we will return to these in the latter part of the book, when we look at how it informed the strategic thinking of the workerists in Italy and the logic of the mass strike. The function of the *negative* played a significant role in how the emancipatory project was conceived, the reality of labour lived, experienced and suffered as *antinomic*, that is, as not at one with itself.[43]

Derrida's suggestion, that we looked at briefly above, was not to sever the link between praxis and production, the realm of shared and shareable labour, but to throw commodification 'out of joint'. His 'deconstructive' solution was to rethink the ontology of labour, and to extract from Marx the idea of a *critical ontology*. He says: 'Marx continues to want to ground his critique or his exorcism of the spectral simulacrum [the commodity form] in an ontology. It is a – critical but pre-deconstructive – ontology of presence as actual reality and as objectivity' (1994: 170). It is an 'ontology' because it involves real movement; it is 'critical' because the real is caught up in the movement of redefinition. This 'critical ontology' means to 'conjure away' the 'phantom' (the commodity form) as 'representative consciousness of a subject' in order to return the representation to the world of labour, to ground it there, to return it to the conditions of an un-alienated emergence. That this critique is 'pre-deconstructive', says Derrida, does not mean that it is illusory or false. Rather, and this is Marx's genius move, this critical ontology of his 'characterises a relatively stabilized knowledge that calls for questions

---

[43] This line of theorising has more recently found profound expression in Karatani's *Transcritique* (2005). In this stubbornly Kantian, rather than Hegelian, Marxism the emancipatory moment finds its locution not in the transcendental movement but in the enduring immanence of the antinomy between noumenon and phenomenon, the space between what is envisaged and what is delivered.

more radical than the critique itself, than the ontology that grounds the critique. One may say that this is where the spirit of the Marxist critique situates itself, *not the spirit that one would oppose to the letter, but the one which supposes the very movement of the letter.*' (Derrida, 1994: 170, 171–2.) How incisive this formulation! To my mind it brings Derrida closest to Marx's eleventh thesis, as Derrida seeks as much deconstructive leverage as he can from the 'aporia' at this point, and sets it against 'the disjointed and dis-adjusted limits' of the contradictory reality of capitalism. There is much to learn from this, as we gradually sharpen the critical-phenomenological viewpoint, that strains at the utopian limit of what cannot yet be named from within a certain economy of language or of representation.[44]

All of which brings us to a central preoccupation of this book, which is the relation of structures and semantics, and we open this first of four instalments on this central theme with the one offered from within Marxist theory. It concerns the phenomenological blockage that accompanies the installation of the commodity form at the point of the recovery of the political promise of social labour. The crucial question, as ever, is about how to envisage redress, what semantic leeway – *what 'movement of the letter'* – might be recovered from the field of structural compulsion.

Semantics and Structures I:
The Movement of Concepts and Structures

One way to navigate the blockage from within Marx's thought, is to retrace what he says about value back to Hegel. We know from the copious notes he took (posthumously published as the *Critique of Hegel's Philosophy of Right*) that Marx struggled through *The Philosophy of Right* in 1843, and although it is clear that what drew Marx's attention were the elements of political organisation, there is a clear homology[45] between the way that Hegel discusses *right* and *value*. The best way to understand what intrigues Marx in Hegel's concept of value as a formal conceptual scheme, is to look at how it straddles the qualitative and quantitative in dialectical form. Value is an abstract, universal, quantitative factor that gives expression to how concrete,

---

[44] Compare here Johan van der Walt's fascinating account of that limit (2014a).
[45] On this homology, see Deranty, 2005.

particular, qualitative moments *relate*. Value is a quantitative factor that *raises* qualitative particularity to commensurability and thus to relationality: on the register of the social, as giving expression to the *socius* itself, value is the very expression-as-quantification of the thing, of labour in our case. We will re-read this argument more gradually; if this gradual approach is both too technical and not technical enough, it is at least compensated by the fact that it takes us through thoroughly familiar ground, as we move quickly through the opening chapters of the first volume of *Capital*.

Capital opens famously with that very conundrum over value. Marx draws out two foundational premises in the way that the theorists of the political economy, Smith and Ricardo, drew them before him. The first is that value is produced by labour and is proportionate to labour time; the second is that exchange is between equivalents. For the worker this translates into the C-M-C cycle whereby labour (C) is sold for the wage (M) that allows the purchase of commodities (C) that will satisfy the needs of subsistence of the labourer. For the owner of money the cycle M-C-M' involves the paying of the wage (M) to buy labour power (C) for the production of commodities that will procure money (M'). But it is unclear how the money invested will produce additional value (M') because surplus value cannot be produced out of the process of the exchange of equivalents. Which is to say that the identical quality of the commodity 'money' in the M-C-M' cycle shows no motive for the transaction.

For Marx, the impasse, between the equivalence supposed in perfect exchange and the non-equivalence required for the creation of surplus value, is breached due to the peculiar nature of the commodity 'labour power'. We come to it in chapter 6: 'In order to extract value out of the consumption of a commodity our friend the money-owner must be lucky enough to find within the sphere of circulation, in the market, a commodity whose use-value possesses the peculiar property of being itself a source of value ... The owner of money does find such a special commodity on the market: the capacity for labour [*Arbeits-vermögen*], in other words labour power [*Arbeitskraft*]' (1867/1970: 164). In the C-M-C cycle in which the labourer moves, the use-value of labour is that it enables his subsistence. Like every commodity its value is determined by the labour necessary for its production. So it is with labour power: its value is the labour necessary to keep the labourer alive and working. That is what the capitalist buys, and he buys it for its value. In Marx's words: 'the labour time necessary for the production of labour-power is the same as that necessary for the production of those means of subsistence; in other words the value of labour power is the value of the means of subsistence necessary for the maintenance of its owner' (168). But now, what for the worker is the simple recursion (C-M-C) delivers labour power to the capitalist as a source of value creation. A certain incision is drawn within 'labour power' in terms of its capacity to be realised. That capacity is contingent on the way in which scarcity has been institutionalised, through the class ownership of the means of production. We will return to this in a minute, though the history of that dispossession that sets the labourer 'free' is well known. For now let us focus with Marx on the conceptual operation. The impasse we mentioned – how is profit made out of the exchange of equivalents? – is breached with the introduction of an internal distinction. The commodity labour power is split, between the capacity to work, or *Arbeits-vermögen* (C1), and its realisation, *Arbeits-kraft* (C2). C1 materialises as C2 only through access to the means of work. The worker is compensated for the abstract-potentiality of C1; C2, *realised* labour power, is what the money-owner buys. And 'it is not the same commodity that is bought and sold, ... neither in quantity, nor in quality.'[46] The value of labour for the worker is the (use) value that keeps him alive; the value of labour for the capitalist is what has been realised in the form of commodities for sale. The difference between C1 and C2 is surplus value. The dual nature of the commodity labour (C1 and C2) is sustained through the class ownership of the means of production, and it is of course property that sanctions capacity and access (C1 and C2 respectively) and thereby organises the field of the extraction of value.

A great deal more can be said about this, but it will have to suffice; we are interested in the insertion of the distinction *Arbeits-vermögen* (C1) and *Arbeits-kraft* (C2) as *internal* to the category of abstract labour – *Arbeit* (C) – that allows the latter, the value-form (C), to do the gathering work, as both distinct from and common to its concrete expressions (C1 + C2). The *form* is operationalised in the *real* processes of the extraction and accumulation of value. The relation between the abstract term and its concrete, 'worldly' expressions, is emphatically not that of a *form* imposed on a basic, unproblematic, 'brute' *content*. Nor is it a relation between layers, a layer of abstraction *supervening* on the layer of concrete labours. If that were the case then a 'release' from the constraint of form would unproblematically release labour to its use-value and humanising function. But it is also not

---

[46] As Gideon Freudenthal puts it (1997: 179). References to the split between C1 (labour power) and C2 (labour embodied in the product) are borrowed from his important paper.

the case that the universal stands in for the particular, in which case the particular would be nothing but the instantiation of the universal. In sum, neither does the particular (as content) exist apart from the universal (form), nor can it be subsumed to it as its mere instantiation. Because then the particular would disappear under the universal, in the kind of subsumption-as-domination that Hegel criticised in Kant's epistemology. In Hegelian thinking, in contrast, the relation between universal and particular is neither subsumption nor supervenience, but refers to a *process* whereby the universal and the particular, the abstract and the concrete, are *brought into relation*. The 'concrete universal' does not *reflect* an autonomous and self-sustaining underlying reality *but moves with it*, mediating and mediated in its relation to particulars, bringing their fragmented reality to reason. And it is as process that it enters Marx's thought too. For the Hegelian that he is, the abstracted universal cannot be the truth of the particulars it subsumes. If it were, then the capture would be total and we would end up with the 'immobile categories of bourgeois thought', in the kind of capture ('captation') that the other great Hegelian, Lukács, identified as the hallmark of bourgeois thought. Kant, the 'speculative philosopher' of the *Critique of Reason* becomes, for Lukács, its supreme apologist.

Of course once the coincidence has been disturbed, with 'mediation' replacing 'subsumption' in the relation between the categories at our disposal and the realities they express, something fundamentally new breaks into meaning-construction. If 'use value' and 'exchange value' stand in relation to 'value' as its variable instantiations, a difference that enables some 'movement' or 'play' within the category is introduced. And with this movement the contradiction is, at least potentially, turned from aporia to passage, but in any case is given some play to recall Derrida. The harbouring of antinomy in the concept of value allows the concept some movement, and action the possibility to *exploit* antinomy, something that was denied on the flat terrain of the exchange of equivalents. But with Marx's theoretical dissection, the 'Vertsand' of commodity-exchange becomes the locus of an inscription that explodes the logic of equivalence on the basis of which the theorists of the political economy had mapped it according to the laws of economic science. It becomes the locus of the inscription of the appropriation of value and thus also of class struggle. The flat expanses of equivalence that organised capitalist exchange are disrupted, and with it is disturbed the immobility of the categories of bourgeois thought, creating the opportunity – without warrant or guarantee – that social labour might be re-collected as *Vernunft*.

If the application of the concepts *Verstand* and *Venunft* appear to be importing too heavy a Hegelian baggage here, let it be noted that Althusser himself, that supremely anti-Hegelian of Marxists, in his 1968 essay 'Marx's Relation to Hegel' undertakes a defence of Marx's method against any 'schematic account'[47] of its relation to Hegel's. For Althusser, Marx's is a move of 'critical extraction', not a mere inversion of the dialectic – not 'the inversion of idealism into materialism', not 'its turning on its head', etc. – but something altogether more conceptually demanding. Though Marx clearly 'owed Hegel the crucial gift of *the* idea of the dialectic' (1968: 174), he did not '*apply* Hegel to Ricardo', says Althusser. To invert the Hegelian dialectic 'can only be a transformation'. It is this transformation of the Hegelian dialectic that Marx 'made work on' Ricardo's labour theory of value (172–3). It involved, suggests Althusser referring back to his *Reading Capital*,[48] a non-Hegelian concept of history, of social structure and, crucially, of the dialectic itself. There results from this a 'new *practice* of philosophy, a philosophical discourse that speaks *from somewhere else* than classical philosophical discourse did'. And most significantly, as Althusser explains the 'point' of the 'transformation' of the dialectic in Marx's hands, it 'was to carry out *a displacement* – to make *something move over (bouger)* in the internal disposition of the philosophical categories', such that 'philosophical discourse changes its modality – speaks *otherwise (autrement)*, which creates the difference between interpreting the world and changing it' (174). To which we might only add – from the point of view of a critical phenomenology – also to *crossing* that difference. Having offered this staggering insight, Althusser recoils: as he 'has pointed out from the outset', he reminds us, he is not interested in any 'phenomenological maieutics'.[49] But Marx *did* engage in such a phenomenological endeavour and crossed the difference – 'between interpreting the world and

---

[47] It is the '5th thesis on Feuerbach' – in which Marx claims that 'individuals ... realise in their practice relations and a conjunction wider than themselves' – which allows Althusser 'to pose the problem of the relations between Marx and Hegel' which 'very schematically' casts *Capital* as the product of 'the Hegelian dialectic as applied on [Ricardo's] labour theory of value' as supplemented by the French socialists' 'theory of class struggle' ((1968/2007: 168, 170).

[48] The 'coupure epistemologique' with Hegelian philosophy in Marx's oeuvre is typically associated with this work.

[49] He begins the article with the statement that he 'renounces rhetoric and maieutics, whether Socratic or phenomenological'. And that he 'shall lay his cards on the table' be they 'what they are ... carry[ing] the stamp of Marxism-Leninism' (1968: 164).

changing it' – in *Capital* where, in the famous section of the 'discovery of the rational kernel within the mystical shell' he says of the *dialectic* that it 'regards every developed [conceptual] form as in fluid movement and this takes into account its transient nature, lets nothing impose on it and is in its essence critical and revolutionary' (1867/1970: 20 in Althusser, 1968: 175).

The argument about critical phenomenology is the subject of the next chapter, in which we will look specifically at the *eleventh thesis* and what it means to cross the difference between interpreting the world and changing it. But already here, in the discussion of the dialectic, in the discussion of the displacement it carries, in Althusser's movement ('bouger') of the categories, and in Derrida's 'slack', there emerges a dynamic *relation* of the concepts to the concrete particularities that are expressed through them, and thereby leeway is given to what is *brought to expression*, the possibilities of *semantic drift*, the relation between semantics and structures and the openness of concepts to history. We saw how the distinction *within* the extension of the term labour power between C1 and C2 allowed movement within the semantic scope, allowing us to observe and make sense of the value form, a traction that simultaneously 'unlocked' the 'cipher' of the commodity and produced a semantic surplus on which value could be differentiated between the two instances. The distinction within the semantic extension of labour power allowed it to move and in that movement to harbour the real processes of the entrenchment, and potential contestation, of value.

With this we come to close this first account of 'semantics and structures' as offered from the point of view of Marxist theory, where arguably the structural conditions that mobilise semantics under the cipher of the 'commodity' are at their most intransigent. Marx offers us a famous distinction that correlates with our own. It is the distinction he draws between *formal and real subsumption*. *Formal* subsumption names the process whereby labour power finds expression under capital's valorisation in the commodity form, in the way that captures the semantic function. *Real* subsumption names the pragmatics of the extraction of surplus value in the history of capitalism, its tectonic movements: the first of these, 'original accumulation', names the historical emergence of the framing conditions of a market in labour, the first sweeping gesture that the institutionalisation of scarcity took under capitalism. A second move of real subsumption refers to the historical conditions of enforcing it in the heartlands (the *Black Act* in England, etc.) and its exportation to the periphery in the colonial dispossessions. A third move refers to the 'creative destruction' (Schumpeter) of labour practices through flexibilisation, unemployment and under-employment, the recalibration of production away from labour-intensive and toward capital-intensive forms, that surround us today. Of course the moves can be described otherwise; however, *eventually* real subsumption comes to consolidate the hold of capital, or as Jacques Camatte puts it, it comes to mark 'the *becoming* of capital as totality' (Camatte, 1988: 45). The *structural* configuration ensures that the reproduction of the labouring classes becomes ever more tightly integrated within the circuit of the reproduction of capital; this is achieved via specific *semantic/conceptual* mediations. And these mediations, as we have insisted with Marx, are both conceptual and historical, formal and real subsumption operating *in tandem*. Formal subsumption acquires a real existence vis-à-vis concrete labours that are subsumed under it as capital extends its hold progressively. Throughout the process it is historical processes that drive the emergence of regimes of truth, of the 'becoming' of capital as totality. At a certain threshold real subsumption achieves a totalising hold of capital over labour; at a certain threshold of the generalisation of the commodity form and the mechanism of price, capital comes to pass itself as the 'truth' of the thing it subsumes.

This is not a complete, perhaps not even an adequate, answer to the phenomenological blockage associated with the commodification of labour and the fetish phenomenon. But for our purposes it is as far as we can go. At stake was the effort to keep an antinomy alive between living labour and its realisation in the circuits of commodity exchange, to give it space in the more accommodating Hegelian conceptual framework. In all this perhaps the language of value does not carry Marx as far as his critical insight would have taken him.[50] It might be that the Hegelian concept of value, for all the mediation and effects it invites, cannot shake off the fetish, if as a formal conceptual scheme it forever expresses the relationality of particular labours (the stuff of concrete social life) in terms of an abstraction, a universality, only ever coincident with their commensurability in exchange. If, that is, labour value's expression as exchange value *cannot* be meaningfully bracketed, for the qualitative to shine through the quantitative, for it to be thought as *both* concrete *and* recognisably social. And yet something significant has been

---

[50] Or to put it in the way that Valerie Kerruish puts it: 'I prefer to say that language does not go as far as Marx wants to go; it does not reach to expressing the *Doppelgänger* of an abstraction' (2007: 11).

granted us. It is the notion that whatever the shortfall of the categories available to us to redraw the boundary between what is contingent and what is necessary, the shortfall is itself contingent, tied in with particular histories, potentially challengeable. Structures and semantics co-evolve in the process of capital's re-valorisation. And that relation between structures and semantics is not unidirectional, in a way that keeps phenomenality circuited to structures. Which also means that the difference between internal and transcendent operations, those that reproduce the structures and those that might put them to question, is intrinsically uncertain at the meta-level. This does not translate into the faith that Karl Polanyi has, that living labour *cannot be* fully externalised, that such a move *inevitably* produces a social antagonism, that there *will* be a 'double movement' in the sense of a defensive storming of the market system by social forces. But while redress can thus be neither foreclosed nor foreordained, our discussion of semantics and structures allows us to see that redress is nonetheless wagered on the same historical-conceptual terrain on which the wrong is inflicted.

1.4

Towards a Critical Phenomenology

Improbable Disclosures

If the previous chapter tracked the trajectories of the 'forgetting' of labour, and the diverse ways in which the emancipatory promise was lost to the mundane violence of the practices of work, the widespread commodification of social life, and the categorical schemata that vacate political opportunity, a critical phenomenology is tasked with recovering what was forgotten. We begin with such deployments of phenomenology as counter-method, as they inform Weil's concept of *attention* and Rancière's of *dissensus*. The emphasis here is on the largely underplayed phenomenological moment in the work of both, the disclosure that *attention* achieves in Weil, that *the aesthetic act* brings to presence in Rancière. The meaning of these insistent efforts at making perceptible is at the heart of a critical phenomenology, critical in the sense that it proceeds *against* the usual path-dependencies. The difficulty is captured in the 'as-if' of courage in Weil, the counter-factual staging of *dissensus* in Rancière. Both Weil's 'attention' and Rancière's ethnographies are, I will argue, profoundly phenomenological endeavours that pit themselves against the self-evidence of what appears as given. It is their unremitting refusal to give in to the 'distributions of sense' currently in circulation that mark them out as political, critical phenomenological undertakings.

*

It is significant that it is principally the language of *rights*, what Weil calls the language of the middle range, that for her is what elides, effaces and forgets suffering. Weil's counter-method breaks into the legal *architecture* of justice and of its distributions of rights-claims and entitlements with a devastating injunction:

> Justice consists in seeing that no harm is done to men. Whenever a man cries inwardly: 'Why am I being hurt?' harm is being done to him. He is

often mistaken when he tries to define the harm, and why and by whom it is being inflicted on him. *But the cry itself is infallible.*[1]

(1989: 286)

And she continues:

> Every time that arises the cry 'Why am I being hurt?' then *there is certainly injustice.*[2]

In order to understand the nature and depth of the injunction we must ask what it would mean to provide an adequate answer to the question 'why am I being hurt?' What is revealing here is not simply that *every* response to the question strikes us as inadequate, but that even to attempt to answer the question is in a significant sense to misunderstand it. I am reminded of an example that Rai Gaita uses in his wonderful book *A Common Humanity*. Gaita recalls an interview in the 1970s during which a French woman who saw a young Nazi officer usher children onto the trains destined for the death camps, described how every day she asked herself the same question, how it was possible for him to do it. She did not mean that psychology, sociology, political science could not have delivered an answer. His behaviour could be explained as a result of fear, duty, or unquestioning obedience to authority, and at one level, says Gaita, this is an adequate explanation. But 'no distance we travel in that direction will take us toward an answer to her question. Hers was a question without answer and someone who offered her an answer would fail to understand her bewilderment.'[3] After every justification has been offered it is *still* always possible to ask the question anew. We might surmise that this 'remainder' tracks the *infallibility* of the cry.

---

[1] The page references to 'On Human Personality' are to McLellan (1989).

[2] 'For if, as often happens, it is only the result of a misunderstanding, then the injustice consists in the *inadequacy of the explanation* ... Affliction is by its nature inarticulate. The afflicted silently beseech to be given the words to express themselves. There are times when they are given none; but there are also times when they are given words, but ill-chosen ones, ... that know nothing of the affliction they would interpret.' (Weil, 1989: 286.)

[3] Gaita, 2013: 39. For Gaita this links to the main argument of the book that 'we are ethically constituted; and this means that we cannot radically prescind from the ethical constitution of our inner lives without becoming unintelligible to ourselves ... To try to describe the inner life without reference to the categories of good and evil would be like trying to describe it without reference to our mortality and our vulnerability to misfortune.' (2013: 53–4)

Back to Weil, for whom to offer to express the question 'why am I being hurt' in the language of rights is an offer of staggering inadequacy. In what she calls 'the middle region' of the discourse and practice of human rights, vulnerability and suffering will fail to invoke anything like an adequate response. She writes this about the language of the middle region in her important late essay 'On Human Personality' ('La personne et le sacré'):

> The notion of rights, by its very mediocrity, leads on naturally to that of the person, for rights are related to personal things. They are on that level.
>
> (1989: 279)

And then:

> Words of the middle region, such as right, democracy, person, are valid in their own region, which is that of ordinary institutions. But for the sustaining inspiration of which all institutions are, as it were, the projection, a different language is needed ... Above those institutions which are concerned with protecting rights and persons and democratic freedoms, others must be invented for the purpose of exposing and abolishing everything in contemporary life which buries the soul under injustice, lies, and ugliness.
>
> (1989: 288)

Weil will contrast the notion of *attention* to the institutional language of the middle range and the appeal to rights. Responsiveness to the cry is undone at the middle region of institutions because the language of institution is a language of generalisation, of reduction and of functionality. Weil does not use this language explicitly, but thematises loss around what she identifies as the 'mediocre' language of *right* and *person* built around the circulation of claim and counter-claim. Rights are concepts that are linked to the logic of exchange and of measured quantity; legal personality to the comparative demand of person to person. Weil prophetically indicts the mass proliferation of rights and rights-holders whose shrillness[4] of claim and counter-claim are heard as they mobilise the language of interest. *Against* these concepts of the 'middle region', Weil interjects *attention*. 'The spirit of justice ... is nothing else but a certain kind of attention' (276), she says. The concept of attention is key to understanding ethical responsiveness.

---

[4] In the original: 'L'usage de ce mot [des 'droits'] a fait, de ce qui aurait dû être un cri jailli du fond des entrailles, une aigre criaillerie [a shrill nagging] de revendication, sans pureté ni efficacité' (1957: 31).

For Weil, *attention* possesses a quality of open waiting; she contrasts this apprehensive phenomenology to the loud proclamation of claim and counter-claim, and the complacent vocabulary of entitlement. In the acute receptiveness of attention something is carried over into manifestation, a meaning is elicited other than that afforded by the languages of the middle range. Weil will offer the tentative language of 'sacredness' – of what is 'sacred in every man' – to capture this heightened sense of responsibility, as geared to the recovery of 'fragile possibilities'. But what does it mean to say that *responsibility has the fragile as its specific vis-à-vis*? It means to disconnect *responsibility* from the structures to which the languages of the middle range subsume it as a question of *accountability*. The tradition of thinking about justice that we have inherited from Aristotle involves an order that holds measured relationships between individuals and goods together,[5] according to an architectonic of reasons, hierarchies and classifications, within which justice-claims find their proper place. In this context, for the 'mediocre' legal language of the 'middle ground' the question would be posed and answered as a question of justiciability and standing. Jurisdiction draws on the institutional constituents of *ordering*. Institutional structures are functionally oriented, and subject positions within them are defined by such functional orientation. That is why they miss the fragile.

Of course hard cases often test these frameworks and structures of expectations of entitlements are re-configured in the process. But the cry 'why am I being hurt?' is not an invitation to such adjustments. If Weil's question 'why am I being hurt?' is unanswerable, and yet the cry infallible, it is because it expresses from the very first instance an imperative which nothing precedes, one that we might call 'axiomatic'. The question is in a crucial sense a question that is prior not just to the sets of concepts that (typically in the form of rights) attempt to answer it, but also to any set of reasons that would justify it as a 'reasonable' question. The phenomenologist, Paul Ricoeur, says this in a tantalisingly short aside in *L'Acte de Juger*:

> We do not accede to a sense of justice except through the detour of protesting against injustice. The cry *'this is unjust'* often indeed expresses a clearer intuition regarding the true nature of society and the place that

---

[5] Starting out from Aristotle's *Politics*, Rancière's *Disagreement* defines political justice 'not simply [as] the order that holds measured relationships between individuals and goods together... [but] the order that determines the partition of what is common' (Rancière, 1999: 5).

violence still holds within it, than any discourse over what justice rationally or reasonably requires.

(Ricoeur, 2003: 190)

Like Weil's this is a phenomenological rather than a normative understanding of justice. For Ricoeur, our perception of injustice comes *before* the theories of justice that might ground it, it appears, startlingly, on a first-person phenomenological register, it takes one by surprise. What is the meaning of this 'before' and the idea that the perception of injustice might surprise our assumptions? The injunction 'this is unjust!' does not invoke as its register any institutional expectational framework with its relative thresholds of violation and disappointment. Like Weil's cry it precedes the middle range language of the institutions and invokes a responsibility that is antecedent to them. I want to insist on the centrality of the dimension of time underlying this. Responsiveness and fragility involve a massive shift in the 'time' of responsibility away from an orientation to the past and recall it in the present-future, whereas institutional responsibility operates a modality of time that defines it primarily in terms of the ability to designate an agent as the author of their actions. It projects the occurrence of responsibility in the aftermath of action ('X *will be* held *to have been* responsible') and is understood as a future answerability to past actions. Structures of accountability inevitably deploy the temporal modality of future answerability, a conditional imputation-back of the wrong to its agent. But this kind of retrospection misses fragility altogether. In one and the same move it institutionalises indifference and belies fragility that requires that it remain alive in the present-future toward the addressee of care.

It is over the question of time, then, that this other hermeneutic of injustice allows us to think the order of responsibility differently with Weil and Ricoeur. And if in asking the question 'what to do about this fragile being?' it rethinks its temporal modality, in the social dimension too, it invokes an addressee that does not find a home in traditional notions of responsibility. As re-oriented to the fragile, responsibility introduces an *incompleteness* here, an asymmetry: it is *always* attentive to the fragile because one can never have exhausted the duty of caring. For Ricoeur 'responsibility refers to the idea of a mandate ... principally with regard to the perishable. Responsibility therefore bears an element of passivity or, if one prefers, of a receptivity that is not devoid of *bewilderment (vertige)* and anguish ... There comes a moment of reflection where the distinction between exteriority and interiority, autonomy and heteronomy, is blotted out.' (Ricoeur, 2003: 190.) To take on this point is to see a reversal in the way the question of ethics is put. Now the static responsibility of the autonomous agent 'to whom nothing can happen', as Derrida put it famously in the *Politics of Friendship*, becomes the responsibility to the fragile towards whom it is irrational to claim that *enough* care has been given, any 'adequacy' here unsettled by the idea of being always-already enjoined or indebted to another. And if that reversal now establishes responsibility as forever in the 'not yet', then its disaggregation into rights and duties pits it *against* the event of its *disclosure as* care.[6]

In sum, what Weil's *attention* draws into visibility the languages of the middle range, as harnessed to function, make disappear. Is it not here that the full impact of the concepts of her 'middle region' hits home? In the *social* dimension legal personality replaces what is most sacred in man with the impersonal ('la personne' she calls it) and with a sociality of distance: what Goffman insightfully captures as the 'dis-attendability' – the continuous interaction *without* attention – on the basis of the role-descriptors that attach to intersubjectivity in institutions. In the *material* dimension specific visibilities and specific stakes are imported, whose adequate specification in the 'middle region' is condition of audibility and success. In the *temporal* dimension with the substitution of time horizons, the irreducible attentiveness to the fragile is reversed in the future-anterior of responsibility *as* accountability.

Incomplete, suggestive, unsystematic, these are fragments of a critical phenomenology that return us to a question whose urgency *attests* to a phenomenality as stake of an ethical and a political demand. Weil was never a systematic thinker, and the fragments she offers us invite an improbable disclosure that strains against what the languages of the middle range seal over in the gesture which is typical of all reductions, the gesture that institutionalises indifference and belies fragility. In Weil, in Ricoeur, in Gaita, in attention, responsiveness and unanswerability respectively, the irreducibility of the question 'why am I being hurt?' persists in the face of the accommodating architectonic of reasons and

---

[6] With the concept of care (*Sorge*) Heidegger introduces a proximity to the other that is always-already the collapse of a certain distance from the other, in the sense that the world is not something I need to cross any subject/object distance to encounter: I start with it, in it, *of it*. Being *is* care and the structure of care is temporality. The coincidence of responsibility and fragility in the notion of care, orients one into the future in an activity directed forever to a 'towards-which'. See also Honneth (2008).

language of the 'middle range', *disclosing 'something as something'* (more on this in a moment) *because* it does not lend itself to a productive deployment by the orders that offer to answer it, as occasion for the reproduction of the systemic logics that they mobilise.

We shall leave Weil now. As we move in the next Part of the book to constitutionalism, we will return to her injunction, but now with a view to generating interpretative mileage out of it. It will be argued in Chapter 2.3 (and then later in the final chapters of Part IV) that the critical achievement of writing obligation, community or solidarity (what we will call the 'dogmatic' resources of juridical thought) into the constitution (Weil's languages of the middle region) is that it introduces a fault line within the constitutional imaginary. The inscription of the aspiration into the mediocrity of the mediating language of rights confronts the promise of obligation, community, solidarity, with the inadequacy of that 'mediation'. Not continuity but tension – or even, to use a more loaded term, contradiction – installs itself there between dignity promised and indignity delivered; between the promise of responsibility and the denial of fragility; between the promise of solidarity and the delivery of 'shrill' contention and claim of right. And where there is contradiction, redress can find traction.

*

If Weil's phenomenology is about troubling disclosure, Rancière's is about contesting the 'distribution of the sensible' (*le partage du sensible*) as he puts it. The distribution of the sensible is 'the system of self-evident facts of sense perception that simultaneously discloses the existence of something in common and the delimitations that define the respective parts and positions within it' (Rancière, 2004b: 12). It is an appreciation of the way in which a world of sensory perception is partitioned and shared within a social structure. Rancière's principal concern is to account for the selective distribution of sense and silence to the oppressed, and to lives deprived of 'worldliness'. There are two cadences that run through Rancière's accounts of working lives. The first is the tireless documenting of the unremarkable features of days lived in numbing routine and insecurity that Rancière records with ethnographic exactitude in *The Nights of Labour*, with an unwavering attention to what it is that the Parisian workers said and wrote during the period between the two revolutions of 1830 and 1848. His immersion in the 'archives of the proletarian dream' allows him to gather often unremarkable details with affection, 'the slow boring of hard boards' Weber might have called it. And Rancière's is a text that records them in a key only just above the level at which these lives daily pass with very little to grant them levity or grace. His concern is to record these histories of labouring lives in their particularity, 'to add his voice to theirs, to hear their voices rather than interpret them, to help them resound, to make them circulate.'[7] Their integration into patterned narratives or sociological extrapolation misses what is unique about them, which also explains Rancière's profound opposition to Bourdieu's sweeping sociological gaze, his opposition to the generalisation of experience in the gathering category of *habitus* which ultimately involves the accumulation of habitual dispositions. To seize by sociological inventory these incongruous speech acts and these hesitant scripts, for Rancière is to do them violence. As Kristin Ross describes the ambition of Rancière's intervention, 'the particular actions and points of view of marginal individuals, when resuscitated with care and attention, reframed and staged can be mobilized against the dominant ideology. Provided, of course, that the right transversals are created' (Ross, 2009: 25).

The notion of the 'right transversals' transfers us to the second cadence. One must tread carefully here because it is a painstaking effort that allows anything like the *political voice* of the workers to emerge from the 'multiplicity of micro-experiences of repartitioning the sensible, a multiplicity of operations that have reframed the place of the worker, the time of his work and his life, the exercise of his gaze . . .' (Rancière, 2009b: 277). 'Place of worker', 'time of work' and 'the exercise of his gaze': the emplacing and timing of what *is given* to the gaze are the prerequisites (transversals) of what may be acted on.

Let us begin with *place*. In Marxist theory, 'ideology' is the lived representation of the conditions under which the exploitation that inheres in living labour is experienced as unavoidable necessity. If those under the grip of ideology dwell in misrepresentation of their place in social reproduction, it is because the place that they find themselves does not allow them to see the structure that allots them that place. The speaking position they occupy carries that blind spot as a matter of its constitution. As became evident in our earlier discussion of commodification, it cannot be shaken off because it informs the very speaking position that labour finds itself in. This point will be vital, later, also to the social dimension of constitutionalism and the speaking

---

[7] Deranty (2003). Deranty's careful reading of Rancière in a number of texts over the years is exemplary.

position afforded to the constitutional subject. The same move that offers freedom locks compulsion in place.[8] The circularity is ideological as Marx understood it, and since it is also structural it allows no redress. If workers are unable *to see beyond* those coordinates, Rancière will put it with arresting simplicity, it is because their 'being unable is the same as their being there'. Then the task becomes to 'split up the tautology of being there' (2009b: 280).

So much for place; what of *time*? Rancière's book is about the *nights* of labour, and the first point of resistance to compulsion involves, in a certain sense, the stealing of time.[9] Since the time of the work*day* imposes itself relentlessly on the life of the manual workers – relentlessly in the way that Weil also described the rhythm that punctuates factory workdays as deafening, and inhuman – what is stolen are the nights. It is at that time that are produced the 'little narratives' that Rancière finds published in the 'numerous and ephemeral newspapers that blossomed' leading up to the revolution of 1848. One of the most remarkable of the diaries is philosopher-joiner Louis Gabriel Gauny's for its 're-invention of the everyday' (Rancière, 1983). It does this (and I simplify greatly here) because Gauny is able to draw a line between his performing certain activities that fulfil his professional life as a joiner and the capacities of seeing, saying and doing that 'fit' that performance (2009b: 275). In the little narrative we find the 'subversion of the performance of inequality'. Not because Gauny can step out of the condition of inequality through the narrative. But because by inhabiting the narrative, the locution of reading and of literature, he subverts its capacity to confine him. Literature forges an imbalance, a break in the fit between an occupation and the sensory frame in which it is embedded. 'What literature endows the workers with is not the awareness of their condition. It is the passion that can make them break their condition because it is the passion that their condition forbade', says Rancière (2009b: 278).

These acts of resistance are aesthetic acts, and as far as the 'exercise of the gaze' is concerned, they are untimely: they unsettle and cut across emplacement and timeframes. Regarding the former, for Rancière a nascent constituent dimension emerges that hinges between the political and the aesthetic, with the aesthetic act disrupting the watertight grip of

---

[8] For Althusser, ideology secures at the structural level that the appearance of the freedom that it promises is not undercut by the truth of the domination that it organises. (See Althusser (1969/2013).)

[9] On stealing time, Ross, 2009: 23.

ideological thinking. For Gauny it is literature that allows him to break with the compulsion of his working life:

> Literary locutions draft maps of the visible, trajectories between the visible and the sayable, relationships between modes of being, modes of saying, and modes of doing and making. They define variations of sensible intensities, perceptions and the abilities of bodies. They thereby take hold of unspecified groups of people, they widen gaps, open up space for deviations, modify the speeds, the trajectories, and the ways in which groups of people adhere to a condition, react to situations, recognize their images.
>
> (Rancière, 2004a: 11)

This is what ties aesthetics to politics, and it is a 'deviant' phenomenology that is forged at the juncture where 'gaps widen', where deviations are 'given space', where 'images are recognised'. A key aspect of that 'reconfiguration' of the system's distribution of the sensible is the 'modification of the speeds', the accelerations and decelerations of the perception of time. But above all, the aesthetic act's claim on *time* involves the introduction of an *interval*: a 'décalage', distancing or disjuncture in the economy of time. It is 'the rift', as Rancière will call it later, 'through which subjects of history pass' (Rancière, 1994: 98). We are faced here with the question of how the time of politics appears, and appearance, he will insist, is always *untimely*.[10] That is, perhaps above all, what allows events to take place not *as instantiations* of this or that, but *as against* the regularities and institutional modalities that would welcome them on the scene. This does not mean that their appearance remains singular and un-interpretable. No, their appearance occurs at the confluence of two worlds – the 'bringing of two worlds into one' as Rancière is fond of reminding us – here of the time of politics on the one hand with its institutionalised regularities and opportunities, and on the other, of that which *surprises* those distributions because it positions itself incongruently to them. I want to insist on this term 'incongruently'. The appearance of phenomena as *against* the register of their ordinary reproduction depends on this positioning. What is at stake for the political, and the appearance of its (temporal) opportunity, is its untimeliness. Rancière is very close to Alain Badiou here and the thinking of the 'event'. Untimeliness informs the event of the disruption – the 'décalage' or

---

[10] In Kirstin Ross's title (see Ross, 2009). A conception that runs close to what is referred to by Negri, and other Marxists, as *kairos*.

'écartement' or disjuncture – of the stream of reassurances through which the extant order reproduces the situation of its ordinary operations. But the 'aesthetic act' resists its integration back into that expectational context; its appearance depends on and constitutes the fissure, the 'écart', the break. Rancière is careful to draw his own account in contrast to what Althusser identified as 'conjuncture', the revolutionary seizing of the opportune moment in terms of the objective conditions of History. Against 'conjuncture' Rancière gives us a conception of political time that can be carved out of the subjective experience of the passing of time through an act of disruption of its rhythm, but one that introduces a contingency that *can* be thematised, shared in language, and acted on. 'Praxis entails a kind of watchfulness or attention to these intermittent manifestations, to the moments when such demonstrations are produced, the moments, in fact, when something is happening' (Ross, 2009: 29). So while the workers, Gauny and the others, remain in the sphere of exploitation, the sensory grip of that reality is nevertheless loosened. A certain 'poetics of knowledge' sets in, Rancière argues, whereby the little narratives are extracted out of the all-subsuming framework that goes by the name of 'workers culture', the sweeping *habitus* of their 'belonging', to appear as statements on, and shifts in, the distribution of the sensible, unsettling and inassimilable. The 'as-if' is what expresses the logic of the extraction of potential from givenness. The 'as if' of the improbable, incongruent disclosures, reveals to Gauny, to the others, the 'something as something' of the appearance of the real claimed *otherwise*.

With this formulation we are now squarely within the field of phenomenology. For the remainder of this chapter, first we will explore the tradition of phenomenology somewhat more systematically, tracing it back to its original statement in Husserl, then briefly discussing two distinct trajectories of its development. Thereafter we will read Marx's *Eleventh thesis on Feuerbach*, the most concise description of the task of critical theory ever articulated, in a phenomenological light. With the critical-phenomenological strain thus identified, we will transfer it across to constitutional theory in Part II.

The Phenomenological Method

The fundamental epistemological innovation that phenomenology introduces is that objective themes on the one hand, and the modality of access to them on the other, cannot be separated: what appears, appears as something to someone.[11] And thus whatever truth value we assign to objects cannot be done so independently of their *givenness* to structures of intentionality. The insight is foundational for Edmund Husserl who made the phenomenological 'breakthrough' at the turn of the twentieth century. Since his point of departure was the modality in which intentional lived experience correlated to its object, the fundamental *problem* of phenomenology was inextricably linked with its most profound *insight*, that of the 'origin' of objects in consciousness. Husserl's many theoretical turns can be linked to his insistence on 'purifying' consciousness of what might be called its 'worldly apperception', in order that it might 'receive' the reality of phenomena unencumbered by its immanent limitations.

The steps of that endeavour are milestones along the fascinating trajectory of the development of his thought, as it centres on the shifting notion of the *phenomenological reduction*, and with it the shift from ontology to epistemology in the imperative that 'Being' must be *made present* to consciousness. In the early 'breakthrough' of the *Logical Investigations* (1900) the 'eidetic' reduction introduced a distinction between an 'empirical' and a 'pure' psychology, allowing Husserl a first form of 'bracketing' of the world, so that the reality of the world could emerge as something different to the consciousness that attempted to know it. A 'bracketing' (Husserl uses the Greek word *epoché*) is not a negation, but a suspension.[12] Husserl invited the bracketing of the receiving consciousness in order to allow the phenomenon itself to come forth. The *General Introduction to a Pure Phenomenology* of 1913 introduced the 'transcendental' reduction, while later Husserl turned to a 'genetic' phenomenology whose emphasis was on intersubjectivity and history. What troubles Husserl as he navigates his phenomenology across this terrain by means of these reductions is at the same time what keeps his attention fixed on the stake: the correlation between acts of consciousness and *the objects that give themselves* in those acts, the

---

[11] The formulation is Heidegger's. I quote it from Hans Lindahl for whom it forms the central axis of the phenomenology of law that he offers in *Fault Lines of Globalisation* (2013).

[12] *Epoché*, bracketing or suspension is the key methodological device. The first step of any phenomenology involves that suspension, and this move is key to Husserl, as it will be later for Niklas Luhmann's grand phenomenological endeavour, the theory of social systems. For Luhmann the bracketing involves the holding of societal complexity suspended, the negative move that sustains the achievement of the emergence of systems of meaningful communication which is the achievement of reducing that complexity.

correlation in other words between *noesis* (acts) and *noema* (objects).¹³ As fundamental a re-orientation of philosophical inquiry as this is, its very inaugurating gesture remains fundamentally opaque in its 'terrifying simplicity': *to return to the objects in question.* Take Husserl's classic definition: '[t]he word *phenomenon* is ambiguous by virtue of the essential correlation between appearing [*Erscheinen*] and that which appears [*Erscheinden*]'.¹⁴ It would not be an exaggeration to say that the whole of phenomenology is contained in the promise and problématique of that 'ambiguity'.

By the time Husserl writes the *Cartesian Meditations* in 1931, the emphasis has moved to *intersubjectivity*: the world is analysed as correlated to the experience of a collective. *Noesis* is a category that engages a collective and is embedded in the context of the *Heimwelt*. The development is traceable to Husserl's insistence to account for the full *extension* of intentional consciousness, of *noesis*, as it appears across its many forms (imagination, memory, empathy) engaging what we might call both the social and temporal dimensions, and the different modes of being of the transcendental subject. And in this context we have another significant shift of the phenomenological perspective in Husserl: it now shifts from being a 'discovery' of the thing in the world, as perceived by an act of consciousness, to a 'justification' of the meaning of its individuation as a phenomenon. By which is meant that phenomena do not just appear to consciousness; their appearance is mediated by a commonality of experience and anticipation, furnished by memory, empathy and imagination. With 'intersubjectivity' having installed itself at the social axis of the meaning of the phenomenon, appearance is constitutively reliant on those associations that 'awaken' the subject to an active intending, associations that are embedded in communal resources, in expectational/motivational structures of the *lifeworld* and its processes of symbolic reproduction. They inform the occasions and modalities of consciousness and provide for the dynamic unity of 'we' identifications.

But now a certain humility attaches to the phenomenological gaze as it radicalises its central methodological constraint in order to generalise it to the intersubjective reception of phenomena. Because any phenomenological description proper must be performed from a *first-person* point of

---

¹³ In the *Idea of Phenomenology* 'the task is just this: within the field of pure evidence or self-givenness to study all forms of givenness and all correlations, and to conduct an elucidatory analysis of them all' (Husserl, 1902/2013: 10).
¹⁴ Quoted in Marion, 1998: 21.

view, each perception achieves only partial givenness, and the question of how the collective might *correct* such partiality becomes a key concern. Husserl calls such first-person perception an *Abschattung*, a simple adumbration. The problem is how to understand the overcoming of the first-person partiality. And because individual acts of consciousness can only deliver partial givenness, Husserl will turn to intersubjectivity to redress that lack of completion, and to set it in history, between 'retention' and 'protension', or more simply between the givenness of what is received as horizon in the *Heimwelt* and the promise of the progress of Reason.

And if along the *social dimension inter*-subjectivity has installed itself, albeit problematically, as horizon of meaning, problems proliferate also along the *temporal dimension*. Consciousness is conceived from the very start as caught up in time, constitutively restless, in a profound sense always-already an alteration of itself. 'Every experience refers to the possibility ... not only of explicating, step by step, *the thing which has been given* in a first view ... but also of obtaining, little by little, as experience continues, *new* determinations of the *same* thing.'[15]

But is this staggering of phenomenality, this postponement of what can only ever appear as incomplete and partial, not now asking too much of phenomenology as *method*? With the correlation now to an *open* intersubjectivity, one in which the givenness of phenomena is never underwritten by anything like the completeness of the receiving structure, Husserl is increasingly drawn to an argument about a *progressive* realisation; even, arguably, a self-correcting process. But what to make of this partial, incremental appearance, that never exhausts the phenomenon, that falls short of granting it signification, that merely postpones its truth? Why insist on intuition as condition of presence if intuition is partial? And does the correlation of appearance with a 'collective' or future – in both cases *incomplete* – intentionality cancel out its promise?

Two lines of phenomenological thinking diverge radically at this point. The first submits the unruly and incomplete category of intentionality to the category of *givenness*, and makes the latter, despite the many difficulties that we saw it encounters, the notion that organises the phenomenological method. This is the route taken by Jean-Luc Marion in his

---

[15] Husserl, 1939/1973: 32, quoted in Lindahl, 2013: 129. In this context we must read Hans Lindahl's trenchant formulation of the manifestation of phenomena as 'reiterative anticipations'. Always in *media res*, legal acts *re*-iterate and *re*-interpret, 'disclosing something as something *anew*'.

profound renewal of phenomenology. I will say something about it also because of its significant insight on method. My suggestion for a critical phenomenology will, however, take a second route, which remains with intentionality as equally co-implicated in organising disclosure. Neither approach, arguably, abandons Husserl's phenomenological project, although Marion might add that Husserl only '*a contrario* renders this [second] path possible' (Marion, 1998: 22). I will outline both orientations beginning with how Marion identifies his methodological departure.

In Husserl's words, phenomenology insists that 'everything that offers itself originarily to us in intuition ... must simply be received for what it gives itself' (1902/2013: 44). Husserl says this with his sight fixed on metaphysics, which would typically posit grounds or conditions for knowledge. But with the phenomenological 'world-disclosure' things are different. Husserl wants to insist on the originary givenness of that which appears in consciousness; originary precisely because lacking conditions or prior grounds. In Marion's words 'the givenness in presence of each thing is realised without any prior condition' (Marion, 2012: 1). 'Phenomenology frees presence from any condition or precondition for receiving what gives itself as it gives itself' (Marion, 2012: 1). And with this we come up against the problem of method. It commits the phenomenological method to letting phenomena manifest themselves. The central promise of a phenomenology for Marion must centre on the concept of *givenness* rather than intentionality.

It is in this context that Marion insightfully calls phenomenology a *counter-method*. Of course phenomenology, 'to be sure, like all rigorous science, decides its own project, its own terrain, and its own method, thus taking the initiative as originally as possible.' And yet, says Marion, 'counter to all metaphysics, [phenomenology] has no other ambition than to lose this initiative as quickly and completely as possible.' 'The methodological beginning establishes only the conditions for its own disappearance in the original manifestation of what shows *itself*' (2012: 9). Marion invites us to see the successive steps and turns in Husserl's trajectory, all the swerving and the 'zigzagging', as his attempts to deal with the paradox that the reductions, intuitions, intentions, fulfilments, 'appresentations', etc., that gave leverage to apparition cannot be conceived as conditions or grounds for it, but must instead be *undone* in the name of allowing the phenomenon to appear as itself. Crucially 'the method does not run ahead of the phenomenon by *fore*-seeing it, *pre*-dicting it or *pro*-ducing it' but instead 'travels in tandem with the phenomenon' (2012: 9). Marion says: 'The phenomenological method, even when it constitutes phenomena, is limited to letting them manifest *themselves.*' Later: 'the phenomenological reduction never reduces except to givenness.' Note the paradox that attaches to the terms 'constitutes' and 'reduces' in the two extracts, a paradox all the more alive as it is bound up with the *acts* of constituting and reducing. Reduction 'leads' the phenomenon towards givenness: '[reduction] leads scattered, potential, confused and uncertain visibles (mere appearances, outlines, impressions, vague intuitions, supposed facts, opinions, etc) to givenness ...' (2012: 15). Marion puts it succinctly: 'The reduction does nothing; it lets manifestation manifest itself' (2012: 10). It is this double movement of performing and withdrawing – the essential phenomenological operation – that 'counter-method' attempts to capture.

As a *negative* methodology, phenomenology on this account engages in the clearing exercise that suspends impurities (empirical psychologies) in a way that lends leverage to the manifestation of things themselves. And 'the reduction must be done in order to undo it and let it become the apparition of what shows *itself* through it, though finally without it' (16). Marion withdraws at this point all conditions of appearance, all pregivenness of the environing conditions of manifestation, the whole phenomenological scaffolding of the 'Als-Struktur' (the as-structure).[16] That is why Marion will downplay Husserl's reduction to consciousness in the name of harnessing phenomenological reduction to givenness instead, turning it, in a fascinating way self-referential and – with all external reference and methodological support withdrawn – only then true to itself.

It is to a second tradition that we turn now, of a *socially weighted phenomenology*, that draws a *constitutive* connection of the appearance of phenomena and the receiving consciousness (the subject of the gaze), in a way that lends itself more readily to the critical turn. It lends itself because it discerns a reciprocity – a *co-constitution* even – between what is presented to consciousness and the consciousness that receives it. Let us recall the main steps of this constitutive articulation. The *noema* (meaning) is tied to *noesis* (act of comprehending), in other words meaning is tied to its reception in consciousness. This reception ties *noesis* in turn to intersubjectivity. There is a key correlation between the *what* of appearance and the structures of intentionality that take cognisance of it and, in that, catalyse its manifestation.

---

[16] Many thanks to Kyle McGee for discussions on this point.

Drawing on the last important work of Husserl's, the 1936 *Crisis of European Sciences and Transcendental Phenomenology*, Hans Lindahl refers to Husserl's careful account of how the phenomenality of the world is situated against a horizon, and is co-experienced by a plurality of consciousnesses, in a crucial way, thus, both 'pre-given' (horizon) and 'co-given' (intersubjectivity). For Lindahl, whose primary concern is to give us 'a first-person plural concept of *legal* order' there is something vastly important in this later work of Husserl's about the plural subject-centredness of the appearance of the world.

> [P]henomenology has insisted ... that a world is *subject-relative*. When describing the structures of the world, one describes its mode of *givenness*, that is, how it appears to *us*, where 'us' denotes both the first-person singular and the first-person plural perspective ... Crucially, it is precisely insofar as the world is subject-relative that it not only 'appears' (to someone), but appears as *bounded* totality of meaning-relations ...
> (Lindahl, 2013: 263–4)

> And crucially, to the extent that disclosure of something as something is also always the co-disclosure of the referential unity whence it is intelligible who ought to do what, where and when.
> (Lindahl, 2013: 126)

The analysis centres on the emergence of the plural perspective as constitutive of what is 'co-given' and 'pre-given' to us as world – the social and temporal coordinates, respectively, of its 'givenness' or disclosure. The moment of subjectivity, the intentional act that receives the given remains significant in the manifestation. If the 'appearance of something as something' is given to or received by structures of collective intentionality, the receiving structure remains active in the manifestation. Furthermore, its active correlation with what appears to it, tied now in a *dynamic unity* of what is given and who receives it, can be thematised in the direction of how the reception might inaugurate reflection on, and reconfiguration of, the latter. And here is the *critical* catch. Given the partial and fragmentary nature of their givenness and manifestation to consciousness (Husserl's *Abschattungen* above referred to 'various perceptual perspectives on objects that shade into each other'),[17] for phenomenology to track the phenomena it must be 'permanently (critically and self-critically) dislocating itself and correcting its course so as to

---

[17] In Gadamer's formulation (1989: 446).

track the phenomena better, to adjust itself to them, even at the price of a self-undermining. Hence it is able "to offer the means of carrying out every possible critique of reason".[18] The emergence of the 'we' is immanent to this process, which also accounts for why it cannot be thought of in advance of those processes, in any sense *a priori* to them.[19]

I will argue that this socially weighted phenomenology leads the way to a *critical* restatement of phenomenology because of the dynamic relation of co-constitution between the meaning of phenomena and their reception in the structures of intersubjectivity; not observed as an objectively existing structure but one that emerges out of its activity of ascribing meaning to phenomena. Two things stem from this. First, this activity of the ascription of meaning engages subjects – in the plural. 'Subjectivity', said Husserl in the *Crisis of European Sciences*, 'is what it is: an ego functioning constitutively only within intersubjectivity' (1936/1970: 172). Secondly, this opening to intersubjectivity triangulates the 'self', the 'other' and the 'world' in a relationship of mutual dependence. *In its transcendental dimension intersubjectivity fashions the world in which it is embedded.* Both suggestions together are key dimensions of *a critical phenomenology*.

But we need a final step before we can make that connection, and it is a step that Husserl could not take. It is only with the *hermeneutical turn* in phenomenology that the phenomenality of Being that was attributed by Husserl to consciousness now finds *its locution in language*. If 'a phenomenon is something that shows itself, or something insofar as it shows itself', as Heidegger famously put it in *Being and Time* (1996: 25), then the phenomenon, says Gadamer, is what manifests itself in language. The publication of Gadamer's magnum opus *Truth and Method* in 1960 marked the arrival of philosophical hermeneutics as a dominant force in philosophy. It argued that manifestation is linguistically mediated; what is given to experience gives itself in language. Gadamer's extraordinary phenomenological contribution was to thinking the disclosure of 'Being that can be understood in language' (1960/1989: 470).

The hermeneutic turn in phenomenology locates the disclosure of the thing, and the event, in language, but this 'self-showing', as it is carried in language, does not in itself carry the *critical distance* that is integral and constitutive of rational interpretation. In fact, arguably, understanding

---

[18] Marder (2014: 19), quoting Husserl.
[19] The *a posteriori*, in Lindahl's theory, emerges in the modalities of responsiveness and questionability, in forcing anew the return to things in question.

coincides with interpretation in Gadamer's work. Interpretation is r separate moment in the disclosure of something as something to so one, it is part of the meaning of disclosure itself. As a consequence of coincidence it is difficult to imagine how one might get behind the disclosure, as it were, in order to query *what* 'shows itself', or, to return to the way Heidegger put it above, the '*insofar* as it shows itself'.

How to understand the gaining of critical distance in the context of these immediate disclosures? Ricoeur, whose important work also finds its place in the hermeneutic turn of phenomenology, picks up Husserl's subject-centredness, the weight afforded to the social dimension: 'The thesis of intentionality', says Ricoeur, 'explicitly states that if all meaning is for consciousness, then no consciousness is self-consciousness before being consciousness of something *toward which* it surpasses itself' (2008: 37). It is perhaps with Ricoeur that we first get that critical aperture, though only *in nuce*; to feel its full force we will turn below to the critical tradition as it was inaugurated by Marx's eleventh thesis. Ricoeur places himself in the line of a 'reflexive' – rather than critical – philosophy, though this reflexive move within philosophical hermeneutics is an intriguing one. It is intriguing because it introduces a critical distance between interpretation and understanding: it extracts the former from the immediacy of the latter. He says: '*[distantiation] frees a second-order reference*'; 'what *must be interpreted*' is 'a *proposed* world that I *could* inhabit' (2008: 82, 83).[20]

To the extent that they lend themselves to the *critical insight*, let us collect some of these suggestions around it, and guide them towards it. The tradition of phenomenology as method has allowed us to return to its Husserlian inheritance and the connection that he draws between disclosure and intentionality, from his initial 'bracketing' of consciousness to the turn, three decades later, to its collective form. 'Intersubjectivity' introduces the element of collective intentionality as methodological presupposition of the emergence of the phenomenon. A virtuous circle installs itself at that point. The bestowal of meaning presupposes a collective intentionality in a relationship of mutual constitution: that is the phenomenological insight, and the reduction to the 'we-perspective' is the condition of disclosure. I would argue that this mutual constitution also introduces a two-way 'questionability', between

---

[20] One of the most eloquent attempts to 'get behind' the disclosure of something as something, can be found in his 2008 'The Hermeneutical Function of Distantiation', in which he tracks the 'positive and productive sense of distantiation' (2008: 72).

disclosure and intentionality. The disclosure of 'something as something *anew*' enables also a reflection of the 'we' is the process, and at this junction the temporal restlessness infects both sides.

The hermeneutic turn embeds disclosure in language and in that way alleviates something of Husserl's anxiety over the fragmentation of personal subject perception. The hermeneutic turn in phenomenology enables us to transfer this as a question of semantics to the relation with structures. Clearly *per se* this does not make it critical. On the contrary, while language may grant continuity to fragmentary perception and accommodate it in an intersubjective medium, the critical moment is lost in the always-already of the accommodation of disclosure in language unless interpretation can be separated from understanding, and the notion of critical distance inserted in the gap. Critique strives to put itself at some distance from the conceptual forms that determine identity and action, if what is given over to 'understanding' (Verstand) by the dominant imaginary is to be prevented from establishing itself as unquestioned and unquestionable context for thought and action. Disclosure and we-identity form a dynamic unity where what gives itself – as disclosure – to the structures of intentionality, gives itself in the modality of a reflexivity that politicises collective identity as the latter rises to receive it. We leave our short account of the phenomenological method poised on intersubjectivity, with the bestowal of meaning to phenomena weighted heavily on the social dimension; and we turn to a fully fledged critical phenomenology that combines with the Hegelian-Marxist legacy.

Elements of a Critical Phenomenology

Marx's *Theses on Feuerbach* were written in 1845 as part of a settling of accounts with the 'New Hegelians' amongst whom Feuerbach was a key figure, and their suggestion that theoretical enquiry alone could serve as an instrument of emancipation. His opposition emerges most clearly in the explosive 'eleventh thesis', in which he famously states that *'[t]he philosophers have only interpreted the world, in various ways; the point is to change it'*. Marx, of course, does not mean that philosophers should cease to try to understand the world; he means that comprehension engages them in a task whose requirements are significantly steeper than ordinarily assumed, and that commit them from the start to practical engagement. The eleventh thesis tells them that their attempt to understand cannot be and should not be divorced and distinguished from an *activity* that has a certain *telos*, that alone for Marx yields objective truth.[21] As he puts it in the second thesis: *'The question whether objective truth can be attributed to human thinking is not a question of theory but is a practical question.'*

The eleventh thesis expresses the key inspiration of critical theory. The tradition of critical theory with its crucial emphasis on practice was later to be linked predominantly with the establishment of the 'Frankfurt School' in 1923, which took a radical turn toward Marxism in the 1930s[22] and remained for over a decade at the forefront of the recovery of Hegelian Marxism. Horkheimer's essay 'traditional and critical theory', a text that despite certain limitations became something of a manifesto, with its emphasis on the 'active element in cognition', stands testament to this.[23] At the juncture of theory and practice neither concept precedes the other: 'the old question – which has priority? – is meaningless as it is posed', insisted Marcuse. For this first generation of the Frankfurt School, the eleventh thesis was a thesis against the reduction of reason to surface understandings that 'interpret the world', and reason was properly deployed in thematising the 'existent' with the view to forging social change. Such thematisation calls forth the facts and events as relevant to the telos of restoring rationality, waged against the irrationalities with which class society is fraught, irrationalities that emerge as contradictions, tautologies and impasses. Waged against the irrationality of a system that promises justice as it relentlessly delivers injustice, the

---

[21] It is questionable whether the eleventh thesis can be said to have been sustained throughout the history of critical thought as its animus. Critical theory today has explicitly in some cases divorced itself from such a premise, and Habermas has argued for a distinction between theoretical and practical reason. Either one can opt for an expansive understanding of critical theory if one can operationalise an adequate notion of emancipation to sustain it, or one can question the inclusion.

[22] The rediscovery of the early Marx of the 'Paris Manuscripts' of 1844, a text that was first published over half a century after it was written, was crucial to the rise of critical theory after the First World War, with its key emphasis on *praxis*, was significant.

[23] The inaugurating move of *traditional theory* involves the separation of questions of fact from questions of value, research from evaluation, description from prescription. In 'traditional theory', conceptual systems (methodologies) that organise our knowledge of the world receive correction according to their own criteria of salience and weight, in accordance, that is, to their capacity to sustain their own internal coherence. The observer perceives her- or himself as passive in the act of reception, as if, says Horkheimer, she or he brings nothing to the process. At the same time the perceived fact stands independently of *the act* that recognises it as fact. For Horkheimer this dual misapprehension misses the crucial insight that 'facts which are presented to our senses' are '*socially preformed* in two ways: through the historical character of the object perceived and through the historical character of the perceiving organ' (Horkheimer, 1932/1976: 200).

aim of the philosopher of the eleventh thesis is to restore a properly human rationality. On the one hand, theory equips practice with its coordinates; on the other, practice situates and re-situates theory within new coordinates that will inform its possibilities anew. A dialectic develops between theory and practice in a dynamic process, that is caught up in history and in the making of history.

'The sentence with which Hegel opens his *Philosophy of Right, as one would open a portal*,' writes Ernst Bloch, 'the fundamental sentence – "The rational is the real; and the real is rational" – carries his Janus face. . . . The *first* part of the sentence . . . is as *revolutionary* as the *second* part is *reactionary* (Bloch, 1986/2018: 129). If Hegel is the thinker of 'becoming', for Bloch, it is because 'Hegel's concept is not a concept of Being but of Being that will be, of Being that places itself in contradiction to all that is fixed' (125). That *other* reading (proposed by the Right-Hegelians) that collapses the rational into the real, and that would, for Bloch, turn Hegel into 'the greatest yes-man in history' is *methodologically untenable*. Bloch reads a profound antinomy ('disruption' he calls it) into Hegel's late masterpiece: 'The positing of disruption in the dialectic of the becoming-for-itself is so great that it transforms Hegel's apology [of *The Philosophy of Right*] into something inconsequential . . . from the point of view of the Hegelian principle itself' (Bloch, 1986/2018: 128). It is this antinomy that Marx carries into the 'theses'. The manifestation of the historical subject as the becoming-for-itself that Marx takes from Hegel to describe the self-realisation of the collective subject,[24] can only work against the conditions of appearance as entrenched in the inimical partiality of class society. The improbable leverage for the self-propelling through history – a 'self', remember, that is denied, that cannot but appear as a class actor – comes from the contradiction that is operationalised through the dialectic. It is what Hegel had distilled down to one sentence in the *Logic*: 'Reality is the unity of essence and existence; in it, formless essence and *untenable appearance* have their truth' (Hegel, *Logic*, §1158). '*Untenable appearance*': what an extraordinary formulation for the subject that seeks the coordinates of recognition in a reality

---

[24] Thesis 3: The materialist doctrine that men are products of circumstances and upbringing, and that, therefore, changed men are products of changed circumstances and changed upbringing, forgets that it is men who change circumstances . . . The coincidence of the changing of circumstances and of human activity or self-change [*Selbstveränderung*] can be conceived and rationally understood only as *revolutionary practice*.

that denies them to it. We confront straight away the phenomenological correlation of collective intention and disclosure on the one hand, and the impasse of reification on the other: the thwarted disclosure, the impaired collective, mirror effects of a profound misrecognition. It is before this denial of recognition that 'works' both ways, that critical phenomenology is set.

The work of bringing to presence is undertaken immanently, tracking 'gradations of Being' along a scale where a manifestation is never more than the expression of a certain *'truce of reason with reality'*, in each case a temporary instantiation of the unfolding of Reason in History. We have encountered a similar notion in Husserl's suggestion of perceptions that 'only achieve partial givenness' above. What has achieved only partial givenness, the 'fawning empiricism', for Lukács, of what appears scattered, fragmented, commodified, reified, will be collected and carried forward in the 'tribunal of reason' (Marcuse). What propels the unfolding (of Reason in History) and accounts for its restlessness is the essential inadequacy of the forms of instantiation, as experienced by those who dwell, and *labour,* under these forms. A *critical* understanding is its own dialectical movement, the displacement of its own constants. Marx, as we discussed in the previous chapter, locates emancipatory potential in the acting on the contradiction, that *appears* to those who work in terms of an experiential deficit, of non-recognition, exploitation, meaninglessness. This is what makes all 'truce' provisional: it is under the weight of that imperfection and thus subjected to the constitutive restlessness of the dialectic, itself defined by Hegel in the *Encyclopaedia* as the 'effective presence and absence of the more perfect in the imperfect' (§ 386). It is the appearance of contradiction, and the acting on the contradiction, the conjuncture of theory and praxis that, in Bloch's memorable formulation, *makes the beams bend* (1986/2018: 128).

This is the inheritance that Marx bequeaths us with the eleventh thesis. We can discern in it the conjunction of the rational and the real the promise of the overcoming of what appears as a positive *real* determination in the light of what *rationally* underlies it as negation. For Marx, in its rational shape the dialectic is a *scandal.* It includes the positive comprehension of the existing state of things and *at the same* time, coincident and asymmetrical, it includes a comprehension of the negation of that state. That is why (as we saw in 1.3) Marx says in *Capital* that the dialectic, 'regards every developed [conceptual] form as in fluid movement' and 'is in its essence critical and revolutionary' (1867/1970: 20). A critical phenomenology finds its site at these joints and fault lines, from where it is able to speak otherwise, allow an incongruous emergence and phenomenality, in the displacements that makes something 'move in the internal disposition of the philosophical categories', a reflexive self-positioning from which it can speak otherwise (*'autrement'*). The *Theses on Feuerbach* provide the clearest statement of how Marx envisages the relation of theory and practice. It can be read in his rejection of pure theoretical work as a means of social change.[25] And it can be read in the fourth thesis, for example, where Marx writes about the 'cleavages and self-contradictions' that circulate at the level of secular society, a society 'both [to be] *understood in its contradiction and revolutionized in practice.*'

If 'revolutionized' appears removed from the more mundane realities of political practice, its key insight applies irrespective: theory measures itself against its ability to rationalise practice, and practice emerges as meaningful with the help of theory. The distinction theory/practice installs a border between the two terms, across which the dialectic operates. The dialectic keeps them combined and in tension. Any *asymmetry* that installs itself between theory and practice can work both ways. A deficit on the pole of practice leaves theory as mere contemplation of, and apology for, the status quo; a deficit on the side of theory leaves practice under-determined. The latter is a more difficult deficit to appreciate, so an example might be helpful; an example, that is, of theory failing to give adequate expression to praxis as self-determined activity. In *The Making of the English Working Class*, Edward Thompson described the communities of hand-loom weavers in Lancashire and Yorkshire at the end of the eighteenth and beginning of the nineteenth centuries that sustained independent forms of production and exchange 'without the distortions of masters and middlemen' (Thompson, 1963/2016: 295) but were unable to protect and maintain those forms in the face of the advancing capitalist economy. Alasdair MacIntyre makes the important point that what these communities lacked was a 'theory that would have successfully articulated their practice' of solidarity in the organisation of production and that would have equipped them epistemologically to resist the supposed inevitability of the defeat of their very own principles of association emerging out of jointly held conceptions of the common good. They lacked the theory that would help them to articulate, as he puts it, 'virtues adequate to the moral needs of

---

[25] 'Just as philosophy discovers its material weapons in the proletariat, so the proletariat discovers its intellectual weapons in philosophy.' (1843)

resistance'.[26] His is a subtle argument that is poised on virtue and invokes an Aristotelian Marxism. The articulation of theory and practice lends a speaking position from within that practice, replete with the moral resources to sustain a working, associational, collective subject position constitutively oriented towards the point of the practice and excellence in its performance. That this is a marxisant radicalisation of the theory-practice nexus is not in doubt, though Marxism would need to be navigated carefully at this point. Because if Marx offers a theory of resistance for the weavers – he was indeed impressed by the militancy of the uprising of another community of weavers, in Silesia in 1844 – it *engages them as proletarians*, a constituency incongruous to them in their professional association, not attuned to the life form that made their engagement and resistance meaningful as oriented to internal standards, and, crucially, one that already assumes the defeat of their form of past life. I am reminded of a similar deficit that Tom Nairn attaches to the 'revolutionary explosion' of May 1968. If 1968 failed, he says, it 'failed because it was too novel, and inevitably dwarfed most of the circumstances around it. It was heavy with a significance too great for our times to bear, a premonitory significance which the events of May could only sketch in outline' (Quattrocchi and Nairn, 1998: 86). How eloquent the incomprehension that attaches to that surge of collective action: of an event that broke with the theoretical models available to interpret it. It returns us to the demand that theory remain in sync with the real historical rhythm of popular mobilisation, that it remain alive and relevant to those processes. The responsibility that befalls theory, once conscious that it lags behind, is to lend praxis expression in terms that are *adequate to it*.

A crucial insight about the unity of theory emerges in this suggestion of the recuperation of reason. In the face of everything that has been said about fragmentation above, theoretical coherence measures itself against the unity that it reads into the situation that confronts it. This dialectical tie is crucial for the role of theory that confronts, under capitalist conditions, a reality riddled with contradiction, in other words of a reality that *cannot* be theorised as a unity. And the importance of this insight is this: the fact that theory in the current conjuncture cannot achieve the level of internal coherence in its encounter with contradiction does not make *it*

---

[26] In the 1994 text, republished as MacIntyre, 1998, at 232. This point is also developed in MacIntyre, 1977.

deficient; instead the recuperation of reason forces the theoretical undertaking not in the direction of *internal* critique and the readjustment of its own methodological assumptions, but in the direction of making-rational the disunity that confronts it, equipped now with the reality-transforming force of *immanent* critique.

The tradition of *immanent critique* associated with Marx finds its opportunity in the irreducible contradictions that it attempts to 'bring to reason'. It is immanent because critique will attempt to navigate this terrain in the historical situation in which *it finds itself*: it is carried in the partiality of contextually situated and historically conditioned perspectives.[27] The contradictory reality it confronts is between the promise of equality and the reproduction of an ever widening inequality; between the promise of inclusion and the reality of marginalisation; between the promise of dignity and the experience of degradation; between the promise to protect the right to work and the generalisation of job insecurity and underemployment; etc. These are contradictions that are experienced and suffered: they enjoin actors normatively in forms of contestation of the reality of their situation. To make sense of it, the contradiction *appears* and is carried in the institutions that inform their situation as workers and as citizens. This involves a performative interpretation of the institutions which is transformative because it disturbs the reproduction of their functional logic. As 'performative' the interpretation carries the meaning that will have to guarantee it in return. All the features of immanent critique are here: located in history, engaging the experiential deficit of actors, normative-institutional, and transformative in the sense of transcending the framework that harbours it. A theory that tracks this practice cannot stand back from this movement. That is why Bloch spoke of a 'humanism that comprehends itself in action', and why the young Lukács wrote in his *Dialectique et Spontaneité* (1925/2001) of 'la praxis qui révolutionne la realité'. And while the strategic deployment of immanent critique will receive a fuller elaboration in the last chapter of the book, we find in the concept the final part to the puzzle of a critical phenomenology, the notion of a theory that becomes a 'genuine force', revolutionising agency (or 'the self-awareness of the subjects') in the social dimension,[28] and in the substantive

---

[27] The reflexive move is emphatically *not* a stepping *outside* the context that might afford an objective (as opposed to class-inflected) view.

[28] And it is renewed and enhanced in the insistence that the unity of theory and practice finds its culmination and completion in the mass revolutionary movement. If today this

dimension establishing that the theoretical elaboration of a state of affairs is indeed a step towards changing it.

At the limit point of a critical phenomenology we encounter the necessity of the factual, of things as they are. Our discussion of the fetish-phenomenon (in 1.3) was about the limit of visibility. The semantic shortfall, which we called phenomenological blockage, was a radical shrinkage, and undercutting, of the reach of critical theory.[29] We saw that for Marx this never really arose as a debilitating question for political action; the advanced reproduction of capital will *not* get rid of its living negation because it is inscribed in its material base and there is a normatively structured lifeworld that will provide traction to the experience of injustice. But this is precisely what, for Weil and Goldmann, could not be guaranteed and what current forms of reproduction of capital effectively withdraw. We will return, though not with Derrida, to re-think the significance of this limit situation for a critical *phenomenology* (its emphasis not on what appears but on what *fails to appear*) in our discussion of political strategy in Part IV. A critical phenomenology of constitutions must engage with these very questions, of what *appears*, what *withdraws* from appearance and what might be *forced to appear*.

Two final points for note before we move to the discussion of constitutionalism in Part II:

First, in the constitutional-theoretical discussions that follow, the question of meaning-construction will be explored not as a question of epistemology or ethics, but at the level of the institutions of law. The construction of meaning is mediated through categories, structures, and conceptual schemes specific to the *ratio juris*. These mediations are abstractions, they select and classify the 'raw' material of observation, individuate events, establish causal connection, generalise specific features of the situation while suppressing others, and in that mediation they configure the real. The processes of meaning construction involve the 'mediation' of factual situations through concepts that read them no

---

connection, with few exceptions, appears increasingly remote, one must remember that for the generation of thinkers that immediately followed Marx and Engels the connection with practice was part of the lived reality of theoretical engagement. See Anderson, 1976.

[29] It confronts us in other words with the limit of its reference. This is what Maurice Blanchot identified as the third 'voice of Marx' (Blanchot, 1986). Alongside the scientific voice (of historical materialism) and the political voice (or the invention of political form) there is a third 'voice', writes Blanchot, that never quite makes it to presence except in the 'void' of 'an absence', and which Derrida will signify with the term *différance*.

longer as series of phenomena but as combinations, mediated and related within larger semantic fields and sub-fields. The creation of meaning occurs in terms of specific imaginaries, with their vocabularies and rules of signification. It also occurs in the context of specific sets of social relations, institutional arrangements and processes of social reproduction. A critical phenomenology of constitutions calls for attention to the fact and the nature of mediation; understands it as historical and therefore as revisable; and in that sense is both attuned to the ways in which social change might be pursued and more importantly attuned to the distinction between what is contingent, and could therefore be thought of, thematised and undertaken otherwise, and what is not. But it will be the intelligibility of the more profound, reflexive, epistemological questions that we have visited in this first part of the book, that set the coordinates for the *reach* of the mediating languages. The adequacy of the latter will be measured, *must* be measured, on their capacity to address the deeper questions about humanity, about dignity and solidarity, and not be re-circuited to their own functionality.

Secondly, the meaning of *collective* agency and action is crucial to the discussion of critical phenomenology (Part I), to the 'social' dimension of political constitutionalism (Part II), and to 'strategy (Part IV). So far I have attempted to show the connection at the level of conceptual analysis; but there is a second level at which the connection between theory and praxis is forged, and this level explicitly links theory to *collective action*, and to what it means to occupy a political subject position in relation to it. And while this is crucially significant for strategic thinking, as we will see in Part IV of the book, the question over the assumption of constituent power by the emergent collective subject, the disclosure of a speaking position that contests the distribution of capacity and agency in democratic capitalist regimes, is already a key question for phenomenology too, even before we look at its operationalisation in strategic thinking. 'The movement of subjectivisation', Rancière puts it well in *The Names of History,* 'operates in the interval between several nominations [of speaking positions] and its constitutive fragility' (1994: 98).

If phenomenology turns on what appears as something to someone, any attempt to extract a critical phenomenology from Marx's theory of *social labour* balances the emergence of its meaning on a collective intentionality-to-be. Lukács' *History and Class Consciousness* can be read as offering such a phenomenological reading of Marxism, in that the undertaking of revolutionary praxis delivers the potential consciousness of a universal class. If the meaning of something – here that of work – is what appears as something to someone, the difficulty that confronts Lukács (and us) is that the collective subject that will authorise this emergence of meaning is not yet in place. The assumption that it *will be* assumes too much. The argument that material development engenders its own crisis, one that beyond a certain threshold will become the vacant site of another form of rationality accommodating another subjectivity (the 'class-for-itself') cannot be warranted. Gorz's critique of economic reason on this point is compelling. The crisis of capitalism will not engender 'the historical subject who will be capable of overcoming it by revealing the contradiction concealed within this development' (1989: 94–5). What is envisaged in this Hegelian unfolding of historical reason is a collective subject that takes reflexive possession of itself in order to *become* the subject of what it *is*. Nothing guarantees this improbable retroaction.

But our critical phenomenological argument about subjectivity can still proceed absent the improbable guarantee. And if it remains aporetic it is no less significant for that. It concedes that the self-realisation of the subject of constituent power remains caught in the thwarted, fragmented, reified systems of meaning that condition political engagement under capitalist conditions. But the phenomenological reading neither *begins* with the political subject's sovereign gesture, nor *posits* the sovereign subject – meta-politically – as seat of properties and capacities. Where action appears fragmented in the truncated forms of social life, in the circuits of commodity exchange, the supposed motivations of utility-maximisers, the naturalised distortions of preference, and the breakdown of association, this fragmentation (or reification as we have called it) transfers from the phenomenon to the observer in the continuity between appearance and receiving intentionality.[30] The stakes are upped. A *critical* phenomenology pits itself against the brute facticity of the 'Verstand', the sobering reminders of necessity, the stubborn givenness of the *is-as-it-is* and of the *fait accompli*. But now, with this, something more significant is wagered. Where action and its subject-position are

---

[30] 'Take bourgeois society,' suggests Horkheimer, 'in which the life of the society proceeds from the economy only at the cost of excessive friction, in a stunted form and almost, as it were, accidentally' (1932/1976: 203). The problem is, he says with extraordinary foresight, that 'contemporary political economics are unable to derive practical profit from the fragmentary questions they discuss' (228).

(as a matter of phenomenology) in a relation of mutual constitution, redress is staked on the postponed meaning of a rational recollection of that activity, such that at the same time restores the *associational* basis of the *human* community. That is its postponed gesture and realisation-to-come of *constituent power*. To this we now turn.

PART II

Political Constitutionalism

2.1

Constituent Power and the Constitutional Distinction

> *The fear of the demos, of the visible will*
> *that needs to be stabilised, turns dialectic into*
> *a movement in a closed house*
> *and leaves it standing still in the domain of law*
>
> Ernst Bloch

The Constitutional Distinction

If 'to speak of constituent power is to speak of democracy', as Antonio Negri puts it in the opening sentence of his important early work *Insurgencies*, the question that constituent power invites from the outset is *how are we to think democracy democratically?* But how are we to make sense of this *double inscription* of the 'democratic' at both first- and second-order levels? It imports a seemingly paralysing unsettledness, a double contingency of sorts, in the offer of choice over choice, of reflection over reflection. And yet its allure and its promise are evident, at least to a radical tradition of constitutional theory that typically returned to the promise of *constituent power* to face up to the following question: If a political society or collective is that which acts through rules of ascription, to what extent can that ascription remain reconfigurable, reflexive, alive to re-definition, open both to operationalisation *and* transcendence by the collective that it names? This is of course also the *problématique* of Marxism, of a certain Marxism that counts Negri amongst its exponents, which self-consciously places the subject of emancipation in *media res*, both bound *historically* to the modalities of an ascription that could not be stepped behind within an order of capital that defined subject positions, *while* at the same time holding on to the promise of an overcoming, and of a genuine *reflexive* process of self-definition.

The idea of the '*double inscription*' of 'democracy' at both level and meta-level generates the following questions of *constitutional* import:

How are we to think democracy democratically as the pure exercise of constituent power? And if that is the aim, does it not jar as prescription for *constitutional* practice, a merger of level and meta-level impossible to achieve at the level of *institution*? The question that this 'merger' raises, in other words, is whether there can be a political-philosophical reading of democracy that holds it apart from, and calls it forth from, the meaning to which the institutional conditions of its exercise confine it. Can the constituent be thought independently, and can it grant a democratic dimension to a theory of *political constitutionalism*?

The theory of political constitutionalism that is advanced in this book takes the distinction between *constituent and constituted power* as the founding distinction of constitutionalism, and holds on to it *not despite* but *because* of the tension between its poles, asymmetrical, non-aligned, aporetic and contradictory: each of these predications carries tension and crisis into the concept of constitutionalism. The customary approach identifies this as the *paradox of constitutionalism*, paradoxical in that constituent power appears to come always-already implicated with constitutional form, the instituting already coupled with the instituted. Political power *must* present itself as conditioned and with it political power is sovereign only, so to speak, under conditions that it is not. Because to be authorised it must be imputed to the constitution that establishes the conditions under which the popular will can be expressed *as* sovereign. Law and democracy are reconciled only via the suppression of a paradox that inevitably impacts on constitution-making as never fully constituent. And that is why, while constitutional theories notoriously hit on an impasse at the threshold of institutionalisation, the founding puzzle of constitutional thinking persists stubbornly and irreducibly.

Take the notorious difficulty that constitutionalism faces in the social dimension when it comes to the *demos*. The problem for democracy is that it *cannot* step behind its starting line to ask the question '*what is the demos?*' because that would beg the question of the constituency of those competent to ask it. Drawing on the important work of Ernst-Wolfgang Bockenforde, Fernando Atria puts it with exceptional clarity: Democracy is the idea that

> state power must be articulated in such a way that both its organisation and its exercise derive from the will of the people or can be ascribed to it. The fact that the rules of ascription are part of what must be ascribed to the people suggests that the people have two modes of action, that there are, we may say, two concepts of the people: an institutional concept and a

pre-institutional one. Institutionally speaking, the people is what acts through the operation of the norms of ascription; and pre-institutionally speaking, the "people" are what wills those rules of ascription.

(Atria, 2013a: 103)

The answers are familiar, as inconclusive as they are tirelessly rehearsed. At the two extremes we have Carl Schmitt and Hans Kelsen: for Schmitt the pre-institutional determination of 'the people' – political, existential – is what breaks the double-bind in assuming the collective as formed independently of and prior to the ascription, whereas for Kelsen the ascription works all the way back.[1] To both we shall return, but for now note that both are attempts to break through the paradox of constitutionalism by denying that the people can occupy both places at the juncture of presence and representation, of being both agent and object of ascription. They are instead in the case of Schmitt placed as concrete, immanent origin, in the case of Kelsen excised as abstract, transcendental condition.

But what does it mean to say that at the heart of constitutionalism there is paradox? And if it is relatively clear *what* the paradox is, what does it mean *that* it is? What does it mean that constitutional thinking departs from and inevitably returns to paradox? And since the Constitution undoubtedly *is*, should the paradox that we discover infecting it be seen as a sign of inadequate theorising, of constitutional theory running circles around itself? If not that, what?

To cut in somewhere, let us propose that there is only paradox if both sides of the distinction (constituent/constituted) are operationalised at once, actualised *in tandem*. But if we accept that as observers we can occupy a place only on one or the other side of the distinction, we might be able to resist the unrealistic ontology of the constitution that condemns it to paradox. The constitution is the site of the coupling of politics and law, constituent and constituted, and therefore straddles the distinction but can be observed and thematised only from one of its poles. Even as juridical reason gains its orientation from the

---

[1] For an exceptional reading of Schmitt vis-à-vis Kelsen, see Lindahl (2007). With Schmitt the constituent remained immanent in the constituted order but was carried as autonomous in *the order of the decision* that should not and could not be reduced to the order of the constituted. The democratic thinking of democracy is then, explicitly in Negri, implicitly in Schmitt, the refusal to collapse democracy into a form, a form that typically in the modern period receives its semiosis in the juridical/constitutional idiom, for Schmitt as *constitutional laws*.

constituent, its unfolding is variously understood in constitutional thinking in terms of internalised solutions that are productive to, and of, constitutional thought; in their impressive scope these internalisations constitute the variety of the modalities of accommodation of democratic will in constitutional reason.

Let us take the distinction *constituent/constituted* as the *guiding distinction*[2] of constitutionalism. To reflect on anything, to observe anything, one must begin by drawing a distinction, says Luhmann, and he designates as *reference* the operation that consists of two elements: distinction and indication. A reference is an operation that posits a distinction and indicates one side of it. The concepts of reference (and self-reference) are understood with respect to the 'operative handling' of a distinction that is posited as a difference and is operated from the indicated side. The constitutional distinction that forms the 'guiding distinction' of political constitutionalism can only be actualised from the side of the 'constituted', and it is from there that the constituent will be observed, thematised and dealt with in practice. A perspective is gradually furnished through repeated operations that cross the boundary. Through these operations the distinction constituent/constituted 're-enters' the field of the constituted. The 're-entry' enables possibilities to be envisaged and what is given can be *thematised* because it can now be viewed in the light of alternatives. It is important to understand re-entry as the 'portal' that it is, first enabling normative theorising of the constitution, theories about the right balance between innovation and stability, between substantive and formal justice, between generations of rights, between rights and democracy. The 're-entry' configures constitutional space. It also fashions hetero-reference (reference to the environment of politics) on the back of self-reference: the 'constituent' is the term of reference for an outside that allows the self-reference of the law to unfold its capacities for resonance while (and because) maintaining its closure, in fact while heightening its autonomy vis-à-vis that externality.

This is still rather abstract, and in the following chapter (2.2) we will develop an analysis of the reflexivity that is particular to the constitution, exploring the logic of normative closure and cognitive openness that is specific to it. But for now we remain with the improbable juncture of the constituent and the constituted as the site where constitutional meaning is generated. On the side of the constituent we have release and

---

[2] For the notion of 'distinction directrice' see Luhmann (1986b).

acceleration of political time; on the side, of the constituted, we have sequence, repetition and the constitutional fixing of time. Where along the *temporal* dimension the constituent introduces a continual provocation that unsettles any one determination or sedimentation of its exercise, the constituted instils path-dependencies that give form to continuities. The tension is productive in all three dimensions of constitutional meaning. On the side of the constituent we have presence and invocations of commonality and community; on the side of the constituted we have structures of representation. Where the constituent along the *social* dimension introduces the much exalted openness to the other, expresses the desire for community[3] and furnishes 'we'-perspectives (first-person plural identifications) with meaning, the constituted operationalises given commonalities. On the side of the constituent in the *material* dimension we have potentiality; on the side of the constituted we have the usual thematics, and variations that forever reactivate known grounds.

It is because of this dissonance that Negri finds in the sedimented forms of the constituted the negation of its constitutive movement. If he approaches democratic thinking from its outer limit, the thinking of revolution, it is because that realm expresses ultimately *the pure form of the constituent*. The tradition of thinking about revolution in the variety of its instantiations typically returns to the promise of *constituent power* to force through a reflexive question that could *not* be asked within the *constituted* order of representation. The key argument in Negri's *Insurgencies* involves how to hold on to the question of constituent power as an expression of the potentiality to break with the logic of capitalist reproduction. It proceeds as a genealogical excavation. At each step of that excavation it confronts the question: 'What is constituent power from the perspective of juridical theory?' At each step the answer is the same: the constituent is belied in the act of giving it expression along the pathways of the constituted. Juridical forms simultaneously 'affirm

---

[3] Constituent power must be understood as 'absolute and unlimited procedure' (Negri, 1999a: 24) that does not seek institutional expression but desires social being, community. 'The desire for community is the spirit and soul of constituent power – the desire for a community that is as thoroughly real as it is absent, the trajectory and motor of a movement whose essential determination is the demand of being, repeated, pressing on an absence.' And in this, his most direct allusion to potentiality, he quotes Aristotle: 'What is potent can be and not be' (1999a: 23). 'Communism is nothing but an activity – an activity and therefore an opening, a radical practical act that connects freedom to desire, desire to sociality, and sociality to equality' (1999a: 265).

and deny' the constituent, he says, and inflict upon it 'every type of distortion' (1999a: 3):

> Constituent power must itself be reduced to the norm of the production of law; it must be incorporated into the established power. Its expansiveness is only shown as an activity of constitutional revision. In this the juridical covers over and alters the nature of constituent power ... This is how the juridical theory of constituent power solves the allegedly vicious circle of the reality of constituent power. But isn't closing political power within representation nothing but the negation of the reality of constituent power?
>
> (1999a: 3–4)

The democratic thinking of democracy, for Negri, thinks the constituent in terms that do not fold it back into the constituted – hence his insistence that we conceptualise the constituent as irreducible to juridical thinking. For Negri, it is the principle of antagonism to that order that in a thinking that sustains itself in the modality of negativity, thinks the constituent as revolutionary. And there can be little doubt that, to some degree at least, it is precisely in the negation of institutional form with all its *pre*-suppositions and *pre*-givens, that the constituent finds its purest expression. 'It is an act of choice, the precise determination that opens a horizon, the radical apparatus of something that does not yet exist, and whose conditions of existence imply that the creative act does not lose its characteristics in the act of creating' (Negri, 1999a: 22). And that is why, Negri reminds us, if Arendt is a profound thinker of constituent power, she found herself both intrigued and repulsed by the principle she had discovered. She was quick to 'deprive the concept of that radical opening that gives it shape' (1999a: 24). Her thought, he says, 'runs into a sort of insurmountable roadblock when she discovers [quoting Saint-Just] that "nothing resembles virtue so much as a great crime: nothing resembles constituent power so much as the most radical and deep, most desperate and fierce negation."'[4] It is not only Arendt that Negri has in his sights here. In an open polemic with the institutionalists, and their more sophisticated epigones like Lefort, Negri declares: '*when strength is institutionalised it is necessarily negated* ... Beyond the apologetic banalities of contemporary institutionalism, any philosophy that even heroically

---

[4] Negri, 1999a: 21. Here, comments Negri, lie the origins of her conversion to classical and conservative constitutionalism. Arendt's fascination with the American revolution was one where, in Sheldon Wolin's words, 'the United States was the beneficiary of a revolution whose genius was its non-revolutionary character' (Wolin, 1994: 32).

has an institutionalist outcome must be refused if we want to grasp the strength of the constituent principle' (1999a: 22–3).

Clearly not all constitutional thinking attaches itself to such unsettledness: at times the *constituent* is excised as mythical origin, as paradoxical or contradictory element in constitutional thinking; at times it is collapsed into the modalities of the constituted without remainder; at times still it is set aside altogether as 'superfluous',[5] ignored as unproductive, or is deployed to justify the refusal to carry the constitutional imaginary beyond the settings that harboured it in the past. These are all mutations that give up on what is most valuable about the constitutional achievement. That is why, if we begin our analysis of political constitutionalism with Negri's radical proposition, and his return to the revolutionary tradition, it is not in order to locate the constitutional achievement in that proposition and in that tradition, but only to reclaim that potentiality for it. To denote, in other words, that the revolutionary tradition carries the élan that runs *within the constituted* as its highest possibility. It is the limit that equips political constitutionalism with the understanding of what warrants the predication 'political'. That is what justifies the emphasis on the constituent as *both* necessary reference *and* as irreducible to the logic of the constituted. Because while constituent power, as the democratic thinking of democracy, engages second-order reflexivity as its pure expression, constituted power is the name for a *first-order* contestability; institutionalisation is what makes possible its exercise, over-determined in all three of the dimensions of constitutional meaning. Of course the accommodation remains *imperfect*, and generates as we will see a certain 'excess' for the post-structuralists, a certain energy for the constitutional democrats and discourse theorists, etc. All this will be visited later in this chapter. And it is in this vein that Pierre Rosanvallon invites us to 'ground [our constitutional] analysis in the complexity of the real and its aporetic dimension [because it] leads [us] to develop an interest in the "very nature" of the political.' In other words to focus on the 'aporetic' antinomies, between the promise of the constituent and its constitutional expression, *as they are revealed in* the historical unfolding

---

[5] E.g. Dyzenhaus argues (2012: 229) that 'legal and constitutional theory should avoid the idea of constituent power. It is unhelpful in seeking to understand the authority of law and the place of written constitutions in such an understanding. In particular, it results in a deep ambivalence about whether authority is located within or without the legal order. Legal theory should then focus on the question of law's authority as one entirely internal to legal order, thus making the question of constituent power superfluous.'

of constitutional formations, throws the political into relief and prevents us from identifying with the forms of 'closed universalism that has made the West blind to its own history' (Rosanvallon, 2009: 546, 547). It is to this history of the constituent we turn next, with a view to a different kind of genealogical excavation.

Theorising 'Constituent Power': A Short History in Four Chapters

Rousseau's Radical Proposition

Rousseau's theory of the 'general will' is the first direct attempt in modern thought to give expression to the radical democratic impulse in constitutional thought. He is the first, in effect, to confront us with the 'enigma' of the general will, testament to the tension that inhabits political constitutionalism from the start.

In the *Social Contract*, Rousseau famously argues that

> If we seek to define precisely the greatest good for all, the necessary goal of every system of legislation, we shall find that the main objectives are limited to only two: liberty and equality; liberty because any form of particular subordination means that the body of the state loses some degree of strength; and equality because liberty cannot subsist without it.
>
> (SC II, 11, 86–7)

The danger associated with 'any form of particular subordination' is the danger of corruption that might affect the 'body of the state'; Rousseau, like Montesquieu, is alive to this risk. Against such subordination, Rousseau proclaims the equal participation of all in the formation of the '*general will*', the name that he reserves for political autonomy and self-rule, a will that famously '*doit partir de tous pour s'appliquer à tous*'. The two key features of the 'general will' are present in this formulation: first the notion of self-determination or freedom that inheres in the legislative function, where the general will expresses itself only in general laws. And second the commitment to equality that orients it constitutively ('it cannot subsist without it') to the 'good for all'. The difficulty of the passage of the universal quantifier from the 'will of all' to the 'general will' is of course the most debated and perhaps intriguing aspect of Rousseau's 'social contract'. Less discussed is a second connection, which links also to his earlier *Discourse on Inequality*, where 'the greatest good for all, the necessary goal of every system of legislation' finds expression in substantive equality and the alleviation of suffering. On a *materialist* reading it is precisely this orientation that allows the *general will* to be distinguished from the *will of all* understood as the aggregation of individual interests. This is the route that unlocks Rousseau's paradox most incisively. On this reading the meaning of political constitutionalism understood as self-government necessarily harnesses it to social transformation in the direction of substantive equality and makes the *sans-culottes* – those whose universalisable will it expresses – its privileged subject. This radical but still faithful reading of Rousseau's constitutional theory makes it a precursor to Marx's and explains his influence on the Jacobins.[6] There is no doubt that the generality of the law was a claim that was originally revolutionary. But it is only a theory of *equality* that did not confine it to the field of formal interchange, that could sustain it as such and provide its stable substance.

We must take this more gradually. In the *Social Contract* a paradox is encountered in the opposition between the generality of the expression of the will and the aggregation of particular viewpoints, interests and needs that would express the 'needs of all'. While the 'generality' of the will and the 'particularity' of the concrete actions of the needy might indeed be contrasted in this way, the 'particular' actions of the needy – and need is nothing if not particular – do not find expression *as such* on a political register as 'particular expressions' of social demands, but can only be carried over into the political if interpreted as the expression of the general will that need will be met, and that no one will go hungry. Rousseau confronts the apparent impasse of the contrast with the triangulation between general will, the will of all, and substantive equality, and in this lies his radical innovation.

The general will becomes an explosive concept even before it enters its Jacobin adventure. It hits several difficulties and objections, most notably the profound disquiet that the promise of constituent power invariably generates in that there is no criterion outside the 'general will' to hold it to. But it is also the theory of radical equality that upsets, and Bloch is right to remark that 'it was not the ideal of freedom, but the ideal of equality before which the incipient bourgeois interests in the French revolution trembled' (1986: 164). The conceptual objection usually put to Rousseau is that the 'general will' wills what cannot be brought before it except as *particular* expressions of need, but must nonetheless be brought into political discourse in terms of *general* prescriptions. One

---

[6] For this point see Goldoni (2017: 13) and Avineri (1968: 41–64). For the 'revolutionary Rousseau' see McDonald (2013).

way around the objection involves an argument from procedure, which may be productively combined with an argument from education. The procedural argument is put well by Klaus Günther: 'the general will represents a position which enables the participants in the process of forming the general will to consider their own point of view from the point of view of everybody else, from the "entirety of addressees".' But of course, Günther concedes, 'this generalised point of view is not there *before* the process begins'.[7] That is why a radical qualification to the proceduralisation is required, which is to argue for a corrective to the process in terms of what, with Aristotle, we might describe as *an education of the will*. This will involve a certain 'de-naturing', whereby the supposed natural inclination of self-love, capricious and egotistical, gives over to a general will that must be 'artificially produced' by fastening onto the publicness of citizenship, law and the irreducible value of association. This is perhaps the key to Rousseau's enigmatic, because premature, suggestion that 'civil association is the most voluntary act of the will'. Civic education intervenes to fill the gap between what is not-yet, but will-have-been the expression of the general will. Amongst the most interesting suggestions here is Patrick Ripley's interpretation that borrows from Rousseau's earlier work *Emile* the formulation '*I have decided to be what you made me*'.[8] The question that presents itself is whether the autonomy expressed in the 'I decide' is fully congruent with the 'you have made me'. And the question becomes even more pertinent if the temporal modality changes and positions the will in the *now*, when it is *ex hypothesi* not-yet that which will have been made of it. Is the 'general will' still a will capable of voluntary acts if it remains to be transformed, since in the now it is stuck in the partiality that prevents it for expressing what is in the general interest? Already we can see *in nuce* here the radical conceptual innovation that Jacobinism brings to the political present, of a revolution that has to speak on behalf of those whose revolutionary will *it will have* carried. They are those who can bring only the 'needs of the body' into the street, and not an argument over just distribution. It is the 'social question' posed *in extremis* by the Paris mob. There is no stepping back from historical responsibility before

---

[7] '... nor is it located in a higher world into which the participants could leap, transcending the particularity of their own specific opinions' (Günther, 1995: 42).

[8] On civic education, with reference not just to *Emile* but also to the *Economie Politique and Gouvernement de Pologne*, see Ripley (2001). See also Ripley (1986).

the demand of the *sans-culottes*, as there is no easy answer to the wager of politics because the demand of meeting social needs *cannot wait*.

It might be useful to refer back here to Arendt's *vehement* rejection of the connection between the general will and the social question. Her 'hellenism', her invitation to contemplate the splendour of the striving for excellence, self-disclosure in action-in-concert, etc., is repeatedly, relentlessly, poised against the sheer burden of the reproduction of material life (*zen*) (1963: ch. 2). Here is her cleansing exaltation: 'At the root of Greek political consciousness we find an unequalled clarity and articulateness in drawing this distinction. No activity that served only the purpose of making a living, of sustaining only the life process, was permitted to enter the political realm ... The "good life", as Aristotle called the life of the citizen ... was "good" to the extent that having mastered the necessities of sheer life, by being freed from labour and work, it was no longer bound to the biological life process' (Arendt, 1958: 36, 37). Of course it is not difficult to embrace the 'good life' if one is 'freed from labour' and from having to contemplate 'sheer need'. But the point is more serious, and Arendt's objection hits out at both of Rousseau's premises, both the meaning of the general will and his radical proposition to found its true expression in the pursuit of equality, his *materialist* proposition, in other words, to found *political* constitutionalism on the *social* question. For Arendt it was Rousseau's invitation to compassion towards suffering that blurred the distinction between the political and the social, and had led to the Terror.

But Rousseau's radical proposition strikes at a higher synthesis: it is that without the orientation to equality the general will cannot transcend the notion of an aggregation of interests and furthermore cannot conceive of itself as general because the connection that makes it general, that grants it political meaning, *is* the common good. And the common good exists in the 'tenderness of the coarsest demand' as Adorno will put it in *Minima Moralia*, 'that no one should go hungry anymore' (1951/2005: 156).[9] The common good coincides with the pursuit of equality and the alleviation of suffering, as Rousseau develops it so powerfully earlier in the *Discourse on Inequality*. And that is why, for him, the irreducible *claim to substantive equality is bound up with the expression of the general will*, and it was precisely that bind that allowed the commutability between the political and the social to be elevated to

---

[9] Or as Rousseau described the heartlessness of reason, which will say: 'Perish if you wish, I am secure' (Rousseau, *A Discourse on the Origin of Inequality*, p. 226).

condition of the constitution of the will. The experience of suffering, the lived inequality of the proletariat and the dispossessed, is what founds Rousseau's radical theory of democracy. In this argument, the 'general will' is bound up with the exercise of constituent power understood as the critique of society and of the injustices it visits on those who are the victims of material deprivation, Robespierre's '*malhereux*' whose voices do not yet carry as general will but who are capable of 'applauding' what is done in their name.[10] As Negri describes the radical claim of the French Revolution, the irreversibility of the definition of constituent power on *the social terrain* is posed here, once and for all.

Of course there are other influential readings of Rousseau's constitutional theory in the direction of more liberal interpretations, and the analysis here has no pretension to intervene in that debate. Instead it picks up from Rousseau a radical argument about the conceptual possibility of the constituent. We might go even further. To this formulation of the paradox of constitutionalism read off his own ambivalence, Rousseau offers us something of a proto critical-phenomenological solution. 'What happens at this point?' Negri throws in a suggestion he does not pursue: 'It happens that the already complex of the dialectic of general will and direct representation is connected to and fuses with a phenomenology of spontaneity' (1999a: 201). That is how it '*reveals* and realises itself' he says. Something profound has been tapped in this formulation, which we might describe as a *phenomenology of constituent power*. And it forms the crux of Rousseau's radical thesis: caught in the force field between channels of political representation and the social demand for equality, the general will emerges in and as crisis, its very iteration forcing it to acknowledge its limitation, and carrying it to confront the radical demand of equality that alone qualifies it as the expression of the generality of the will. This is a demand it can never fully meet. But in the process the general will implants itself as a critique of society, and as a forever renewed gesture to carry that critique. If one might be allowed the anachronism, this is Marx's eleventh thesis carried in the radical claim of the Jacobins.

---

[10] 'Les malhereux m'applaudissent' famously for Robespierre. Later another famous socialist, Jean Jaurès will proclaim: 'I am with Robespierre and go and sit next to him at the Jacobins.' The pertinent question 'can the subaltern speak?' was asked by Gramsci, and later by Spivak.

The Jacobin Constituent Moment

When on 17 June 1789, the deputies of the Estates General, convening in Versailles, declared themselves the National Assembly, *no longer assembled at the behest* of the Monarch but as representatives of the people of France, political modernity was born in a sweeping exercise of constituent power as an act of *self*-authorisation. As Chris Thornhill describes it in his exceptional historical sociology of constitutionalism:

> At the beginning of modern socio-political order, the claim that state institutions were authorized through constituent power was presented as a symbolic caesura with pre-existing patterns of public coercion. In many respects, the concept of constituent power did indeed describe a great division between modern and early modern political order.
>
> (Thornhill, 2011: 205)

As 'the spiritual enthusiasm' generated by the 'glorious mental dawn' of the caesura and as the gesture of this self-positing, 'thrill[ed] through the world',[11] constituent power assumed historical form. And while even at the moment of its emergence, its meaning was fraught with ambiguity, the French Revolution unambiguously posed the problem that the epoch had to work out, as Hegel knew well: constituent power confronted it with the meaning of the political realisation of freedom. From that moment on, as Negri summarises the development of western constitutionalism, 'constitutional thought becomes the effort to resist it' (1999a: 206).

From the outset, then, the release of constituent power is bound up with the principle of its own expansion. This can be tracked along all the dimensions of its meaning. That the revolution imported a new *temporality* is obvious. It was an event that the preceding constitutional situation could not have anticipated; it carried a radical innovation that accelerated political time. Along the *social* dimension it threw into ongoing contention the logic and structures of representation and as the logic of representation came into sharper confrontation with the principle of democracy, it carried the improbable promise of the direct expression of the will of the people. Along the *material* dimension – and we saw already how Arendt abhorred this – it merged the political question of the exercise of public power with the social question of the meeting of need. Let us say something more about each of the

---

[11] In Hegel's memorable words from *The Philosophy of Right* (1820/2015: 47).

dimensions in turn, because they express the meaning of the exercise of constituent power and its extraordinary historical manifestation.

Originally Lafayette had been commissioned to draft the text of the Declaration with a view to transferring the inspiration of 1776 into the French context. But by June 1793 the US Constitution's 'life, liberty and the pursuit of happiness' had become explicitly restated as the triad of the *tricolor*: liberty, equality, fraternity.[12] 'Consequently the radical already socialist accent of the French revolution' by the time of the Jacobin ascent and under the influence of Babeuf's 'society of equals' effected a crucial reversal, of securing freedom by means of equality, thereby also elevating fraternity, for Bloch unequivocally by June 1793, as the 'heritage of the tricolor' (Bloch, 1986: ch. 19). Along each of its axes – temporal, material, social – a threshold of radicalisation was crossed with Jacobinism. Our interest is what this threshold-crossing means for constitutionalism: what it allows us to comprehend in relation to the constitutional distinction.

Take time first, in its constituent significance. We can trace it in terms of its acceleration and density, as the revolution drove itself forward at frenzied rhythms and unprecedented intensity. 'From the conquest of the Bastille to the days of the Germinal,' writes Negri, 'in the entire revolutionary trajectory of the masses, temporality has as its target the entire, absolute realization, in the political as in the social, of the democratic process' (1999b: 195). Along the temporal dimension the meaning of the revolutionary constituent comprehends *time as intervention*,[13] and therefore around the distinction whether it is opportune or not. The orientation of constitutional time reverses radically from the past to the future.[14] With the revolution, laments Tocqueville in *Democracy in America* (volume 2, 331), 'the past has ceased to throw its light upon the future, and the mind of man wanders in obscurity'. And of course if one finds widespread a preoccupation with the inauguration of the revolutionary event, the question of what will bring it to a close is posed with ever greater urgency. If, as Negri reminds us, Napoleon, with 'inimitable, ironic arrogance' declared: 'Citizens, the revolution is determined by the principles that began it ... the revolution is over' (1999a: 2), he was

---

[12] The formula had been proposed in June 1793 at the Club des Cordeliers under Danton and Desmoulins.
[13] The formulation is borrowed from Rancière, who is referring to Alain Badiou: 'Time is nothing more than intervention' (Rancière: 1989).
[14] It was 'a legacy preceded by no testament', as Rene Char memorably put it (Char, in Arendt, 1963: 217).

certainly not the first to have declared its termination. Already in September 1791, nearly two years before the ascendancy of the Jacobins, the moderates in the divided and battered National Assembly were desperate to pronounce that the time of constituent power was over. 'The Revolution is finished,' said Le Chapelier in September 1791, 'as there are no more injustices to overcome, or prejudices to contend with.'[15] The radical phase of the revolution did in fact come to a close in 1794 with the fall of the Jacobins. Immediately the Thermidoreans dismantled the regulations fixing a maximum price for essential goods by the 'commission of subsistence'; this led to a collapse of stocks and rampant speculation. The 'hunger barricades' were set up by the sans-culottes in May 1795 in the Faubourg Saint Antoine in the Bastille area, and they echoed with the slogan 'Bread and the 1793 constitution'.[16] To stem the reaction the Convention adopted the decree proposed by Sieyès 'against seditious gatherings'. The insurrection was defeated in a bloodbath.

The reference here of the insurgents to the 1793 Constitution is significant. On 24 April of that year, Robespierre had introduced to the Convention an amendment of Condorcet's *Declaration* in the direction of what he described as an 'arrangement required by the interest of humanity', to establish a progressive basis of taxation[17] and 'mutual assistance'.[18] The Constitution of 1793 – sometimes referred to as '*la constitution selon Rousseau*'[19] – was drafted by Robespierre, ratified by the Convention but never implemented. It remains the constitutional document that most clearly institutionalises the 'crossing' between the

---

[15] Quoted in Jaume (2007: 71). For a more extensive account see Jaume (1989).

[16] I refer here to the extraordinary retelling by Negri, in *Ghostly Demarcations*, of a (later) incident first relayed by Alexis de Tocqueville in his *Recollections*. 'We're in a lovely apartment on the Left Bank, seventh arrondissement, at dinnertime. The Tocqueville family is reunited. Nevertheless, in the calm of the evening, the cannonade fired by the bourgeoisie against the rebellion of rioting workers resounds suddenly – distant noises from the Right Bank. The diners shiver, their faces darken. But a smile escapes a young waitress who serves their table and has just arrived from the Faubourg saint Antoine. She's immediately fired.' And Negri concludes: 'Isn't the true spectre of communism perhaps there, in that smile?' (Negri, 1999b: 15).

[17] Is there 'any principle more obviously derived from the nature of things and from eternal justice,' he asks, 'than one that obliges the citizens to contribute to public expenditure progressively, in accordance with the advantages they draw from society?'

[18] 'The committee has also forgotten to quote the duties of fraternity which unite all men ... and their rights to mutual assistance' (68).

[19] Goldoni, 2017: 19 referring to Bodineau and Verpeaux, *Histoire constitutionelle de la France* (2013) at 13.

political and the social. On the side of the political it establishes commutability between the individual and the collective, so that with reference to suffering '[t]here is oppression of the social body whenever a single one of its members is oppressed. There is oppression of each member whenever the social body is oppressed' (sect. XXXIV). And it comes closer than any other document in declaring a right to resistance: 'resistance to oppression' as direct 'consequence of the other rights of man' (sect. XXXIII). But its main contribution is its direct regulation of the 'social question': 'Public assistance is a sacred debt; Society owes subsistence to unfortunate citizens, whether in procuring work for them, or in ensuring the means of existence to those deprived of the ability to work' (sect. XXI). *Art XI*. The support essential to those who lack what is necessary is a debt owed by those possessing superfluous means: it is for the law to determine the way this debt should be acquitted (Robespierre, 2007: 69–70). There are other examples, regarding progressive taxation and what we would call today 'social protection'. In all cases substantive *social equality becomes the constitutional good that orients political capacity*. Political rights form the substratum of social rights, equality is declared continuous to freedom, and constituent power becomes redirected to the social question. As the political flows into the social it forces commutability between the two, as the concepts of freedom and equality transfer freely between the political to the social.

If the Jacobin constitution of 1793 grapples to institutionalise the momentum and the insurrectionary élan of the Revolution it will of course only ever capture it imperfectly. What interests us from a constitutional point of view is precisely the meaning of this *imperfection*. It is perhaps at this liminal point, where constitutional promise is delivered inextricably bound up with crisis, that something of the paradox of constitutionalism comes more obviously into relief. If, to use Bruce Ackerman's exhausted formulation, we could call the Constitution of 1793 the *constitutional moment* par excellence of modernity, it is a failed exercise of constituent power in a most instructive way: it delivers crisis rather than synthesis. And yet, in crisis, it gives traction to the constitutional promise of democracy. We must turn once again to the notion of the general will to make sense of this.

The concept of the general will is bequeathed to the revolution by its 'patron Saint', Rousseau, in all its ambivalence. It must reconcile within itself the generality of the will of a people, and on the other hand the particularity of the demands as they find concrete expression in the assemblies at the local, sectoral, cross-cutting levels by the Cordeliers, the Commune, the Jacobin club, etc. How will Rousseau's abstract hypothesis of the omnipotent 'general will' carry the radical political practices of the assemblies and the societies and claim constituent power in that carriage?[20] And at the same time reach down to include within its ambit the claim of those who bring nothing to political presence but dispossession and need? The suggestion that carries over from our discussion of critical phenomenology, in Part I, gains traction from the ambivalence and locates the general will *as emergent in and as crisis*, finding expression in the very framework of iteration that the iteration transfigures. The crisis is not in the opposition between 'the spirit and letter', between the constituent and the constituted, but, borrowing from Derrida, 'a thinking that supposes the very movement of the letter'. For the first time this thinking sets before us *historically* the relation between semantics and structures that occupied us earlier (in Chapter 1.3). It sets the problem of the constituent before us in a way that invites Hegel's intriguing attempt to read the *real*, radical acceleration of the revolution in terms of the unfolding of *reason* in history. But for the Jacobins, caught in its momentum and without the benefit of hindsight, there is no transcendence of the contradiction they are caught in, and the rupture they instigate could not have been 'more furious'. It is often recalled that as the war of the First Coalition of the European Monarchies against revolutionary France raged at Fleurus in June 1794, 1,300 were guillotined in Paris in six weeks between June and July of that year during the period that became known as the Terror: the system of emergency government and summary execution put in place during year II under the auspices of the Committee of Public Safety and the Revolutionary Tribunal. With his own fate on the line, Robespierre attempts to justify the action of the Committee, with 'devastating clarity and fatal purity': 'Citizens,' he proclaims in one of his last speeches, 'did you want a revolution without a revolution? ... Who can mark ... the exact point at which the waves of popular insurrection *should* break?' (Robespierre, 2007: 79). 'The Jacobin tragedy', says Negri, 'consists in their incapability to see the fabric on which Rousseau's enigma exploded ... When clashing with the real they are prisoners of a violence that they do not understand, and that they cannot avoid' (1999: 212).

[20] Negri concludes that 'Rousseauism is a lexical form and a perspectival image in which the mass movement finds an opportunity to advance its project. To be faithful to the theory does not matter much; what matters is to find in it the polemical stimuli that allow the fundamental moves forward' (1999a: 203).

Well, that is one way to deal with Rousseau's gift to the Jacobins. In any case, how fascinating this dynamic read back into Rousseau, one that can transfer key insight into how the paradox of constitutionalism became productive for the Jacobins. And if it is indeed with the French Revolution that the principle of constituent power explodes onto the scene of European history, it is the Jacobinism of year II that captures in practice the crisis of the general will that materialises as constituent power, overwhelming the institutions with a temporality, and a novelty, that cannot be contained. Much of the discussion of the *time* of the constituent inevitably spills over into the *what* and the *who* of constituent power, the question of its content and its subject. And here the rupture is pronounced, determinations fought over and materializing through processes whose innovative intensity and violence still astounds. The constituent here explodes the distinction between the political and the social in a radicalisation of democracy that sweeps their mutual demarcation and limitation asunder. Our short genealogical account here attempted to track the expression and subsequent radicalisation of the principle of constituent power. Now, with Hegel, we track its recoil.

Hegel and the French Revolution

Hegel, like Kant, was a fervent spectator of the unfolding revolutionary events in Paris, and was 'stirred ... [by the] spiritual enthusiasm [that] thrilled through the world'. That which had entered history with the revolution, he wrote, shattered the epoch's 'patient acquiescence' and its 'calm satisfaction with the present' (in Ritter, 1984: 44). For Hegel, the French Revolution posed the problem that the epoch had to work out; philosophy would be called to unlock its positive meaning in order to grasp its age in thought. This is what would 'raise philosophy to its own time', making sense of – *making graspable* – the event before which it stood. And for this it could not fall back on the old historical categories to grasp what emerged in its novelty, because the old forms are not *adequate to it*.

In his extraordinary essay 'Hegel and the French revolution', Joachim Ritter transfers the problématique of the dissonance between constituted and constituent power to Hegel's reading of the revolution and to a 'reality' that is out of joint with the 'formality' of its representation. Ritter writes: 'in the ostensible perseverance of the old forms and in the semblance of historical continuity ... reality may be driving on anarchically... while the "vitality of the present day" is prevented from

CONSTITUENT POWER, CONSTITUTIONAL DISTINCTION 169

grasping itself in law.' (1984: 46) The dissonance brings us to what is most important, most intriguing about Hegel's pivotal identification of *the real with the rational*. 'To comprehend what is, this is the task of philosophy, because what is, is reason', claims Hegel famously (1820/2005: 11). That is why to grasp the constituent moment of the revolution becomes for him 'the task before which the age was unconditionally set' in Ritter's elegant formulation. The magnitude of the difficulty of meeting this task is astounding. It is not an exaggeration to say that Hegel would struggle with that revolutionary form-giving for the rest of his life. In 1819, he will write: 'I have passed thirty years in this eternally agitated time of fear and hoping, and I hoped that for once this fearing and hoping would be done with.'[21] Hegel's agitation is obvious. For him, philosopher of *becoming*, the passage is *arrested*: the revolution offered no lasting political solutions or 'political organization' that might have given it expression. It carried the novelty of the demand to think freedom in the form of equality but it gave that demand no 'substantive determination', and institutionally no 'order' that might accord with it. In other words, if the revolution is 'the process through which the Idea must pass in order to realise itself' (1828/1980, III §38) the realisation is deprived any legible form. What is presented unequivocally was the profound inadequacy of the old forms to which there could be no return. (Hegel's damning critique of the Restoration as a pathetic attempt to re-route the new back into the redundant forms of old is a case in point.) But now what to do with the historical expression of this pure, and non-transcended, *negativity*? How to comprehend the challenge that it confronts philosophical thought with one that is constitutively oriented to giving positive *rational* expression to the unfolding of the *real*? The event of the revolution has 'constituted itself in emancipation from all pre-given historical orders' (in Ritter, 1984: 50), severed itself from the historical framework that can now only claim it back (as Restoration) by misreading it. But what does it – the negative – *mean*, rationally? Ultimately, *The Philosophy of Right* will give it the meaning of what *will have been* the result of its synthesis in, the semantic order of the *democratic* constitutional state. There the ground of the state is the power of reason realising itself as will (1820/2002, §258).

But that was later. And we are still in the early 'Tubingen period' that only comes to a close in 1793, and Hegel is still enthralled to a Revolution that has entered its year I, with the Girondins outlawed and

---

[21] Quoted in Ritter (1984: 43).

the Jacobins taking over the Convention. The Terror is progressively unleashed. How is philosophy to 'greet and know' this 'new emergence of spirit' if he is to stay true to his premise that 'in the Revolution the abiding world-historical substance brings itself to an actual present political realization' (Ritter, 1984: 54)? Here we encounter Hegel's critique of the inability of the Revolution to give rise to the form that might contain it in a lasting institution. Its perennial driving on, its unremitting actuality, is unthematisable except as a meaningless lashing out of violence and as terror. With the revolutionary trajectory spiralling out of control, with 'reality ... driving on anarchically', what would approximate the real to the rational? Instead, 'the vitality of the present day' is prevented from grasping itself in law. In the 'broken middle'[22] where the philosopher finds himself confronted with the negative there is neither the option of a return to the 'perseverance of the old forms' nor the option of a form-giving in which to 'express, contain and comprehend' the 'vitality'. In terms of the former, 'the ferment where Spirit has jolted' cannot be sealed over, and there is no retreat from the principle that has entered world history. To lift itself to a comprehension of the 'jolt' that thrills the Age is the challenge. We might say, with Ritter, that the discontinuity introduced in history 'goes unresolved in all the tensions and antagonisms of the period', and that resolution therefore only comes later. But there is something remarkable, here, about the formlessness of the constituent principle as it is *enacted* by the Robespierrists, something remarkable about its non-iterability. We will return to Marx for this. But for Hegel what might have dignified the violence with meaning? Even in 1807 in that more comprehending text that is the *Phenomenology*, he is appalled by the 'fury of destruction' (359) and by the 'sheer terror of the negative' (362). This is unmediated pure negation and brings about death without significance 'like splitting the head of a cabbage', in his memorable metaphor in the *Phenomenology* (§590), with no meaning to dignify it. For Hegel the Jacobin notion of an unmediated popular sovereignty as the sublime unity of the people (à la Rousseau), and as principle of universal freedom, entailed the destruction of the actual institutional organisation of the world.[23] In *The Philosophy of Right*, the fanatical, destructive excess of the Jacobin terror is what follows their attempt to

---

[22] As the Hegelian philosopher Gillian Rose described the site of 'diremption'.
[23] On Hegel's 'superficial' reading of Rousseau and on 'refusing to honour his debt to Rousseau' see Shklar (1976: 207) and Ripley (2001: 146).

carry the abstract idea of absolute freedom into a world whose institutions prevented its realisation since for Robespierre the structures of representation thwart the positing of the will of the revolution.[24]

It is probably fair to say that Hegel does not resolve the conundrum of the Jacobin expansive principle of constituent power. Except as negativity, as that which was summoned as the antithesis of the feudal order. The brokenness of any current political experience, its arbitrariness, the *ad hoc* at work, is summoned to *a posteriori* rationalisation that endows meaning to what was not and could not have been present to those performing the work of transcendence.[25] If the dialectic marks 'the presence of the perfect in the imperfect' as Hegel puts it in the *Encyclopaedia*, one encounters nothing of its essential restlessness in the revolutionary moment, no meaning to a transition that goes beyond itself, except the *a posteriori* historical seal of the reason of state having realised itself as will. So much for that momentous event, the Jacobin constituent event, spiralling out of control, consumed by its own intensity, now *post festum* finding its meaning in the 'concluding' chapter of the Thermidor which is of course *anything but* a culmination.

Marx on Constituent Power

It is with Marx that the radicalism of Rousseau's thought is returned to the masses, and constituent power restored as subversive principle at the core of critical thought.

Marx's original critique of Hegel's treatment of the constituent principle is in the *Critique of Hegel's Philosophy of Right*, the early text that consisted of notes he took while reading *The Philosophy of Right* in the summer of 1843. If for Hegel there was no positive meaning that can be attached to the multitude's self-positing gesture of constituent power, Marx's interpretation returns to Rousseau's legislative function to argue, against Hegel, that the subjection of the executive to the legislative function makes possible the expression of constituent power. 'The representative constitution is a great advance, for it is the open, genuine, consistent expression of the condition of the modern state. *It is the*

---

[24] According to Robert Wolker, Hegel 'regarded Robespierre as having brought Rousseauism to its dreadful climax' (Wolker, 1998: 48).

[25] As Gorz puts it well: 'where history is a process unfolding a meaning at the end of time, from where it calls upon the multitude of its alienated, mystified, aborted and mutilated historic manifestations to transcend themselves towards it' (Gorz, 1982: 17).

unconcealed contradiction' (1843/1979: 75). For Marx the widening of the franchise to include all classes, and without the moderating influence of the executive on the legislature, would sublate the state-civil society contradictory articulation in the direction of a radical-democratic self-determination. 'Electoral reform within the abstract political state is therefore the demand for its dissolution, but therefore also the dissolution of civil society' (1843/1979: 121). An expanded legislative function would accommodate the unleashing of class antagonism so long as the function wasn't sheltered, à la Hegel, by a corporatist edifice that secured its subordination to the internal workings of the executive state. 'By raising the representative system from its [State-bound] political form to the universal form', he writes to Arnold Ruge, 'by bringing out the true significance underlying this system, the critic at the same time compels this party to go beyond its own confines, for its victory is at the same time its defeat.' With *On the Jewish Question*, however, the suggestion of a smooth passage from political emancipation (universal suffrage) to human emancipation is abandoned.

By the time of the *German Ideology* in 1846, communism is identified as a humanism in action, 'the real movement which abolishes the present state of things. The conditions of this movement result from the premises now in existence' (1846/1970: 94). The revolution gains its traction from conditions in place, and this immanent resistance transforms the constitutional basis on which the organisation of productive forces stands. 'This resistance, this strength, are constituent power' (Negri, 1999a: 224). 'The communist revolution', continues Marx, 'is directed against the preceding mode of activity, wage labour, and abolishes the rule of all classes with the classes themselves, because it is carried through by a class which no longer counts as a class in society, is not recognised as a class, and is in itself the expression of the dissolution of all classes' (1846: 94).

The logic here is well known: under conditions of the generalisation of capitalist industrial production the capitalist system itself elevates the proletariat into the position in which it can for the first time in history *potentially* assume the position of universal class. The assumption of that subject position marks the 'dissolution of all classes' and the 'founding of society anew'. In the *Poverty of Philosophy*, Marx will describe the dialectical movement thus: 'Economic conditions had first transformed the mass of the people into workers. The domination of capital has created for this mass a common situation, common interests. This class is thus already a class as against capital, but not yet for itself. In the struggle ... this mass becomes united and constitutes itself as a class for itself.' He asks: 'Is it at all surprising that a society founded on the opposition of classes should culminate in contradiction, the shock of body against body, as its final denouement?' (1845/1936: 145-7).

Throughout the turmoil of the 1840s, in the political writings of that period Marx treats the proletarian revolutions – from the ascendancy of the Jacobins and the insurrections of the Year II and III up to the 1848 revolutions across Europe – as the unfolding of a permanent constituent power, in which 'the [bourgeois] constitution of labour ... opens to an immanent and continuous alternative characterised by the ever new aperture of constituent power' (Negri, 1999a: 224) understood both extensively in terms of its permanence, and intensively in terms of accelerations, crises and 'offensives'.

But it is in 1852 with *The Eighteenth Brumaire* that Marx fastens on and explodes the constitutional distinction in its Hegelian reconciliation. With an eye on the historical curve ushered in with the French Revolution, Marx tracks first the ascending phase during which 'audacity mounts, one goes over further: constitutionals, Girondins, Jacobins', and then the descending phase during which 'the constitutionals conspire against the constitution, the revolutionaries seek to be constitutionals, the omnipotence of the National assembly gets bogged down in parliamentarianism'. This is the phase in which the 'phrase wins over the content'.

Here is the famous text:

> The social revolution of the nineteenth century cannot draw its poetry from the past but only from the future. It cannot begin with itself before it has stripped away all superstition about the past. Earlier revolutions required recollections of past world history in *order to dull themselves to their own content*. In order to arrive at its own content, the revolution of the nineteenth century must let the dead bury their dead. There the phrase went beyond the content – here the content goes beyond the phrase.
>
> (1852/1979: 106)

How does the duality phrase/content tie into the *problématique* of the constitutional distinction? Marx achieves the tie through metaphor, but then, as Althusser once put it, what language is *not* metaphorical that attempts to track a displacement? 'Phrase' is signifier for the language that lends itself to iterating the constituent; 'content' that which overflows it. Marx's injunction is against the summoning the new in the language of old, against falling back on the 'dulling' vocabularies of old. This, the most semiotic of Marx's texts, invites what Derrida calls the 'fissuring' of historical signifiers in order that the new content might burst through. The historical path dependency of the constituted past is subverted, the stake is the iterability of the constituent new.

It is perhaps unsurprising that what fascinates Derrida about Marx's text is the logic of a certain retroactivity, that he will link to the promise of democracy. From Blanchot's short text 'the three voices of Marx' he borrows the second, political, 'voice', which does 'not carry meaning but a call, a decision of rupture ... bound to an impatient and always excessive demand, since excess is its only measure' (Derrida, 1994: 33). Carrying a meaning would have integrated it back into the interpretative schemata of old and their untroubled exegeses. What is to come is 'not described or foreseen in the constative mode, it is announced, promised, called for in the performative mode' (1994: 103). If this language is to carry the displacement it is because it carries an 'originary performativity', Derrida tells us, and 'a performative interpretation is an interpretation that transforms the very thing it interprets' (1994: 51). Link the performativity with the promise and we are in Derrida's preferred idiom of a 'democracy-to-come', not a future democracy in the future-present, not a regulative ideal in the Kantian sense or a utopia: 'still a future-present, ie a future modality of the living present' (1994: 64–5). And later, democracy envisaged in the 'gap between an infinite promise and the determined necessary and necessarily inadequate form of what has to be measured against that promise'. And 'a promise must promise to be kept, not to remain abstract but to produce events, new effective forms of action, practice, organisation and so forth' (1994: 89).

This is where the spirit of the Marxist critique situates itself, not in the spirit that one would oppose to the letter, but one that supposes *the very movement of the letter*. We explored this under 'semantics and structures' earlier, (in 1.3); now it comes to connect to the expression of constituent power. If the 'content is to go beyond the phrase' as Marx wants, it is because 'it will exceed form, it will overtake signs. But paradoxical as it seems it is this unleashed overflowing, at the moment when all the joints give way between form and content, *that the latter will be properly its own* and properly revolutionary. By all logic, one ought to recognise it by nothing other than the excess of its untimely dis-identification, therefore by nothing that is presently identifiable.'[26] Marx writes in the *Eighteenth Brumaire*:

---

[26] Derrida (1994: 171). He continues (174): 'Marx remains a glorious, sacred, accursed immigrant chez nous. He belongs to a time of disjunction in which is inaugurated laboriously, painfully, tragically a new thinking of borders, a new thinking of the home and the economy.'

> The tradition of all dead generations weighs like a nightmare on the brains of the living. And just as they seem to be occupied with revolutionizing themselves and things, creating something that did not exist before, precisely in such epochs of revolutionary crisis they anxiously conjure up the spirits of the past to their service, borrowing from them names, battle slogans, and costumes in order to present this new scene in world history in time-honored disguise and borrowed language.
>
> (1852/1979)

This is how to understand the 'anachrony of the revolutionary present' of Derrida's beautiful formulation; anachrony because nothing *predicts* it. If the revolutionary present is *untimely* in this sense, it is not just because 'time is out of joint' as Derrida was so fond of reminding us, but because it is in advance of its proper expression, we might say, and in excess of the situation that defines it in the 'borrowed language' of the past. The *meaning of the constitution that it generates appears to have to guarantee it in return*. The constituent is caught up with the constituted in this reciprocity, expressed for Derrida as a future anterior, but in any case a temporal 'co-implication' we might suggest that cannot be accommodated in linear succession, or in giving conceptual precedence to either term.

And yet it is arguably in the very last writings on the Paris Commune that Marx gives us the most concise, and brilliant, account of constituent power in a clearly political key, that is, in terms of its expression in a political form to which it gives rise and in which it finds expression- the simultaneity of giving form and finding expression capturing what is essential about the constituent. *The Civil War in France*[27] is Marx's text that comes in the wake of the Commune, that astounds Marx for its invention of a new political form whose unfolding is the constituent power of labour's organisation. The political form is at last discovered as an *emergent form of labour's own self-government*. The seizing of power by the workers occurs in March 1871; in the final week of May, just over two months later, and after a week-long battle, twenty-five thousand workers have been massacred in the streets of Paris by the army stationed in Versailles. The massacre will claim more victims amongst the

---

[27] See *The Civil War in France: Address of the General Council of the International Working Men's Association*, 1871. Within a year of its publication, the pamphlet had been translated into French, Russian, Italian, Spanish, Dutch, Flemish, Croatian, Danish and Polish and published both in newspapers and in pamphlet form. All references in this section are to this work (1871/1972).

Communards than the whole of the Franco-Prussian War, significantly more than the Terror. If the barbarity is unremitting it is because the moment of worker self-organisation had been so subversive. For Marx this had been the expansive principle of constituent power in all its *potentia*: formative, ruptural, unarrestable. And crucially, at the same time, it is that which gave 'thoroughly expansive political form' to the 'self-government of the producers' (1871: 210). 'The Commune was to serve as a lever for uprooting the economic foundations upon which rests the existence of classes, and therefore of class rule. With labour emancipated, every man becomes a working man and productive labour ceases to be a class attribute' (1871: 212).

Marx wrote a new Preface to the *Manifesto*, a year later. 'However much that state of things may have altered during the last twenty-five years, the general principles laid down in the Manifesto are, on the whole, as correct today as ever.' And yet something astoundingly new had entered history with 'those *Parisians storming heaven*':[28]

> In view of the practical experience gained in the Paris Commune, where the proletariat for the first time held political power for two whole months, this programme has in some details been antiquated. One thing especially was proved by the Commune, viz., that the working class cannot simply lay hold of the ready-made state machinery, and wield it for its own purposes.

If it is indeed that 'the social revolution of the nineteenth century cannot draw its poetry from the past', as Marx put it in the *Eighteenth Brumaire*, it is because the past – Marx reads this so accurately from Hegel – cannot avail the language to give it adequate expression. It is generally the fate of completely new historical creations to be mistaken for the counterparts of older, and even defunct, forms of social life, to which they may bear a certain likeness. It was this inadequacy that we explored earlier as the categorial deficit of a language whose reach became the stake of the question that, to return to Hegel, philosophy asked of its age. With the Commune the rhythm accelerates; the signifier runs ahead of the signified. Like language every revolution tends to travel beyond its bounds, says Terry Eagleton.[29] The epoch's poetry is to be found in its future. If we might borrow a line from the Commune's quintessential

---

[28] From Marx's letter to Kugelmann, 12/4/1871.
[29] Eagleton, foreword in K. Ross, 1988: xi.

CONSTITUENT POWER, CONSTITUTIONAL DISTINCTION 177

poet, Arthur Rimbaud, '*La poésie ne rhythmera plus l'action; elle sera en avant*'.[30] In this phrase Rimbaud gives us the 'absolute metaphor' of the age, to capture 'the poetry of the revolution' leaning into a future that has not yet given it its semiosis.

If in May 1871 Rimbaud proclaims from the barricades that 'the invention of the unknown demands new forms', for Marx the Commune 'at last discovered' the 'political form under which to work out the economic emancipation of labour'. It is a 'political form' that catches Marx by surprise because of its *emergent* nature. The breach is not exhausted in the iconoclastic moment (what Hegel described as the 'negative' in Jacobinism); instead the 'fissured signifiers' of old are given a new content in an ongoing dialectic of form-giving. With the Commune the problem of the inadequacy of the categories, the problem of the shortfall that we have been discussing so far, gets caught up in the unfolding of action whose élan moulds them as appropriate to its unfolding, the moment of form-giving coincident with the praxis of the Communards. What fascinates Marx about the Commune is that the form runs *alongside* the workers' re-organisation of production in a moment of democratic self-assertion. 'When the Paris Commune took the management of the revolution in its own hands; when plain working men for the first time dared to infringe upon the governmental privilege of their "natural superiors," ... the old world writhed in convulsions of rage at the sight of the Red Flag, the symbol of the Republic of Labor, floating over the Hôtel de Ville' ; 'this was the first revolution in which the working class was openly acknowledged as the only class capable of social initiative'; '[t]he great social measure of the Commune was its own working existence'. (All quotes from 1871/1972.)

The concept of *autogestion* that the Paris Commune inaugurates in modern history is what in constitutional theory is signified by *constituent power*. It is born with the Jacobins, and it is claimed by the workers themselves with the Commune. Marx sees it as the emergence of political form, a form that might allow communism to break with the dilemmas that accompany the seizure of State power. Marx is adamant in the late

---

[30] [Poetry will no longer give rhythm to action; it will be in advance.] From a letter to Paul Demesny. In the same letter he identifies the poet with Prometheus ('le poète est vraiment voleur de feu') Rimbaud speaks of the poet as 'chargé de l'humanité' ('responsible for humanity'). The formulation 'absolute metaphor of the age' belongs to Catherine Ross (Ross, 1988: 66).

writings on the Commune: 'The working class cannot simply lay hold on the ready-made state machinery and wield it to their purposes. The political instrument of their enslavement cannot serve as the political instrument of their emancipation' (1871: 196). To this final work of Marx's on the political phenomenology of emergent form, link most profoundly the spontaneism of Rosa Luxemburg and the praxis philosophy of Georg Lukács.

*

What has the radical tradition bequeathed the thinking of constituent power? We have traced this problematic through the eruption of the French Revolution, the radical constitutionalism of Rousseau, as it informed the thinking of the Jacobins, as it found expression in the 'negative' in Hegel's constitutional thought, as it developed in Marx's work in discussion with Hegel's dialectic: in its continuous development from 'unconcealed contradiction' of a full-blooded legislative expression, through the 'real movement' of the *German Ideology*, the iconoclasm of the *Eighteenth Brumaire,* to the spontaneous, emergent form-giving *autogestionnaire* moment of the Paris Commune. The tradition of 'constituent power' carries into the twentieth century. First in Weimar, notoriously with Carl Schmitt in the clear contradistinction between constitution and constitutional laws. The people for Schmitt are the unconstrained force, the unity of the initial presence that is the source and subject position of the constitution. (How, asks Schmitt, can Kelsen *begin* with a norm?) Later, constituent power emerges in the discourse of the *operaismo* and *autonomia* currents of Italian Marxism especially as the thinking takes a 'political turn' with Tronti and Negri. To some of this we will return in future chapters when we discuss constitutional strategy, and the relation between semantics and structures that forms a key *problématique* of the book. But the genealogical excavation of the constituent must now be drawn to a close.

Before we do, let me insert a final comment on the *fear of the political* in its expression as constituent power. In the standard formulation, if 'constitutionalism gives legal form to the political, it is so that the abysses and the temptations of the political are banned'.[31] Derrida famously

---

[31] Ulrich Preuss, quoted in Lindahl (2013: 210).

objected to constituent 'presence' and to theorising radical democracy as pure or immediate presentation, as inexorably leading to a fellowship of terror: for Derrida it involves the inevitable shading between radical democracy and, coming full circle back to Arendt, to totalitarianism. Regis Debray describes the convergence well: '*Totalitarianism* serves much the same function in the arsenal of our political science as fanaticism did in that of the Enlightenment or totemism in primitive anthropology: it is both an excuse for mis-recognition and a rite to ward off evil' (Debray, 1983: 11). And for Bloch: 'the fear of the demos, of the visible will that needs to be stabilized, turns dialectic into a movement in a closed house and leaves it standing still in the domain of law' (1986: 125). The oft-repeated, uncritically received assumption that the exercise of the constituent shades into terror, the Commune negates by its own extraordinary reassertion of the wager of collective praxis.

*

The concept of political constitutionalism, I have argued, draws constitutively on the distinction between constituent and constituted power. If constitutionalism is the form of the distinction that holds the two poles together, we have looked at how the 'constituent' imports the irreducible measure of potentiality at its one pole. The other pole unfolds that potentiality along the temporal, social and material pathways of the 'constituted'. It is to the second pole, of constituted power, that we now turn. If one begins from this side of the distinction, there are two ways in which the reference across to the constituent can be effected. The difference is significant and has significant repercussions in how we make sense of constitutionalism. In the first case the constituent is overdetermined by the constituted, absorbed and sealed over. We will discuss this in the next section under the title 'eclipsing the constituent'. In the second case, of imperfect accommodation, the constituent is sustained as foundational reference for the varieties of political constitutionalism. Here the accommodation (of the constituent in the constituted) remains 'imperfect' but is mobilised as an asymmetry between the two terms. This informs the varieties of political constitutionalism that we explore in this part of the book. In each case they come up against a fundamental limitation. In the following two chapters (2.2 and 2.3) I attempt a restatement of political constitutionalism as antinomic, with an emphasis first on the formal dimension (2.2) and then the substantive dimension (2.3).

Theorising 'Constituted Power': Eclipsing the Constituent

The theory of *'ideal types'*, Max Weber's major heuristic innovation, was always going to sit uncomfortably with the interpretative openness of his hermeneutical method. Μέθοδος (the composite μετα–οδος) is a second-order undertaking, introducing reflexivity (μετα) over the route (οδος) one takes. Ideal types are imported, by Weber, at the meta-level in order to open out the inquiry at the first-order level of the construction of meaning. Weber is well aware that contingency cannot obtain at both levels, and he identifies the problem as that of the 'double hermeneutic', a formulation that expresses that precise concern that contingency cannot be kept alive at *both* level and meta-level. And yet that is precisely what his major *hermeneutical* gesture invites. His way out is to sacrifice contingency at the meta-level. Weber's methodological innovation of 'pure' or 'ideal' types is one of the clearest attempts to contain the contingency at the second-order, that is to delineate and to hold distinct the methodological question *as* a question of levels. Method is clearly designed to hold on to the conditions of asking the questions and holding on to the sharp differences drawn out between types; the phenomena observed will only ever be approximations of those types. Walled in and insulated in their purity and ideality, these interpretive forms cannot be both deployed and queried; they are not the *stake* of the question one asks about society, but its *condition*.

There is something deeply disquieting about the splendid isolation of the ideal type. Because it impacts on Weber's commitment to a comprehending sociology, whose object is the meaning of social action, and whose hermeneutical insight *must* be that it remain reflexive about its own comprehending. There can be no escaping the double hermeneutic of comprehending, that immediately migrates from the meaning that action has for the social actors performing it, to the meaning it has for the actors' social-scientific observers. The hermeneutic moment travels spontaneously from level to meta-level. But as the hermeneutic crosses both levels it *unsettles* both levels, because understanding must involve the retrieval, not the stipulation of meanings. And Weber finds himself caught in the double bind, on the one hand of navigating a (hermeneutic) contingency that, if alive at both levels, would overwhelm comprehension, and on the other, a reduction to ideal types that pre-empt comprehension and impose an unshakable path-dependency. The promise of reflexivity is blocked at this juncture; here the critical nerve of Weberian sociology is dulled, holding rationalisation to the formal order of methodological types and of hierarchies, comprehension strictly circuited back to it. Where, at the first level, action only ever acquires meaning in terms of its proximity or deviation from given ('ideal') forms, form overdetermines the observation. And there can be no dialectical moderation at the meta-level because ideal types are by design immune to such moderation. The givenness, and immunity, that these ideal forms are furnished with, carries a heavy price. Because what would it mean to contest the ideal type in the light of what it helps bring to question? What *explanandum* would discredit the *explanans*? Any dialectical tie between the levels is cut at the root. The *explanandum* will be carried by a methodology that has inserted its *a priori* as always-already accommodating of any impure instantiation. The promise of a *critical* sociology is sacrificed to this methodological immunity.

Marx's answer to the problem of critical theory, that the categories available to us fall short of the task – a task always measured *normatively* of course, because Marx's rationalisation, unlike Weber's, is either emancipatory or it *is not* – is *not* to stipulate them and to wall them in to a theory of pure types. His answer is instead to open them out reflexively to the political, and to release them into history; rationalisation for Marx is inevitably partial, historical, provisional. And if the 'rational' falls short of its emancipatory function, history will not guarantee, as in Hegel, the coincidence of the *rational* and the *real*. That is the wager, and the steep and irreducible risk that reflexive engagement takes in Marx.

Weber would have known Marx's wager, as he would have known that his ideal types allow him to cut the corner methodologically. It occurs to me that in those later, pre-Weimar years, dominated by deep disagreement over the meaning and possibilities of the constitutional settlement, something of the ineluctability and bankruptcy of bourgeois thought enters his disenchantment discourse. The profound immunising gesture of his sociology will have pitted him directly against Rosa Luxemburg's insistence that every political struggle was a struggle over its boundaries. Against her radical proposal for the constitutionalisation of council democracy, and against the writings of his close friend Georg Lukács with whom he breaks over the constitutional question, Weber finds himself defending a disarming moderation. Lukács, for his part, in that enigmatic masterpiece that is his *Theory of the Novel* written in 1916, places Weber's category of the comprehension of the meaning of social action at its very centre only to show the impossibility of navigating it. He speaks of the *abnormality* of a comprehending sociology in a world of *convention* whose all-embracing power marks the 'embodiment of recognised but meaningless necessities'. Weber himself is at his melancholic best in the wonderful last lectures, 'Science' and 'Politics as a Vocation', where the term 'vocation' is emphatically returned to activities whose demands can never fully be met. Weber's key question and insistent preoccupation throughout the early writings had been the 'moral' relationship between human beings and their work with the advent of capitalism, where the term 'vocation' had been reserved for the form of work driven by the profit motive, which was barely morally tolerable, let alone worthy of a 'calling'. By the time of the 'vocation' lectures the problematisation of social action has acquired a negative slant, experienced under bourgeois conditions, as an instrumentalisation writ large. Rationalisation may be path-dependent, but the path circles back on itself. There is a claustrophobic consequentiality in this that leads him close to Lukács of *The Theory of the Novel*. (*History and Class Consciousness* doesn't appear until 1923.) And it would not come as a surprise if the allusion to the 'firebrand spirit' in *Science as a Vocation* wasn't in fact a generous gesture to his erstwhile friend, while the *in pianissimo* of his wonderful passage isn't offered in the spirit of a redemption of sorts. Here is the passage:

> The fate of our times is characterised by rationalisation and intellectualisation and above all by the 'disenchantment of the world.' Precisely the ultimate and above all, by the most sublime values have retreated from public life either into the transcendental realm of mystical life or the brotherliness of direct and personal human relations. It is not accidental that our greatest art is intimate and not monumental, nor is it accidental that today only within the smallest and intimate circles, in personal human situations, *in pianissimo*, that something is pulsating that corresponds to the prophetic *pneuma*, which in former times swept through the great communities like a firebrand, welding them together.
>
> (Weber, 1918/1946: 156)

Beautifully as it culminates in these last lectures, it would not be unfair to query whether the famous humility of Weberian sociology, expressed in the retreat into value neutrality, is not in fact a sweeping gesture that positions and immures an unquestionable methodology. And might it not be said, counter-intuitively perhaps, that Marx's is the true humility, that departs from the *crucial inadequacy* of the categories available to historical thought, including his own thought. What, in *that* light, does it mean to step, with Weber, outside the dialectic of theory and practice in a way that insulates the question of method from the vagaries of history?

*

Earlier, first in Chapter 1.2 then in Chapter 1.4, we approached the question of method by way of Marx's wager. Here the question of normativity, imported through the eleventh thesis and the refusal to accept rationalisations that circuit possibility to the disenchanted world of capital, furnished a theoretical undertaking that had the odds stacked against it from the start. Here the critical undertaking would, methodologically speaking, need to claim its ground since the conditions of asking the question were obscured by the operation of bourgeois thought. It was what we visited as the impasse of the 'fetish phenomenon', that concerned the conditions of asking the question of emancipation because it installed itself at the very point of the recovery of meaning and could therefore not be stepped behind. *How to extract a question of method from this, as capable of upholding an emancipatory thinking, was the quintessential question for critical theory.* How to insert reflexivity against the false necessity of the commodity form and sustain a conceptual scheme that is embedded – because all thought is *historical* thought – in the very conditions it aspires to overcome.

If the constituent in Weber's thought is disarmed and carried in the reduced reflexivity of the ideal-types, Hans Kelsen, Weber's great interlocutor in the constitutional debate of early Weimar, takes a more direct methodological route to excise the constituent altogether from the 'pure theory' of law. Kelsen's solution pushes the paradox of constituent power far enough back to the outer limit of the legal system that it merely shadows without ever intruding. As founding hypothesis, the 'constituent' becomes merely a conceptual *a priori*, retaining nothing of its excess or boundlessness, and at no point breaking back into the order of the constituted. Kelsen famously invites us to see the 'coupling' of the juridical and the political, the constituted and the constituent, in terms of a founding hypothesis (the '*Grundnorm*') that authorises the first constitution (the foundation of the legal order) as valid. Clearly this is counterfactual: the first constitution is an act of political self-authorisation not legal validation, and yet it inaugurates an order of validity whose problematic beginning does not carry through subsequent performances. That is Kelsen's paramount concern and key methodological innovation. The constituent neither intervenes in the order of the constituted nor has any dialectical relation with it: facticity and validity do not articulate, the former remains nothing but the latter's external reference, an underdetermined situation that awaits to be granted 'objective' legal meaning by legal science. The 'constituent' remains temporally isolated at the point of origin, having inaugurated a system of law that no longer requires it, a system organised through chains of validity and thus 'constituted' through and through. The necessary animus of the constituent remains external, as the political impetus to change or apply that whose objective meaning can never be anything but legal.

The language of validity in all cases surrenders self-constitution – the constituent democratic moment – to the constituted order. For the Kantian that he is, Kelsen's theory remains pure to the extent that it pivots on the juridical condition, an 'as-if' that sustains it in its purity. In the purity of the General Theory of Law, *the active will finds expression in constitutional reason*, and with it the representation of the political event constitutively yields to the imputation of objective meaning to it. Thereby attribution is stripped of an external reference and the 'juridical condition' (Kant's *rechtlicher Zustand*) is doing all the work. What, then, if anything, remains of our 'double inscription' that requires a certain simultaneity of the constituent and the constituted? The problem remains alive for Kelsen only at the outer limit of his theory. Of course this is not a negligible concession: the hypothetical validation of the founding act, the originary constituent act, cannot be passed over because the transcendence returns to haunt the theory in the notorious difficulty he has, and theorists who followed him have had, with the problem of 'revolution'. The revolutionary act of self-constitution, in the postcolonial setting typically, remains a performative tautology, the act of self-institution, paradoxical and uninterpretable at the moment of its happening, since the condition of interpretation, the interpretative schemes of validity, is not yet in place. The problem confronted also those judges who were called to pronounce on jurisdiction and found themselves caught up in the paradoxes of recognition, most significantly in the Australian case of *Mabo* where the question of what authorised the very speaking position of the judge came sharply in to view. Kelsen's grand architectonic scheme offered them nothing as they stood before the novelty of a constituent act. Kelsen's is, instead, what with Luhmann we might call an achievement of 're-entry', a result of repeated operations that mobilise the claim of validity. But in the present, absent the retroaction, how can the purely performative terms of the judges' 'we hold', stand as the guarantor of its own performance, or the judge pronounce on her own jurisdiction? There is nothing in the modality of the present-future that might grant the subjective act of constituent power its objective meaning as constitutional law. The *Grundnorm* is a hypothetical validation of a founding act that could not be interpreted as such, that is, could not have claimed its objective (legal) meaning in the now.

But this is perhaps a small price to pay for having displaced the constituent dimension of constitutional law. In the circumstances the *Grundnorm* is called upon to do the work of keeping law's founding moment legal: its hypothesis an *a priori* – an as-if – that diffuses the temporal paradox that the supreme legal act of founding a constitution cannot be imputed to a body that is capable of law-making. Representation of the will and imputation of the will stand mutually constitutive at this point; the oddity of this mutual constitution is that it *cannot* be accommodated in temporal terms. Representation and imputation operate with different temporal modalities, requiring at once a *representation* of the will that *is* in the present and only in the present can it be the ontologically and normatively privileged site of collective action, and yet it *is* only by being *imputed* back to a people whose will it is, and thus re-calls a fore-structure that gives it meaning as will (since a will requires a willing subject). From the material point of view, validity determines content, formal descriptors and institutional facts; from the social point of view, points of allocation and address of decision-making are formally instituted; from a temporal point of view chains of authorisation hold the system in place, as it were, synchronically and diachronically. Validity never articulates with any 'facticity' because in all three dimensions it over-determines it: facticity, the world of 'brute facts', remains forever validity's external reference. The constituent moment evaporates into the hypothetical of the as-if. This transcendental argument, and the containment of the constituent that it underwrites, are thus caught up in contradiction. Of course where there is contradiction there also potentially arises political opportunity to force it at the level of critical theory and at the level of political practice – more on this later.

At the antipode of Kelsen's argument but with a striking symmetry in the logic of the suppression of the constituent by the form of bourgeois law we find Evgeny Pashukanis. What Kelsen elevates to the achievement of legal science Pashukanis indicts as the deep ideological function of bourgeois law. But the effacement of content by form is drawn out in strikingly parallel manner by both. Pashukanis' profound insight of the relation of form and content, is that content is eclipsed by the form of law. And crucially that this erasure is constitutive of law as a formal system. It is by absenting the underlying content, the material relations of production, that law attains to its form in the same way that in Kelsen the validity of the law collects the objective meaning of the underlying facticity into what is formally law and what underlies its 'purity'. For both theorists, the gesture that organises law is the same one that excludes its material base. Law's exclusionary function is founded on nothing but its own ongoing articulation, immunising what may count as a possible evolution of its thematics from any challenge that might have emerged from the material reproduction of social life or in terms of alternative configurations of individual and collective identity. The constituent is sealed over, in Kelsen as a function of the purity of thought, in Pashukanis as a function of immunisation of bourgeois law from the contradiction-laden terrain of social reproduction.

*

In the seminal theories of Weber and Kelsen, constituent power was variably eclipsed, suppressed and excised as a question of method. We remain with the methodology of thinking the constitutional question and turn to Chris Thornhill's important work in the sociology of constitutions: Thornhill adopts a historical-functionalist method, that eclipses the constituent in the way in which it suggests a reading of constitutions as adaptive and adapted to functional continuities.

> The first wave of modern constitutional formation was deeply marked both by the fact that rights prefigured constituent power, and that rights subsequently internalized a model of constituent power within the political system, or even approached an ongoing *surrogation* of the norm-giving functions allotted to constituent power. From the beginning, rights imposed a juridical structure on constituent power, and they ensured that constituent power impacted on laws in a form that was strictly filtered and systemically pre-selected. In each respect, the relation between rights and constituent power meant that, although defined as the external source of the state's legitimacy, *constituent power was immediately translated* into an internal organizational formula for the political system, and the actual externality of this source remained a projective fiction of the state's inclusionary self-construction.
>
> (Thornhill, 2012a: 389, emphasis added)

For Thornhill the *surrogation* of constituent power by rights is understood as a vital element in the adaptive societal functions of constitutionalism. If, at least with the Jacobin constituent interregnum, constituent power made a brief appearance on the scene of history enabling an independent conceptualisation of political constituency and self-determination, it is 'the dialectical configuration of constituent power and rights in early constitutionalism ... [that] played the most far-reaching role in the formation of the political system as a separate societal domain, in which political power could be applied across society in positive and autonomous inclusivity' (2012a: 389). The 'institutions of constitutional rule' become, in the functionalist perspective, 'embedded elements of adaptive societal reflexivity' (2012a: 373). Thornhill's important contribution tracks the shifting articulation of political power in society from the state to *rights*. Where the exercise of political power in society earlier found expression in the semantics of the state (which, in Thornhill's words, provided an arrangement for 'the general and inclusionary circulation of power' (2011: 391)), political power becomes increasingly correlated with the function of rights. 'These rights are neither the rights of states nor the rights of persons: they are rights in which power articulates itself after the catastrophe of statehood' (2011: 392).

We will not be able to understand the logic of this 'surrogation' – the gesture that always-already internalises constituent power as what carries and propels evolutionary adaptation – unless we take a short look at the *functionalist method* first. Functional analysis has the advantage over causal analysis of being able to navigate problem-complexes, and to answer questions of indeterminacy connected to complexity. Its fundamental reversal is that it begins with effects, in order to assess the range of causes that bring about those effects. Luhmann speaks of the *'uncertainty relation'* in functional matters between causes and effects: and explains that *both* causes and effects *cannot* be thematised at once. His functional analysis shifts the sociological perspective to effects. 'What matters,' he says, 'is not the law-like or more or less probable relation between certain causes and certain effects but rather the establishing of the functional equivalence of several possible causes from the perspective of a problematic effect' (1962: 627, 623). And with this he can transfer his key methodological perspective onto what interests him most: the relations between systems and their environments. Here the domain of functional equivalence spans the 'variation possibilities' that the system can locate for itself vis-à-vis its environment, possibilities, that is, 'of change, substitution and replacement' in it (1962: 626). Taking the cue from Luhmann, Thornhill will suggest:

> Observed in this way, we can see that the recent transformation of constitutional law reflects a deep functional continuity with earlier patterns of constitutional norm formation. Constitutional law always condenses an inclusionary structure for the political system of society. But the inclusionary pressures to which the political system is now exposed necessitate legal norms that cannot be explained through reference to a single national will. As discussed, the task for sociological analysis of

constitutions is to interpret the changing form of constitutional law as a refraction of changing pressures for inclusion, and to observe constitutional law as a set of norms that are adaptively produced, under particular circumstances, by society's need to preserve a distinctive political domain.

(Thornhill, 2016: 28)

Luhmann's functional analysis orients sociological analysis to a comprehension of how systems secure the *adequate* handling of complexity, which means that it is oriented to the equivalence spectrum for change: 'variation possibilities' as he calls it. It is what drives Thornhill's analysis towards the substitution possibilities that allow the political system to secure adaptation and inclusion. The substitution of constituent power for rights is how constitutional ordering responds to the inclusionary challenges of a political system no longer homologous to national societies and therefore no longer able to locate the exercise of political power in national political constituencies. The co-implication of democracy and rights is uploaded to the supranational, in functional continuity with earlier patterns, but reconfiguring their internal balance, and in effect subsuming constituent power to rights in the name of preserving a distinctive political domain that is able *adequately* to respond to the new pressures exerted on it (See Thornhill, 2016: 30).[32]

But there is a significant unquestioned assumption behind the smooth passage between functional equivalents. It is the question: *what is the measure of that adequacy?* Functionalism must import a quasi-normative premise at this juncture, despite itself. For Thornhill, 'the yield of a sociology of constitutions' also 'allows to illuminate the probable normative structure of modern society, and even to indicate that deviation from certain constitutional norms might (for reasons that are not normative but sociological) be undesirable and might *jeopardise* the basic resources and structural form of society', or later the 'reliable politicisation of social exchanges' (2011: 376). Let us interject to ask: what is the meaning of the disclaimer, and the sociological (rather than normative) appeal not to jeopardise existing structures, or the reliability of social exchanges? And

---

[32] Significant to appreciating Luhmann's departure from the tradition that names Durkheim and Parsons amongst its protagonists, is his insistence not to subsume function to the relationship between cause and effect. Where sociological functionalism took function to be the maintenance of social structures and of social order as such and thus re-conceptualised it as a cause of sorts, i.e. the cause for the stabilisation of social contingencies, Luhmann will argue that 'the function is not a special case of the causal relation, but the causal relation is an application of functional order' (1962: 626).

if, as suggested earlier by Thornhill, 'to observe constitutional law as a set of norms that are adaptively produced, under particular circumstances, by society's need to preserve a distinctive political domain', the questions of what qualifies as 'need', what marks it as 'distinctive', what shrinkage of political space is compatible with 'preserving' it, are all *normatively weighted questions*.

If there is a normative model that a sociology of constitutions proposes, suggests Thornhill, it 'has the distinction' of 'not being afflicted by the deductive aporia afflicting rival lines of inquiry' (2011: 376). The key problem of the latent normativity that seeks its footing and justification in functionalist methodology, is that it begs the question of *the measure of what is adequate*, be that adaptation, complexity-reduction, resonance-capacity, or inclusivity. At this point functionalism runs into an impasse it cannot resolve. *The point is that adequacy is a normatively mediated concept*. What social formation is adequate, adequately inclusive, adequately 'adapted', adequately resonant, etc, is an irreducibly political question. If the constituent is always-already expressed through rights, how might a political question over the adequacy of that surrogation be posed? Functionalism can only ever respond to that question by eliding it, or perhaps we might put it, the question of constituent power is a question that sociological functionalism is methodologically poised to miss.

*

In the tradition of political constitutionalism the distinction between politics and law, between will and reason, between democracy and rights, or, in their more abstract formulation, between constituent and constituted power, is configured as an *asymmetry*. Varied as are the forms in which the *constitutional distinction* is thematised, the constitutional perspective is cast from the point of view of the pole of 'constituted power'. As Castoriadis puts it, *the imaginary constitution of society* 'is something that can be presented only in and through the institution, but which is always infinitely more than the institution' (1975: 112). Political constitutionalism is the name for the articulation of the institution with deeper normative dynamics (the 'infinitely more'). We will indeed see that what qualifies these institutional articulations as instances of political constitutionalism is the promise of the constituent that is held to, in all cases, as the constitutive vis-à-vis. In the complexity-deficit between the constituent and its institutional expression – what we have been calling the asymmetry between constituent and constituted – we have both the containment and the promise of politics, and between the two the possibility of traction. Political constitutionalism holds the promise that the asymmetry will be productive: the constitution offers to give 'the people' the vocabulary to furnish democratic experimentation while simultaneously containing and delimiting the field. If it achieves both imperfectly, then that imperfection is what gives constitutionalism its élan: in indeterminacy it harbours responsiveness to the dynamism of the political but a responsiveness that remains within the ambit of constitutional reason.

There are important variants along the range of political constitutionalism and we will visit instances, though not systematically, nor in the form of any typology. What qualifies them as instances is that the 'constituent' and the 'constituted' are held together and it is their conjunction that sustains the constitutional point of view, their articulation that gives it play, and their dialectical movement that gives it unity. In all cases the constituent pivots on the constituted, gains purchase from it and in a crucial way *returns to it*.[33] Path-dependence harnesses the constituent to the logic of institution that alone lends it unity and expression. Here one encounters the tradition of *jurisgenesis*, which spreads the constituent into a community's ongoing normative contention over continuous (constitutional) time, and gives rise to the variety of American republicanisms. One also encounters the integration of the constituent into *constitutional dialogue*, with the discursive turn. And of course *critical theories of rights* committed to keeping the constituent alive in the modalities of destabilisation, or *in extremis* as dangerous supplement, are also key expressions of the imperfect accommodation of the constituent in constitutional discourse.

As we proceed to look at the formal and substantive dimensions of political constitutionalism in Chapters 2.2 and 2.3 respectively, and also later when we look at strategic deployments of political constitutionalism, we will return to these important statements. The main impetus in political constitutionalism that came with the 'procedural turn' as the new basis of the legitimation of constitutional arrangements, places *constitutional dialogue* at the centre of processes of democratic will-formation. Tied predominantly with the (second) Frankfurt School and the leading figure of Jürgen Habermas, the expression of the constituent is couched in a systematic theory of discourse that subtends democratic practice as

---

[33] I have explored elsewhere the constitution's thwarted promise of carrying the constituent per se; Christodoulidis (1996), (2003), (2007).

sustained and underpinned by the law. The key formulations that have infiltrated debates on the public sphere ever since are those of 'co-originality' and 'co-implication', both denoting a simultaneity and originary co-dependence of rights and democracy, and of public and private autonomy. But it is in radical theories of rights that political constitutionalism finds some of its more subversive expressions.

'The proletariat takes the bourgeoisie at its word', Engels famously declared with direct reference to the French Revolution, to human rights and to bourgeois natural right. And Ernst Bloch who quotes him, continues: 'In most respects the bourgeois revolution [of 1789] was unquestionably more bourgeois than revolution ... but it still contains that concrete utopian form of a promise that the real revolution can hold onto.' 'This is the stipend of human rights', 'anticipatory of humanity', and 'pointing far beyond the horizon of the bourgeois world' (Bloch, 1986: 174). Bloch's was an intriguing renewal of the natural rights tradition that attaches the juridical articulation of rights to deeper political and ethical societal resources. This line of thought that draws from Bloch's profoundly unorthodox Marxism is renewed in the work of Costas Douzinas for whom natural right was the creation of revolutionary thought, an act of Promethean rebellion, as he puts it. The transcendent position of natural law retains the 'radical potential of right' for the present, availing a claim to truth above what common sense establishes as its existent possibilities.[34] Of course one must take care here to distinguish the radical tradition of natural right from rights-discourses committed to the reproduction of exchange-dependent processes of societal formation.

We will return to these Leftist restatements which are set against the more tempered analysis of co-implication, and certainly set against the unremarkable banality of zero-sum competitions between constitutionalisms 'political' and 'legal'. Immanent in the constituted forms but transcendent in their capacity to subvert those forms, this 'critical' or 'constituent' theory of right must navigate a complex field with subtlety, and inform the strategic uses of law. But if there is significant strategic opportunity in this critical take on rights, there are also significant limitations, and strategic deployments must remain alert to them. 'What a colossal deception,' writes Marx in *The Holy Family*, 'to have to recognise under the aegis of human rights the modern bourgeois

---

[34] See Douzinas (2000). In the same tradition inspired by Bloch, see also Kochi's important work (2019).

society' (in Bloch, 1986/2018: 48). In this, as in much else he wrote, Marx does not assign to human rights the role of epiphenomena of economic relations. Built into the very logic of immanent critique the normative values they embodied, could provide a language to register not only economic exploitation but more broadly *degradation* and therefore leverage to transcend the system that inflicted it. In Foucault's work too, famously and quite explicitly in the later work, there is a reliance on rights as immanent to the field of political struggle, and important recent work has tapped this rich field, as in Ben Golder's suggestion of reading Foucault's rights as 'counter-concepts' against the way in which liberal theory has thematised and deployed them[35] (Golder, 2015). There is mileage in a constituent politics of rights.

The point to keep from the discussion of asymmetries is that the realm of institutions (the dimension of constituted power) is what provides the constituent with traction. The traction and the antinomy is what harbours a critical phenomenology in the field of constitutional thought. But there is nothing obvious, spontaneous or warranted about its conditions of emergence. What is achieved politically through such deployments should not be traded readily, and the achievement of political constitutionalism must guard, first, against its collapse without remainder into the institutional framework, and, secondly, against the market deformation of constitutionalism, explored in Part III, with the smooth expanses it avails to the circulation of rights, the commensuration of constitutional values, the immaterial constitutional dialogue, the easy jurisgenesis of the constitutionalisation of soft global law.

---

[35] For Golder, '[Foucault's] invocations of rights are strategic in this *incongruous* sense as they are situated within the spaces of political formation but are intended to resist and go beyond that formation, to transcend it' (Golder, 2011: 295) (see also Golder (2015)).

2.2

Constitutionality

Prolegomena

I suggest that we understand *constitutionality* as the modality of *law's self-reflection*, or, to take Gunther Teubner's famous title,[1] *constitutionality is 'how the law thinks' about itself*.

Already controversially this statement suggests that the law *thinks*, and that *it* thinks about *itself*: to cast the law as both agent and object of scrutiny, it has been objected, involves a circularity that does not allow scrutiny to get off the ground. In this chapter we will treat the circularity not simply as productive but as constitutive of the meaning of the 'constitutional' as *autopoietic*. To answer the 'epistemological' objection we will follow Luhmann in his theory of how legal meaning is generated, and we will navigate (and also circumvent) a great deal of theoretical complexity, in order to arrive at an understanding of how legal operations at the first-order are controlled at the second-order, constitutional level, in the way in which they are organised, framed, sanctioned and reflected on, and thus how constitutional meaning is generated across all three dimensions: social, material and temporal. This, I will argue, is what systems theory may offer constitutional thinking that in the face of globalisation sweeping away the constitutional givens, finds it so extraordinarily difficult to answer its identity problem, the question 'what is the Constitution?' The answers we get range from theoretical *a prioris*, to unsustainable assumptions about constitutional culture, to meaningless zero-sum contrasts between political and legal constitutionalism, to weak and tentative delineations couched in the language of so many pluralisms and of a creeping constitutionalisation, all of which surrender the political dimension of the constitution and belie what the constitution is so obviously about: unity, framing, entrenchment, foundation, fixity, orientation and rationalisation.

---

[1] Teubner, 'How the law thinks: toward a constructivist epistemology of law' (1989).

The analysis proceeds from, and deepens, the understanding of constitutionalism that in the previous chapter was identified as 'political'. If, as was argued in Chapter 2.1, what defines 'political constitutionalism' is the asymmetrical deployment of the 'constituent/ constituted' distinction, in this chapter we look at the modalities of that deployment. How precisely does constitutional reflexivity navigate uncertain and complex environments in terms of that distinction? We will explore how the complexity and uncertainty is managed – 'reduced' in systems-talk – along the three axes, material, social and temporal. And we will not lose sight of how, in the process, the border between the constituent and the constituted runs *within* the constituted as its highest possibility. The 'constituent' grants it restlessness, aspiration, and the measure of its adequacy. Constitutionalism as *reduction achievement*, Luhmann reminds us, *must* provide adequate complexity, an exigency that he measures in functional terms. We argued above (in Chapter 2.1) that this functional approach begs the question of adequacy. We will, instead, attempt to restate that adequacy in *political* – normative – terms, but without losing sight of the Constitution's functional reach.

We have become accustomed to differentiating between forms of constitutionalism: political, economic, social, etc. Constitutionality is the name for the way in which law's relationship to the other spheres, or systems – politics, economics, etc. – is always, constitutively, mediated and accomplished through a self-understanding. This makes self-reference pivotal, and with it, I will argue, constitutionality the condition both of the law's openness to other spheres and at the same time the condition of its own closure as a (complex) system. Systematicity does not precede the openness to other spheres; in systems theory, the legal system is only ever a system vis-à-vis an environment, and in that vis-à-vis, self-reference and other-reference are actualised *in tandem*. It is this that gives law's self-observation (or constitutionality as we are calling it) form and meaning.

*

First let us dispense quickly with the unhelpful circularity of theorising 'legal constitutionalism' as pitted against 'political constitutionalism'. It is clear, and will become clearer as we look at the self-referential deployment of constitutional reason, that all constitutionalism is, and can be nothing except, legal. In the theories where the contrast is deployed, it is intended to connote an opposition between political constitutionalism in its 'democratic' overtones and the 'juristocracy'[2] of rights adjudication by constitutional courts. The contrast has spawned a thousand variations. Suffice it to say that it is a category mistake to collapse constitutionalism into the function of adjudication as a matter of *theory construction*. It is when Court-centred analysis raises its ambition to the level of a theory of 'legal' constitutionalism that it confronts questions that it is categorially incapable of answering. Whether courts act as 'guardians' of the constitution, whether they uphold its fundamental commitments, whether they enhance or deplete democratic forms of conducting politics, are all contingent not definitional matters. Pick any one out of a myriad examples here: what does it mean to celebrate the US Supreme Court as the embodiment of constitutional reason in the wake of *Citizens United*? Such cases typically send American constitutional theorists into a spin, wistfully seeking *ad hominem* arguments about virtuous judges of the likes of Brennan, Holmes or Warren, or imaginary ones like Hercules.[3] From theoretical construction to zero-sum institutional competition between courts and legislatures, 'legal constitutionalism' revels in its stifling introversion.

We will instead pursue a theory of political constitutionalism that *is* legal, with the radicality that the notion of self-reference brings to the formulation, and in which both rights and democratic discourse have a role to play. This is an understanding of constitutionalism which is set with democracy as its specific vis-à-vis and therefore *must* navigate its reference to its political environment and the challenge of democracy, deprived of which it would have nothing to observe, nothing to thematise and nowhere to go. To remove the constituent from the equation is to deprive constitutional thought of the distinction that founds it. How the latter has played out historically in the 'evolutionary achievement' that is modern political constitutionalism can best be observed, to begin with, in the dynamics of the co-evolution of the legal and the political system in the context of the nation-state.

*

---

[2] The reference here is to Hirschl (2007).
[3] Alternatively the venture is backed, in a more 'pragmatic' vein, by supplementary, if anaemic, arguments about the capacity of constitutional courts, as per Michelman, to 'pick up voices from the margins' (1988) and where such arguments are dismissed even by theorists of discursive inclusion – Habermas, for example, teases: 'Michelman is apparently guided by the intuition that the discursive besiegement of the Court by a mobilized society gives rise to an interaction that has favourable consequences for both sides' (in 2001: 73).

The 'modern' story of constitutionalism understands constitutionalism as a result of, and compensation for, the functional differentiation of the spheres of law and politics. Returning to the American and French revolutions, Luhmann traces constitutionalism's conceptual innovation: a legal text first fixes the terms of a political constitution and with it there occurs 'a legal establishment of a political order [whereby] one saw the political order as a legal one' (1990b: 178). For Luhmann constitutionalism is a reaction to the functional differentiation of a political and a legal system that could no longer be identified with one another, subsumed to one another or incorporated in some hierarchy under an overarching natural right to rule. The *evolutionary achievement* of the constitution emerges with the positivisation of law and the democratisation of politics with the advent of modernity. This occurs at a crucial point of the co-evolution of the differentiated sub-systems of law and politics, when the democratic self-determination of 'the people' becomes coupled to the semantics of the Nation State and given expression in its law.

With an eye as always on *function*, Luhmann turns to this largely 'autological' text that is the constitution, and comments on how remarkable it is that as a result of *political* revolutions *legal* restrictions were imposed on the powers of all organs of the State as well as on the omnipotence of Parliament. The priority of the constitution above all other law meant that the constitution now positioned itself as measure of the legality or illegality of all laws, and with this the law itself now enters a state of contingency: it could be legal or illegal. While politically the unity of the system could perhaps still be defined territorially, this could no longer be on the basis of the old formulae but only as a difference between ruler and ruled, which, under democratic conditions, breaks the tautology 'I decide what I decide' with the formula 'I decide and am bound by what I decide', which holds together, in an improbable balance, the legal and the political. For Luhmann, it is this difference that forms the specifically political decision-making process that claims sovereignty for itself.

In all this there has been, claims Luhmann, a displacement of temporal perspectives (1990b: 192). The overwhelming orientation to the past that characterised pre-modern society is displaced by a new openness to the future made possible in the new constitutional order. Openness to the future means that the law foresees its own changeability and controls it by placing all law under constitutional scrutiny. And this is achieved through a continuous 'structural coupling' with the political system, that enables the law to reach out to politics and establish, for itself, that it is giving a people a means of expression of its sovereign will. It can also reorient the law to the future by tapping the 'not-yet' of politics, the openness of politics to the future and resist the closure that would suffocate it. In enabling the coupling it renders tolerable the paradox of the incommensurable logics that couple around it, captured in that improbable formula of the unrestrained power of self-restriction. That, after all, is the very paradox that constitutional thought forever returns to, that of reconciling self-rule and law-rule, and it is what animates democratic representation. The constitutional paradox, 'unfolded', comes to underpin all constitutional possibility. In the process of attempting to reconcile themselves with it, both political and legal systems can 'see' themselves represented in the concept – 'their' self-description as the Democratic Constitutional State.

While a long tradition of political thought inclines us to see only a unified politico-legal system, evoked to a large extent by the concept of *the State* which has both a political and legal status, 'our proposition will be', says Luhmann, 'that there is not one system under the heading of the concept of the state but that there are two different systems, both operatively closed, having different functions, different codes and different code-dependent programmes ... The concept of the state becomes an artificial device for holding together what has emerged as the self-reinforcing dynamics in the political system and the legal system' (2004: 364, 365). These are 'self-reinforcing' dynamics that do not, however, combine in a unity notwithstanding the 'organisational and semantic movement' which integrated politics and law found in the great codifications of the eighteenth and nineteenth centuries, as well as the idea that the function of the State to guarantee freedoms in terms of the law.[4]

Reference to 'self-reinforcing dynamics' is crucial here. It is the articulation, the mutual exposure that allows, for each system, the consolidation of their respective semantics, and this consolidation stabilises the respective domains. Key concepts, emergent self-descriptions, provide the vocabulary with the help of which are structured both the self-organisation of each system and its outward reach. It is around this

---

[4] While the positivization of law and the democratization of politics support each other reciprocally and they have left a significant mark on both the political system and the legal system of today, ... it is impossible to see politics as an ongoing interpretation of the legally fixed constitution', no matter how much political capital is generated from readings of the constitution, or how much legal decisions are guided by politically desirable consequences (Luhmann, 2004: 364).

emergent constitutional semantics that democracy and law manage their self-reproduction under the aegis of the constitution.[5]

*

The 'articulation' between legal and political systems just described falls under what Luhmann terms 'performance'. In a key trichotomy – *function, performance, reflection* – that organises the field of functional differentiation, *performance* is the term that captures the contribution that one functional sub-system makes to the self-reproduction of another. In the co-evolution of politics and law through the constitution, the forms of structural coupling that the constitution offers support the systems' mutual performance. If performance describes the inter-systemic interface, *function* describes the relation that each functionally differentiated system has with the overall system of society.[6] *Reflection,*

---

[5] Luhmann adds a word of caution to his important account of how constitutionalism has transcended the 'evolutionary achievement' that was the national constitutional order, that will be relevant in our later discussion (Chapter 2.4). As politics are endlessly confronted with problems that can no longer be referred to questions of sovereignty, and as law is no longer predominantly about the regulation of conflict but increasingly geared to the production and programming of specific outcomes, 'perhaps', Luhmann says, 'we are deceived in our fascination for the Constitution and the acknowledgement of its value, the introduction of a guaranteed hierarchical final instance [Hochinstanz] and the daily recourse to it, ... about how far advanced we are on a path that has long left behind these foundations' (1990b: 215).

[6] What is the function of the law according to Luhmann? According to the 1981 'Die Funktion des Rechts' the function of law consists, merely, in the stabilisation of expectations, an account developed from the *Rechtssoziologie*. Law's function is there described as the 'congruent (consistent across all dimensions) generalization of structures of expectation' (1972: 40ff or 24ff) since law, functionally understood, 'attains selective congruence and therefore forms a structure of social systems' (p. 77). At this time of the *Rechtssoziologie* of 1972 Luhmann develops his sociology of law around a functional definition of law as a *structure*, rather than a system, functional in the sense of contributing to the establishment and maintenance of congruence across expectational structures in society. While this function is broadly maintained in later writings, the re-conceptualisation of law as a *system* in society, rather than a structure of it, comes with an internalisation of mechanisms of meaning-generation on the one hand, and an externalisation of function on the other that occurs across, and thus has to reckon with, system/environment differentials. With the 'autopoietic turn in his theory, Luhmann's suggestion for the function of law, is that it be viewed in conjunction with 'the exploitation of conflict perspectives for the formation and reproduction of congruently generalized behavioural expectations' (Luhmann, 1988b: 27). Law achieves order by 'using the possibility [better: occasion] of conflict for a generalisation of expectations in temporal, social and substantive aspects' (Luhmann, 1986b: 121), a formulation he subsequently repeats in (Luhmann, 2004).

finally, turns the observation inward, as *intra*-systemic, to the reproduction of the system itself.

Take the combination of 'performance' and 'reflection' that is key here: the reciprocal dependence (*performance*) of the legal and political systems across the boundary and under the sign of the constitution is always mediated by self-reference (*reflection*). The systems do not lend themselves to commensurate syntheses. In their mutual cross-reference across the systemic boundary, systemic communications couple around common concepts – signifiers that travel between the systems – but the meaning-alignment is always, and could only ever be, internal. Significantly for the theory of reflexivity developed here as deployed in political-constitutionalism, the concept of *constituent power* is a key organising reference across the two systems.

Luhmann will insist that the constitution in its function of securing a stable coupling of the two systems over time is an *improbable* achievement. What makes it improbable is the fact that to secure their coupling each of the two systems needs to adapt and organise its own semantic resources *adequately* so that expectational structures can be reproduced in a stable rather than random manner, although its own projective vocabularies, sensors and activations can only ever *approximate* other systemic constructions in its environment. The concept of the system's 'adequacy', or its (own internal) 'adequate complexity', captures and measures *functional resonance*. As Thornhill explains it, resonance centres on the 'adaptive functional element which the political element of modern society generates for itself', as a means through which the political system 'simplifies' and 'adaptively orders its functional structure' (2012a: 376). The constitution sustains a coupling between law and politics that is reproduced over time as productive to both systems; 'improbably' as we said because it demands that each system adjust its own internal complexity adequately in order to secure functional resonance across the systemic boundary with a system in its environment that it can neither control nor predict. The form of coupling that as part of the performance of each system secures the stable reproduction of both, is called '*structural coupling*' and plays a key role in systems theory. With 'structural coupling', a functional system can take certain structures in its environment for granted and rely on them (Luhmann, 2004: 441). At the operational level, law's coupling with politics, expressed as its performance, involves its coupling on a continuous basis ('structural'). Thereby the legal system impacts on the function of the political system, which is the reproduction of society through *collective decision-making* processes, decisions taken against the background of conflictually held positions. At the same time the legal system relies on the political system to furnish (collective) conflict perspectives that will allow it to fulfil its own function of generalising normative expectations across society. Both systems depend on each other and must presuppose certain cognitive and normative structures as key to their functioning, which they cannot themselves produce. The lasting forms of structural coupling sustain 'performance' at these 'junctures'. Differentiation and coupling, function and performance: key categories that underpin and sustain the reproduction of society.

Self-Reference

The claim that thinking about the constitution involves distinguishing between first- and second-order levels of norm creation is certainly not novel. Even for theorists drawn to the pragmatic tradition of the Common Law, adverse to the conceptual architecture of civilian jurisdictions, one finds a concession to a basic form of systematicity. Famously amongst legal theorists of this tradition, H. L. A. Hart's description of the law as 'the union of primary and secondary rules' involves the articulation of first and second orders. 'Secondary' rules for Hart are 'on a different level from the primary rules, for they are all *about* such rules' (Hart, 1961: 92, original emphasis). The importance of these rules lies in their relation to primary rules in the way that establishes a legal *system*. Hart argued that the transition from more 'primitive' to more sophisticated systems is marked by the development of this second layer of norms, and that the articulation of layers, primary and secondary, is what accounts for the development of the legal system under the exigencies of – not his word – complexity. Secondary rules allow the recognition of primary rules as rules of the system: they thus perform the elementary *constitutional function*, of establishing system-specific criteria of identification and selection of rules as *structures* of the system. They fold the system back upon itself through establishing criteria of identity, or 'recognition', including also rules of change which orchestrate how the unity of the system might sustain its identity over time. Constitutionality is here for Hart the condition of possibility of a legal system, and the supposedly notorious 'circularity' of the argument – that 'recognition' is effected by actors always-already 'recognised' as capable of granting it – is in fact the inevitable condition of any system that operates through self-reference. Systems, Luhmann would argue, 'exploit' such tautologies and paradoxes, turning virtuous what critics of Hart would see as a vicious circle; a point made already without the use of systems theory by scholars like Neil MacCormick, who argued that it is precisely that circularity that allows legal institutions to develop in relations of mutual support with political institutions (MacCormick, 1981).

If the articulation of levels grounds constitutionality as condition of the legal system in Hart, it reaches highly sophisticated expressions in continental legal theory. For Kelsen, that most systematic of philosophers of law, constitutionality underlies imputation, establishes constitutional recall, grants validity, and with it 'objective' legal meaning to subjective acts which, in the process, are selected as elements of the system. That it needs to be kick-started through a hypothesis (the *Grundnorm*) is, as we saw earlier, an inevitable feature of self-reference that at some point must breach the fundamental tautology that it is law that validates law. Luhmann has no time for that 'unnecessary' and 'unlikely construct' of Kelsen's; for Luhmann law's positivity inheres in circularity that law is what the law says it is. The fundamental tautology of the legal system, as he describes it, is that the law is the law because it is the law. This tautology is 'exploited' by the law itself to create cognitive openness, and thus responsiveness to a changing world, on the back of the normative closure that underpins it *as* positivity, guaranteeing its independence from any 'super-regulative' instance like morality, reason or nature, and based solely on its own self-reference.

*

The foundational notion of *reference* is the term that Luhmann uses for difference-based observation. To reflect on anything, to observe anything, he says, one must begin by drawing a distinction, and he designates as *reference* the operation that consists of two elements: distinction and indication. 'If one wants to thematize the unity of a difference one must determine both sides of the distinction.' We had a first brief look at this with regard to the 'constitutional distinction' in the previous chapter. A reference is an operation that posits a distinction and indicates one side of it. The concepts of reference (and self-reference) are understood with respect to the 'operative handling' of a distinction posited *semantically* as a difference. It is the semantic counterpart, as it were, to the operations of *social* systems that are systems of meaning.[7] With time,

---

[7] In Luhmann's typology living systems involve the autopoiesis of life, conscious systems involve the autopoiesis of consciousness, and social systems involve the autopoiesis of meaning. See Luhmann, 1986c, for a concise summary.

'difference-specific social systems develop', that build up the internal complexity that will allow programming and selectivity based on connections, differentiation, and classifications.

Let us take a systematic look at how 'self-reference', radicalised in Luhmann's systems theory as *autopoiesis*, occurs at the first-order level of law's operations, and at the second-order, constitutional, level. Luhmann gives us a typology of self-reference that includes 'basic' self-reference (*basale Selbst-Referenz*) at the first level, reflexivity *stricto sensu* and reflection (*Reflexivität and Reflexion*) at the meta-level. It is a complex and technical discussion, and I will simplify considerably, with an emphasis on what is relevant to the constitutional function.

At the first-order level 'basic self-reference' is at work in the autopoiesis of the system, in how elements of the system (for us legal communications) produce new elements of the system. It involves the creation, in the system, of everything that the system uses as an element; the closure of the system depends on these elements being linked recursively. Communications are coded as a positively or negatively interpreted proposal of meaning: something is claimed/argued/decided as being legal or illegal (without the possibility of a third option). The self-reference here inheres in the fact that communicative offers are tested on criteria that the system itself avails and controls.

Self-reference at this first level is necessary but by no means sufficient to the task facing a system of law. The further operationalisation of that procedure allows the system to build up its own (internal) complexity in order to become adequately responsive to the environment. The generation and structuring of internal complexity requires self-reference to operate at higher levels, that Luhmann identifies with the terms 'reflexivity' and 'reflection'.[8] *It is here that is located the constitutional function.*

Take reflexivity (*Reflexivität*) first. Similarly to Hart's analysis, second-order rules of change establish the conditions according to which new primary rules can be introduced or older rules amended, at the many levels at which rules of change are prescribed by our legal systems: at the level of 'constitutional amendment', that is the conditions under which the constitution can be revised, at the level of making changes to legislation, at the level of the powers of government to vary legal standards within areas of jurisdictional competence, or to individuals to vary their

---

[8] It is not in his book on law, but his earlier *Social Systems*, which serves in the way of Kant's 'prolegomena' and Marx's *Grundrisse*, that Luhmann develops his most useful and systematic discussion of self-reference. The discussion here draws from that book.

legal status, say through contract or marriage. It is similarly with a view to observing the control of change within the legal system that Luhmann imports the more demanding concept of 'reflexivity'. At stake is the way in which '*Anschlussfähigkeit*' (usually translated as linkage-capacity) is operationalised in law, that is how the system's development – because what is *not* change in the law understood as a temporal system? – is brought and contained within a stabilising structure of selection. How is change in law, in other words, sustained as functional to its continuation? Law is a system of incessant *change* that must deploy that change to consolidate and *stabilise* societal expectations. And that is why at the level of reflexivity the constitution, 'the search for connection' – the search for what sets in sequence and in motion – must configure what selections will bring the contingency under control.

If 'reflexivity' is to answer the question 'how is law to organise its self-reference?' in *procedural* terms, it must step back from the continuous linkage and reproduction of events of legal communication and acquire some measure of distance from it. Distance is what sets observation apart from its object. At the 'basic level' of legal reproduction we had minimal distance, enough simply to ensure the connectivity of operations. But constitutionality operates at a remove from the level of operations, brings that connectivity to the fore as a question in its own right, in order to control the system as unitary, as rationally bounded and as one. Systems gain distance[9] – and constitutional scrutiny would be meaningless without it – 'if they make the distinctions that they use as differences accessible to themselves as unities' (1995a: 440). The possibility of self-reflection turns on this gaining distance. Constitutional observation may now fasten on and pronounce on the legality of 'legal' (first-order) operations. 'We speak of self-reference in regard to process when the unity of what is complex is re-entered using the means of the process' (1995a: 451). It is through this '*re-entry*' that the system gets the requisite distance that furnishes it with reflexivity, and although the notion itself of 're-entry' is demanding, the constitutional procedures it includes are familiar. The constitutional review of legislation would be a good example. The constitutional discussion about the legality of law, whether it is over the deployment of legal criteria to determine entry (standing),

---

[9] If the legal system is a system *a posteriori*, as Joxerramon Bengoextea put it insightfully in an early piece (Bengoextea, 1994), it is because constitutionality performs the gathering work of integrating *new* elements *back into* existing structures that are renewed even as they are re-embedded.

authority (jurisdiction), inclusion (*res materiae*), etc., in each case involves re-entries. This means that a discussion in law about the legality of something must meet legal thresholds and use legal tests of admissibility for what can count as such a discussion. We can see re-entry as an application of the process to itself, a folding-back of legality on itself. It is what gives the unity of the process value within the process. One encounters in these examples elementary procedures becoming integrated into more complex ones. With second-order selectivity (selection of selections) connectability is managed and law's responsiveness becomes organised as the process gains in complexity.

'Reflexivity is a very general principle of differentiation and intensification [that] allows processes to guide and control themselves' (1995a: 454) says Luhmann, and what is noteworthy in this formulation is that his two terms 'differentiation' and 'intensification' name contrasting tendencies. Running alongside the increase in complexity (that differentiation brings) but tempering it, he identifies a second achievement of constitutionality in the notion of *entrenchement*. Modes of selectivity gradually acquire a guiding function, and while they remain possible to challenge they become increasingly difficult to change, once the connectivity value also links back to the value of stability and the rule of law. Possibilities of connection are established, and strengthened through re-iterability, to the detriment of those that are suppressed – in fact 'connectability excludes almost all conceivable linkages', says Luhmann (1995a: 283). Rigidity sets in in place of plasticity, and in the name of something that we value as constitutional. Self-reference understood here still in its *procedural* dimension, navigates the risk of transcendence on the one hand, of pure tautology on the other, and thus keeps 'reflexivity' both internal and productive. Productive because a certain 'distance' has now been purchased and it is possible reflexively to deploy legal processes as unitary, to observe them (at a meta-level), and to draw decisions about them. 'Reflexivity' focuses on process, on the deployment and 'exploitation' of temporal perspectives, and thus also on the changes of structures. Structures are re-configured as legal processes unfold, reflexivity tapping the resources of adaptation and containing the dynamic of change. We will need the final form of self-reference fully to understand constitutionality but already there are important conclusions to draw regarding what is variable and what not at the level of structural selection, and regarding the steering capacity of law in respect of *hierarchisation* and *entrenchment*.

*

If *'reflexivity'* captures the procedural side of constitutionality, the way in which law thinks about itself through the staggering and articulation of procedure(s), we now turn to the third form of self-reference, *reflexion (Reflexion)*, to understand how the law thinks about itself-in-its-environment. Reflection is what subtends 'self-observation', and as the system builds up such self-observations, they crystallise into self-descriptions, and a certain level of constancy is gained in respect of the ways the system sees itself in an environment. A key function of the constitution is contained in this, for which we will reserve the term *rationalisation*. Together *hierarchisation, entrenchment* (which we have analysed as aspects of *Reflexivity)* and *rationalisation (Reflexion)* render the *formal* dimension of constitutionality: they are the three functions that we take as comprising it.

We find *'reflexion'* at the confluence of two routes. Earlier we had identified it in the 'trichotomy' of differentiation, alongside performance and function, as the system's relation not to society (function) nor to other sub-systems (performance) but *to itself*. Now we encounter it again via the route of the modalities of self-reference, as we pose the constitutional question: how does the legal system organise its self-reference and *thereby* its reach into its environment? Or, more simply, how does it observe and describe itself as a system in an environment? Constitutionality, after all, is the term for the way in which the legal system *organises its self-reference*, the dialectic of closure and openness, in a world to which it must respond and do so *adequately*. Reflection brings the 'self' of self-reference fully into view as that which can be identified as such in the context of a distinction between the self and its environment. Reflection, in other words, is the moment in which the subject of autopoiesis becomes conscious to itself; it is how constitutionality enables law to think about itself.

Of course *all* legal communication, not just constitutional discourse, operationalises a system-environment difference. Legal communications, at the most basic level, are communications *about* an environment: Did an economic transaction occur? Was it intended? Did factors make its execution impossible? All legal communication thus involves 'the continual internally reproduced double orientation to what the system identifies as itself and as environment', an environment that, as in the case of all systems that are functionally differentiated, calls upon it to *perform a function* only in relation to which the system, too, can invoke it (the environment) at all. This, for Luhmann, would be the rationality of a first-order observer, 'quite *unideal*', he says teasingly with Habermas in his sights and [at that first-order level], 'without an option of non-rational operations'. We arrive at the 'more demanding conceptuality' of *'reflection'* at the level of second-order observation. Again re-entry is involved: 'the system must take the distinction self-reference/external reference as its basis and carry this distinction over into its self-reference' (Luhmann, 1992). This makes it aware, as it were, of its own differentiation and is the operation that secures its unity – a gesture that is at the source of all formalisms. It will do this by linking up internally its own key concepts – its self-descriptions – that mediate reference to its environment (the forcefield of social antagonism) and thereby organise and order its *other-*reference. Both references – to self and to the environment – are actualised simultaneously.

Remember that if Luhmann proposes that we take up the sociological perspective through the concept of the system, it is not to designate it, the system, as a privileged object, but to situate insight, and observation, in the context of a difference. And for this, Luhmann suggests that one begin with the concept of the system, not as a particular type of object, but as a particular distinction, the distinction between system and environment. 'A system is the form of a distinction, possesses therefore two sides: the system (as the inside of the form) and the environment (as the outside of the form). Only the two sides together constitute the distinction, constitute the form, constitute the concept. ... As distinction the form is closed.' And intriguingly: 'The boundary between system and environment separates the two sides of the form, marks the unity of the form and is for this reason not to be found on either side of the form. *The boundary exists only as an instruction to cross it* (1992: 69). With this 'instruction' we are returned to the realm of operations, of how form (as the difference between system and environment) is *produced.* 'Re-entry' is key to 'reflexion' as it was, previously to 'reflexivity'. The re-entry of the system/environment distinction back into the system accomplishes that the distinction between system and environment returns in the system as the distinction between self-reference and other-reference. The system operates by means of the continual reproduction of the difference between self-reference and other-reference. That *is* its autopoiesis.

'Reflexion' indicates the higher level of control that is attained by social systems orienting themselves to themselves. In 'reflexion' a system 'orients its operations to its own unity' using as guiding difference not the 'before/after' of reflexivity but that between system and environment. A distance of a different kind is achieved in this manner. The system can see and handle itself – that is, its own complexity – as a unity, identifying

and exploiting all the while the difference between itself and its environment. Not all systems are capable of self-referential operations at this level, but the legal system is, and the term reserved for it is *constitutionality*. The continuity between the reflexive (constitutional) level and the ordinary level of legal operations is assured because it can become itself the object of legal communication when the question of constitutionality is raised explicitly. At such moments constitutionality acquires operative significance, informational value and corrective value.

The self-description of the law as constitution makes it possible to condense and concentrate the self-reference of the legal system. Luhmann suggests, in other words, that the legal system turns this self-description into the accompanying meaning reference of all the operations that purport to be part of the self-reproduction of the legal system because they are consonant with, and under the authority of, the constitution. The consonance is sporadically tested in constitutional cases, though for the most part its claim runs silently alongside the operation of the system that through reflection now closes the circle of self-reference, because only what is constitutional is legal. We do not need to dwell on the question of what level of recursion achieves autopoiesis;[10] all we need to establish is that constitutionality gives the system closure and contains its centrifugal tendencies and the pressure towards variation by condensing its semantics, consolidating constitutional value, and securing re-iterability. The function of rationalisation is thereby performed, consolidating the law's self-understanding of itself-in-an-environment, in a way that sets it vis-à-vis the political and allows the re-entry of the politics/law distinction into law.

*

What conclusions are we to draw from the above? How does our discussion of constitutionality at the formal level help to think about our 'guiding distinction' of political constitutionalism, the distinction between the constituent and the constituted? On the side of what is *constituted* as procedure and as unity of the legal system, we have entrenchment and hierarchisation ('reflexivity') and rationalisation ('reflexion'). These are the hallmarks of the constitutional. What they enable is reference to an environment as the basis of law's own

---

[10] In Teubner's early work, it was the recursive operations of the system that allowed self-descriptions to emerge, *gradually* reaching the threshold where autopoietic closure was achieved.

autopoiesis. The reference carves out the space of potentiality, in relation to which the systemic operations will drive the system's inherent temporary instabilities to new states of (always temporary) stabilisation. The system/environment distinction exists as an instruction to cross it, Luhmann told us. The legal system is thereby constitutively oriented to the environment, and constitutionality allows it to organise and deploy that constitutive orientation. Constituent/constituted is the distinction that enables the 're-entry' of politics into legal discourse, the unfolding of self-reference in the direction of renewal.

'The difference between difference and identity', says Luhmann, 'is instituted as it were across the difference between actuality and potentiality, to control the latter within the former's operations' (1995a: 66). What is (constitutionally) say-able, do-able, thinkable is a selection achievement and the distribution of opportunities of deployment and resistance are strictly coupled to variation possibilities of given selections. Potentiality, the spectrum of the constituent, relates asymmetrically to what the system entrenches constitutionally, and to what it might rationalise as opportunity. The constituted installs itself at the point of the creation of the meaning of what the constitution is (actuality) and what it might become (potentiality). The constituent is meaningful as asymmetrically related to this range of determinations.

Against Habermas and the co-implication of democracy and rights, or any dialectical articulation between them, Luhmann's radicalisation of self-reference as it applies to the 'constitutional distinction' thinks the articulation of law and politics as only ever activated from the inside, the side of law. There is no co-implication in this, no plane to accommodate a synthesis. Instead, the simultaneous reference to the self and to the other, to system and environment, makes possible the observation of that which spans self-and other-reference, the unity of their difference, *from the inside*. The projective constitutional vocabulary means that what is referred to as constituent power is never more than the unfolding of self-reference of the constituted, never more, that is, than its 'accompanying self-reference'. It is, however, made productive for the system in providing an outward reach, the opportunity to unlock the unproductive self-reference that 'what is constituted is what is constituted' (or that 'law is what the law says it is'). It is crucial for Luhmann's theory that '[s]elf-referential systems acquire information with the help of the difference between referring to self and to something else, and this information makes possible their self-production' (1995a: 448).

And with this we come to the 'phenomenon of meaning', here of constitutional meaning, that centres Luhmann's grand *phenomenological endeavour*.[11]

> Meaning appears as a surplus of references to other possibilities of experience and action. Something stands in the focal point, as the center of intention, and all else is indicated marginally as the horizon ... Reference actualises itself as the standpoint of reality, referring not only to what is real ... but also to what is possible (conditionally real) and what is negative (unreal).
>
> (1995a: 60)

The phenomenological description is related back to a problem-related functional analysis. Every meaning reformulates the *compulsion* to select implied in all complexity, and every specific meaning qualifies itself by suggesting specific possibilities of connection and making others improbable, difficult, remote, or temporarily excluded. Meaning is consequently the rendering of complexity, indeed a form of rendering that, wherever it attaches, 'permits access at a given point but that simultaneously identifies every such access as a selection' (1995a: 60–1). And if 'connectability', as we saw, 'excludes almost all conceivable linkages', it is because complexity must be reduced if it is to be navigated. There are vast constituencies left unthought and untouched in their complexity, and it is the achievement of reduction that certain selections can be actualised against all that does, and *has to*, retreat from presence. The phenomenology of that which emerges is tied to indifference toward all that must be suspended in order to allow the emergence. The law remains a field of reduced complexity in an expanse of high societal complexity, and the selections that constitutionality mobilises in the form of reflection and reflexivity sustain that border between what the legal system is and what is politically possible for it, in terms of processes of linkage, connection and suppression. It is how legal meaning emerges under the aegis of the constitution. It is to this that we turn now.

The Dimensions of Constitutional Meaning

We begin with a relatively uncontroversial account of the three dimensions of the meaning of the 'constitutional'. In the *social* dimension the

---

[11] On his own characterisation of systems theory as a phenomenology, see Luhmann (1990a). An interesting paper on Luhmann's debt to Husserl is Paul (2001).

question is over the subject that the constitution names; in the *temporal* dimension the question is over the constitution's ability to recruit the past in its expectation-binding operation for the future; in the *material* dimension the question is over the threshold of *unity* that gathers it (the legal system) as a meaningful whole. All three involve systemic reflexivity; all three dimensions involve how 'the law thinks about itself'. These are *threshold requirements for ascribing constitutional meaning* because we associate with the constitution the constitutive functions of providing unity for the legal system, normatively binding certain key expectations for the future, and naming the subject of popular sovereignty. In this sense they are the essential forms that *constitutional reflexivity* takes.

For political constitutionalism, the emergence of constitutional meaning is effected against a horizon of the constituent. *If* the temporal question asks how *present* constitutional expectations might bridge constitutional pasts with the radical openness to the future; *if* the social dimension involves the question of the *self* of 'self-determination', or of popular sovereignty; *if* the material question involves the achievement of *unity* for a system that renews itself through the open contingency of democratic law-giving and yet must retain its identity over time; *then* in each case these questions are asked in terms of the structural coupling between law and politics. Constitutional reflexivity here, along all three axes, is constitutively oriented to the political. It is in each case *political* contingency that needs to come under control, the *political* subject to find expression. Law's expectational structure in the context of political constitutionalism inclines it in the direction of the democratic/political imaginary, and as bound constitutively to the constituent/constituted distinction.

Combining the dimensions is key because meaning cannot *appear* along one dimension alone. The three 'can be analyzed separately', says Luhmann,[12] 'but they *appear together* in meaningful communication' (1995a: 86). 'If meaning is complex enough, [factual/material references] must adapt themselves to complicated interdependencies with temporal and social meaning references' (1995a: 74). But this *joint* appearance should not detract from the fact that '*specific* semantics [to each] have emerged to regulate performances of differentiation – above all a semantics of time, ... and a semantics of the social' (1995a: 89). In what follows we discuss these

---

[12] The *locus classicus* of Luhmann's discussion of meaning-construction remains the second chapter of his *Social Systems* (1995a) (see Chapter 1.1). I have used the terms 'material' and 'substantive' interchangeably to denote the dimension of the '*sachlich*'.

semantics, their structural function, the meaning-combinations they enable (and occlude) in the specific form they acquire as *constitutional* categories.

We will look at what constitutional reflexivity signifies, and how it organises the (legal) system's self-reference – at the *formal* level – as a 'reduction achievement'. What it achieves at the level of 'reflexivity' (*stricto sensu*) is entrenchment and hierarchisation, as we saw. The system's capacity to control these processes, to define itself through them, involves 'reflexion'; constitutionality is the name that 'reflexion' takes in the legal system. What is achieved at the level of 'reflexion' involves how the system operates its dual reference to itself and to its environment. It is this aspect that we elaborate now, and for the rest of the chapter. On the 'formal' side meaning is constructed – through phenomenological *reduction* – in a way that is specific to, and constitutive of, constitutionality, an *achievement* that first enables the disclosure of 'something as something', constitutionally speaking.

The Material Dimension

In the material dimension of social systems are included *all themes* of meaningful communication. After all, explains Luhmann, 'the expectation of expectations is only possible through the mediation of a common world to which expectations are identically attached' (1995a: 62). The sharing of the 'common world' must however face the fragmented world disclosure of systems of meaning, the '*unitas multiplex*' (Teubner, 1993) of a world of system-specific competing semantics.

Along the material dimension of legal meaning, selections take the form of roles, programmes and values. *Roles* are abstractions that allow legal personality to become a point of address and attribution of action in the legal system. Correctness of behaviour is lifted from the personal context and fixed at the impersonal level, at which level rules ground the normativity of expectations of individual action through impersonal criteria of correctness that displace the personal reference. *Programmes* fix expectations through *rules*, which fall into two categories: goal-oriented and conditional.[13] In a conditional programme a condition is stipulated and kept invariant so that whenever that condition is seen to be fulfilled, the consequences appended to it are activated. This is the form of programming most typical to law, the 'if p then q' formula. In a

---

[13] Luhmann, 1986a and 1977: 110–13.

goal programme on the other hand, the system selects a goal, and uses it as a rule for selecting causes that can bring it about.[14] At the constitutional level, typically programmes select and activate *values*. As part of goal-oriented programming, the value provides orientation, whereas when it comes to conditional programming, a value typically plays the role of a *negative limit*, in the form, say, of the prohibition of the violation of dignity, of free speech, etc. We will return to this at length in the next chapter (2.3).

This does *not* mean that free-floating political and ethical values directly impact on law. The problem with values, says Luhmann, with Carl Schmitt of the *Tyranny of Values* weighing on his mind, is that they do not specify their own hierarchy for cases of clashes, leaving open the question of hierarchy as a question of preference; moreover, while they may furnish rules of preference, they do not specify the content of preferable action across systems.[15] In *Social Systems*, Luhmann writes:

> [v]alues are general, particularly symbolized rules of preference regarding states or events ... Actions can also be evaluated as friendly, right, polluting, as expressing solidarity, readiness to help, racial hatred ... But the fact that actions can be brought under the positive or negative description, the ascription of value tells us nothing about the rightness of the action.
>
> (Luhmann, 1995a: 433)

The reason that they 'tell us nothing' is that, for Luhmann, values are crude, poorly selective devices for reducing complexity. Because they allow too much interpretative leeway, values contribute very little to the stabilisation of expectations and the reduction of contingency.

But with this concession, Luhmann is sacrificing a precious insight which he had offered us previously with the concept of 'reflexion'. And if against Luhmann's rushed dismissal, we concentrate on the *intra-systemic* importance of constitutional values, a very different picture emerges. The function of the constitution is to manage the interdependencies of concepts, rules and values in a way that preserves coherence and organises the law as a system. The law's generalisations in the material dimension, that is, roles, programmes and values, are

---

[14] This is a formula increasingly apposite to the interventionist type of law. Luhmann adds that 'these two fundamental types of program are jointly exhaustive. But they can be combined in numerous ways and embedded in each other, so that it is often difficult to assign concrete programs to the one type or to the other' (Luhmann, 1977: 111).

[15] For the difference between programmes and values, see Luhmann, 1995a: 432ff.

mutually dependent and determine each other reciprocally: roles are operationalised through rules or become points of attribution through rules and values, and rules depend on the existence of self-descriptions such as roles (Luhmann, 1972/1985: 70ff); rules activate values, which they either directly 'carry' (as a matter of operative fact) in conditional programming, or rely on for their interpretation in goal-programming. Moreover, revisability in the material dimension depends on the fact that some of the expectations remain constant as the structural backbone that allows the system to make sense of change. As the law evolves, roles, programmes and values shift and, what is more, their dynamic interplay and interdependence also shift. The rise of formal rationality and the uprooting of legal relations from their pre-modern *Gemeinschaft* context, as well as the reversal of this evolutionary trend in the 'post-liberal' era, are reflected in a mutually re-enforcing re-negotiation of *values* (certainty and justice), a shift in *programming* (a retreat of conditional and an expansion of goal programming) and a 're-materialisation' of *roles* (from the all-inclusive legal personality to more concrete *loci* of attribution of rights and duties).

Now this is a lexicon that spans the sociology of law in its entirety, and I refer to it only in order to make a much smaller point: that the unity of the law, as articulated and secured at the level of the constitution, operates to re-embed a legal system's generalisations and distinctions between levels in ever new contexts. In the process, of course, there will be centrifugal forces undermining law's unity. Divergent uses of discretion and shifting interpretations of rights are precisely centrifugal forces of this sort. *But heterogeneities of this kind demand aggregations at higher levels,* and that is what constitutionality achieves. Against this move of differentiation there is a force of *'redundancy'* at play, Luhmann argues, that sets thresholds of 'tolerable' – for the system – variation. The unity of the law then depends on this gathering-in of new elements. Elements will appear 'incongruous' or they would have no information value for the system: information requires that the system be 'surprised' in some way. But the Constitution *gathers in* this variety around its existing categories and descriptions, which are re-embedded as the legal system goes on, and they are re-embedded in terms of the dynamic interplay of levels (roles, programmes, values): the constitution must secure unity for the legal system in order to guarantee that it will be reproduced *as one. And values play a crucially significant role in this process, strengthened through recursion, and thereby acquiring orientation-value for the system.*

More specifically, Luhmann borrows from information theory the term '*redundancy*' to denote the system's tendency to reduce the element of surprise within it. A system exhibits redundancy 'in so far as it supports itself in processing information on what is already known ... Every repetition makes information superfluous which means, quite simply, redundant' (1995b: 291). The legal system is paramountly a redundant order. In processing information on the basis of what is already known it supports itself and self-referentially assimilates what is new to what already exists.

> Cases that require a decision are concrete cases and that means they are different from each other. They provoke the system into acknowledging their differences. Argumentation picks up on that provocation and transforms it into redundancy [in terms of programmes and rules] that are tested, condensed and confirmed in relation to a greater number of possible applications. Argumentation evidently opts for redundancy, for economy of information and surprises.
>
> (Luhmann, 1995b: 291)

In 'opting for redundancy' ('opting' because it *could* do otherwise) legal argumentation overwhelmingly reactivates known grounds. Information becomes confirmed in subsequent operations, and gradually becomes entrenched in self-descriptions, acquiring orientation value for new arguments and condensation value for the system. Of course the assimilation cannot be complete. The system needs to react to a changing environment, and to this effect '*variety*' comes into play. Significantly, the practice of distinguishing and overruling 'occasionally invents new [grounds] to achieve a position where the system can, on the basis of a little new information, fairly quickly work out what state it is in and what state it is moving towards' (2004: 291). The reason why it requires 'a special effort' to shake the redundancy of the system and stretch its imagination is because the system tends to 'reduce its own surprise to a tolerable amount and allow information only as differences added in small numbers to the stream of reassurances' (ibid.). In all this, and marking the moment of unity, is a certain 'gathering' *rationalisation* around organising principles. The unity of the system is strengthened through redundancy, and conversely undermined – and in limit cases even eroded – if the new acts of interpretation can no longer be imputed back to its organising principles. And it is here above all that the *constitutional function* becomes manifest. The constitutional function is necessary if the balance between redundancy and variety is to be maintained as productive for the system, allowing the activation of known grounds in every expansion onto new terrain. A balance has to be achieved on both fronts: externally because otherwise the legal system loses its responsiveness; internally because it must maintain its unity, minimise incongruence, mistakes, deviant interpretations – a minimisation that is necessary if it is going to perform its function and provide stability of expectations.

We are on familiar constitutional terrain here.[16] But what does it tell us about our two key questions, of how to understand: firstly the generalisation of *constitutional* expectations in the material dimension, and secondly the relevance in this context of *political* constitutionalism? Let us take the two questions in turn.

Let us re-iterate that the constitutional function in the material dimension has to do with managing the unity of the system – a system that must navigate its development in a complex environment that has a centrifugal impact on it because it pressures it to develop internal variation to meet new eventualities. If the generation of heterogeneities demands aggregations at higher levels, as we said, the constitutional response involves the re-alignment between the levels of generalisation: *strict* re-alignments of concepts and rules to programmes and values. Rules must mobilise legal concepts in consistent ways, and with the help of these concepts, distinctions can be stored and made available for a great number of decisions. For Luhmann, concepts compound information, thereby producing the redundancy required by the system. But these concepts too must submit to condensations further up the hierarchy of norms. After all 'the referential structure of meaningful objects or themes can only be used in a condensed form. Without this condensation, the burden of selection would be too great for connecting operations' (1995a: 96). Repeated usage condenses in *self-descriptions* that acquire orientation-value in the system and allow the emergence of structured complexity. We saw earlier in the chapter how 'reflection' deploys self-descriptions to 'unfold' self-reference in the direction of better knowledge of the environment. Perhaps *the most important thing* to hold onto along the material dimension is that unity holds together, in a set order, *higher levels of values* with lower levels of programmes, and

---

[16] It is stated for example by Ronald Dworkin in *Law's Empire* as the requirement of fit that drives and contains law's constructive interpretations if they are to maintain its integrity, a commitment largely forgotten by Dworkin himself in the later *Justice for Hedgehogs*, and clearly lost in the ululations over proportionality of his epigones.

then concepts, whereby 'plurality is related to unity as symbolized by it' (1995a: 93). The ordering secures that lower levels are informed by higher levels, interpretatively, and that they do not transcend limits of violations set at those higher levels. The final alignment to values preempts and pre-determines the system's handling of its environment, its resonance-capacity, its receptivity to change, adaptation and 'learning'.

With this we come to our second question: what is the significance of this insistence on unity for *political* constitutionalism? This can be appreciated in contrast to a constitutionalism that is *reactive*. The reactive mode, with the priority that it gives to adjustment, comes at the expense of the *normative* hold that the constitutional structure has on the future. In particular when it comes to values, the reactive mode withdraws their pre-emptive significance. In the final chapter of this part (chapter 2.4) we will track the undoing of the constitutional achievement in the modalities of constitutionalisation, constitutional pluralism and proportionality, where in its reactive modality the constitution simply comes to sanction market distributions. (Later, in Part III, we will see how this underwrites the dominance of market constitutionalism.) What *political* constitutionalism still has to offer in the material dimension is the rationalisation of the disparate elements under systems of values as symbolic generalisations that are democratically sanctioned and normatively held onto as a matter of political choice and commitment. Values then equip expectations embodied in programmes and roles *in advance with normative thresholds*, immunise those expectations from 'learning', and project them as disappointment-proof into the future, to bridge discontinuities, to align them to values, to select and retain references that lend themselves to generalization according to those values; in a word, to *give form* to potentiality[17] in a normative vein.

The Social Dimension

The social dimension of the constitution concerns collective subject positions, the 'we' of popular sovereignty, and the institutionalisation of plurality. The legal and political systems are along this dimension 'structurally coupled' via the 'hybrid concept' of 'the people'. It is the concept

---

[17] The difference between identity and difference is instituted across the difference between actuality and potentiality, 'in order to control the latter within the former's operations' (Luhmann, 1995a: 66).

that enables, in each system, a specific handling of complexity. From the point of view of law, and in order to mobilise the concept of the people, the constitution adapts the democratic reference to a 'judiciable content'.[18] This presupposes drawing the conceptual lines that form its *external* (constituency) and *internal* (dissent) *boundaries* around which it defines itself and in terms of which it collects itself. The first question, of constituency, relates to the constitutional determination of *relevant* plurality; the second question relates to what processes deliver the unified will, both in terms of how consensus is achieved, and how *representation* organises it.

Let us begin with the *distinction between consent and dissent* except visit it, contra Habermas, from a *phenomenological* perspective. From a sociological point of view, the *coming-into-play of plurality* must contend, first and foremost, at least since Talcott Parsons formulated it, with the problem of 'double contingency', and the way in which contexts of expectations develop that ground social meaning as a matter of culture, value systems, interactional settings, etc. But we might ask a *different* question that approaches the emergence of plurality, the 'we-perspective', from a different angle. Luhmann argues that the possibility of communication, and the possibility of understanding, is organised along the social dimension through a basic distinction between consenting/dissenting. If it seems odd to link understanding to this distinction in a *constitutive* way it is because we usually assume that understanding precedes the distinction 'consent/dissent' and that the distinction merely organises a response. But Luhmann invites us to take it one step back, to *the threshold of meaning-generation* in the social dimension. 'Only when dissent can emerge as a reality or a possibility, has one occasion to interject the two-fold horizon of the social', he says. Thereby 'what is social in meaning themes is experienced as reference to interpretive perspectives', and this introduction of plurality, quite obviously now displaces the notoriously 'monological' subject: 'the social dimension enables a constantly accompanying comparison with what others can or would experience and how others could position their actions' (1995a: 81). This 'accompanying comparison' is carried alongside the meaning of plurality in terms of the consent/dissent distinction.

---

[18] 'The Constitution [to this purpose] uses terms like "the people" and refers thus to politics ... [Such] references to politics establish the structural coupling ... [by making it possible] for law to reduce concepts to a judiciable content' (Luhmann, 1990: 193).

If the distinction consent/dissent subtends the social dimension in organising the 'accompanying comparison', it takes a specific form in the legal system. The introduction of 'judiciable content' to consent/dissent that marks the point of legal *institutionalisation* takes the form of *'the third'*; the third is *ex hypothesi* the 'disinterested party' on whose projected consensus the success of the legal communication depends.[19] Luhmann's is of course not the first phenomenological effort to turn to the 'third' as condition for the appearance of legal meaning. Alexandre Kojève, in his *Esquisse d'une phenomenologie du Droit* (written in 1943 but published posthumously), argued that the only way to determine a situation as juridical is when a 'disinterested and impartial third person intervenes' in the interaction between two. Without such an intervention it would be impossible *phenomenologically* to distinguish a juridical situation. Kojève says: 'the essence of right is manifested in and by the interaction between two human beings, A + B, which necessarily provokes the intervention of an impartial and disinterested third, C, and whose intervention annuls the reaction of B opposed to the action of A' (1943/1981: 28). We may query the terms 'provokes' (why would a disinterested third 'necessarily' be provoked?) and 'annuls' (perhaps Luhmann's term 'exploits' might better capture how the law deploys the conflict between A + B for its own 'generalising' purposes), but it remains that Kojève is driven by the need to determine what constitutes a proper 'juridical interest' and how it emerges by the interjection of the 'third' who 'intervenes for purely moral or theoretical reasons in order to cause the reign of justice' (ibid.).

Institutionalisation is achieved as a consequence of the introduction of third parties; it is with the introduction of the 'third' *that the shift from the interactional to the social-systemic context of law is primarily effected.* An expectation becomes legal in that it is assumed to be backed by the expected consensus of third parties (Luhmann, 1972/1985: 73), the introduction of whom as 'normatively co-expecting' means that the expectation context is now first abstracted from the concrete interactional setting and first cast through a system-specific referent.[20] What is interesting and controversial in this analysis is that the achievement of legal institutionalisation secures stabilisation in *substituting for consensus*. For Luhmann,

---

[19] For a comprehensive discussion of 'institutionalisation' and 'the third', but without reference to Kojève, see the early *Rechtssoziologie* (Luhmann, 1972).

[20] An expectation is legal (necessary but not sufficient) only if third parties *normatively co-expect it*.

Habermas' quest for consensus hits upon both epistemological and practical impasses. On an epistemological level, he says, 'my consent is consent only in relation to your consent. But my consent is not your consent, and there is no objective argument or rational ground that would finally guarantee that coincidence' (1995a: 75). What is worrying for discourse theory, practically, is that the achievement of consensus is both unlikely and crucially *fictitious* under conditions of complexity and social acceleration. Under such conditions we encounter a certain de-synchronisation of political time from actual political practices, in a way that impacts crucially on democratic deliberation and the formation of the political will, both the key elements of a consensus theory of politics. Hartmut Rosa has offered us important insights in this direction.[21] We will return to Rosa when we later discuss (in 3.2) how the de-synchronisation has become productive under market constitutionalism.

For our current, more limited, purposes, however, suffice it to reiterate how the achievement that is the creation of legal meaning depends on normative closure and institutionalisation, in the temporal and social dimensions respectively. And that the introduction of the normative co-expecting third party, epitomised by the judge, is key to the social dimension. The constitution comes to sanction this 'accompanying reference' that alone secures legal meaning, typically in the form of constitutional jurisdiction. The loosening or abandonment of the 'third' under conditions where globalisation has loosened the opportunity or need for this constitutive sanction, undoes the institutional achievement of political constitutionalism in the social dimension and loses it, as we will see, in the proliferation of fora, the choice of jurisdiction, the varieties of 'law-shopping' and, more generally, in the cross-cutting currents of global pluralism.

Variously asked as the question over the 'self' of self-determination, the 'we' of the 'we hold', etc., the institutional achievement of political constitutionalism is not to lose sight of the subject of constituent power but to circumnavigate the meaninglessness of a 'formless forming' of the subject à la Schmitt, the idea in other words of a pure, because

---

[21] The thrust of Rosa's critique of dialogic forms of democratic theory is that they neglect the temporal preconditions of democracy and therefore fail to grasp the current crisis of democratic self-determination under the acceleration of globalisation. Due to the acceleration of social change and the 'contraction of the present', i.e. the shrinking of the time-spans for which social expectations and conditions for action remain stable, background conditions become increasingly contingent; instead of providing yardsticks for the decision-making process, they become complicating factors. See indicatively Rosa (2005).

unconditional, assertion of the 'we'. The achievement of political constitutionalism is to hedge in the double contingency of the question '*who decides who decides?' enough* for it to be asked meaningfully. In this the constituent loses its 'formlessness' and *the addressee is constituted from the site of address*. It also means that we take the question of *constituency* – who is included in the 'we' – and the question of *representation* – who speaks for the 'we' – together.

In traversing the 'genealogy of constituent power' in the previous chapter, we saw that the notion of constituent power, as expression of the direct will of the people, gave leverage and legitimation to political constitutionalism. The aspiration and the urgency to deliver the will of the people unmediated was for many, as we saw, coincident with 'terror'. But if the recourse to the actual, unmediated, will of the people mattered so much it is because the gap that opens up between the presence of the people and their representation in political institutions is impossible to justify on democratic grounds. For all the problems that the Jacobin constituent 'solution' entails, it is uncompromising in not collapsing it: hence the dictum of admiration of the young Marx: '*Die gesetzgebende Gewalt hat die Französische Revolution gemacht*' ('Law-giving power has made the French Revolution').[22] And it is the absence of the constituent power of the people since then that Rosanvallon captures well in the opening lines of *Le peuple Introuvable*, when he speaks of the absence that haunts the history of democratic representation. For Rosanvallon, while democracy and popular sovereignty have represented for two centuries the 'obvious horizon of the political', our democratic regimes 'sont bien marquées par la déception, comme si elles incarnaient un idéal trahi et défiguré'[23] (Rosanvallon, 1998: 9). And it is undoubtedly the case that, with the exception of the brief interlude of Jacobin Constitutionalism,

> the notion of constituent power that came to maturity in France in and after 1789 resided in the principle that the normative basis of the political system needed to be founded, *not* in the external factual will of the people, but in a complex of norms by means of which the political system *excluded* the people as a concrete aggregate of social agents.... *Once declared by its representatives, then, the will of constituent power fell fully silent*, and the people (nation) were conclusively expelled from further exercise of power.
>
> (Thornhill, 2011: 219)

---

[22] In Marx's *Kritik des Hegelschen Staatsrechts*.
[23] 'Democracies have been marked by deception, as if they embodied an ideal betrayed and disfigured.'

With the 'expulsion' of the people political processes are immunised from social-material processes. We began with this expulsion in Arendt's work. A society replete with needs was only to be represented at the political level as external to the latter, denied and expelled in the process. Democracy, action-in-concert, worldliness became signifiers through which the projective constitutionalist vocabulary addressed the social in order to supplant it: a functionalisation of democracy in the direction of reproducing legitimacy for the political system, coupled with a careful excision of the social question. It is not only Arendt, of course, for whom this circumvention of the social is vital. She is in good company here. Claude Lefort, in synchronised retreat with Castoriadis from the leftism of the *Socialisme ou Barbarie* years, designates the political as an empty space,[24] one might project, partially in order to protect it from the social forces that would otherwise overwhelm it. 'Only the intelligence of the political [du politique]', he says a year after the publication of *Democracy and Political Theory*, 'could get us out of the positivist rut that Marxist theory and the social sciences had kept us in' (Lefort, 1987: 190). What is evacuated in this flight from presence effects a substitution in the sphere of political power. Thornhill put it eloquently: '[o]nce declared by its representatives, then the will of constituent power fell fully silent.' The question is whether such a substitution without remainder ('fully silent') is an expression or a negation of 'presence'. If, one imagines, representation can only be adequate if it keeps the side of the constituent *alive*, if it remains responsive to 'presence' rather that substitutes for it – so that constituent power is *mediated* constitutionally rather than eclipsed – then the question that political constitutionalism is called to answer is what precisely does it mean to ask the question: 'when is constitutional representation *adequate?*'

Again, a great deal turns on this question of adequacy, but now, in this discussion of the *subject* of popular sovereignty, there is more (constitutionally) at stake than ever. The quandary revolves around the fact: that the difference between presence and representation tracks a deficit (of the latter vis-à-vis the former) that is constitutive of its meaning. The deficit is not merely endemic in all forms and instantiations; it is in fact constitutive of

---

[24] For Lefort famously 'the reference to an empty place ... implies a reference to a society without any positive determination, which cannot be represented by the figure of a community' (Lefort, 1988, original in French 1986: 226). For Lefort's formulation of democracy's institution of the locus of power as an 'empty place', see Lefort (1988: 16–19 and 1986: 303).

the meaning of representation that it 'falls short' of (presentation or) presence. That is what makes the question over the adequacy of representation so perplexing: that the measure of adequacy would be the degree of proximity (of representation to presence) and yet at the point of approximation it would cancel it out as *re*-presentation (and for Lefort et al. that spells 'terror'). Popular sovereignty involves a substitution of representation for presence before which any talk of adequacy simply folds in on itself. We saw the aporia in the *affirmation* of the general will in Rousseau; the same aporia in Sieyès' *retreat* from democracy. If the aporia is resolved in the theory and practice of *autogestion* (as we will see in Chapter 4.3), it would be fair to say that the resolution has not engendered durable forms.

Given the conceptual tensions and antinomies harboured in representation, our usual imaginative shortcuts and shorthand metaphorical formulae typically fail us. The notion that plurality is 'funnelled' through representation in order to enter the decision-making processes; or the spatial metaphor that identifies it at the intermediate level; or even the notion that it is a nodal point in a circuit of transmission: none of these metaphors capture anything of the internal contradictions of representation as it measures itself against what it might mean, aspirationally, for a people to articulate their collective will. And perhaps it is against the background of such internal antinomies that the market imaginary scores one of its great successes. Market thinkers find opportunity here to cut through the complexity of political representation with the false humility of 'choice'. In place of the layering of the formation of the will, with its need to rely on a logic of representation that can only succeed at the expense of the democratic imperative in its pure form, market constitutionalism proposes to circumnavigate these structures through the signalling function of the price mechanism. The price mechanism simply inscribes individuals' autonomous choices, as it were, and the market has no need whatsoever to rely on the mediating structures of representation, or worry about their 'adequacy'. Consumer choice and open markets become its functional equivalents in 'market constitutionalism'. The democratic co-option that we will visit in Chapter 3.2 relies on this circumnavigation whose success lies in the simplicity and directness of that substitution.

We will look at this later. For now let us stay with political constitutionalism and the difficulty we might have with the predication 'political' along this social dimension where representation is doing *all* the work of 'gathering', 'funnelling' or 'transmitting' our political voices to the institutional fora. Borrowing a thought from Nicos Poulantzas,[25] might one counter-suggest that representation involves the structuring of a plane of political mediation that is crucially *relatively autonomous* from material processes of social reproduction, and as relatively autonomous should not be understood as a 'transmission belt' or as continuous to either civil society or the reproduction of relations of production? Here is where the relevance to representation might be tracked, understood in terms of the logic(s) of mediation and 'condensation', as lending constitutional form to political action, identity and conflict and endowing them with constitutional meaning. This is neither an 'empty place' nor a fiction; it is underlain by the materiality of political practices, but it is a space where practices are first concretised *given* the symbols, categories, thematisations, that are available and operative at that level. Let us keep this from the analysis: that the level of political representation is independently form-giving, because it strictly couples the struggles of civil society, its plural voices and identities, its conflicts and demands, to the political medium of expression that at the level of political constitutionalism finds expression in and as representation. This is the Constitution's reduction-achievement in the social dimension. 'Achievement' because it is form-giving; 'reduction' because the form is (always-already) tied to particular semantics of consent and dissent and to procedures that stipulate the conditions under which actions might aggregate or collective capacity for action might be recognised. And yet, in spite of the alignments, reductions and form-giving, the constituent *is* maintained throughout the process as far as this paradigm of political constitutionalism is concerned, because what is given form to is the projected presence of the people in the democratic moments of its expression, and the form is only *relatively* autonomous from the underlying dynamics.

To close this discussion about the social dimension here is Pierre Rosanvallon again, this time in his critique of the two 'closed' universalisms of Habermas' and Rawls' normative political theories. Our concern, and his, is how the constituent subtends the social dimension in the paradigm of political constitutionalism is the sense that the democratic

---

[25] 'If political practices bearing on the State *traverse* its apparatuses, this is because they are *already inscribed* in that state framework whose strategic configuration they map out. Of course popular struggles ... stretch beyond the State; but insofar as they are genuinely political they are not really external to the State. ... [Struggles] are always *inscribed* in power apparatuses which *concretize* them and which also condense a relationship of forces. ... Thus the dominated classes and their particular struggles have a *specific presence* within the structure of the State.' (Poulantzas, 1976: 141, emphases added.)

moments forever unsettle the constituted. That is not how Rosanvallon puts it, but it is how he too means it, and what he sees downplayed in the smooth universalisms of the liberal mindset:

> Both [universalisms are] founded on the refusal of the tensions and structural ambiguities of the democratic ideal. They set aside the complexities underpinning the history of Western democracy. They swept away the intellectual doubts that were the very motors of investigation into the nature of democracy from its earliest moments in the United States, France or England. First of all, democracy is founded on doubt about the very nature of a regime based on the 'people.' *The 'people' can only exist in a democratic regime through approximate and successive representations.* ... Popular sovereignty has difficulty expressing itself in representative institutions that do not call it into question in one form or another.
>
> (Rosanvallon, 2009: 546)

The Temporal Dimension

The crucial distinction that defines normativity – 'what does it mean that expectations are experienced with the "ought" quality?' (Luhmann, 1972/1985: 23) – is not that between the normative and the factual – the 'ought' against the 'is' – but that between the normative and the cognitive. Normativity involves a pre-commitment, a determination of an expectation of the future that will not be discredited if it is not, in fact, met. Normative expectations are, in that important sense, *disappointment-proof*.

> Expectations are experienced and treated as cognitive when they are adapted to reality in the case of disappointment. For normative expectations the opposite holds: that one does not reject them if someone acts against them. ... The expectation is fixed and any discrepancy is held against the actor. ... Accordingly norms are counterfactually stabilised behavioural expectations. ... the symbol of the 'ought' expresses primarily the expectation of such counterfactual validity.
>
> (Luhmann, 1972/1985: 33)

If disappointment-proof expectations are what characterise normative systems, law, as a functional sub-system of society, 'claims a specific use of normativity for itself' (Luhmann, 1988b: 27). Law provides the internal systemic guarantees that 'stabilize normative expectations through regulating their temporal, material and social generalization' (Luhmann, 1995a: 91). Law guarantees reliability of normative expectations under recognisable, systemically stipulated, conditions that are organised and backed constitutionally. When it comes to the temporal dimension of constitutional meaning, the focus is on the constitution's ability to recruit the past in its expectation-binding operation for the future, and in the process to guarantee the unity of the legal system. This involves a specifically constitutional use of normativity.

Let us re-state, then, that at the level of legal operations, the law operates through provisions that are binding for the future, that is, that are not *tested* by the acts they determine. The essence of normativity is that it involves a pre-commitment to holding on to an expectation of the future that will not be discredited if it is not, in fact, met. This relatively easy differentiation becomes more complex when we look at the distinction between normative and cognitive at both first- and second-order levels. 'There are four possible combinations with two-level reflexivity' (Luhmann, 1972/1985: 39). At the second-order level, we can expect either normative or cognitive expectations normatively *or* cognitively. This is hugely significant to our discussion of political constitutionalism and its difference from market constitutionalism. And although the shift from the former to the latter will only become fully manifest in Part III of the book, we can already identify here, along the temporal dimension, how high the stakes are.

Let us see why. If the function of normative expectations is to provide for stability in the face of discrepant events, how are we to understand disappointments *at the second-order, constitutional, level,* that might force normative systems to change their distributions of 'normation' (Luhmann's term) and thus learn? Because by and large law stabilises normative 'expectations' and the constitution provides a kind of second-order normativity, whereby normative expectations may be normatively expected under recognisable, systemically stipulated, conditions. The constitution secures and underwrites the *structuring and handling of normativity*. But structures can be 'disappointed' too, says Luhmann, and they can be disappointed for good reason, when they fail to achieve (everything is, of course, functional through and through with Luhmann) a proper balance between their delivery of a 'bearable complexity' in the specification of problems (the cognitive domain) and their adequacy in terms of providing stabilisation and continuity (the normative domain). In situations where it no longer makes sense to hold on to normative expectations, the structure of expectations must *yield to constitutional 'learning'*. This will involve a receptivity at the level of structure, away from a stubborn normative holding of normative expectations to the cognitive holding of normative expectations, open to learning and adaptation.

It is worth noting that Luhmann poses the question of 'constitutional learning' as a question of constitutional *adequacy*. He writes the following in the *Rechtssoziologie* of 1972, two years before Hayek's sweeping celebration of the 'market as discovery procedure' (discussed below, Chapter 3.1); 1972 is still too early for the wholesale switch towards the cognitive that is the mark of the success of the market paradigm. And although later he will associate globalisation with a decisive shift from the normative to the cognitive, the early work still reflects an important ambivalence:

> Society can regulate the retention of a compromise between the *necessities* of adapting to reality and expectations by aid of this differentiation [between normative and cognitive]. It can institutionalise behavioural expectations as cognitive and will not reproach its members for their adaptation of expectations to the reality of action as long as the *interest in adaptation* predominates. It will transfer expectations to the normative sphere and articulate them there if the security and social integration of expectation are the highest priority.
>
> (1972/1985: 34, emphasis added)

Luhmann will add that 'structural risks will also increase with the increasing complexity of society and this increase must be met by heightened differentiation between cognitive and normative expectations' (1972/1985: 34). And while the criteria of the balance are *not* yet coincident with the 'interest in adaptation', a curious language of 'risk' and imperatives ('must be met') invites judgement over what is an *adequate* response to increasing complexity: whether it is to continue to treat security of expectation as 'the highest priority' or whether to switch to the cognitive holding of normative expectations.

The question that arises crucially for a *critical* constitutional phenomenology is this: how do we *know* that we are confronted with a failure to achieve the proper balance? Remember that the distinction between cognitive and normative expectations was not drawn semantically but functionally, as a solution to the problem of how to deal with the adequacy of expectational structures. And the distinction, as we saw, related to the handling of the experience of disappointment. The problem also relates to the threshold at which the consistently disappointed normative expectation is no longer maintained but discredited. These were all questions that the constitutional function of normatively holding to normative expectations was meant to block. The value of the constitutional staggering of levels was precisely that it prevented the disappointment of an expectation turning into a discrediting of the structure.

For example, if workers normatively hold that they will not be fired if their strike is legally protected, they do not expect the result of their strike to be the revision of the system of labour protection. Something counted as a disappointment *given* the operation of a reduction at the level of structure. For the structure to *give* in the face of disappointment of the expectations it furnishes, does not normally account for the way we understand its operation as constitutional.

Except that sometimes it does. And it does, as we will see with the Laval/Viking jurisprudence with socially devastating effects. It is clear at this point why the question of *adequacy* is a normative question, because it is a normative question whether we are prepared to allow the constitutional protection of work to yield and learn from markets, or, in Luhmann's own terms, whether we treat 'the security and social integration of expectation as the highest priority' and as a steadfast commitment to expectational structures even where they clash with market optimisation. The key question that arises at the constitutional level of selections is how to combine normativity and cognition, and it is here that the demand of a political constitutionalism is that that combination can only be democratically decided, which means also that normativity at the second-order level is democratically buttressed.

*

This chapter used Luhmann's writings to put forward an analysis of constitutionality, or constitutional reflexivity, by combining the typology of self-reference ('basic self-reference', 'Reflexivity' and 'Reflexion') with his account of the generation of (constitutional) meaning along the three dimensions of meaning (material, social and temporal). In the discussion of self-reference we have looked at how the autopoiesis of law that occurs at the level of operations ('basic self-reference') is observed and controlled at higher levels. And how, then, at the level of 'reflexion' the system determines its own identity in relation to its environment. Key to the analysis is how the 'constitutional distinction' is used to steer internal processes. I argued that in the paradigm of political constitutionalism what accounts for the constitutional dimension is the introduction of the meta-coding according to the guiding distinction constituent/constituted, and that this meta-coding inclines the constitutional, constitutively, in the direction of the political. I then returned to the three dimensions of constitutional meaning to show how this incline, this unfolding of the constituent from the point of view of the constituted, operated in all three dimensions to accomplish the reduction achievement that is the political constitution: 'rationalisation' through the language of constitutional value in the material dimension; self-determination in the social dimension through the control of consensus and constituency and the structures of representation; and entrenchment of normativity in the temporal dimension, that is, the normative (democratic) holding of normative expectations. The constitutional achievement was to grant the legal system internal complexity 'adequate' to the coupling with the environment. The adequacy, the reflexivity, the 'way that the law thinks about itself in its environment', are all measured on a political register. Because, it was argued, the question of adequacy cannot be contemplated on purely functional grounds, outside a normative register.

If this chapter looked at constitutionality as a formal achievement, the next chapter (2.3) concerns the substantive dimension of political constitutionalism. It centres on the 'social question' as its central pillar, and looks at social rights and specifically the protection of work. We move now from the formal to the substantive, from form to content, to look at the values that inform the social constitution, and the way they inform its 'rationalisation'. Departing from the notion of the 'dogmatic' and the very particular form of foundation it introduces, we look at how the emergence of the constitutional tradition of labour protection has drawn constitutively on the legal-dogmatic resources of solidarity and dignity, and coupled them structurally to democracy.

2.3

Labour, Solidarity and the Social Constitution

> For when confronted with the question 'What justifies labour law in economic terms?', we are prompted to ask ourselves: 'What justifies such a question?'
>
> *Alain Supiot*

Constitutional Value and the Dogmatic Question

At the point of entry let us state, as 'prolegomena', two fundamental premises that I assume fundamental for any theorisation of *social rights constitutionalism*. The first we visited in the previous chapter, and involved the formal side of constitutional reflexivity as institutional achievement: it was argued that the institutional form, as *constitutional*, involves constitutive assumptions about entrenchment, hierarchisation and rationalisation. A commitment is constitutionally *entrenched* when it can only be modified through political decisions as mandated through constitutional amendment procedures; *hierarchy* elevates constitutional provisions above ordinary institutional activity of the legal regulation of economic and social life; and *rationalisation* means that norms make sense in the light of constitutional values.

In this chapter we visit a second set of connections, this time substantive rather than formal. This second, *axiomatic*, premise, to be discussed below is that *social* rights give institutional form to *solidarity*, best conceived as a *dogmatic* constitutional value, whose instantiations are never exhaustive but only ever approximate and provisional determinations of its meaning. The term dogmatic and its axiomatic function will be discussed in the next section.

The formal/substantive distinction is a useful way to analyse constitutional complexity. The term 'formal' as applied to the constitution captures the internal dimension, the way in which meta-level constitutional rules *of recognition, jurisdiction, change*, etc., organise the deployment of legal discourse. In the typical gesture of self-reference that is at the root of it all, they enable the law to 'think about itself', as we put it earlier. But the inward reach of self-reflection ('reflexion' above) takes its opportunity from the outside: what systems take to be their environments. It is only such *other-reference* that enables self-reference: after all, jurisdiction depends on *something* being in need of regulation, legal concepts need to attach to *thematics* in the world, personality needs to find its *subject of attribution and address*, rights need to represent *interests*, etc. This is where the 'substantive' comes in. The inside/outside distinction unfolds the law's operations, making both sides possible in that unfolding, internal and external, formal and substantive, *actualised together*.

If the substantive names that 'crossing' – of law *to* that to which it refers – we cannot and should not lose sight of its intrinsic connection to the formal. Looked at as a question of constitutional reflexivity (Chapter 2.2), the relation between the formal and substantive sides of the deployment of constitutional reason concerns *how the law structures itself internally in order to organise its conceptual reach into the world*, or what we might identify more specifically as its social and political environments. And just as the formal dimension involves the processes that organise the internal pathways that give expression to constitutional reason, the substantive dimension involves the forms of *structural coupling* of law to its political and social environments, where *meaning selections* can be taken partially for granted and deployed to build more stable patterns of reference to those environments.

As 'prolegomena', these constitutive conjunctures, first on the formal level with the three aspects of the reflexivity of constitutional thought, and then on the substantive level, with the forms of reference to law's environments are key mirror dimensions of law's *phenomenology* in its systems-theoretical form.

Of the three 'formal' functions it is the last, rationalisation, that most clearly connects constitutional reflection to the substance of what is being reflected on. The use of constitutional values, *formally* entrenched as a matter of political decision and placed hierarchically above the ordinary processes of law, rationalise the field of law's application. As a point of normative regress within constitutional discourse, values are where constitutional reason finds its source, and therefore function as the limit of the reach of constitutional reason back to its sources. Hence their axiomatic status in the substantive dimension as horizon of constitutional thought. The constitution can perform the function of rationalisation by virtue of constitutional values. They are hermeneutical depositories of sorts. In themselves they are in need of determination: they need to be instantiated, the abstract rendered concrete in the particular occasions of their application. At that level, of application, they are in systems-theoretical terms 'poorly selective'. Further forms and devices for selection need to be mobilised through practical reasoning. At the same time they delimit the range of what can count as a valid selection; what transcends the limit falls outwith constitutional authorisation.

In this chapter we will discuss the constitutional value that is most central to the social constitution: *solidarity*. It informs the deployment of constitutional reason and introduces the limit beyond which constitutional reason cannot travel. The concept of the 'dogmatic' captures that limit; but as such its institutional meaning is incomplete. As abstract value and dogmatic resource, solidarity needs to be instantiated, concretised, given institutional presence and organisational form. Social rights are key such instantiations, themselves calling for further concretisation through selections in the practice of constitutional discourse and jurisprudence.

Before we explore all this, two caveats:

First, as ever, there are important limits to this political-phenomenological endeavour to be conceded. We cannot suggest that the constitutional iteration will provide anything like full expression: whatever the dividends of the recourse to social rights, they will be 'disciplined' to the semantic reach of the 'implementing' rules, and the relative inertia of the institutional imagination. The law, as we have repeated Luhmann's formulation often, is a *reduction achievement*. The *achievement* refers to the generation of meaning; it refers to the opportunities of deployment of legal reasoning, the instantiations, concretisations, or, as we will go on to discuss, its determinations. But the achievement is one of *reduction* (of complexity). Whatever the constitution provides as means for protecting solidarity from market impingement, they will be over-determined by the particular selectivity of the medium, the limits that are placed on content, time and subject-positions that comprise its referential reach, and they will be immunised towards a range of alternatives.

A second important caveat is over antinomy. The critical constitutional argument of the book takes antinomy not as pathology, but as productive. Antinomy inserts itself between the aspiration encapsulated in constitutional value and the reductive forms of its instantiation, including crucially the language of *rights*. If the processes of constitutional reasoning do not, in fact, allow the smooth passage from the abstract to the concrete and from the general to the particular, this does not mean that the argument about constitutional value, in this case solidarity, is cancelled in the processes of its 'realisation'. The antinomy that inserts itself in the chasm that opens up between the two levels, does not give the lie to the promise of social constitutionalism. Instead, antinomy gives hermeneutical traction to solidarity, intrinsic to the *ratio juris* as a question of its very deployment. And thereby it also gives meaning to the redress of unnecessary suffering, that is, meaning, where otherwise there would be meaninglessness.

*

Alain Supiot's *Homo Juridicus* is a restatement of *law as social hermeneutic*; the *hermeneia* referred to is unique to juridical reason and sustains the dignity and autonomy of the *ratio juris*. Its achievement is to provide the shared symbolic medium that *binds* by 'interposing shared meaning between people' (2007: xxiv). It is here that Supiot locates the anthropological function of law which marks the ambition of the work. The function of law is a function of *binding*. On the one hand the law 'connects infinite universality to finite existence', our material to our spiritual existence; on the other hand it binds to others through sustaining a symbolic function. In this social dimension, what the law achieves, across societies and history, is to generate forms of this bond, and by means of which, also, a reciprocity that rests on obligations assumed. 'Binding' and 'interposing', reciprocity and obligation: words that, for Supiot, sustain at the foundational level the meaning of 'the human' and of 'the common' *in tandem*. In mining a deep hermeneutics, Supiot is offering us a radical recuperation of juridical reason. The juridical is recovered as distinct from, and as irreducible to, the various reductionisms of law to scientific or economic reason, and guards against its harnessing to historical determinisms or deconstructive undoing. Importantly, the *recuperation* goes hand in hand with the radical *critique* of law, including of course the critique of rights. And while we will return to Supiot on the question of *dogma* with a view to exploring how the commitment to both recuperation and critique might be upheld, we will need first to look briefly at the *question dogmatique* in the tradition of thought from which Supiot draws, and in which Pierre Legendre is a key figure.[1]

Legendre invites us to think of 'ce qui se monstre mais qui se ne démonstre pas' – that which appears but is not demonstrable. Key to this disclosure is that the dogmatic is situated pre-interpretatively, setting in place the conditions of interpretation. It is in that profound sense axiomatic and heteronomous. Axiomatic because nothing precedes it; and heteronomous because it cannot be questioned. For the Legendrian that he is, Supiot also takes 'heteronomy' as sustaining the legal-hermeneutical exercise. At a pre-interpretative level it furnishes those pre-understandings that set in place the conditions for interpretation. And these conditions, for the hermeneutical enterprise to unfold, cannot be questioned. The dogmatic in that sense installs an *unquestionability* that is not merely productive, but at the root of the very autonomy of juridical reason. In its properly symbolic dimension heteronomy enables disclosure of a world. It is disclosure that is at stake in the function of the dogmatic because the dogmatic sets the *limit points* that sustain the symbolic order. To question the conditions is to unpick what is axiomatic to the symbolic order and can only be performed at the cost of the symbolic order and *economy* of representation coming undone, which spells meaninglessness.

The concept that most crucially subtends and sustains the order of intelligibility as a *human* order is *dignity*. *Dignity is axiomatic* in that respect and Muriel Fabre-Magnan offers an important insight when, taking the cue from Giambattista Vico's *La Science Nouvelle* (1725), she designates it 'as a principle self-evident as to be able to serve to provide a means of demonstration'. For our preoccupation with disclosure this is crucial. 'One cannot demonstrate or define it, one can only show it. . . .

---

[1] Peter Goodrich has provided one of the few serious engagements with Legendre's vast oeuvre – or this 'non-school or institutionally diasporic species of legal critique' as he characterises it (2009: 302) – which is largely unknown in Anglophone scholarship. 'Resistant to systematization, hostile to students and disciples alike, prolific yet inaccessible or at least complicated in style, arcane and at the same time grandiose in range of reference and titles of works, Legendre is almost impossible to classify, let alone to translate' (299). 'We need, we are compelled, as human beings to attach to images of identity and community that will bind us to a place, a group, an order of being while exteriorizing our fears of emptiness and non-being onto the outside and alien, the different and other. So the argument as to the anthropological significance of the norm goes and it operates across the vast corpus of Legendre's work to analyze the psychic function of scripture and Text, of word and image, of dance as a choreography of human places and social being, of rites of solemnization, of dogma as such' (300).

La dignité de la personne humaine est le dogma premier, l'axiome de base au fondement du système juridique, en réalité son but ultime [The dignity of the human person is the principal dogma, the basic axiom at the foundation of the juridical system, in reality its ultimate aim]' (2007: 10). The dogmatic function of the law sustains the field of reference of human commonality;[2] it treats that commonality as the accompanying reference in all deployments of legal reason.

Where does a *critical* legal-constitutional project stand in relation to the sources and stakes of unquestionability of the dogmatic? For Legendre it is clear that the critical project sits uncomfortably with his understanding of the law as an institution that relays significant and valuable cultural goods, through the juridical hierarchy of sites of enunciation and mobilised through institutional roles. For him the hermeneutical recovery of legal meaning is pitted against (at least) the *postmodern* take on critique understood as the radical play of interpretations that cut away at the coherence of law; his argument being that such 'radicality' cuts it adrift, self-defeatingly, from its own symbolic premises, the logic of institution and identity that sustains the subject in the social. Legendre insists that the collapse of the heteronomy of the symbolic – of 'dogma as such' – will entail the loosening of the binding function of the symbolic. But we must be cautious here and resist generalising this dismissal, because there is a profound lesson to be learnt from the 'unquestionability' attached to the dogmatic for a critical constitutionalism.

It will take returning to a more openly political approach, taking the example of 'dignity' and extending it to 'solidarity' as its complementary axiom. And it is best to approach this as a phenomenological argument, of what provides the conditions of phenomenality, of how a field of hermeneutical enquiry can be disclosed and sustained on the basis of what constitutes its most elevated horizon. Our priority is with the resources of interpretation that the dogmatic releases. Where dogma does the work of sustaining the discursive space by setting in place the non-negotiable mainstays of the common, the work of legal hermeneutics is to unfold the dogmatic resources, with Supiot, *as interdiction and as judgement.*

We need to take the two terms *interdiction* and *judgement* severally and in their combination. Interdiction is a wonderful term for the

---

[2] 'La dignité de la personne humaine est en effet comme un axiome indémontrable et indérogeable, et sans doute même aussi indicible' (Fabre-Magnan, 2007).

equivocation it carries, as that which on the one hand *resists, stems and interrupts* and on the other mediates: *inter-dicts*. On the one hand it refers to the sense of 'diction' that *mediates* by carrying meanings 'between' ('*inter*') registers: from politics, ethics, economics, etc., to law, and back. On the other hand it refers to the sense of *preventing* (stemming, interrupting) the subjection of the logic of one medium (law or politics) to that of another (economics). There is something profoundly urgent in this latter function of interdiction. The *non-negotiability* of the fundamental values of reciprocity, solidarity and community that underlie what it means to *belong* in a world, are installed and enshrined at the level of the dogmatic as the mainsprings of human association. Only thus are they vested with the unquestionability that make them conditions rather than objects of question, pre-understandings, pre-dispositions, guiding orientation, however we might describe the hermeneutic enterprise of calling them forth-as our constitutional culture's symbolic resources- in renewed acts of interpretation. Interdiction names the refusal to put them to question.

Here Supiot looks to Weil, in the first of two 'contradictions', for a different reconciliation of the 'unconditional' and the 'critical'. Weil writes:

> A value is something that we unconditionally accept. ... [A] system of values in the instant that it orientates our life, is not accepted subject to conditions, but purely and simply accepted. ... At the same time, we cannot abandon the attempt to understand them since this would mean ceasing to believe in them, which is impossible because human life cannot exist without orientation. Therein resides a contradiction which is at the very heart of human life.
>
> (Weil, 1941, quoted in Supiot, 2007: 70)

'This contradiction', adds Supiot, 'is the driving force behind human thought' (2007: 70).

Weil's 'set of values', as dogmatic, are not accepted subject to conditions, because it would normatively make no sense for something to have installed itself behind the orienting set of values as *their* condition. Rather we are already invested in the value set. A demand is thereby placed on us for an understanding of how their requirements will be met in the midst of competing interpretations and particular dilemmas. Reciprocity, solidarity and obligation, as dogmatic resources, are elevated to the level where they furnish normative orientation. There is no stepping outside (the system, the horizon, the dogmatic) because there is nowhere to go normatively. This was the function of *interdiction*. But as internalised, Weil's first 'contradiction' becomes productive to juridical thinking. The 'conditions' – that were meaningless as *conditions of* the 'system of value' – now become conditions of its proper instantiation, of our interpretative choices regarding applications that remain, unavoidably, underdetermined, complex and contradictory. They become productive on an internal register as suspended between the two poles of interdiction and judgement. As *judgement* they inform the move from the universal to the particular that is condition of all practical reason; they authorise actualisations and determinations of value. It is at this point that interdiction links with *judgement*, the first term setting and clearly delimiting the context for the exercise of the second which takes effect at the level of renewed instantiation. We will have opportunity a little later to look more carefully at the Thomist idea of *determinatio*. Suffice for now to describe judgement through the function of specification, concretisation or instantiation, of the abstract value resources in specific, particular, occasions. In all this 'dogma' remains the name for that which is not lost, for that which after all its actualisations, particularisations, balancing, is, in spite of it all, never lessened.

In their combination, interdiction and judgement attach a very particular meaning to critique understood as the recuperation of law as dogma that is *instantiated* rather than re-invented, modulated or undermined through its critical invocation in judgement. A productive tension now installs itself at the juncture of closure and under-determination, calling forth the interpretative practices that enjoin us in community. In the interstice that opens up between dogma and its productive deployment in interpretation, Supiot sets the opportunity-structure of legality as both limit and occasion. He says: 'The law hedges in every new beginning and at the same time assures its freedom of movement' (2007: 58). If hermeneutics always opens on a horizon that cannot be transcended, the notion of the dogmatic as origin and limit is rolled out in every new interpretation. Juridical reason is deployed within the set of values it enacts as fundamental presuppositions to it, and the key concepts it mobilises it already presupposes as deep premise, foundation and reason.[3]

---

[3] It is perhaps more difficult for an English readership to appreciate the subtlety of the dogmatic approach in the absence of the distinction that Supiot relies on to make his argument, between *droit* and *loi* (*Recht* and *Gesetz* in German, *nomos* and *dikaio* in Greek). The non-coincidence between *loi* and *droit* subtends the reflexivity of law, the

We have reached here an important watermark in the argument, but there is one qualification that Supiot makes, that must be heeded. The rootedness of the juridical in what Weil above called 'system of values' (and what Supiot in *Homo Juridicus* carefully traces as inventory of the normative across eras and civilisations) cannot be severed. And it *is* severed in the varieties of positivism that circumscribe law within the realm of facticity. Such a '"science" of law would not allow the issue of the reasons (and unreasons) of law to be addressed' (2007: 71). The legal positivist's claim is similar to that of 'the technical expert who claims that the science of technical objects forecloses the issue of their use and purpose'. This view of laws as management tools falls down on each of the thresholds that Supiot has set for juridical reason.

A different genealogy, one that is not explicitly recalled in *Homo Juridicus*, might accommodate Supiot's objection to the varieties of positivism in a more familiar idiom. Like in Aristotelian virtue ethics, dogmatic values are not negotiable: they define something of the teleology of what it means to realise a life worth living, which removes from the list both arbitrariness and the need for any further or meta-level justification. They are emphatically not preferences or desires, and thus clearly to be set apart from any utilitarian or optimisation calculus. They are the normative foundations that make normative reasoning meaningful. Dogmatic thinking is reminiscent, and in one important sense crucially so, of the Aristotelian thinking that informs Lon Fuller's fine book *The Morality of Law* and the distinction that he insightfully draws between the morality of aspiration and the morality of duty. Fuller argues there, in a comprehensive, to my mind, pre-emptive rebuttal of the positivist conception of law put forward by Hart, that standards of excellence underlie our understanding of certain practices (and the concepts we employ to designate them) so that an appreciation of those standards is constitutive of what it means to understand them. Law, claims Fuller, is one such concept, its internal morality constitutive of its meaning. And here Fuller introduces an important twist: while in their nature as aspirational such standards cannot be reached, not only do they remain operative in any proper understanding of the practice, but they

---

latter giving it content, the former ensuring the *closure* that gives *ratio legis* its circumference and leverage, that therefore alone does the work of *containing* interpretations as instantiations *of law* as opposed to the open play of language. This insistence on closure relates Supiot's theory via Legendre, explicitly, to a concept of the 'mytho-logic'. We will not follow him there, to the revelatory discourses of foundation.

also introduce a crucial cut-off point and resist inversion. If a practice falls below a certain threshold in terms of that standard of excellence it can longer claim to instantiate that practice. Both the framing function of dogma and the disjuncture between Law and laws-as-management tools is present in this constitutively 'moral' reading of the legal. Both Fuller and Supiot are keen to stress that if law is to be seen as a tool or technique it *is* that only in the light of the *purpose* it is there to serve, or as 'defined by the representation that governs [its] manufacture'. Take a spade for example: one can of course use it to kill a rat. But here the proper function of the object is missed, and therefore, as with any functional definition, the object misread. In a similar vein Fuller was perplexed by Hart's supposed *reductio ad absurdum* of his theory, in the 'inner morality of poisoning' counter-example. For Fuller, law was a technique that gained its meaning in terms of the aspiration that governed it: to bring human behaviour under the governance of rules. To sever it off from that aspiration was to subvert its meaning, not dissimilar to defining spades as rat-killing devices.

Supiot never mentions Fuller so all this may be no more than mere conjecture. If Supiot's thinking of law moves him towards the tradition of natural law it is certainly not encumbered with the conservative limitations of Fuller's, but more akin to that other, emancipatory, tradition in which Ernst Bloch's *Natural Law and Human dignity* still stands as the exemplary instance. Essential to Bloch's pursuit of the 'unclaimed heritages' of the natural law tradition was to reclaim the promise of human dignity found in its 'intention'. It is the dignity that Bloch finds in the young Marx's call to 'overthrow all relations in which man is a degraded, enslaved, abandoned or despised being', and the notion of an 'unclaimed heritage' resonates with what Adorno called the '*grosse Blockmusik*', Bloch's unflinching orientation to a 'humanised nature and a naturalised humanity'.

But let us return to the dogmatic. If Supiot wants to couple judgement with interdiction it is because across their contradictory articulation they act as both enabling and immunising factors for the hermeneutical work of the critical jurist. The enabling function of the dogmatic harnesses it (always-already) to the deeper structure of commonality, and furnishes the interpretative range afforded to *dogmatic* determination. Dogma offers the context which cannot be transcended but also that which cannot be collapsed without a radical loss of meaning. 'Interdiction', in its productive equivocation, returns us on the one hand to the power of language to tap the deeper resources of community and reciprocity, as deliberatively and interpretatively deployed, and on the other to install itself as antagonistic to the various reductionisms, whether these are of the 'law and economics' varieties with their attendant quantifications of value, or the various forms of systemic enfolding into old and new varieties of positivism.

The coupling, now, of interdiction with judgement, asks what it means to locate the constitutional value at the level of dogma, as extended, unfolded, *instantiated*, in terms of the discourse of rights, not as their correlative but as source of their proper meaning and measure of their proper deployment. And the answer to this question confronts us with the antinomy that resides at the very heart of the concept of social rights, as instantiations of an ideal of solidarity the demands of which they can *only ever partially* express. And it is at this juncture that a second invocation of contradiction, by Weil, needs to be heeded. Supiot does not address this second meaning directly, but it is of paramount importance to the *antinomic* conception of social rights constitutionalism. Contradiction in this second sense attaches to the distinction, internal to juridical imaginary, between *law as a language of the middle range*, and *law as a dogmatic resource*, where the latter, as we have seen, taps the deeper recesses of human embeddedness.

How is responsiveness undone at the middle range of institutions? The language of institution is a language of generalisation, of reduction and of functionality. As a language of *generalisation*, it introduces selective suppressions; classifications at once actualise and suppress possibilities. As a language of *reduction* it introduces simplification; the reality of that simplification is best captured through the idea of a reduction of *complexity* through which the language of law fashions the key concepts that have an exclusionary effect in that they stand in for the more complex environments that they displace. And *functionality* introduces linkage; institutions offer possibilities of connection. Linkage-capacity of concepts enable combinations and circulations that in turn provide for systemic constructions and the reproduction of expectational structures. Note how an institutional achievement emerges concisely, simply, and in the selectivity that conditions its emergence how it walls itself against alternatives. Expectations will reproduce it for what is given visibility by it alone, and what not.

Weil does *not* use the language of systemic achievement and exclusion but thematises that exclusion around the reductive language of *right* and *person*, the circulation of claim and counterclaim. Rights are concepts that are linked to the logic of exchange and of measured quantity; legal personality to the comparative demand of person to person. (She speaks prophetically of the mass proliferation of rights and rights-holders whose shrillness we encounter in our Europe of optimising, of calibrating, of balancing.) Against these concepts of the 'middle range' Weil interjects *attention*. We looked at the concept in Part I. Here our concern is with the chasm that opens between the levels, of justice at foundational level and how it is cashed out in claims of right at the middle level. The insistence on deploying the language of justice at both levels is important for the critical project because it inscribes solidarity and dignity into the rights-language of the middle range and by doing that it introduces *a fault line within* that institutional language. The inscription of the aspiration into the 'mediocrity' of the mediating language of rights confronts the promise of solidarity, of dignity, with the inadequacy of that 'mediation'. In this we have not a continuity but a tension between dignity promised and indignity delivered; between the promise of responsibility and the denial of fragility; between the promise of solidarity and the delivery of 'shrill' contention and claim of right. This opens it out as a field of immanent critique. And while it would be inaccurate to claim Weil for a field that has developed out of the Hegelian-Marxian dialectical tradition, Weil develops something akin to it with her emphasis on the idea of theory as practical, engaged activity. For politics, she says, the problem 'comes to this: to find, in conditions as they are [necessity], a form of society which would conform to the demands of reason and which at the same time would take into account necessities ... A method as materialist as this is absolutely necessary if good intentions are to be changed into actions' (Weil, 1978: 130).

The ambition of the suggested *dialectic of interdiction and judgement* that mobilises the dogmatic resources of *ratio legis* measures itself against both suggestions: that of any direct, mechanistic or deductive derivation of the particular from the general, and of any suggestion that legal decisions might be produced ex nihilo, as per Schmitt,[4] a pure

---

[4] '[As] justified by the specificity of the normative and arises since a concrete judgement must be made of a concrete fact, even though the only available evaluation criterion is a general principle of law. Accordingly, every decisional instance entails a transformation ... every transformation entails an *auctoritatis interpositio* ...; the very essence of judgement is the fact that there can never be absolute declaratory judgements. With regard to the content of the decisional norm, each constitutive and specific decisional moment entails something new and foreign. *Normatively speaking, the judgement is born out of nothingness.*' (Schmitt, 1922/1985: 41).

decisionism rushing to fill the particularity void. This is the terrain that the discussion of *determinatio* attempts to navigate.[5]

The idea of *determinatio*, which we will return to with reference to practical dilemmas later (in 3.4), captures the logic of instantiation, along the direction of how these principles are concretised. Institutional logic intervenes here, and the logic of reduction – the institutional achievement of reducing complexity – is a key part of it. The pragmatics of instantiation is what we come to know and practise as law. The logic of specification is not the logic of balancing. *Determinatio* in the beautiful simplicity of its pure directionality captures the connection between furnishing judgement (with content) and providing thresholds and limits as to what might count as moments of heteronomy that the dogmatic offers to juridical reasoning.

Let us then draw some of the threads of the 'dogmatic' together before we move to the connection to solidarity in the next section. If there are echoes of our earlier discussion of Fuller in Supiot's insistence on the dogmatic, they concern the operation of the aspiration/duty distinction as sustaining and subtending the sphere of legality. Both jurists' reference to the 'aspirational' and 'dogmatic' taps the rich field of legal interpretation as a sphere of striving, of aspiration and of commonality, that is ultimately about protecting the human bond. In the as-if of the 'rational' and the aspirational inhere the standards of excellence of legal practice that as such cannot be exhausted but only striven towards, never guaranteed and therefore always open to renewal in interpretative undertakings.

Law as a social hermeneutic attempts to restore a proper vocabulary to the field of human association. It performs the function of an interdiction, as we said, as that which on the one hand resists, stems and interrupts and on the other mediates. In carrying connotations of 'separating', 'forbidding' and 'mediating', it is, to reclaim an abused term, interstitial. 'Interdiction' returns us to the power of language not just as a tool – though of course it is that too – but as commonality, and antagonistic to the various reductionisms of the constitutional imaginary

---

[5] Values, or what the Aristotelian philosopher John Finnis famously identified as 'basic goods', express at the abstract level our human commonality. In this context the idea of *determinatio* captures the logic of instantiation, along the direction of how these principles are concretised, too under-determined to provide situation-specific answers, but is also exclusionary, in providing thresholds of interpretative options. Finnis' reference to the 'basic goods' as *pre-moral* is pertinent here (Finnis, 2011).

to the logic of instrumentality and the logic of price. In the face of reductions or simplifications into generalised commodity exchange, legal reason, Supiot is keen to argue, recovers the 'sense of measure', which is above all a 'human measure'.

That is the first insight that the dogmatic offers us in the reflexive equilibrium between interdiction and judgement, the former delimiting the context to which the latter offers instantiation. The second, more troubled, and troubling insight, that we drew out interpretatively from Weil, concerns the problematic of instantiation: her insistence that rights name claims of the 'middle range', that they are forever inadequate instantiations, markers of an imperfect passage. The whole discussion of the antinomic nature of social constitutionalism that follows attaches to this point. It is an antinomy that holds between the dogmatic of solidarity and the language of rights.

Homo Juridicus, Laborans

In its original juridical sense that dates from Roman law, *solidarity* was the term for what was effectively a technique of holding co-responsible all those who played a role in the generation of a certain risk (Supiot, 2013: 99). 'The Roman legal concept *in solidium*', adds Hauke Brunkhorst, 'means an obligation for the whole: joint liability, common debt, solidary obligation' (Brunkhorst, 2015: 2). The original solidary 'asymmetrical' obligation is 'sublated' in the direction of *reciprocity* (p. 60), and this sense of reciprocity is generalised with the advent of the social state, which introduced the pooling of the risks of existence and gave solidarity the organisational form of social security and public services, to which one contributed according to one's resources and benefited according to one's needs.

That the crisis of social rights constitutionalism marks today the decline of solidarity as *organisational* form does not, for Supiot, mark also its decline as dogmatic resource. After all, 'the social state is simply one moment in the long history of human solidarities which have taken multiple forms, none of them neither definitive nor guaranteed' (Supiot, 2013: 99). This is because solidarity underpins and sustains juridical reason in a way that is never exhausted by any one of its (organisational) instantiations. Supiot captures this with the concept of *dogmatic*, in the way that we have so far expounded it. In its hermeneutic function, dogma furnishes the conditions of intelligibility and at the same time marks the limit beyond which *hermeneia* is undone. This notion of limit point is, as we said, important; one might think of dogma as that which prevents passage to a *different* register to measure the adequacy of law's solutions. In this gesture of self-reference, *law turns its reflexivity back on itself as dogma* and thereby resists the 'truths' of market veridiction.

We discussed this self-referential closure as the way in which constitutional reflexivity is made possible, expressed in the modalities of entrenchment, hierarchisation and rationalisation (Chapter 2.2). In terms of the last of the tree functions, solidarity as *constitutional value* orientates teleological and systematic interpretation; it furnishes its particular instantiations in legal practice with meaning that will indeed be open to re-interpretation, but also marks the point beyond which no such (re-) interpretation can travel without giving the lie to the meaning of the value. In terms of its institutional realisation solidarity underwrites social and labour protection and the obligation of social security, legally buttressing them with forms of objective liability. The forms that the institutional support may take is negotiable, but the value the institutional forms support is not: solidarity affords constitutional protection to collective forms of representation and action and collective procedures. We need go no deeper into the function of institutional instantiation, protection and warrant than to look at the sources of vulnerability that form solidarity's specific vis-à-vis. To understand solidarity as the foundation of the social state and the founding commitment to mutualise the risks of existence through the provision of social protection, is to appreciate the gesture that understands societal valorisation as irreducibly collective, where even those less exposed to risks bear a duty of responsibility given that they partake as beneficiaries of the totality of social production.

Against the vagaries of market activity, solidarity recast as 'dogmatic' resource, installs at the root of the properly juridical a certain unquestionability: to constitutionalise solidarity in the forms of social rights, of social protection and social insurance, means, at minimum, to introduce it as axiomatic and non-negotiable interdiction. 'Collective self-determination' sanctions collective capacity for action in the forms of freedom to associate, to bargain and to strike. The institutions of social insurance and public services offer collective defence against the risks of existence: together they offer the institutional realisation of solidarity, historical and therefore contingent, and subtended by legal dogma. And while it would exaggerate the function of social constitutionalism to suggest it has ever *resolved* the contradiction between democracy and capitalism, it has had demonstrable capacity to shelter democracy from capitalist excess, imbuing democratic institutions *within* the economy with force, and enabling the recognition of the constituent role of *virtue* in the economy. It is but a symptom of the pathological expansion of total market thinking that to understand and theorise the economy by means of democratic and moral categories is either seen as some kind of category mistake, or folds into the a priori 'truths' of rational action thinking. We will return to this too. Let us simply say that when George Herbert Mead spoke of 'the working hypothesis in social reform' as the application of intelligence to the control of social conditions,[6] he was talking about the economy as an expression of *democratic* life, and social policy in terms of the reciprocal recognition of vulnerability and dependency, and was certainly not invoking the banalities of rational action thinking.

*

Reminding us that the Philadelphia Convention that set out the principles of post-war society preceded the creation of the UN and its Declaration of 1948, Supiot in his recent *L'esprit de la Philadelphie* (2010a) returns to the constitutional protection of work set out in the Declaration. And he returns us crucially to the relationship of work not in its character of transaction but in terms of the thicker notion of association. The latter is the constant that runs through the work arguing that there is no defensible theory of value production other than 'adapting the economy to the needs of human beings'. Supiot's is a fully fledged normative theory of a constitutional-social hermeneutic, reaching down to include, decisively, unapologetically and crucially, the social dimension. For Supiot the human condition is, to reverse Arendt, constitutively tied to the dignity of labour.

The main principles that Supiot draws from Philadelphia are the following: First, the Declaration neither revealed nor uncovered fundamental principles but *affirmed* them. It is an affirmation explicitly 'dogmatique' – in the way 'dogma' underlies the anthropological function of law, as we saw above. Secondly, the affirmation constitutes an act of *reason*; its rationale: no durable peace can be established except on the basis of social justice ('un paix durable ne peut être établie que sur la base

---

[6] 'In social reform, or the application of intelligence to the control of social conditions, we must make a like assumption, and this assumption takes the form of belief in the essentially social character of human impulse and endeavor. We cannot make persons social by legislative enactment, but we can allow the essentially social nature of their actions to come to expression under conditions which favor this.' (Mead, 1899: 370.)

de la justice sociale'). Thirdly, it pivots on the foundational concept of *dignity*. The Declaration establishes dignity as the fundamental principle that subtends (informs and rationalises) all other principles and rights. To breach it, breaches the entire juridical order ('la dignité humaine est un principe sur lequel on ne peut pas transiger sans remettre en cause l'ordre juridique tout entier' (2010a: 22)). At stake is nothing short of the 'reification' of man (ibid.). Fourthly, it is dignity – as supreme – that informs and makes sense of the articulation of the principles of liberty and security, not the other way round. It is dignity that ensures the proper balance between the two subordinate principles. As such, it underlies the following four commitments: (i) to non-commodified labour; (ii) to collective rights (freedom of expression and association); (iii) to solidarity, as tied explicitly to the redress of poverty; and (iv) to social democracy, linked directly to the redress of *needs*.

The essence of the Declaration is in the understanding that the organisation of the economy is subordinate to social justice, a subordination that Supiot argues was already present in the 1919 constitution of the ILO in linking durable peace to social justice; but the restatement of its fundamental principles after the Second World War in the Declaration of Philadelphia enhances this in two directions. First it gives it global reach in affirming that all human beings enjoy the protection of liberty, dignity, economic security and equal opportunities. Secondly, it makes the realisation of social justice thus understood the 'central aim of all national and international politics' (24). And with this we come to Supiot's central claim: that it is the inverse perspective that currently dominates the actual processes of globalisation. The objective of social justice has given way to the free circulation of capital and commodities. The priority of ends to means has been reversed. And instead of indexing the economy to human needs and finance to the economy, the economy has been indexed to finance and people – as 'human capital' – to the service of the economy (25). The stated objective of his book is to track the great inversion that appears to have abolished the lessons of the 1914–45 period. And its normative point, to argue that despite this collapse and inversion 'the spirit [of Philadelphia] retains all its pertinence' (25), disappointed, one might add, but as a *normative expectation* not thereby discredited. It is this affirmation that sustains the work.

Supiot argues that 'the market, if it is to function well, must be limited by rules and institutions that ensure the security of human, natural and monetary resources' (Supiot, 2007: 94). Note in this the implicit reference to Karl Polanyi's three 'fictitious commodities' of work, nature and money. *Disembedding* is not a word that is used by Supiot, but it resonates well with the severing of law from its dogmatic anchor. More interesting, however, is the hidden reference to the logic of Polanyi's 'double movement'. Like for Polanyi, for Supiot too the exposure to the market generates compensatory gestures and the need to shelter certain fundamentals of existence. Inherent tensions and resistances to marketisation abound: 'certain things resist their transformation into commodities, because they retain, e.g., the mark of the person who created them'. Or, '[s]pecial domains of law have developed (labour law, social security law, [etc.]) in order to accommodate the elements that fall outside the sphere of the calculation of individual interests' and rational utility maximisation, though 'the effectiveness of such props is constantly diminished by the progress of free trade and the opening up of national frontiers to the circulation of capital, goods and services, which obliges States to reduce these props or adapt them accordingly' (Supiot, 2007: 100). However we assess the link to Polanyi, and society's self-protective gesture against market exposure that is the 'double movement', there remains in the recuperation of juridical reason an urgent and important message. In the face of reductions or simplifications into generalised commodity exchange, against the collapse of juridical personality, and against the incipient 'Market Leninism' of the neo-liberal turn in the European Union (Glasman, 1996; Supiot, 2007), Supiot is keen to argue, recovers the 'sense of measure', which is above all a 'human measure'. To rediscover this sense of measure one must place anew man's destiny at the heart of the system of evaluation of economic performances, re-orientating them to a longer temporal horizon and against the acceleration of short-termism.

Supiot answers the constitutional question of labour protection, above all else, as a question of protecting solidarity at the collective level, and dignity at the individual. There is a developing constitutional jurisprudence of dignity and it would be dogmatically wrong and strategically imprudent to ignore its growing significance. For Supiot it is not just a question of strategy, though it is undoubtedly that too, but crucially a question of the very foundation of law. As fundamental constitutional aspiration and dogmatic resource, the protection of solidarity and human dignity sets a standard against which all interpretation of law must measure itself. Constitutional interpretations that are supposed instantiations of general principles and yet give the lie to those principles are deficient laws, to be righted as unconstitutional. Where the relation between principles and their instantiations is eroded and the dialectic is broken, any possibility of making sense of the law as a rational enterprise disappears with it.

Let us keep from the dogmatic the sense of rootedness in the sources of human reciprocity, that Weil called *l'enracinement*. And let us locate there the meaning of solidarity. According to the thesis of law as social hermeneutic, a community of sense is *inscribed* in dogma. We asked: if what is 'dogmatic', in ordinary language, is what we take on faith, in what sense can it underpin a social hermeneutic that informs and undergirds nothing short of the creation of meaning, the pursuit of autonomy, and the critical project? The answer involves a particular articulation of interdiction and judgement. This lifts *solidarity* up a level, to the realm of that which provides legal thought with its horizon and animus, while claims of right fall into the sphere of its fallible and reversible determinations. The asymmetry between the obligation and the right installs itself as source of legal meaning and as lever of juridical reason. Any assumed correlativity between obligation and right is here replaced by the *tension* generated by the asymmetry between the dogmatic resource and the 'mediating' categories of rights that purport to realise it (Weil's second 'contradiction'), a tension that calls forth the interpretative practices that enjoin us in community: never as affirmation of right (those 'shrill claims' Weil called them) but as invocation of a deeper reciprocity. Which is also to say: if community is always an aspiration, its modality always the 'not-yet', the form it receives in the institutional practices falls short of its realisation; community is instead lived and experienced in the form of a deficit as well as the imperative to overcome it. That, at least, was what Weil's 'courage' invoked, the faith that the space was recoverable against all the facets of necessity that conspire to seal it off and place it beyond reach.

Social Rights Constitutionalism

The Radical Marshall

In his seminal lecture of 1949, 'Citizenship and social class', Thomas Marshall argued that successive waves of rights – civil, political and social – should be conceived along a continuous trajectory as markers of society's struggle to contain and *overcome* the latent and hidden injuries of class. The final category in this linear succession were social rights, which were tied to the efforts of 'political power to supersede, supplement or modify operations of the economic system in order to achieve results which the economic system would not achieve on its own, …

guided by values other than those determined by market forces'. His theory engaged a 'secondary system of industrial citizenship', where syndicalist activity assumes 'the guise of an action modifying the whole pattern of social inequality' (Marshall, 1950/1992: 28). Keen to remain with Marshall's normative argument about citizenship, but missing its critical message, social rights advocates have offered to 'resolve' the contradiction between democracy and capitalism and have variously invoked, rationalised and deployed social rights *as continuous* to civil and political rights. But all too often these 'accommodating' syntheses are shown to be captive forms of thought, forms of the reconciliation-cum-subsumption of democracy to capitalism. Let us see more gradually why, and how, the critical message of Marshall's argument might be restored.[7]

The 'continuity argument' between civil, political and social rights appears to stumble early on the objection that the successive categories of rights involve different bases of justification. To argue for their continuity misses the fundamental opposition between the rationales of entitlement and liberty, underlying civic rights, participation, underlying political rights, and need satisfaction, underlying social rights. For those objecting to continuity, where not actually zero-sum, rights might at best align in a relationship of mutual limitation, or mutual correction. Take the varieties of the argument popularised under the rubric of the '*tragedy of the commons*': with its connotations of overstepping and inexorability, it stands as a warning against *hubris*. The lesson conveyed is that rational action – taken unquestionably as coincident with the maximisation of individual returns – cannot guarantee the sustainability of the commons. Where the pool of common resources is freely available because bereft of the sanction of the exclusionary device of individual property, individual motivations, typically greed, will obstruct sustainable use; then social rights will give free rein to need that, inexhaustible and unchecked, will lead to the raiding of the common pool of resources through overfarming, overfishing, etc. Property and civil rights typically come to the rescue as framing conditions to what the requirements of ordering the commons might require: property rights protect from the potentially overwhelming demands carried by social rights, and protect also from political rights, the apparent risk here being that the motivation of politicians to promise too much to electorates to secure re-election, makes democracy an inappropriate register and means to achieve any

---

[7] This section summarises the argument made in Christodoulidis (2017).

kind of equilibrium, let alone the delivery of efficient outcomes. Against the hubris of organising a society solely on the principle of need satisfaction, the rational response is to understand the individual (negative) rights as trumping social (positive) rights.

The response to the 'tragedy of the common' thesis has typically been to thin continuity between the rights to the point where compatibility is secured. In their much quoted and admired book *The Cost of Rights* (1999), Stephen Holmes and Cass Sunstein argued in favour of the *budgetary* continuity between categories of rights. The 'negative rights/positive rights distinction' turns out to 'be based on fundamental confusions', they argued, for 'all legally enforced rights are necessarily positive rights' (1999: 43). Every first generation civil/political right is exercised in the shadow of public enforcement: the right to vote requires a publicly funded polling station, the right to property must be protected by fire fighters and the police, contracts would be useless if creditors could not instigate a public judicial procedure against a defaulting debtor, etc. (1999: 53, 13, 48). In fact the 'opposition between "government" and "free markets" turns out to be largely spurious' (1999: 64). Finally, a budgetary perspective of rights undermines the notion that some rights are non-derogable, or 'absolutes', for if rights imply budgetary costs, then their enforcement engenders opportunity costs, and in a world of scarce resources a 'no-compromise attitude will therefore produce confusion and arbitrariness and may, on balance, disserve the very rights it intends to promote' (1999: 125). Clearly, for all its self-proclaimed honesty, good sense, and widely professed wisdom, this is a remarkably superficial argument. This 'budgetary' argument that establishes continuity by stringing together the shared *surface* characteristics of rights offers an argument for continuity-cum-elision. Where the difference of kind (of social rights vis-à-vis individual rights) is transfigured into a difference of degree, their *differentia specifica* – their eidetic specificity – collapsed, they are forced to blend seamlessly into the long postscript of the political, then social, accommodations of capitalism. And with this blending-in, the very thing that social rights name, *solidarity*, is supercoded to capitalist determinations and thereby cancelled out. To argue that both social and property rights are 'positive', 'institutional', 'costly' and 'social' is hardly controversial but certainly inattentive to the redistributive demand at the heart of the clash of their respective essential justifications. Unless an argument is offered that writes re-distributive demands into property relations, in the way, say, of deviationist doctrine or 'the commons', the 'social' nature of the property rights regime remains comfortably immune to the demands of solidarity.

A second, highly popular, statement of the continuity thesis explains it in terms of a *justiciable* constitutional guarantee to individuals of all rights across the three categories. The important point to take from this is that the recognition of social rights as individual actionable entitlements and as '*authentication*' of individual demands are at the same time forms of *blockage* of collective claims of distributive equality and societal needs satisfaction as a political-democratic question. Simply stated, social rights are *not* individual entitlements to societal resources, actionable in Courts. The commitment to solidarity and dignity, as informing the protection of health, housing, work, education, etc., is not to be, and should not be, cashed out as the State obligation to provide a diabetes sufferer with treatment (*Soobramoney* in 1997), a homeless person with a home (*Grootboom* in 2000) or the inhabitants of the Soweto with free water (*Mazibuko* in 2009). I refer to South African cases here for a reason: 'activist'/transformative constitutionalism has rarely been as insightfully developed as it was in the post-apartheid constitutional jurisprudence, that had to face up courageously to such dilemmas.[8] The Court struggled with what would have been an unworkable and unjust constitutional practice of allocating limited societal resources on a 'first-come, first-served' basis that would make a mockery of the political responsibility of government to all its citizens. While the proper limits of the reasonableness of judicial review waged for over a decade in both the courts and the academy, the constitutional consensus gradually emerged that 'it is impossible to give everyone access even to a "core" service immediately. All that is possible, and all that can be expected from the state, is that it act reasonably to provide access to socio-economic rights',[9] and within the available resources 'to achieve a progressive realisation' of social rights (Davis, 2008: 687). The question of judicial oversight of governmental action in the direction of meeting urgent social needs has been recommended, rightly, as a further constitutional commitment to the protection of social rights. That such political responsibility be directed to distributive justice and conform to the ideal of solidarity is what social rights constitutionalism demands, and of course there is an important place for justiciability in this; but that actionable individual rights is its proper *modus operandi* misconceives it as an individual entitlement, and miscasts continuity on the back of that misconception.[10]

---

[8] See Karl Klare's influential statement to this effect in (Klare, 1998: 146).
[9] *Minister of Health* v. *Treatment Action Campaign*, 2002 (5) SA 721 (CC) at para. 35.
[10] For Fernando Atria (2015), successes in securing the justiciability of social rights are nothing but toothless victories at best, at worst a sign of how their political leverage has been wasted, in his terms of how the 'political meaning of social rights properly so-called

In Chapter 3.4 below we will look at two further ways in which social rights have been integrated, as continuous to civil and political rights, into the logic of the reproduction of capital: the first is in reconceptualising social rights as 'capabilities'; the second is in incorporating them into 'proportionality'. But let us pre-empt and suggest at this point already that all four of these counter-proposals for the 'continuity' of rights involve a crucial surrender of the social constitution. They are surrendered, first, when they are strung alongside their more robust property- and civil-rights counterparts in an argument about budgetary continuity, especially in the face of the obvious realisation that such sovereignty has been handed over to creditors and markets; secondly, in the inflationary invocation of social rights as justiciable individual rights; thirdly, as harnessed to capabilities to facilitate 'market access' and enhance market participation; fourthly, as flattened out in the relentless weightings and calibrations of 'proportional' balancings. All four 'accommodationist' positions did indeed address the question of continuity *institutionally;* and it was at the institutional junctures that the understanding of continuity in fact hangs *and* falters, whether it be the continuity-as-commensurability of the 'budgetary continuity' argument, the toothless corrective of the *social* market, or the attribution of proportionate weightings. In all cases continuity is cast on a register where market allocations always-already skew distribution, where *re*-distribution comes too late, where the recuperation of what is owed to the producers of value is obscured and undercut.

Against the various problematic syntheses of rights, we ask what it might mean to allow *their contradictory articulation* to be played out in constitutional practice. The argument that follows is not an abandonment of Marshall's argument about continuity but its (improbable) restatement in the framework of fundamental antinomy. To hold on to continuity in the face of the contradictory articulation of categories of rights gives antinomy its epistemological significance.

Let us insist then on the fundamental, if controversial, premise that social rights are incongruous to capitalism and its particular structures of

---

has been defeated'. The contradiction that besets the category of rights replicates the contradiction between two competing logics of resource allocation: on the one hand on the basis of what is revealed as merit in the free play of market forces and on the other on the basis of social need or entitlement as conferred through democratic choices. This is a real contradiction between individual rights and social rights that cannot be sealed over or harmonised, but instead sustains their political potential (Atria, 2015: 605, 603).

opportunity and reward. Where the market does *all* the work of allocating value to resources amongst possible uses, the distribution of resources with the explicit aim to meet needs is, from the point of view of market thinking, *irrational*. This incongruity made the 'accommodations' problematic, incapable of managing the fault line between democracy and capitalism except by subsuming the former to the latter. What does it mean to insist on the incongruity, and to act on this assumed 'irrationality'? In essence, I suggest that if social rights are beset by the contradiction between capitalism and democracy, that we explore the significance of their constitutional iteration, as enunciated, that is, with constitutional force, and as unyielding to the various accommodations we explored above. With the urgent appeal not to displace the antinomic significance of social constitutionalism, we might begin to conceptualise how the insistent strategic use of social rights may import a real contradiction, the Hegelian/Marxist moment of the *Dasein der Widersprach*, from which the system cannot retract. To focus on antinomy is to pick up from Hegel, with Marx, not the drive to culmination and synthesis, but the self-undermining moment of contradiction, of thought hitting upon its limit *given* the categories available it. Let us look a little more gradually about what this means, and why antinomy matters.

*

When we discussed the 'forgetting of labour' in Chapter 1.3 we identified a 'deficit' along three registers: ethical, political and philosophical. The political deficit withdrew from labour its constitutive political demand; the philosophical deficit withdrew the possibility of its comprehension outside the logic of utility maximisation; the ethical deficit withdrew recognition. The deficit in each case points to a shortfall of the categories available to us to make sense of the processes of value production and social reproduction, the mismatch between the categories of thought and the modes of social being. Their emergence as contradictions marks the crisis-points of articulation, of expressibility and of intelligibility. Examples abound: where it *is made to appear* that there is no other rational way to organise the economy than through markets, political-democratic alternatives are eclipsed as a matter of 'reason'. Necessity takes the form of the 'unaffordability' of social protection, antinomic because it occurs in the midst of a general increase in resources that derives from expanded capitalist reproduction. The antinomy *appears* in the life of those who toil to generate value for the market, is experienced as the injury of massive job insecurity and stagnant wages, and can emerge as the injustice of the withdrawal of recognition. In each case, then, the critical task is to discern in the situation the antinomy that might acquire hermeneutic traction, be signified as injustice, and acted on as such. It is here that the constitutional contradictory iteration of social rights constitutionalism with market thinking, propelled by the former's unwavering insistence on solidarity, may provide the leverage.

At none of the junctures on which the withdrawal of meaning occurs is a communicative-'agonistic' stance capable of redressing the usurpation of value or the withdrawal of speaking position. Recognition, dignity, solidarity can only be interpreted as *antagonistic* to the given economies of representation, the recognition orders, the given distributions of contingency and necessity, what Rancière with such insight called the '*partage du sensible*'. The antinomic here, expressed by Rancière as 'dissensus' elevates contradiction as condition of staging of political subjectivities, where the collective is not thought of in terms of identification but of enactment. We can transfer this insight of Rancière's to radicalise Marshall's, in the only way that does justice to his argument about continuity, one that could not have foreseen at the time the paradigm change brought about by the totalising ideology of the market. If Marshall argued for the continuity of generations of rights as a means to overcome the injuries of class, it is because the form of continuity that culminates in social rights can be read back across the preceding generations to disturb received distributions. This would be effected *by means* of political rights. With respect to the dialectical unfolding of rights, each successive generation promises a moment of transcendence of its predecessor. There is a clear message in Marshall *against* the priority of market allocations and *for* a synthesis that projects back along the path of its culmination a different logic of distribution: these are the points along the path where the sequential turns *transversal*. As we proceed to radicalise Marshall we appreciate the role that the 'dogmatic question' plays in holding fast to the semantic resources that inform each stage in the transition from civil to political, then to social rights in terms of which the succession is also a culmination that strains towards the promise that citizenship holds, holds in the modality of the dogmatic, and therefore as irreducible to successive manifestations. It is a promise that only transcendence (of class) through the contradictory articulation of rights might deliver. For the radicalised Marshall continuity is understood as antinomic or not at all.

A useful practical example might be provided by the right to strike. In the cases *Laval* and *Viking* (that we will discuss at length in Chapter 3.4), the social right of Scandinavian workers to act to protect the significant achievements of decades of social and labour protection was deemed disproportionate vis-à-vis the economic rights of entrepreneurs to move their capital and hired labour around, in a classic case of the race to the bottom. Emboldened, perhaps, by this new constitutional mindset of the CJEU, the 'employers' group' at the ILO - in a move that created a protracted deadlock particularly conducive to the interests of capital – challenged the settled interpretation of Convention 87 and decades-long jurisprudence that the constitutional protection of the freedom of association *extends* to the right to strike.[11] Note how clearly the collectivist and individualist paradigms diverge here to fall on either side of this dispute. Understood as a *political right*, freedom of association enjoins democratic and collective categories and is therefore inseparable from the right to strike as the collective-democratic expression of its exercise. Furthermore as a *social right* it carries the ideal of solidarity into the picture. But as an *individual right,* freedom of association attaches to the individual's right to – or not to – associate, and is in fact inimical to collective democratic expression and, ultimately, to the extent that it may undercut collective agreements and trade unionism, a clear move to 'de-socialise' freedom of association. Pooling the rights and their interpretations here achieves nothing except an insidious commensuration, and the right, as a social right, needs to be understood and exercised, *against* market-driven harmonious and proportionate realignments, in its *contradictory* articulation to individualism.

As we will discuss at length in Part III, a series of political, and therefore reversible, decisions have constructed, buttressed and underwritten the collapse of the constitutional imaginary into its market form. There has been nothing necessary about this construction or its protection; in fact it marks the increasingly desperate attempts to protect the market even from itself.[12] The result has been an insidious constitutionalisation of soft instruments, a creeping, rushed and unsystematic campaign to shore up monetary union that receives the aegis of the constitutional, backed by the noxious exercise of proportionality as optimisation according to market metrics. The suggestion for an antinomic constitutionalism, that will be more fully developed in Part IV,

---

[11] See Novitz (2003) and La Hovary (2013).

[12] What, one might ask, *from the market perspective,* allows one to draw the line, in the way that Mario Draghi drew it, between *usual and unusual market turbulence* that licenses the ECB's highly selective and arbitrary decisions over the grant of liquidity?

invites us to insert 'social rights' in the gap between normative language and social experience, to enable the hermeneutic traction I suggested earlier, to provide a measure against which suffering is experienced not as necessary, but as a wrong. The suggestion is, in other words, to import constitutional contradiction and to act on it.

Semantics and Structures II

An important discussion in analytical philosophy over the *normativity of concepts* offers a semiotic route, and significant insight, into the suggestion to invoke and act on constitutional contradiction. The discussion takes its cue from an older debate in analytical jurisprudence over rule-defeasibility and semantic scope. Hart asked famously, what does it mean for legal concepts to have 'open texture'? His distinction between the 'core of certainty' and the 'penumbra of doubt' introduced, ever so reluctantly, into jurisprudence something of the pragmatic dimension of language against the dominant assumption that the proper use of terms could be settled on *criterial grounds*, on the basis, that is, of the identification of the necessary and sufficient conditions for the proper deployment of legal concepts. Against such formal closure, Hart argued for the 'relative indeterminacy' of the meaning of legal concepts and of the defeasibility of rules. Moving freely between the two – the first captured under 'open texture' proper, the second under relative ignorance of fact and relative indeterminacy of aim – Hart offered us a contestation of the closure of legal meaning on the basis of meta-criteria, introduced Wittgenstein's challenge into legal thought, and thereby awakened jurisprudence *from* its 'noble dream' of formalism *to* the pragmatics of linguistic usage.

This is all familiar territory in analytical jurisprudence, endlessly rehearsed, refined, footnoted. A particularly interesting aspect of the discussion over the normativity of concepts carries, in turn, a challenge to Hart's earlier challenge. Drawing insights variably from the writings of those who have followed in Wittgenstein's footsteps, mainly McDowell, Kripke and Putnam, it re-opens the question of what it means to follow a rule as a question of semantics, or rather of the semantic extension of legal concepts contained in a rule. *Against* Hart now, it is argued that to think of a rule as applicable across the range of its ordinary coverage, but defeated in the exceptional cases where a 'penumbra of doubt' spreads over new 'facts' (not automatically subsumable under the old categories), or where the 'indeterminacy of aim' of law calls for a *judgement* over defeasibility, conflates the issues. Because it leaves Hart working with the assumptions of the 'criterial' thinking he has jettisoned: the rule applying automatically (without judgement) in easy cases that fall straightforwardly within the extension of its terms, and in hard cases, most obviously when there is 'indeterminacy of aim', only there inviting judgement, that is external to the semantic extension of the rule. A useful way to cut through the confusion is to focus on the semantic question alone, of what is the proper extension of the concept deployed by the rule. And this designation is an interpretative question that turns, as McDowell notes, on what counts as a proper criterion for a correct designation. However we answer that question, its focus is clearly on an expanded notion of semantic disagreement, the disagreement in other words over the legal concepts' proper extension. And here there can be no *a priori* criteria that will fix the semantic range across which a legal signifier might be floated, none that might insulate the term from normative disagreement over its meaning. Is it correct to designate capital punishment as *cruel*? Does the freedom of *association* extend to industrial action? Do the managerial practices deployed by Amazon in its warehouses amount to a violation of *dignity*? Does women's domestic labour fall under the concept of *work* for purposes of social protection? These are cases of semantic disagreement – over what cruelty, association, dignity and work *mean* – and the answer is not given by recalling a set of criteria of proper use or, with Hart, making some *prima facie* decision over what falls on either side of the core/penumbra distinction that will decide the defeasibility of the rule. Instead the contest is over the semantic extension of the rule's linguistic terms, and what the contest calls forth is *semantic judgement*, one that engages the interpreter normatively in the exercise of identifying the meaning of the concepts' reference. The focus shifts away from the rules and turns to the concepts. Justification is called for regarding the applicability of a concept (and only indirectly the defeasibility of a rule). The question now becomes: what might be understood as the exemplary (or paradigmatic) instantiation of the concept, and what might count as adequately similar to fall within its range? – one and the same questions inviting judgement over the meaning of the term and the applicability of the rule that deploys it. In the words of one of the more eloquent exponents of this position: different views of what it means for something to be 'x' stand in substantive *and* semantic disagreement (Stavropoulos, 1996). The suggestion that concepts are normative is fully endorsed. Against a view that normative contestation is possible only by virtue of concepts that have been deployed on criterial grounds, with Brandom, Kripke and others, normative contestation is moved one step back, into the meaning of concepts involving *judgement* over the appropriateness of their deployment.

This is not to heed to Fredric Jameson's (playful) invitation 'to rethink everything through once again in terms of linguistics!';[13] nor is it to treat semantic disagreement in the way that analytic philosophy draws reason and language together to do it, in isolation from the material contexts in which it plays out. But the analytical discussion gives us an important handle on this *semantic surplus* that accommodates contestation over proper designation, with no meta-criterion available to settle it on criterial ('necessary and sufficient') grounds. It is a short step from there to theorising how contradiction grafts itself onto these constitutional semantics, accommodated in the 'surcharge', harboured in disagreement over the extension of the constitutional terms, introducing a contested signification that works all the way down (an essential contestability,[14] if you like, writ large). That this expanded semantics opens out to dialogical and democratic uses, to inform a politics of interpretation is incontrovertible, even if it is far from the agendas of most of the participants in the debate we visited. What accounts for the settledness of legal meaning given that there are no longer rules that fix semantic designation in watertight ways? 'Surplus' strains against such settledness, as it does against the very ordinary inertia that largely contains and circumscribes the semantic reach of legal concepts through the operation of selection and condensation, the systemic features of law that we have used the term 'redundancy' to denote. Legal concepts are 'specifications' that circulate within a relatively stable 'context of usages' and 'make precise what is problematic in the *quaestio juris*'. They are 'self-descriptions' in Teubner's sense that make possible the mobilisation of specific and largely self-reinforcing connections within the systemic parameters of law. We have seen how the reduction achievement that is constitutional semantics operates (in Chapter 2.2) as re-iterations that consolidate the semantic extension of legal terms, so we do not need to repeat that here. This limited range *nonetheless* avails a context in which antagonism *can* inscribe itself as constitutional contradiction. The dynamic of this inscription?: the context of redundancy on the one hand, the semantic surplus on the other. Despite the forces of inertia that

---

[13] Jameson, *The Prison House of Language* (1972) quoted in Eagleton (2020: 142).
[14] On 'essentially contested concepts', see Gallie (1955). My own argument here is not that all constitutional terms are essentially contested, but that it is in their nature as signifiers that they could be.

stabilise and entrench semantic designations, the interpretative question of what counts as a concept's proper designation cannot be fixed through any set of formal descriptors and cannot be foreclosed. If this opens out to the possibility of a politics of interpretation it is *not* because suddenly everything is up for grabs, but because *what is* (up for grabs) is an interpretative question over the proper or exemplary extension of a concept. As far as a *critical* viewpoint is concerned, first a normativity carried in the question over point or purpose 'infects' description, and therefore what is critical grafts itself across the divide between ought and is, as we have insisted all along. Secondly, it allows for a politics of interpretation that by exploiting contradiction might find its purchase in an expanded semantics. Of course, from a legal point of view, contradictions would be seen as anomalies to be ironed over, whether in the name of coherence, integrity, predictability, or the stability of expectations. But a semantic surplus accommodates them as meaningful even as they are transient, as sites of contestation over what needs to be seen as exemplary. We insist on those apertures, suspended as they are over the evolving constitutional imaginary, in the full ambiguity of the term 'suspended', of being both held and withheld.

2.4

Constitutionalism Adrift

Constitutionalisation and Pluralism

Buoyed by the move to the transnational level, largely released from its confinement in the State form, constitutionalism has in the last couple of decades come unmoored from its traditional settings to become something of a floating signifier on the transnational scale. The nautical metaphor[1] is not altogether unconnected to the flows of capital. The new semiosis of the constitutional involves a productive coupling of two terms, constitutionalisation and pluralism, in a series of articulations that have been largely successful in overhauling the constitutional debate in its totality. In that context, constitutionalisation, a concept bereft of a referent, has been for reasons of its under-determination productively coupled with the concept of *constitutional pluralism*. My interest in this chapter is with *constitutionalisation* as a process of 'becoming-constitutional', the conditions of that process, the criteria of ascription of constitutionality and its constitutive articulation with *constitutional pluralism*.

The European constitutional project is paradigmatic in this respect: crisis-prone, reeling from social to democratic deficit and back, driven by a vision (if we can call it that) of economic integration without economic solidarity, it appears to have been improbably successful in fashioning itself as a *constitutional* settlement *a posteriori*. The name it gives the process of 'settling' is *constitutionalisation*. The name it gives to the radical disagreements that beset it is *pluralism*, a compensatory term[2] for the enfeeblement of democracy at the European level. But if 'constitutionalisation' and

---

[1] Supiot had once suggested the idea of the 'ancre flottante', a device whose function is not to hold in place but to control and contain the drift (Supiot, 1990: 491). But in a field of moving significations even that assumption may be asking too much.

[2] The term 'compensatory constitutionalism' has been used by Peters (2006), though my argument has no truck with hers.

'constitutional pluralism' are the answers variously provided, what is the question that they are the answer *to*? In Chapter 2.2 we identified three dimensions of constitutional meaning: in the *social* dimension the question is over the subject that the constitution names; in the *temporal* dimension the question is over the constitution's ability to recruit the past in its expectation-binding operation for the future; in the *material* dimension the question is over the threshold of *unity* that promises to gather the legal order as a meaningful whole. These are threshold requirements for ascribing constitutional meaning. And yet, in the current situation in Europe they too appear unsettled, and subject to a number of extraordinary developments in all three dimensions. In the absence of a collective, democratic subject to drive it, the *a posteriori* dynamic ascribes subjecthood to a European demos *as configured* through the process, messianic in promise,³ and possessing the characteristics *imputed back* to it. Thus, in the social dimension, *because* no constitutional subject can be ascribed as locus and agent of constituent power, the subject is fashioned out of the process itself, in a kind of backward projection. In the temporal dimension, one encounters no framing function, and, startlingly now, no actual need for one: just a gradual solidification of what the process produces, constitutionalisation as sedimentation. In the material dimension, finally, one encounters an incremental process of capital accumulation and a submission of social protection to the logic of competition, increasingly, in the current more ruthless phase of its acceleration, in terms of the competitive alignment of national systems of labour protection. As far as our current discussion of concept-formation is concerned, this fragmentation, this *denial* of unity, is graced with the name of legal pluralism; and as productive to the logic of the integration of capital that the EU now seems incapable of reining in, let alone reversing, the integration it propels forward is graced with the name of 'constitutionalisation'.

---

³ In capturing that 'messianic' logic undergirds constitutionalisation and guarantees the 'success' of the process of the advent of a European Constitution as built into the process, Joseph Weiler was perhaps more prophetic than he realised when he wrote, in a book that defined the academic debate for a decade, that what emerged from the Treaty of Rome in the 1950s was already 'a constitutional legal order the constitutional theory of which has not been worked out, its long-term, transcendent values not sufficiently elaborated ... [It was] the beginning of the first truly Europe-wide constitutional "hearkening" of an act to which the peoples of Europe and its member states had already said, in one way or another, "we will do"' (Weiler, 1999: 8).

We will return to focus specifically on Europe later, in Chapter 3.3. With our sights now on 'transnational' constitutional theory in general, its inability to draw *any* useful distinction between 'juridification' and 'constitutionalisation' is instructive in this context. The first problem is that since constitutionalisation is seen (and can only be seen) *as reactive*, the notion of something being constitutional *via* a *framing function* becomes nonsense. In our previous discussion on the formal aspects of constitutionality (in Chapter 2.2) we had conceptualised constitutionality in a way that grants it a certain 're-iterability' through self-descriptions, and a structured complexity all of its own. This is sacrificed in the shift we are tracking.

We will explore the dimensions of constitutional meaning in the new dispensation. In the course of this analysis we will see how 'constitutional pluralism' and 'constitutionalisation' become mutually enabling, and conjoined in supra-state formations. A radical rethinking of the relation between constitutional semantic and constitutional structure is effected in the process. We will explore the meaning and the effects of these various forms of enablement, as well as the new form of legitimation they invoke. The possibility of holding on to a concept of the political will, of a theory of justice, even of normativity, becomes increasingly tenuous in the new dispensation, with legitimation migrating accordingly to link with output and growth. We will end up with a tentative account of what success means in the context of this creeping constitutionalism that paves the way nicely for its market co-option, less in the sense of historical, and more of logical preconditions.

We begin with *constitutionalisation*, the constitutional curiosity that is the incremental, fragmentary process of *becoming-constitutional*. In our previous discussion of political constitutionalism we identified the key constitutional function in the temporal dimension of expectation-binding for the future, as definitional element of normativity. There the term 'constitutional' connotes *a framing function*, which *pre*-selects what is to be recognised as valid and what can be contested legally. Extended to the material dimension, the same framing function is expressed as unity, again the *pre*-selection of instances that conform to higher principles as a matter of content, typically as instantiation – rather than negation – of value, with contradictory instantiations deemed void, struck down or referred back to legislatures. The notion of 'systematicity' straddles both dimensions – temporal and substantive – of political constitutionalism in the above sense.

Against that background, what does it mean to talk of constitutionalisation as ongoing process? If constitutionalism traditionally denotes a certain articulation of the political and the legal, the legal sanction of the democratic will, where might one look now for that normative achievement? In an important contribution, Martin Loughlin identifies 'constitutionalism' as the term used for the attempt 'to subject the exercise of all types of public power, whatever the medium of its exercise, to the discipline of constitutional procedures and norms' (Loughlin, 2010: 47). If we concede the weakening or collapse of political opportunities of framing, does constitutionalisation not appear question-begging on two important fronts, significant because constitutive of the constitutional in two directions, externally with politics, internally in law? The first involves the articulation, or coupling, of the legal and the political; what appears question-begging about the coupling is that the *political will* is not given expression except, as we said, *a posteriori*, and as conceptualised *post festum* it could not have willed at all. The second involves the fundamental question of what gives law its systematicity; in this context it is an oxymoron to talk of the function of framing as taking place *a posteriori*. It is the last point that links directly to the second of our terms, *constitutional pluralism*.

To call a constitutional order *plural* is, at least *prima facie*, contradictory. As Thornhill puts it, 'the constitution is *the point of final normative regress* in the system' (see 2012b). Such regress is what systematicity requires, and systematicity is the distinctive feature of the legal order, or at least it was for the vast range of legal formalisms, that defined law through its systematicity and thus, with the same move, against 'plurality'.[4] Against the intransigence of older formalisms, the constitutional question has now been 'answered' in large outwith such attempts to think it through in terms of the concept of law itself. The storming of traditional 'unitary' constitutional imaginaries by constitutional pluralism suggested removing the old fixities, and led to a renegotiation of constituencies, competencies, operative levels and structures. The notion of a constitutional project-in-the-making was greatly facilitated by the notion

---

[4] It is perhaps indicative that the first round of agonising over the difficulties of sustaining such gathering orders at the transnational level came from legal theorists versed in these traditions. Neil MacCormick famously confronted the question over overlapping and non-hierarchical legal systems in his 'Beyond the Sovereign State' (1993) and some years later 'solved' it by accommodating whatever plurality he could in the notion of a 'commonwealth' (1999), which entailed a pluralism of sorts.

of constitutionalisation as ongoing, at which point the coupling becomes mutually productive: pluralism gains its point of purchase in constitutionalisation that imports a certain openness to the future, and constitutionalisation gains its justification from its ability to accommodate the plural. The becoming-constitutional comes to dominate the new space and imaginary.

There are three forms that constitutional pluralism typically assumes, and the coupling with 'constitutionalisation' is significant in all three. The *first* form assumes a pluralisation of *levels*; and it comes in the production of 'decisively non-holistic forms of constitutionalism', as Neil Walker puts it, in which constitutional norms are produced at varying levels. The paradigmatic case is 'multi-level constitutionalism', but also here find their niche the 'open method of coordination' and other forms of 'soft' law whose *hardening as constitutional* installs itself at crucial junctures of the market system to produce, as we shall see, the 'flexible rigidities'[5] of market constitutionalism. The *second* form involves the pluralisation of constitutional *registers* at the transnational level as pertaining to different functional spheres of transnational exchange and interaction; as a result we have constitutionalisms of the 'economic', 'political', 'legal', 'social', 'security', etc., varieties.[6] The division of labour is 'functional' in the sense that in each case the *sectoral* constitution is constitutively oriented to meeting the exigencies of the regulation at the transnational level of the economy, the lifeworld, politics, or security, whatever the field. In that sense the proliferation of constitutional registers involves the separation off of the 'economic Constitution' and the 'social Constitution' from the 'political Constitution'. The *third* form comes in the varieties of *societal constitutionalism* which in many ways is a radicalisation of the above process of the differentiation of sectoral constitutionalisms. Except that the 'significant other' for the 'societal constitutionalism' variety is the national state, so its inaugurating move involves the severing off of the 'constitutional' from the 'statal' and its return in capillary form as appropriate to the logic of social fields.

---

[5] The term is borrowed from Hyman (2006b).
[6] See Tuori (2010) and Tuori & Tuori (2014) for significant formulations. As far as Europe is concerned, it finds pertinent expression in the Lisbon agenda, where the initial commitment to 'competitiveness, social cohesion and sustainability' of the European social model has now given way to the subsumption of the latter two terms to the former, with labour migration issues also increasingly framed in terms of competitiveness (Chapter 3.4 below).

Positioned as challenges to monism and the notion of unity, pluralisms must negotiate a difficult boundary. Accounts of pluralism that stretch the containment of plurality beyond breaking point of what the system can accommodate as variety, cease to be plural orders and give way to entropy. Alongside the proliferation of pluralisms that in their impressive range stretch the 'monist', or at least centripetal assumptions of constitutionalism, there are the runaway pluralisms, the varieties of 'constitutionalism from below', though to the extent that they involve *institutional* experimentation they are different in kind to those that resist the institutional achievement *tout court*.[7] However labile the forms there must be some solidity left to the predication, if what is plural is to pivot on what is constitutional. We will not explore these many pluralisms at any length. We will come across a number of them again when we move later to 'experimental governance', but the ambition is not to provide anything like an overview or mapping of the panegyric endorsements of pluralism, nor to point out the conceptual difficulties that attend its definition. Instead our concern remains with whether we are able (and under what conditions we are able) to hold on to the signifier 'constitutional' in the new dispensation. Further, to hold on to the normativity that attaches to 'political constitutionalism' and explore whether it might carry to the transnational level. In the way we have developed its meaning, it was the asymmetry between the constituent and the constituted that yielded constitutional meaning. The risk which constitutional pluralisms assume, and sometimes explicitly endorse, in effect decouples the constituent from the constituted and undoes the achievement that is political constitutionalism. We will be concerned exclusively with theoretical attempts to hold on to the notion of the constitutional in its normative import against its collapse into cognitive adjustment, and the celebration of the 'energies' that collapse supposedly releases.

*

---

[7] See Falk (1999) addressing the role played by social movements in constructing an alternative vision of globalisation to neo-liberalism, which has now generated an extensive literature across a range of disciplines. From a constitutional perspective de Sousa Santos (2015) and others have sought to ground in constitutionalism from below 'grassroots resistance to neoliberal institutions and initiatives for alternative legal forms'. See also Gill (2003).

As far as the constitutional debate in Europe was concerned, an important early theoretical encounter with pluralism was Ingolf Pernice's concept of *Verfassungsverbund*, introduced in the mid-1990s in the wake of the German *Maastricht* decision, to capture in the idea of a 'composite constitution' the novelty of Europe's experiment of multi-level constitutionalism. In his careful account, Neil Walker offers a subtle terminological clarification: 'Where the more usual term *Staatenverband* refers to a compound of states, *Verfassungsverbund* seeks to capture the same sense of a composite arrangement, but one whose genetic code is constitutional rather than statal' (2011: 144). The 'deeper message' of this shift for Walker, 'is that once "constitution" rather than "state" is understood to be the governing regulatory category', pluralism's vicious circle turns virtuous. The problem, that states are seen as the form that structures the collective normative order in an exclusive and exclusionary way, now, with the shift to the interaction amongst constitutions, gives way to a productive tension. 'The fuzziness of boundaries' becomes the space where are negotiated the 'establishing, organizing, sharing and limiting [of] powers' (ibid.) and multi-level constitutionalism becomes the name of what accommodates continuity and complementarity of the exercise of public authority in Europe. Circumventing the agonising attempts to square legality, sovereignty and the European experiment, we can now comprehend 'sovereignty as pooled' 'so that at the level both of cultural identity and of institutional function and loyalty the relation between the state and the supranational platforms are not to be regarded in either/or, zero-sum, terms, but rather as an interlocking, overlapping and positive-sum whole' (2011: 145).

If constitutionalism had involved – constitutively – an articulation between law and politics, (constitutional) reason and (democratic) will, the normative hierarchy of the legal system and the 'heterarchy' of the political process, then multi-level constitutionalism, having abandoned any constitutive orientation to the democratic and the constituent, gains whatever leverage it does from the 'fuzziness' of boundaries, the 'renegotiation' that the multi-level invites under the universalising sign of the constitutional (rather than the statal). In the process what is installed is a constitutionalism without democracy, where 're-negotiation' substitutes for democracy and where constitutionalism is propped up on the back of that substitution. It is indicative in this respect that a decade and a half later, Pernice insisted that *irrespective of the failure of the* 'constitutional treaty' of Lisbon to receive democratic endorsement, his 'composite' constitutional arrangement be nevertheless understood as an instance of multi-level constitutionalism.[8] What does it mean for constitutionalism to extend its reach precisely in order to compensate for the loss of democratic leverage? With this we come to one of the ways in which the achievement of political constitutionalism gradually becomes eroded and undone at the supra-state level. We see it reflected in the very justificatory base of constitutional pluralism: where constitutionalism is the achievement of a certain coupling of law and democracy involving the asymmetrical coupling of the constituted with the constituent, the 'pluralism' of constitutional pluralism provides a functional equivalent in the absence of democracy and of constituent power.

Neil Walker's important contribution to this debate revolves around the theorisation of constitutional pluralism as a decoupling of constitutionalism from the order and imaginary of the Nation-state. In an important article that was to become a key point of reference for 'constitutional pluralism', he says:

> A rehabilitated language of constitutionalism would meet these challenges through a version of constitutional pluralism. Constitutional pluralism recognises that in the post-Westphalian world there exists a range of different constitutional sites and processes configured in a heterarchical rather than a hierarchical pattern, and seeks to develop a number of empirical indices and normative criteria which allow us to understand this emerging configuration and assess the legitimacy of its development.
>
> (2002: 317)

Conceptually, as argued by Walker, in order to capture the full range of the 'constitutional experience' and imagine the full range of constitutional possibilities within the new plural order, *constitutionalism and constitutionalisation* should be conceived of not in black-and-white, all-or-nothing terms but as questions of nuance and gradation. There is no unitary template in terms of which constitutional status is either achieved or not achieved, but rather it is approximated in terms of a set of loosely and variously coupled factors, which serve both as *criteria* in terms of which forms of constitutionalism can be distinguished and as *indices* in terms of which modes and degrees of constitutionalisation can be identified and measured (2002: 339–40). And with reference to the question of

---

[8] Pernice further urged 'a more pragmatic approach, a purely technocratic improvement of the primary role of the EU by simply amending the existing founding treaties' as the 'European way of salvaging the Constitution of Europe.' (Quoted in Ming-Sung Kuo, 2009: 581.) See also Walker (2015) and Berman (2012) for significant contributions.

constitutional definition, nearly a decade later, he says '[i]n the final analysis, if one is to overcome this opposition one must look beyond the reductive commitments ... of even the most thoughtful of the state-centred and multi-level positions. It must be asked whether something more general is at issue that is capable of being acknowledged ..., and which can therefore serve as a common point from which to investigate their differences' (2011: 152).

Walker approaches the question 'in functional terms' (152). No 'common point' can be retrieved unless the main difference between the positions can be cast as a difference between 'conceptions of the *constitutional means* necessary to *ends*'. For any position to qualify as constitutional it has to align itself to that relationship between means and ends, and offer an adequate answer to how competing means might realise given ends. It must couch itself in that (means-ends) functionality, or rule itself irrelevant against the (meta-constitutional) register of what can be understood as properly constitutional. With this move both the meta-question of what is properly constitutional is installed through function, and constitutional pluralism finds expression *in and as* the split perspective. Constitutionalism is installed at the level of the *concept* whose *conceptions* give expression to plurality. The perspective is constitutional because it is fixed on the constitutional function ('what means will realise the end?') and, as split, it is accommodating of plurality. Key to all this is to identify the relevant *end* as beyond question, or *as beyond constitutional question*, let us say, since what subtends constitutional reflection cannot at the same time be put to question by it. And Walker here commits to a *political* concept. 'Constitutionalism serves a deep and abiding function in human affairs, namely the meta-political function of shaping the domain of politics broadly conceived' – of literally 'constituting the body politic' (2011: 152). At stake in constitutional reflection is the *'common interest'*, object of collective decision-making and measure of its correctness, and, as under-determined, the common interest imports an 'open, indeed a reflexive quality'. It allows no *a priori* stipulation of appropriate level, relevant constituency, correct balance between 'collective and individual goods or preferences'. Conceived as 'the ultimate end of the constitutional project', 'common interest' allows the project sufficient grounding in respect of the proper function of *constitutional* engagement and sufficient contestability to allow for constitutional *pluralism* at the level of determinations. Because, Walker says revealingly, 'one *cannot stipulate in advance* or treat as permanently resolved what are the appropriate sites for the pursuit of the common interest, or what are the appropriate terms of engagement between these sites' (2011: 152, my emphasis). His suggestion is to fix the function of constitutionalism, to preserve it as 'placeholder', and to orient plurality *to* it. In order to help the constitutional ideal along its migration away from the state as 'jurisdictional container of the common interest', Walker invites us to shift *from* framing *to* function as a more adequate criterion of the meaning of the constitution, and to tie that function to the pursuit of the 'common interest as the ultimate end of the constitutional project' (2011: 152), at least 'in matters concerning the organisation and regulation of collective decision-making' (2011: 160). That pursuit cannot be pre-figured or contained in one exclusive site; the reflexive question of what serves it best is the constitutional question par excellence. The reflexive question is installed at the level of concept and it is unfolded in contested practice in terms of its conceptions.

Democracy is no longer definitive of constitutional function; the constituent retreats to be replaced by 'reflexivity' as oriented to the 'common interest'. Now the unity of the constitutional project is cast and held together by function. The constitution, as concept, remains under-determined in order to span all its instantiations, but determined *enough to* orient all conceptions of the constitution to the necessary and sufficient function of the pursuit of the 'common interest', maybe even the 'common good', harbouring diversity and allowing constitutional practice both to remain the same – as concept – and be contested – as conception.[9] But note now how, with the turn to function, a certain slippage becomes manifest. It is clear that the function that Walker sees as constitutive of the constitutional is not the usual function of *framing* the political process, the jurisdictional containment, the expectation-binding for the future. To the extent that these bindings cut away at the reflexivity

---

[9] This is distinctly different an approach to the relation between concept and conception to that provided by Wittgenstein's concept of '*family resemblances*'. The introduction of the latter allows a certain loosening of the hold of the 'concept' over the 'conceptions', or the general category over its concretisations, since it is no longer the case that the former ('concept') sets the necessary and sufficient conditions that need to obtain for the inclusion of the latter ('conceptions') under its ambit. For an analysis of Wittgenstein's notion, see Mulhall (2001). With 'family resemblances' no set of features need to be shared by all instances: instead 'overlapping resemblances pass from one case to another via intermediate cases' (Mulhall, 2001: 84). The notion relies on there being a significant overlap between cases where the criteria of what can be deemed significant need not meet any closed list of conditions.

appropriate to the realisation of *the common good* across spaces, sites and configurations of the collective, they can only be conceived as unnecessarily restrictive of constitutional reflexivity and constitutional function. But here lies the fatal equivocation of the 'placeholder' function, that it throws the process open to *functional equivalence*. As set *against* the reductive logic of political constitutionalism with its unquestioned framing assumptions, the openness of constitutional pluralism *with only function to define it* leaves it wide open for the market to assume the function. Market constitutionalism offers to perform the same function of 'determining the common interest' with the tried and tested instrument of *price*. Which is to say that *for a normative theory of constitutionalism the problem with the reliance on functional definitions is that they invite functional equivalents*. Where constitutional pluralism leaves the constitutional constitutively pinned to function alone, the co-option proceeds with a speed and a magnitude that is astounding, as we will discuss in the next part (Chapter 3.2) when we look at how market capture moves from the economic, to the democratic and then to the epistemological level. But we can give one example already of how easily functional concepts travel the stretches of equivalence, even before we come in the next chapter to Hayek, and to his lesser acolytes.

The example comes from systems theory. Drawing on Teubner's influential defence of legal pluralism in 'the global Bukowina', Alberto Febbrajo offers an analysis of 'instruments of inter-systemic regulation', instruments, that is, that manage relationships *between* systems by balancing external expectations and internal operations of variation, selection and stabilisation. Febbrajo identifies three 'instruments'. The first of these is the 'Constitution', and here he echoes Luhmann's familiar analysis of the Constitution as site of the structural coupling of the legal and political systems; the second is the Market as the 'instrument' that couples law and the economy. Democracy is the third instrument, and for it Febbrajo reserves the rather grander function of coupling the legal system (proper) to 'external legal cultures'.[10] It functions, he says, not just to produce consensus but also to sustain a variety pool for innovation in law.

Febbrajo's key question is this: given these intersystemic connections, what happens when the 'regulative control exercised by law and politics

---

[10] Not that 'culture' was ever one of Luhmann's preferred terms; for Luhmann, 'culture was one of the worst concepts ever created' (quoted in Stäheli, 1997: 127).

on economics through the instruments of intersystemic regulation becomes unsustainable or impossible because of the reduced role of the state and the absence of credible alternatives?' (2011: 290). And his diagnosis: 'The present crisis of legal regulations could be seen as the result of the weakening, not only of the state and of its role in society, but also of the circular malfunctioning of its [sic] three instruments of intersystemic regulation: constitution, market and economy. These instruments, no longer supported by credible state semantics, ... could reinforce, instead of reducing, the reasons for their own failures' (293). Giving a further spin to the idea of 'soft' law, Febbrajo talks of the emergence of a 'sort of "liquid" constitution, destined to be constantly re-shaped by the current cultural factors and explicitly based on a kind of "multilateral compromise" which is not able to define higher level of values in order to stabilise the frequent variations of the lower values' (294). Febbrajo describes this flight as *a new kind of constitutional pluralism* that confers 'a minimum of constitutional stability to a confused and contradictory reality' (294).

We can draw some interesting conclusions from Febbrajo's analysis, an analysis that has been variably replicated along similar lines across a significant range of sociological functionalism, complexity theory, and crucially also, as we shall see, the theory of global governance. The coupling of the constitution *with* democracy and *with* the market (as definitive of performance and reflexivity) gives way to a new functional distribution between variation, selection, re-stabilisation; and this substitution invokes an evolutionary thinking in which normativity has no place. If, for Febbrajo, the market comes to the centre of the 'intersystemic regulation' it is because it is the market that 'constantly selects forms of behaviour and decisions through the autonomously-changeable determination of prices and, thanks to its recursive closure it does not destroy for the future the choices that it has excluded' (289). In a revealing division of labour amongst the three 'instruments' (market, democracy, constitution) the all-important function of *selection* is thus reserved for the market and the logic of price, that of variation for democracy – remember its function is to sustain 'a variety pool for innovation' – and that of stabilisation, unsurprisingly perhaps given that the function of law is to stabilise expectations, for the constitution. Look at how the logic of *functional equivalence* has, in the process, seamlessly set in: regulation can be performed by any of the instruments interchangeably. And once functional equivalence between constitution and market has been established, given the increase in external complexity, it is the market to which selection can be entrusted to send self-correcting messages and convey information. The constitution enters the picture only to stabilise those selections, as an afterthought providing sanction for those distributions;[11] while additional levels of cognitive self-reflection are called for on its part, which inevitably means it tempering its normativity and leads to a pressure to learn from markets. This is the main argument developed in Part III of the book. Here we simply catch a first glimpse of how a concept of constitutional pluralism that is constitutively tied to function, offers itself up to equivalence with the market. Released from the 'no longer credible' semantics of the state, how readily the semantics of constitutionalism are floated in signifiers without referents, cut adrift in order that they may attach themselves to shifting correlations of global processes of market integration.

*

'Globalization' says Teubner, 'above all means that functional differentiation, first realized historically within the nation states of Europe and North Africa, now encompasses the whole world.'[12] Teubner will concede an asymmetry to this uploading of differentiation to the global level: 'Certainly not all subsystems have globalized simultaneously, with the same speed and intensity. Religion, science and the economy are well established as global systems, while politics and law still remain mainly focused on the nation state' (Teubner, 2012: 42). As a result, 'the staggered nature of globalization produces a tension between the self-foundation of autonomous global social systems and their political-legal constitutionalization' (43). In the old dispensation, as we saw, a functional definition coupled law with politics in the 'evolutionary achievement' of the modern constitution, which gave the legal system a democratic underpinning, the political system a means to organise the formation and expression of the will of the people to pursue the common

---

[11] Febbrajo's suggestion is to connect the three instruments – Constitution, Market and Democracy – in a form of *hyper-cyclical linkage*, a concept famously linked with Teubner's early work. In *Law As An Autopoietic System* Teubner had argued that systemic autopoiesis was achieved only at the point of 'hypercyclical linkage', that closes the cycle of self-reference and thus internalises all relations between elements, structures and processes of a system. For the notion of the 'hypercycle' and its role in the self-referential closure of autopoietic systems, see Teubner (1993).

[12] Such 'realisation' at the global level is far from given, and has in fact been fiercely contested as far as the periphery is concerned. See in particular Neves (2001) on the concept of 'allopoiesis'.

good, and both systems the opportunity to condense their semantics in this coupling. But since 'not all subsystems have globalized simultaneously, with the same speed and intensity', the shortfall of the political system means that the pursuit of the 'common good' cannot be uploaded to global circuits as a matter of politics and democratic will-formation. And if for a moment we assume that that is a good thing, in the name typically of a new reflexivity that supposedly does not take constituency for granted, *what is one to make of the 'good' that has no 'common' to predicate it in terms of its democratic determination*? It will be of course market thinking that will cut the damoclean knot of this stifling introversion. It is little wonder, in the context, that the theorisation of global *justice* finds itself in an unprecedented impasse.

Take Thomas Nagel's influential article on 'the problem of global justice' (2005) as a case in point. In it he argues that the 'circumstances of justice' presuppose a 'commonly authorised sovereign power' which is lacking in our globalising world. Where the requisite political structures are absent, absent in other words the conditions of political constitutionalism, the conditions of any robust sense of economic justice are similarly absent. Nagel borrows from Rawls the notion of the 'political conception' of justice to argue that, since State sanction is a necessary condition of social justice, the function cannot be sustained at an international level that lacks the mechanisms for collective will-formation necessary for the determination of the common good. If (re)distributive justice cannot be uploaded to the transnational level it is because at that level there is no constitution to sanction the political-public conception of the common good. Where such constitutional processes at State level yield forms of collective self-binding that impose duties on citizens, at the transnational level such duties can only be conceptualised as incidental costs of the interaction of actors in world markets. Thinking the processes as isomorphic simply produces conceptual incoherence for Nagel. On the back of this staggering of social justice at national level and of 'mere economic interaction' at supranational level, comes an *absolution as unwarranted as it is alarming*: 'If one takes this political view, one will not find the absence of global justice a cause for distress' (2005: 121).

How are the conclusion and absolution reached? Let us take the argument more gradually. Nagel contrasts the 'cosmopolitan' with a 'political' conception of justice 'since it is exemplified by Rawls's view that justice should be understood as a specifically political value, rather than being derived from a comprehensive moral system, so that it is essentially a virtue – the first virtue – of social institutions'. On the political conception, 'sovereign states are not merely instruments for realizing the pre-institutional value of justice among human beings. Instead, their existence is precisely what gives the value of justice its application, by putting the fellow citizens of a sovereign state into a relation that they do not have with the rest of humanity, an institutional relation which must then be evaluated by the special standards of fairness and equality that fill out the content of justice' (2005: 120). Nagel is not the only political philosopher to be drawing out the contrast between a looser interaction of the international markets variety, on the one hand, and the more exacting standards of republican citizenship (he calls it *political*) that invokes obligations of treating others justly.[13] The higher demands of justice, tied to the political constitution, determine the *grounds* of justice and *on that basis* its *scope*. Justice as *grounded* in state constitutions cannot extend its *scope* beyond state borders. It is because the relation of justice is constituted in domestic orders that *no vector of right* can carry it beyond the border except as knowledge, that is, in cognitive terms.

Nagel will not, of course, deny that economic interaction occurs globally; what he denies is that such interaction generates obligations of justice. For those working largely within Rawlsian parameters, such as Thomas Pogge, Iris Marion Young, Charles Beitz, Onora O'Neill and many others,[14] interaction outwith the national constitutional setting generates obligations of justice because it generates associative bonds by virtue of its density. Nagel similarly does not deny that distributive outcomes are dependent on institutions of global governance. Cross-border economic interaction is heavily regulated, and Nagel himself approvingly quotes Anne-Marie Slaughter's work on government networks, which 'link the disaggregated subparts of sovereign states sharing common competences and responsibilities'.[15] But he is quick to point out that these 'newer forms of international governance share with the old a markedly indirect relation to individual citizens and that this is morally

---

[13] David Miller is another. See the debate with Andrew Linklater in Dannreuther and Hutchings (1999).
[14] Indicatively Beitz (1999); O'Neill (1986); Pogge (1989); Young (2004).
[15] In the *New World Order* (2005) of 'disaggregated statehood' governmental functions can be performed by a number of regulatory agencies, pragmatically invested in the operation of decentralised networks of legislation, regulation and adjudication. Significantly for Slaughter this networked governance is not devoid of 'constitutional norms' located at the level of a 'hypothetical global polity' (Slaughter, 2005: 27–31). We will revisit these in the chapter on governance (Chapter 3.2).

significant' (2005: 139). What *is* morally significant is that 'a global or regional network does not have a similar responsibility of social justice for the combined citizenry of the states involved'. And the reason they don't is because these forms of global governance do not involve institutions that actively involve people's wills as instruments of democratic will-formation. And since the juridical condition of political justice obtains only at nation-state level, the constitutional thinking of global justice involves shoring up existing patterns of distribution of competence, rather than re-configuring them.

The argument somewhat perversely leads Nagel to the logical conclusion that since the 'circumstances of justice' cannot obtain at the transnational level which is placed beyond such institutions, 'mere economic interaction' – which would likely include wage competition, social dumping, the competitive alignment of systems of social protection – be left unabated and immune to considerations of social justice and redistribution since the more exacting 'heightened standards of economic justice' cannot *ex hypothesi* be met at this level. Until such time as a 'world state' of some description emerges to mediate the conflicts and submit them to the political conception of justice it must remain 'mere economic interaction'. Nagel presents the staggering – of economic justice and 'mere' economic interaction – in terms of a defence of democracy where it *can* obtain: a legitimate coercive structure of justice entitlements and allocations obtains at the level of the democratic State sanctioned by the constitution. Justice is something we owe through our shared institutions only to those with whom we stand in a strong political relation. Under those terms *only* is an associative obligation generated. Interaction in the circuits of economic trade and the global organisation of production is denied the 'associative' status. So that outwith those processes and structures sanctioned by the 'political condition' there can be no legitimate entitlement to enforce just distributions, and therefore 'no need to distress'.

What remains unacknowledged in this strict division of conceptual labour, the demarcations of political justice against cosmopolitan justice, or socio-economic justice versus 'mere economic interaction', is that it misreads the deep continuity and interdependence in global material production, 'which inspires', as A. J. Julius puts it in his formidable critique of Nagel, 'projects for shaping outsiders' action to insiders' purposes' (2006: 190) in a way that gives the lie to the 'moral significance' of which side of the border the production occurs. Economic connectedness reaches across the spheres that Nagel separates, of political obligation and the sphere where duties of justice are not owed. But the continuity of material interdependence extends exploitative and manipulative relations across the world of material production, and to draw a boundary between those we recompense with socio-economic rights and those we do not looks somewhat more sinister than merely naïve in this light.

Very much like Arendt's treatment of the 'social question', Nagel's conceptual frame and the rigidity of his divisions and delineations drive him into a corner that leaves politically un-addressable the Age's most pressing demand to extend justice to the world's exploited and dispossessed. The 'political condition' of his theory of justice is not aimed at politicising distributive justice but at shoring up existing distributions. He is right not to want to dignify the fragmentary and disaggregated instruments of global governance – the networks of central bankers, rating agencies, antitrust regulators, finance ministers, security commissioners, insurance supervisors, etc. – with the term 'constitutional' in its 'political' dimension. But this leads him to deny that associative obligations are institutionally generated at the transnational level, 'thick' with significance, and with often devastating effects on lives. To classify these as 'mere economic interaction' denies them the gravity that they *de facto* possess. All of which leaves us with a grave problem of definition that links directly with the symbolic currency of the political constitution. On the one hand there are those, like Nagel, only prepared to recognise the political concept (that grounds associative obligations) where collective procedure of will-formation undergird it. On the other there are those who are prepared to extend the scope – or 'extension' – of the concept of constitution on the back of supra-state *functions*, whether that be the 'stabilisation of expectations' (Febbrajo), the replication of functional differentiation (Teubner) or the pursuit of the 'common good' (Walker) at the transnational level.

Between the narrowness of the first and the expansiveness of the second approach, a more careful constitutional trajectory can be navigated, so that the specific achievement that is the constitution be lost neither to the introversion, and consequent irrelevance, of the first, nor the under-determination and risk of substitution carried by the second. There is nothing that as a matter of definition (functional or otherwise) ties the constitution as institutional achievement to *national* constituencies. But that does not mean that it can be floated indiscriminately in the circuits of the transnational. Instead we must see that the concept of the constitution carries both institutional limitation and the promise of a constituent reflexivity as fundamental to it. The constituent promise requires the institutional reduction to ground it – in what Luhmann called its 'reduction-achievement'. We have seen all this in the successive chapters of Part II, where we looked at how constitutional reflexivity is tied to the logic of institution in both formal and substantive ways. In its formal dimension we described constitutionality in its framing function as underpinning the *unity* of the system in the relatively precise terms of holding fast the criterion that decided inclusion (or identity) of what did and what did not belong to the legal order (what is *ultra vires*, what is unconstitutional), of allowing variety (in containing rules of change and delimiting legitimate interpretative scope), of allocating jurisdiction. There are a number of ways to re-describe what framing means and how it is effected, how the terms are set, and of course none of them allow for watertight containment; there will always be room for interpretative adjustments, for revisiting and renewing these norms through novel interpretations. And while distinctions here can be made between rigid and flexible constitutions, or regarding specific provisions like basic rights, in its formal dimension, *constitutionality as such, as coincident with reflexivity itself, cannot be put to question* reflexively, which means that the formal and substantive dimensions are definitive, not contingent. If the *formal* dimension defines constitutionality in the direction of delimiting the constitution's reach and its operation (entrenchment, hierarchy, rationalisation), in the *substantive* dimension it institutionalises value at more general levels, so that the multifaceted determinations or instantiations of value effected in legal operations can refer back to them. Along this substantive axis, and this is the crux of it, the constituent moment must be understood as enshrining the deep-seated values of dignity, solidarity and equality, and operationalising democratic categories in the definition of participation, protection and production.

The *loss of the concept* of the constitution – and the loss of the orientation-value it offers – leaves the thinking of justice confounded, outwitted at the juncture where it is generalised across orders. The asymmetry that is generated between economic concepts that are successfully uploaded and normative concepts that are vacated at the national border, leaves constitutional thought at sea, oscillating between the alternatives outlined above, of its strict coupling to the semantics of the state, which leaves injustice unaddressed and unaddressable in the global context, or its loose coupling to those semantics to the point where the constitutional is undercut as an institutional achievement in its own right, lost to 'plasticity' and to functional equivalence, and harnessed to market expansion.

In the second part of this chapter, and our third instalment of the 'semantics and structures' thread that runs through the book, we will discuss at greater depth two key theoretical points, already encountered in the analysis above, regarding the relation of the semantics of the constitution and the structures of *global* society. The first has to do with the *loss of concepts*, in our case the concept of the political constitution, where the operation that 'loses' them is their deployment as 'floating signifiers'. The second has to do with 'learning processes' and *the distinction between cognitive and normative expectations* that will become key to the analysis of the paradigm change of constitutionalism. It connects to how functional equivalence sacrifices the normative hold that the constitution offers, and thereby disconnects from justice.

Semantics and Structures III

One way to explain the undiminished hold of the symbolic currency of constitutionalism is to see it as a case of what Reinhart Koselleck calls 'asymmetric counter-concepts' (Koselleck, 1989/2004: 155ff). These are concepts that morally disqualify those who oppose them by introducing 'a depreciative meaning' that functions for their adversaries 'as a linguistic deprivation'. (The distinction between *Hellenes and Barbarians* is a classic instance.) As a result of its expansive use as a 'fighting political concept' and as part of a 'victorious offensive', the constitution, writes Marcelo Neves referring to Giovanni Biaggini's 'Die Idee der Verfassung', has become 'a contextually unlimited metaphor' in the high seas of globalisation. 'Contextually unlimited' means decoupled from its structural and institutional grounding. As a result, writes Neves, 'it has become unrecognisable as a semantic artefact and no longer refers reflexively to a specific social structure' (Neves, 2013: 7). The decoupling empties it of content and floats it well beyond its formal and substantive coordinates in plural and labile forms.

A *floating signifier* is one that does not attach unambiguously to a *signified*, but where, instead, 'either an over-determination or an under-determination of signifieds prevents it from being fully fixed' (Laclau, 1996: 36). For the father of modern linguistics, Ferdinand de Saussure, signifiers attach to specific signifieds and the sign takes form as the associative link between the signifier and signified. A sign's 'meaning depends on its relation to other words within the system' (*Course in General Linguistics*). From Saussure we know that every system of signification (of which language is a principal instance) is a system of differences. Signification is differential inscription. To name an identity is to draw out its difference within the system where every linguistic identity will be purely *relational* vis-à-vis all the others, in what he calls *langue* to denote the latent structure in ordinary language. The set of contrasts between signs is how signs derive their meaning.[16] And because identity is constituted as difference within the relational field, it enters into relations of equivalence with all the other differences of the system, and the term 'enters' denotes the dynamic nature of that relationality as differences are carried in the spontaneity and unpredictability of speech acts, Saussure's *parole*, re-configured and renegotiated in the changing semiotic network of their linkage. Naming something as 'x' – deploying signs in linguistic usage – mobilises at once both a logic of difference and a logic of equivalence. The context of language, the *articulation* of difference and equivalence, is mobilised in every operation in which linguistic signs yield meaning.

When signifiers lose their attachment to particular signifieds, to particular contents, when they become disconnected from the specificity of difference, then they can be floated across greater stretches of equivalence. They ride on ambiguity and extend their semantic reach across a broader field. We might say that their *extension* grows at the expense of their *intension*. Where a purely differential content would attach a signifier to a single signified, an equivalential move loses that correspondence in a certain slippage on the symbolic plane, one that opens the signifier to a variety of re-articulations.[17] A particular signifier comes thereby to represent an 'equivalential chain', and the more it gains on the plane of equivalence, the more it loses its specificity on the plane of difference.

How far can we travel across the expanses of equivalence to ever remoter constituencies (regional, global) and temporally to accelerated processes well out of sync with actual processes of will-formation, before the 'constitution' – that key 'condensing symbol' as Walker puts it so well – is emptied? This is the dilemma at the heart of 'constitutionalisation' and 'constitutional pluralism'. Beyond a certain threshold, where equivalence overwhelms difference, the concept of the constitution is subjected to a radical loss of meaning. It is a loss of the normative hold on the language and therefore also an evacuation of *a point of view* itself.

---

[16] As the translator of Saussure's *Course in General Linguistics*, puts it in the introduction, '[t]he essential feature of Saussure's linguistic sign is that, being intrinsically arbitrary, it can be identified only by contrast with coexisting signs of the same nature, which together constitute a structured system' (intro to Saussure, 1983: x).

[17] We know from Jacques Derrida that with the renegotiation of such specificity (between speaker, listener and observer) the possibilities of interpretation and reinterpretation become radicalised.

We will witness it in the long discussion of market constitutionalism in the next part in terms of a fatal loosening of the normative hold that is implicit in the constitution and the *imaginary* specific to it. Significant to a discussion of redress is the opportunity of *recuperation*. One aspect of our discussion of strategy in the last part of the book involves how the retrieval of the symbolic currency of constitutionalism (a stubborn insistence on its political dimension) might be effected and acted on, in the face of the collapse of normativity that confronts us in the new dispensation, the gradual displacement of normative expectations by cognitive expectations in the processes of social learning we associate with globalisation.

But all this will come later. For now let us look more closely at how the accelerated rhythm of globalisation forces a *misalignment* between the constitutional semantic of political self-determination and the structures of market expansion, a misalignment that aggravates under the momentum it generates.

Samuel Moyn has given us a useful account of this misalignment in the description of the semantic displacement and profound co-option that accompany what he calls the process of 'historiographical absorption' in the field of human rights (Moyn, 2010; 2012). Moyn's interest is in the 'invention and breakthrough' of the category of human rights, and his methodology combines a reading of the '*scalar history*' of rights, with the emphasis on the geography of their application, with their '*salience history*', with the emphasis on their 'prominence as a language of struggle', which in turn connects to the 'privileging of one moral optic or mode of engagement in the world over others' (2012: 125). It is the combination of these two histories, he says, that might explain how human rights 'came to fit the imagination and re-orient the actions of large swathes of people ... and legitimate one sort of moral world over another.' On the first historical register, of scale, he invites us to look at the 'scalar leap of human rights' and ask what propelled them to go global as they did; on the second, to look at the processes through which a certain semantics *supervenes* on another to gain leverage. In Moyn's more precise formulation, this involves a process of *historiographical absorption*. It is a process whereby pasts are 'invented' or at least re-signified and summoned in alignment to current configurations, events called upon to find their place in, and offer justification to, present developments. The process involves the annexation of what used to be independent fields. The supervenience itself, and the combination of histories of scale and salience, yields important dividends to how we understand the dynamic relation between semantics and structures.

The most clear example of 'historiographical absorption' involves how human rights became cast as part of the continuing unfolding of older legacies, or, as Moyn puts it more accurately, older legacies were 'called upon to find their place in the history of human rights'; legacies such as humanitarianism and anti-slavery that 'had a fascinating and venerable historiography long before human rights did' (2012: 130) and before they were annexed as the 'pre-history' of human rights. But how productive this anachronism became!

A 'global' discourse of human rights was hoisted out of it, gaining traction and leverage from a humanitarianism that had gone global earlier in terms of the anti-slavery campaigns: scalar and salience histories combine here to propel human rights onto the global scene. A profound misreading of the past – 'where humanitarianism powered anti-slavery activism, rights claims figured only very marginally in it', Moyn remarks (2012: 131) – allows the human rights discourse to 'piggyback' on humanitarianism in order to go global *in retrospect*. But the significant hermeneutic traction gained from this new-found continuity carries its costs. Humanitarianism involves 'identification with traumatised victimhood', making 'cruelty the worst thing we can do, not solidarity the best thing we can achieve' (2012: 135).

For our purposes there are two things to take from this.

The *first* is captured well by the argument about salience, scale and the anachronism that comes with 'historiographical absorption'. The 'hermeneutic traction' that is granted to human rights through this new history of salience, makes humanitarianism and victimhood their accompanying reference. In the process the *summum bonum* of the 'common good' is substituted for the *summum malum* of the infliction of injury as accompanying reference to the deployment of rights. A language of compensation rather than participation sets in, capacity mutates to need, and pity comes to replace solidarity as the organisational basis of collective redress. It is the redress of suffering rather than of exploitation or domination that carries the semantic weight, and re-orients redress away from the thinking of political capacity and self-determination, and in the direction of what is now increasingly thematised as 'bare life'.[18]

The *second* thing to note involves more specifically the question of *social rights*. That very same scalar leap to go global privileged one subset of rights (typically property and civil) against the other (social and

---

[18] In this respect of course Agamben's work is heavily indebted to Arendt (1951); for a critique, see Rancière (2004c).

economic) and thus undercut the latter as foci of collective self-determination, which they *had* been *before the rescaling*. This is more specifically what 'absorption' in (historiographical) practice 'achieves': their effective de-socialisation, their severing from collective structures, corporate identities and collective capacities. And Moyn describes this well when he writes: 'Even as post-Cold War politicians have been dealing welfare states their final indignities, recent historians have followed an enthusiastic public discourse in making international human rights, not welfare states, the goal of world war II' (2012: 135). The point is that social rights never carried the achievement of social protection on their own; social protection was carried in the organisational form of the social state, in the corporatist achievement of industrial democracy, in the provision of social services. So that the 'fabulous retroactivity' that the 'historiographical absorption' delivers, that installs social rights as the means of redress of suffering, eclipses their proper meaning and political leverage. The scalar leap disconnects them from political capacity and the democratic expression of solidarity. Solidarity is indeed the obvious casualty of these 'absorptions' as it is lost to the national systems of social and labour protection at the same time at which it is asserted in the weak and pallid forms of its global (humanitarian) expression. As rights go global while local welfare is left behind, entrenching the priority of human rights with the very move that 'de-socialises' them, histories of salience supervene on histories of scale and semantics are reconfigured as they are driven forward by structures along trajectories that gradually hollow them out, that no longer see them as continuous to political rights and thereby sever the meaning of (social) solidarity from (political) association. This was the point about constitutionalism and rights becoming floating signifiers: at the point of their 'scalar leap' to the global level, salience is reconfigured, specificity is sacrificed, and the terms are lost to equivalence.

*

In his 1971 essay 'Die Weltgesellschaft',[19] Luhmann predicted that globalisation, or as he put it at the time, the emergence of 'world society', will gradually lead to a comprehensive displacement of normative expectations by cognitive expectations, and that the reliance on law and politics that once enjoyed a certain 'evolutionary and functional primacy' in societies will be replaced by a primacy of science and technology.

---

[19] Luhmann (1971); cf. Luhmann (1997).

He predicted that between the two types of expectation there would be both a displacement and a blurring: a displacement to the extent that, with the advent of world society, normative expectations are guaranteed less and less by a functionally differentiated legal system; and a blurring to the extent that any clear primacy afforded to normative expectations by the legal system comes under pressure of adaptation and 'learning'. But of course learn from disappointment is precisely what normative expectations do *not* do. Unlike cognitive expectations, which are discredited when they are disappointed, normative expectations are held on to counterfactually. There would be no meaning to the normativity of an expectation that one's dignity will not be violated, if every time a worker was subjected to degrading treatment she 'learnt' from the degradation and shifted her expectation. What is true of all normative expectations, applies to legal expectations par excellence. By the time we reach the level of the constitution, the normative hold has been strengthened significantly: at the constitutional level normative expectations are normatively expected, sanctioned in terms of rigidity, entrenchment and the axiomatic assertion of constitutional value, as we saw.

All of which means that only a significant structural shift will allow for normative expectations to mutate comprehensively into cognitive expectations. This is the shift that, Luhmann tells us, 'world society' ushers in. He will approach the developing mis-alignment of constitutional semantics and global structures, unsurprisingly, as a question of complexity. For him, 'if the level of complexity changes, the semantics that orients experience and action must adapt to that change, otherwise it loses its connection to reality' (Luhmann, 1980: 22). For his problem-oriented functional analysis the disruption of the fit between the meaning of the constitution as attached to nation-state structures and the post-sovereign structural formation to which it is transferred, is emphatically not an abandonment to 'floating' signification; it is instead a *productive* mis-alignment that will re-orient a constitutional semantics-in-crisis to emergent structural patterns. In other words, when the embeddedness of the (constitutional) semantics in the social structures that they give expression to, is troubled, the ensuing *strain* between semantics and structures calls forth a re-alignment of the former to the latter, *always in the direction of an adaptation of semantics to the new configuration of structure*. Luhmann is not worried about such mutations: if cognitive expectations flood in to fill the gap of what used to be a matter of political decision, the shrinkage of politics places it conveniently out of harm's way. But for us, and for *a defence of political constitutionalism*, the reflexive equilibrium of the cognitive and the normative cannot be abandoned to evolutionary realignment. We will look at what options that leaves us with below.

For the advocates of the varieties of constitutional pluralism, constitutional cosmopolitanism and (as we will see in Chapter 3.2) experimentalist democratic governance, the paradigmatic shift that loosens the grip of normativity is treated as opportunity for new voices, new themes, new arrangements, to enter the scene, all carried in the inflationary idiom of the new constitutionalisms, as we saw. For our pluralists, falling over themselves and each other to keep constitutional semantics abreast of the rapid flows of global exchange, the theoretical task becomes the breathless pursuit of 'relevance', an openness expressed in the willingness to learn and to adjust. This is 'constituent power' for the neo-liberal age: pluralism is the term to which constitutional theory turns to replenish its depleted political energies, away from the older definitions and hierarchisation of priorities and commitments, the many trappings of state-'constituted' power. The loss of normativity is never anything but a gain in terms of cognition; any counter-suggestion becomes a sign of outdated theory, redundant semantics, intransigence, naïvety. And if the objection is raised that constitutional pluralism must fix at some level what is constitutional about the plurality it introduces, the response is typically to remain reflexive about that question, even if that reflexivity now exercised at both level and meta-level leaves theory-construction as deadlocked as it is exuberant. Set against the well-defined and highly hierarchised nested neo-liberal asymmetries – the domination of the economy over collective life, of the market over any concept of the political economy, of finance over production, of services over industry, etc.[20] – it is no wonder that the emancipatory gains of constitutional pluralism have been trifling.

But if constitutional pluralism responds to the 'strain' between the constitutional semantic and the structure that threatens to supersede it by surrendering the semantics of constitutionalism to the structural drift of globalisation, that is not Luhmann's argument. For Luhmann the strain is held to in the name of the achievement of constitutionalism. As far as he is concerned, the asymmetry between *Gesellschaftstruktur* and *Semantik* is productive because it sets in motion a certain dialectical movement to overcome the semantic 'shortfall' in the direction of its adjustment

---

[20] For an analysis of these asymmetries, see Magri (2008).

to – and correction vis-à-vis – the corresponding social structure, and to *rehabilitate normativity*. The semantic adjustment is tied up with the processes of systemic 'self-description'. Unless a certain resonance-capacity is secured, the complexity deficit between system and environment becomes too vast to manage. Correction is triggered when the system's observation of its environment falls short of what would allow it *adequate* adaptation; adequate when it comes to functional systems is measured against what it means to perform a function. To adequate responsiveness, the system must manage the tension between variety and redundancy which is the distinction in terms of which it manages complexity. If it leans too much in the direction of redundancy it loses responsiveness to a changing environment; if it leans too much in the direction of variety it stretches or undermines its self-understanding. Which is all to say that complexity deficit is intrinsic to system formation and maintenance, and that therefore the 'shortfall' we have been discussing, to which constitutionalisation and pluralism are the supposed remedies, is constitutive of the system. The shortfall finds expression in the self-descriptions of the system, in constitutional concepts, that help it to navigate complexity and which carry its self-understanding, and these concepts-as-self-descriptions are reiterations in new contexts that enable durability and furnish a memory of past selections to guide present ones. And if durability and re-iteration matter more as far as law is concerned, it is because it is the function of law to generalise expectations of meaning in the direction of reproducing and entrenching normativity.

A key insight thus differentiates Luhmann's position from the free-wheeling pluralisms we discussed. On the one hand, yes, the constitution's reflexivity that he identifies with openness to learning and to correction, names the rapid, always path-dependent, reconfiguration of a semantics that were stuck at state level, where normative and cognitive expectations were still calibrated on the assumptions of national constituencies, thematics and times. Only in this way will the outdated semantics of the system achieve the required *resonance* with the environment whose increase in complexity they are, functionally, required to meet. This is what makes the asymmetry affirmative, what puts the productive spin on the *strain* between semantics and structures in Luhmann's evolutionary take. And yet, for all the emphasis on the constitution's adaptability to shifting structures and for all the evolutionism, Luhmann will not concede a wholesale substitution of cognitive for normative expectations in the name of a supposedly adequate theorisation of globalisation. The new semantic openness, managed at the level of self-description, is managed with a view that the 'reduction achievement' that is the constitution not come undone, that it does not lose its specificity in the particular ways it has of reducing complexity, and that variety stretches the institutional imagination only so far so as not to relinquish what is constitutional about the perspective it sheds on the world.

In the final chapter of *Law as a Social System,* written over two decades after 'World Society', Luhmann describes the rapid shift away from expectations that are held to counter-factually and are instead forced to 'learn' in global society, and the repercussion of this shift for the function of the legal system in the face of the 'constant stream of disappointments' to which law is 'constantly called to adjust' (468). In the tension Luhmann now reads a *risk* that he sees the law of global society as being called to confront, and in confronting to assume as its own. He will nevertheless insist, against all those who call for rethinking the function of law as having shifted altogether to coordinating processes of market adjustment (more on this in Part III), that the law must at its core build on normative expectations.[21] With no external guarantees lending themselves to such a task, Luhmann will concede a state of heightened risk, of law losing control of its handling of the normative/cognitive balance. The crucial question connects to the self-observation of the legal system, the constitutional function par excellence, and he asks 'how capable is law of recognising its own risk'? It is a challenging question given the structural drift that 'imposes high temporal instability in norm structures', that in the social dimension experiments with changing constituencies and networks, and that in the material dimension has significantly increased 'variety' (experimentalism) at the expense of redundancy (stability). The problem at the heart of this is 'finding legal forms which are compatible with the autopoiesis of law, with its specific function and the peculiarity of its coding' (2004: 473), its capacity in other words to translate the demands placed upon it into its own concepts, in particular as the law increasingly adopts 'an incremental approach which depends largely on incidental events and tries to solve issues unsystematically... If there are ever to be legal concepts which are socially adequate, they will have to be found through a testing and re-testing of solutions to establish potential

---

[21] For Renner, through recourse to 'regulated self-regulation ... and the unquestioned adoption of economic criteria for risk-evaluation, law has undermined its own basic capability: that of creating and stabilising normative expectations' (2011: 104). And yet 'even the law of the knowledge society must at its core build on normative expectations' (2011: 103).

eigenvalues of the legal system in modern society' (2004: 473). Law's 'own risk' is the risk of undoing its 'reduction achievement' understood as the self-descriptions and linkages by means of which it *holds itself* at the level of internal consistency *against* the patterns of environmental complexity it selectively calls itself to manage. Here the emphasis is on legal validity as a lever and anchor of inner consistency, and the law's *eigen-values*, ultimately its constitutional *eigen-values*, the point of normative regress in the system that underwrites and directs the possibilities of internal self-reference. If 'today the legal system is hampered in expressing its own risk appropriately in its normative texts' it is because 'the normative texts have to be hermeneutically useful and interpretatively valuable in accordance with the normative function of law' (2004: 475). In the end, for Luhmann, it is function alone, expressed through the specific use of normativity, that can form the basis for the reflexivity of law. Luhmann's final word on law navigates tensions, paradoxes, varieties of differentiation, dynamics of exclusion and inclusion, and it might be read as suggesting that these forms of selectivity and selective visibility are productive for law if they can counter global law's own risk, of the collapse of normativity into comprehensive learning and rapid adaptation to markets. We might identify here an element of normativity, however ambivalent, in Luhmann's position, something of a 'normative turn' in systems theory has more recently placed a special emphasis on differentiation and discovered a different role for constitutionality in a global context.

*

A series of questions arises at this point for a critical theory of the constitution.

If it is a 'complexity deficit' that constitutes a system in the first place, allowing it to individuate and sustain itself vis-à-vis society's overwhelming complexity as an 'island' of reduced complexity, *at which point does the shortfall, which is constitutive of constitutional semantics, become a problem for it?* When, in other words, does the successfully instituted self-description become the problem? *How* is the aforementioned 'loss of connection' *signified*? What is the semiosis of this asymmetry *given* the semantic path-dependency as radicalised in systems theory, if it is that very path-dependency that is in question? What does it mean to register the 'suspicion' that in 'the increase of complexity' the language has been left behind, that the new structural givens (*given as what?*) have not-yet been adequately thematised?[22] Another way of putting the same objection, closer to functional analysis, is to ask: what does it mean to speak of the emergence of the *problem calling for a language to describe it?* Absent the language, what makes it a problem? What, in all this, is the meaning of the 'strain' and of the semiotic deficit between the semantics of the Constitution and the structural conditions brought about by the transnationalisation of capitalist activity *that puts the constitution's fit to question?*

A second set of questions suggests itself at this point, and we might interject to ask: *why* are we to make sense of the semantic shortfall, this asymmetry between semantics and structures, as *felicitous? Why felicitous?* If *strain* captures something of a non-coincidence between semantics and structures, the answer cannot simply be that, however the strain is intimated, the semantic *will be* restored in the direction of a renewed adequacy, that equilibria *will be* re-calibrated and achieved.

Let me restate the two sets of questions above in the form of three injunctions, that will function at this stage of the argument only as *placeholders*. We will need to explore how market constitutionalism has reconfigured the constitutional field before we can appreciate their import and begin to develop and answer them. But they have already arisen for us in the discussion of the strained relationship between the semantic of constitutionalism (Chapters 2.2 and 2.3) and the structural drift associated with globalisation.

Injunction 1. The 'inadequacy' of semantics vis-à-vis structures is not a factual given but an interpretative question laden with normativity. What strain we discern between semantics and structures depends on the answer to the normative question of adequacy and of its measure. A critical phenomenology attaches the phenomenality of the strain to these normative dynamics.

Injunction 2. If there is a strain between semantics and structures we can redress it either by adapting the semantics to the structures or by deploying the semantics to stem the structural drift. At this juncture a critical phenomenology links to strategy.

---

[22] The answer that Urs Stäheli gives to this question is that 'speaking about a distinction between social structures and semantics has to be read as a distinction that is always-already re-entered: this highlights that *social structures themselves are a semantic construction if entered on the semantic side of the distinction*' (1997: 138, emphasis added).

Injunction 3. Indeterminacy and contradiction are internal sources of strain for the semantics of the constitution and have an important effect on structures. For a critical phenomenology contradiction is a significant semantic resource.

Regarding the *first injunction*: It is foundational to a critical phenomenology to ask under what conditions something emerges as a problem, which transfers in the current context to the question *under what conditions do we observe a strain between semantics and structures*? In a situation of complexity, every phenomenological reduction – an operation at the very heart of systems theory – (re)-configures the distribution of what is signified and what denied signification. What puts to question the available constitutional distribution between the two, and by what measure we will decide the adequacy of the available constitutional semantics – that is, whether or not they are critically lagging behind – is itself a question laden with normativity. Luhmann's answer here will short-circuit the more complex hermeneutical set-up to functional analysis and collapse the critical-normative question of adequacy. What does this mean? It means that with function driving the thinking, the 'adequacy' of the semantics, and any deficit between constitutional semantic and structure, will be measured on functionality. The function of law, however re-described, invariably turns on the 'exploitation' of conflictual perspectives carried semantically, to reproduce, re-iterate and stabilise expectations. As a result any asymmetry within the concept (of the constitution) between the memory it mobilises and the innovation it introduces (how far it can be *floated* in the way we analysed it above) will always lean in the direction of stabilisation, given the function. Overwhelming in that sense is the 'time-binding' function of the concept,[23] and it is against that function that any adequacy, and shortfall, will be measured. The impulse of innovation is felt in the direction of variation as dictated in the last instance by function, which means also equipped with a relative immunity to surprise.

In Thornhill's concise formulation and defence, functional analysis seeks to correct the foundational 'reductivism' of normative inquiry, the deductively constructed models of normative constitutional theory, and

---

[23] On the 'time-binding' function of concepts, see Koselleck (1989/2004), although Luhmann would likely be reluctant to pursue Koselleck's politically loaded suggestion (Stäheli, 1997: 129).

to re-orientate it toward reasons that are not normative but sociological, and more specifically to 'embedded elements of adaptive societal reflexivity' (2011: 373). If what is offered, insightfully, by Thornhill's sociology of constitutionalism is its proximity to societal processes whereby societies recursively apply and reproduce their power, the 'yield of a sociology of constitutions', in my reading of it, has a latent critical-normative dimension. Because Thornhill's functional analysis is attentive to 'deviations' from norms 'that might jeopardise the basic resources and structural form of society', that 'might undermine their ability to use political power as an autonomous facility' or 'relinquish their capacity for a reliable politicisation of social exchanges' (376). In this language of what might be 'jeopardised', 'undermined' or 'relinquished', in the language of 'reliable politicisation' and the maintenance of political capacity, something akin to a *critical* constitutional perspective is raised above the blind conformity to adaptive pressures. And although Thornhill would be unlikely to extract something blatantly normative from all this, the question of adequacy does provide leverage to qualify questions such as the following *as constitutional*: do social dumping, the undercutting of the right to strike, or the abusive exercise of managerial prerogative and degrading forms of underemployment, *constitute problems* that call forth a normative constitutional semantic to deal with them, or do we abandon them to the *structural* drift of a neo-liberal globalisation that treats them as occasions of 'creative destruction' in capital's unflagging pursuit of its own valorisation?

Regarding *the second injunction*: If we agree that the question of adequacy is a normative question, then it is crucial to the critical perspective to resist the phenomenological drift that evolution entails, and to forge out of these constellations the opportunity to put a brake to semantic drift. It is against this evolutionism, of the strain as productive to – and as opportunity for – adjustment, rather than as irreducible antinomy, that a *critical* project of constitutionalism will measure itself. It is true that with the threat of a comprehensive shift of the constitutional terrain, the question of holding on to the semantics of solidarity and dignity becomes more improbable, even as it becomes more urgent. The relative autonomy of semantics from structures, their field of 'politicisation' in Koselleck, allows us interpretive leeway at this juncture. In the context of the constitutional question over *adequacy*, the elevation of solidarity – as *dogmatic* resource – to constitutional value at the substantive level, and the constitutional entrenchment of its non-negotiability at formal level, express the political achievement of social rights constitutionalism, the *decision* to hold on to the aspiration of solidarity in the face of all that the market presents under the sign of necessity. Decision is the key term here, and one that at this juncture *resists* the shift and the reconfiguration of constitutional semantics, pitting political constitutionalism *against* its market varieties that collapse the space of political decision (to protect work) by submitting its claim to 'truth' to the veridiction of the market.

A somewhat incongruous reading of systems theory might sustain a critical perspective at this point. Society begins to understand and describe itself as global, for Hauke Brunkhorst, 'when [it] recognises *itself* as a world society in its description'.[24] Could it be that a specifically constitutional operation might renegotiate a different semantic reach for the constitution? Not because a societal perspective might be comprehensively fashioned out of it; to recall one of Luhmann's many playful variations on the theme, 'society is observable because it is unobservable' (2002: 87) because, in other words, any attempt to observe it must include a phenomenological 'bracketing' or *epoche* and therefore its inevitable partiality. Society is an object of self-observation and self-description that will never coincide with itself. And yet we might identify constitutional *moments* – to deploy a near-exhausted semantic – of political self-thematisation where society 'dis-identifies' with the dominant self-understandings, shakes off the self-evidence of its self-description, to recover 'the submerged sense that society is never just society' (Thornhill, 2007: 513). This is the challenge whose 'yield' would be a critical systems theory. The challenge will need to wait for now; it will be addressed later (Chapter 4.2) and its yield is likely to be modest.

The *third injunction* invokes the logic and the language of immanent critique, and we will explore at some length what it means to 'constitutionalise contradiction' in the last chapter of the book. At this stage, and looking back to the argument made about the forgetting of labour in Chapter 1.3, we might identify a key gesture of immanent critique in the usage of 'a concept to reach beyond a concept',[25] to effect a dialectical dis-identification, to bring about a negative moment that is sustained as such.[26] Sustained, that is, against the grand synthesis that locates any semantic shortfall of the present not as an expression of the intrinsic

---

[24] Brunkhorst, quoted in Neves (2013: 21).
[25] In Adorno's formulation, as quoted by Cordero (2020).
[26] This will be a key argument of constitutional strategy in the book's final two chapters.

inadequacy of our categories of thought but as a mere stage in the inexorable historical processes of their sublation, in the way that they find expression in structural transformation, to couch the history of capital integration in a constitutional language that is relativised and pluralised enough to meet the task. With an emphasis on what is 'critical' and on the use of the 'negative', we might discern in the 'decoupling' of the constitution from its embeddedness in a 'specific social structure' a certain loosening of the semantic artefact from its surrounding structure that may indeed give reflexivity some 'slack' at the juncture. Koselleck's thinking about *Begriffsgeschichte* focuses on what *semantic innovation* is brought to the structural anatomy of modern society (Koselleck, 1989/2004: 75). His suggestion introduces 'an inflection in the way we engage with concepts: from coherent unities of meaning ... to a complex web of heteronomous significations that have the semantic capacity to register social-historical experiences, as much as the performative capacity to participate in shaping the direction of [structural] transformations' (Cordero, 2020: 11). We might take from all this a co-evolution between semantics and structures in terms of *a reciprocity that works both ways*, both embedding semantics in structures, as well as allowing semantics to move structures along different paths. It is what would make the constitution a 'fighting political concept'. At stake is both to preserve the genealogy that tied the term constitution to revolutionary foundation and intrinsically to emancipation, while at the same time disassociate the semantics of the constitution from its structural over-determination and its diminishment in terms of performance.

*

If this is all moving us along too fast, it also throws into perspective the essential argument of this book. To take stock of where we find ourselves, let me repeat the root quandary of this chapter over how the new constitutional imaginaries cut themselves adrift from the formal and substantive dimensions of the constitutional achievement.

With constitutionalisation as *emergent* quality of the constitutional, constitutional function – still tentatively orientated to the common good, whatever that means under conditions of radical pluralism – is tied to adequate responsiveness to contingencies as they arise, and the constitutional achievement is a process of incremental sedimentation. Manifold sites and processes of law-making operating in the absence of state-constitutional principles acquire constitutional standing if they can be seen to still be 'framed' – whatever that now means – and guided by principles of legality, proportionality, rationality, etc. Alongside this comes an entrenchment of norms which acquire constitutional standing through recursive operations, or through generalisation as benchmarking. Staggered, fragmented and disjointed processes are uploaded to constitutional standing. Unconcerned with pedigree and fixated on output – tasks of 'managing, shaping, constraining political power' after the fact of its emergence – the new constitutionalism forces us to re-think the constitutional in terms of a process where '[g]radually the layers of common normative principle thicken; they come to be argued for and adapted through a mixture of comparative study and a sense that they are (or are becoming) obligatory'.[27] And with this any constitutional blockage is turned productive, the paradox of the democratic and social deficits 'unfolded' in what is becoming the *evolutionary achievement* of a transnational or global constitutionalism, with pluralism substituting for democracy and constitutionalisation substituting for constitutionality.

With this totalising inclusion we have come full circle. The constitutional form is pluralised and becomes inclusive, pluri-vocal because it is fragmented, a plurality superimposed on a shifting correlation of 'demoi' and constituencies, which resist singular designation. Combining with this surface plurality, we have the advent of an economic constitutionalisation that proceeds by recasting its subject and its unity (the constitutional order) not as conditions but as end-products of a process of becoming-constitutional. With its in-built guarantees and bootstrapping, and nothing to hold it to its principles, constitutionalisation proceeds uninterrupted, dislocating, realigning and internalising all obstacles, infinitely labile, and thus functionally harnessed to market expansion. We began our discussion of the relation between semantics and structures in Part I with the semantics that 'forgot' labour, and we revisited it above, on constitutional terrain, in order also to insert three injunctions that will inform, in the final part, a strategic thinking of constitutionalism. Constitutional thought faces a crucial theoretical-political choice in the face of the structural drift to globalisation: on the

---

[27] Kingsbury, 2009: 32. Not so for Martti Koskenniemi, for whom, internationally there is no equivalent to the common good defined by domestic constitutional laws 'beyond the languages of diplomacy and positive law whose very fragmentation and indeterminacy provided the starting point for the search for an (implicit) constitution' (Koskenniemi, 2007: 1). This may be little more than a rushed rhetorical flourish since it is profoundly question-begging how the 'search' for the 'implicit constitution' will 'seek its starting point' in the 'fragmentation' it must, as constitutional, seek to overcome.

one hand, to adjust it to the structural drift of so many compensatory constitutionalisms with their elisions, covering-up and covering-over; or, on the other hand, of a stubborn refusal to submit the constitutional semantic to re-signification, an insistence, in other words, to hold on to the dogmatic connection and the sources of normative commitment.

PART III

Market Constitutionalism

3.1

Market Trajectories

From Differentiation to Fragmentation

A long tradition of social theory that includes Durkheim and Parsons, tells the story of the advent of modernity as a story of the shift towards a differentiation of functional domains. For Luhmann, '[t]he evolution of this highly improbable social order required replacing stratification with functional differentiation as the main principle of forming subsystems within the overall system of society' (Luhmann, 1986b: 318). Modernity was marked by a new configuration of the nature of the social bond as a type of solidarity that Durkheim termed 'organic', and correlative to a new division of labour and pluralisation of value spheres. The differentiation has to do with the gradual autonomisation of spheres and logics of social action, the development of separate semantics for the differentiated fields, and with their principle of linkage – 'solidarity' in Durkheim – being largely reconceptualised in the process.

Even though from the very beginning the social theories of modernity divided over whether the study of society should be undertaken from the viewpoint of conflict or of equilibrium, the answers that so radically divided them were, arguably, answers to the same fundamental question: *'how is social order possible?'* For conflict-theorists, Marx paradigmatic amongst them, the question was posed in the face and against the background of class conflict that made it improbable for contradictory dynamics to find expression in the form of order. For equilibrium theorists, Durkheim paradigmatic amongst them, the question was posed in the face and against the background of double contingency. In the case of double contingency the question of order acquired a higher pertinence in the wake of the acceleration of dynamics of division of labour. The answer, argued equilibrium theorists, must seek its improbable locution in the field of societal differentiation, or the autonomisation of societal spheres and domains.

In this section we follow the well-travelled path of differentiation with our gaze on the question to which it is the answer. If 'men, down to the present time,' says Durkheim, 'have conceived moral forces under the form of religious allegories,' what would it mean to 'disengage them from their symbols [and] present them in their *rational nakedness*?' (1925/1961: 11). The question goes deeper than merely asking about what substitutes for religious feeling once societal values have been denuded from the 'allegories' that had sustained them. Instead it asks what makes the substitute order an order of value *at all*? Because if the 'forces' that sustain social solidarity are stripped of value-content, what holds society together as a rational order at all for the purposes of its maintenance and reproduction? The question is asked of both terms: *'rational'* and *'order'*.

The question over the possibility of order originates with Durkheim, and is formulated as sociology's key question by Parsons.[1] With systems theory it is confronted as a question of complexity and reduction. To put it summarily, the disciplining of the double contingency of communication is the *reduction achievement* of social systems. How communicative domains or spheres generate meaning is contingent on processes of systemic differentiation. As far as law is concerned, with the generalisation of expectations as disappointment-proof across contexts of value and across social strata, we have first a narrowing of legal thought, its immunisation towards the contents of normative orders that it becomes differentiated from (religion, morality, politics) and its uniform extension across society. *Reflexivity* is tied to reproducing positive law under the sign of validity; the reproduction of *positive* law, as pared back from particular normative orders and immunised against broader social dynamics and conflicts, guarantees the *function* of generalising expectations; and this function, performed uniquely by the law, is what underpins its *differentiation*. By withdrawing to the formal side of social interchange the law becomes the guarantor of rational order. Through the lens of functional analysis we see how reflexivity organises the internal meaning-processing achievement that we know as modern law by navigating the forcefield of complexity and in the process organising law as a differentiated, self-orienting, self-observing domain of reduced complexity. As Luhmann summarises it:

> Our definition of the concept of law can no longer be conceived of in ontological, but, instead, in functional, terms. ... It is precisely the

---

[1] Especially in Parsons (1951) and in Parsons and Shils (1951).

> *functional* reference to congruent generalisation that enforces this non-identity under complex, rapidly changeable structural conditions of the societal system: law can no longer simply *be* that which it should *achieve*. . . . 'Justice' as ethical principle is now placed outside the law.
>
> (1972/1985: 174)

Note, however, how as a direct result of differentiation, how *thin* the 'material' dimension of law becomes after the divestment of shared value: in other words, once '[j]ustice' as ethical principle is placed outside the law. Also note, to return to Durkheim's quandary over the possibility of order, how 'disengaged' this law becomes 'from its symbols', how disembedded from contexts of communal belonging and valuation. And if law is now, to paraphrase Durkheim, 'present[ed to men] in its *rational nakedness*', what is it about it that still underwrites its *ordering* function and its rationality? The answer is of course that it is precisely that 'nakedness' that secures the function. The reproduction of normative expectations becomes less and less dependent on societal relations of power, political consensus or political standing, shared values or individual motivational structures. As Luhmann puts it, 'the temporal, social and material generalisation of behavioural expectations is increased to the extent that their congruency . . . can be secured only . . . by high indifference towards every kind of individual structure of motivation' (1972/1985: 169); and therefore, counter-intuitively, by their very 'rational nakedness'.

As we close this brief account of the organising idea of functional differentiation, and what it means in terms of how we understand the place of law in the differentiated structure, let us stay for a moment with Durkheim's ambivalence. If modernity confronts us with the proliferation of differentiated spheres of activity, or in his terms the radicalisation of the 'division of labour', two dilemmas emerge for us in answering his question *'how is social order possible?'*, and both concern how improbable an achievement social order is.

The first dilemma is that due to the acceleration of the division of labour the differentiation that *makes* modern society, beyond a certain point comes *undone as fragmentation*. Famously Durkheim identified the threshold that marked the line between differentiation and fragmentation as *anomie*. We borrowed the term 'performance' from Luhmann (as underlying the heterarchical relation between sub-systems) to denote that differentiation needs to be clearly understood as a relationship *not of fragmentation but of linkage*. In Luhmann's historical analysis, it was the 'constitution' that allowed the structural coupling and dynamic co-evolution of the legal and political systems of modernity. Durkheim's anxiety that comes with overstepping, combines with what Luhmann describes as the precarious architecture of function, performance and reflexivity that underwrites modern society's principle of linkage.

The second question that Durkheim offers us revolves around his own key term, 'solidarity', by virtue of a typology that he introduces to thematise the social bond ('mechanical' versus 'organic'). The answer to the question of order *as* a 'solidarity' that runs alongside differentiation was always going to be precarious, under the proliferation of differences and their re-absorption into the dynamics of class conflict. In the face of atomisation, the 'rational nakedness' of value, and the mobilising force of self-interest, lurks this question: what in the new era makes organic solidarity a *solidarity*? In the end, Durkheim himself will acknowledge the devastating effect of this question, as André Gorz reminds us too when he writes:

> [T]he functional integration of individuals will prevent their social integration, ... and will exclude their forming reciprocal relations based on co-operation, for the purpose of achieving common objectives according to common criteria. Their organic solidarity does not exist for *them* as a lived relationship. It only exists as such for the outside observer.
>
> (Gorz, 1989: 43)

To the first of these questions we return immediately below. The second question, over solidarity, its experience and eclipse, suspends itself insistently over our whole discussion of 'market constitutionalism'.

*

The question of solidarity may not be at the forefront of Luhmann's concerns as he expounds the virtues of differentiation, in an argument whose quasi-normative premises are as obvious as they are problematic. For him the dividends of functional differentiation connect to the gains in complexity, and the new dynamics of inclusion, freedom and equality that they deliver. His defence of rights is paradigmatic in that respect; its most sustained expression remains his *Grundrechte als Institution*. In this early work of 1957, human rights become the devices through which modern differentiated society secures both the liberty and equality of its citizens by way of securing their participation across the range of its functional domains. Luhmann traces the functional differentiation of modern society and the emergence of the semantics of fundamental freedoms and human rights as parallel and complementary historical processes. The entrenchment of the latter protects society from the threat of regression into de-differentiation. For example, the freedom of religion protects society from a possible fusion of the religious and political systems, in the creation of a theocratic system. Similarly, economic freedoms prevent the fusion of the economic and political systems in the form of command or state-run economies. The function of human rights relates to the maintenance of autonomous societal spheres and facilitates the inclusion of individuals in all of them, in the sense *at least* that one's partial (or non-)inclusion in one system (say through *economic* deprivation) is prevented from spilling over into others (say the right to *political* participation, or access to *education*). In the careful orchestration of function and performance, human rights become institutionalised in law in a way that reproduces them for the whole of society and at the same time sustains its differentiation.

The normative meaning of functional differentiation, as institutionalised through human rights, plays out across the three registers of *inclusion, freedom* and *equality*. Inclusion is 'partial' and 'multi-functional'; partial because it concerns particular aspects of one's individuality (citizen, legal subject, economic actor, church-goer, pupil, etc.) and multi-functional because it traverses systems as the individual is only *transitorily* involved in any one of them. The transitory nature of the individual's embeddedness in any one context, 'the indestructible possibility of moving from one thing to another', realises inclusion and freedom in tandem in the key idea of *passage*. If for Ernst Bloch in 'the *homo religiosus, homo oeconomicus, homo politicus,* and all that rigmarole of Latinised men, the list of which we could string out indefinitely, there is grave danger of mistaking them for something else than they really are: phantoms which are convenient providing they do not become nuisances',[2] for Luhmann, 'the unity of the world is not the unity of an assemblage ..., but rather the unavoidable, indestructible possibility of moving from one thing to another – not an aggregation, but rather a correlation of meaningful experience and action' (Luhmann, 1977: 411). And we might recall also Gadamer's beautiful aside in *Truth and Method* about the experience of 'moving' and of passage: 'The self-awareness of the individual', he writes, 'is only a flickering in the closed circuits of

---

[2] For the materialist Bloch, 'the man of flesh and bone, reuniting them all simultaneously, is the only real being' (Bloch, 1986/2008: 125).

historical life' (1989: 276). To this Luhmann would add that the closure of those circuits is sealed by the self-reference of the differentiated expectational structures; whether the 'flickering' affords anything substantial enough to furnish the experience of recognition, self-awareness and the holding of subject positions is a question that is unlikely to trouble Luhmann's notion of the individual as 'homo aviator' across the manifold of systemic opportunities.

In any case the *dividends* that Luhmann draws out relate to all three ideals of inclusion, freedom and equality under modern conditions of complexity. The modern form of inclusion runs alongside the modern concept of freedom and of equality. Freedom as unimpeded participation in the autonomous fields; equality because one's social status neither qualifies one for nor impedes inclusion: all subjects are equally entitled to rights and protections. The self-presentation (a key concept in *Grundrechte*) and mobility of individuals is guaranteed by the institutionalisation of human rights in a way that is essential to social recognition. They are protective of the 'symbolically-expressive dimensions of free action ... and are concerned with the general right to free development of the person' (1957: 79).

As far as equality is concerned, there is no pretence that it will go anywhere beyond the most formal of conceptions. Equality means simply that no institutionalised discrimination should prevent access of all citizens to all systems. 'The principle of equality is to be conceived as a principle of *selective indifference;* only relevant features or inequalities have to be reckoned with in the process of inclusion' (1990: 278). Selectivity concerns what inequalities may be taken as pertinent *given* the demands of functional differentiation and modalities of inclusion. The message that was clear in 1957 is later reinforced in *Law as a Social System* in 1993, where

> the analysis permits us to subsume the right of equality within the general normative area of human rights and to consider it even as a paradigm of human rights ... human rights are correlated with modern society's structurally required openness toward the future. If every single individual needs to get free access to all function systems and if at the same time their inclusion can only be regulated within the function systems themselves, *since one can only decide what is to be conceived as equal or unequal on the basis of functionally specific criteria* ... Functionally seen, human rights serve to keep the future open for functionally specific autopoietic reproduction.
>
> (2004: 115–16, emphasis added)

In the classic gesture of abstention, equality attaches to equal human status and substantive equality of the meeting of needs is relegated to the economic sub-system and left to *its* devices. The answer to complex equality is answered instead as a question of liberty (equal access to all systems) and differentiation (its demands too complex to be handled at the societal level). The meaning of social rights, for Luhmann, is in tune with the formal notion of equality as conceptualised independently of needs. The right to work is only ever referred to as the free choice of employment, where 'choice is free and exit is possible' (1957: 91) and free access to a variety of professional roles (1957: 131). Any other, fuller, needs-driven, concept will be rebutted as incursion and signal of de-differentiation, as sign of the political system's encroachment on the economy and the 'absolutizing its own perspective'.

Let us take from this an important point about the way in which the *semantics* of subjective human rights dovetail with social *structures*, in this case the communicative openness of society and the role-structures through which people participate in its multiple functional spheres. Importantly for Luhmann, the institutionalisation of human rights involves the self-limitation of politics, its containment in, and withdrawal into, its own *proper* domain. Both moments of inclusivity and exclusivity are achieved *in tandem*, rights acting to accentuate the positive inclusivity of the emergent political system of modern society, and on the other hand to 'exclude some spheres of social exchange from the purview of the political system altogether', 'acting to police the boundary between the political system and its social environments' (Thornhill, 2014: 363, 364). It is this boundary-policing that informs Luhmann's scarcely hidden normative claim against de-differentiation, a claim that he will never be able quite to square with his expressly sociological, as opposed to normative, perspective, and which, especially in his critique of the politics of the Green Party in Germany in the 1980s, assumed shrill tones.[3]

*

What are the repercussions of *globalisation* for the functional differentiation of societies? Gunther Teubner's highly influential *Constitutional Fragments* (2012) offers the following diagnosis: 'Globalization above all means that functional differentiation, first realized historically within the nation states of Europe and North Africa, now encompasses the whole

---

[3] See in particular the concluding chapters of his *Ecological Communication* (1986a).

world. Certainly not all subsystems have globalized simultaneously, with the same speed and intensity. Religion, science and the economy are well established as global systems, while politics and law still remain mainly focused on the nation state' (Teubner, 2012: 42). 'The staggered nature of globalization produces a tension between the self-foundation of autonomous global social systems and their political-legal constitutionalization' (ibid.: 43). Teubner raises the question of this 'tension' to point out that the 'constellation' that was possible in the nation state between law, politics and the regulated field (sub-system) has come undone; that there is 'no counterpart' to it 'in the global context'; and that 'global self-foundation and national constitutionalization' – the global economic and the national political for example – 'are irrevocably drifting apart' (ibid.: 44). The discrepancy between 'globally established social sub-systems and a politics stuck at inter-state level' can only lead to 'the constitutional totality break[ing] apart' to be 'replaced by a form of constitutional fragmentation' (ibid.: 51). 'The comprehensive structural coupling' that Luhmann famously identified as an 'evolutionary achievement' in the constitution of nation-states in modernity, he says quoting Luhmann, 'clearly has no equivalent at the level of world society'. We have instead a 'new phenomenon: the self-constitutionalization of global orders without a state' (ibid.: 53). This forms the basis of Teubner's theory of [world-]'societal constitutionalism'. For Teubner, with the new societal form of 'self-constitutionalization of global orders', the constitutional function might be uploaded from national to global level, with an emphasis on constitutional *function* as definitive of what it is to have a constitution. We will return to this.

One of the earliest texts to query the elevation of functional differentiation to the global scale, was Marcelo Neves' profound attempt to argue that once generalised at the global level the autopoiesis of law becomes an 'allopoiesis'.[4] He argued that Luhmann's individual does not travel well in the world periphery, where functional differentiation at state level had not already facilitated the smooth passage between fields of her inclusion. The periphery is not differentiated, says Neves, and as a result it harbours 'expanded and intensified' forms of exclusion,

---

[4] See also Neves (1992). And although one can only speculate here because the references are sparse, I would not be surprised if Luhmann didn't write that fascinating final chapter of his treatise on the legal system (2004), the chapter that refers the reduction-achievement of law to World society, with Neves' objection in mind.

resulting in the releasing and generalising of destructive consequences which act against the validity of differentiating legal codes and against the constitution based on the rule of law and which represents the structural coupling of law and politics. This is not about a mild meta-difference of inclusion and exclusion in Luhmann's terms, ... , but rather about the generalised phenomena of exclusion that questions and threatens functional differentiation, the autonomy of law and constitutional normativity.

(Neves 2001: 261)

Over a decade later, in *Transconstitutionalism*, Neves will revisit the argument of exclusion on the global scale again as an argument about pathologies of differentiation. He describes the 'hypertrophic growth' of the economic system against 'the atrophic propensity' of the legal and political systems (2013: 33). With the balance thrown off kilter functional differentiation does not hold. This leads to 'systemic corruption' which leaves the legal system incapable of self-reproduction and operative closure. The mechanism of structural coupling that maintained stable patterns of mutual conditioning between systems comes asunder with the *corruption* of the constitution, with the effect that the economic system colonises the field. Economic efficiency becomes the 'contingency formula' for both politics and law displacing their own 'contingency formulae' of justice and legitimacy respectively; reciprocal *performance* is replaced by uni-directionality; even *reflexion* – Luhmann's term for systemic self-reference – is colonised, with economic thinking transplanted into the way that the law 'thinks'. Constitutionality at that point is floated across stretches of equivalence made possible by the generalisation of contingency formulae and the wholesale export of economic metrics and semantics to other fields. The 'normative turn' comes with Neves' insistence on 'constitutional normativity' that is not lost at the global level, as long as what he calls a transversal rationality might be maintained in the thinking of 'transconstitutionalism'. Transversal rationality is an attempt to sustain at the global level something of the normative function of the constitution by restoring some form of structural coupling at the reflexive level, a move that also characterises Teubner's global constitutionalism.

*

We thus arrive at the crux of the argument about functional differentiation which 'uploaded' to the global level surrenders its achievements and generates an asymmetry that, like cancer, having achieved an initial incursion in a system, proliferates under its own momentum. This is what we experience as the generalisation of economic reason. The 'absolutising' of one systemic rationality – the economic – once elevated above those of the political and legal systems, instrumentalises them and in the process magnifies the inequality that functional differentiation had promised to exclude. The massive asymmetry between the economic system on the one hand, and the legal and political systems on the other, cannot be addressed as a matter of design, which is why the subsumption of political systems to the logic of capital has not been met with any countervailing gesture, no force in the other direction of states reclaiming their national economies. Drawing on what has been said so far we can attempt to discern why.

Functional differentiation, as we said, names the rationalisation of spheres of activity on the basis of specialised functions, and leads to an increase in complexity in the differentiated spheres that the adequate performance of that function makes necessary. A careful architecture of mutual performances organise the field of functional differentiation, with demands on the reflexion of systems in terms of self-limitation and the maintenance of proper boundaries. If the new rationalities of the economy, of politics, of the range of differentiated spheres, remain meaningful in this precarious dispensation, it is because as differentiated they discipline the double contingency of action that would otherwise spell meaninglessness. In all this, *functionality* (as principle of differentiation), and as answer to complexity, walks a fine line. As aligned to differentiation it is purportedly experienced as inclusion in functional spheres, and, as the proponents of differentiation would have it (Durkheim, Parsons, Luhmann), delivers the dividends of a flourishing, multi-faceted agency. But if the division of labour names an interdependence, the maintenance of order must avoid the risk that interdependence splinter into fragmentation. And this is precisely what happens with globalisation.

The question of justice is vulnerable to scaling up because the scaling up causes differentiation to collapse into fragmentation. Differentiation names *a principle of connection* that holds the parts together meaningfully – as differentiated and therefore as maintaining a relationship both to the whole and amongst themselves. Fragmentation on the other hand simply means *scattering*; it marks the move away from the whole and towards brokenness. Differentiation breaks under the weight of an asymmetry between an economic system and the legal and political systems, where the former's organisation of the global flows of capital depends on the exploitation of the latter, still largely stuck at state-level. This deficit is no temporary, and transient, anomaly; it is instead *structurally* built in to *the architecture of global capitalism*. In the case of Europe the asymmetry shows in the unevenness of the integration of national markets (through the fast-tracking of economic integration) as against the fragmentation of states' systems of social protection. At the level of 'world society' it is seen in the hugely successful creation of 'global turbo-capitalism' against the multi-fragmented processes of political trans-nationalisation. In each case the asymmetry is vital and productive for the integration of capital and the extraction of profit. Where the economic system overwhelms (and the political underwhelms) the transnational is already largely colonised by the economic logic it is supposed to 'impact' on. The idea that a transnational system, *whose very logic of connectivity* (the 'trans' of the transnational) *plays out that of competition* (amongst national systems) and comparative advantage, might nevertheless act to rein in what sustains it, makes no sense at all. We are depressingly familiar with the ways in which the transnational is organised along the lines of managing 'preparedness for the market' – through the 'un-protecting' of labour, the suppression of wages and undercutting of trade unionism, the rolling back of the main costs of labour reproduction back onto labour, etc. The relation between capitals and states is crucial here, and the asymmetry propels the creation of margins of profit in terms of the 'race to the bottom' where social protection afforded by states are costs and where any attempt to hoist it, social protection that is, above national level is systematically undercut. Spectacularly here, more than any other sphere of legal thinking, the reflexivity of the legal and political systems is short-circuited back into the market paradigm by taking for granted the 'redundancy' of any older problématique that might have invoked democratic arguments about participation in production, 'co-determination', or any sense of virtue when it comes to economic relations. For the most part theorists of social rights and labour law appear incapable of thinking past labour market optimisation (see Chapters 3.3 and 3.4), and the power asymmetries in relations of core and peripheral states become part of the 'rationalisation' of the global economy. In the meantime the systematic pauperisation of the periphery daily jettisons large numbers of skilled and semi-skilled workers into what used to be called the 'reserve pool of the unemployed', to compete for casual labour with the ever-increasing flows of illegal immigrant labour. The pattern is generalised across the board, always driven by the demand of maximisation of financial returns, and in each case re-specified to the institutional logic of the field.

Of course, at the level of theory, many of these examples can be discussed further, explained otherwise or away, and the assessment of what political publics on the global scale might achieve cannot and should not be underestimated: global economic action inevitably generates global constituencies of addressees and therefore also global challenges.[5] It is not my purpose to pre-empt any of those discussions. My modest aim of this reference to constitutional fragmentation was to identify an asymmetry that is constitutive of the logic of extraction of surplus value under conditions of globalisation, and thus structural. And to insist on the consequence this has for systems-theoretical analysis, namely that the thesis of mutual cognitive adaptability between systems relied on a symmetry that is now buried under a different principle of organisation, where the move from national to transnational politics is significantly impacted upon, if not actually organised, by the economic logic it will then be called on to mitigate. The economic system, having successfully harnessed the state to a system of global competition, simply 'exploits' it in the direction of its own aggressive expansion.

The collapse of differentiation into fragmentation is what will allow the market to collect fragments into the principle of circulation and append them to its circuits, to re-organise and align the fragments to its own very particular logic of optimisation. This is what the generalisation of economic reason means, offers and entails, as it is carried in the varieties of differentiation. It is to the generalisation of market thinking that we will now turn, and to its most incisive champion, Friedrich von Hayek.

The Generalisation of Economic Reason: Hayek's Legacy

Hayek's seminal 1968 lecture 'Competition as a discovery procedure'[6] delivered with the explicit intention of 'considering competition systematically as a procedure for discovering facts', was staggering in its influence to the rise of the New Right during the eighties, and more broadly in the way in which it helped to shift the social and political imaginary of

---

[5] Or pure negativity. If, that is, the logic of global capitalist expansion, as race to the bottom, pits the economic against the political systems, then the learning process can only assume the form of anti-capitalist struggle. It may be that a number of political mobilisations of our time, including the October 2019 outbreak of the anti-systemic movement in Chile, provide evidence of this.

[6] Originally: 'Der Wettbewerb als Entdeckungsverfahren'. Translated and reproduced in F. A. Hayek, 'Competition as a discovery procedure' (2002) 5(3) *Quarterly Journal of Austrian Economics* 9.

advanced capitalist societies. There are, of course, other significant texts poised on the breach; we take Hayek's as exemplary. The lecture comprises five parts; two provide an attack on trade unionism and on macroeconomic management; two capture the promise of the new freedom, on an epistemological register. Between the two sets the theory of 'catallaxy' provides the pivot for the move from the former set to the latter. Is it incidental that Hayek's lecture culminates in a defence of the generalisation of economic reason to the field of social value production, that is, the sphere of work? We might usefully begin with that.

Hayek's text contains a scathing attack on trade unionism and the catastrophic effect that he claims the 'rigidity of wages' has had in systems of industrial relations like Britain's with its 'most deeply rooted, and most all-encompassing trade union movement, which through its wage policy had succeeded in conserving a wage structure that was determined much more by considerations of "justice" than of economic appropriateness' (1974/2002: 20). For Hayek, a wage structure that becomes 'rigid' prevents the economy's adjustment to altered circumstances, and the movement of workers among the branches of industry. The structure does not 'learn', committed as it is normatively to politically entrenched 'achievements' of collective bargaining and outmoded considerations about 'fair' price. The task of debunking these falsities and anachronisms is not made easy, complains Hayek, where an idiom of working class victories 'confers an aura of legitimacy on the antisocial and destructive practices that they cause' (ibid.). Hayek attacks trade unionism for favouring entrenched interest on the one hand and for being economically wasteful on the other, unions respectively anti-democratic and economically detrimental. The attack is levelled both on *economic* and on *democratic* grounds: Trade unions are anti-democratic because '[w]e cannot go on much longer closing our eyes to the fact that the interest of labor as a whole demands that the power of individual trade unions to maintain the relative position of their members against other workers be removed' (1974/2002: 22). They are economically wasteful because their stubborn resistance to risk-taking (the risk that real wages may fall absolutely) leaves workers stranded in economically destructive rigidities. A waste of opportunity in the name of 'social justice', an outmoded concept, for Hayek, that ordinarily involves the imposition of uniform values on a plurality and diversity of perspectives on justice. Later Hayek will claim: 'The real exploiters in our present society are not egotistic capitalists or entrepreneurs, but organisations which derive their power from the moral support of collective action and the feeling of group loyalty' (Hayek, 1979/2002: 96). 'It is a strange dialectic', noted Bruno Latour in another context, 'that brings the exploiter back to life and buries the gravedigger' (Latour, 2012: 8).

While much of what was presented by Hayek in the confrontational terms of the attack of the New Right that he spearheaded has gradually morphed into cooler varieties of global market necessitarian thinking, with new distributions of necessity and contingency on that scale, the effort fully to reduce labour to its commodity form continues to be pursued unabatedly, if unremarkably, by Richard Posner and other champions of the Law and Economics movement. The identification of trade unionism with 'cartelisation' is a key feature of such analyses that celebrate the reduction of the *ratio juris* to the logic of price. We do not need to dwell on the flattening banalities of Law and Economics, the paucity of theory, the barbarism of reduction. If we choose to focus on Hayek, it is because Hayek is a profound thinker of the market, and we will only be able to gauge, and resist, his very particular influence if we recognise the epistemological acumen of his powerful and devastating epistemological reduction, though of course that is not his term. The other reason for this focus is in order to appreciate the staggering of an argument for the market first made on economic grounds, which then migrates to a theory of justice and democracy, finally and crucially to an epistemology (or in his terms 'a discovery procedure'). It is on these ultimate grounds that the generalisation of economic reason receives its epistemological warrant.

So let us reconstruct Hayek's theory of the market in terms of the series of moves that track what we have called the generalisation of economic reason: the *first* involves the collapse of the political economy into its market form; the *second* involves its democratic redemption in an argument that allows 'unplanned' market allocations to displace a society's constitutive political orientation to meeting needs and re-orients the thinking about 'social justice' in the process. But neither of the moves on the economic and democratic registers would be possible without a *third* move, which undertakes the epistemological defence of the market, on which the generalisation of its reason depends and which upholds and redeems the substitutions at the other levels. The three steps of market 'capture' – economic, democratic, epistemological – will help us to structure the following chapter (3.2) on the consolidation of 'total market thinking'. But first things first.

The collapse of the political economy into its market form proceeds through Hayek's influential argument against the management of the economy. His impatience is notable as he takes on Keynes and macroeconomic management, to criticise the 'irresponsibility' that that tradition has bequeathed its successors: 'We are harvesting here only what the founder of this fashion has sown, since we are naturally already in that "long run" in which he knew he would be dead.'[7] The irresponsibility lies in directing economic thinking to the meeting of social needs and is reflected in *political* efforts to correct prices and income in the name of some at best nebulous, but for the most part disingenuous,[8] commitment to '*social justice*'; the latter 'is a principle that cannot be implemented in general without destroying the foundations of the market order' (1974/2002: 17). Against deploying democratic categories in the running of the economy, Hayek will argue that a *democratic society* cannot be run through a command structure. 'An economic system in which everyone received what others felt he deserved could not help but be a highly inefficient system, quite apart from the fact that it would also be an unbearably tyrannical one' (18). The justification for using the price mechanism, then, 'is solely that it shows individuals that what they have previously done, or can do now, has become more or less important, for reasons with which they have nothing to do' (17).

In Hayek's re-telling of the story, efficiency, justice and freedom *remain* the clear stakes of the game, but in relation to each of those values, the Left's commitment to social democracy shows itself to be cumbersome, partial and 'tyrannical' respectively. The power of Hayek's text lies above all in that reversal, whereby the foundational commitments of the Left to justice and democracy are co-opted or undercut, leaving them looking outdated, politically oppressive and philosophically naïve. The move allows Hayek to collapse the notion of a political economy into its market form *in the name of* individual freedom from the collective command structure and egalitarian inclusion, and for that matter also of democracy. If the scope of democratic citizenship needs to be scaled back and claimed back from its alleged corporatist deformation, it is because the form of 'political' intervention that the latter mandates substitutes for the plurality of individual choices a uniform system of objectives. As the argument unfolds it gradually mutates from 'democracy' to 'rationality', and from the political

---

[7] Hayek, 1974/2002: 20. The sarcastic aside refers to Keynes' famous statement in the 1923 *Tract on Monetary Reform* in which, having established that the economy *can* slip into an *under*-employment *equilibrium*, his retort ('in the long run we are all dead') was directed at mainstream economists who argued that the economy will eventually return to a point of equilibrium if only we were willing to wait long enough without interfering. Hayek's is an insistent renewal of the argument for abstinence.

[8] 'In practice it has had virtually only one [meaning]: protecting some groups of people from having to descend from the absolute or relative lifestyle they have heretofore enjoyed' (Hayek, 1974/2002).

to the epistemological register. The political economy – politically directed and mandated on the one hand, on the other involving hierarchisations of needs on the basis of uniform criteria – involves the 'tyrannical' imposition of societal choices and value systems on individuals, an imposition that cannot be sustained as rational and finds no footing in the field of knowledge. The market order, in contrast, for Hayek, offers both.

*

If the rigidity of the wage structure is what infuriates Hayek, and social policy initiatives impairing market functionality what 'exhausts' him, the argument that he offers for 'competition as discovery procedure' pivots on the notion of 'catallaxy' and coupled with it the institution of *law*. Hayek invented the term 'to describe the order brought about by the mutual adjustment of many individual economies in a market. A catallaxy is thus the special kind of spontaneous order produced by the market through people acting within the rules of the law of property, tort and contract' (Hayek, 1976/2002: 108–9). But to introduce competition at the very root of society's attribution of value to resources, in order, that is, to place competition *behind* the starting line as initiator and motor of 'discovery' and as judge and measure of social value, he has to perform what is in effect an *extraordinary elision*. The elision functions to sustain *and* obscure the gesture of closure that sets his conditions of market 'openness' and reflexivity. He performs this clearing act in relation to the question of *scarcity*.

It is wrong for economic theory, Hayek says, to proceed 'from the assumption of a "given" quantity' of scarce goods. 'Which goods are scarce, or which things are goods, or how scarce or valuable they are, is precisely one of the conditions that competition should discover: in each case it is the preliminary outcomes of the market process that inform individuals where it is worthwhile to search' (1974/2002: 13). Against the 'givenness' of goods and their relative 'value' or plenitude, Hayek will insist that *no given assumptions of scarcity should or can precede their discovery* through competition. But there is an inversion in this. And Hayek will have been familiar with the objection that economics *begins* with the *institutionalisation of scarcity*.[9] The form of that institutionalisation in market economies is to recognise private property in

---

[9] On this formulation, see in particular the early American institutionalists Veblen and Commons. For the institutionalists the emergence of law was never a spontaneous development from individual interactions but involved a constitutive institutional dimension.

natural resources. The objection that scarcity already presupposes institutionalisation, and that the institutionalisation of scarcity is achieved through property title, can be traced at least back to the *German Ideology* where Marx argued that scarcity is properly understood as the *result of* property title that enables a logic of exchange dependent on the exclusionary nature of property title: the legally buttressed capacity to control access to resources. Hayek will only ever respond with the unquestioned givenness of at least *that* institution. And clearly there have to be *some* givens for market discovery to lay claim to its field, to deliver however 'preliminary' certain outcomes, in order for competition to get *any* traction. In all this Hayek's 'catallaxy' (as he is 'pleased to call market order, to avoid using the expression "economy"') carries its *a priori* assumptions lightly. But for all its assured 'thinness' vis-à-vis institutional form, market capacity does presuppose property title and therefore a prior institutionalisation of scarcity, without which any micro-economic possibilities of individual market activity and 'discovery' could not get off the ground. Of course, once on its way, the attribution of value through demand and supply allows a renegotiation of the distribution of scarcity amongst resources. But this is an attribution and re-negotiation of value *given property relations,* not a discovery of 'which goods are scarce and which things are goods'. Somewhere on the fork of this binary, of this double bind as condition *and* object, the promise of competition as discovery comes theoretically undone. (As Keynes once put it with relation to Hayek, 'an extraordinary example of how, starting with a mistake, a remorseless logician can end up in Bedlam'.)

With each turn of the argument, Hayek's defence of the market seeks a firmer footing on epistemological ground. He argues that the discovery of social value cannot seek legitimation *in political decisions* because they necessarily lack the requisite basis in adequate information, and for that reason too cannot claim legitimacy. Market freedom is insistently pitted against the arbitrariness of politically mandated orders and their ranking of objectives.[10] With the argument about competition as discovery procedure, Hayek can lay claim to the field of contingency (regarding the choice of values and their relative weights) in a way that secures

---

[10] 'All members of an economy – conceived of as a consciously managed organization – must serve the uniform hierarchy of objectives in all their actions' and all 'effort is directed toward a uniform order of objectives, are to an extent completely irrelevant for the complex structure consisting of the many individual economies. . . . The market order does not serve a particular rank ordering of objectives.' (1974/2002: 14)

'openness' and further unleashes innovation and wealth-creation. And he can claim this *against* political macro-management. Contrast it, he invites us, 'with the two advantages of a spontaneous market order or catallaxy: it can use the knowledge of all participants, and the objectives it serves are the particular objectives of all its participants in all their diversity and plurality' (1974/2002: 14). Against the 'uniformity' of democratically ranked economic objectives, Hayek will introduce the 'heterarchical' as roughly functionally equivalent to the 'democratic' and as inviting 'pluri-vocal' forms of fluidity. In the next chapter we will encounter these substitutions again in the nearly messianic status they have acquired in the literature on democratic governance.

Catallaxy designates 'a special kind of spontaneous order produced by the market through people acting within rules of the law of property, tort and contract' (1976/2002: 109). It is at this juncture that we discern *the constitutional function of law* and the very particular way in which Hayek offers a re-conceptualisation of constitutionalism as supporting the structure of the 'Great Society'. The constitutional function of law is to support private property rights, ensure that returns accrue to those who make investments in the process of discovery, and guarantee freedom of access to markets. The function of these 'abstract rules of just conduct' is that 'by defining a protected domain of each [individual], [they] enable an order of actions to form itself wherein the individuals can make feasible plans' (1973/2002: 85–6). At the same time as supplying institutional support for the 'motive power' of individual economic actors,[11] they impose limits on group and sectional interests that would work to impose distortions; the power of such groups will require limitation by general rules of law. The rules are thus negative in tenor, they place prohibitions on the intrusion of collective logics of action on individuals, and they sanction agreements. Crucially (and revealingly), for Hayek the 'traditional Rights of Man – freedoms of speech, of assembly and of association – must be reconsidered so as to *sterilise them against collectivism*: they have only one valid objective: they are intended to protect individual liberty in the sense of the absence of state coercion' (1979/2002: 86–7). The 'real issue' behind the protection of freedom of association now having 'become the freedom of the individual to join or not to join a union' given that the 'sole cause' is 'as often as not' an attempt by the union 'to force unwilling workers to join' (1960/2013: 268). If the

---

[11] I have borrowed the expression from Simon Deakin.

constitutional function of law secures catallaxy in the form of the rule of law, negative freedoms and the protection of property, it is complemented by an evolutionary account of the law as social learning, as captured in his celebration of the *common law*, which is for him a body of distilled wisdom 'by which the spontaneous order grows', and requires legislative intervention only exceptionally where some distortion has arisen.

*

The informational value tied to conventions and the tacit normativity they carry connects to a second hugely important argument that supports the epistemic argument for the market. It has to do with the signalling function of price. 'The curious task of economics is to demonstrate to men how little they know about what they imagine they can design', Hayek will write in *The Fatal Conceit* (Hayek, 1988/2013: 76). Already in the 1968 lecture, '[A]ll economic decisions are made necessary by unanticipated changes, and the justification for using the price mechanism is solely that it shows individuals that what they have previously done, or can do now, has become more or less important . . .' (1974/2002: 17). The price mechanism encodes knowledge about scarcity and the price signal shows people to adjust their behaviour. Thus it operates as an 'information transmission system' which aids agents to overcome coordination problems. No other process is 'conceivable which would in the same way take account of all the relevant facts as [does] the pricing process of the competitive market' (Hayek, 1935: 143).

Now this argument about pricing rehearses earlier insights by Ludwig von Mises and owes much to the Austrian School of Economics. Mises offers the key insight that the attribution of value to resources is the work of *subjective preferences* of agents, and answers in that way the question that had perplexed classical economists from Smith to Ricardo over the *objective* determination of value. No planning authority is able to lift itself above the order of subjective attribution to substitute for the collective and several distribution of value amongst resources and possible uses, as this is invested in actual participatory activity of individuals and inscribed in the market. If at the basis of the economic knowledge of a society is the knowledge of the opportunity costs of resources, argued Mises, then no planner's *shadow pricing* of any given stock of resources can replace the subjective expectations about returns as expressed in the autonomous and decentralised activity of individual decision-makers. The subjective conferral of value to the whole range of social objects, and consequently the subjective nature of the 'data' of the social sciences, points towards an inductive, conjectural method to the approach of patterns of human behaviour. Shadow pricing on the basis of statistical, etc., information, both Mises and Hayek argue, will incur a loss of information. The process of competitive price formation, involves the discovery and utilisation of knowledge that no one can know in advance or in its entirety. The argument against planning is then an argument against the arrogance of a 'constructivist rationalism' (Hayek will call it) that assumes the 'view from above' and in socialist economies corresponds to a progressive abuse of reason.[12]

It is with respect to the argument about pricing that Hayek performs a significant departure from Mises and offers an argument that delivers a formidable if often ignored insight. With respect to pricing, Mises had offered a 'calculational' argument, or, rather, pointed to a calculational impossibility regarding the aggregation of knowledge. He argued that because resources and preferences are not static, relative prices are in constant flux, and as a result simulating market pricing 'from above' is a calculational impossibility. If a socialist system is an 'anti-economy', as he was fond of saying, it is because the epistemic problem involves the root calculational limitation regarding assigning scarce resources to competing ends. In the context of this argument, Hayek introduces his great conceptual innovation that directs the market as an epistemic device to the most valuable of social resources, human knowledge. His significant advance on Mises is to turn to the market *not as a solution to the problem of the calculability of knowledge but to its generation*. Knowledge as a resource is generated in processes of participation in market activity that brings to the sphere of what is knowable and known otherwise unarticulated, otherwise irretrievable knowledge. What competition as discovery procedure discovers is information that is *embedded*, in local and tacit contexts, and *embodied*, in practices now called forth as agents hone their skills and talents in market participation.

What the market therefore discovers for Hayek is information extracted from its embeddedness in latent structures of tacit knowledge, and in the pre-understandings embedded in tradition and in fleeting

---

[12] And as Manfred Streit comments in laudatory mode, 'This question must be asked, last but not least, because market prices are the result of contracts whose initiation, negotiation, and execution depend in many ways on expectations of a conforming behavior among actors who frequently are strangers to each other' (Streit, 1993: 223). See also Gray (1992: 23).

economic environments and unarticulated assumptions. It is knowledge that is embodied because constitutively linked to skills and practices and – to the extent that Hayek is centrally concerned with the marketability of those skills and practices – to entrepreneurial insight. These are portrayed by Hayek as *lifeworld* practices, embedded in forms of life, expressed in intuition over choice and value, both mobilising expectations and pre-understandings from pools and inventories that would otherwise remain untapped. There is also a concern here with *practical knowledge*, an emphasis on 'skills and abilities' 'in many regards always unique' that 'will not only (and not even primarily) be skills that the person in question can recite in detail or report to a government agency'[13] that primarily contribute to the reproduction of society and on which it evidently depends. They cannot be 'recited or reported' as long as they remain untapped. They are first called forth and given significance through market activity, the references here easily inclusive of what Gilbert Ryle called 'knowing how', Michael Polanyi 'tacit knowledge' and Michael Oakshott 'traditional knowledge'. The information embedded in market pricing, since it is not the property of any one market participant, is a sort of holistic knowledge of the whole society, a *public patrimony* as John Gray puts it well (Gray, 1992: 7).

In this light, the gathering concepts of economic theory that inform, for Hayek, spurious macro-management dependent on coarse reductions and collective signifiers, are clearly insufficiently attentive to the embeddedness of micro-economies and individual orientations towards values. Participatory engagement will carry tacit knowledge, in that it cannot be second-guessed and cashed out in terms of simulations or projected assumptions. It is instead knowledge constitutively tied to microorientations, incentives, attributions and mobilisations of agents. The discovery by individuals of *embedded information* during competitive interaction is the motor of the process of spontaneous *adjustment* whereby the market reorders itself in response to changing circumstances. For Hayek, this form of economic order has crucial advantages insofar as it allows for the harnessing of the knowledge possessed by all the individual participants – knowledge which in a society based on an

---

[13] 'Rather, the knowledge of which I am speaking consists to a great extent of the ability to detect certain conditions – an ability that individuals can use effectively only when the market tells them what kinds of goods and services are demanded, and how urgently' (Hayek, 1974/2002: 13).

advanced division of labour is widely diffused and cannot be known to any centralised bureaucracy.

Participatory engagement in the process itself is necessary to reveal a greater level of detail about such contingencies as what use-values – at any given moment – can be sold as commodities and what values (understood as an expression of relative scarcity) these will have. Such information is transmitted to individual participants via *price signals* in relation to which they reflexively orient their behaviour, discovering further facts about themselves (each individual's particular combination of skills and abilities) which again cannot be fully known in advance (1974/2002: 13). What is certainly lost in this win-win account, is any concern with those lacking requisite skills or resources, those that are thereby inhibited from participating for lack of 'talents' to hone or commit. For them, unbridled markets simply reproduce and perpetuate structural inequalities in life-chances, a redundancy that fast traverses the spectrum of economic activity, democratic participation and the distribution of rationality in the way that Hayek has recast them as continuous.

*

Distinct lines of critique suggest themselves along each of the three steps of the generalisation of economic reason: the gradual elevation of the market to organising principle of the economic, the democratic and the epistemological domains respectively. It is with the capture of the epistemological domain that Hayek finally *achieves* the generalisation of economic reason.

The first line of critique refers to the collapse of the political economy into its market form. It involves a moment of coupling and one of decoupling. The coupling is with the legal form of property title, on which the *institutionalisation of scarcity* depends. The form that institutionalisation takes in market economies is the recognition of private property in natural resources. Scarcity presupposes institutionalisation, and the institutionalisation of scarcity is achieved through property title; property title is what releases goods into the circuits of the market. Only on the back of this coupling – which imports the logic of commodity from the very start – can the market gain traction as discovery procedure, to then furnish Hayek's thesis that innovation is realised through the competitive activity of entrepreneurs constantly searching for unexploited opportunities, that knowledge of the self is most profoundly disclosed in the process of adjustment to market circumstances, etc. An elision sustains the edifice of justification. That is why it is simply not true that 'which goods are scarce, or which things are goods, or how scarce or valuable they are, is precisely one of the conditions that competition should discover' because there would be nothing to discover if the distribution of scarcity had not already received the sanction of the institution of property. But the *coupling* that brings commodification to the very heart of the discovery of 'value' in production, effects at the same time a *decoupling* of production from the values of democracy and solidarity which are constitutive of social labour and organise production as a collective, human, undertaking. Hayek's move has rendered these ideals inimical to competition and *thereby* also to the determination and allocation of value. The economy is cleansed of its political dimension in the only proper understanding of it as a *market* economy, a move as noxious as it is arbitrary.

The second line of critique refers to the use of the principle of the market to supplant the principle of justice. The spontaneous order alone underwrites the justice of distributions. The distributional results of the spontaneous order of market activity are not intentionally planned by anyone, so *however unequal the resulting burdens*, they are not directed by or to specified persons since the effects of market activity on particular individuals is unknown. The injunction 'this is unjust' is not available where the loss suffered is accompanied by a loss of concepts to name the injury: where economic activity takes place in a field marked out by non-negotiable coordinates, in the way one would understand the play of natural forces, the term 'coercion' and the term 'justice' appear something of a misnomer in this light – 'chimerical' in Hayek's idiom.

This re-signification of the field of political rationality has devastating effects on the pursuit of social justice by societies attempting to meet some of the social costs of the unbridled operation of markets through systems of social security and social rights. Again, this argument meets an inflexible counter, in terms of what Hayek is not prepared to permit even at compensatory levels. For him the inequalities and concentrations of power and wealth which arise from the operation of market forces produce their own solution by incentivising those who, by misfortune or otherwise, fail to profit from the system. Even if certain gains and losses accrue by chance leaving some with 'undeserved disappointments', he concedes, ex-post redistribution of resources blunts incentives for individuals to invest in their own skills and efforts. Interventions which might have been justified from a 'market perfecting' point of view as far as Hayek is concerned block the *process* of competition as discovery which, as we saw, provides the means by which dispersed knowledge and information are put to use: hence, 'attempts to "correct" the order of the market lead to its destruction' (Hayek, 1976/2002: 127, 142).

Not unlike *The Road to Serfdom* that preceded it by over two decades, *The Mirage of Social Justice* is an uncompromising polemic against the Left, impatient, superficial, shrill. It attacks the 'instincts' of 'altruism' and solidarity as too deeply 'imbedded in our purely instinctive or intuitive reaction' to hold up to reason, 'a great obstacle to the development of the modern economy' (1976/2002: 96ff). Hayek's attack on the notion of 'social justice' is blistering here. Its 'chimerical quality' is exhibited foremost, in his view, by the unintelligibility of the counter-concept it measures itself against. Injustice, says Hayek, is properly understood as a vice of human action: to be the victim of injustice is to have some wrong done to one by some intentional or negligent action of another acting subject. Social inequality is not unjust because, on the one hand, 'societies' are not themselves acting subjects that might be blamed for committing injustices, and, on the other, humans, who *are* acting subjects, *can* commit injustices by breaching obligations transactionally assumed, but *cannot* be blamed for having intended the distributions of good and bad fortune that are the results of those transactions. Inequalities therefore which are clearly not the intended result of any action cannot be injustices, and social justice talk is conceptually confused.[14] How unremitting this quasi-Kantian rebuttal: to the extent that what is installed as market activity involves the 'catallaxy' of general rules, we cannot be held responsible for the effects that those rules will have. Why? Because since the distributional results of the spontaneous order are not intentionally planned by anyone, and the considerable range of inequality produced affects 'unspecified persons', that is, the effects on *particular* individuals is unknown, then supposed economic *coercion* can be no more conceived as a restriction of freedom than natural obstacles can. And this applies even though *we know* that markets produce inequality, and Hayek himself will not doubt it for a second. In that absolution the opportunity structure of equality is thereby left uncompromised. Hayek's was a 'non-zero-sum game whose rules have the objective of increasing the

---

[14] Hayek, 1976/2002: 31–43, 62–100; and more generally, 1976/2002, chs 8 and 9. One is reminded here of Hans Magnus Enzenberger's poem *Cold Comfort*: 'We have learnt to our dismay/ that there is no justice/ and furthermore, to our even greater dismay/ from informed sources beaming with satisfaction/ that nothing remotely like it/ can, should or ever will exist' (from *Selected Poems*, 1978, trans. D. Constantine et al., Carcanet).

payoff but leave the share of the individuals partly to chance' (Hayek, 1974/2002: 16). To this facile absolution, Neil MacCormick offers a comprehensive rebuttal, delivered with characteristic eloquence:

> Those who seek to restore the market know that properly working markets generate considerable ranges of economic inequality. No such inequalities are or need be intended by any of the market's participants. But those who deliberately set about restoring a market-based economic order must be deemed to intend just such inequalities, for a person is deemed to intend what he knows to be the foreseeable outcome of his act. That one cannot foresee who will make the gains and suffer the losses is irrelevant to the issue of responsibility. If I give a hand-grenade to a madman en route to the theatre and people get killed, I cannot afterwards excuse myself by saying that I couldn't foresee who would be killed.
>
> (1989: 48)

The third line of critique refers to the elevation of the market to principle of veridiction. Hayek argues that the 'truth' of the economy is to be found at the micro-level, since 'the coarse structure of the economy can exhibit no regularities that are not results of the fine structure, and those aggregates or mean values, which alone can be grasped statistically, give us no information about what takes place in the fine structure' (1974/2002: 11). The contrast between 'coarse' (macro) and 'fine' (micro) is key to Hayek's argument. The macro-level of economic *theory* cannot and should not claim truth value for the regularities it discovers, regularities that at best condense, when they do not actually distort, the 'results of the fine structure' of market exchange. It is a violation of that fine structure that is inflicted at the macro-level by the use of averages, aggregates and mean values grasped statistically. Hayek's attack on macro-economic thinking has profound implications for economic theory in general. If (macro-)economic thinking is pseudo-science for Hayek (not only is the latter less 'scientific' than the former, but that it can 'in the strictest sense... make no claim to the name of a theoretical science' (1974/2002: 11)), it is because he denies that passage is possible between the level of competition at the micro-level and the generalisations that operate at the macro-level with the use of aggregations, collective categories and the 'spurious' extraction of data that they enable. In the *Theory of Complex Phenomena* (1964) Hayek argued this point in the context of a theory of complexity, suggesting that 'pattern predictions' are, at best, rules of thumb generalising and keeping constant across stretches of time assumptions that were always subject to being belied by the inexhaustible production of concrete data and the constant generation of information at the level of the 'fine structure' of market exchange. This relative inertia of the macro-structure vis-à-vis the vast diversity and incessant movement of its micro-level substratum explains why economic science will forever only imperfectly replicate the workings at the micro-level, like a mirror of distortion never achieving anything like a level of independent reflection and adequate theorisation at the macro-level.

The answer to Hayek on this point must be that the micro and the macro do not represent levels of reality where the former *nestles* within the latter. Bruno Latour makes this point well in his critique of what he calls 'anti-zoom': 'It cannot be said that the small and the short lie *within* the large and long, in the sense that the largest or the longest contain them but with just "fewer details". … The longer narrative does not contain the "shorter" one at all; it instead re-iterates all the elements differently.'[15] The move that *must both be made and obscured* by Hayek involves this transitivity, 'reiterated' as smooth passage between the two levels. But the assumed congruence between the levels is precisely that: *assumed*. It is a fiction that naturalises the macro as the plural organisation of the micro, the long run as a succession of short terms, the invisible hand not *handling* anything at all! But we are getting ahead of the argument. Let us stay with Hayek's epistemic move and justification at the heart of the thesis of 'competition as discovery procedure': the expectation of transitivity between *micro-* and *macro-*levels in which the concepts organising the *macro* do so in the most benign imaginable way, reflecting without overstepping the 'gathering' work they are meant to perform, and thus upholding competition at the micro-level as that which alone yields true outcomes. And let us confront it for the ideological work it performs.

*

Mid-way through his lecture ('Competition as a discovery procedure'), Hayek performs one of his signature dismissals, aimed implicitly at *critical theory*. Except that there is a supposed humility about this one, couched in a language of obvious pragmatism and epistemological modesty. Hayek writes:

> The only reason we use competition at all has as its necessary consequence the fact that the validity of the theory of competition can never be

---

[15] Bruno Latour, 'anti-zoom' (2014) as quoted in Moncrieff (2016: 106). I owe this point to Lilian Moncrieff.

empirically verified for those cases in which it is of interest. It is of course possible to verify the theory on preconceived theoretical models; and in principle we could also conceivably verify the theory in artificially created situations in which all the facts that competition is to discover are known to the observer in advance. In such a situation, however, the outcome of the experiment would be of little interest, and it would probably not be worth the cost of conducting it. When, however, we do not know in advance the facts we wish to discover with the help of competition, we are also unable to determine how effectively competition leads to the discovery of all the relevant circumstances that could have been discovered. All that can be empirically verified is that societies making use of competition for this purpose realize this outcome to a greater extent than do others – a question which, it seems to me, the history of civilization answers emphatically in the affirmative.

(1974/2002: 10)

A humility of sorts attaches to the argument of Hayek's: he calls on no meta-theory to justify it, invoking simply the empirical affirmation of success for 'societies making use of competition'. The 'coarse' level of macro-economic theory achieves nothing except at best a broad-stroke replication of the finer workings of the micro-level, but more likely a distortion of those workings by grasping them by means of aggregates, averages, mean values and statistical information, the many ways that theory always already misrepresents the field of its intervention. The 'preconceived theoretical models' of the extract capture Hayek's contempt for their supposed 'verification' that can be nothing except the distortion of the understandings (*Verstandnisse*) mobilised in the finer structure. The organising (Hegelian) distinction between 'understanding' and 'reason' is reversed, nothing except distortion can be delivered at the 'tribunal of reason (remember Marcuse), and critical theory carries the hubris of a 'constructive rationalism' that substitutes for the understandings that market actors genuinely bring to competition as discovery procedure.

This epistemological 'honesty' and 'modesty' lies at the heart of Hayek's defence of market thinking. What it misses is that the development of the activity of micro-capital occurs in, and is *mediated* by, the macro-institutional frame of property relations and the movement of capital at the macro-level. The relation between macro and micro occurs as their dialectic rather than the one-way projection of the micro onto the level of the macro, that for Hayek comprehends the latter as its always imperfect representation. As Gregor Clunie puts it eloquently: 'If we are unable to construct more than minimally useful understandings of macro-economic processes, then the Marxist understanding of capitalism's macro-irrationality (issuing from the micro-rational behaviour of capitals) is not only unprovable, but indeed fundamentally nonsensical. If we are unable to *know* capitalism in the aggregate, what could it mean to say that it was *irrational*?'[16] The macro-irrationality of capital, *the collective process* with its contradictory logic of motion, its very particular distribution of the benefits and injuries of class, of advantage and disadvantage at individual level, and of contingency and necessity at societal level, are experienced and suffered as *fate*, that is as beyond redress.

It is perhaps at this point of intervention over theory construction, that we see Hayek's enduring and devastating contribution. His invitation to remain attentive to the diversity of micro-transactions, to their irreducible plurality and heterarchy as an epistemic demand, against theory's imposition of uniformity, allows for generalisation only in the thinnest sense, as market self-organisation. In the process he allows himself not only *a smooth passage from the 'micro' to the 'macro' but also in a genius move, to the 'meta'*. The market's promise is to collapse the top-down logic of organisation and to release societal energies down heterarchical routes and trajectories not as a prescription of market thinking but as its very redemption – democratic and epistemological.

The generalisation of economic reason that subtends his argument is of course never acknowledged as a generalisation, that is a move of selection, that both actualises and suppresses aspects of the reality it observes. In the market paradigm he expounds, the 'macro' is only ever a kind of replication at a higher level of the micro across the three dimensions of its meaning: as neutral arbitrator of value (material), as vehicle of autonomous action (social), and as investment of expectation (temporal); what elevates the market into privileged site of societal rationality is the move of obfuscation along all three dimensions, where the selective reductions at play are hidden from view.

In the *material dimension*, his invitation is to observe the micro-dynamics of the transactional allocation of value to resources, to their optimal usage and to the question of their scarcity. Valorisation as market allocation is the principle of selection; the question of social value receives its content and metric from the market choices of agents. What is highly selective about this reduction is that it relies on a prior institutionalisation of property rights and of commodification, that withdraws the space for any account of the common good, of fair price, and of social justice, independent of the micro-decisions of market allocations.

---

[16] I quote from the unpublished manuscript of his outstanding doctoral thesis at the University of Glasgow.

In the *social dimension*, there can be no macro-subject, for Hayek, and no corporate or collective identity that is not reducible to individual identities. It is the rational choice of self-determining social agents that determine the relative use-value of all societal resources. What is highly selective about the reduction here is that the paring down of agency to the *homo economicus* involves its radical divestment from the associations that define agency, a reduction that, as we know from Marx, and from Polanyi, it took massive amounts of coercion and discipline to mobilise. What is suppressed is the rationality of social citizenship, of economic solidarity and the forms of agency that the democratic organisation of production invokes and fosters.

In the *temporal dimension*, Hayek's invitation is to disarticulate the long-term into *momentary* decisions over marginal utility of the use of resources as embodied in individual transactions. The long term consists of a succession of short terms, or better, the integration without remainder of the long term into the short term. If (as John Commons put it in 1924) capital is ultimately 'the present value of the expected beneficial behaviour of other people', the *time* of capitalism is cast in that particular modality of the present-future. This highly conjectural modality of the present-future ('the present value of future behaviours') cuts across a range of temporal scales and modalities and configures them otherwise. Its 'achievement' is that it re-aligns heterogeneous time frames, rhythms, experiences of time, differentially experienced and lived, and installs 'transitivity' amongst them. Of course what is privileged in the process is short-termism, because considerations of marginal utility lose their bearings in the long term and against a horizon of uncertainty. But what matters is that a metric is installed which is coinage for market valorisation. To then generalise that temporal modality as paradigmatic, to immunise it (to 'black box' it) by placing it at the base of the process of capitalist reproduction, inflicts a massive selective operation of actualisation and suppression of time that goes unacknowledged. What is suppressed takes the form of market externalities, the risks and costs that find no expression and whose solution therefore must be postponed in time.

We have covered a lot of ground with Hayek, and he has helped to understand what brought about the paradigm shift to market thinking.[17] The elevation of market thinking to privileged site of societal rationality

---

[17] The exemplary analyses of this shift remain; Polanyi (1944) and Foucault (2004). In the 1978-9 'Birth of Biopolitics' series of lectures, Foucault traces with rare insight how during the eighteenth century the market shifts from being the object of regulation to become the 'site of veridiction' for the exercise of public power ('raison d'état'), reconfiguring the proper range and limits of public law in the process (2004: 38ff.).

involved Hayek in a line of argument that both points to its superiority vis-à-vis politics but also crucially that naturalises it by undercutting alternatives at the root. The conceptual move is one of selection *and* suppression, presentation *and* obfuscation, negating the contingency of problem-setting, sidelining the reflexivity and surrounding it with false necessities. We discussed the excision of political decision-making from the determination of economic outcomes; the attack on macro-management, and his aggressive rejection of the democratic organisation of production. For Hayek these applications are constitutively misconceived, and any notion of democratic production and economic solidarity can be nothing but a manifestation of *irrationality*. In their stead Hayek will elevate the *market* as impersonal aggregator of self-directed actions, guarantor of a self-equilibrating and self-enhancing system; guarantor of freedom as autonomous actions; egalitarian in its impersonal modality; participatory in inviting engagement. It is this false promise that will be seized by the governance theorists to whom we turn next.

3.2

Total Market Thinking

In the previous chapter we discussed *functional differentiation* as the principle that organises modern society, in the tradition initiated by Durkheim, developed by Parsons and radicalised by Luhmann to name but a few along its long trajectory. Differentiation, associated with the maintenance of the proper boundaries of systems, ensured that the legal, political, economic, etc., systems maintained consistent forms of coupling. Our own concern with political constitutionalism has been a concern about how these forms are organised under the sign of the constitution, in a way that allowed a particular constitutional reflexivity to emerge.

Functional differentiation has been weakened and undercut on two fronts: the *first* involves the shift from *differentiation to fragmentation*, which we discussed in the previous chapter. Differentiation is a principle of linkage, and beyond a certain limit it breaks. We discussed the threshold, and the form that the brokenness takes, as well as the use of the market to collect and integrate the fragments into its circulations. The *generalisation of economic reason* marks the moment when the fragmentation turns productive for market constitutionalism when the market's principle of circulation installs itself at the meta-level where previously the careful balance of function, performance and reflexivity orchestrated the co-evolution of systems as a matter of functional differentiation.

The *second* undercutting, to which we now turn, involves not brokenness but *substitution*. If functional differentiation is undercut when the principle of linkage collapses, it is also undercut with the generalisation of functional equivalents. If sub-systems are differentiated on functional grounds, then each sub-system must perform a function *uniquely*. If it does not, then, by definition, the principle of *its* differentiation *from* the other sub-systems is lost. The systemic challenges that the legal system faces are replicated at the transnational level, because global function systems must each be understood to perform a unique function also in a functionally differentiated *global* society. If, at that level too, systemic performances can be jointly or, more likely, severally met by other systems then the very achievement of functional differentiation is undercut. Differentiation is thus undercut not only with the fragmenting of the principle of linkage, but also with the generalisation of functional equivalence. 'Under the regime of functional differentiation each functioning system controls social inclusion by itself', wrote Luhmann about the national constitution (2004: 488). *Key to the rise of 'total market thinking' has been the generalisation of the logic of functional equivalence.* In this chapter we explore the logic of this substitution as it is effected through the operation and under the sign of *governance*.

We will turn to the meaning of governance, variably described as 'democratic', 'constitutional', 'new' and 'global', in the next section. Before that, something more needs to be said about functional equivalence, not just because without it the extraordinary rise of the governance paradigm could not be appreciated, but for another reason too. The logic of *substitution* can only be appreciated in the light of the paradigmatic innovation that the functional method imports at the level of social analysis and the radical shift towards problem-centred analysis under conditions of complexity that it effects.

The next section of the chapter looks at the rise of new governance and distinguishes two phases, the first coincident with the meteoric rise of the ideology of the New Right in the 1970s and 80s, the second tied to globalisation and the emergence of the network-society. This part of the text builds on the discussion of the collapse of the political economy into its market form that we already visited with Hayek. The forms of corporatism and association that sustained the political economy as a field of productive organisation, and engaged economic, democratic and ethical values in the process, become evacuated in order that the economy be aligned to undiluted market equilibria. In the process of this evacuation, association is offered up to accumulation, and the move is buttressed through the 'democratic co-option' that comprises the second step of market expansion. With it not only does market thinking co-opt democratic thinking in the modalities of 'democratic governance' but it deprives the co-opted of the language in which democratic resistance to it might be couched. It is not difficult to discern in the loss of terms the successful operation of hegemony. The final move that totalises market thinking as the horizon of possibility comes with the 'epistemological co-option' that establishes the market as the forum of veridiction for the 'knowledge economy'.

The New Worlds of Governance

Hayek's theory of 'competition as discovery procedure' provided key theoretical leverage to the free market ideology that stormed the political imaginary in the late 1970s, and was put to effect first by the Reagan and Thatcher governments. Against the loudly proclaimed 'failure' of Keynesian macro-economic planning, the new priorities for the State were pared back to, first, the control of monetary policy with a view to securing a stable macro-economic environment, and, second, to the policing of the political and social unrest that would follow the widening of the inequality gap, the shrinking of welfare provision and the clamping down on trade unionism. The champions of the New Right persuaded their political audiences that the dividends of growth spurred on by the release of the entrepreneurial energies would 'trickle down'. The achievements of industrial democracy and of economic solidarity were abandoned as if, in a profound sense, *anachronistic*.[1]

Such was the *new reckoning*.[2] It involved the paradigmatic *shift from government to governance*. Focused on micro-processes and interactions, and furnished with the philosophy of rational choice and decision theory, new governance was seen as a solution to the complexity- and overload-induced inertia of the bureaucratic regulatory state, promising a more efficient, responsive, heterarchical and pluralistic pattern of rule. The shift from government to governance is effected in, roughly speaking, two waves that follow distinct logics.

The *first wave* focused on the state. The emergence of new governance as a *solution* depended on a narrative that understood 'regulatory fracture' as an inevitable pathology and expression of changing state functions. There were two prongs in the attack on the state. First, the post-war regulatory state had been *corporatist* in organising state action and had formulated public policy by reaching out to societal associations of organised interests and collective identifications, with a view to settling disputes, typically wage agreements in collective bargaining processes. As we saw earlier with Hayek, the theorists of the New Right *denounced* the privileged inclusion and entrenchment of the political capacity of particular representatives of economic and professional interests as economically dangerous and democratically suspect. In one blow, social welfare reform and associational democracy were attacked for philosophical

---

[1] For this argument, see Glasman (1996).
[2] The allusion is to David Marquant's important book with that title.

naïvety and political prejudice. Second, the idea that the regulatory state could monitor and combine with the work of policy-makers and social-welfare reformers came under increased attack as embodying the discredited aspiration of command economies. It is wrong, however, as is sometimes argued, that this was an attack on the full range of the functions of the state, or that it led to its demise. Through monetary policy, the state would remain a necessary facilitator and guarantor of a stable macro-economic environment, and a moral force behind identity-formation and community.

This first wave of the emergence and consolidation of governance, spearheaded in Britain, was thus coincident with the radicalisation of the agenda of the New Right, and was launched on the axes of marketisation[3] and rational choice. The turn to governance introduced during this first wave under the Hayekian mindset, with the elevation of the market to society's final arbiter of the distribution of value to resources amongst possible uses, ran up against the limits of its rationalising capacity. The 'under-socialisation' of the market needed to be corrected, and the theoretical response here was typically sought in attempts to turn the market away from the 'neoclassical' economic model of an 'asocial' and 'apolitical' market[4] and the organising blind spot of the *homo economicus* that 'arrives' to economic activity with 'exogenously formed' preferences. The form that the 'socialisation' of the market takes is informed by insights, on the one hand, of 'bounded rational activity' that came from behavioural economics (Simon, 1957; 1991) but which found their way into the theories of the market in the 1990s,[5] and on the other of cognitive psychologists in the 1980s and 1990s on decision-making behaviour in the context of risk. But the gains in complexity did not come only in the form of resituating economic motive, but also in the form of theorising market activity away from the 'spot-trade' form of exchange and in the direction, on the one hand, of 'embedded' (Granovetter, 1985) long-term and continuous relations of trust, and, on the other, of their entanglement with social institutions, a 'new institutionalism' that would allow a richer understanding of both organisational patterns of markets

---

[3] 'The dominance of governance theory that places the market at the centre of its regulatory design has been relatively unabashed over the decades since the 1980s, and even the current financial and economic crisis does not yet seem to have induced its demise. At the same time we see that the engagements with "market" as governance category are untiring' (Zumbansen, 2015: 119).

[4] See Julia Black's important intervention (2013), indicatively pp. 405ff.

[5] For useful accounts, see Klaes and Sent (2005) and Bevir (2010).

and the structures of motivation that inform economic agency. The move is a move toward 'embeddedness', away from the market as formal mechanism and towards its location as 'market *place*'[6] in particular contexts. Both correctives to the 'under-socialisation' of the market give market thinking new impetus, and were influential in the new orientation of market analysis to *networks*, with a special emphasis on how *information* is discovered through social networks, and not merely available, as Hayek suggested, to participants in 'transparent' markets.

As we proceed to explore the 'democratic co-option' in the next section we will ask, what does it mean to have a socially adequate notion of the market? The real question that is posed ultimately to advocates of market-socialisation, is what happens to the 'beauty of the price mechanism' once the complexity that had been shorn in paring social value back to market pricing, is re-introduced through re-socialisation in the range of 'market places'?

That question can wait. In the meantime let us look at how in the face of these multiple challenges, the *second* wave of governance, that took hold in the 1990s, involved a partial retreat from the individualistic creed and the privatisation agenda, and its re-launch in terms of *joined-up governance*. Governance now shifted policy-making towards *networks*. The discovery of networks as a new organising platform for society, making available new points of entry of actors in policy processes, and new, fluid, patterns to coordinate activities and allocate resources, comes with an emancipatory idiom that changes the political imaginary. New spaces of participation, new understandings of 'stake-holding' (more on this in a minute), the mobilisation of fragmented, cross-cutting, plural, mutually re-enforcing and cross-fertilising identities, the whole set of 'multi-perspectival' politics is hailed in to inform the processes of joined-up governance. They come with a new emphasis on the meaning of social activity as embedded in social institutions; on the appropriateness of solutions to the complexity of the receiving field,[7] on flexibility and responsiveness,[8] and the celebration of *'democratic experimentalism'* as a source of innovation. Also, significantly, we now have the acknowledgement that complex problems, like insecurity, social exclusion, or

---

[6] Black (2013) on 'understanding markets not as abstracted entities but as locations – market places – where encounters between those engaged in exchange are organised and structured by social institutions and social networks, which in turn they shape' (427).

[7] For the exemplary formulation of responsiveness, see Teubner (1983).

[8] See in particular Nonet and Selznick (1978).

unemployment, can be 'wicked'.⁹ It is at this point that *functional analysis* is invoked as the methodology best placed to address them.

The notion of a 'wicked problem' entered the stage of social science in order to direct inquiry to *complex* problems understood as being 'unique' and contestable as to their definitive formulation, problems that could not be solved *as such*, but that could be tackled *more or less* successfully. Success here relates to the extent that the side- and knock-on effects might be reined in, for example by preventing a spillover of the effects of unemployment from pushing social exclusion beyond manageable limits.[10] (On a more critical reading, that there is no question of solving them *as such* becomes clear when we look at the structural role that unemployment plays to the constitution of a market in labour.) Governance re-orients itself to the task of meeting the demands and this means that it must be *responsive* in the sense of *unencumbered by democratically assumed priorities and pre-commitments*. To respond to a wicked problem is to look for equitable solutions; and at this point a deep-seated empiricism, *ad hoc*, pragmatic, problem-centred, stands in for theory construction, the latter perceived as too encumbered with the *a prioris* of framing conditions and rigidities of politically held pre-commitments.

*

As with any paradigm shift, explanatory frameworks rose to organise the evidence around a new configuration of *explanans* and *explanandum*. The successive waves of governance involved significant shifts in the *forms of analysis and explanation*, where formal modes of analysis gradually came to pervade. Governance becomes constitutively coupled with forms of knowledge-production that by centring the focus on outcomes and effects seek solutions in terms of synchronic models of *functional* analysis, while bracketing historical-*causal* forms of explanation.[11] The turn to functional analysis marks a theoretical shift of staggering significance. A short comment on methodology will show why.

The best way to understand functional analysis is to see that its point of departure involves a switch of perspective from cause to effect, since,

---

[9] For a definition, see Bevir (2010: 77).
[10] See Bevir (2010) and Rittel and Webber (1973).
[11] We briefly discussed functional analysis above, in Chapter 2.1.

to borrow a phrase from Isabelle Strengers, 'no cause has the power to prescribe the way it will cause' (Strengers, 2011: 356). In view of the inability of causal analysis to navigate complex situations and problem-complexes, and in order to answer questions of indeterminacy connected to complexity, functional analysis switches the *leading perspective*. In this reversal the point becomes to hold on to effects, and scrutinise the adequacy of causes to explain those effects. Luhmann speaks of the *'uncertainty relation'* between causes and effects: if the observer fixes, and holds firm to, a cause, in other words if she treats the cause as lending the leading perspective, it will be possible to discern a number of effects; if an effect is held constant a number of possible causes becomes discernable. Luhmann insists that *both* causes and effects *cannot* furnish the leading perspective *at once*: 'a clear and simultaneous identification of a cause and an effect' is impossible (1962: 628). His recommendation of functional analysis shifts the sociological perspective to effects. If the shift in leading perspective opens up a domain of variables of what can serve as the cause of a certain effect, it is the span of this domain that Luhmann calls the *equivalence domain* (1962: 624). This is not a domain of comparability but of interchangeability: as functional equivalents, variables (the 'coordinate causal factors') are mutually substitutable. This is precisely the achievement of 'equivalence functionalism'. For Luhmann what matters is not the law-like or more or less probable relation between certain causes and certain effects but rather the establishing of the functional equivalence of several possible causes from the perspective of a problematic effect (1962: 627, 623).

But this re-orientation to function detaches explanation from history. And for all the gains in complexity there is a deep *depoliticisation* that accompanies the shift to functional analysis. This will be better appreciated if we contrast the *functional* to the *genealogical method*. Neither take problem-construction for granted, in both cases no givenness is afforded to a 'problem' and no naturalness attaches to it. The genealogical gaze is directed to the past conditions that allowed something to *emerge as a problem*; for functional analysis, the question was how the *problem is construed* as the domain of equivalence between what appears as a problem vis-à-vis the range of solutions proffered (the unity of that difference, that spans the two poles of problem and 'its' solutions, is what defines the function). But if in both cases problem-construction is the stake rather than the condition of asking the question, the methodologies thereafter radically diverge.

The *genealogical* coupure cuts into historical trajectories to look at how at crucial junctures certain options were discarded and certain options were installed as conditions of the full range of further developments. If genealogy is a history of the series of interpretations, it is also a history of how things have come to be seen as objective. The genealogist is tasked with 'recognis[ing] the events of history, its jolts, its surprises, its unsteady victories and unpalatable defeats', says Michel Foucault (Foucault, 1977: 144), in order to understand the 'hazardous play of dominations' against what comes to install itself as the apparent objectivity of the present. That is why Foucault's emphasis is on the events of history, and why genealogy is the marker of disruption – a contingency read back into histories to destabilise them at the junctures where they assert objectivity and constitute themselves as a knowledge.[12] The genealogical method holds the historical framework itself to question in a way that both exposes the points of foreclosure on which current certitudes draw and directs historical insight back to the discarded histories of those certitudes. Genealogies unsettle the spurious naturalness, unearth the tacit assumptions, keep alive the contingency of interpretations at level and meta-level, disrupt the framework of explanation and thus the search for solutions in terms set by the theories that caused the fracture.

If genealogy directs its gaze to the hidden causalities that direct history's disclosures and silences, functional analysis displaces causal explanation altogether. It positions itself in the present-future instead and in that temporal modality alone, and not by looking back over history, does it address the unity of the problem *and* the solutions. In other words, functional analysis locates its contribution as the holding together of what is identified as a problem *given* the range of functionally equivalent options that offer it solution. Both poles are alive and contemporary in this vis-à-vis. It is arguable, clearly, that functional equivalence is indeed one way to respond to the false necessity of reasons given and states of affairs assumed. But only at the price of those structural assumptions that keep the functional range in place and the formulation of the problem intact as the source of the variety of solutions. And with it comes the disembedding of the problem from the context of historical and hermeneutical conditions. Genealogy was the methodological attempt to recover the dynamics of problem-setting, with an eye to the

---

[12] It is remarkable how little of the genealogical insight survives in the governmentality literature that arose as a consequence of the destabilisation of the causal chains that read developments in terms of necessary historical trajectories.

contingency of what is selected and what discarded in the process. That is precisely the methodology that functional analysis needs to bracket and what, in effect, pits it squarely against genealogy, despite a certain proximity in how they both envisage the contingency of reading effects into causes. The methodological innovation that functional analysis imports to the thinking of governance is staggering in the way it thinks the unity of problems and solutions, and of 'stake-holding', and judges adequacy and responsiveness, in terms of output-legitimacy.

The Democratic Co-option

The question of democracy focuses our discussion of governance on subject positions and the 'collective action problem'. We navigate the field by exploring key concepts that sustain it: the question of constituency, the structure of representation, the definition of the common good, and the notion of stake-holding. The first three concepts informed our discussion of political constitutionalism in its formal (constituency, representation) and substantive (common good) dimensions, in Chapters 2.2 and 2.3 respectively. The final concept, stake-holding, is the organising concept of 'constitutional governance' that effectively displaces the other three, index of the move from political to market constitutionalism.

Take *constituency*: it is significant that while the *first wave* of governance gained its leverage from the critique of the national (bureaucratic) state, with the *second wave* and the shift to the *global* flows of capital and organisation of production, the structures of governance also migrate to the supranational level. The first wave was marked by the fragmentation of the state political system's 'publics' but was mostly contained at that level. But with the generalisation of economic activity across national borders, the proliferation of networks now connects directly upward to the rise of regional blocks (second level)[13] and global governance (third level).[14] Of course there are differences and shifts of emphasis at each level; but the contribution of the new logic of governance is understood as largely uniform at all levels, geared to the facilitation of inclusion of new social actors alongside the emergence of new forms of expertise and processes of knowledge-production, and the rise of new forms of policy. Their implementation will undoubtedly engage the state, but how best to designate the relevant constituency is no longer taken as given.

[13] Indicatively, Sabel and Zeitlin (2012).
[14] Indicatively, De Búrca, Keohane and Sabel (2014).

While this new reflexivity is welcomed by the theorists of governance, there can be no doubt that the reconfiguration of constituency wreaks havoc to the structures of *representation*. It undercuts the subject-position of 'citizen' and the institutions that organise political capacity and transfer decision-making to the representative political institutions. It is uniquely revealing, in this respect, that the displacement and undercutting of representation are celebrated first and foremost as an achievement on a *democratic* register, expressed in the literature as a call for the *strengthening* of democracy. One would have thought that the disaggregations, fractures and evacuation of political representation would have been conceded as a blow to the capacity from a 'people' to form a will and transfer that will to the state for implementation. Not at all. Instead the literature on new governance is resplendent with references to empowerment, 'bottom-up' deliberation, experimentalism, all clearly distinct from the stale and inward-looking cul-de-sacs of national democratic regimes and of states that have become poor aggregators of their citizens' interests. State regulatory functions, most notably in relation to the economy, are now exploded from within, and harnessed to transnational frameworks where the national does not impede and where supposedly nothing is taken for granted. Networks and self-interested corporate actors emerge below, above and around the state institutional formations, so that the political is called to be re-thought in terms of this proliferation of subject-positions that cut across the traditional forms of representation. The re-launching of the function of governance runs alongside democracy as shorn of its national impediments, no longer beholden to the 'imperfect aggregations' of planning or the 'coercive transfers' of national welfare systems, pluralised as 'demoï-cracies'[15] or other such absurd neologisms, and increasingly circuited to market dynamics at the transnational level.

Both renegotiations, of constituency and representation, to be credible as democratic undertakings, must connect to the pursuit of the *common good*, to which any adequate concept of democracy is constitutively oriented. And here key to the paradigm shift from government to governance is the largely successful attack on the notion of the common (or public) good as tied to the state, understood as the institutional form

---

[15] Initially Nicolaïdis (2003), 'Our European Demoï-cracy: Is this Constitution a Third Way for Europe?' in Nicolaidis, Kalypso and Weatherill. But now also Jan-Werner Muller, 'The Promise of Demoi-cracy: Diversity and Domination in the European Public Order' (2010).

of the organisation of the national community. It was part of the post-war settlement that the social-democratic political consensus was expressed and enforced by the state, which secured the implementation of the popular will as expressed through national legislation. With the acceleration of the global organisation of the economy, with 'regulatory fracture' at the level of the state, the exercise of public policy migrates to supranational levels, and with it migrates also the guiding democratic idea of the public interest. The migration heralds a 'new freedom': the breakdown of the hierarchy of rule allows a new 'heterarchy', and with it a new structure of regulatory competition,[16] a new freedom of jurisdictional allocation, and new opportunities of forum-shopping and 'forum shifting' (Braithwaite and Drahos, 2000).

In our discussion of the social constitution in Chapter 2.3 we explored how the substantive dimension of political constitutionalism connected to the values of solidarity and democracy as a question of the constitution's *dogmatic* function, instantiated in their institutional expression, non-negotiable mainstays of the meaning of the common good. Institutions, as Alasdair MacIntyre powerfully argued in *After Virtue*, embody a moral philosophy and a distinctive rationality, and their collapse comes at a cost. The cost is that with the migration to supranational settings commonality is begged, and what is 'common' about the 'good' loses its bearings. We explored this at length in Chapter 2.4, in our discussion of constitutionalism coming 'adrift'. The disarticulation of the 'good' from the 'common' collapses the meaning of what the two terms hold together, and the 'good', now institutionally adrift from representative structures of will-formation, comes to attach itself to a shifting pattern of commonality and constituency. The problem with the new 'pluralisms' in whose context the 'good' is now floated, is this: pluralising simultaneously both what is 'common' and what is 'good' of the guiding distinction of public policy, leaves the terms distinguished from each other and singularly underdetermined in themselves. What was irreducible (because 'common') about the 'public interest' was disaggregated in the first wave of governance through rational choice assumptions attributed to individuals, and the generalisation of micro-level analyses, then, in the second wave, harnessed to shifting patterns of stakeholder constituencies. With the 'good' losing its immanent connection and embeddedness in what was common, the 'common' now a sign for *any* discernible commonality of interest, the 'public interest' can do little

---

[16] Indicatively Slaughter (2009), Picciotto (2011).

gathering work of its own as loosely coupled to processes of dislocation and realignment on a global scale, too readily co-optable, too easily outwitted.

The grand project of de-structuring the common that is undertaken as new governance, gains its leverage and justification from the fact that it is effected on fluid terrain, on which governance professes to optimise the flow of streams, to counter bureaucratic inertia, to fragment rigid structures of decision-making and re-align processes to more flexible models of horizontal relationships within and between networks. Networks typically involve negotiated forms of coordination in 'horizontal' rather than hierarchical patterns. If what is supposedly win-win about governance in all this inscribes itself predominantly, as we said, on a democratic register, it is because what is celebrated is inclusion and democratic experimentation, the coordination at many levels of government achieving multi-level 'integration' at the levels of locality, region, nation, as well as supranationally. The cultivation of diversity and the respect for subsidiarity at the material level, contests the uniformity of solutions imposed across constituencies with the gains in flexibility offered by open-ended standards, flexible and revisable guidelines, and the commitment to decentralised experimentation as generative of 'new knowledge': exchanging results, relating experience, benchmarking performance, and sharing best practices. On the temporal axis, all this in turn marks a significant increase in *responsiveness* – a term that understands politics in reactive mode to the new exigencies of heightened complexity and uncertainty. An emancipatory idiom mediates the rise and rise of governance: new governance, alternately, though often also cumulatively, is celebrated as *participative, collaborative, deliberative, responsive, experimentalist, recursive, reflexive, revisable, multi-level, etc*. The exuberance is unabated; but perhaps enough has now been said of it.

It is remarkable how difficult it is to hold onto any political signifier on this terrain of slippage. Take the instructive attempt by Claus Offe to provide a topography (Offe, 2009). The value of 'governance' for Offe is that it is able to navigate and synthesise a number of 'several simplistic dichotomies that inform the social sciences',[17] including the likes of state/society, political/economic action, structure/process, domestic/foreign, subject/object, etc. Their synthesis and (circum-)navigation involves a sobering fastening onto problem-solving, that avoids the tendency to

---

[17] Offe (2009: 553), quoting Jessop, 'The Rise of Governance and the Risk of Failure: The Case of Economic Development' *International Social Science Journal* 155 (1998): 29–45.

'over-aggregate' phenomena, but instead deals with them *as they appear*. His suggestion is to locate 'governance' at the middle point between, on the one hand, government, which refers to the 'shrinking realm of manifest state power', and, on the other hand, the 'private and civil society sphere' where '"spontaneous" coordination of action ... occurs through associative as well as market transactions'. But the notion that governance applies to phenomena that fall *between* State and Market perspectives involves a *curious ontology*, given that the range will be thematised in mutually exclusive ways by market and state. How something emerges as a problem, what conditions its emergence as a theme, and what path-dependency grants it meaning, are tied to the mutually exclusive frameworks of market and state, and their own mapping of what falls within and outwith. This is a boundary that can only be observed from the inside; in the case of the market it distinguishes between what can be priced and what constitutes an externality, and in the case of state policy-making, what falls within and outwith the regulation of the common good. Nothing mediates or 'interdicts' (we might say with Supiot) 'total market thinking' and state-planning in order to set up the 'range of phenomena' on a commonly delimited plane 'in between' as relevant to the logic of governance. Instead, the latter must 'bridge and blur' to fashion a space for itself, and the equivocation here between associative and market grounds is indicative of a functional turn, away from 'deficient state capacities' and towards 'its [governance's] greater problem solving capacity' (Offe, 2009: 554). In particular, Offe is interested in adopting the identification of the 'collective action problem' from the governance scholarship: the 'horizontal problem', as it is customarily put, of the 'production of collective goods' (Offe, 2009: 556). His invitation is to address the problem of collective action by releasing it from redundant patterns and attaching it instead to fluid conceptions of *stake-holding*.

So let us turn to this concept squarely, to look at how the new paradigm offers 'stake-holding' as the category that redeems new governance *democratically*, as placeholder of the new 'openness'. Stake-holding, a concept that we have already repeatedly encountered, is an organising category in new governance thinking. For Gráinne de Búrca 'the two most crucial features of an experimentalist-governance system, and those without which the system will fail in addressing the problem, are (1) the broadest possible degree of stakeholder participation compatible with effective decision-making, and (2) effective and informed monitoring' (De Búrca, 2010: 227). If stake-holding gives us the answer to the 'collective action problem' it is because it successfully breaks with the concept of 'representation' and the traditional structures that tied it to the institutions of government. As organising concept in the new dispensation – the 'stake-holder society' – the concept of 'stake-holding' promises reflexivity in two directions: regarding the determination of the problem (*stake*-holding) and regarding the determination of the subject position (stake-*holding*). It is indeed reflexivity that holds the clue here for how governance is expressed, and redeemed, as a democratic achievement. It is in the name of the democratic questioning of stake-holding, that reflexivity is invited regarding both *how* to understand the problem and *who* has a stake in its solution. The notion of 'representation' is thereby *destabilised* in the direction, supposedly, of more democracy. Stake-holding as an organising category of new governance allows an insight into how new governance effects a reconfiguration of democratic politics along temporal, material and social dimensions. Let us look at this more closely.

The *time* of governance with its staggered, incremental, step-by-step approach, both recursive and revisable, locates itself in the modality of the present/future and avails itself of 'learning'. Learning is released from the single-track path-dependencies of old, of overbearing structure and over-bearing theory. Learning, as we know, involves a loosening of normativity to the extent that disappointed expectations – over what is *at stake* – are not held onto, but are discredited in the face of better knowledge (we will return to the normative/cognitive distinction later in this chapter). An older democratic politics, one insistent on the mandates that a people had entrusted to its representatives in government, involved no such surrender: a normative commitment was something that one intended to hold onto. Implementing the mandated word was the test of the truth of representation. But governance, as Supiot writes, 'implemented as programmes of self-adjustment to received signals in real time, is incompatible with keeping one's word'. Governance shifts the temporal modality to become, instead, a question of 'the capacity of human beings to adapt their behaviour to changes in the environment in order to survive'.[18]

But stake-holding allows a reconfiguring also of material and social givens. Along the *material* axis the stake is re-thematised, and the 'interests' that constellate around it are held up to re-negotiation. In the self-proclaimed heavily *pragmatic* social theory that new governance locates itself, institutional fora enable practices of negotiation and settlement (in participatory councils, in processes of 'social dialogue', etc.) where, to use the words of one of its champions, 'interests values and

---

[18] Supiot (2017: 28). And he adds: 'The replacement of government by governance is an expression of a new cybernetic imaginary' (30).

[the] institutions [themselves] can always become the starting point of their redefinition' (Sabel, 1994: 158). Reflexive stake-holding of this kind, reflexive here over the definition of the 'stake', will additionally draw from local contexts as apposite to the truly participative thrust of new governance: its key is the horizontal articulation of particular interests and knowledges as opposed to any top-down imposition: 'heterarchy' rather than hierarchy. If in the temporal dimension stake-holding re-directs democracy to learning, and in the material dimension explodes fixed interests in the direction of democratic re-negotiation, it is in the *social* dimension that it secures its democratic pedigree par excellence: structures of representation are no longer the starting point or vehicle of representation, but stake-holders emerge reflexively in re-negotiations of fixed subject-positions – of corporate, class or national identities. The reflexivity of stake-holding becomes the democratic corrective to representation, in the direction of better knowledge. Might one object here that it does not take great sociological insight to discern that those with specific and targeted aims, those with clearly staked out interests and the leverage to press them will do better in the competition over the definition of stakes and of holding them? Perhaps this objection is too obvious. Let us stay with how governance theorists understand the stakes.

With governance introduced to carry the organising concepts of politics into the new, post-state, dispensation, the term 'common good' is divested of its *differentia specifica*, floated across the boundaries of public/private, citizenship/market, and lost to the field of equivalence where it names everything and nothing in particular. But what at the semantic level collapses the meaning of political terms, at a second, *functional*, level, mobilises them as functional equivalents within governance's problem-solving vernacular. Different aggregations and optimisations arise here to harness governance to problem-solving as pragmatic, sobering, objective, and crucially free of the collective irrationalities and biases that riddled the 'collective action problem' when it used to be cast in corporatist or class terms. The 'collective action problem', the democratic question *par excellence*, is now recast in the modalities of stake-holding. With collectivity and 'the common' adapted to more flexible figurations, the scope of governance expands, and with it the operation of functional equivalence between problem-solving mechanisms with little more than optimisation and efficiency left as criteria for its success.

Because governance releases 'collective action' from fixed constituencies and channels of representation, governance comes to identify with democratic experimentalism, involving the explosion of given subject positions, individual and collective: a reflexivity is supposedly imported at the very level at which these subject-positions used to be taken for granted, taken, in other words, as *entry points to* the democratic game rather than as *results of* it. New governance invites new pluralities and reconfigures the plane of societal association. Except that these are also now pluralities without history. Divested of such encumbrances, *stake-holding* can only but *mutate into an economic category*. The radicalisation of the point of entry into stake-holding is at the same time a dramatic reduction of political capacity. In the wake of the collapse of collective categories and corporate identities, the stake-holder is invoked and called forth in the only way possible, as *utility-maximiser*, as self-interested rational chooser, whose affiliation to the stakes of social and political action can only be external. With stake-holding replacing self-determination, the 'self' having been cut free from the register in which macro-identities and stakes were mutually constituted, the loss of collective categories and corporate identities is a loss with many facets, involving: (i) the loss of the value of *participation as such* in collective practices; (ii) the loss of the social meaning of democratic participation at the level of the *constitution of collective identities*; and (iii) the loss of the language of antagonism, as it gives way to the language of competition, sometimes dignified as agonism. In the substitutions effected, the *eclipsing* of democratic thinking is tied to its alleged 'experimentalist' *affirmation* as governance. Undertaken as reflection on what it *means* to be a 'stake-holder', the reflexive move destabilises traditional assumptions and structures of representation in the name of a reflexive exercise ('what are the conditions of thinking about stake-holding?'), an affirmation that is harboured in and therefore no longer critical of the vast global field of power asymmetries, comprehensive exclusions and strategies of rendering populations redundant, in other words, *stake-less*.

In the discussion of stake-holding, in its severing off from given speaking positions, structures of representation and non-negotiable guarantees of commonality or the good, governance has operationalised and celebrated a vacuous reflexivity that hands over stake-holding to those in the best position to define and pursue the stakes. Democratic governance is a myth because the predication 'democratic', neither qualifying nor anchoring, becomes instead a sign of a self-referential operation that has internalised all its criteria in order that governance be able to define for itself what is democratic about it, and hands itself over freely to the hegemony of entrenched advantage. And if the objection is ever raised that this re-launching of governance elides a theory of justice to which it might be held, it is suggested that the undertaking itself, gaining leverage from – but no longer captive to – its pre-suppositions might fashion its own theory of justice, again, reflexively.[19] With this forever renewed gesture of inclusion, the 'empty signifier' of governance becomes the sign of the field of equivalence, installing itself as horizon of every possible instantiation of democracy and justice. As experimentalism writ large, 'new governance' ticks all the boxes. Such organisation is precisely what is being secured in this succession of slippages. It is this usurpation of language, this loss of terms, the collapse of critique into affirmation in the modalities of the forever renewed, meaning-depriving inclusion, which come to sustain and buttress the myth that is democratic governance.

The Epistemological Co-option

The Logic of Equivalence: Substitution and Unaddressability

In his pioneering work *La politique des grands nombres* (1993), Alain Desrosières argued powerfully, and controversially, that social statistics don't measure a world of 'brute fact' but generate it in the process of measuring it. For Desrosières, a complex relationship exists between modalities of representation and the production of statistical information, and he deploys the term 'space of equivalence' to capture something important about the way in which the latter is harboured in the former. If the production, processing and use of statistical social data ignore the 'conventions of equivalence' that carry the interpretative choices, local conventions, idiosyncrasies and particular pre-understandings that underlie and mark the generation of social meaning, then the connection that would have granted statistical reason functionality and value is severed. The problem is that a false comparability is projected onto the heterogeneity and diversity of those practices, and this move carries its own risks. Significantly, a latent normative dimension inheres in the use of the instruments of measurement. As Desrosières puts it, 'the "undisputable facts" which [statistics] are summoned to provide (but which they themselves contributed to authorising) do not themselves provide for the modality of their discussion' (Supiot, 2010a: 81–2, quoting

---

[19] For this suggestion, see De Búrca: 'Another possible answer is that the philosophy of experimentalism – which is premised on the recursive, deliberative, and inclusive working out of shared solutions to common problems – should over time produce its own theory of justice, since our theories of justice derive ultimately from the exercise of public reason' (De Búrca, 2010: 238).

Desrosières). In *Governance by Numbers,* Supiot renews Desrosières' warning about the way in which the 'governance by numbers' is premised on forgetting the 'conventions of equivalence' that produced the very facts that statistical analysis deploys. An important discussion about the politicality of the 'conventions of equivalence' and the indicators that undergird them has developed in France both around a defence of juridical thinking as against economic thinking by Supiot, and against the collapse of economic thinking into market reductionism by Robert Salais and his collaborators. 'The founding idea of the economy of conventions', explains Desrosières, 'is the plurality of the logics of enterprise, not reducible to a single objective', and what they challenge is 'quantification as criterion of facticity or reflection of the real as independent of its conditions of inscription'.[20] Conventions of equivalence introduce an irreducible measure of *interpretation* because an agreement (often latent) is required to establish what is equivalent. To ignore this is to miss that substantive choices underlie and inform the use of instruments that measure equivalence and convergence. With the severing off of measurement from the conventions that furnish it and onto a single metric, a different politics of instruments is introduced that abstracts measurement from the interpretative understandings that embed it, with all the substantive *effects* that this has on understandings of what was reconfigured, what was at stake, what was sacrificed, or what can be re-visited and revised, for the participants in economic life.

The most pertinent instance that we face today concerns the use of *indicators* as a technology of *global* governance. Principally associated with scholarship emerging from the New York University, the theorisation of indicators as technique of global governance has been at the centre of literature both facilitative and critical of policy-making. Spanning an extraordinary range that includes public actors such as the World Bank or the US State Department, NGOs such as Freedom House, hybrid entities such as the Global Fund, and private sector political risk rating agencies,[21] indicators are used to compare and rank states for

---

[20] As Desrosières puts it in his 'Une analyse politique des statistiques publiques': 'L' idée fondatrice de l' économie des conventions', 'a été la pluralité des logiques d'entreprise, non reducible a une seule objective', 'la quantification comme critère de factualité ou de reflet d'une réel independent des conditions de son enregistrement' (2014: 219–20).

[21] The use of indicators as a technique of global governance is increasing rapidly. Major examples include the World Bank's Doing Business Indicators; the World Bank's Good Governance and Rule of Law indicators; the Millennium Development Goals (which inform many indicators); many OECD indicators and rankings; the indicators produced

purposes as varied as deciding how to allocate foreign aid or investment and whether states have complied with their treaty obligations. According to a broadly accepted definition,

> An indicator is a named collection of rank-ordered data that purports to represent the past or projected performance of different units. The data are generated through a process that *simplifies* raw data about a complex social phenomenon. The data, in this simplified and processed form, are capable of being used to *compare* particular units of analysis (such as countries or institutions or corporations), synchronically or over time, and to evaluate their performance by reference to one or more standards.[22]

The key elements in this definition are 'simplify' and 'compare'; simplification is based on reductions of complex situations on the basis of criteria of salience. Indicators 'measure', for example, the level of respect for the rule of law in a given country in a given year in a way that may be represented by an indicator such as the 'rule of law index'. That simplification can involve *aggregation* of data from multiple sources, and it will certainly involve *filtering* that excludes certain data. The criteria are used to abstract key features and keep them constant across situations, which in turn allows the comparability of the situations; comparisons produce data which are fed into processes of decision-making. To understand indicators as technologies of governance is to look at the ways in which they enable its operationalisation across the board: at the level of processes of standard-setting, decision-making, but also, for those of a more radical bend, *contestation* in global governance.

I mention this last point about contestation because the advocacy of indicators does not come devoid of some *angst*. In a book under the eloquent title *The seductions of quantification*, Sally Engle Merry, a key member of the NYU global governance team, calls attention to the 'disparity between qualitative, locally informed systems of knowledge

---

by Transparency International, by Freedom House, and by consultancies specialised in advising investors on political risks; and the US State Department's Trafficking in Persons indicators. Human rights indicators are being developed in the UN and regional and advocacy organisations.

[22] IILJ Working Paper 2010/2 Rev, Finalised 08/02/2011, available at www.iilj.org/publications/documents/2011.8.IndicatorsasaTechnologyofGlobalGovernance.pdf: 'The goal of this collaborative project is to develop a shared theoretical perspective among many scholars working in different parts of the world and on different indicators in order to develop a broader and more nuanced theoretical perspective on the role of indicators in global governance. This process involves comparison across indicators and among countries. Through comparison of these focused studies of different sites, indicators, and processes, the team will create a general theory about how indicators work in action.'

production and more quantified systems with global reach' (2016: 3) of the kind that indicators for policy formation and governance produce. '*Beneath* the truth of quantified knowledge', says Merry, 'lies the complexity of the local, the interpretative, the subjective', and the reference to 'beneath' in the above invokes a layering on which a great deal hinges. It is a layering that hints at a continuity and resonance between the levels, between the greater complexity of the local and the reduced complexity of the knowledge that indicators yield. Merry does not identify the gap as a complexity deficit but as a disparity between the quantitative (indicators) and the qualitative (local practices). It is clear that as bridging devices between the need to govern and the need to remain sensitive to the regulated field, indicators must meet exigencies on both sides. Her solution to the deficit that concerns her is to offer a bridge to the local and the interpretative in the form of an 'ethnography' of sorts. The indicator-based knowledge must be *adequate* to the underlying stratum, and for Merry a more careful ethnography might deliver that adequacy, and counter 'data inertia'. It must reflect 'the social and cultural worlds of the actors and organisations that create them and the regimes of power within which they are formed' (2016: 4–5). The attentiveness includes a *genealogy* of the construction of indicators, presumably to alert to blockages and simplifications and address the opacities that attend quantification. Her stated aim is 'to make indicators' particular ideological and structural biases more visible' (2016: 26). Merry's self-proclaimed '*critical*' take on indicators commits to at least remaining alert to those built-in biases, and alert to the need of revisability even, or especially, where the structuring assumptions are tacit.[23] Because in all cases a degree of selectivity is exercised by the compiler of the information in terms of the choice of indicators, the relative weight ascribed to them, the margins available regarding (smoothing over) data unavailability, a selectivity in turn significantly magnified when it comes to composites which aggregate a variety of indicators or cross-cutting compilations. Across the spectrum of this selectivity, the critical theory of indicators invites qualifications and revision opportunities: 'The theory or idea embedded in an indicator may be developed or reframed by

---

[23] In particular one might ask: 'a particular feature of global governance indicators is the way they *tacitly* embody theories about both the *appropriate* standards against which to measure societies (or institutions) and the appropriate ways in which to measure compliance with those standards' (p. 6, my emphasis). More generally to the question: 'How do the conditions of production influence the kinds of knowledge that indicators provide?'

its users or by other actors in ways that differ from anything intended by the producers' (2016: 11). Her 'indicator activism' finally demands that indicators be 'paired with context-rich qualitative accounts'.

The angst, protestations, contestations and qualifications notwithstanding, *there can be no critical theory of indicators*. Indicators are not 'paired' with qualitative accounts because they *stand in* for them: the relation is one of substitution. An indicator is a device of simplification. Its adequacy is not measured in terms of its proximity to the phenomenon it substitutes for. In roughly the same way in which representation cannot reach back into presence to measure its 'adequacy', indicators substitute for the practices they measure, and their own adequacy is measured on their functionality. In other words, the delivery of indicator-based good governance invokes its own criteria of adequacy. Indicators, in themselves and in their combination, provide a layer that is exclusionary to the substratum that they measure (I will explain this), one *ab initio* harnessed to a logic of functionality. The functional method, as we discussed, measures problem-construction against a range of proposed solutions. It does not excavate it (problem-construction, that is) in either a genealogical or ethnographic vein, back to the meaning of practices. A second-order exclusionary function is one that by definition you cannot 'get behind' in order to return to the first-order data because the signal that a revision is needed, that the data have been rendered 'inert', that suppressions have ironed over significant particularities, etc., cannot *ex hypothesi* be received at the level of exclusionary reasons. Their function was always to simplify and in simplifying to suppress 'context-rich qualitative accounts': the semiotic regime of indicators does not lend affordances of text to accommodate context-richness, because that would be at the expense of their own functionality.

None of this is to say that no dividends accrue from the use of indicators and the functional method, and Merry is well aware of this. It is of the very essence and functionality of indicators that they abstract, facilitate, suppress and generalise. The acknowledgement that the 'transformation of particularistic knowledge into numerical representations that are readily comparable . . . in numerical form, . . . carries a distinctive authority' (2016: 11) is why they are produced as, and used as, markers for larger policy ideas and what has made them a key feature of governance. The dividends take the form of '*uncertainty absorption*'. As Merry describes the term:

> 'Raw' information typically is collected and compiled by workers near the bottom of organizational hierarchies; but as it is manipulated, parsed, and

moved upward, it is transformed so as to make it accessible and amenable for those near the top, who make the big decision. This 'editing' removes assumptions, discretion and ambiguity, a process that results in *'uncertainty absorption'*: information appears more robust than it actually is ... The premises behind the numbers disappear, with the consequence that decisions seem more obvious than they might otherwise have been.

(Merry, 2016: 32, quoting Espeland and Stevens)

And of course uncertainty absorption is crucial to the way that cognitive and normative expectations are related, and more obviously to changes in the logic and form of legitimation. The success of an indicator is measured on its output, and its adequacy – and therefore revisability – works in that direction only. If its adequacy was measured on the complexity it had reduced, and which it substitutes for, then it would absorb no uncertainty, because the uncertainty would linger and return to cancel it out. In any case 'returns' of this kind are impossible for *exclusionary reasons*. These are *negative second-order reasons*, that is reasons to *not* act for a reason, reasons in other words *not to return* to first-order reasons.[24] That the deployment of devices and the reasons they embody 'strips meaning and context from the phenomenon' is precisely what was intended and is implicit in the logic of indicators: they are constitutively oriented to *uncertainty absorption* and as such a functionality that has nothing to do with recovering interpretive practice or re-routing attention back to the pre-quantification state of a practice.

This is, finally, why the call for 'indicator activism' is at best a call to refine the tools of simplification and recalibration, and why a *critical* approach in this context – a call for an enhanced reflexivity – is a misnomer. The function that attaches to indicators is constitutively that of simplification, quantification, comparability, and it is only *in terms of* and *not over* these functions that their reflexive reach is measured.

The Hidden Normativity of Indicators

If indicators are operative across a widening spectrum of *global* governance, they have also become increasingly relied on as *constitutional method* at the *European* level where the political dividends of the reliance on 'benchmarking' and 'good practice' remain considerable. With the asymmetry built into the architecture of the Union between the

---

[24] The concept of exclusionary reasons is famously developed by Joseph Raz (1990).

hard-wiring of negative integration at the European level and the respect of subsidiarity at the level of the national institutions of social solidarity, governance practices are mobilised to fill in the gap. We will explore all this in the next chapter (3.3) where we will expand on the metaphor of the 'gap', the discrepancy it names, and the resources that it mobilises to fill it. All this, with special reference to labour, is to come; let us foreground it, however, with the use of an example that is typical of the shift to governance and speaks volumes about the way in which what I am calling the market's 'epistemological co-option' of the field of labour protection is effected. It addresses the 'wicked problem' of unemployment. And it looks at how governance mobilises a set of indicators to address it.

The European Employment Strategy of *optimising employability* is an exemplary instance of the 'constitutional method' of coordination (OMC). I draw here from Robert Salais' analysis.[25] Registered job-seekers in the United Kingdom are obliged to accept job-offers made (temporary, rotation or even 'zero-hours') or they lose their 'job-seeker' (unemployment) benefit, and this acceptance removes them from the list, and thus from the statistics. While the acceptance of a series of short-term jobs does nothing for the prospects of being integrated into employment, or in the case of 'zero-hours' contracts even of receiving a wage, it removes job-seekers from the statistics with the effect that they appear as new 'entrants' when the short-term employment terminates. As a result of this the indicator of 'long-term unemployment' is improved. The United Kingdom thus scores better in the bench-marking and thus its policies appear more effective. The endorsement of 'best practice' translates in the Europe-wide adoption of systems of action in national policy that maximise the indicator in question. 'What', interjects Salais, 'does an employment rate measured independently of the quality of the jobs making it up actually mean?' (Salais, 2004: 113). Whatever it 'means', what it achieves is significant: it allows different normative models to compete according to indicators that in practice favour certain models and in particular the liberal market model. The performance indicators that head the list of employment strategy, relate to employment levels and the aspirational targets set in Lisbon (70% employment for the population aged between 15 and 64, 60% among women, etc.) '*Any* work counts, whatever its length, hours per week, status, etc, in other words its quality. ...

---

[25] Salais (2004) and (2006).

Indicators, initially called "effort" indicators are intended to measure the efficiency of action plans from three points of view' (Salais, 2004: 109). The three are 'prevention' (improving employability), 'activation' (participation in employment policy measures) and 'return to employment'. National sources are designated to provide the figures for the accounting frameworks that are then 'harmonised', processed and compiled, by Eurostat. 'Harmonisation' here works to steamroller over differences between countries that have long been investing in educating and training their labour force (who therefore enter the labour market later) and those who have not, the latter scoring much higher on the '15–24' category employment rates, whereas investing countries lose out. But more crucially, the category of 'individual employability' disconnects employability (speed of return to employment) from vulnerability (the falling back into unemployment), a disconnect that operationalises a skewed metric that covers over the simple truth that if employability and vulnerability increase in parallel there is in fact no improvement in the employment rate. But, beyond that, 'the *exclusive* focus on employability is explained by the particular nature of European policies.' The EES targets the optimum functioning of the labour market,

> which leads to a particular conception of prevention. Prevention is only supposed to be triggered once individuals enter the labour market. The preventive efforts within employment, which are in practice undertaken in enterprises, sectors, or areas and that should be encouraged (training in employment; more secure career paths; collective bargaining on the modernisation of enterprises) are excluded as they are seen as curbs on market adjustment in this new normative model.
>
> (Salais, 2004: 111)

We can discern three separate moments with regard to the process of uprooting the understandings of work and employability from the 'conventions of equivalence' and the interpretative context of their embeddedness. The *first* involves *abstracting* from evaluative contexts that give meaning to practices, that furnish, in other words, understandings of what ties means to ends, what ends practices entail, what is taken as fulfilling them, what counts as success and failure; *the second* is of submitting those abstractions to the logic of aggregation, comparison and *scoring* in order to identify which practice is 'best'; and the *third*, finally, in a moment of '*re-entry*', of re-importing best practice back to the regulated field.

We begin with the *first* moment, of *disembedding*, where two key 'transplants' from economic science are transferred over to organise the field of the governance of employability. The first is the identification of *'best practice'* and the second is the *'principal–agent'* problem. The notion of 'best practice' is borrowed directly from the management of firms.[26] In order to remain competitive, businesses orient their own internal organisation towards best practices and this requires them to *identify* innovative practices, *transfer* them into their own organisational structure and *motivate* their personnel (new management techniques play an important role here) to adopt such practices in order that they be efficiently implemented. The motivation strategies take us to the second, 'transplant', which is key to the philosophy of new public management as it underlies 'good governance' at all levels. It involves the transfer into policy production of the solution to the *'principal–agent'* problem. With the separation of ownership and control in the corporation arose the problem of the delegation of discretion to those who exercised control on behalf of the owners. Managers were often perceived as following an agenda that increased their own power base and professional standing to the detriment of the interests of shareholders. And the solution that rational choice theory suggested to counter the non-alignment was a structure of incentives that would bring the two sets of interests into line. Second-wave 'new governance' carried over this insight from the private sphere into the formation and implementation of public policy, on the assumption, naturally, that public officials could be usefully understood as service providers and citizens as service users. Running alongside this development was a softening of the public/private distinction, a new awareness, as William Simon puts it, that 'public problems now seem to call for the same contextualizing and adaptive capacities in government organisations' as shown in the 'continuously self-revising organisation ... in the private economy' (Simon, 2015: 31).

In a classic case of what Keynes called the 'fallacy of misplaced concreteness', in both of the above instances the nexus of problem and solution is exported intact from the business environment to that of public action and policy. A generalisation of motive, expectation and rationality is effected across the two contexts, importing assumptions about self-interest and utility-maximisation from the economic to the political sphere. No effort is made to justify why the terms of internal organisation, hierarchies of decision and implementation strategies at the level of the firm might be *naturally* replicated at the level of public

---

[26] See Salais on the transferral (2004: 287ff.) and more generally Salais 2004, 2006 and 2011.

governance. Nor why the correlation between indicators and objectives that might be identified at the level of the firm, whose *raison d'être* is the pursuit of competitiveness, profit, cost-reduction and productivity, can simply be transferred across to displace objectives in systems of industrial relations tied to a variety of practices each with their own governing assumptions and criteria of excellence, assumptions about democratic involvement, representation and association.

The first moment, of disembedding is the one that also troubled Sally Engle Merry. The promise of 'quantification' involved a cost that is visited on the particularities that are left behind, the local meanings and associations of the first-order that might have informed alternative readings. How improbable that an 'ethnographic' or 'genealogical' approach might – as 'indicator activism' would have it – disrupt such *naturalisation which is sanctioned with the mark of measurement rather than interpretation*. The extraction of data from practices such that they can be generalised, involves their uprooting from the particularity of labour practices which are tied to forms of collective action-in-concert with their own emphases and understandings. We confront the damage, then, that what is left behind in these selections cannot be recovered. This is not to invoke some hidden communitarian agenda; it is to capture something of the nature of *practices* as replete with evaluation and as *sensitive to their point*, in the way that Alasdair MacIntyre, for one, so powerfully captures their meaning; and in the way in which Desrosières, earlier, spoke of *conventions*. Contextual understandings go to the very core of what it means to identify salience. To generalise, then, is to introduce across the diversity of local practices a range of meanings that *must* be shared and yet can *only* be shared by doing them violence. To generalise 'job satisfaction' or 'job security' involves abstracting from particular contexts of expectations, the forms of association, the particularity of local institutional forms that embed them in cultures with their own histories, normative assumptions about the balance between work and leisure, the importance of professional status, the connection between work and education or the acquisitions of skills, etc. But even less obviously, evaluative indicators carry reductions of a more invidious kind that apply also to prima facie objectively measurable phenomena such as employability or unionisation.

In the first move, understandings that inform practices are removed from the local contexts and imaginaries, and abstracted on a scale of general equivalence with the help of indicators. The generalisation disembeds because it lifts instances of practices out of the context that endowed the relevant concepts (job status, job satisfaction, job security) with meaning. The *second* move installs the benchmarking procedures in order to identify 'best practice': imparities and asymmetries are measured on the scale of quantification and receive a score. At this stage, of *scoring*, indicators introduce comparability across fields and across national systems.[27] It is here that a second reductive 'moment' becomes manifest. Comparability introduces commensuration. The identification of 'best practice' invokes a criterion of best, but that normative criterion is removed from any context that might allow an interpretative choice, balancing or judgement. What is best is what gets the highest score on the basis of indicators that are both *exclusionary of the complexity they speak to*, and not themselves subject to any balancing of their *respective weights*. In a deep way statistical information establishes normativity here in furnishing expectations that are disappointment-proof. But this is not the normativity of political self-binding. It is the hidden normativity of the blind spots and elisions that accompany the deployment of indicators.[28] It is disappointment-proof at the deep level at which these reductions establish *what is fact*; facts can be related, configured and calibrated, but not contested as facts. At the level where these facts circulate, the instruments that have configured them as facts are not put to question. The scale of equivalence that establishes them as facts is presupposed, otherwise there would be no comparability and thus no circulation. Key here is that modification is possible at the surface level of their combination and circulation and not the deep level of their constitution. And with this we have the most effective and unchallengeable form of market capture, unchallengeable because constitutive of both the problem and the possibility of its solving.

The third *final moment, of re-entry*, is that of implementing 'best practice' by importing it back to the system that is found to be falling behind 'best practice', that no longer has *anything* to do with the instrumental rationality that orients means to ends *given* interpretative frameworks,

---

[27] Salais develops an argument to the effect that the mutation of bench-marking from the level of the competition amongst firms to that between national policies in the context of employment, imports a 'brutal reduction' that turns bench-marking into little more than a scoring method, which, in the absence of any hierarchy of implementation, sets up a degenerative game between the supra-national and member-State level: 'degenerative' because the game-theoretical 'rationality' draws from the skewed instrumentality of indicators transferred across contexts (Salais, 2004: 287–9). Also Salais, 2006: 109, 113, 114.

[28] Samuel Jubé's work is exemplary here. See in particular Jubé (2009).

and *everything* to do with cutting costs and maximising returns. 'Best practice' needs to be *re-embedded* in national systems of public policy. To be re-embedded involves a process of 'learning' that requires first of all *traction*, because learning involves a selective *yield* of the particular normative expectational structures of the receiving field. And what is risked with the displacement of those (normative) structures, what is risked at the threshold of re-entry, is the generation of *meaninglessness*. If what is effective and what is efficient have come undone from the *telos* or point of the practice that informed their meaning in the first place, then what does it mean for it to reinstate itself now, *a posteriori*, as measure and register of efficiency, of the relation between means and ends? Effectiveness, adrift from particular contexts of instrumental action and their particular understanding of instrumentality, will only ever appear as reduced to the economic logic of cost-cutting that set off bench-marking on its way in the first place. 'What does it mean for a solution, any solution, to be *adequate*?' we asked earlier. The question is never answered except by default in the form of the floating signifier 'best practice' and its relentless invocation. With every relay another layer, and with it a thickening not just of opacity but counter-intuitively also of normativity, if Benedict Kingsbury is to be taken at his word.[29] The 'best' of 'best practice' becomes circuited to the criterion of *optimisation* whereby the cycle of disembedding achieves perfect closure. At this point, in other words, the market enfolding becomes total; another chapter in the continuing story of capitalist economies extracting surplus value from the operationalisation of productive asymmetries.

The Eclipse of the Political Constitution

With this we have come full circle. The epistemological co-option, mobilised by the logic of governance, installs the range of possibilities, the circumference of what is thinkable as common good and as collective action. Governance displaces the political on both the registers of democracy and of epistemology. It supplants democracy with stake-holding, inserting an agonism without history at the level of how a society organises its material reproduction through democratic categories and at the junctures of what it means to think and act politically. And it

---

[29] 'As layers of common normative practice thicken, they come to be argued for and adopted through a mixture of comparative study and a sense that they are (or becoming) obligatory' (Kingsbury, 2009: 32).

sanctions this at the epistemological level with the withdrawal of the language in which labour, value, and the moral economy might have found expression outwith what can be cashed out in market terms. What emerges as rational governance and what recedes from intelligibility, what establishes itself as politically rational and what is rebutted as politically naïve or insane receives its sanction within market coordinates.

As we return to the question of constitutionalism, and track the shift from political to market constitutionalism, we return to *constitutional function*, to draw, finally, certain insights together about the meaning of market constitutionalism in terms of the significant leverage it gains from the emerging paradigm of governance, away from the *normativity* of the political constitution and towards its forever renewed *cognitive* adaptation. To ask the question over *constitutional governance* is not to ask the question whether the predication 'constitutional' is warranted, but more worryingly it is to ask the question of what, if anything, keeps the two terms from folding into each other, in an implosion that reconfigures political space in its entirety.

With only a few stubborn exceptions, constitutional theorists have variably been turning to the *fait accompli* of the constitutionality of constitutional governance having been re-set. To gauge the mood of the debate in German constitutional theory we may usefully turn to Christoph Möllers' hugely influential writing, that contrasts two *paradigms* at the constitutional level: one 'private law framework of public institutions' and its opposite, 'a public law framework of public institutions'. The former relies on the 'heterarchical' making of the law, horizontal articulations rather than any top-down imposition of political *will*, it pivots on *relationality*, 'spontaneous coordination processes', and is typically seen as 'self-emergent' (Möllers, 2004: 335). At the (sliding) threshold of what is retained as rational and what is superseded in the constitutional processes of realignment, what typically gives is the 'traditional public law framework', that, we are reminded, 'still invokes hierarchy' and defines law as 'the result of a political process, which is ... intentionally steered' (2004: 337). While 'transnational legal discourse' invokes both frameworks, and while the trend is clearly the 'application of a purely private law framework', 'an adequate theory' of constitutionalism, Möllers insists, 'needs a dialectical synthesis of both approaches [and] lives up to its tensions and contradictions' (2004: 337). Note the language of adequacy again, this time combined with 'dialectical synthesis'. Maybe Möllers is right, and perhaps such a 'synthesis' is on the cards. But in the *interregnum* there is dialectical standstill. And in place of the traditional framework of political constitutionalism (Möllers' 'public law framework of public institutions'), with its constitutive link to 'the political process' and commitment to 'steering', we have only dislocation at the points at which the 'old' seeks its rational accommodation, with the result that its organising tenets are left at sea, impossible to accommodate in the new, cast away as redundant, and 'irrational'.

*

The shift that most revealingly tracks the comprehensive move from political to market constitutionalism is the shift of constitutional expectations from a normative to a cognitive register. We have looked, with Luhmann, at the rapid shift away from 'expectations that are held to counter-factually' to those that are forced to 'learn' in global society, and the repercussion of this shift for the function of the legal system in the face of the 'constant stream of disappointments' to which law is 'constantly called to adjust' (2004: 468). *Responsive* regulation and 'regulation by information' emerged as instances of the overall shift, and Teubner's important early work on *reflexive law* was an instance of such responsiveness, involving a careful re-thinking of the balance of the normative and the cognitive in terms of the performance of law as instrument of regulation. He argued against an unthinking incursion of law's normative demands into societal domains whose own logic would thus be thrown out of kilter, and in favour of rethinking normativity in terms of a more self-conscious attempt to learn and understand the regulated field. For Luhmann such responsiveness overstated the law's reflexive reach. But whatever their differences, the effort was all about sharpening the instrument in the direction of better knowledge that might improve the *normative* aims of regulation, whatever the new balances of the normative and the cognitive under conditions of increased complexity. As we moved our discussion, however, to the hidden normativity of indicators, the practices of bench-marking, and the way in which regulation was reconfigured in social constellations such as networks, the attempts at calibration turn into something altogether more sinister: the *displacement* of normative by cognitive expectations. Riding the heightened complexity but at the same time eliding all nuance, emerged the vastly simplified message of new governance: that *political* decision-making vested with normative legal force could not and should not be deployed directly to deal with complex situations and 'wicked problems'. Under the auspices of 'democratic' or 'good governance', a rapidly expanding body of policy-driven literature dispersed its insights across society, suggesting 'regulation by information' in place of direct regulation with its 'command and control techniques', and inviting a change of structures of incentives through the provision of suitable information, or linking regulation by information to 'regulation by networks'.[30]

Concerned not to surrender the normative achievement of political constitutionalism, we turn finally in this chapter to explore the equivocations that attach to the signifier *constitutional governance*: the specific figuration that it offers of the normative and the cognitive, of what is to be insisted on as normative against what is to be learnt as cognitive, of what resists against what yields. We looked at the deployment of law's very particular form of reflexivity – its *eigen-reflexivity* so to speak – under 'constitutional reflexivity' in Chapter 2.2 Constitutionalism is not introspection, though it is that too; but in its selective and self-controlled exposure to its environment it controls its learning processes in the light of its normative commitments. With globalisation and the emergence of governance, it was the deployment of this particular reflexivity that comes under threat. The question that faces political constitutionalism is how to reconcile the situation of heightened complexity that confronts it, with the *function* of the law and the specific use of normativity tied to it.

In this context what does it mean to identify a strain in the constitutional handling of the two types of expectation? As ever with Luhmann, the answer is asked as a question of complexity. It is an important premise of systems theory that as soon as the system/environment difference is established, the system begins to develop internal differentiation in a recursive manner. Reflexive mechanisms arise internally to the system in order to allow it to respond to its environment by referring environmental 'unstructured' complexity to its own 'structured complexity'. The function of the legal system, and the achievement of constitutionalism, is to keep control of this reflexive unfolding and the differential between the levels in check: the balancing, Luhmann calls it, between variety (increased openness to environmental stimuli) and redundancy (relative indifference to them). Everything in systems theory turns on these complexity-differentials (*Komplexitätsgefälle*), and on sustaining them in productive deployment. To that goal systems manage

---

[30] See the work of R. Dehousse (and comitology more generally) in Ladeur (2004: 139–41).

their own cognitive openness in the face of increasingly demanding environments, and management here means controlling their resonance-capacity through their own control of normativity. It is here that the recalibration of the normative/cognitive balance may take its toll on function. Under conditions of globalisation the *functional* achievement of law becomes increasingly unstable because of heightened complexity. If the control of the 'complexity-differential' is weakened, then the law's function to generate and guarantee stability of expectations (and to control and immunise against conflict) is jeopardised.

Thus, as far as systems theory is concerned, the risk that the demands placed on law by globalisation is that they threaten a *pathological* asymmetry between 'over-complexity' with regard to the system's cognitive expectations and 'under-complexity' with regard to its normative expectations, an undermining of its own stabilising mechanism that presupposes adequate levels of 'indifference'. At stake is the constitution's ability to control and turn functional the complexity gap, the self-managed balance between the two levels of complexity. The appropriate reflexive mechanisms for processing cognitive expectations, even of this level of complexity, must rely on the law's use of normativity. Normative criteria guide selection of relevant information, and learning processes are those that keep both sets at play and manage the relation between them. This balancing exercise can lean decisively to the side of environmental complexity, but a limit point will eventually be reached to law's ability to deploy normativity as condition and filter of learning – its own modulating cognitive expectation structures that we called 'reflexivity'. In the face of the rapid expansion of markets, at stake is law's ability to reproduce its own repertoire of reasons vis-à-vis the market's. The constitutional hold on its reflexivity is challenged in the direction of a radical uncoupling, and overwhelming by economic givens, that risks losing the distance that allows law's particular resonance, and risks abandonment to unqualified market adjustment. That abandonment is precisely what is celebrated in the varieties of 'constitutional' governance as *total market thinking*, and to this 'celebration' we, finally, turn.

*

Where for Luhmann the shifting correlation of the normative and the cognitive in the advent of global law is replete with risks, and where for Teubner it calls for a new constitutional sensitivity to the proper limits of the system, no such ambivalence thwarts Karl-Heinz Ladeur's ambitious launch of his 'post-modern', ultra-liberal project of constitutionalism.

His is a market-constitutionalism that is sweeping and unapologetic. If we conclude the chapter with his theory of governance it is because of the totalisation of market thinking that it relies on and effects. His defence of market constitutionalism is pitched above the level where a rational, political objection to it might be articulated. In a move of *inclusion* that disarms and wrong-foots all objections to it, it installs itself at the meta-level, facilitator and guarantor of a competition to which it provides the conditions and by virtue of which it secures its immunisation.

Ladeur's argument is deeply indebted to Hayek, whose theory Ladeur radicalises with the explicit intention of re-launching the *knowledge society*.[31] He renews Hayek's ambitious move to build the 'discovery procedure' on competition, one unencumbered by top-down regulatory direction, or any command structure that will inevitably be found lacking in requisite complexity. The constitution has a special role to play under conditions of globalisation, the latter appearing in Ladeur's work above all as opportunity. Constitutional governance is constitutively oriented to knowledge production and the permanent generation of innovation.

Like all hegemonic moves, Ladeur's prescription does not expend with *democracy* but instead redefines it in order to call it into line. He offers a theory of democracy detached from *hierarchical* concepts of the state and popular sovereignty, shorn of collective categories of action, no longer beholden to outdated concepts of will-formation, or stultifying assumptions about the state as a representative of the notion of the common good,[32] and with competition rather than consensus at its centre. The formation of the general will is read off dynamic societal processes of self-binding, self-observation, and observation of others through a *heterarchical* model. He says:

> [T]he concept of democracy can ... be reformulated more to the effect not of consenting to a basic stock of rules and principles. It is instead the practical, heterarchical, distributed social network of networks among citizens producing 'overlapping consensus', in the sense that citizens are in practice involved in differing networks in differing roles, and a heterarchical organized stock of linkages and co-ordinations arises from their

---

[31] 'The pressure for change under which the political and legal institutions of post-modern societies are emerging is not produced primarily by globalization processes, but is instead connected with the basic transformation of the economy into the "knowledge society"' (Ladeur, 2004).

[32] 'The state and the legal system should follow some meta-rules or principles, which could reformulate the public interest at a much more abstract level than in the past' (Ladeur, 2004).

overlapping permeability to each other, that enables a 'polycontexturally' distributed self-observation and observation of others by the various patterns of actions produced, continually feeding the associated 'pool of knowledge' with novelty.[33]

The 'network of networks' and the associated productive possibilities is so 'openly dimensioned' that far-reaching inclusion of citizens is guaranteed. Ladeur renews Hayek's message against state-political management of the society. His is an understanding of the constitutional imaginary rediscovered in the cognitive modalities of openness, heterarchy and experimentalism and as circumventing the encumbrances of justice and democracy. Ladeur's *constitutional* theory is a variation of Hayek's, though thinner in institutional density. Hayek's catallaxy had put the emphasis on the rule of law in order to secure the constancy that the market required for 'individuals to make feasible plans', and negative liberties and property title provided the institutional frame for the spontaneous order. This established the relationship of law to the *self*-organisation of society. Like Hayek, Ladeur is keen to make the connection between the self-organisation of society in terms of new knowledge and the structures of law supporting it, but now upscaled to the level of the operation of networks. His own conception of fundamental rights as *'negative liberties'* understands them as mechanisms for 'distributing decisional rights' in order to enable the self-reproduction of society under conditions of uncertainty. Echoing that other Hayekian insight, Ladeur argues that negative liberties allow for 'seizing' the *implicit knowledge* dispersed in society which can then be used for decision-making, in the direction of permanent innovation. As long as individuals are relieved of liability for remote consequences of their action, spontaneous cooperation and coordination between individuals constantly produces new patterns of orientation and resources of knowledge, which, of course, as Adam Smith knew, will also be beneficial to third parties: 'Trenchantly formulated, from a sociological perspective, the function of "negative" liberties actually consists in multiplying possibilities of action for others.'[34]

---

[33] Ladeur, 2004, at 107 (footnote omitted); see also Ladeur, 1999 at 40.

[34] Ladeur (1999: 37). This is emphasised especially regarding the right of property. For Ladeur, the right of property, even more than other liberties, is characterised by a reflexive form geared to producing new property which is also beneficial to others as employees, buyers, founders of new businesses, etc. (Ladeur, 2004: 24).

But for all the debt to Hayek, a crucial difference destabilises Hayek's most important juncture in the guise of expanding it; it is what sends Hayek's generalisation of economic reason in the direction of total market thinking. With *catallaxy* Hayek had attempted to capture *the market-constituting moment of law*. The constitution provided the framework structure and support for the elevation and generalisation of market thinking. But in Ladeur the market is elevated *above* the constitution in an argument that directly celebrates it – the market – as orchestrating *a 'second-order' discovery procedure*. To put it, then, in the terms that Möllers offered us above, Ladeur takes the 'private law framework of public institutions' as condition – rather than pole – of any dialectic and as framing the discovery process of a market society. At this point Ladeur also parts with Luhmann's suggestion of constitutional *function*. As we saw, Luhmann's continuing defence of the function of law was tied to its specific use of normativity; it remained that of 'making the formation of expectations possible in a society that is becoming more and more a problem for itself' (it is interesting that Luhmann here credits the formulation to Ladeur) (Luhmann, 2004: 467, fn. 14). Luhmann was careful to hold on to the function as that of systemic stabilisation of normative expectations. But for Ladeur, no such 'blocking' devices of stabilisation should be allowed to get in the way of innovation. Instead, 'the competition of institutions is an important prerequisite for rational regulation' because

> [a] second-order discovery procedure ... not only produces criteria for individual decisions but enables – through the competing patterns of social institutions, including the alternative between public and private rules – the optimisation of social norm systems. The criterion of market-defined efficiency is introduced as an argument in political decision-making procedures at national level, but also as an object of practical options by market actors and of self-organization of regulatory patterns that spontaneously form on that basis.
>
> (2011: 93)

In Ladeur total-market thinking seals itself in a move of self-reference – what Teubner in earlier work called 'hypercyclical linkage' (Teubner, 1993). Ladeur's is an elevation of competition to 'second-order discovery procedure' and with it the subsumption without remainder of constitutional reflexion to market thinking. Where for both Hayek's and Luhmann's more tentative accounts of the market-constitution complex, differentiation mattered as a principle of societal formation and the constitution performed a key function in that respect, now, with

Ladeur's radicalisation, the function is collapsed and competition does all the work of releasing society to face up to uncertainty. 'Constitutional governance' will play an important mediating role if the potential creativity of the 'new systemic collective intelligence is [to be] liberated' (2011: 77). In accordance with the fundamental laws of the 'society of individuals', the cognitive self-organisation of society has to be given priority. This second-order imperative carries the only (quasi-) normativity in all this, and the self-organisation of regulatory patterns will do all the work of coordinating processes of continuous market adjustment in the only moment of self-reflection that Ladeur is willing to dignify as constitutional. Because, for Ladeur, law is based on the 'institutionalisation of the distributed search and experimenting processes' of a society which defines itself by an unknown future. Note that at every step what informs 'self-reflection' is not judgement (on the basis of norms) but optimisation (of those norms): cognitive self-regulation is only ever cognitive innovation, and normativity is eclipsed, albeit the holding of collective standards, collective-democratic determinations, or its inscription in common practices and values.

This is self-immunising in its vacuity for certain; but one might still query what 'collective intelligence' will be 'liberated' out of a constitutional governance no longer oriented to tapping the tacit knowledge of a society, but of networks in which knowledge is now, as per Ladeur too, increasingly inscribed. We have already mentioned that the turn to networks was largely an attempt to rethink social interaction beyond the theoretically rushed rational-action templates, for which any form of *bounded* rationality was already a pathological expression, and Ladeur joins the chorus of second-wave governance theorists in their rejection of the '*homo economicus*'. Against the classical view of laissez-faire capitalism, Ladeur argues that 'it does not lead us very far' under post-modern conditions, to reduce the economic system to the dynamic that can only be defined by reference to an individual through whose search for wealth and power the economy acquires the necessary leverage for 'self-aggrandisement'. For Ladeur, the problem is of course neither capitalism nor the uneven aggrandisement of the economic system at the expense of others. The problem, instead, has to do with blockages in the renewability of the economy's knowledge base. And this, ultimately, is because capitalism and the renewal of society's knowledge base are mutually constitutive under conditions of economic incentivisation.

Whatever the other weaknesses of this sweeping diagnosis, it fails to capture Hayek's second major insight that we discussed earlier concerning the distinction between information and calculation, the market for Hayek possessing informational rather than calculational value. But networks are technologies of calculation, and they are useful *precisely because they remain inattentive* – opaque, 'black-boxed', etc. – to the generation of meaning through individual participation in market activity. For Hayek, as analysed earlier, what competition – as discovery procedure – discovers is information that is *embedded* (in local and tacit contexts) and *embodied* in practices, called forth as agents hone their skills and talents in market participation. Unperturbed by these finer distinctions, and drawing on literature on the network society, Ladeur develops an argument about the organisation of knowledge under post-modern conditions that perversely takes the network – which is, after all, the paradigmatic form of 'black-boxing'[35] – as a 'new form of knowledge production' (2011: 79) and links it to the paradigm of 'regulated self-regulation' or 'negotiated regulation', the 'organisational framing of the knowledge processes' (2011: 78). The foundational theoretical motivation for turning to networks was a concern to account for the mechanisms that secure the *second-order stabilisation of social formation*, whether these be thought in terms of the containment of contingency, or the countering of uncertainty. That is the *function* on which the credibility of *causes* in measured. And Ladeur can celebrate in all this the release of a 'collective intelligence' ushered in by

> a new paradigm of multi-faceted cognitive constructions that operate beyond clear criteria and well-defined targets, and the accumulation of solutions generated on that basis ... a new constellation [that] demands a reflexive secondary observation focused on the explicit preservation of the multiple character of the new modelisation processes in order to avoid 'lock-in effects'. Evaluation *ex post*, and not a refined approach of steering *ex ante* will be necessary for the new control-project of post-modern society. The post-modern legal system should opt for a *renvoi* of the cognitive problems to societal actors and at the same time it should be more attentive to the meta-rules of societal knowledge generation and their limits.
>
> (2011: 91–2)

A '*renvoi*' indeed, of catastrophic proportions, as those on whom the catastrophe is visited struggle to deal with the 'cognitive problems' it engenders, the law-like release of market *forces*, with no interpretative

---

[35] For the importance of 'black-boxing' for knowledge production see McGee's fine interpretation of Bruno Latour's theory in (2014).

yield, and no critical redress. A 'renvoi' of the 'cognitive problems' in the exacting terms of the externalisation of the costs of capitalism, a system that, as Negri and Guattari put it some years ago, has 'reigned idiotic and supreme' (1990: 172) over growing class inequality in the metropolis, over the pauperisation of Europe's periphery, over the continuing devastation of the South. And the 'cognitive problems' that have been 'handed back' to the 'societal actors' involved, relate to the unintelligible and unacknowledged sacrifice inflicted by a financial crisis for which Ladeur suggests a 'new refined *ex ante* steering' approach in terms of 'new modelisation processes' out of which, presumably, cognitive value will be extracted and significant material value will be delivered to those cognisant enough to opt for 'non-homogenised financial instruments' that avoid 'lock-in effects'.[36]

In all this, the grand scheme of abandoning the normative foundation of political constitutionalism in the name of better knowledge and the challenge of uncertainty, releases the 'collective imagination' along capitalism's path dependencies, options blocked through the selective opacities and the new materialities in this Right-wing variation of Actor-Network Theory disconnected from the materialism of needs. The endorsement of networks introduces selective opacities at key junctures of justification and redress, while negative rights shield market outcomes from egalitarian correction.

---

[36] This is key to Ladeur's 'solution' to the comprehension and prevention of financial crisis, as expounded in Ladeur (2011).

3.3

Europe's 'Social Market' and the Disembedding of Labour Protection

> Cato knew from the Greeks that empire is hurry,
> and dominion never goes to the phlegmatic –
> it was hard to be Demosthenes in his stone-deaf Senate:
> 'Carthage must die,' he roared . . . and Carthage died.
> He knew that a blind man looking for gold
> in a heap of dust must take the dust with the gold,
> *Rome, if built at all, must be built in a day.*
>
> Robert Lowell, Marcus Cato

What the Rome Treaty inaugurated, what set the European project on its course and fuelled its rapid acceleration, was an original asymmetry, a coupure into the fabric of European societies. It cut into the political economy in order to replicate at the European level the radical separation of the political from the economic system, that was the hallmark of the liberal settlement of post-war Germany. But once uploaded to the transnational, European, level, the separation generated an asymmetry between the differentiated systems, the economic system uploaded to the transnational level and the political system left tied to democratic processes and solidarity-based institutions at the national level, an asymmetry that assumed its own momentum. The magnitude of the breach and the effects of the asymmetric configuration of supranational and national, can only be appreciated in retrospect. This chapter will explore those effects, that have gradually led to the *disembedding* of Europe's economy from its society.[1] As 'ordoliberalism' was stormed by 'neoliberalism', to the detriment of what the post-war consensus had allowed to function on a human scale, this was a disembedding that became increasingly difficult to control, let alone reverse. We are today depressingly

---

[1] Karl Polanyi's profound argument about 'disembedding' has, promisingly, become central to critical literature on the European Union. Amongst the best, Glasman (1996), Joerges and Falke (2011).

familiar with the way in which the institutionalisation of the separation between market economy and social protection was set on a trajectory where it became productive for capital, to the point where the profit margins have become staggering and the effects devastating. It is not the way the story of the European Union is customarily told, to focus it on asymmetry, on breach, on time, and on the surplus value extracted from the processes of evasion and elision that it sets in motion. But with hindsight, it is nevertheless what holds the key to the European misadventure.

The split that sets European 'integration' on track invests both the level of conceptual determination and the level of material reproduction. At the former level it concerns how negative and positive integration are to be related *both* across the originary split between the economic and the political and across levels national and supranational. The latter secures how the competition amongst national systems of social protection is productive of surplus value. We will track the combination of levels, conceptual and material, in the twists and turns of the unfolding of the European process of market integration, through a periodisation that is neither particularly original nor, I think, particularly controversial. The first period, from Rome to Maastricht, sets the basis of a social market economy under the auspices of an Ordoliberal 'economic constitutionalism' that separates the market-economy from state-social protection and entrusts the oversight of their 'synergy' to the European Court. The European Community releases its subject – the *homo economicus* of the ordoliberal mindset – into a market stretched across national boundaries, offering Europe's workers free circulation and expecting the market to deliver their *optimal location* amongst jurisdictions. The Maastricht Treaty inaugurates a second phase that promises democratic/political citizenship in an 'ever closer Union', and delivers it in 'social dialogue' and the (light-touch and reluctant) regulation of social and labour protection. The Lisbon Treaty inaugurates a third phase of market acceleration and short-termism in the face of crisis, with the entrenchment of the new economic governance, which morphed into something new and pathological with the advent of sovereign debt, with the insolvent states forced into securing price stability at the expense of their own peoples' lives and livelihoods.

Our particular reference throughout this short history is to social and labour protection. The Ordoliberal founding moment inflicts the crucial separation between market action and social protection; with Maastricht we have the launch of EU labour law, largely as labour market regulation; with Lisbon, the turn to governance brings its own challenges and diminutions. Such genealogies and lineages, their mutual demarcations, reciprocities and overlaps remain at the centre of the debate over the current state of the 'social market' of Europe: of what was envisaged and what it has become. The first, ordoliberal, 'constitutional moment', looks at the inaugural gesture of this development *in tandem* of State and market, their parallel positioning in an embeddedness of sorts and their harnessing in the direction of a 'social market'. What, I argue, might have been the achievement of differentiation at the national level nevertheless fractures under the weight of its transferral upward, to the European level, where the achievement of differentiation yields to the asymmetry of negative and positive integration. That is the first of the three 'constitutional moments' we explore. The second concerns substitution, and the regulatory competition that is initiated with the turn to the 'soft constitutionalism' of the second phase. With the third 'moment', the *degenerative* 'constitutional moment' of the Laval/Viking jurisprudence (in Chapter 3.4) we have a hardening and a radicalisation of market constitutionalism in Europe. This transition is partly reflected in and explained by the change from an ordoliberal to a neo-liberal mindset, in a process in which the qualification 'social' of Europe's 'social market' has been variably re-absorbed, re-qualified and collapsed into the market it was meant to predicate. The brutality of the 'social market's current deformation in the new functionalism of the Europe of austerity, I will discuss in the following chapter, in terms of the competitive alignment of the national systems of social protection.

Europe's Social Constitution: 'Moments' and Milestones

In the wake of the Second World War, 'social market economy' became the sign for the synthesis between an efficient market economy and a new role for the state and state law, and came to underpin the social model of the young German Federal Republic. This ordoliberal heritage was inscribed in the founding of the European Community in the separation of the economic from the political dimension, and their re-articulation by means of a juridical structure designed to manage their different dynamics and competing modalities on the basis of an unwavering commitment to protecting competition. Sustaining its architecture was the de-coupling between the supranational economic integration and the national social constitution (Scharpf, 2002). The differentiation found support in the 1956 Report (which came to be known as the 'Ohlin Report') commissioned from the ILO, that recommended that social policy should remain within the purview of national states while supranational institutions were given the role to ensure cross-border movement of economic resources. Free trade in the common market would ensure that the economic growth produced would deliver benefits across all member states, and no separate measures would need to be mobilised politically to equalise the social costs of market activity to different states. In fact, according to the Ohlin Report, political institutions at the national level would be better positioned to distribute the benefits of growth, especially when 'account is taken of the strength of the trade union movement in European countries and the sympathy of European governments for social aspirations'.[2] These insights found their way into the Spaak Report of the same year, which formed the cornerstone of the Intergovernmental Conference on the Common Market (and Euratom) in 1956 and led to the signing, on 25 March 1957, of the Treaties of Rome.

Phase 1 (1957–1992): The Era of Foundation

The first decade of the EEC was characterised by nearly complete inaction in the field of social policy. With the exception of the commitment of equal pay between men and women, no attempt was made to set common social standards for all member states except to the extent necessary to prevent specific circumstances of unfair competition. Distributive measures were left to the national states, and, if these varied among states, that was seen as reflecting levels of productivity that the internal market would operate to align. In any case, the European level of governance was not to be burdened with political tasks; it was there to secure a system of undistorted competition, leaving questions of redistribution to the national level.

It was only in 1974, and following Willy Brandt's initiative to give the common market a 'human face', that we have the first Social Action Programme. 'In ambition, at least', notes Ruth Dukes, it 'reflected the first efforts of the EEC toward the creation of a European labour constitution, understood in the Sinzheimerian sense as entailing the use of labour law to democratize the economy', although it did fall 'rather short of the mark'.[3] If this was a historical moment where organised labour was finding a foothold in Europe, it was to be short-lived. By the late 1970s

---

[2] Report by a Group of ILO Experts, 'Social aspects of European Economic Cooperation' (Geneva, ILO, 1956), para. 210.

[3] Dukes (2014). For an analysis of economic constitutionalism in its original (Weimar) Left-wing conceptualisation, see Dukes (2008).

the Programme had stalled more or less completely. And while in 1973 we had the creation of the European Trade Union Confederation (ETUC), no attempt was made for the representation of trade unions within the European institutions; prioritisation of national interests meant that there was very little room for coordinating common points of view across the unions, or the development of joint European influence.[4]

The reinvigoration of the internal market project came with the market-making initiative of Jacques Delors in the mid-80s with the removal of legal and fiscal barriers to freedom of movement on the one hand, and on the other with the recognition of the need for a 'European *social* area' as a necessary adjunct to the single market. The 'legendary' 1985 Commission White paper on the completion of the internal market 'signalled the advent of a new era' (Joerges and Rödl, 2004). With the 'Single European Act' of 1986 the EEC significantly expanded its legislative competence in the social field. Most important amongst the social policy initiatives here (always against the persistent exemption of the United Kingdom) was the signing of the Charter of Fundamental Social Rights in 1989, non-binding in itself but accompanied by the second Action Programme which carried compulsory provisions regarding working time, health and safety and posted workers, though nothing relating to collective labour rights.

During this period there is significant jurisprudence of the ECJ that, in line with the ordoliberal design, appointed itself as a constitutional court overseeing the integration of the market. During the 1970s we had two revolutionary decisions by the Court: the first was the decision over 'direct effect' which made the decisions of the Court directly implementable by the nation states. The second was the doctrine of the supremacy of community law over national law, including national *constitutional* law. Combined, the two doctrines allowed the Court to determine for itself the question of its own competence, and thereby lift itself to the position of Europe's constitutional court. National jurisdictions still entrusted with social policy and labour protection were now bound by superior community law directly enforceable within their jurisdiction,

---

[4] 'European employers in particular have no interest in advancing positive integration or European-level social intervention; with respect to common social policies that go beyond market-making, their interests are best served by non-decisions – i.e., by what intergovernmentalism is most likely to produce on its own. Also, with employers unavailable as European-wide interlocutors, unions, while fundamentally interested in supranational economic and social regulation, are thrown back to their national organisations and national economic and institutional interests.' (Streeck, 1995: 37)

and the negative liberties entrenched at constitutional level acquired constitutional standing and were thereby fast-tracked against positive liberties enacted at state level, and prioritised in cases of conflict. A few years later, a third decision came to seal the constitutionalisation of EU law, though this time it was a decision of a national constitutional court. In its 1993 decision on the Maastricht Treaty, the German Constitutional Court delineated the 'essential competencies' that fell within its own jurisdiction and by that very move granted functional legitimacy to the European Union to pursue the supposedly politically neutral economic integration, in a further chapter of the negotiation of the economic/political boundary. But with this we are already within the second period of 'ever closer Union', to which we now turn.

But before that, something to take note of: The 1979 *Cassis de Dijon* decision of the ECJ was an opportunity to expose national legislation to the economic rationality test – no longer through the lens of anti-discrimination, but something altogether different that quietly inaugurated a more radical form of market thinking. What stands in the way of the freedom of movement of goods, and therefore contravenes the law, is no longer the discriminatory treatment by a state in favour of its own products, by customs duties, etc.; it is now its very own laws and sovereign determinations, upholding standards, etc., *even where those are non-discriminatory* as such. Gradually this logic of protecting the movement of goods comes to provide the template for the other three freedoms. With the ascendancy of economic reason under the principle of undistorted competition, by the mid 1980s all state regulation of economic activity becomes increasingly thematised under that prism, with direct effect on the public provision and guarantee of goods and services insofar as they were seen as 'anti-competitive regulation'. The path has been cleared so that by the time we enter the EU's third period with the decisions in *Laval* and *Viking,* private holders of capital acquire the power to substitute for political publics in deciding, with the sanction of the CJEU, what counts as the preferred collective solution to the labour protection of Europe's workers.

Phase 2 (1992–2007): Maastricht and the Completion of the Internal Market

The treaty of Maastricht in 1992 inaugurated a second phase, during which the promise of an 'ever-closer union' brought a neo-functionalist mindset to prevail, as the harnessing of the European project to monetary union generated tensions that became very difficult to contain (Offe, 2013: 598). The project of monetary union, notoriously set in motion without a 'break facility', was superimposed on socio-economic diversity and discrepant economic strength amongst member states in the newly created 'eurozone'. The 1990s brought with it an immense increase in regulatory effort, to the point that Giandomenico Majone memorably spoke of the emergence of a 'regulatory state' at the European level.[5] The internal market initiative forced the Commission to operate a dense network of committees (of national administrative experts, independent scientists and representatives of economic and social interests) and to promote and coordinate national certification bodies and European standardisation organisations. Most of this was incompatible with the vision of a European economic constitution of the Ordoliberal vision. This much is undisputed according to Everson and Joerges: that 'intense regulatory activity documented mistrust in the self-regulatory potential of markets, and a quest for ever more coordination. As much as national and member state interests may have coalesced around the internal market programme, the intense juridification and re-regulation that followed in its wake was not simply unloved but also intensified the demand for the legitimation and control of Europe's burgeoning administrative structures' (Everson and Joerges, 2019: 414).

As far as Europe's 'social deficit' in the field of social policy is concerned, a limited market-correcting reservoir of policy was introduced, clearly short of anything like full harmonisation, but aiming also to protect the capacity of nation states to exercise national policy in the name of *subsidiarity*. The main form that the regulation of social and labour policy takes during this period is the constitutionalisation of 'social dialogue' and flexible forms of harmonisation that establish 'minimum standards' of labour protection.

Social dialogue was introduced with significant fanfare (under Articles 138 and 139 of the EC Treaty). On issues of social policy the Treaty obliged the Commission to encourage 'dialogue between management and labour' that would 'lead to relations based on agreement', both regarding legislative proposals and, if action was to be taken on these

---

[5] 'Majone's regulatory state, by contrast, is concerned with market failure, but has a normative basis within the effort to maximise the economically-defined welfare of consumers and citizens. In Majone's view, the non-majoritarian institutions of European regulatory politics and the majoritarian institutions of the Member States are complementary to one another.' (Everson and Joerges, 2019: 411)

proposals, on the content of the legislation. Dialogue was to be at the centre of the European social model, a 'driving force behind the economic and social reforms', especially where the dialogic form was geared to 'implementing a vision of social justice as a process of reconciling the divergent interests concerned rather than as a predetermined product' (Maupain, 2005: 89). And yet from the outset this was a 'social dialogue' fraught with problems. It stumbled first and foremost on the issue of 'representativity' (Davies, 2005). Neither was there effective representation of workers at the European level, so that there was no guarantee that affected parties would have a say in the dialogue, nor was the question of the representativity itself subject to and thus determined reflexively in processes of dialogue.[6] 'Social dialogue' remained anaemic in the absence of decisive procedural guarantees, or of bargaining structures that would have regulated bargaining outcomes, and was largely abandoned after Lisbon.

In 2001, a new reform agenda was launched with the publication of the 2001 White Paper on European Governance by the Commission and the term *governance* made its decisive entry onto the European scene.[7] The Social policy Agenda of the years post-2000 was, consequently, couched in terms of measures that were largely persuasive rather than mandatory in character, with an emphasis on soft law and the principle of subsidiarity. The term 'soft law' is used to describe a multitude of non-binding governmental instruments including recommendations, opinions, Green Papers, White Papers, informative communications, action programmes, guidelines and notices. If Community measures were deemed necessary, resort should be had preferably to framework directives and not to regulations. The guiding idea was that where legislation at European level was problematic, because of considerations of subsidiarity, or because agreement across member states could not be reached, soft law instruments could be used instead to encourage cooperation and the achievement of a commonality in goals and standards. According to what was by now 'the operational *Grundnorm* of new European economic governance'

---

[6] Some of these questions were identified by Keith Ewing in (1995): 'Democratic Socialism and Labour Law': 'What is the bargaining unit?' 'Is any threshold of support required?' 'What is meant by the employers' "duty to bargain"?' 'How are disputes on these issues to be decided?' See Ewing, 1995: 24. Ewing raises his questions in respect of trade union recognition within the UK, but they are also relevant to the matter of social dialogue at the European level.

[7] See European Commission (2001), 'European Governance. A White paper' COM (2001) 428 final of 25.07.01. See also 'Enhancing democracy in the European union. Working programme', http://europa.eu.int/comm/governance/work/en.pdf.

(Giubboni, 2018: 9), coordination involved the setting of minimum standards. The rules laid down at the supranational level set minimum standards of protection which member states had to comply with, while free to maintain or introduce higher levels of protection. This was, in other words, setting *a floor of protection*; the logic of positive integration and upward harmonisation of national systems of labour protection was the business of national social states. It is with the third phase, and following *Laval* and *Viking*, that 'floor' mutates to 'ceiling' of what protection national social policies can afford before they are outlawed as 'disproportionately' burdensome to the flows of cross-border economic activity.

Phase 3 (2007–): The Regulation of Crisis

The third phase of integration involves what Claire Kilpatrick calls the 'displacement of social Europe' (2018). The enlargement of the EU in 2004 and 2007 did not just generalise a market-friendlier mindset, but allowed disparities in wage costs and labour standards to be operationalised as a major source of the extraction of surplus value. Since 2007, the Treaty of Lisbon inaugurated a third phase of market acceleration and short-termism, significantly coupled with the governance of the financial crisis. Lisbon left the Social Chapter and the Employment Chapter of the TFEU largely unchanged, but endowed the Charter with legally binding force. Social dialogue was accorded less significance in the Lisbon Treaty; the Europe 2020 strategy was addressed to poverty reduction and away from participation. Otherwise we have a near-complete exhaustion of legislative initiatives in the field of social policy, coupled with a massive proliferation of emergency measures that elevate the policing of the crisis into a default constitutionality of sorts, *ad hoc*, erratic, particularistic, reversible. In terms of social policy, deregulation and flexibilisation continued to dominate as solutions to the problem of unemployment, and their institutionalisation continued to be operated as coordination policies, except now coupled with a punitive policing regime under the 'European semester' which 'promotes close policy coordination among EU Member States and EU Institutions', including assessment of the *Scoreboard of key employment and social indicators*. The scores are analysed by the Commission for compliance with Europe 2020, and lead to the issue of country-specific recommendations based on the assessment of the 'national reform programmes' by the Commission. A whole discourse of 'benchmarks' and 'targets', of learning processes' and 'best practices' are – as we saw above and will return to below – mobilised around this process.

Alongside these labile processes there 'hardens' a regime of EU governance in the form of policing by means of the 'excessive deficit procedure', the surveillance and balancing mechanisms and the imposition of conditionalities and adjustment programmes, that ensure the smooth operation of monetary policy. Concerned that eurozone governments could not be entrusted to deploy their competences in ways that would ensure price stability, and in the face of 'moral hazard' problems like those presented by Greece and the weaker economies of the south, 'conditionalities'[8] were introduced as *ongoing* measures of control by the Commission of the economic and fiscal performance of member states; no longer simply the catastrophic 'enforceable conditionalities' under Troika supervision, but now also, as Fritz Scharpf describes them, of a 'precautionary' variety (Scharpf, 2016: 5). Something of a 'constitutional deficit' arises out of this 'management' of crisis, the constellations of measures that take the form of legal and para-legal interventions, the unconventional discretionary judgements and measures of the ECB over the granting of liquidity and market interventions; and the whole array of ersatz laws, the soft instruments, *ad hoc* decisionism that are the hallmark of authoritarian governance. But the constitutional deficit takes a more direct form when it comes to the Memoranda of Understanding (MoUs) as key instruments of conditionality, which are clearly incompatible with the competences of the European Union. *Formally* because they include measures regarding public health, the administration of justice, the sale of state assets, the determination of salaries or the organisation of social security, all of them issues for which the European Union is simply not competent. *Substantively* because the conditions that they impose are in breach of international, European and national fundamental rights standards.[9] Finally we have the radical

---

[8] See the excessive deficit procedure (EDP) and the macroeconomic imbalances procedure (MIP).

[9] The High Level Mission that visited Greece in 2011 on behalf of the ILO, reported on the 'exponential' rise in the use of part-time and 'rotation' contracts, as well as the emergence of large numbers of 'discouraged' workers. The concern is not only that wages established by collective agreements have been slashed. Also, employers have now won the right not to pay collectively agreed wage rates, if they can secure the 'agreement' of workers to accept less and to sign away minimum terms and conditions of employment. From a strictly juridical point of view, since the new Greek government is committed to upholding fundamental social rights it should clearly conform to international legality: the Constitution of the ILO and to international labour conventions ratified by Greece, but also to the EU Charter of fundamental rights and to the Social Charter of the Council of Europe. Apart from exceeding the competences of the Union, the directives of the troika contravene these international social laws.

inadequacy of national courts' constitutional scrutiny, the bloody-mindedness of the CJEU's decisions *Laval/Viking*, *Ruffert* and then *Pringle*,[10] the subsumption of constitutionality to conditionality, the randomness of the deployment of that floating signifier par excellence: proportionality. These are all markers of the *absence* of law, not of its proliferation. We will return to these developments, albeit briefly. They are the result of what Wolfgang Streeck calls the 'frivolous experiment' (2015) to realise a market economy emancipated from all political bonds. It is important that they are documented for the injury of labour devaluation that they visit on the working people of Europe, and the punitive demolition of the field of association and community that they effect. But this form of punitive social re-engineering is important for our more narrow purposes of conceptual analysis, of what European constitutionalism means today.

In the short history, above, we have looked at the inaugural gesture of the asymmetric positioning of state and market in the early phase of European integration, which arguably took the cue from Ordoliberalism to fashion a social market that relied on a number of tenets: (i) the bracketing of majoritarian democratic preferences as they were expressed in the political systems of the nation-states in favour of the operation of the common market understood solely in terms of negative integration and as based on a synthesis of economic science and formalist rules; (ii) the reliance on the same democratic institutions when it came to the systems of social protection; (iii) the reliance on a strong judiciary to 'constitutionalise' the process. The problem with the European Union, as Scharpf rightly observed, is that it pushed for the dismantling of national solidarities without being able to build solidarity at the supranational level (Scharpf, 2002). With the move to the ever-closer union after Maastricht, a neo-functionalist mindset prevailed and, as the harnessing of the European project to monetary union generated tensions difficult to contain, the spectre of sovereign debt came to add a new chapter to the shifting dialectic of markets and states. The first tenet – that required the rule of law and justiciable criteria – has largely come undone; the second tenet, social protection, becomes improbable for a number of barely (or non-) solvent debtor states to deliver; the third tenet, judicial independence, has morphed into a self-delegation of extraordinary power, where the Court of Justice hails practically unlimited jurisdiction in the guise of

---

[10] Case C-370/12 *Pringle v. Ireland*, judgment of 27 Nov. 2012.

proportionality. *Laval* and *Viking* in 2007 and 2008 heralded the new dawn of total market thinking.

While we will return in the last chapter (3.4) to some of the more extreme pathologies of the totalisation of Europe's market integration, we will not delve in the history of the successive steps, not least because there is much excellent specialist literature on the various turns. What the remainder of this chapter will offer instead is a more detailed account of two constitutional moments: one pertaining to the genesis and the legacy of Ordoliberalism that underlay it, and one pertaining to the logic of new governance, installed during the middle period and accelerated during the third. A genealogical reading of the first moment shows how a hidden asymmetry in the architecture of the European Community became highly productive to capital by immunising market-making from market-correcting policy. The second constitutional moment marks the point at which Europe's constitutional achievement is undone, in the way we broadly described it in Chapter 2.4, but now specifically under the sign of the 'new EU governance'.

Crucial to both these moments is that they reflect within the European constitutional trajectory the logic of fragmentation (that we explored in Chapter 3.1) and substitution (in Chapter 3.2). The staggering of the ascendancy of market thinking in the European Union proceeds crucially through a moment of *fragmentation*, which allows what we called the 'generalisation of economic reason' across spheres (political, social, work, etc.) and a moment of *substitution*, which allows market thinking to establish itself as locus of veridiction, arbiter of all solutions, iterations of policy and their possible alternatives. Fragmentation and substitution map onto the two constitutional moments, of genesis and acceleration, respectively. In the first instance, the ordoliberal balance between the *differentiated* systems of politics, law and the economy (with the careful orchestration of respective function, performance and reflexivity) *fractures* as it comes up against a different differentiation, of levels this time, national and European. As a result of the fracture, the 'generalisation of economic reason' is mobilised through the fast-tracking of economic freedoms (negative integration) while the political and legal systems, stuck at national level, can offer nothing to rein it in, maintain proper systemic boundaries, or offer positive integration. Despite its aspiration to offer solutions at the European level, Ordoliberalism remains stunted at that juncture. And the *guarantee* of inclusion that functional differentiation offered the individual (the dividends that Luhmann read into differentiation, remember) in the various sub-systems of European society, becomes instead the *opportunity* of inclusion through *market access*, an inclusion offered and thwarted in equal measure. It is at this point that the second moment, of substitution, delivers the process over to capital through a series of elisions, slippages, and reconfigurations under the aegis of 'new governance', the market now spanning the field of equivalence on which policy solutions are proffered in the labile forms of 'democratic experimentalism'. The question of legitimation, too, as we will see, is recast on this re-assemblage, where the withdrawal of democratic and political categories from the field of the economy run at supranational level, leaves the possibilities of political identification – collective and democratic – stranded at national level. With nothing to hold on to, no intermediate associations or solidarity-based institutions, entry into the public sphere spirals down into the fanaticised nationalisms that abound around us.

The Ordoliberal Synthesis

'Founding ideology' is the formulation customarily used for what came to underpin the separation of the economic from the political dimension of the European Community, and their re-articulation by means of a juridical system designed to manage their different dynamics and competing modalities. The ideology was that of *Ordoliberalism,* and it emerged in pre-war Germany out of the 'Freiburg School', a loose and heterogeneous grouping of German academics around the influential figure of Walter Eucken. In their Manifesto of 1936[11] the *Ordo* group borrowed the notion of the 'economic constitution' from the Leftist writings of Sinzheimer and Neumann as 'the general political decision as to how the economic life of the nation is to be structured' (Joerges, 2005) but reversed it to couch the separation of politics and economics, state and market. The economic *ordo* was to be conceptualised as independent of the state's *democratic* constitutional institutions.

The imperative of the separation of market and state derives from the Freiburg School's founding, pervasive antipathy towards the state, which drew, at least in the 1930s and 40s from an opposition less to Soviet planning, as is often assumed, but to National–socialist economic

---

[11] 'The Ordo Mainfesto of 1936, signed by Franz Böhm, Walter Eucken and Hans Großmann-Doerth (English version in Alan Peacock and Hans Willgerodt (eds.), *Germany's Social Market Economy. Origins and Evolution,* New York: St Martin's Press, 1989: 15–25).

thinking,[12] though in respect to that, too, caveats have been inserted.[13] We can leave this dispute to historians. Let us instead stay with the 'progressive' and 'humanising' impulse of the founding as it emerges from the *social* market thinking of the ordoliberals. If the ordoliberal legacy is today so fraught with disagreement as to its role in providing the coordinates for the journey of European integration, it is because of the original ambivalence that it harboured, between its commitment to social justice and its profound suspicion of the state. There is indeed clearly an anti-state impulse in ordoliberal thought that finds expression in the faith in a market-driven integration of civil society. But while we can legitimately speak of a certain ordoliberal *state phobia* in the context of a social economy emerging from the wreckage of the National-Socialist State-run society, it would be anachronistic to generalise it to the kind of neo-liberal anti-welfare state paroxysm that the later, *neo-liberal*, turn engendered – a turn that one might chronologically place without too much distortion with Hayek's influence during his Chicago years. This is a subsequent state phobia *away* from its ordoliberal roots and harnessed to the anti-regulation agenda.[14] To do justice to Ordoliberalism, we must bracket the all-too easy rejection of 'statist' constitutionalism and the blanket phobia that displaces a more careful scrutiny over the threshold of appropriate steering. We *can* retrieve such nuance, arguably, in ordoliberalism's complex synthesis of social justice and market distributions. The ambivalence which is 'resolved' by neo-liberalism by the collapse of social justice into market distributions is still held on to in ordoliberal thinking as productive, however tenuous and fragile.

Difficult as it is to extract a coherent philosophical position out of the writings of the Ordoliberals – and how could it be otherwise in a group that

---

[12] This is at least the argument that Keith Tribe (1995) makes forcefully. He says: 'If we insist on reading the writings of the 1940s primarily as a critique of socialist planning we are in danger of going seriously astray' (1995: 207).

[13] The strong support of Eucken for Papen's government and the ties of Muller-Armack and von Stackelberg to Nazism are all in point.

[14] It is well captured in the following short extract from Foucault's 1979 series of lectures at the Collège de France: 'Against the inflationary critique of the state, against this kind of laxness, I would like to suggest some theses ... In the first place there is the thesis that the welfare state has neither the same form, of course nor, it seems to me, the same root or origin as the totalitarian state, as the Nazi, fascist or Stalinist state. I would also like to suggest that the characteristic feature of the state we call totalitarian is far from being the endogenous intensification and extension of the mechanisms of the state; [the totalitarian state] is not at all the exaltation but rather the limitation, a reduction and a subordination of the autonomy of the state, of its specificity and its specific functioning ... in relation to something else, which is the party.' (Foucault, 2004: 190)

included the fiercely republican Roepke, the deeply conservative Eucken, the Nazi-sympathising Muller-Armack, etc. – certain key elements nevertheless underpin the *Ordo* philosophy; key amongst them is a commitment to an 'undistorted system of competition'. Ordoliberalism came with an emphasis that this would serve social justice and social security in a way that pre-figures the current discourse of the 'social market'. In this sense, the *economic order* which they envisaged was meant to be *socially embedded*. By the end of the war, a significant 'ordoliberal' literature had appeared, drawing attention to the uses of economic instruments to impact upon the 'calculating machine' of the market[15] and to moderate the effects of the functioning of the price mechanism.[16] In 1948, Muller-Armack identified a number of *conditions* for the emergence of a *socially guided market economy* to add to the priorities already clearly articulated by Eucken regarding the pursuit of anti-monopoly policy and the control of cartels: they included the participatory structure of business organisations, the extension of social insurance, the introduction of minimum wages and measures to forestall the misuse of power in the economy. The role of law here is important, including interventionist law, although how exactly it was to be squared with the non-impairment of the market mechanism was left perhaps under-theorised.[17] In any case, *per* Joerges, 'the dual commitment required in their view the institutionalization of specific, albeit interdependent, orders, viz, a legally-structured order of industrial relations and of social security along with a legally guaranteed economic ordo, the "economic constitution"' (Joerges, 2005).

Wilhelm Roepke was, amongst the ordoliberals, perhaps the most radical exponent of social embeddedness, denying economic matters to be autonomous, but presupposing instead a 'meta-economic, social integration' for which he reserved the term *soziale Integration*.[18] '*Es gibt keine Autonomie des Wirtschaftlichen*', he insisted.[19] And unlike classical liberalism, per Roepke neither is a strict separation between the

---

[15] In von Stackelberg's formulation.
[16] Important contributors to this debate were A. Lampe, H. Mendershausen and F. A. Lutz. See Wegman (2010), Joerges (2005), Tribe (1995).
[17] 'Muller-Armack's proposals in 1947, for instance, involved no reflection on the economic implications of the social policy measures that he there outlined. From the viewpoint of the late 20th C, this is a rather serious oversight. It would appear that the Ordoliberals were mute on this point; where the constraints of the market economy intersect with the social conditions required for its functioning.' (Tribe, 1995: 239–40)
[18] Roepke in 1951, quoted in Wegman (2010: 92).
[19] Roepke in 1961, quoted in Wegman (2010: 91).

social and economic to be safeguarded, nor should economic integration be conceived as *pacemaker* for social and political integration. In order to preserve society, he argued, sufficient integration outside the competitive market is required. Roepke understood social integration as a basic condition of economic integration, and argued for a steadfast law-based order and a code of norms, principles, rules of conduct and moral concepts. There are the elements here for the thinking of the *moral economy*. Without state intervention and a society organised around values and institutions that do not reduce to personal advantage, the cultural and ethical practices around which coordination depends would break down. Roepke argued that 'the capitalist impregnation of all sections of life in our society is a curse that we must banish, and the free expansion of the economy must not lead to the perversion of genuine human values.'[20] The staving off of proletarianisation had to involve institutional solutions 'in forms of life and work', instantiated in legal forms of liberal interventionism aimed to 'protect small and medium sized property holdings'. Roepke understood institutional protection to extend to the guarantees for forms of participation in the economy, the support to independent farmers, but further also as aiming to 'revive pride in work and in professional standards, combat the feeling of human rootlessness' (Roepke, 1937/1951: 119). His prescriptions were directed toward the institutional recognition and support of 'human scale' communities and productive organisations and this to a large extent, implicitly perhaps and more in the economic argument rather than a full-blown moral one, by sheltering forms of activity and community from commodification. In an argument that foreshadows the *capabilities* argument, these were institutionally sustained and guaranteed opportunity structures for participation in the economy.

The market system for Roepke is intrinsically anarchic, a predicate he clearly wants to contra-distinguish from 'chaotic'. He begins the *Lehre von der Wirtschaft* with the question of how order might be created out of an anarchic system, and it is to this 'central question' that the coordination of production and distribution by the price system is the answer. It is wrong, he insists, to contrast the capitalist system by profit and the socialist by needs; it is important to see needs as intrinsic to both systems, and the market as the system that reveals needs of its consumers. 'In an unalloyed competitive system the production plan

---

[20] In his early *Die Lehre von der Wirtschaft*, Vienna, 1937, quoted in Glasman (1996: 52).

originates with an agent, namely the consumer, whose right cannot be lightly dismissed.'[21]

We might usefully summarise the ordoliberal 'synthesis' between the economy and the state, with an emphasis on the embeddedness of the social market, in terms of the following three tenets:

The *first* tenet refers to a system of general and predictable rules; a clearly formalist law and impartial state order achieved the very particular synthesis of juridical thought and economic science. There is commitment to regulation (Roepke called it 'liberal interventionism') and in all cases a commitment to a strong anti-trust law to protect markets; the ordoliberal ideal of the economic constitution does indeed presume a vigilant state. The commitment to formalism and the rule of law insulates the synthesis of law and the economy from majoritarian preferences, discretionary politics and democratic oscillations. For Eucken, clearly, *Ordo* is the name given to the economic system of a free market economy within a legal framework of institutional rules,[22] a 'rule of law' type ideal rather than historically contingent order. Key to the institutional order is the emphasis on competition law and the insistence on keeping the economic chances of all market participants equal at any time. Lawyers and economists' cooperative efforts converge to draw the line, and sustain it, between unfair and permissible competition. For Eucken the rise of cartels and monopolies was the key danger for the constitutional order, and 'complete competition' was its ideal. In all this, the main principle of the social order is bottom-up: rules of just behaviour, or economic fairness, emerge from repeated interaction between economic actors, buttressed by a law that sustains the opportunity structure and transactional character of that order.

Secondly, ordoliberalism came to be constitutively tied to the ideal of the *social market*. Understood irreducibly through its social dimension, the social market combines as a matter of definition with social institutions. It concerns a socialisation of the economy that contained key social mechanisms for the *organisation of production* but differed radically from the welfare state as conceptualised, for example, by the Labour governments in the United Kingdom. In his exceptional study of German

---

[21] Roepke (1937/1951: 185), quoted in Tribe (1995: 214).
[22] For Eucken the market is conceived as a structured process 'in which proportion and balance persist'. 'Ordnung, die dem Wesen des Menschen und der Sache entspricht, d.h. Ordnung, in der Mass und Gleichgewicht bestehen'. Quoted in Wegman (2010: 93).

economic history, Keith Tribe describes the difference as the 'distance separating social marketeers from market socialists' and quotes Roepke's stark denunciation of the Beveridge Plan in his *Civitas Humana* of 1944 'as a gigantic machine for pumping the national income about, ... with its highly complicated system of pipes, screws and valves ... *It is the extreme logical result of a proletarianised society*' (Tribe, 1995: 240). The difference is significant and it requires us to take a step back, to see how the first tenet of ordoliberal theory, above, articulates with the second, the commitment to social institutions. Maurice Glasman describes as 'a fundamental fallacy' to identify 'the ideology of the social market as a freely competitive capitalist economy' (Glasman, 1996: 51). With an emphasis on Roepke's protection of intermediate institutions and forms of organisation, on Alexander Rustow's defence of progressive taxation, and on Eucken's incentives and structures within the economy in pursuit of societal goals, Glasman sees in Ordoliberalism the theorisation of the market as a structured process, where '[e]conomic activity was embedded within a self-organised society which imposed non-negotiable costs concerning democratic participation in economic decision-making and the necessity of negotiation' (Glasman, 1996: 52).

Thirdly, the ordoliberal programme of safeguarding the economy from the political system with the help of law is, unsurprisingly, entrusted to Courts. Important decisions about the nature and limits of intervention are to be referred to Judges, not legislators, as guardians of '*functional Ordnungsrecht*', says Hauke Brunkhorst, quoting Mestmaecker (Brunkhorst, 2014: 41).

We began this chapter on the constitutional design of the European community by reading Ordoliberalism, the social model of the young German Federal Republic, into the founding moment of the European Community as it came to underpin the separation of the economic from the political dimension of the union, and their re-articulation by means of a juridical system designed to manage their different dynamics through a commitment to competitive processes. But now comes the moment of uploading it to the transnational level, *as foundation* of the European polity. 'As a concept, Ordoliberalism appeared particularly apposite to integration', explain Joerges and Rödl (2004). 'Ordoliberalism's core message concerned the taming of discretionary politics. Politics and law should establish a 'system of undistorted competition', a formulation that found its way into the Treaty of the EC. 'In the ordoliberal account the Community acquired a legitimacy of its own by interpreting its pertinent provisions as prescribing a law-based order committed to guaranteeing economic freedoms and protecting competition with supranational institutions. ... At the European level governance should not be burdened with political tasks' (Joerges and Rödl, 2004: 6). The eclipse of political constitutionalism is sealed by a further substitution: that of legislative for judicial organs. If 'law and economics' have become 'Europe's hidden curriculum',[23] it may however be premature to ascribe it to Ordoliberalism as such. But it is also true that the Ordoliberal differentiation of economics, politics and law left the linkage vulnerable to the neo-liberal turn. As the *differentiation* that was precariously sustained in the ordoliberal *credo* was transferred to the supranational level, it resulted in *fragmentation*. In European integration is exhibited the story of differentiation, fragmentation and then the generalisation that will collect the fragments within the purview of the market.

Let us read this trajectory back into the ordoliberal founding of the European Union. If it is the *embeddedness of the social market*, in the varied and complex structures of association that surround them, that characterises Ordoliberalism, what are the effects of the '*Grundentscheidung*' that transfers it upward to the European level? If we are to assume the claim credible that Ordoliberalism provided the European Community with its founding principles, what happens to the constitutive embeddedness of the social market once it is thinned out in order to be lifted to the European level? If the argument is that the move is to establish the economic constitution on a plane cleansed of state control, then the argument misunderstands the ordoliberal position. To appreciate the specific dynamic of the relationship between state and market, as deployed and thematised in the ordoliberal economic constitution and the social market, one must avoid the marked tendency to look at the relationship of market and state in zero-sum terms; assumptions about the 'demise' of the state in the face of the rise of market operations are indicative of this. This simplifying assumption mis-reads both the continuing role of the state as well as the state-like condensation of political power in the governance mechanisms of the European Union. Instead let us summarise the key features of Ordoliberal thinking as they might apply to the European story with an eye to the lines of fracture. The European project is launched as an economic project. The autonomy of the economy becomes institutionalised through negative integration and the protection of competition. The economic freedoms are given

---

[23] Brunkhorst explains, 'With the establishment of the economic constitution in 1957 ... instead of subsuming the economic under the political constitution the political constitution was subsumed under the economic constitution.' 'This', he says, quoting Claus Offe (2003: 463), 'is Europe's "hidden curriculum"' (Brunkhorst, 2011).

priority; national markets are opened; self-regulation frees the emergent domain of action from democratic or political input. Its processes are founded in law and shielded against political input, discretionary national policies and any form of protectionism, now in the name of anti-discrimination. Social protection does not disappear, but in the new architecture it is entrusted to member states in the name of subsidiarity. We might even stretch to suggest that state-administered social policy is conceived as an aspect of the organisation of production, not as a welfare net or compensatory gesture for social costs suffered by the operation of economic activity (as in Roepke's critique of Beveridge's Welfare plan, above). If this first (pre-Maastricht) phase of the European integration can be called its ordoliberal moment, it is because these key features are in evidence. A robust formalism upholds economic rights in the 'synthesis' of valid law and economic science. Economic policy is guided by law and justiciable criteria. Such justiciability is guaranteed by the gradual constitutionalisation of rights by the European Court of Justice in the principles of direct effect, supremacy, pre-emption and self-empowerment. The key difference from the ordoliberal paradigm is not that social protection is abandoned: on the contrary it is 'entrusted' to the national states in the name of its rootedness in welfare traditions of social and labour protection.

And yet something significant *has* changed with the uploading to the supranational. The social dimension in no longer constitutively tied to the logic of production as guaranteeing the social conditions of people's participation in work. The labour market is, instead, released from the relative immunity previously afforded to it from the vagaries of price; it is harnessed to economic freedoms and *in that modality* trans-nationalised. This development is highly significant. We will need to wait until the next chapter to see the magnitude of the effects. But it is seeded in the logic of the transferral from social embeddedness to transnational exposure, a transferral that destroys the careful synthesis and justificatory basis of Ordoliberalism. The problem, to summarise, is that the initial separation of spheres (economic and statal) crosses with a second separation, of levels (statal and supra-statal), in a way that instead of ensuring the 'fit' and mutual accommodation of the two distinctions, fractures the fragile ordoliberal understanding of the first.

New European Governance and the Social Constitution

With the ordoliberal promise of an 'embedded market' lost to transnationalisation, Europe had to react to the 'social deficit' that followed. After Maastricht, a limited market-correcting substantive body of regulation was introduced establishing 'minimum standards' of labour protection, in line with the commitment to state-level exercise of social policy in the name of *subsidiarity*, and the complementary only introduction of European-level procedural solutions in the form of 'social dialogue' on the one hand, and on the other the flexible harmonisation of 'new governance'. The main form it took was the *Open Method of Coordination*, installed in 2000 to become the main engine of constitutionalisation of social policy. As a key device of democratic governance, it mobilises bench-marking across an extensive list of indicators which are offered for synchronising and coordinating the various processes, in particular for streamlining the 'social protection' OMCs with those of 'employment' and 'economic policy'. Its theoretical champions suggest that 'practical policy discourse' in the terrain of OMC 'has been (or is likely to become) significantly unencumbered by ideological baggage, and more open and reflective'[24] and have 'explicitly interpreted the OMC and the EES as examples of the idea of experimentalist or directly-deliberative governance'.[25] In respect of coordination, OMC appears only marginally to limit the sovereign exercise of political power by member states, handing over to Europe what are nominally coordination issues and leaving the substantive political choices to the states. But the ambition is larger, and 'EU added value' accrues in terms of the use of the motor of negative integration, whereby the coordination of national systems become locked in a mutually re-enforcing cycle with the protection of economic freedoms across the Continent. The case for OMC runs something like this: The transplantation of substantive principles and foundational notions of the constitution from national to supranational levels stumbles on a variety of problems, notoriously that of constituency or demos with the deficits and paradoxes that attend it. But the procedural solution promotes a 'thinning' of constitutional principles to allow them to span the European political space across the diversity of its political cultures and constitutional understandings. This allows the bypassing of 'thicker' constitutional solutions on the supranational scale and instead delivers a 'functionally limited' EU constitutionalism centred on entrenched market-liberalisation norms and administered by a set of formal EU institutions, and the existence of a dense and complex system of multilevel governance spreading into all fields of policy. The case for

---

[24] Simon (2015: 22), quoting Trubek and Mosher (2001).
[25] Simon (2015), referring to Trubek and Trubek (2004) and Sabel (1994).

OMC, and the constitutionalisation more generally of 'soft law', claims a space in between the 'high' forms of constitutionalism and the extensive spread of governance by suggesting an *articulation* of a novel kind, and with it a legitimacy on a different register. 'High forms' would have included the preservation of unity as strict hierarchisation between levels, and the formal exercise of constitutional review. Instead what now becomes operationalised is the distinction between hard/soft (or high and low) forms as constitutive of the field of governance that claims for itself the porosity of the boundary between those forms. A productive synthesis is proposed that works in both directions: as a response to the rigidities of high forms of constitutionalism the open method provides 'softer' and 'voluntaristic' forms of policy-making, contextual meanings, fleshed out in local contexts, and pre-emptive of the stalling of the European project where national sensibilities, typically over the protection of labour standards, often made moving forward politically charged. At the same time, in their placeholder function, the 'higher forms' keep the OMC's centrifugal impetus in check, containing within the ambit of a set of values and principles that *as form* circumscribe, undergird and inform content.[26] The mutual enablement in both directions (between OMC processes and fundamental rights) offers a version of constitutionalisation of 'soft law', such that would allow the holding up of current practices against the principles they instantiate. The generality of the principles allows the maintenance of *variety* at the level of concrete regulation, and their *entrenchment*, simultaneously, the confirmation and re-establishment of the core commitments underlying the unity of law.

What makes the above 'synthesis' possible is the *wholesale proceduralisation* of governance: the purely procedural OMC can then be seen to achieve the productive containment of the tension between the 'high forms' – statements of fundamental and universal rights – on the one hand, and limited European competences on the other.[27] It aspires to the

---

[26] OMC processes could be used as a way of giving concrete contextual meaning to the various rights set out in the Charter. OMC could constitute a suitable vehicle through which the general and abstract guarantees of the Charter are given flesh in particular settings and the context of particular policies; Charter rights could be used as 'ideal norms' in relation to which the outcomes of the OMC processes would be appraised, and as means of stimulating reform or revision of the standards which emerge when the outcomes are considered substantively unsatisfactory (De Búrca, 2003: 431).

[27] In the words of one of the most eloquent advocates, what this involves is 'a strategy which leaves a considerable amount of policy autonomy to the Member States, and which normally blends the setting of guidelines or objectives at EU level with the elaboration

articulation between a level of principle that must remain at a level of abstraction such that it may command loyalty across political/constitutional cultures and understandings, on the one hand, and a level of instantiation that both maintains the link to the principles and meets the contextual, local, 'thick' expectations of actors, and delivers at the level of governance, on the other. The way that this articulation remains alive to both levels is because it is realised in procedural terms; not through normative determinations (of the traditional disappointment-proof kind) which are, on top of everything else, also too top-down, but through *reflexive* determinations that are that because they are 'open to learning'. And with this all relevant targets are hit: as learning processes they both reflect changing perceptions and invite contestation, revision, local instantiations – in a word, democracy. The word is *fluidity* and *institutional experimentation*: civil society with its fluid and overlapping understandings and priorities finds a voice in the labile forms of the OMC, which *remains both 'open' and regulatory* at the same time, at the intersection of European and national orders. These national orders must remain open to the best practices of the other national partners, and this recognition of what is 'best' is not a *political* concession but a matter of *correct measurement*.

In all this the law itself is nothing but *passage*. No normativity grounds it. In its comprehensive proceduralisation, the constitution provides only leverage to the accelerations and adaptations of the cognitive '*self*'-organisation of society, so 'openly dimensioned' that it is hard to fathom that any *self* might be hoisted out of all this at all, either around stakeholding (by assertion, elision or default) or around some conception of the 'common good', now a-centric to the point that defies assemblage. That normative value is surrendered and that problems proliferate at these junctures does not worry the proponents of constitutional governance because the solution of the problems can be postponed, with the grand collapse of constitutionalism into an *ongoing* cognitive project, running alongside shifting sovereignties and re-conceptualisations of political space in the dynamic constitutionalisation of soft law (see Chapter 2.4).

---

of Member State action plans or strategy reports in an iterative process intended to bring about greater coordination and mutual learning in these policy fields' (De Búrca, 2003: 419). And she asks: 'Is there a way for constitutional values to be reflected and protected within soft law (and open method of coordination – OMC) processes, other than as flexible policy standards, capable of being revised in any direction?' (430).

The obvious way in which the relationship between constitutional principle and governance practice is secured, and 'blockages' in the assumed and necessary dialectic relationship of the two levels avoided, is by treating constitutional values and principles as declaratory, as aspirational, and therefore as 'soft'. A crucial conflation is mobilised at this point. Where the governance practices cannot seriously be said to instantiate a constitutional principle, say those of the protection of *dignity or democracy* in work, the principle is deemed 'less prescriptive'; such principles 'fail to establish themselves as real recognised standards'; or 'their aspirations have abated'.[28] Here the argument that general principles make possible a certain variety of concrete interpretations is collapsed into another, quite different, argument, that declaratory principles are to be contrasted with *jus cogens*. But this is elision and subterfuge. That constitutional principle, or constitutional value, is articulated at a higher level of generality and abstraction makes it no less binding for that: principles are not for that reason deficient norms. They do not 'abate'. They are the normative bases that inform constitutional practice (see Chapters 2.2 and 2.3). If the governance practices don't stand up to the constitutional principles then they are legal mistakes, to be righted. The failure to address them gives free rein to what eventually becomes the collapse of political constitutionalism as a normative project. Note how insidious the logic of the hollowing out: at the ground level of the operation of indicators a soft *'juridification'* – understood in managerial terms of alignment to best practice gradually *morphs into 'constitutionalisation'* in the absence of any barrier of level-differentiation that might have insulated the latter from the creeping process of endless recalibration. This constitutional deformation is more often acclaimed than criticised, as a 'sort of "liquid" constitution, destined to be constantly re-shaped by the current cultural factors and explicitly based on a kind of "multilateral compromise"' (Febbrajo, 2011: 294).

In our earlier discussion of the 'epistemological co-option' associated with the use of *indicators* as instruments of mediation, we saw that the problem was understood as a problem of rigidity that sets in at intermediate levels, because indicators are inattentive to the wealth of the

---

[28] 'Formally, the [2000] Charter is merely a solemn proclamation by the European Parliament, Council and Commission ... It was at one point hoped that, although the instrument is not as yet legally binding, it could provide a new source of reference for the courts in the exercise of its [sic] fundamental rights jurisprudence. This aspiration has abated ...' (Novitz, 2005: 228).

contexts that they index, too reductive and too coarse. That is what troubled Sally Engle Merry: that meanings do not 'carry' without distortion across the qualitative/quantitative divide, the divide between the context-rich practice and the reductive mediation that carries it into the field of regulation. Indicators are fictions but they come to stand in for, and become indistinguishable from, the elements that form the substance of society: practices, with their histories, their moral economies and their productive organisations. Merry's 'solution' misread the magnitude of the challenge she diagnosed. The technology of indicators is the 'coinage' that introduces comparison and circulation, what sets governance on its tracks. It cannot be 'tempered'. Quantification is the reduction that establishes comparability, and it severs, as it is meant to, the criterion of 'best' from particular sets of normative commitments, both those explicitly contained in the text of constitutions, and those inherent in moral economies and local understandings.

But what is more pertinent to us at this point, is that mediation is problematic at the other 'crossing' too. Indicators not only select out what is salient and suppress the rest at the first interface of practice and measuring instrument; they also impact at the other interface between measurable performance and constitutional principle. If on the first interface of mediation the problem is that the mediating instruments reduce the understandings they are meant to reflect, on the second interface they distort the principles they are meant to instantiate. At both interfaces the interpretative question is lost. At the first interface it was lost, as we saw, as a matter of the exclusionary function of the mediation: the indicators cannot be refined in the light of the very thing they substitute for. At the second interface it is lost because the substantive principle is *already* proceduralised, in order that it can be compared, balanced and optimized. The criterion of 'best' constitutional practice is severed from the normative commitments that are explicitly contained in the text of constitutions, and all that remains 'constitutional' in the new dispensation is the *method* (of coordination) of those commitments. We will need to look at proportionality in the next chapter before the full import of this hits home, but already the constitutional undercutting is manifest. Maybe the most indicative manifestation comes with the impossibility of asking the following question: *What is constitutional about the competitive alignment of national systems of social protection?* We could ask the same question more simply: *Is the OMC constitutional or unconstitutional?* If that question appears meaningless it is because we have lost the constitutional register on which to ask it. *Measured* against the constitutional value of dignity, 'social dumping' – or the competitive alignment of systems of labour protection – *is* unconstitutional. But that is not an available injunction in the constitutional dispensation where constitutionality is in effect coincident with its comprehensive proceduralisation, a move that internalises and absorbs any independent criterion of proper *'measure'*. If the OMC is 'the EU's constitutional method par excellence', it is because constitutionality is conceived of *as* procedure and *as* coordination: what is constitutional is delivered by the constitutional method in that modality, of the comprehensive collapse of substance into procedure and procedure into functionality. It is this slippage that loses the constitutional register, and ushers in another kind of 'veridiction' in the precise terms that Hayek offered earlier. Remember Hayek modestly suggested that 'the history of civilisation emphatically affirms' the success of societies 'using competition' to discover their truth, and that is 'all that can be empirically verified'. We will return to the appeal to the 'empirical' and to facticity immediately below. But to Hayek's suggestion as to what might be 'emphatically affirmed' about Europe's social constitution we might counter this: Where information-gathering aligns itself to competition through benchmarking, comparators and metrics, *key objectives of public action* become divorced from the public good and thus of the ends of promoting social welfare and guaranteeing social protection, and are instead cut adrift as values to be pursued independently of ends. But competitiveness is not a natural principle of human flourishing; only as underlying economic growth is it valuable, and then only if harnessed to achieve 'improvement of living and working conditions' or 'economic and social progress', as Agustin Menendez puts it insightfully.[29] In the same way, he adds, financial stability is valuable as harnessed to social aims of full employment and higher living standards; it is not properly the 'higher objective' that it was declared to be in *Pringle* (Menendez, 2017). But once the link is severed, economic growth is floated as competitiveness and financial stability as price stability, cut off from the principles of social constitutionalism against which they might be measured, *best practice* becomes an 'empty signifier' as it scales the plane of equivalence, released as an *eigen value* in the circuits of capitalist expansion. The relationship between means and ends is reversed at this point; and in the constitutional 'solution' of optimisation, the *question* to which it is

---

[29] I borrow this argument from Agustin Menéndez' important critical work on European Governance; see Menéndez (2017).

the solution forever slips away and back into the self-fulfilling promise of market veridiction.

*

We conclude our account of the loss of concepts and of the proper register of social constitutionalism on a *phenomenological* note, on what *appear* as the relevant facts, that are submitted to comparability, that test the success of constitutional practice. Here, like earlier, we turn to the important work of Alain Desrosières on the production of statistical data. Desrosières invites us to contemplate the connection that exists between the configuration of public space and statistical reason that ordinarily is assumed as a technique to aggregate and process facts. He writes: 'The construction of a statistical system cannot be separated from the construction of equivalence spaces that guarantee the consistency and permanence, both political and cognitive, of those objects intended to provide a reference for debates' (1998: 324). How revealing these terms: 'political' and 'cognitive', measuring the 'permanence of the objects of reference'. Desrosières is inviting us to understand the complex relationship that exists between political spaces of representation and the production of statistical information, and he deploys the term 'space of equivalence' to capture it.

La politique des grands nombres is an account of the genesis of statistical reason and its development from the seventeenth until the twentieth century. Rather than posit the notion of *probability* as central concept, as one would expect from a theory of statistical reason, Desrosières takes the notion of *expectation* as key. The notion of 'expectation' introduces the *social* dimension as methodological condition, and with it comparability becomes tied to social histories. He does this, he explains, because the notion of expectation captures a duality between a *subjective* and an *objective* element that in various forms persists throughout the history of statistical reason. On the *subjective* side it captures the awareness of a knowledge deficit that undergirds and advances statistical reason – *What are the chances of the safe return of a ship? What are the chances of the success of an inoculation?* – and allows the judgement of a number of people to coalesce around it. The key question asked on the subjective side is: under what conditions might the necessarily incomplete knowledge nevertheless merit a warrant, *furnish* an expectation? On the *objective* side it was a question of uncovering the regularities that *really* obtain. For Desrosières it is Adolphe Quetelet who is the key exponent here, offering a 'calculus of averages' as an instrument involving objective measurement designed to reduce the heterogeneity both of particular objects and of particular judgements. Quetelet, and later Galton, says Desrosières, understood their work as 'opening up a new continent for the objectification of causality – that of a partial, statistical causality' (1998: 329). The notion of a 'partial causality' is revealing as it strains to express Quetelet's conviction that there *were* regularities, and that it was important to 'approach [their] reality' (336). Later systems of social insurance were to be built on the objectivity of these regularities, and the transformation of individual chance into stable collective objects, necessary for the institutional endeavour, hinged on those averages.

Desrosières tells a long and fascinating story of the development of statistical reason as the shifting articulation of the two dimensions, and by the time we get to the election of Roosevelt in the United States in 1932, statistical reason has expanded and entrenched, with a vast array of population and business censuses organised, and the creation of a national (federal) statistics to back economic intervention involving surveys, representative samplings and national accounts, organising the knowledge required for state regulation. Desrosières notes something in passing, that is hugely significant for our own analysis. He mentions that during this period, with the New Deal on the table and state regulation underway, it was the *federal* territory of the United States that was seen as the *pertinent totality* for the aggregation of the information. Let us stay with this term, pertinence. It is this pertinence that answers the question of scale and delineates the space of the relevant conventions of equivalence; in this *the proper constituency for aggregation of information was tied with a political judgement as to the proper constituency for the regulatory intervention*. In this pertinence subjective (judgement) and objective (probability) combined, facticity runs alongside the political, inextricably.

Why is 'pertinence' – the emphasis on what is *thought* as relevant constituency – so important for (Desrosières' and) our own argument about Europe? It is because of the correlation between relevant information and appropriate intervention. It is because the delineation of the space of *economic information* ties directly with the delineation of *economic policy*, in a coincidence where neither determination precedes the other. This internal link impacts on *taxonomy*, categorisation and indices, that is, the terms of reference, on the vocabularies of encoding of objects, on the opportunities and limits of their contestability; all relate to the macro-social framework of reference. The information thus produced is already correlated to what might be thought as the possibilities of intervention *given* the macro-social frame of reference, the pertinent constituency.[30]

Take unemployment again, where it is clear that the nature of measurement ties to the function of the network of connections, assumptions and records that inform it. We saw this earlier, in the way that benchmarking worked to privilege the more flexible systems of employment. In France, says Desrosières, 'polemics on the assessment of unemployment have been triggered at regular intervals, every two or three years from the mid-1970s on. . . . these polemics on the realism of the equivalence created at a given moment by an institutional and cognitive network show that such networks are never definitively fixed.' As far as France was concerned, 'the idea of a clearly definable and measurable unemployment was clearly integrated into the network of common representations'. Networks are made of 'stabilized connections of routinized equivalences' that form the 'discernible set of bonds that make things hold' (333). From the point of view of this set, 'these certainly were realities' (332).

Two things are notable when we transfer these thoughts to the European case and discussion of unemployment, and its procedural regulation through the OMC. The first is that these 'routinised equivalences' 'that make things hold' is what comparability abstracted *from*. The interpretative nature of the conventions of equivalence was bracketed. The diagnosis of the problem, and the solution to it, called for conventions of equivalence and, instead, received a metric. Remarkable about this is that it was the very disembedding of information from any particular 'network of

---

[30] Compare Negri's invocation of the *Europe* of producers as pertinent constituency in the following: 'Now, only a political, economic and social Europe, a strong union of this area, can shape the mediation of the expansive interests of the new mode of producing and the urgent necessities of resistance to the power of world financial corporations. *Only Europe is an area adequate to the federalist constitution of the common good* . . . Why is it that only now we recognize ourselves as federalists? Why, for at least 20 years, have we hindered rather than supported the development of productive autonomies? Why didn't we succeed in quickly identifying the characteristics of the new mode of producing? Why didn't we succeed in inventing a syndicalism of the "diffuse factory"? Why did we endure the construction of the produced common good as if it concerned an enemy, instead of anticipating its development and being able to represent its articulations and needs? . . . From now on it's a matter of going forward united. It's a matter of re-inventing and experimenting with the programme of the new left from the very bottom, on the basis of the exceptional (but exceptionally, gravely dangerous) situation that is our Veneto. Here labor has changed, here today subjectivity, once again, has its "laboratory." Long live autonomy.' ('Letter from Toni Negri to the Venice meeting of the European counter-network & its allies', Rebibbia prison, Rome, 10 September 1997.)

equivalence' that meant that these 'certainly were realities!' It was their disembedding that made them that. The exclusionary logic of re-embedding, calibrating and generalising that we discussed at length in Chapter 3.2 is what allows the measuring of unemployment and employment policy to be floated across spheres of equivalence that sever it from the sets of bonds that make things hold.

But there is a second thing to note, and it concerns this revised *correlation* of *information* garnered from conventions floated transnationally and the *intervention* they allow at that level. If statistical information was gathered at the time of the New Deal from the whole of the US territory it was because the intervention was planned at federal level: *economic information* tied directly with the delineation of *economic policy*. Similarly, if 'during the period 1950–1975 an effort was made', 'at least provisionally', Desrosières qualifies, 'to unify the economic and social debate around a common language, this was the language of planning and Keynesian macroeconomics, of growth and national accounts, of the sociology of inequalities and its statistical indicators' (333). And, as he argues at length in *Prouver et gouverner* (2014), it was also the unified and stable language of state-backed collective bargaining over salaries in the context of an egalitarian and redistributive welfare system. With the OMC, the turn to proceduralisation and bench-marking, and with 'harmonisation' through the market, comes the unravelling of these stable vocabularies and the 'networks of equivalences' that framed statistical knowledge, the 'discernible set of bonds that make things hold'. Now things fall apart; the centre does not hold. The collapse of the frames of equivalence that sustained it casts macroeconomic planning as meaningless, the objects and measurements that circulate in the internal market deprived the reference that grants them meaning. Comparability requires traction and it gains it in the mirror of intervention, where alternatives and options first *appear*. The wholesale proceduralisation of the OMC, and the competition *of 'frames of equivalence'* that marks the moment of disembedding of social and labour protection, is a comparability that lacks a referential frame, a comparability without history and without register. It is the move that delivers the labour constitution over to the market, and is at its core a moment of withdrawal and destruction of meaning of the practices it arbitrates. It is a 'creative destruction' in the sense that Schumpeter understood the renewal of capitalism. The competition of frames of equivalence delivers labour protection to the market and is what underwrites the deformation that is Europe's market constitutionalism.

3.4

The Deep Commodification of Labour

You have disgraced yourselves again.

W. B. Yeats[1]

Laval/Viking Jurisprudence

The 'quartet' of the *Laval/Viking* decisions, all decided by the Court of Justice of the European Union within a period of two years (2007–2009)[2] heralded a 'constitutional moment' of far-reaching significance that has shaped the field of labour protection and Europe's *social* constitution. It is a *degenerative* constitutional moment. Its impact has been to unsettle the difficult articulation between the national and transnational constitutional orders of labour protection. It was clear then, as it is now, that the launch of EU Labour Law with Maastricht, during what we identified in Chapter 3.3 as the second phase of European integration, was never going to be smooth. From the start, EU Labour Law understood itself as the regulation of the European labour market (the same shift in the self-understanding of labour law as labour market regulation had occurred in the United Kingdom in the 1980s).[3] This placed EU Labour Law in a

---

[1] It was with these words that W. B. Yeats reacted to the rioting at the performance of *The Plough and the Stars* held in 1907 at the Abbey Cathedral in Dublin. The 'again' was referring to a previous incident of mass rioting on the occasion of the performance of J. M. Synge's *The Playboy of the Western World*. Yeats himself made this comparison explicit when addressing the masses at the performance: 'You have disgraced yourselves again. Is this to be an ever-recurring celebration of the arrival of Irish genius? Once more you have rocked the cradle of genius.' (In Anne Miller, *The Independent Theatre in Europe: 1887 to the Present*. New York: Ayer Publishing, 1972, p. 291.)

[2] Case C-341/05, *Laval un Partneri Ltd* [2007] ECR I-11767; Case C-438/05, *International Transport Workers' Federation and Finnish Seamen's Union v. Viking Line ABP and OÜ Viking Line Eesti* [2007] ECR I-10779; Case C-446/06, *Rüffert v. Land Niedersachsen* [2008] ECR I-1167; Case C-319/06, *Commission v. Luxembourg* [2009] ECR I-4323.

[3] See Dukes (2014) on the shift, and Deakin and Wilkinson (2005) as one of its most ambitious instantiations.

difficult 'middle' position where it faced a difficult relationship at either interface: with the ILO which now held to (a limited but) *substantive* set of principles, and with the national systems (organised in their majority according to principles of *political* constitutionalism) that established social and labour protection as a matter of national-democratic decision-making. The earlier phase of the constitutional jurisprudence of the European Court had reflected both the difficulty of boundary-maintenance, but also a deference to what the Treaty clearly identified as matters that fell under member state jurisdiction. Not always coherently, and certainly with a dose of self-restraint on the part of the ECJ, the fragile architecture had been upheld during this time. It took the constitutional moment of *Laval/Viking* decisively to collapse what for a decade before it had been quietly eroding, and to subsume labour protection to the logic of market optimisation. Let us look at the steps of this degeneration, both in terms of its effects on the institutional architecture of labour protection in the European Union, and also at the conceptual level, in terms of the *deep commodification* of labour.

Laval concerned a Latvian company that won a contract to renovate school premises in Vaxholm, Sweden, using its own Latvian workers who earned about 40 per cent less than comparable Swedish workers. The local branch of the Swedish builders' union opened negotiations with Laval's Swedish subsidiary (Baltic) in order to extend the relevant sectoral collective agreement to the posted workers and negotiate wages for them. The Swedish Building workers' Union demanded that the company provide comparable wages and conditions to those of Swedish workers under the construction sector collective agreement. Following Laval's refusal to enter into such negotiations, the building workers' union organised an effective blockade of Laval construction sites, followed by sympathetic industrial action by the electricians' unions (all permissible under Swedish law), which eventually resulted in Laval's Swedish subsidiary going into liquidation. Laval brought an action in the Swedish courts. The firm sought a declaration that the industrial action was unlawful, and compensation from the unions for the losses it had suffered. The Court referred questions to the Court on the interpretation of the Posted Workers Directive (PWD) and Article 49 EC, on the freedom to provide services. The CJEU found that as rates of pay were not laid down in Swedish legislation (and as Sweden had furthermore not availed itself of potentially applicable derogations under the PWD), the provisions of Article 3 of that Directive were not applicable, and that an extension to posted workers of the host country's employment conditions at issue was therefore not possible.

Viking concerned a Finnish company wanting to reflag its vessel (that sailed the Helsinki–Tallinn strait) under the Estonian flag in order to enter into a new collective agreement covering its crew. The International Transport Workers federation (ITF), known for its long-standing campaign against the use of flags of convenience, instructed its affiliates not to enter into negotiations with Viking Line, thus frustrating the latter's efforts to reduce crewing costs. Viking sought an injunction in the English High Court, alleging that the ITF circular (which had been issued in London) violated its free movement rights under EU law and more specifically that it breached Article 43 of the TFEU *on freedom of establishment*. The CJEU was thus asked to rule on a series of questions exploring the extent to which collective action should be subject to Union law. The CJEU held that such actions could not be considered to fall outside the scope of the freedom of establishment as laid down in Article 49 TFEU: the explicit limitations on EU action as regards the right to strike in Article 153(5) TFEU were not decisive as member states had to comply with Union law in the general exercise of their competences.

Both cases turned on what construction the CJEU would give to the articles protecting freedom to provide services (*Laval*) and freedom of establishment (*Viking*). The Swedish case, *Laval*, raised the additional issue, addressed at the very outset by the Court, on how to interpret the Posted Workers Directive. (PWD).[4] The main objection to the Court's competence to decide the case stems from the basic architecture of the distribution of competences between European and national level. The Court held that although the member states were free to regulate the right to strike, they were obliged to do so in accordance with Community law, including the free movement provisions. In summary, then, the Court found that EU law *did* apply to the cases; it applied in a way that implicated *trade unions directly*. It found *that collective industrial action was a restriction on fundamental freedoms* and so presumptively unlawful unless it could be justified and was *proportionate*.

We will focus on these four key issues[5] and bypass some of the complexities of the cases, not merely because excellent elaborate analyses

---

[4] Given the well-established rule that directives cannot have horizontal direct effect meant that Laval could not rely on it in its action against the union.
[5] Identified by Barnard (2012a).

are already on offer,[6] but also because our interest in the decisions is more narrowly confined to how they drive European constitutionalism to an extreme market form:

1. *Does EU law apply to the right to strike?* In the constitutional architecture of Europe, the right to strike, whether explicitly or under the freedom of association, is for the member states to regulate. Article 153 of the TFEU repeats this premise by excluding EU competence in respect of the right to strike. The Court's self-authorisation to extend its jurisdiction relies on a move on the broader plane: strike action, *as a whole*, does not fall outside EU law because 'nation states must *also* still comply with Union Law' (emphasis added).
2. *Does EU law apply directly to trade unions?* The Court here embraces horizontality unreservedly to establish that EU law can be invoked by employers, circumventing states, directly against unions.
3. *Do strikes impede free movement?* Relying on the 'market access' argument the answer is yes. '*Market access*' changes the presumption: it makes strikes *prima facie* unlawful, and reverses the onus on to the unions to show that they have acted proportionately.
4. *Should strike action be proportionate?* The Court answers this positively as a demand to 'reconcile and balance' and places the onus on the unions to engage in action that is 'appropriate, necessary and reasonable'. The key supplementary question *'proportionate to what?'*, the Court answers 'as suitable to achieving the objective' and not beyond what is necessary to achieve it. It is not for the unions themselves, but for courts, to deem whether other means were not at the disposal of the unions, so that strike action be indeed the 'last resort'.

The first two questions concern how the Court understands the demarcation between the social and the economic; the second two involve a recalibration and a co-option. The first two involve the act of laying bare, the necessary condition for the systemic operations proper; the second two, expressive of that operation, collect the pieces in the inclusionary move of market realignment, or, of deep commodification. We will look at this more gradually, the first two steps in the remainder of this section, the second two in later sections of this chapter.

The question whether EU law extends to the right to strike is quite straightforwardly answered by the Treaty in the negative, which also

---

[6] Amongst the best here Davies (2008); Barnard (2012b); Kilpatrick (2009); Bercusson (2007).

means that it is beyond the CJEU's jurisdiction to pass judgment. But the Court will perform one of its signature moves, in the same performative gesture that allowed it to claim jurisdiction in earlier constitutional moments and elevate itself into arbiter of the question of its *competence*. The problem for the Court was that by constitutional design that competence in cases of social and labour protection was reserved for national courts. As if that wasn't conclusive, a clear jurisprudence stemming from the Court's important previous decision in *Albany* had established that collective agreements between management and labour 'with a view to improving conditions of employment' fell outside the competition rules contained in the EC Treaty.[7] The reason is clear: the fact that from the very beginning, as we saw in Chapter 3.3, social protection was allocated to the states and market integration to the European level created, by the very principle of that allocation, the obvious problem that the results of collective agreements had to be excluded from anti-trust scrutiny. The problem stems from the fact that collective agreements are obviously restrictive of competition, by precluding employees selling their labour at a price below that set by the agreement. The justification for such agreements is that they establish a minimum threshold of social protection for workers in a specific jurisdiction. But once differential protection is introduced across jurisdictions there arises a conflict between the social imperative of the protection of workers and the market imperative of competition. To protect subsidiarity and the economic/social architecture of the European Union, since *Albany* was decided in 1999, there developed a clear jurisprudence that granted collective agreements a clear immunity from anti-trust scrutiny and ring-fenced national systems of worker protection from the reach of EC internal market law.[8] For that reason it is clear that *Albany* upheld an outright incompatibility, an immunity from anti-trust scrutiny, *not a balancing*: collective agreements were deemed to fall outside the scope of the Treaty freedoms *notwithstanding* the inherent, and obvious, restrictions on competition that they entailed. The trade unions' argument in *Viking* and *Laval* was that the right to take collective action was

---

[7] Case C-65/96, *Albany* [1999] ECR I-5751.
[8] It could be added that the very rationale of passing the 'Posted Workers Directive' discussed in *Laval*, was to maintain the immunity of national systems of social protection once cross-border activities became generalised and could thus potentially trigger European law applications. The Directive could be seen as safeguarding worker protection as the domain of national competence by guaranteeing non-discrimination between national and foreign workers.

analogous to what *Albany* had protected: collective action was always going to infringe Articles 43 and 49 and should therefore be exempted from assessment under those Articles; in both cases, though perhaps particularly in *Viking*, the unions argued that the Court should resolve this conflict by holding that the right to strike was outside the scope of the free movement provisions.[9]

The Court had nothing so confining in mind. But to give itself a clean break from *Albany* it had to interpret it narrowly to refer specifically to collective bargaining and not to extend to collective action. Equally importantly, the Court considered that the exclusion of social rights from the scope of the competition rules did not exclude them also from the scope of the articles on economic freedoms. It was contended that there was no need to confront the question in the harsh terms of an *Albany*-type incompatibility.[10] On the other side of the – now *apparent only* – clash, the right to strike is 'after all not absolute; it always comes with restrictions'. The incompatibility is thus argued away and the terrain opened up as fertile for balancing and proportionate limitations.

The second question involves the Court in an extraordinary interpretation of *horizontality*. The Court's concern, as Anne Davies explains it, is that the removal of barriers to free movement imposed by states might be 'neutralised' if private parties could create barriers of their own to which Community law did not apply (Davies, 2008). As Catherine Barnard argues, this interpretation of the Court is in essence 'an extension of the doctrine of *vertical* direct effect, with trade unions being liable in the same way and to the same standard as states'. But this commits a systemic mistake because the primary function of a trade union is to protect the interests of its members and, unlike a state, not to promote the broader interests of society as a whole (Barnard, 2012a). The Court, according to Barnard and other commentators, makes a mistake in its horizontal interpretation by assuming that unions can and should be called upon to serve the public interest. It is on this basis, as against the

---

[9] A pre-emptive move in *Viking* treats as fundamental that 'it *cannot* be considered that it is inherent in the very exercise of trade union rights and the right to take collective action that [the] fundamental freedoms will be prejudiced to a certain degree' (*Viking* § 52). *Viking* includes a more detailed discussion than *Laval*, and a clearer rejection of analogy with *Albany*.

[10] Advocate General Maduro opined, and the Court agreed (Viking §§ 48–53), that there was no incompatibility between fundamental freedoms and the Community's social policy objectives, as there may continue to be in the more narrow template of the competition between collective bargaining and competition rules.

public interest, that the Court will measure the reasonableness of their actions; which also explains why the Court has no qualms in allowing itself to substitute for the unions in the exercise of that judgement, uniquely positioned as it proclaims to be outside partial affiliations and alignments.

More needs to be said about the decisions, and in fact we will reserve the discussion of 'market access' and 'proportionality' for later sections. For now, let us take from our brief discussion three key points. The *first* is the extraordinary performative gesture of the Court to expand its jurisdiction into a field that it was constitutionally barred from. The *second* is the horizontality of application that treats states and unions as functionally equivalent obstacles to moving capital and services freely around. The *third* point also involves a reversal: *Laval* turns the protection afforded by the PWD *from floor to ceiling*, above which member states cannot go lest they restrict the right to free movement. Together these three legal innovations have far-reaching consequences into the way in which Europe's labour constitution[11] is understood. To appreciate the gravity of these decisions, a gravity accentuated by the fact that the Court quite openly acknowledges the magnitude of what is at stake in its allusion to the 'overriding public interest' to 'protect workers in the host state against possible social dumping', we need to see these developments against a radical reconfiguration of tensions, stakes and alternatives in the context of a decisive market turn and the 'deep commodification of labour' that it effects. A number of delicate – and in retrospect fragile – balances were sustained by the architecture of the relation of rights and freedoms, social protection and economic integration. As was discussed in Chapter 3.3, in the initial split of the 'economic' from the 'social' in the architecture of EU constitutionalism, was ingrained an argument about sustaining and enabling the social dimension *as distinct,* categorically so, *from* the processes of 'negative integration'. Social protection increasingly came to be seen in terms of insulation of national systems from European processes of integration. It is against this background that we must appreciate the *Laval/Viking* jurisprudence for what it is: a significant reconfiguration that does not replace the architecture but hollows it out to the point at which its constitutive, however tenuous, tensions collapse and a new 'synthesis' is proposed in which the old contrasts lose their bearings, and the dilemmas become aligned to the projected win-win

---

[11] I borrow the term from Ruth Dukes' exceptional book (2014). See also Roedl (2009).

outcomes of market integration. That they are not seen as losses, but as new accommodations, explains why the court does not shy away from naming the 'stakes'; why social rights and economic freedoms are seen as largely coincident in the new accommodation; and why the argument is defended in the name of inclusion and 'access-justice'.[12]

As the profound effects of the cases began to sink in, changing the constitutional landscape of labour protection in the member states as they did, the controversy they sparked invoked a response by the Commission, that in 2010 urgently sought to 'address the objective of reducing tensions between national industrial relations systems and the freedom to provide services', on the grounds that 'continuing legal uncertainty could lead to a loss of support for the single market by an important part of the stakeholders and create an unfriendly business environment including possibly protectionist behaviour'.[13] The legislative initiative was undertaken at EU level (Monti II) to mitigate them, in an attempt to insulate domestic collective action from EU law liability. The suggested solution was relatively unremarkable: to increase the margin of appreciation of local courts in the name of subsidiarity. The initiative was defeated. The fate of this legislation, argue Mark Freedland and Jeremiah Prassl in 2014 'suggests that an initially promising legislative avenue for reconciliation has become an impasse, no doubt in part because of the negativity, even at times the understandable paranoia, which the Viking and Laval case law has generated in Member States'. As a result of that 'moribund attempt by the European Commission to address the balance struck in Viking and Laval through legislative action' (Parents, 2014) *Laval/Viking* case law continued to play a key role in EU law, with legislative intervention at national level deadlocked. In the intervening period what did change was how much more adept at creating posting scenarios[14] employers became and how regime-shopping flourished in the wake of the *Laval/Viking* jurisprudence.[15] Practices of illegal posting were rife, workers were posted to live under unsuitable conditions in mass accommodation facilities, or posted

---

[12] For this term, see Micklitz (2018).
[13] Memorandum, pp. 9 and 14, quoted in Goldoni (2014).
[14] Nicola Countouris and Samuel Engblom explore such scenarios (including temporary work agencies designed exclusively to supply posted workers aimed at undercutting local working conditions) in Countouris and Engblom (2014).
[15] The overall posting in the period between 2010 and 2016 rose by 63% with 2.3 million cases of posted workers in the EU (1% of total employment). Data available at https://ec.europa.eu/social/keyDocuments/.

through 'letter box companies' that would declare bankruptcy at the first hurdle. In the meantime the issue found itself at the top of the political agenda of the European Union.[16] After two years of debate, the Revision of the PWD was voted in the European Parliament in 2018, introducing limitations to the time of posting, changes in the rate of pay of posted workers, and other measures. It is premature to tell how effective the Revision will be in dissipating the frustration, and to achieve its stated aim of a 'better balance' between market freedoms and social rights. My suggestion is that the articulation is structurally locked, and therefore unaddressable from the point of view of the aspired 'completion' of the single market, a deadlock which also explains why the primacy of economic freedoms over social rights remains stark over a decade after the decisions were handed down.

To the structural problem we shall return, as we shall to the deeper reconfiguration that this functional intersection between national and transnational constitutional orders has effected on the constitutional imaginary. We will explore it in the direction of *market access* and *proportionality* weightings. But first we must see how the deep commodification of labour has been pursued not only along judicial but also along *legislative* routes in the Europe of austerity.

The New Functionalism

In one of the most memorable passages of *The Great Transformation*, Karl Polanyi describes a memorable reversal. Echoing, to some extent, Marx's argument about primitive accumulation and the laying of the foundation of capitalist economies, Polanyi famously writes '*Laissez-faire was planned; planning was not*' (1944: 147). If the *Laval/Viking* jurisprudence of the CJEU aimed to release the new energies of capitalist expansion in a renewed race to the bottom, and if the comprehensive proceduralisation that was mobilised through the OMC aimed to channel those energies without thwarting opportunity through labour market 'rigidities', the grand effort at *laissez-faire* at European level has been far from self-sustaining. In the wake of the crisis that accompanies the third, current, phase of European integration, post-*Laval* and post-Lisbon, a vast machinery of regulation and enforcement has been introduced to sustain the European market. The new functionality that

---

[16] It dominated Macron's election agenda with 'travailleurs détachés' having become a synonym to 'social dumping' in France.

pervades the European Union finds expression in the deluge of *Ersatz* law, the 'six-packs' and 'two-packs', the EFSM and the EFSF, and the full range of measures that sovereign debt loan assistance has assumed. It includes the constellations of measures that take the form of legal and para-legal interventions, the unconventional discretionary judgements and measures of the ECB over the granting of liquidity and market interventions, the whole array of soft instruments, the *ad hoc* decisionism, and the punitive refusal of liquidity. And while not the whole range of authoritarian governance can be dignified with the term constitutional, given the forces of *constitutionalisation* and the shifting ground of what counts as entrenched and what not, it is difficult to know what is.

Already with the launch of the Lisbon strategy in 2005, the OMC 'hardened' in the hands of the Commission, no longer the mechanism of reflexive harmonisation and of mutual learning through the exchange of good practice, but an instrument of 'colonization of the welfare state by the economic policy making process'.[17] The cause of the crisis was attributed to the slack in budgetary constraints and inefficiency of the soft coordination that had allowed overspend in welfare budgets and reluctance to implement social reform. Enter *the European Semester:* Introduced as a major form of macro-supervision of economic policies and performances this 'hybrid meta-coordination framework yoked together hard and soft law processes' or rather 'put hard law mechanisms at the service of soft instruments' (Costamagna, 2018: 12), forcing guidelines and recommendations on wage-setting and other nominally national competences.[18] The effect has been staggering.[19] The European Semester introduced new scoring systems ('social scoreboards') and sets of indicators to 'monitor societal progress'. By forcing through policy objectives of budgetary discipline, and the 'reduction of welfare dependency', the aim of the Semester has been to coordinate the

---

[17] Chalmers and Lodge, 'The OMC and the European welfare state', quoted in Costamagna (2018: 11).

[18] See Salais (2013), Kilpatrick (2018) and Dawson (2018) on 'the displacement of social Europe'.

[19] Take one instance: for three consecutive years between 2013 and 2015, Council Recommendations were addressed to France to reduce the cost of labour 'to ensure that developments in the minimum wage are supportive of competitiveness and job creation', leading France to pass (by executive decree) the infamous industrial relations act of 2016, weeks before it faced a fine by the Commission for missing its deficit targets. Examples abound.

competitive alignment of national systems of social and labour protection.

The sovereign debt crisis introduced a new wave of transformation and degradation of social Europe as financial assistance was made dependent on conditions of comprehensive structural reform on the part of debtor states. *Memoranda of Understanding* were key instruments of macro-adjustment, and introduced conditionalities clearly incompatible with the competences of the European Union. All this is well known and its effects have been devastating. I have attempted to say something about those effects in my 'Europe's Donors and its Supplicants: reflections on the Greek crisis' (2017), written during the resistance and eventual capitulation of the Greek leftist government to the diktats of the Eurozone. I will not repeat that argument here; I will simply end this short account of the ersatz constitutionalisation of the Europe of crisis, the new functionalism of EU governance, with a note on how it continues to receive the unwavering support of the CJEU, and how difficult its commentators find it to disentangle themselves from market thinking.

The Irish case of *Pringle*[20] was emblematic in this respect. Against what the TFEU (Art. 125) explicitly establishes as the 'no-bail-out clause', the absolute prohibition of debt-financing between member states, the Court argued that conditionalities secure the prime purpose of *price stability* within the EMU in ensuring that debtor member states will be subject to market discipline in maintaining sound budgetary policy. The European common interest, the endorsement of which becomes a requirement for assistance, is measured on the axis of stability, discipline and austerity. What are the grounds of reversing the clear meaning of the bail-out clause? For Paul Craig, leading EU lawyer, 'economic reality renders the neat juncture between purpose and interpretation of Art 125 a great deal more tenuous. . . . The blend of text, background purpose and teleology that constitutes the very essence of legal reasoning' (Craig, 2013: 9), and this is what *Pringle* exhibits. Other scholars are lending their weight to this line of argument, so that the dominant position is one of praise for the efforts of the CJEU to maintain monetary stability. A functionalist reading of this euro-securing decision harnesses the European constitutional imaginary to the leitmotif of conditionality against current and future political democratic alternatives.

---

[20] Case C-370/12, *Pringle v. Government of Ireland, Ireland and the Attorney General*, 27/11/2012.

But *price stability* is not a telos. Restoring *competitiveness* is not a telos. They are merely instruments, or functionalities, in a certain understanding of the economy. We should not use terms like *teleology* cheaply; the term cannot be hollowed out to simple and blatant functionality without diminishing the concept of constitutionalism. For those who remain sceptical of the breathless pursuit of market discipline, there may still be some comfort in a formalism that resists such *telē*. 'A sadly diminished legal discourse', is how Michelle Everson puts it, surrenders the constitutional imaginary to the *faits accomplis* of economic science. Here is her comment:

> *Pringle* fails on all counts. In a Europe of uproar and revolt against austerity regimes, as well as of counterpart fiscal trepidation, or popular unwillingness to commit to a European community of solidaristic fate, the *fait accompli* judgement, expounded without reference to social context, and unfolded only within the technical minutiae of a sadly diminished European legal discourse forecloses potential for proper evolution of a socially-responsive European constitutional tradition. At the same time, in all of its manic vacillation between formalism, literalism, teleological referencing and purposive re-statement of that referencing, the judgment similarly fails to connect with any form of constitutional-legal tradition, leaving itself open to the accusation of legal trickery in the politicised service of a brute functionalist rescue of the Euro.
>
> (Everson, 2015: 480)

Forms of managerial legal thinking are hurriedly enacted to shore up stability in the modality of *ad hoc* responsiveness and under the sign of *emergency or necessity* as interchangeable states.[21] Emergency comes to stand for the time-frame within which society must be reproduced, and necessity becomes the other side of the coin, since any form of resisting it (necessity, that is) has come undone along the temporal dimension and the pace of market choices. This is akin to an order of policing, what Walter Benjamin called 'law-preserving violence'. The givens of market integration

---

[21] I say this because emergency and necessity name different things. *Urgency* refers to the need to take decisions outwith the normal timeframes and procedural requirements that secure adequate deliberation. *Necessity* refers to the absence of alternatives. What happens when urgency and necessity collapse into each other around the notion of exceptionality? For one thing the horizon of political decision-making recedes. The need to act at once to avoid calamity (urgency) meets the diminution or elimination of options (necessity); the circumvention of democratic deliberation becomes the way in which emergency is managed.

prevent any politically mediated evolution of the European polity that remains neither adapted nor adaptable to the variable steering demands of the core and the periphery of the Eurozone. If the very idea of constitutionalism involved in its conception and development a co-evolution of the political and the economic around the organising concepts of the juridical, a 'sadly diminished' European constitutional discourse under the sign of emergency now forecloses the potential for a responsive constitutional sensibility. The problem, as is so often the case where battles are won by default, is in the difficulty of discerning and establishing the battle lines. The *loss of language* becomes clear in the constitutionalisation of austerity. We have noted this loss already at various turns. We encounter it again in our discussion of proportionality where *taxonomy*, with its careful architecture of hierarchy and emphasis, is collapsed into commensuration and balancing. It is to this that we now turn.

Proportionality as Market Exposure

Laval and *Viking* were received as landmark cases in Europe's national courts and as they were absorbed into national discourse and practice they significantly changed Europe's constitutional landscape, aligning stances and expectational structures in member states.[22] They triggered a half-hearted initiative (defeated as we saw) by the Commission, bent on *'prevent[ing] solutions being unilaterally sought at national level'* while sustaining an increasingly hollow commitment to subsidiarity. Because what might subsidiarity actually *mean*, and what would 'subsidiarity review' actually *review*, in the context where the *protection* of labour at *national* level is the very thing that is struck down as *protectionist* at the *European* level? How, given market integration, might subsidiarity carve out a space for itself when its constitutive claim to difference coincides with the negation of the harmonisation that 'EU added value' promises, or better that *is* its added value. 'Added value' is what accrues by the shrinking of labour protection. It is delivered by the material organisation of Europe's market integration as downward

---

[22] For Charles Woolfson the rulings of the Swedish Labour court subsequently to the CJEU decision 'seem to confirm that the "Swedish model" has, at the very least, been significantly redefined if not fundamentally altered in the light of *Laval*' (Woolfson, 2010: 335). For the austerity-struck countries, already devastated by the undercutting of the unions, the effects have been nothing short of catastrophic. See Koukiadaki and Kretsos (2012).

levelling of the social protection it entails and sanctions. Subsidiarity is a call to alignment, and subsidiarity review is left with little to do except record market discipline.

Some of the ripples of the tectonic change even reached the CJEU, where there was a partial acknowledgement that it had perhaps gone too far, and a certain (though never overwhelming) unease, as evidenced by its effort to re-operationalise proportionality as a *reconciliatory* device between freedoms and rights. Perversely the need was already clearly acknowledged in the text of the *Viking* decision in the recognition that 'the [Union] has not only an economic but also a social purpose' and that 'the rights under the provisions of the Treaty on the free movement of goods, persons, services and capital must be balanced against the objectives pursued by social policy'; that the freedom of establishment *may* be restricted where what is involved is the pursuit of 'a legitimate objective compatible with the Treaty and is justified by overriding reasons of public interest'; and while 'the right to take collective action for the protection of the workers of the host state against possible social dumping may constitute [such] an overriding reason of public interest' (§103), nevertheless continue the judges in *Viking*, the unions' exercise of the fundamental right to strike in pursuit of 'the legitimate public interest objective of worker protection' needed to be '*proportionate*' (§103). The Court returns to the need to mobilise proportion against the fear of democratic excess and to rein in the disproportion of strikes. Again the expectation that *strike action be proportionate* is perverse. A strike is an *assertion of a political conception of justice*, it is not an offer to proportionate weighting. In any case, the decisions in *Laval* and *Viking* received a gentle rebuke,[23] for adopting a 'hierarchical relationship between fundamental freedoms and fundamental rights in which fundamental rights are subordinated to fundamental freedoms, and for not realising that 'the proportionality enquiry cuts both ways'.[24]

Proportionality has a history longer than the Constitution in Germany, according to Dieter Grimm (2007), and while it goes back to the Prussian administrative courts of the late nineteenth century, it was with the famous case of *Lüth*, in 1958, that it came to inform constitutional jurisprudence whenever the court has had to review laws limiting

---

[23] In AG Trstenjak's restatement of the proportionality principle in *Commission* v. *Germany (occupational pensions)*.
[24] See Syrpis, 2011: 225–7 and passim for a useful analysis.

fundamental rights. With *Lüth*, says Ernst-Wolfgang Böckenförde, the 'balancing' conception of proportionality came to take up a place alongside the classical model of the proportionality test in German constitutional review, but its function changed. It came to be thought of as constitutive of a norm rather than interpretive of a (pre-existing) norm, 'meaning-giving' (Sinngebung) rather than clarifying meaning (Sinndeutung).[25] By the time the principle is exported outside Germany, the *'balancing'* component has become *definitive*. In his seminal article of 1987, Alexander Aleinikoff explains the method as realised in 'a judicial opinion that analyzes a constitutional question by identifying interests implicated by the case and reaches a decision or constructs a rule of constitutional law by explicitly or implicitly assigning values to the identified interests'. What made this method uncontroversial for the author was its 'resonance with current conceptions of law and notions of rational decision-making'. (Aleinikoff, 1987: 944–5, 960.) It is the emphasis on 'rationality' and balancing as its pivot that has propelled 'proportionality' to inform how constitutional review is organised. The most influential theoretical work on proportionality to date is Robert Alexy's *Theory of Constitutional Rights* (2002) introducing the key notion of *rights as principles,* and *principles as optimisation requirements.*

Anticipating much of what was to follow, in *Between Facts and Norms*, Habermas warned of profound 'methodological errors' when it came to the deployment of proportionality. His 'hostility' to 'balancing' is typically pared down to a few, albeit weighty, objections: that balancing abandons the language of normativity proper, of the distinction between right and wrong, for the language of the more-or-less, of adequacy and inadequacy; that it dilutes rights into goals, policies and values, the latter used by Habermas interchangeably in his critique; that because 'there are no rational standards for it, weighting takes place either arbitrarily or unreflectively, according to customary standards and hierarchies' (1995: 259); that it thereby collapses the 'firewall' of rights-protection and the *deontological* understanding of rights; and that it

---

[25] Böckenförde in *der Staat* (1990), quoted in Van der Walt, 2014b: 361. And as Johan van der Walt puts it in his important work on *horizontal effect*, it was indeed *Lüth* that 'bequeathed horizontal effect jurisprudence to Europe' with its 'insistence that the sovereign's law apply everywhere and to everyone' (Van der Walt, 2014b: 357).

abandons criteria of rationality either to random balancing or to 'irrational rulings' (1995: 253–61).[26]

Alexy's response to Habermas is to outflank him by elevating proportionality to *constitutional method as such*. His *Theory of Constitutional Rights* has spawned a thousand applications, though much of the theoretical work clusters predictably around the perennial question of the legitimacy of constitutional review, with all the narrowness that entails. His elevation, however, of proportionality to constitutional method is hugely important for what it tells us about constitutionality in the way we have defined it: the *reflexivity* involved in how *the law thinks about itself*, its limits and possibilities and, in the process, also the environment that confronts it with its competing imperatives, the dilemmatic structures of its demands. Alexy describes a structure of constitutional principle that remains reflexive to the extent that it performs the balancing acts required of it, and can do so proportionately. It is hard to exaggerate the importance of proportionality in his theory, as it informs every aspect of his answer to Habermas' critique on the one hand, and on the other fastens on to the theory that law is a 'special case' of rational argumentation, a position he so influentially defended as an internal position within the Habermas-inspired paradigm of legal theory (Alexy, 1989). It is interesting that Alexy conjoins the two, arguing *against* Habermas' critique of proportionality *in terms of* rational argumentation. For Alexy, 'balancing' is not an alternative to, but an integral expression of, rational practical discourse. Against Habermas' objection that proportionality abandons the language of 'rightness' for the language of 'adequacy', he argues that both are facets of the claim to correctness, except that his, as a proposal for understanding how constitutional rights apply to real situations, involves balancing rather than 'subsumption'. Against the charge of 'randomness' he presents the careful architecture of proportionality as structured inquiry, and the variability it introduces is nothing but the responsiveness of that architecture to the complexity of the demands confronting it. What is 'customarily applied' is not in terms

---

[26] As usefully summarised by Greer: 'According to the "hostile" view, [balancing] should be regarded as an irrational and illegitimate renunciation of law in favour of a largely arbitrary judicial discretion, difficult to justify according to the ideals of democracy, respect of human rights, and the rule of law and, therefore ripe for elimination from the legal process. Alternatively, the "sympathetic" view maintains that, although the current judicial practice of balancing may be difficult both to describe and to defend, the concept of balancing, when properly understood, is neither irrational nor illegitimate.' (Greer, 2004: 413)

of unthinking repetition but carries the full weight of the hermeneutical method; and if the 'firewall' is not present in the form of trumping defences, it is no less protective for that, because proportionality will only accept interferences to the basic principles where they carry enough justificatory weight, and serious violations of rights (that the 'firewall' was there to protect from) do not carry such weight, or very rarely do. Finally, Alexy's theory of proportionality preserves the primacy of autonomy by preserving the primacy of practical reasoning over deontology, as George Pavlakos, one of Alexy's most careful readers, argues convincingly (Pavlakos, 2011: 153). It is the argumentation that mediates and allows the specification of abstract values in contexts of action that realises autonomy, as opposed to a deontological assignation of values to reasons from the outset. The processes of determination, in other words, presuppose and realise the values as appropriate to (concrete) contexts of action.

In all this it is Alexy's *rational rehabilitation of proportionality* that has won such admiration. The principles that comprise 'proportionality' are what they have been since *Lüth*: 'suitability', 'necessity' and 'proportionality *stricto sensu*' or 'balancing'.

> All three principles express the idea of *optimisation. Constitutional rights as principles are optimisation requirements.* As optimisation requirements, principles are norms that require that something be realized to the greatest extent possible, given the legal and factual possibilities.
>
> (2002: 47 and 2003: 135)

Optimisation carries the 'claim to correctness' and thus the 'test of public reason' that of course, in the tradition of both Habermas and Alexy, redeems validity claims in the *intersubjective* processes of *communication* geared to consensus. The way that it is undertaken 'given the legal and factual possibilities' grounds it in law as 'special case' of practical rationality: it is within the constraints of the extant legal order and 'given the legal and factual grounds' that optimisation works, close to the ground of application on a case-by-case basis, and as expressive of constitutional rationality itself. That is why proportionality is claimed not as a compromise of but as the very *realisation* of practical rationality. The fact that it is undertaken by Courts provides the added value because Court-based proportionality enjoys superiority to the balancing that occurs in legislatures: while both rely on argumentative and discursive processes, and subject them to the 'test of public reason', judicial argument relies exclusively on such processes *to the exclusion of the decisional element*, and all the arbitrariness of political or majoritarian preferences, that characterise legislation.[27] The argument about 'optimisation' is pitted against decisionism.

*

To begin to see what is wrong with this grand synthesis, we can follow a less trodden, though I think productive, route that takes its lead from the ancient notion of *appropriate judgement*, an Aristotelian idea bequeathed to us through Aquinas' notion of *determinatio*.[28] This has involved, since Aristotle and Aquinas, the move from general to particular, from principle to concrete application. At the most abstract level, values express our human commonality; they define something of the teleology of what it means to realise a life worth living, which removes from the list both arbitrariness and the need for any further or meta-level justification. In Aristotle's defence of the *virtues*, they are not negotiable as such: what remains negotiable is their instantiations. They are emphatically not preferences or desires, and thus clearly to be set apart from any utilitarian or optimisation calculus. They are the normative foundations that make normative reasoning meaningful. The idea of *determinatio* captures the logic of instantiation, along the direction of how these values are concretised. Institutional logic intervenes here, and the logic of reduction – the institutional achievement of reducing complexity – is a key part of it. The pragmatics of instantiation is what we come to know and practise as law. But *determinatio* in the beautiful simplicity of its pure directionality captures the connection between furnishing judgement (with content) and providing thresholds and limits as to what might count as reasonable interpretation. Direction and threshold-setting: like in our earlier discussion of the 'dogmatic', these are key moments of heteronomy that present themselves to juridical reasoning.

Now this is not the language of Alexy or the proportionality champions so why should it concern them? Because Alexy *is* keen to embed

---

[27] This involves, in Alexy's argument, the insulation of legal-reflexive balancing from political decision-making; constitutional scrutiny here receives some insulation from the rough and tumble of political bargaining, or the circumventing of proper reflection through majoritarian decisions, making the court its ideal forum. I will say no more here about this familiar, tired, debate.

[28] The most faithful expression in modern jurisprudence is in Finnis (2011) but it arguably also informs Lon Fuller's discussion of the 'two moralities' (Fuller, 1964). The most insightful application of Aristotelian thought about appropriateness to the modern context, as it comes up against the problem of complexity, is Klaus Günther's *Sense of Appropriateness* (1993).

his theory of principle in contexts of application, hence his constant reference to 'the legal and factual possibilities' (above). It is here in fact that he claims significant mileage for his theory: if proportionality analysis is necessarily at the heart of reasoning about what principles require in *real* contexts it is because 'unlike rules, principles are not yet related to the factual and legal possibilities of the world (Alexy, 2002: 59). At every turn we are reminded that proportionality (as optimisation) subtends the application of principles in the 'real world', it mediates their reach and their intensity in concrete situations. Always the reference to the crossing, between abstract principle and concrete case, and proportionality becomes the signifier for it. Weight is contextual and 'interferences' are weighted in concrete contexts of application. Proportionality subtends and informs the move: the principle *will acquire relative weight only in context,* and proportionality informs how the conflict of principle will be read, and decided, in the situation where it applies.

And it is here that the unravelling begins because proportionality ultimately conflates determination with optimisation.

What is constitutional about the reflexivity of optimisation? Might this simple question breach the self-immunisation that proportionality achieves and remind us that proportionality delivers its dividends only by abstracting from *constitutional function* that, as we discussed in Chapter 2.2, involves entrenchment, hierarchisation and rationalisation? Rationalisation, we argued, involves holding up constitutional *principle* to constitutional *value.* Constitutional reflexivity operates and is delivered along this *unbroken line of normativity.* The adequacy of any constitutional solution is measured on that line. It is against this measure that proportionality falls short.

In discussing the 'material dimension' of constitutional meaning in Chapter 2.2, we followed Luhmann's suggestion that 'every *determinacy* presupposes carrying out a *reduction* and every observation, description and conceptualization of determinacy requires giving a system reference' (1995a: 177). Where the reference is the legal system, normativity is tied to its particular reduction-achievement, reproducing disappointment-proof expectations (normative) or 'expectational nexuses' – amongst them roles, programmes and values – which are used in 'individual interactions but extend beyond them in their meaning references'. There is no suggestion here of abstracting normativity from contextual appropriateness; far from it. These expectational nexuses *that operate at different levels of abstraction* are differentiated and then combined in forms of interdependence between levels.[29] Of course Luhmann is aware that abstract values, as such, do not determine appropriate outcomes. 'On the highest attainable level of establishing expectations', 'where one works only with – or talks only about – values ... one must renounce all claim to establishing the correctness of specific actions' (1995a: 317). But 'values are not without importance for the way in which expectations are anticipated. The importance arises from the *difference between programmes and values*. If they are to perform their specific task in the best possible way, programs often must be formulated as highly complex, variable and unstable with regard to details' (1995a: 318, emphasis added). We have here – between values, programmes and specific interaction – a staggering of generalisation. At the level of programmes one indeed encounters 'ordering schemata with much greater complexity' than values because programmes operate at more concrete structural levels. But they only operate as programmes because they constitute forms of mediation between the level of values – insufficient to determine their own appropriateness in interactional contexts – and the particularity of those interactions. Programmes occupy the middle ground: they hold the promise of responsiveness to increasingly complex environments while securing and maintaining the stability (or expectability) of expectations. They *are normatively held* and they equip normative expectations at the more concrete levels.

For proportionality exponents this is precisely the point at which 'proportionality' cuts in. Proportionality operates at the level of programming – the level of *principles* – to mediate the distance between values, that are insufficiently selective to provide answers, and concrete situations that avail no criteria for the complex balancing that constitutional judgement requires. But what we described above as a 'channelling down' of normativity (along the *vertical* axis of values-programmes-interactions) is not, emphatically not, what the advocates of proportionality have in mind. Optimisation is its own principle, it does not come encumbered with overbearing value and overbearing normativity. Proportionality travels light as optimisation rather than determination. And to do so, the differentiation between constitutional values and constitutional programmes is collapsed into the difference between constitutional values and constitutional *goods*. The difference between constitutional value and constitutional good is highly significant. As far as the logic of *determinatio*

---

[29] 'The coherence of the synthesis must have a meaning extending beyond interaction in order to be convincing within interaction' (Luhmann, 1995a: 423).

is concerned, in performing the function of mediation, programmes must maintain their continuity to values, otherwise the function of determination is lost. The *vertical* linkage along the axis of normativity is what connects back to values, and a degree of abstraction what differentiates them from values. Against this, proportionality as optimisation must concretise values in order to assign them relative weights in precise situations of competition, but that operation is now over-determined by the functionality of producing a result, a balancing. The plane of commensurability that alone enables the assignation of relative *exchange* value (if not 'exchange' what is the meaning of the 'relative'?) is organised as proportionality. And here constitutional principles circulate as constitutional goods *because* their normative connection to value is broken. What has thereby been broken is the logic of *determinatio*, as concretisation that seeks its truth *irreducibly* in the normative dimension. The normative – what a political society *holds on to* democratically as its normative commitments – flips over into the cognitive. 'The Court shifts abruptly,' as Toni Marzal puts it eloquently, 'from a Herculean balancing of values framework to a seemingly innocuous and purely factual review of Pareto efficiency' (Marzal, 2017: 622). The question becomes a question of the efficiency of regulation, albeit 'better' or 'smart' in the way the Commission defines it. To regulate 'better' or 'smarter' involves cognition, not normativity; the imperative to 'legislate better' invokes metrics, not values. Market veridiction becomes the only possible means to authorise the rational calibration of optimisation as involving the economic logic of marginal utility that now carries constitutively into law the logic of the economic system in its market variant, which, as we know from Hayek and his lesser acolytes, involves as definitional 'the study of human behavior as a relationship between ends and scarce means which have mutually exclusive uses' (Becker, 1976: 1). The adequacy of the constitutional solution is measured not on normativity but on functionality.

It is noteworthy, with regard to this suggestion of 'Pareto efficiency', that Lon Fuller was first to denounce 'law-as-managerialism' some decades before the more famous discovery of the 'managerial mindset' by Koskenniemi. Fuller describes the problem as the fundamental inapplicability of the principle of marginal utility to legal thinking. That principle, by which we make the most effective allocation of the resources at hand in achieving whatever objectives we set for ourselves, for Fuller contradicts law's constitutive orientation, its 'inner morality'. 'It is with the word "utility" that the economist draws a veil over his failure to discern some economic good that stands above all particular goods and serves to guide the choice among them ... an empty container for every kind of human want or striving' (Fuller, 1964: 17). Utility floats across contexts; and 'in default of some highest good we resort to the notion of balance; the achievement of an ultimate end the ceaseless shifting from one end to another in search of optimisation' (1964: 19). How apposite this reference to, and denunciation of, economic efficiency by the theorist of 'the morality that defines law', although it is clearly anachronistic to draw Fuller into a debate about proportionality!

It is in contrast to a normative/political concept of constitutionalism that can be read *the price* of conceptualising principles as optimisation requirements. Optimisation is tested horizontally, on the plane of conflicting principle, not vertically, as fidelity to what it concretises. Of course proportionality theorists will be quick to point to the dividends of leaving behind the realm of the 'tyranny of values' (à la Schmitt) and the 'radical' choice they entail, for the relative comfort of a balancing that might be *tested* to deliver rationally justifiable results. And it is becoming clearer how in the idea of proportionality the development of market constitutionalism achieves one of its more deep-seated guarantees, and how this achievement informs the deep commodification of labour. No longer beholden to the overbearing constitutional *values* – insufficiently selective, deontological, intransigent, etc. – the move to *principle* frees up constitutional reason to differential and optimising application, in a way that meets the requirements of complexity and the invitation of the new pluralisms, cosmopolitanisms, etc. But in the process constitutional reflexivity gives up what is constitutional about it. Proportionality is a *flattening* device that collapses constitutional value into constitutional good by collapsing the vertical normative link. In the 'concrete' contexts where proportionality is called on to deliver appropriate judgements, we see now that the process of 'concretisation' is no longer tied to the values themselves – 'how the protection of the *dignity* of work is best *instantiated* in the concrete situation' – but to the logic of their calibration – 'how the dignity of work is best measured against freedom of establishment in the concrete situation'. The concretisation is driven by the need to discover the level at which they are best balanced, or 'optimised'. The judgement as to whether the value is worth giving up, to what degree, is not informed by the value itself, since by definition it is insufficient to inform its instantiation, but by a logic of optimisation that involves both concretising the value at the appropriate level *and* deciding the competition amongst the values thus concretised. In fact, quite clearly the judgement can only follow the reverse logic: the best balance also determines the level at which the values were best concretised in the first place. In other words: given that the application of law is not a case of simple subsumption of particulars to general categories, but of appropriate judgement, proportionality comes to pervade and organise the reach of constitutional principle into that world of particular situations and dilemmas, and mediates the processes of giving content to the formal principles. In this way proportionality comes to guarantee its own performance by controlling selectivity at both the level of posing the problem and of answering it. *Determinatio* is over-determined by proportionality, with optimisation doing all the work.

Significantly, once proportionality has proven itself through optimising the dividends at the level of concrete application, it can then move back up the list and confirm its other achievements. If the key move that sustains proportionality is that it is the guarantee of its own performance, then *of course* it also stands up to 'the test of public reason'. Its invulnerability is guaranteed at all levels. And it also provides the justification for why it can sever itself off from political decision-making. If social protection does not meet the threshold equilibria projected by optimisation, then its curtailment can be justified on rational rather than political grounds. Neither deontology, with its overbearing demands and 'firewall' obstinacy, nor normativity, with its resistance to learning, should stand in the way of constitutional reflexivity that turns away from the normative and towards the cognitive, because, as we said already, to assess relative weights and optimise balances can only turn on a question of knowledge, not political will.

Compare this to that other reading of constitutionality that ties it to political constitutionalism. There the severing of good from value *is the sign of breach of constitutionality not its realisation*. Values are markers of what should not be sacrificed, names of what could not be put into circulation. The irreducible (vertical) connection between value and principle, that maintained the link to the sources of value and dogmatic mainstays of constitutional reason, allowed values and principles to be differentiated on the level of generality. Determination meant something in that linkage which underwrote constitutional method. Determination is not a free-floating procedure that randomly tracks options and balances them. It *becomes* that once the constitutive linkages are breached. The transmutation of constitutional values into constitutional principles, that under the prism of optimisation turns them into constitutional goods in order that they may circulate and compete as preferences, renders them co-extensive with principles of market competition.

Proportionality judgements depend on the profound internalisation that they organise. The promise of proportionality in Alexy, remember, is that of optimisation: 'that something be realized to the greatest extent possible, given the legal and factual possibilities'. Proportionality in one stroke both guarantees the optimisation of that 'something' and gives it content (as optimised) and nothing external can disturb the flow of that short-circuiting. Which is why it is difficult to make any sense of the acknowledgement of the 'givenness of legal and factual possibilities' on the expansive terrain of its exercise. 'Legal possibilities' proliferate on the back of proportionality, they do not constrain it. But the reference to facticity and the supposed limit that it imports is perhaps more interesting, and revealing. Because we know by now that what one comes to read as the 'givenness of the factual' depends on how one reads the constitutional situation, how interpretative frameworks contain and sustain factual situations, how the normativity of concepts strains against that containment, how structures harbour conflicting semantics. Our specific quandary, to which proportionality came to the rescue, was the 'politically intractable' clash between workers' social rights to maintain dignified conditions of work, and the economic freedoms of entrepreneurs to reflag their ships and move their capital around. To attach proportionate weightings to those actions, stakes and objectives, the factual situation had to be *read*, and it could only be read in terms of the proper meaning of association, the relation between association and action, what it means to strike 'in sympathy', all of them factual givens laden with normativity. Proportionality re-negotiates everything – legal and factual – across the board, and the 'factual and legal givens' are the result, not the condition, of its exercise. The demand and argument for the 'un-protecting' of labour *as* comparative advantage marks a departure that is made possible with *the circulation of 'social protection' or the 'dignity of labour' as only two amongst many constitutional goods*. They are circulated alongside, and *on a par* with, other constitutional goods like property rights and freedom of establishment, the coordinates of their competition undone from any overall framework. Theorising solidarity or dignity as *dogmatic* resources of constitutional thought meant precisely that they could not be cashed out as constitutional goods. If the question of value returns us to the dogmatic sources of the *ratio juris*, constitutionality as proportionality cuts away at the very integrity of constitutional thought.

Let us conclude our discussion of proportionality with a note from the Greeks, not the tragic genre as one might expect in this context, but with comedy. Proportionality finds its first, extraordinary, instantiation in Aristophanes' *The Frogs*, in the scene where Aeschylus and Euripides are locked in a contest over the comparative weight of their poetry. The weight is tested on a scale before which each of the tragedians stand. Every time they speak the scales register relative weights and Aeschylus' scale, without fail, proves the heavier. The Olympian god Dionysus is the appointed 'judge', though arguably it is a case less of judging than of ascertaining weights – a cognitive rather than a normative exercise as we have been describing it. Nevertheless, it is clear from the play that when the contest is over, Dionysus 'prepares to decide' (v. 1411). The 'principle' of decision in favour of greater weight, the god explains, depends objectively on the things weighed. It is not a case of random or irrational ascription *ex deus machina*; the decision is reached on objective criteria. He gives an example: a verse with 'water' in it is likely to turn the scale because things wetted are heavier than when they are not (v. 1386).

Market Access as Social Dumping

It is fair to say that the 'race to the bottom' instigated by the *Laval/Viking* jurisprudence was met with no shortage of angst. At the level of institutions we encountered its expression already in the self-contradictory assertion in *Viking* that 'possible social dumping may constitute an overriding reason of the public interest' (para. 103); in the subtle protestations of the Attorney General in *Commission v. Germany;* and in the Commission's largely mute attempts in *Monti II* and in the *Revision of the PWD* to achieve a 'reconciliatory' rather than a subsumptive relationship between economic freedoms and social rights. But like any effort that pushes against structural assumptions and structural lock-in, there has been little give.

The angst, however, finds its more obvious outlet in legal-theoretical work that emerged in the wake of the CJEU decisions. Here a not unprecedented *malaise* descends on those keen to defend the social rights of the Nordic model in the name of *social democracy*. It was Lenin who first attacked the 'Mensheviks of the West' and the 'labour aristocracy' in the name of 'the masses of the workers':

> The Mensheviks of the West have acquired a much firmer footing in the trade unions; there the narrow-minded, selfish, case-hardened, covetous, and petty-bourgeois 'labour aristocracy', imperialist-minded, and imperialist-corrupted, *has* developed into a much stronger section than in our country. . . . We are waging a struggle against the 'labour aristocracy' in

> the name of the masses of the workers and in order to win them over to our side; we are waging the struggle against the opportunist and social-chauvinist leaders in order to win the working class over to our side. It would be absurd to forget this most elementary and most self-evident truth.[30]

Today the pan-European labour movement, 'the masses of workers', finds its spokesmen in the voices emanating from the 'new' member states. Except that the solution offered lies not in the Soviets, but in the Market. History, said Marx memorably in *The Eighteenth Brumaire*, repeats itself first as tragedy, then as farce.[31]

Here is the standard expression of the argument against the privilege of labour protection:

> I would like to argue that it is artificial to separate economic considerations from social considerations in the context of free movement. In consequence, I maintain that EU free movement law itself has a social dimension, which should be taken into account when 'social rights' are being invoked against internal market freedoms. It is necessary to probe into claims of social rights before attaching to them the full moral claim which the use of the adjective 'social' entails. Social rights are intellectual constructs which can be perceived not only as protecting weakness, but equally as instruments of domination and expressions of power on the part of those who possess them. Only those who have a 'right' have a voice in a legal system such as EU law, which is based to a large extent on the idea of promoting rational self-interest and private enforcement.[32]
>
> (Leczykiewicz, 2014: 307)

---

[30] In Lenin's *'Left-Wing' Communism: an Infantile Disorder* in the chapter 'Should Revolutionaries Work in Reactionary Trade Unions?'

[31] Echoing Engels: 'it really seems as though old Hegel, in the guise of the World Spirit, were directing history from the grave and, with the greatest conscientiousness, causing everything to be re-enacted twice over, once as grand tragedy and the second time as rotten farce.' (Letter to Marx, 3/12/1851)

[32] In Mark Freedland and Jeremiah Prassl's account of this view, 'as the national reports show, Member States' social policies differ widely in their levels of protection of individual autonomy and it is therefore not inconceivable that some are in fact protectionist rules, that is to say, rules which restrict the private autonomy of other market participants and are thus prima facie open to scrutiny by European Union law. The main criticism of the judgments in Viking and Laval, then, is, according to this view, *the Court's failure to articulate* the supposed social benefits of the resulting intra-Member State wage competition, and free movement law more broadly, for the citizens of the Union's "new" Member States, whose lower labour cost give them a significant competitive advantage in penetrating new markets.' (Freedland and Prassl, 2014: 1–10)

This view reflects an argument made some time ago by Damien Kukovec in a 2010 lecture, and later (in Kukovec, 2015). I quote from the former:

> Like Wittgenstein's duck-rabbit picture, what appears as economic is social and what social is economic, depending on the angle from which we see the dilemma. The debate could just as well be framed in terms of social rights of [Estonian] workers against the [Finnish] interpretation of the freedom of movement provisions which ignores their realisation.[33]

For Catherine Barnard, Britain's leading EU lawyer, Kukovec 'puts succinctly' a necessary 'caveat'. 'The precedence of the economic over the social is not necessarily a bad thing for developing a social dimension of the European Union in the general sense, since opening up the markets will benefit the Estonian workers, improving their prosperity and thus giving effect to the aspiration originally expressed in art. 117 EEC' (Barnard, 2012a: 123) though she will qualify this endorsement.[34] It is not coincidental, in this context, that those who are to gain 'market access' from the decisions are the first to attack the contra-distinction between the social and the economic. The (social) right to work of the Estonian or Latvian workers sacrifices the (social) right of the privileged Nordic workers to increased protection. The clash is no longer between rights and freedoms, the social and the economic, but between those who are prepared to work for half the wage and those who are not. And yet after all the qualifications, and the caveats, there remains something profoundly disturbing about 'the merit' of a 'duck–rabbit' understanding of the interface of the social and the economic that *pivots* on market access understood in its functionality of sustaining a downward spiral of lowering wages (social dumping); and to assume market access in this modality as *sole* guarantor of *both* social rights (for Baltic workers) *and* economic freedoms. Perversely, for this line of argument, since a social dimension exists within the very framework of the internal market freedoms, Europe's social market appears realised, not undercut, by 'social dumping'. In an earlier chapter we suggested how difficult it was

---

[33] D. Kukovek, 'Whose Social Europe?', talk delivered to Harvard Law School (16 April 2010), SSRN, http://papers.ssrn.com/sol3/papers.cfm?abstract_id=1800922.

[34] 'While this argument has much merit, it distracts from the general thesis of this article, namely that in terms of preserving the integrity of national social systems, the *Viking* judgment is severely damaging to rules developed by the states in the social field – the very area over which the initial Treaty of Rome settlement deliberately gave autonomy to the states – because fundamental (EU) economic rights take precedence in principle over fundamental (national) social rights.' (Barnard, 2012a: 123)

for the predication 'social' of the ordo-liberal 'social market' to do any independent qualifying work. Now we have full recursion: the social dimension of the market is delivered through market integration *as social dumping*.

To understand the recursion, and with it the slippage of Europe's labour protection into total market thinking, we need to say something more about the concept of 'market access'. The key shift in European law that opens the door to this radical reconfiguration of the economic/social interface, is the shift from its previously held *anti-discrimination justification* to a *'market access' justification*, that occurred in the early 1990s with *Saeger*.[35] Under the anti-discrimination rationale, host countries were obliged to extend the same protections to migrant workers as they afforded their own. This was a key principle of equal treatment. It was also the rationale that protected democracy. In Sweden, in Finland and in Germany decisions about the balance of the economic and the social had already been taken on democratic grounds. The decisions over key thresholds – of how far solidarity would limit the level of the extraction of profit – were politically taken. And the anti-discrimination rationale meant that this threshold would be generalised for all workers in the country, citizens and migrants, a generalisation that gave expression to constitutionality. As Barnard puts it, '[s]o long as the Court adopted a discrimination-based approach to the interpretation of the four freedoms, non-discriminatory national social policy remained protected from a potential incursion by the single market provisions' (2012b: 119).[36] With 'market access' the test of constitutionality is flipped on its head. Under the market access rationale, the focus shifts to the effect

---

[35] Case C-76/90 [1991] ECR I-4221, para. 12: Article 56 TFEU required 'not only the elimination of all discrimination against a person providing services on the ground of his nationality but also the abolition of any restriction, *even if it applies without distinction* to national providers of services and to those of other Member States, *when it is liable to prohibit or otherwise impede* the activities of a provider of services established in another Member State where he lawfully provides similar services' (emphasis added).

[36] 'The Court's embrace in the 1990s of the Säger "market access" approach (more recently referred to as the "restrictions" approach), in place of the discrimination analysis, threatened to undermine the careful balance between the preservation of national labour law and EU rules on free movement. While the non-discrimination model adopts a comparative approach looking to see how both nationals and migrants are treated (and only if there is a difference in treatment is there a potential illegality), the market access/ restrictions approach considers the perspective of the out-of-state actor only. It asks whether the national rule hinders/restricts the ability of the out-of state actor to gain access to the market or to exercise freedom of movement.' (Barnard, 2012b: 201)

of the national rule on the out-of-state actor and the question becomes whether the system of protection of the host country does not act to restrict the ability of out-of-state workers to exercise 'freedom of movement'. The market access test results in provisions of national social policy being placed in potential conflict with the European Union's four freedoms (which of course benefit from the supremacy of EU law vis-à-vis municipal law) and deemed unconstitutional for that reason. Note, finally, in the context of this comprehensive change an interesting variation on a formal jurisdictional matter that acquires a new relevance and renews the connection between freedoms and rights. It used to be a fundamental condition that in order to activate EU law, and to claim a right under it, one had to show a link with a cross-border element. With 'market access' the criterion is reversed; the triggering effect is not the connection (with a cross-border element) but the *potentiality* of it. It is now the *denial* of (market) access across borders – that is, the very *lack* of a cross-border element – that activates the 'right', and provides standing.

The difficulties that the social-democratic Left have had with the 'duck–rabbit' thesis, that folds social into economic rights, is the outcome of the comprehensive internalisation that is effected as the total-market paradigm. We have witnessed how social rights became a signifier for inclusion in the labour market, an inclusion effected at the expense of other workers, in the case of *Viking* of the sacked Finns of the reflagged vessel, whose own social right to work was sacrificed at the altar of comparative advantage. In the process 'social Europe' became coincident with the integration of its internal market, and in the unfolding of this relentless process, the language of redress was lost to market thinking and the 'frictionless' flows of capital. Exasperated labour lawyers found themselves defending the 'labour aristocracy', and as a result an embarrassed silence gradually extinguished the legitimate protestation against the injury. What we have witnessed is the democratic and epistemological 'co-option' (Chapter 3.2) as played out in the particularities of these dilemmas, and what they engendered was a *loss of the language* which would carry the critique of social dumping. Against the comprehensive uptake of market thinking as horizon of every determination *and* every alternative to it, the play of mirrors and the duck/rabbit conundra, the answer is in the most modest demand: *uphold democratically enacted law*. The answer *cannot* be in the terms that the capitulation to the market makes available, the false transparency of its givens, the ideological function that places something – the market – *as lying altogether beyond question.* Critical theory must clear the space to ask the question in terms not already co-opted by the totalising move.

*

We remain with the interface of the social/economic distinction. If we cross it under the prism of 'market access' from the economic to the social, and argue that economic participation, however achieved, delivers social rights, we end up with social dumping. But we can cross in the opposite direction, this time from the social to the economic. It is in this other crossing that we encounter the *capabilities* argument. If we enhance social rights, the argument goes, then we enhance economic participation, turn the vicious cycle of social dumping virtuous, and we might just end up with a market that delivers adequately, even something akin to the 'social market' as originally envisaged.

Let us be clear that the capabilities argument, for all its virtues, relies unwaveringly on the market system as the mechanism that will optimally distribute societal resources amongst possible uses.[37] Once it is acknowledged that the conditions of general competition will never obtain empirically, the efficiency of markets becomes questionable, and it is at that point that capabilities theory locates its intervention. But what remains unquestioned and unquestionable for the capabilities-centred overhauling of the defence of the market, is its clear superiority against planning. The capabilities approach is an attempt to correct, or consolidate, not substitute, the range of *information* that is available through the price mechanism. And the enhancement has to do with addressing – at the level of structure – the opportunities that economic actors *actually* have of revealing their preferences through their choices. Opportunity-structure is what the capabilities theory is about: equality, as equal basic capability, measures itself against the promise of equal participation. And 'constitutionalized *social rights* can be thought of as the juridical instantiation of the concept of capability' (Deakin and Wilkinson, 2005: 345).

---

[37] We have explored this argument at length in Chapter 3.1 with an emphasis on Hayek. As David Campbell summarises it succinctly, 'in the neoclassical conception of the operation of the market, economic actors reveal their preferences through the choices they make and, if the market conforms to the conditions of general competition, a Pareto optimal equilibrium representing a perfectly efficient allocation of goods will be established' (Campbell, 2013: 199).

THE DEEP COMMODIFICATION OF LABOUR

In the last four decades the pervasiveness of market thinking has, as we saw, colonised the ways of thinking about labour law *as* labour market regulation, its effectivess, or the 'crisis' that has beset it, routed back to its very *idea*. 'Labour law is widely considered to be in crisis' begins an important publication in the field under the title *The Idea of Labour Law*. It asks 'the most fundamental question: what is labour law for?' (Davidov and Langille, 2011: 1). One obvious answer, one would have thought, is that it is *for* providing protection to work and to working people, but that is not the answer sought, or the one 'prevalent': it is *for* the regulation of the labour market. And if labour law is in crisis it is because of inefficiencies that call for market-correcting measures. It is here that 'capabilities' effect and measure their intervention.

Let us put it at the outset: any theory that treats the market as its point of departure and basis of justification, must *contend* with what the following assumptions – that sustain market thinking – *conceal*

The equilibrium assumption conceals a constitutive excess of labourers over the available level of employment.
The value assumption conceals the contingency of the value set that the market generalises as value *simpliciter*.
The efficiency assumption conceals the increase in inequality that the market engenders.

Let us begin with the *equilibrium assumption*. 'Capitalism begins not with the offer of work but with the imperative to earn a living,' says Michael Denning in a fascinating paper (Denning, 2010: 80). And Marx reminds us in the *Grundrisse* that the free labourer is a virtual pauper; if the capitalist has no use for his *surplus* labour, then the worker may not perform his *necessary* labour. In the mismatch between the *contingency* of the availability of work and the necessity of its performance, is played out the fundamental injustice of the capitalist 'institutionalisation of scarcity'. And Marx reminds us that the higher the productivity of labour, the greater the pressure on the means of employment, the more precarious therefore the condition of the labourers' existence (since it is dependent on the sale of their labour power). The general law of capital accumulation suggests that over time more and more workers will become unable to re-insert themselves into the reproduction process.[38] This is as alive today as it was when Marx described the 'relative surplus

---

[38] 'The working population produces both the accumulation of capital and the means by which it is itself made relatively superfluous; and it does this to an extent that is always

population'; if anything it has been radicalised under two conditions. The first radicalisation can be tracked along what Schumpeter called the 'creative destruction' stage of the 'business cycle', as capitals attempt to deflect losses onto one another through closures and bankruptcies. In the crisis that ensues capital finds labour power available to it at discount prices, which is today expressed in the endless 'flexibilisation' and 'casualisation' of labour (see Chapter 1.3, above) and the other forms of the 'rationalisation' of the labour process. This includes the range of ways in which surplus value is extracted through the realignments and supersession of existing combinations of capital and labour. The permanent 'crisis' of labour law receives a more sobering reading in this light, as both endemic and productive to capital. The second radicalisation involves the creation of *redundant populations*, those whom the processes of *real subsumption* have forced out of the circuits of global production. I refer to those workers who find themselves beyond the pale of the historical dialectic between capital and labour, whom global capital needs as neither consumers nor producers, and who are therefore redundant even as far as exploitation is concerned.[39] Manuel Castells puts it like this:

> For the mass of the world's population the primary concern is to avoid irrelevance . . . Because exploitation *does* have a meaning for the exploited. The danger is, rather, for those who become invisible to the programmes commanding the global networks of production, distribution and valuation.
>
> (Castells, 2004: 29)

The value assumption is what *naturalises* conditions specific to market thinking, and turns historical, therefore contingent, assumptions about value, motive, self-understanding or association into the lexicon of economic freedom and formal equality. Naturalisation operates at the level of meaning construction, and sustains market capture at the foundational level of epistemology. The argument as it affects the reflexivity and rationality of the constitution is at the heart of this book. If I mention the value assumption here, it is to show how capabilities theory cannot but endorse the reductive theory of value because it aspires to *price*

---

increasing' (Marx, 1867/1970: 625). See also Benanav and Clegg (2014) for an acute analysis.

[39] 'Under capitalism the only thing worse than being exploited is not being exploited' (Denning, 2010: 79).

information more adequately; and in order to price, one must take the *currency of value* as given.

If the equilibrium assumption depends on making invisible the question of the constitutive excess of labour, and the value assumption to naturalise market value, the *efficiency assumption* must face up to the question of inequality. Here capability thinking comes into its own with its promise to enhance market participation. Amartya Sen's work has been at the centre of the general attempt to invest in the capabilities of the poor to engage in economic activity in order to address the problem that there are actors who do not possess the practical capability to pursue their interest – or to take action – within the market system as it stands (Sen, 2009: 7–8). According to the theory of capabilities, uncontrolled (or 'disembedded' markets) deplete human resources, and thus threaten the very conditions on which markets depend for their operation. The answer comes in the form of a participation-enhancing *social market*, and social rights as enhancing capability underwrite the empowerment.

Social rights play a key role in this conversion. While the market, as harnessed to capitalist production, grants societies a significant increase in productivity and innovation, it also effects a significant increase in social inequality and social exclusion, with the very real threat of generating vicious circles that cause the depletion of the human resources it requires. For capabilities-theories, social rights are conceived as an answer to the inequality and the depletion. If capitalism privatises the gains and socialises the costs of running the economy, social rights offer ways to meet those costs of the operation of markets and guarantee the conditions of participation and meaningful citizenship. Where 'negative rights' underpin and sustain liberty in the sense of a demand that the state not encroach on private spheres of activity, in a complementary gesture social rights sustain 'positive duties', demands on the state to meet the population's needs for education, healthcare, sustenance, housing, etc., *without* which personal autonomy or meaningful participation in society would remain fundamentally unrealised, and *with* which, endowment can realise advantage which in turn enhances macroeconomic performance.

For a position that seeks to situate itself in the vanishing interstice between market-enhancing and market-correcting logics, its space of intervention was always going to be narrow, though not its ambition, which Supiot describes well: 'that the notion of capacity would constitute at the European level a *common normative reference*, that would be coherent with legal developments and that could guide the efforts at redefinition of social citizenship in the context of the disintegration of the protections and solidarities that issued from the age of industry' (Supiot, 2009b: 161–2). Its privileging of market over political allocations in the final instance leaves it vulnerable from the Left, while the fact that its prescriptions *must* involve some welfarist leverage in order to materialise opportunity-structure for the powerless and therefore cannot avoid regulatory 'coercive transfers' leaves it tainted for the Right. Theorists on the Right have of course for a long time argued that under conditions of the separation of the political and the economic systems it becomes nonsensical to attempt to redress deficits on the supply side of the economy with political devices like social rights (Luhmann, 2004: chapter 12). And from the point of view of the market, the objection is understandable that 'the social welfare function can be identified only by government action. However we define it, we must use governmental computation processes to identify social welfare and if we are to put our welfare conclusions into practice, we must use government power to alter the outcomes of voluntarily agreed exchanges' (Campbell, 2013: 204). For those who criticise capabilities from the Right, then, capabilities theorists have merely moved coercion one step back: from government action directly imposing coercive transfers (against those voluntarily assumed by market players) to engineering 'social conversion factors'. And all engineering, however far *back* one takes it, involves a compromise of what is 'voluntarily assumed' through market choice. Once in the market paradigm, correcting it becomes question-begging.[40]

But it is not our concern to intervene in that debate. And to the extent that the *capacitas* argument now occupies a central position in the discourse on Europe, claiming its leverage from Article 3(3) TEU regarding the (highly competitive) 'social market economy', a formula that was formally introduced into Europe's constitutional parlance to 'correct' the neo-liberal tilt in the constitutional project, the intention is admirable. Our concern is more that the battle is lost in advance – for both pragmatic and conceptual reasons – under the weight of 'total market' thinking.

If 'constitutionalised social rights' are indeed, as proclaimed, the 'juridical instantiation' of capabilities, capabilities-thinking endows them with an ambition much greater than merely operationalising them at the margins of the redress of the economic system's violent enactments

---

[40] 'It is not possible to have a concrete policy towards specific choices that is amorphous' in the sense of an abstention from imposing patterns because, to promote opportunity, one must in the end 'have a policy that pursues a particular goal of advantage to the economic actor in respect of a particular pattern of consumption.(Campbell, 2013: 207).

and costs, 'to blunt the harsh edge of market forces on the fabric of social life' (Rittich, 2008: 110). Instead they are called on to mediate the requirements of market entry and alleviate the brutality of market 'optimisation' in the form of social dumping. At a time when the question for Europeans tempering 'actually existing Europeanisation' (Hyman, 2006b), the agency-enhancing market participation that the capabilities approach promises, if it is going to mean something over and above participation *simpliciter* in the race to the bottom, must counter the relentless re-organisation (which as Samuel Jubé rightly says is *disorganisation* (2009)) of labour relations under the pressure of maximising returns for capital. It is difficult to know in the midst of all the short-termism what would *entice* the owners of productive capital in the European Union to play the 'long game' and forego the immediate maximisation of the returns for their capitals in favour of the promise of a market-enhancing capabilities regime that cuts against current market allocations. The problem is compounded by the fact that the main adjustment factor in the competitive race is the devaluation of labour. 'Restoration of competitiveness and profitability' is the goal behind the policies of internal devaluation, the abolishing of collective bargaining on wages, the reduction of trade union power, the liberalisation of professions and the flexibilisation of employment. In this complete reversal it is not simply that the means-end relationship between capabilities and competition is severed; it is in fact that under conditions of austerity it is the very systems of social rights protection that are instrumentalised – aligned competitively – to enhance competition. The enhancement of competition hinges on the depletion of rights and capabilities. The dialectic on which the capabilities argument depends turns *negative* at the point of this *axial turn*, if we can borrow the term from Adorno. The promise of growth through competitiveness, under austerity, effects an insidious recursion, that leaves capabilities thinking undercut at its core.

But if capabilities theory stumbles on pragmatic grounds, its commitment to market thinking arguably stumbles on a conceptual problem too. It can be accounted for in the *temporal* dimension. Why are capabilities worth investing in? Because, we are told, they bolster the conditions needed for the economic actor's effective participation and ability adequately to reveal preferences through choices. This enhancement impacts positively on the range of *information* that is available through the price mechanism. Capabilities re-orient our attention to 'the process by which preferences and endowments are formed' (Deakin, 2009: 19) but these processes take time. During the time they take, the invisible hand of the market must be stayed, while the conditions of information are restored. The delay depends on a valorisation that must be immunised from market pricing, *while* it delivers. What alternative valorisation, then, for this postponement? A suspicion arises that the question is begged. If capability is a corrective to how agency is 'priced' in the market (now) then the real difficulty is to conceive how we will *know* when agency might *optimise* a projected capability and a projected value (in the future) *against* its current pricing, since it is pricing that delivers knowledge. And even if in the medium and long term, agency enhanced by acquired capabilities will indeed deliver higher profitability, how would we *know* when 'conversion factors' have delivered optimally, and significant future *thresholds* have been reached; at what point in time, in other words, is the investment in capabilities to be cashed in? The price mechanism is after all that which cannot be second-guessed, and that, for Hayek, was its abstract beauty. On this reading, 'total market thinking' defeats capabilities as market-internal attempts to correct its allocations.

PART IV

Strategies of Redress

4.1

The Constitutional Situation

Taking Stock

In our analysis so far, two lines converge. The first line, developed in the first part of the book, sought to establish the conditions of a critical phenomenology. The focus was on what emerges as a problem, the conditions of that emergence, and what in turn sustains those conditions; the critical effort was to submit all three moments to question. The sections on semantics and structures that run through the book turn phenomenology towards hermeneutics, that is, towards thinking about meaning and interpretation. At stake is the loss of terms for redress. As normative expectations become increasingly displaced by cognitive expectations in the modalities of governance by information and the optimisation of outcomes, the key question that must be held on to, I argued, is what are the conditions of iteration of something as a problem such that a *political* solution might be sought. At that point a critical phenomenology is read into Marx's eleventh thesis, a thesis that resists reading solutions off situations in fragmented and closed forms of 'understanding the world' – the positivisms that express the depleted forms of the *Verstand* (Hegel's term for the absence of dialectical thought) – but reconfigures the problem to which a solution might be adequate in the direction of expanding potentiality, or what we call *constituent power*.

The reference to constituent power brings us to the second line of argument that traverses the book. It has to do with the defence of political constitutionalism against its market deformation. Political constitutionalism is defined in terms of the juncture of the juridical and the political, with all the limitations and opportunities that this coupling engenders. With market constitutionalism the integrity of the *ratio juris* surrenders to market thinking in a profound process of co-option. We have explored the two paradigms in the mirror Parts II and III of the book, with a bridging chapter between the parts looking at how constitutional thought came adrift of its constitutive orientation under the pressure of a globalising market, and laid bare to be re-configured by it. The effects were traced more broadly and (in the third chapter of each part) with regard to the meaning and the protection of work.

This final part of the book picks up the inspiration of critical phenomenology and ties it to constitutional strategy. If the question is reclaimed back from the way it has been circuited to market solutions, then it can lend itself to answers that are strategically deployed in the direction of redress. Let us then, again, pick up the thread of political constitutionalism in order that we may tie it to strategy.

*

In the modern story of political constitutionalism as historical, *unfinished* project, the constitutional theorist begins by drawing a distinction: between politics and law, between will and reason, democracy and rights, or in its more abstract formulation, *between constituent and constituted power*. However the distinction is configured, what is constant is that the poles articulate, and that their articulation is characterised by tension. Constitutionalism is the name for that articulation and that tension. Political constitutionalism consequently gives us the vocabulary to furnish democratic experimentation and simultaneously delimits the field of experimentation. If it achieves both imperfectly, then the imperfection itself carries the mark of the logic of institution in all three dimensions of its meaning, with its offer of 'containment' first of social antagonism in the concept of the unity of the 'people', then of political stakes in constitutional thematics, and finally of political time – *kairos*, opportune time or intervention – in the cast of constitutional renewal. In the imperfect delimitation, this strained containment harboured responsiveness to the dynamism of the political. In the specificity of constitutional language, necessarily reductive of the scope of political meanings, it secured both renewal and stability. This 'imperfection' in both directions, guarantees that there will always be tension, and constitutionalism straddles this tension with the promise of self-determination on the back of what it sanctions as conditions of that self-determination in terms of relevant constituency, containment in rights- and property-regimes, what is negotiable and what is fixed. Luhmann, with the help of the concepts of structural coupling, would call this the constitution's selective release of the future in, respectively, social, material and temporal dimensions; the unsettledness of the meaning of the constitutional text tracks something of the restlessness of the political. This in turn allows political constitutionalism a claim on *the constituent* in the various modalities, irreducible to the *constituted*, the former poised asymmetrically to the latter. It was these 'imperfect accommodations' of a political constitutionalism that we first encountered in Chapter 2.1, restated in Chapter 2.2 with regard to the *formal* dimension of its reflexivity, and in Chapter 2.3 with respect to its *substantive* dimension: the full political implications of the 'social question', the dogmatic value of solidarity that underpins it, and the way in which it operationalises political-democratic categories in the constitutional definition of participation, protection and production.

Globalisation came to strain that containment. As capital was released from its relative confinement in national political economies, set free to maximise its returns by circumventing social states and systems of national protection, a large-scale compensatory gesture takes effect with constitutionalism's *plural* explosion on to the global scene. If political constitutionalism finds its coordinates in the articulation-in-tension of politics and law, the new paradigm leaves it without its constitutive tension. Instead we have horizontal proliferation. What coinage precisely sets something in circulation as constitutional is not specified, but then pluralism tells us that it shouldn't (Chapter 2.4). Against alleged hegemonic understandings, hierarchy-building, privileged political imaginaries and the rest, pluralism invites plurality also at the level of definitions: no privilege to any one of the criteria of the constitutional. In the varieties of 'democratic' and 'experimental' governance 'democracy is stirring' proclaim its advocates (Sabel, 2001: 121), with the promise to 'release' political voices from the straight-jacketing of the state. And it is perhaps because of the way in which such a variety of oppositional discourses to the state find expression in constitutional pluralism, that certain broadly emancipatory projects are allowed to coexist so seamlessly with neo-liberal forms, in their common endorsement of the opposition to state-centred and centralising constitutionalisms. Release from the confining normative claims of the state and its monopolising of the common good propels the pluralists; hatred of the state joins libertarians and anti-state activists in a common cause so that constitutional pluralism is celebrated across the board as adapted to a multiplicity of loyalties, identified with 'democratic experimentalism', constitutively linked to 'democratic experimentalism', 'polycentric governance' and 'cosmopolitan' awakenings, a move that often combines with Habermas' discourse principle in its democratic instantiation. As Thornhill summarises the mood in European legal theory: 'The focal shift towards pluralism reflects the underlying sense that, if the EU has a constitution, this is a constitution that is not exhausted in legal texts, and that only comes to light through analysis of the correlation between legal formation, patterns of conflicting motivation, claims to juridical primacy, and embedded societal processes of legal dislocation and realignment' (Thornhill, 2012b). In all this, the impasse is turned productive, the paradox of the democratic deficit of the European or the global Constitution 'unfolded' in what is becoming the *evolutionary achievement* of a global constitutionalism, with pluralism substituting for democracy and constitutionalisation substituting for constitutionality.

We explored the rise and rise of market constitutionalism in Part III of the book, first in terms of the undercutting of differentiation with the generalisation of economic reason (Chapter 3.1), then the mutation of political constitutionalism into constitutional governance (Chapter 3.2), and finally its European trajectory in terms of the abandonment of social and labour protection to the market (Chapters 3.3 and 3.4). Key to the market turn was the entering into regulatory competition of national systems of social and labour protection in the form of law-shopping or forum-shopping. The rise of market thinking involves a comprehensive shift of the constitutional imaginary from a political to an economic register. The unprecedented and currently unquestionable prevalence of economic reason involved the colonisation of what was previously the constitutional achievement of coupling constituted with constituent power. Now, in effect, the constituent dimension of constitutional reason folds under 'total market thinking'. A response to such a comprehensive dislocation must involve a strategic re-orientation of constitutional thinking. That is what will be argued in this final part of the book.

*

We must forestall a lingering objection to the 'naïvety' of a return to a robust sense of political constitutionalism. Already in the 1970s, with the rise of the New Right, the rationality of democratic outcomes was challenged and the market was offered as a means to circumvent the problems of democratic overload, corporatist interference in the economy, and the necessary shortcomings of state bureaucratic organisation, constitutively unable to coordinate the information necessary to run society. For the New Right, the market would ensure rational allocation of resources, and the truth of economic science would replace the inefficient, cumbersome and fallible processes of democratic determination, in society but most obviously in the economy. As Glasman recalls the attack by the proponents of the free market, 'social democracy was attacked on philosophical, political and empirical grounds as undemocratic, unpatriotic and unfeasible' (1996: xiii). If that was the situation in the 1970s, by the time we come to the second wave of governance (Chapter 3.2) 'correct theory' has taken on the heuristic of networks and has relaunched itself not just to eclipse social-democratic thinking as anachronistic, but to re-discover democracy in the modalities of experimental governance, and to re-situate it in a 'socialised' market.[1] We have seen all this at length, both at the level of concepts, and at the level of European constitutional policy and practice. The consolidation of the market turn insists on a different thinking of the constitution that cognisant of the truths of economic science would avoid the naïve commitment to outdated theory and the anachronism of the paradigm of political constitutionalism. Let us dispense with this 'critique'.

The promise of market constitutionalism, in the moderate and the radical forms that we have encountered it, is that by abandoning normativity (of democratic conceptions of justice) for better knowledge, it will be better placed to navigate *uncertainty* for a society caught up in complex times. The shift from normative to cognitive expectations and from government to governance, and the many ancillary shifts that surrounded them, all keyed to the same promise. But the promise is belied at the encounter with uncertainty because, faced with it, market constitutionalism cannot hold: the articulation of market and constitution comes undone. Or, more accurately, the *interface of constitution and market* comes apart under the strain at both poles. The encounter with 'uncertainty' destabilises 'market constitutionalism' in the sense in which the terms *hold together*. To see why we should approach the interface between market and constitution from both sides in turn: let us attempt it first from the side of the latter pole, that of the constitution.

---

[1] In the field of labour, 'if for Sinzheimer and Kahn Freund legal sociology and anthropology were the disciplines with the greatest potential to shed light on the empirical operation of legal rules ... Today economics is more prevalent and the challenges it poses at a methodological level are of a wholly different order' (Deakin, 2007: 1170). If for Supiot *homo juridicus* implies a constitutive orientation to anthropology (as evidenced by the book's subtitle: 'the anthropological function of law'), for Deakin the rise of economic thinking displaces the insights of legal sociology or anthropology, a displacement that of course imports an anthropology all of its own. As Polanyi famously put it with reference to Adam Smith, never had a misreading of the nature of man had such an effect in mobilising a fiction of agency to underwrite the market system.

In something of a prophetic work written in 1924 under the title *Legal Foundations of Capitalism*, John Commons identified 'the transaction' as the fundamental unit of legal analysis and the economy as the adaptive network of transactions. As an analytical category the transaction is the name for what occurs as economic life, 'an electron not an atom' he says revealingly (1924: 8), that captures the capitalist system in motion. It is movement which constitutively defines it since *capital* is nothing else but 'the present value of expected beneficial behaviour of other people' (1924: 28). Commons explains this motion in terms of the articulation of actual markets ('every store, every factory, every railroad', he says memorably) with legal structures, an intriguing variation of how we have thematised and understood structural forms of coupling between systems. But Commons' article is remarkable not simply because of his account of entanglement of legal and economic structures as they couple in the zero-points of transactions, but also because we can read into it a *displacement* that occurs at those junctures: what we might think of as the destabilisation of the legal form under the weight of what it is asked to carry. What Kyle McGee extracts from Commons in a remarkable short paper (2016) is a logic of substitution whereby 'economic contrivances outstrip their transactional grounds and come thus to unground their own legal and political foundations'. The substitution begins to show itself with the extension of market devices, as the production of incorporeal variations (market returns based on fluctuations of prices) destabilises and gradually reverses the meaning of property. Since they exist only as anticipatory, and since the credit system and business initiative are built around them, value is displaced onto the probability that something will come to pass, and property title comes to sanction contingent market devices that stretch the logic of the institution. From this McGee will move to a larger argument about the meaning of grounding, and the reversal that is effected when it is the grounded (in this case the economic transaction) that reconfigures the ground (the legal structure). As he puts it, 'the ground is summoned and rendered' by the operations of what is contingent on that ground (McGee, 2016). From Commons and McGee we can move the argument of the substitution of grounding for ground to market constitutionalism, and its paradigmatic case of constitutional governance. It is for the same reason that Commons gives, that constitutional governance, under the logic of its 'cognitive' expansion over fields that property is constitutively ill-equipped to sanction, loses the meaning of what it is to constitutionalise. One would need to look in detail at how law is increasingly oriented to 'uncertainty' to fully appreciate this, but in any case, by the time it comes to the modelling of financial instruments to deal with uncertainty, the economy has indeed nominated itself as cause of all effects, so that the predication 'constitutional' becomes at best an empty signifier, floated across a range of forms and forces, independently qualifying nothing at all. When it is itself subjected to the competition of 'public law frameworks' (Möllers in diagnostic mode, Ladeur and Kingsbury in acclamatory mode in Chapter 3.2), it simply folds into market thinking.

But if the 'constitutional' pole does not hold independently in order to ground the 'discovery procedure', as Hayek famously suggested its role in 'catallaxy', neither does the pole of the market independently fulfil the promise of knowledge retrieval. To see this we will need to look at another distinction, that between *restricted* and *general economies*. Drawing on Hegel (and Bataille), Derrida defines a 'restricted economy' as the system which cannot tolerate an excess which it cannot absorb. It is with reference to the handling of 'excess' that the 'restricted economy' is different to a 'general' economy for which excess does indeed possess meaning.[2] The distinction that matters to the argument about the market, is that between an excess that is meaningless and is therefore *externalised*, and an excess that remains a surplus, is retained as opportunity, and is therefore *potentialised*. The hegemonic gesture that elevates the market to meta-arbiter of the meaning of selections (in Hayek, Ladeur and the lesser acolytes) would need to accommodate this distinction but *cannot*, because the market can operate *only* as a restricted economy.

Let us move to the field of meaning-construction to see why. Meaning relies on difference to enable the acquisition of information. This is familiar ground, as is the consequence that what is processed as information leaves an infinite amount unsaid and unmarked – further operations will tap this terrain on the basis of connections based on other distinctions within the system's – *every* system's – 'contingency formula' that designates the way in which something becomes meaningful for the system (as legal/illegal, true/false, cost-effective or not, etc.). Look at how the distinction between what is potentialised and what externalised operates at this point: what remains surplus to current selections has a

---

[2] For Georges Bataille, from whom Derrida borrows, 'sovereignty' is the locus of the expenditure of such excess. Sovereignty possesses a meaning, for Bataille, that is not always-already preserved (as it is in Hegelian 'synthesis'). See Derrida (1976).

meaning for the system both as option against which current selections can be measured, as well as opportunity for future selections, to be accessed by new 'crossings' of the contingency formula. What makes the system dynamic is that it sets itself against a horizon of what is potential for it; not, therefore, exhausted in the static terms of current selections (as some positivisms would depict the legal system) but as opportunity for future linkages, the system's not-yet actualised possibilities. All of this, quite sensible, account of meaning-construction, depends on a distinction between what might be retained as the horizon of future selections ('potentialised') and what is 'externalised' as mere 'noise'. Noise is not retained in the modality of potentialisation, by definition, because it *means* nothing. So it is with the market: its potentiality is marked and exhausted on *what it can price*, and what it can price also as the expected future behaviour of people. That is its 'contingency formula', it marks the limit of what is potential for the system, and it marks the definite (and severe) limitation of its cognitive reach. To return to our distinction, the market offers externalisation *as if* it were potentialisation, and in that 'as-if' lies its promise and its lie.

More would need to be said to substantiate the argument on the side of the market, but perhaps enough has been said to introduce a fundamental doubt about the preparedness of a theory of market constitutionalism to survive its collision with uncertainty. On the 'law' side of the constitution/market interface, the constitutional promise cannot hold on to its institutional achievement to reduce and discipline the field of uncertainty, because the grounded shifts the ground, the implosion of constitutional form is lost to variety and adaptation and finally to the complexity of its environment. Here the constitution is nothing but slippage, endless re-configuration, the labile forms of the *ex post* sanctioning nothing. On the market side of the interface, the market cannot deliver its promise because it can only ever deliver a restricted economy, not the 'general economy' that might have offered the cognitive gains promised by the theory. Compromised on both sides, market constitutionalism can only limp along for so long while still holding the promise of responsiveness to uncertainty. On the 'constitution' side, having sacrificed the normative control of expectations that might have mediated market exposure, it can only encounter uncertainty by submitting it to a 'contingency formula' that is not its own, but the economy's. On the market side, offering to propel knowledge society through pricing, blind to what has been externalised and thus already missed as knowledge. And as it proceeds tripping on both fronts over both of these constitutive limitations, it is a sign of hubris that it is launched by its champions to take on nothing short of the challenge of uncertainty, with which it frontally collides and before which it surrenders.

It was Frank Knight who, in a 'profound critique of the omniscience of perfect markets',[3] in the early 1920s drew with rare insight the distinction between risk and uncertainty, the distinction, that is, between dangers which, as risks, may be usefully submitted to probabilistic reasoning and those which, as uncertainty, cannot. He writes:

> We may use the term risk to designate measurable uncertainty and the term uncertainty for unmeasurable uncertainty ... the practical difference between the two categories risk and uncertainty is that in the former, the distribution of the outcome in a group of instances is known (either through calculation *a priori* or from statistics of past experience) while in the case of uncertainty this is not true, the reason being in general that it is impossible to form a group of instances, because the situation dealt with is in a high degree unique.[4]

It is because uncertainty is 'unmeasurable' that Luhmann fastened on to the concept of *risk* in order to hold on to normativity (Luhmann, 1993), and insisted that law must be able to observe and control risk in an attempt to reproduce itself as a system of expectations in environments of uncertainty *where all that is disappointed is immediately discredited*.[5] This was to suggest that the concept of risk, as a first-order uncertainty, could be strictly coupled to law, whereas uncertainty, at the second order (the riskiness of risks as it were) could not lend itself meaningfully to legal operations. Joyce Appleby in *The Relentless Revolution: A History of*

---

[3] For Salais: 'C'est Knight qui, par une critique approfondie de l'omniscience du marche parfait, a pose le premier les jalons nécessaires pour fonder en théorie les constructions de l'incertitude que peuvent entreprendre les acteurs économiques' (Salais and Storper, 1993: 22).

[4] Knight, 1921: 233. Knight was a leading figure at the LSE during those years when Hayek was there as a young scholar. For Knight's influence on Hayek in the pre-war years at the LSE, see Joshua Rahtz's review of Angus Burgin's *The Great Persuasion: Reinventing Free Markets since the Depression* in (2014) 89 NLR 137. For Knight, capitalism breeds deformed subjects: 'it could sustain itself only to the extent that it consisted of individuals whose behaviour departed from the norms it incentivized' (quoted at 140).

[5] Not so for Ladeur, for whom uncertainty is opportunity and the springboard for knowledge generation. He argues that 'uncertainty is from the outset integrated in the complex settings in which it is produced, and which have to be organised in a way that allows for productive operation with its phenomena by introducing new reflexive moments of design, modelling, of self-revision and of monitoring.'

Capitalism, argued that from its inception capitalism was based on the founding insight that 'no one was explicitly in charge of an entrepreneurial economy' (2010: 248), an insight of Smith's renewed in a rigorous form by Hayek. It is an insight that must remain the system's least acknowledged if trust in the system is to be maintained, and which goes some way to explaining the urgency around 'uncertainty absorption' that we discussed with reference to indicators. But the marketisation of risk does not lessen, it increases uncertainty, as a vicious cycle sets in when we rely on the market's 'restricted economy' of risk to face up to uncertainty. Uncertainty resurfaces as the risk over the pricing of risk, and there isn't even anything particularly Hayekian about all this, no information to be garnered through the 'beauty' of pricing in contexts where uncertainty remains intractable and unknowable. Insurance becomes the name of a substitution, the logic of how one makes profit from loss. If the loss is certain, insurance yields certain profits; if the loss is catastrophic, the profits will be vast. A whole new lexicon has emerged to mitigate this insanity, and with the sudden realisation that no one is in charge, a complex body of meaningless macro-supervision is mobilised to assess and impose reasonable levels of risk-taking, whatever that now means, fashioning 'appropriate risk appetites', mobilising ratings, 'macro-prudential supervision', etc. All of this is fertile ground for a renewal of the appetite for theorising governance, and we are back to where we started, recalibrating, experimenting, black-boxing and the whole ludic repertoire of new governance. But enough perhaps.

At this point we might instead insert a reminder that it was in response to uncertainty that national systems of social insurance were created. It was because, unlike risk, uncertainty did not lend itself to calculation, that solidarity amongst people demanded that its burden be shared. As Supiot explains it, 'the Social State introduced the pooling of the risks of existence and gave solidarity the face of organizations – those of social security and public services – to which one contributed according to one's resources and benefited according to one's needs' (Supiot, 2013). The organisation of social insurance was a response to uncertainty. Social insurance orients our expectations to the future and the idea of social insurance expresses the normative commitment of a society to meet the uncertain risks facing its members as a *collective* undertaking that guarantees the fundamentals of a dignified life. It is this normativity, and this commitment, that are lost in the disaggregation of uncertainty into risk. In the case of uncertainty, as Knight put it, 'it is impossible to form a group of instances' to which the future outcome can be distributed, though under the category of risk 'distributions' of contingency are possible. The significant difference between the categories is why it is paramount to hold on to uncertainty as being irreducible to risk. Whereas calculable risk can be incorporated in systematic prediction in the short- and medium-term, uncertainty cannot.[6] Except that once the distinction is collapsed and the drive to commodify all risk becomes pervasive, the radical contingency that uncertainty names is re-introduced back into risk as a meta-level contingency, in a way that submits to the price mechanism of the insurance market the whole range of future contingencies. Let us insist on the basic *disutility* of uncertainty, and, with Bruno Latour (1988) its *irreduction*: disutility as resistance to economic leverage; irreduction as signifying a profound incompatibility with the logic of commodification and the extraction of surplus value. And to insist instead that the collective response to uncertainty turns on the constitutionality of the systems of social protection, that dignified post-war societies, in whatever organisational form we give them today as a matter of political-democratic decision, and of constitutional strategy, not market surrender.

Communicative and Strategic Constitutional Action

Now thinking about the constitution in strategic terms will immediately come up against a number of objections. The most obvious emanates from the theory of rational discourse and the transferral of the concept of discursive rationality to the context of constitutionalism. More specifically, when Habermas enjoins citizens 'critically [to] appropriate the constitutional mission' it is because they can identify its mission as their own, insofar as the constitution establishes practices of deliberation that might provide citizens with reasons that determine their action that they can accept because they have contributed to. In *The Theory of Communicative Action*, Habermas identifies inclusionary processes of reason-giving as a form of 'communicative action' because they aim at reaching understanding and consensus (1984: 99). He contrasts communicative action with strategic action, because whereas the former is

---

[6] While at the time of writing it is too early to draw conclusion about whether the COVID-19 pandemic affected public attitudes to radical uncertainty, it is beyond question that a massive burden of expectation was placed on state structures, not markets, to protect society. As the saying goes, as there are no atheists on a sinking ship, there are no free marketers in a pandemic.

oriented to reaching understanding, the latter is 'oriented to success' (1984: 288). Those who engage in strategic action do so with a view to achieving their own goals *through* the decision of the other (1984: 285). To explain the difference Habermas falls back on the theory of speech acts, and the distinction between illocutionary and perlocutionary made famous by Austin, that he rather too easily correlates with communicative and strategic: in communicative action 'participants pursue illocutionary acts without reservation' (295) whereas the *perlocutionary* has an 'internal relation' to strategic action, because it both presupposes and distorts the 'inherent telos of speech' to the extent that perlocutionary acts aim *not to persuade but to influence* (1984: 289–95). On the back of this, Habermas draws in stark terms the distinction between communicative and strategic action:

> Whereas in strategic action one actor seeks to *influence* the behaviour of another by means of the threat of actions or the prospect of gratification in order to *cause* the interaction to continue as the first actor desires, in communicative action one actor seeks *rationally to motivate* another by relying on the illocutionary binding/bonding effect of the offer contained in his speech act.
>
> (Habermas, 1983: 58)

The strategic 'distortion' leads from communicative to instrumental reason, and from rational deliberation, inclusive of subject-formation, to a different 'polemical' logic of winning: through manipulating if need be instead of persuading. Truth-seeking is contrasted to manipulation, self-motivation to other-causing, with constitutional reason proper, of course, falling on the side of the illocutionary.

This all may appear straightforward, and to the extent that Habermas' influence on constitutional thought has been staggering, even self-evident. With the cards stacked against it, constitutional strategy is pitted against the constitutive connections between deliberation, consensus, and truth, and in constitutional theory to democratic self-determination, connections that comprehensively situate constitutional reason in the discursive paradigm. And what makes the task to rescue 'strategic' thinking as a form of rational action, is just how formidable the ambition of Habermas' projection is, that ties constitutional function all the way back to the uses of language ('universal pragmatics') as coupled with the openness of discourse ('the ideal speech situation'). The emphasis on the 'illocutionary', the motivation to persuade rather than win, traverses the whole line of argumentation as directed constitutively to consensus, guarantee of the truthfulness and correctness of statements. And it transfers to the constitutional plane where 'communicative offers' receive their institutional expression as basic constitutional rights that we 'mutually accord one another', accounting for the emergence of a 'we perspective' as sustained by the constitution. No entry point for strategic action in the smooth expanses of the operation of consensus. Here is Habermas:

> Under the pragmatic presuppositions of an inclusive and non-coercive rational discourse between free and equal participants, everyone is required to take the perspective of everyone else and thus to project herself into the understandings of self and world of all others; from this interlocking of perspectives there emerges an ideally extended 'we-perspective' from which all can test in common whether they wish to make a controversial norm the basis of their shared practice.'
>
> (Habermas, 1999: 58)

The deliberative situation sustains norm-creation, and by extension constitutional practice. According to his famous formulation of the discourse principle, only those norms are valid to which all possibly affected persons could agree as participants in rational discourse. The term 'all possibly affected persons' refers to the position of addressee. The counter-factual 'could agree' situates all as addressor of the norm. This coincidence of the speaking positions premises the bindingness of our law on a rational, self-reflexive move. Habermas explains: 'As legal subjects they must anchor this practice of self-legislation in the medium of law itself; they must legally institutionalize those communicative presuppositions and procedures of a political opinion- and will-formation in which the discourse principle is applied ... *In this way the discourse principle acquires the legal shape of a democratic principle*' (Habermas, 1995: 458). '[T]he modern legal order can draw its legitimacy only from the idea of self-determination: citizens should always be able to understand themselves also as authors of the law to which they are subject as addressees' (1995: 449). And thus, finally, as Klaus Günther puts it, '[t]he democratic process is distinguished from all other forms of legitimisation of norms in unifying the notion of citizen and the notion of legal person in the concept of the deliberative person' (Günther, 2001: 11), engaging the citizen in a form of *rational self-binding*.

There are three distinct moments in this conceptualisation of public discourse that we can separate analytically as three levels. The first refers to the condition of universal pragmatics; the second to the procedural conditions that underlie and guarantee its openness; the third concerns the passage of the deliberative into institutional practice. Habermas' grand synthesis depends on the internal articulation of the three levels.

The level of language use: Meaning emerges at the level of the pragmatic conditions of the relations between speakers; the semantic content of a speech act is tied to the pragmatic dimension of the (act of) utterance. These insights are at the root of the theory of *universal pragmatics*, which Habermas developed with Karl-Otto Apel in the 1970s, which refers to the base-level conditions of the use of language. The theory suggests a transcendental structure that all use of language *already* presupposes. 'Anyone acting communicatively', says Habermas, 'must, in performing any speech action, raise universal validity claims and suppose that they can be vindicated' (1979: 2), which means that every speech act, constitutively, involves the raising, recognising and redeeming of validity claims.[7] The implicit claim in any communicative offer is that the offer is comprehensible, true, sincere, and in the context that it is offered, right or appropriate for it. Should the speaker be questioned over any of these aspects, her failure to justify the truth, sincerity, etc., of her speech act would lead to 'performative contradiction'. The universal pragmatic infrastructure of speech underlies what it *means* rationally to engage in communication.

Note that there is a basic normative dimension even at this groundwork level of entry requirements into communication. It attaches to a claim to justification that needs to be met.[8] It is Habermas' vital insight that the felicitous performance of communication already imports normative criteria at the ground level of its 'grammar', 'a morality that makes language possible' to paraphrase Lon Fuller's famous formulation about law. Participants in communication, says Habermas, 'can neither understand nor misunderstand one another unless there is a presupposition of rationality' (Habermas, 2005: 86). Seamlessly the normativity of the entry conditions of communication spreads upward: the practice of communication oriented towards mutual understanding requires that interlocutors take up an attitude of *mutual recognition* towards one another (defeasible

---

[7] In contrast, for Luhmann communication should not be reduced to 'communicative action' which 'registers the participation of others either as mere affect of this action or as normative implication in Habermas' sense' (Luhmann, 1992b). In his own theory of communication, Luhmann treats the 'communicative act' (Mitteilung) as the middle term in the triad information/communicative act/understanding.

[8] Which 'imposes a series of non-optional moral standards upon communication that function as constraints enabling the practice that is communication. See Pavlakos (2007a) for an extensive analysis.

of course to the measure that they may be proven deceived) in which they regard each other as *equals* with respect to their capacity for rational speech and rational evaluation of speech. This is why communicative action 'always already presupposes those very relationships of reciprocity and mutual recognition around which *all* moral ideas revolve in everyday life no less than in philosophical ethics' (Habermas, 1983: 130).[9]

The level of reaching consensus: The *ideal speech situation* sets the parameters within which speech acts can circulate under conditions of uncoerced communication in order that practical judgements can be reached about norms that we give ourselves, transparent and reflexive through and through. According to Habermas' famous formulation of the discourse principle, only those norms are valid to which all possibly affected persons could agree as participants in rational discourse. This coincidence of the speaking positions of addressor and addressee does away with any need for external justifications, and premises the bindingness of norms on a rational, self-reflexive move.

On this model, communicative action comprises both an *illocutionary* act by a speaker and a rationally evaluative (yes/no) position taken by a hearer concerning the acceptability of the 'validity claims' implicit in what is said. The success of an illocutionary act in establishing an uncoerced agreement depends on the hearer's 'rationally motivated approval' of what is said (Habermas, 1983: 134). At this point the connection back to the pragmatic conditions of speech is direct. And Habermas will argue that 'a speaker owes the binding force of his illocutionary act ... to *the coordinating effect of the warranty* that he offers: namely to redeem, if necessary, the validity claim raised with his speech act' (Habermas, 1984: 302). In this way the internal constraints imposed by the goal of reaching agreement lead to a form of *rational accountability* to which speakers hold each other, and the practice of criticising and justifying claims ('discourse') gives rise to a distinctive form of rationality, which Habermas calls 'communicative rationality'. The circulation of validity claims in all cases concerns 'illocutionary' acts,

---

[9] Apel will go further. Apel tries to capture this normative requirement of all agency and perception via language by employing what he takes to be the prescriptive dimension of Discourse-ethics (*Präskriptive Dimention der Diskursethik*). According to this thought, there is a dimension of discourse which goes beyond the narrow boundaries of speech and language and extends upon agency (and perception). This dimension rests upon a moral/ethical *Grundnorm* which prescribes that: 'All beings who are capable of communicating via language ought to be acknowledged as persons' (in Pavlakos, 2007b: 122).

communicative offers to persuade, not to influence. The latter motive would turn the logic of action from communication to strategy.

Agnes Heller puts it very well in an early critique where she suggests that Habermas ascribes to reason what Marx ascribed to the proletariat: that it was the addressee of history in the important sense that in overcoming its constitutive partiality (the move that Marx famously describes as from the 'in-itself' to the 'for-itself') it would grant itself the universality that would solve the 'riddle of history' (Heller, 1982). In one respect Heller is overstating the analogy. But in another she is spot-on: the self-reflexive restoration of reason keeps alive the Hegelian theme that informed the first generation of the Frankfurt School, while at the same time allowing Habermas to unburden his theory from any materialist implication as far as regards identity and action. It allows him to keep the ideality of the theory at a remove from the material conditions of its instantiation, whereby conveniently Reason stands corrective to the fragmentary and exclusionary nature of its actual expression in history. Like for Marx, a certain teleology is built into History, a drive to a progressive cleansing from impurities, from the 'colonising' impulses of systemic logics, from the exclusions and the silencing of those who are the proper addressees of Reason. And yet, as the swathes of those redundant populations of the globe swell, those whom the global organisation of production requires neither as producers nor consumers and – more appositely to this discussion – whom the construction of global law requires as neither addressors nor addressees of norms, the question of what might include them in the situation of dialogue, if only to challenge their exclusion, is devastatingly begged.

The level of institutionalisation: The third step involves the institutionalisation of the procedure through rights that underwrite participation in the public sphere. It was Robert Alexy who initially proposed the 'special case thesis' for law ('*Sonderfallthese*'), elevating the law as a special case of practical reason, capable of harbouring the operation of public reason (Alexy, 1989). From this, significant dividends accrue on two fronts. *Firstly,* law shores up processes that promise to ground the correctness of normative statements on consensus, even where the latter remains forever only potential (the agreement of all is practically unattainable).[10]

---

[10] This of course is only one in a range of problems! Equally problematic for Luhmann is to 'impute to communications an inherent, quasi-teleological tendency to consensus. If that were the case everything would already have been over long ago and the world as silent as it once was' (Luhmann, 1992b: 72).

Habermas will concede: discourses take place in particular social contexts and are subject to the limitations of time and space. Topics and contributions have to be organised. Law has a vital role to play here. *Secondly*, institutionalisation matters because it sustains individuals' participation in the public sphere by sanctioning both capacity and autonomy. On both fronts *institutional measures* are needed 'sufficiently [to] neutralize empirical limitations and avoidable internal and external interference so that the idealized conditions always-already presupposed by participants in argumentation can at least be adequately approximated. The need to institutionalize discourses, trivial though it may be, does not contradict the partly counterfactual content of the presuppositions of discourse' (Habermas, 1995: 92). Look how much is packed into this passage: institutional measures filter out ('sufficiently neutralize') empirical givens; these givens would be 'limitations' to the rationally unfolding discourse; they are limitations because they stand in the way of 'always-already' presupposed conditions of engagement as implicit in language use (as underpinned by 'universal pragmatics' and guaranteed through the 'ideal speech situation') the facilitative institutional passage, albeit necessary, is 'trivial'; and in any case does not 'contradict' the ideally stipulated conditions of discourse.

What does Habermas offer to address these elisions? If the institutional site for public reason indeed avoids the regress (there must be some limit to processes of reflection) and circularity (that would submit the conditions of reflection to reflection) and instead institutes the *enabling conditions* of public discourse it does so by way of reducing the social, temporal and material conditions, speaking positions, thematics and timeframes, that condition democratic debate. Habermas offers the justification in his magnum opus *Between Facts and Norms*, which developed the institutional theory in the direction of co-implication of democratic dialogue with rights. The main difficulty that discursive rationality faces at this juncture (by Habermas' own admission) is the problem of *institutional thickness*, and the blockages, *a priori* and blindspots that accompany it. Habermas had already signalled this early on: if 'communication is [to be] neither hampered by external contingent factors, nor by constraints which are internal to the structure of communication itself' (1973: 255) it needs to be protected externally and shored up internally. To secure the latter, *internal* function, and live up to the promise that the discourse will be *adequate* (to delivering uncoerced consensus), Habermas suggests replacing the criterion of actual consensus with that of *'well-grounded' consensus* as criterion of truth: 'The meaning of truth lies not in the circumstance that some consensus is actually achieved, but rather in this: that at any time and in any place if we but enter into discourse, a consensus can be achieved under certain conditions which prove this to be a well grounded consensus' (1973: 239). To protect it from *external* manipulation and strategic deployments, on the other hand, it must install the conditions of the constitutional conversation, in which participants offer only *illocutionary* contributions to a debate over the common good. In *Between Facts and Norms*,[11] a theory of rights has been elaborated to deliver both promises. What Habermas secures with the third, *institutional*, step that his book delivers in a grandiose way, is to integrate, totalise and immunise the theory of discourse by way of what we might call the *constitutional situation*.

*

The notion of the 'situation' is a concept developed by Alain Badiou to describe a totalising inclusion. 'All thought supposes a situation, a structure, a counting-for-one, whereby the presented multiple is consistent, numerable', says Badiou in his important work *Being and Event* (2007: 44). With the idea of a 'situation' Badiou captures the moment of containment, of gathering-in, which is effected through 'criteria that limit what is presented, that is, what *qualifies for inclusion* in the situation they describe' (2007: 13, emphasis added). The threshold objection to carrying Badiou's analysis over into discourse theory is that Badiou's term 'situation' aims to name a closure, and Habermas aims to institute openness. And yet note how the entry requirements into the open processes of will-formation carry their own limitations and how compensatory moves *shore* up 'containment' in the public sphere, in a way that is broadly similar to Badiou's reference to 'what qualifies for inclusion'.

First there is the question of the criteria of what counts as 'well-grounded' consensus. 'Well grounded', procedurally correctly enacted norms bind us as addressees of norms whether we did *in fact* agree to them or not. The fact that we *could* or *would* agree (the terms 'would' and 'could' are interchangeable here) under conditions that would make our consensus rational, that is, under conditions of unfettered communication, is all that is required, and this requirement is institutionally underwritten. In the process, the coincidence of addressor and

---

[11] And in a series of articles in constitutional theory that have acquired canonical status, see in particular Habermas (1999) and Habermas (2001).

addressee receives an institutional warrant, as sufficient condition. But the problem that the counterfactual ('would agree') intimates does not go away. Once it is conceded that the conditions of discourse that would have adequately underwritten consensus are far from guaranteed in *actual* settings, and that 'ideal' consensus *must* give way to 'well-grounded consensus', the concept goes into freefall. The ideal situation holds the promise that, should the real conditions be improved in the direction of the ideal situation, and should certain thresholds (though these are typically only reflexively stipulated) be met, the consensus will be *well-grounded*. Note the series of slippages involved: it is *actual* conditions of engagement that stand in the way of the aspired-to inter-subjectivity, consensus and truth; these can be procedurally propped up or improved in the direction of the *ideal* speech situation; but ideal consensus is by definition aspirational and therefore unattainable, and thus must give way to the more modest ambition of a 'well-grounded' consensus; conditions for what counts as 'well-grounded' cannot and should not be imposed *a priori*, therefore must emerge dialogically, reflexively, from actual practice, the very practice that we've just been told requires the constant corrective of the ideal. And the substitution of real for ideal continues at each step of the way, standing in for participation, while the 'ideal' is doing all the work of redeeming the promise of inclusion. This is what installs the constitutional situation, in Badiou's sense, as that which includes and exhausts *within* the situation all possible legitimate alternatives, including alternatives *to* it.

We might ask at this point whether this is not what the first generation of the Frankfurt school called *affirmative theory* to denounce the kind of reformism whose language promises to overcome what its operations can do nothing but affirm. If with affirmative theory comes a 'distinct loss of critical power' it is because of how the three 'steps', above, articulate. First, the communicative offers that qualify as contributions to the public sphere are illocutionary, 'always-already presupposing conditions of engagement as implicit in language use' and therefore carrying into communication the transcendental condition of reason. Secondly, the democratic conversation must meet conditions of unconstrained exchange and remain reflexive about those conditions. Thirdly, the constitutional framework underwrites those conditions through buttressing public and private autonomy and the exercise of rights. Democracy and rights, co-original and co-implicated, sustain the dialogic paradigm. And yet this pure affirmation taps a profound source of unease. Under conditions of the mass deterioration of peoples' life-chances under global neo-liberalism, what does it mean to fold the conditions of acting, and acting-back, into these structures and configurations of participation as aspirationally held? For those who have launched projects of transformative constitutionalism on the terrain of this synthesis, one may be justified in querying why the dividends are so meagre. And justified to ask more generally: who, apart from the beneficiaries of the status quo, is to gain from this accomplished counterfactual, the projection of the smooth expanses of co-implication? Strategy comes too late on this homogenised – communicatively moulded – terrain. Who stands to gain from such syntheses which so radically, and devastatingly, leave nothing outside the co-implication for resistance to find purchase?

*

If this final part of the book is to reclaim a notion of constitutional 'strategy', it must reclaim some *purchase* for strategic thought in the smooth inter-traffic of law and democracy, and *traction* for it in the grand syntheses of the constituent in the constituted, against their co-implication that makes sure that negation and antagonism disappear 'in the flattest of transcendental horizons' as Negri puts it (1999a: 21). Strategic reason is not a rejection of communicative reason, as Habermas contra-distinguishes them, but positions itself incongruently to it, resistant to the gesture of inclusion that characterises affirmative theory. As an entry point, we test the limits of the inclusion through three test cases, in each case *a speech act offered in the modality of illocution*, as Habermas would want it offered, that tests the framework of its inclusion. In each case, we will observe a breach; in each case the inclusionary framework does not hold, and with it the constitutional situation cannot deliver on its promise. Strategic thinking finds its point of inscription in the breach.

Speech act 1: '*You do not interest me*'. The phrase updates Rousseau's devastating statement in the *Discourse on Inequality*: 'perish if you wish, I am secure'.[12] For Simone Weil, it is the statement that 'no man can say

---

[12] The statement appears in *The Discourse on Inequality* following Rousseau's discussion of Hobbes who disregards man's 'innate repugnance to seeing a creature like himself suffer'. Rousseau contrasts 'compassion' to 'reason'. 'Reason is what turns man back onto himself; reason is what separates him from everything which upsets and afflicts him. It is philosophy which isolates him. Thanks to philosophy he says in secret at the sight of a man suffering: *"Perish if you wish; I am safe."* Nothing troubles the calm sleep of the philosopher and drags him from his bed any more, other than dangers to all of society.

to another without committing a cruelty and offending against justice' (Weil, 1957/1989). But what does it tell us if performed in *illocutionary* mode as a response, say, to an appeal made by another on one's privately owned resources? The whole gamut of theoretical debate and denial of what duties we owe to others, from the redundant populations of the starving, to the 'boat people' drowning on their desperate journeys to reach European shores, is testament to how 'alive' the illocution under question is. It is at least as old as Cain's question in the Bible: '*Why should I be my brother's keeper?*' Can we take comfort that language structure will not sustain it, that its assertion might appear as a 'performative contradiction' of its transcendental conditions? But what condition of the universal pragmatics of language use would defeat it? Would it be its sincerity, its truthfulness, its appropriateness, or the requirement that it calls for further justification? What might disqualify the illocutionary statement that cuts human solidarity at the root? And if, as we suspect, it isn't disqualified at the level of entry-conditions, what defeats it at the level of its 'redemption', if, as Habermas puts it, 'a speaker owes the binding force of his illocutionary act ... to the warranty that he offers: namely to *redeem* if necessary the validity claim raised with his speech act' (1984: 302). At this level of the offer of warranty, justifications freely circulate to defeat the claim that solidarity is owed, that compassion matters, let alone the duty to meet social needs, trumped by some variation or other of the 'tragedy of the commons' thesis (à la Hardin in Chapter 2.3) or the unavailability (à la Nagel in Chapter 2.4) of a claim to justice at the global level.[13] This 'redemption' of the validity claim 'you do not interest me' is abundantly available to compound the injury of the withdrawal of solidarity.

Speech act 2: 'Do you understand?' At one level this is the quintessential illocutionary offer of the communicative paradigm. On a different reading, it is the very thing that throws into relief the distinction between the strategic and the communicative, and the dynamic of its crossing. Remember that for Habermas a relation of reciprocity, even *recognition*, can be read across the relation of accountability that expectations extend between speakers. I borrow the argument here from Rancière, who in the

---

One can slit the throat of his fellow man under the philosopher's window with impunity; he has only to put his hands over his ears and argue with himself for a little while in order to prevent nature, which rebels within him, from identifying with the one being murdered.' (Rousseau, 1755/1992: Part 1)

[13] Nagel (2005); indicatively also Miller (2020).

third chapter of *Disagreement* turns Habermas' argument against him. He invites us to think of this question – '*do you understand?*' – addressed by managers to workers in workplaces throughout the world. It is, he says, 'a false interrogative'. Its function is not to elicit a response but to establish 'who is the boss', to pre-empt, or regulate, the threat of disagreement. 'Do you understand?', says Rancière, tells us that '"to understand" means two different, if not contrary, things: to understand a problem, and to understand an order' (1999: 45). It makes it known to the addressee of the question that there 'is no dissenting view that does not, in some sense, constitute a misunderstanding' (Russell and Montin, 2015: 545). One might imagine Habermas seizing the opportunity to point here to a clear instance of the *strategic* use of language, aimed at influencing, rather than persuading, a veiled threat, a leading question. But this would be to miss Rancière's point. In a perverse way the question *is* an illocutionary moment aiming at mutual understanding, but what changes is the relation of reciprocity that in Habermas invokes, remember, the *equality* of participants in the communicative exchange. What the question tests is the capacity of the worker to understand it not as an equal but as a subordinate. Rancière's challenge defeats Habermas' claim that participation in dialogue carries critical import per se, in order to turn the question into one over the very existence of the situation of dialogue, of who is entitled to take part, and – in the direction of emancipatory practice now – how the *site* of the communicative exchange might be reconfigured to stage 'dissensus' or the 'eventhood' (Badiou and Rancière are very close at this point) of a different distribution of speaking positions and of meaning.

Speech act 3: '*You understand*'. By this formulation I intend to capture an *unwarranted* inclusion in the situation of discourse. The affirmation 'you understand' addressed to those who position themselves consciously as outsiders, is a performative extension of the jurisdiction of the speech act. I have here in mind those who might contest rather than answer the previous question 'do you understand?' with a yes/no; those, in other words, who might resist the 'false interrogative' of that question and the relation of subordination in the distribution of speaking positions that it entails. The affirmation 'you understand' removes any meta-level injunction to the inclusion, and extends jurisdiction (the connotation of law and standing is apposite here). I have in previous work attempted to make a case for the unwarranted inclusion in the situation of dialogue as *the objection that cannot be heard* (with particular emphasis on the courtroom, in Christodoulidis, 2004); Hans Lindahl arguably offers an invitation to resist law's gesture of inclusion with the theory of 'a-legality' (2013) to which we will return in Chapter 4.3. For now, and with our focus on extracting a strategic orientation from the constitutional accommodation that includes us all *anyway* in an open society of interpreters of the constitution, offering our 'illocutionary' speech acts of the interpretation of *our* law, 'you understand' marks the gesture of an inclusion *at once* unwarranted *and* uncontestable.

Three speech acts, three different challenges to the *constitutional situation* as it finds expression in a theory of communicative rationality. The challenges are not exhaustive. They are not even exemplary. They are simply cases where the distinctions between illocution and perlocution, communication and strategy collapse. And as such they force a breach in the totalising framework of the constitutional *situation*, reclaiming constitutional reason as *evental site*, as Badiou would call it. Strategic thinking finds its point of inscription in the breach. Perhaps enough has been said to give strategy due credence to a thinking about the constitution. *Strategic thinking* is relied on to counter the hidden exclusions and the theoretical moves that aim at distributions of what is rational and what irrational within the constitutional domain, and thereby place what is disqualified as altogether beyond question. It is relied on here to bring back an unapologetic *political* dimension to thinking the constitution and resituate the constitutional point of view on the distinction between the constituent and the constituted. As a *critical* project it is committed to excavating the emancipatory potential of political constitutionalism. And finally as a critical *phenomenology* it focuses on the conditions of the emergence of meaning, as attached to practice and therefore also to the *wager* of practice. It is keyed to the specific intelligence and intelligibility of the constitution, that doesn't mutate to conform but holds the field, in order to reclaim the possibility of self-determination, and of the iteration of what is just, in a context where that possibility has not been wasted as market adjustment.

Strategy, Critique, Redress: Opportunities and Limitations

We will limit ourselves here to a relatively brief and programmatic statement of what is to follow. In the light of key *priorities* that inform constitutional strategy we look at three possible *deployments*. We outline first the priorities and then the deployments.

The first priority for strategy is to gain *traction*, and to gain relevance. A return to a political understanding of constitutionalism, especially one that turns on its critical axis, must navigate ambiguous terrain, deceptively smooth, fragmented to the point that much of the constitutional vocabulary, of the 'common good', of 'solidarity' and 'dignity' finds little purchase. The question becomes how to mobilise the categories on the fluid or liquid terrain of market constitutionalism where they slide vacuously. As Daniel Bensaïd put it in 'the return of strategy', '[t]o believe that fluid forms – *organizing in networks* and the logic of affinity groups – escape the subordination to capital is a grotesque illusion. *Such forms are perfectly isomorphic* with the modern organization of computerized capital, flexible working, the liquid society, etc' (Bensaïd, 2007: 8, emphasis added). How to gain traction on this terrain that co-opts and reconfigures the language of critique, is a key consideration for strategy. Numerous examples of such co-option have already been analysed: the right to work as endless flexibilisation, the right to associate as the undercutting of unionisation, the demand for solidarity (for the Estonian workers in *Viking*) as their right to work uninsured, the 'common good' as market access, etc.

The second priority for strategy is how it inserts itself in the *history* of constitutional practices, locating itself in lines of continuity with understandings of those practices, maintaining the connection with the constitutional imaginary and people's investment in it. 'The ideal' – suggests Bloch with freedom, equality and fraternity of the *tricolor* in his sights – 'precisely as valid and as necessary, must be historically mediated, and it must be possible to demonstrate that they [liberty, equality, fraternity] have their tendency and their possibility in the course of history', if they are to provide 'a penetrating, concrete critique of a degenerated and discredited realization, a realization that would be better called a defeat and makes itself known as such' (Bloch, 1986: 198). The question for the renewal of critical strategy is to understand and reflect this historical inheritance, 'tendency and opportunity'. Part of the challenge with such appeals for our discussion is that this inheritance ties *critical* constitutional theory, on the one hand, to the state as the form of the political organisation of society, and, on the other, to the political economy as site of its material reproduction, where both constitutive references are undergoing rapid forms of reconfiguration. Neither of these two constitutive references – to the state and to material production – can be taken today to have the meaning they had for previous generations of critical theorists. The demand as received from Marx, that theory address the historical conjuncture it finds itself in, remains one of critical theory's most valuable legacies, and such an effort today would demand that we turn – as far as the political economy is concerned – to the modalities and expressions of capitalist renewal in its new forms of flexible accumulation, the staggering growth of financialisation, the fragmentation of labour and the new forms of its exploitation; and – as far as the state is concerned – to the new functions of the state in the era of global flows, the new linkages of states and capitals, the articulations and disarticulations of state steering functions, etc. This involves a significant re-orientation of the constitutional viewpoint to the new modalities of organisation (and dispersal) of economic and political power. Connecting back to the inheritance is not to romanticise our constitutional pasts but to suggest an approach in genealogical mode, that 'excavates' and exploits the ambivalence of those pasts, challenging the foreclosures that set current certitudes on their way, the most comprehensive of which we explored in the conditions of installing the market paradigm in the 1970s (Chapter 3.1). This also means not ignoring that the state entertained a coeval relation with capital, or that it framed the organisation of industrial relations to facilitate the extraction of surplus value. But in its constituent social dimension, the constitution also operationalised democratic categories in the definition of participation, production and protection, a connection lost once the constitution is surrendered to market veridiction, or uploaded to the supra-state level where, as we have seen at length, the loss of the democratic ways of thinking about work has been comprehensive. And where a variable process of concept formation at the two levels, statal and supra-statal, appears incapable of transferring leverage upwards to arguments about dignity, job security, health and safety guarantees, at the transnational level of the constitutionalisation of employment.

The third priority orients strategy neither to the field that receives it, nor to history, but turns it inward, to what we have described as constitutional '*reflexivity*'. Here what is at stake is a critical strategic thinking about the *limitations* of the constitution's own particular intelligibility and intelligence. *First*, critical theory's connection to *praxis* must negotiate what we might identify as the constitutive limitations of the institutional; because institutions reduce the contingency of human interaction, they entrench models of social relationships, and, in doing so, hedge in imaginative political uses and opportunities. *Secondly*, critical theory's *dialectical imagination* comes up against the dominant (and severely anti-dialectical) paradigms, on the one hand of law's heteronomous dependence on politics and the exception (Schmitt, Agamben); and, on the other, of its autonomous or 'pure' self-reproduction (Kelsen), which places politics at the antipode of law, and re-conceives law as non-political, a gesture that for Kelsen gives it its autonomous meaning and attraction. *Thirdly*, the very particular *mediation* of legal meaning is achieved through the ways in which it puts concepts in connection and in sequence and oversees application through the regulation of procedure. *Fourthly*, if genealogy calls us to unpick the law at the joints at which it establishes and renews its repertoire of reasons, it must first confront law's powers of 'homology' and the unique ways it has to marshal the past in support of current arrangements, radically limiting our ability to re-imagine or dis-entrench it except in piecemeal ways.

Given these priorities, the following three chapters track three possible deployments of constitutional strategy: in the direction of 'militant formalisms' (Chapter 4.2), 'strategies of rupture' (Chapter 4.3) and immanent critique (Chapter 4.4). What differentiates the three deployments is that each operates a different balance between the constituent and the constituted. In the case of *formalism*, the weight is on the constituted dimension while the constituent orientates the strategic deployment largely externally (or at the meta-level). In the case of *rupture*, the constituent expands to the point of near eclipsing the constituted dimension, though it must hold on to it as its necessary negativity. In the case of *immanent critique*, the constituent and the constituted are placed in contradictory relation. Which is also to say that strategy does not invoke the priorities or engage the deployments in a cumulative way, but navigates them.

The argument about function and stabilisation, about 'homology' and variability, is what we will discuss in the next chapter (4.2) in the context of a first deployment of constitutional strategy. It will suggest – on strategic grounds – a critical appreciation that not all formalism is to the detriment of the dis-empowered and that political-strategic considerations are crucial to determine to what measure formalism might be deployed to hold on to key commitments of dignity and solidarity, to redress injustice and oppression, and that *militant formalisms* might be harnessed against the permeation of governance imperatives.

Formalist strategy will be distinguished from two other deployments that we will call *ruptural* and *immanent* respectively. Where institutional opportunity yields to the system's structural givens to the point that it is vacated or undercut; where legal homology overwhelms; where legal mechanisms of deadlock offer only 'involution' – the endless splitting up and splintering off – and no transcendence; where systemic givens always-already impinge on opportunity by providing the coordinates of any possible actualisation: in all these cases a *strategic decision* is called for whether to *play the system* or *to confront* it.

This will be the subject of Chapter 4.3, where we explore the tradition of anti-systemic struggle that experiments with new, emergent political forms. It is here that the constituent moment confronts the constituted as its negative, since the extant forms are precisely those that thwart its expression. This logic of *rupture* finds political expression in the tradition of *autogestionnaire* workers' politics. It makes an appearance in that final, explosive text of Marx's tribute to the Paris Commune, *The Civil War in France*, and finds more systematic expression, if 'systematic' does not belie the phenomenological novelty, in the writings of Luxemburg and Sorel. It is what in the more recent past broke into the European scene during the 'Polish summer' of 1980. And it is what we are witnessing, as I write, in the extraordinary *constitutional innovation* that is being pursued in Chile.

The final form of strategy in our typology is that of *immanent critique*, and it is developed in the book's final chapter (4.4). It generalises the argument that was already made in Chapter 2.3 with regard to the social constitution. There we argued with regard to solidarity and dignity for a concept of the social constitution as *antagonistic* to the settled understandings of the social question as far as constituted power was concerned. *Immanent* because drawing on resources that the system itself makes available, this form of constitutional strategy finds its opportunity in the constitutional situation where norms of equality solidarity, dignity instantiate a dynamic of transformation *because* they are belied in the forms in which they are sanctioned and enforced. The axiomatic of equality is inscribed in structures of hierarchy and advantage constitutively unable to deliver it. Take the constitutional right to work, for example, which promises all citizens a means to realise their productivity. Between the structural conditions of a system that requires a necessary level of unemployment to control inflation and sustain a *market* in labour, and the promise of a political society to realise the productivity of all its members, a contradiction arises that allows neither reconciliation nor resolution *within* the system; immanent critique promises to exploit politically what is otherwise forever externalised ('hard on crime', 'war on drugs', etc.). It locates itself in the discrepancy between what is committed to constitutional text and what is delivered as constitutional practice, fashioning out of that deficit a claim against exploitation and an injunction against the withdrawal of work, not a request for its optimal market allocation. Its injunction is an injunction against suffering. The tradition of the *material* constitution, invites us to begin with the thought that those who produce value in a society also determine its disposal, and that *to act on the contradiction* – as emerged in the fraught articulation of social rights and capitalist interests – is to act against the usurpation of value and the denial of a speaking position to the producers of value. It may take the form of dissent against the integration of interests by the agents of capital as orchestrated through the European Union. Or, in the constitutional key more generally, it may take the form of the stubborn assertion of social rights, of constitutional warrant, against their elimination through 'total' market activity. In all cases immanent critique intervenes to change the coordinates within which questions are asked, and in which they can be answered, and thus has the *real* effect of expanding political opportunity.

We insisted, when discussing the shortfall in Chapter 2.3, on this *experiential* dimension of suffering because it is this dimension onto which the antinomic grafts, as a *practical*, not a logical, contradiction.[14] The constitution, as a matter of its very definition, functions to secure the unity of the system of law, and that is what makes the connection active between value and the more concrete levels of their instantiation. Because the connection is active and because the constitution harbours a contradiction in that connection, that it can neither suppress nor contain, it is for that reason transformative. That is the logic of immanent critique that we inherit from Marx. The problem – that Marx captured with the notion of ideology – was how pervasively the dilemma was placed out of question, how demanding it was to level the charge against naturalised market distributions on a political register. He argued that immanent critique required an experiential register, for it to be compelling, an experiential deficit in order for the contradiction to be acted on and acted out. Contradictions emerge at the point at which the law as tied to the processes of the material reproduction of society couches in the *universality* of its categories the *partiality* of its distributions. In that context, redress is carried in the modality of immanent critique.

---

[14] Not because, as Husserl put it in the *Crisis*, 'all reflection undertaken for existential reasons is *naturally* critical' (1970: 60); nor, as per Ulrich Beck, can we assume that 'a public *emerg[es]* not on the basis of consensus of decision but *out of dissent* about the consensus of decisions' (2006: 339) because what counts as 'dissent', and the scope of reflexivity, overstates the capacity of the constitutional subject under market conditions to make sense of the constitutional situation that confronts it, the intelligibility, even, of the situation *as* constitutional.

4.2

Militant Formalisms

Formalism as Strategy

It will come as little surprise that the most widespread defence of formalism sees it as a safeguard against the exercise of political power. Martii Koskenniemi speaks for many when, in *The Gentle Civilizer of Nations*, he defends a 'culture of formalism' as entailing 'that there must be limits to the exercise of power, that those who are in positions of strength must be accountable and that those who are weak must be heard and protected'. The 'culture of formalism' denotes 'a culture of resistance to power, a social practice of accountability, openness, and equality whose status cannot be reduced to the political positions of any one of the parties whose claims are treated within it' (2001: 500). If this justification is, for good reason, shared amongst liberals, the appeal of formalism can be extended to critical theory too, even where it is not invoked by name. Important examples can be found in the field of social rights constitutionalism. The first refers to *social action litigation* (SAL) of the type that was developed in India in the late 1970s and early 1980s. In the space of two years alone (1980–82) over 75 SAL writs were fired by social activists to the Supreme Court, vastly extending the normative reign of rights and the administrative review of executive action in the direction of social protection and the alleviation of poverty. The right to life, for example, protected under the Indian constitution (Article 21) was interpreted to encompass the right to a trial, to dignified treatment and to legal aid. Upendra Baxi documents the 'explosive assertion of judicial power in the aid of the dispossessed' and quotes the words of the Chief Justice from *Kesavnanda*: 'this court is not intended to be the arena of legal quibbling for men with long purses. It is made for the common people' (Baxi, 1985: 111). Perhaps most importantly, the development of SAL from the late 1970s onwards helped create the procedural conditions that would allow the Indian Supreme Court to hear cases of particularly disadvantaged groups if they were brought by a public-spirited citizen or organisation. The tradition of SAL was closely linked to the prior tradition of *public interest litigation* (PIL) that was developed in the United States involving, significantly for our argument about strategy, 'fruitful innovations in technique', typically relating to the claiming of *locus standi*, and the uses of procedure to pursue substantive claims (Trubek, 1979). In his seminal work, Roberto Unger renews some of these lines of argumentation. A diversity of 'possible institutional forms', he says, 'shed an oblique but revealing light ... from the point of view of complex enforcement and structural injunctions'. 'New forms of procedural interventions have arisen', he argues, with a particular focus on the *class action lawsuit*, forcing 'a different adjudicative practice with agents, methods and goals, different from those of the traditional style' (1996: 4). Examples of the strategic use of formalism abound, and we too have encountered one that was significant in our discussion of the *Laval/Viking* jurisprudence of the CJEU. Wolfgang Streeck in the aftermath called for a 'democratic departure from the life threatening sedation provided by cheap level capitalism', towards a commitment to democratically enacted *law;* and Christian Joerges' solution to the degenerative moment of CJEU jurisprudence was a militant formalism, an attempt to hold the line through a formalist argument as a direct counter to the functionalism of 'integration': 'I fear', he says, 'that there is no third way here except the stubborn insistence to protect the achievements of Finnish law in this case.' 'Respect Finnish law', he insists, and 'respect the efforts of trade unions to coordinate labour interests transnationally' (Joerges, 2011: 4).

Formalism announces law's autonomy from politics and economics in a move of self-reference and normative closure. If Kelsen is its greatest theoretical exponent, it receives its most radical expression in systems theory where it is radicalised as autopoiesis. We have explored at length how the autopoietic legal system organises its reflexivity and develops its internal complexity on the basis of the gesture of closure that is at the root of all formalisms, expressed in the tautology that '*the law is what the law says it is.*' With all the caveats in place, we can see the value here of a formalism that both provides for the foundation and underwrites the integrity of the legal system. We described this in terms of *constitutional function*. The function can be performed because the constitution provides the formal criteria (of 'entrenchment', 'hierarchisation' and 'rationalisation', Chapter 2.2 above) that sustain the achievement of reduction and linkage and hold it back from merging with market thinking. And if the emphasis here is on *reduction and linkage*, it is because reduction, like in every phenomenology, organises the emergence of legal meaning, and linkage *selects* the criteria for future operations (on legal, *not* economic grounds) that sustain the system in increasingly complex and uncertain environments. Of course globalisation transforms the context of constitutional reference. But to respond to a transformed context is not the same thing as to evacuate the constitutional achievement.

Our aim in this chapter is not to defend formalism as such, but to think of it as a valuable resource for strategy. The important point about strategy is over the question when to deploy formal mechanisms of closure against the erosion of democratically enacted law, and when to release the formalist hold over the institutional imagination for more political and politicised uses. Political constitutionalism, we have said, is defined by the asymmetrical relation between the constituent and the constituted, and the formalist tendency is to organise the constitutional imagination around the pole of the *constituted*, maximising what Luhmann calls the 'redundancy' of the system, against the 'variety' of its more experimental deployments. The modest argument made here for constitutional strategy is to allow the distinctions (redundancy/variety, constituted/constituent) to find their proper constellation and concrete expression in particular historical circumstances and dilemmas, in the 'conjuncture' as Marxists would have it, therefore not as a matter of pure theory but of political judgement, which is, again, at the definitional level what qualifies it as critical theory.

But how to carry this thought productively into particular contexts? I have in previous work suggested the terms 'homology' and 'deadlock' as key features of formalist constitutional thought (Christodoulidis, 2009). *Prima facie* they both name pathologies. But if one connects them to constitutional strategy they may offer some markers for how to navigate the terrain of market constitutionalism on which we find ourselves, in the direction of restoring elements of political-democratic capacity against the implosion of constitutional thought that we have described.

Homology describes law's tendency to privilege redundancy over variety. To secure its function, the legal system needs to maintain a relative balance of stability and innovation, or, more precisely, to reproduce structures of normative expectations through controlled innovation. Innovations can only be grafted on what already exists, and what already exists sets the thresholds of what might count as relevant information, what and under what circumstances may count as a 'surprise' in the legal system, that might in turn lead it to vary expectations. But one must appreciate that the balance of variety and redundancy, what is new and what is business-as-usual, can only lean so far in the direction of variety without jeopardising the function of the law that must at some level meet the exigencies of the rule of law, which in this context means that more experimental political uses of the constitution will at some point yield to protected expectations. The way that this affects the potential of critical constitutional strategy is decisive. In its development, to paraphrase Luhmann, *law overwhelmingly re-activates known grounds*. Granted, there is nothing deterministic about the givenness of context (contexts *are* re-configured as selections are made) but it is also counter-productive to exaggerate the leverage that critique is afforded under the conditions of normative closure and legal self-reference. The pattern of what can be varied, what contested comes heavily pre-determined, not because the borders of law are heavily policed (though they are that too) but because structures of expectations release opportunities of variation selectively on the back of what is entrenched as invariant. There is room for a useful deployment of strategy here to hold on to productive redundancies *when* these matter to protecting values. It is in this sense that homology, the name of the deep, structural inertia of the legal system that stands in the way of critical re-appropriations, might nonetheless be strategically important when it comes to holding the line against market erosion.

If 'homology' is about repetition, sedimentation, coherence and the stabilisation of expectations, mechanisms of deadlock serve to 'lock in' solutions, typically through rules of jurisdiction and standing, the distribution of competences, and rules or practices of unamendability. The example of the constitutional situation in Chile is an exemplary case of deadlock,[1] characterised by Fernando Atria's as the 'cheating constitution' (*La constitución tramposa*). Devised by the constitutional lawyers at the Catholic University of Santiago under the firm steer of Jamie Guzman and the oversight of the Pinochet regime, the constitutional deadlock survived Chile's return to democracy in 1990 and such was its design that it remained in place throughout a series of vehement political movements, locking in capitalist structures and making political change impossible except in piecemeal, and for the most part unremarkable, ways. The staying power of the constitutional situation was secured – and

---

[1] Chile is the country that pioneered the Washington consensus in the Americas under Pinochet. Having overthrown Salvador Allende's socialist government, the military junta suppressed all societal resistance to the installation of the 'market utopia' under the supervision of the 'Chicago boys' and permitted the clean slate to be introduced for the inscription of the 'total market'.

I will be very brief here[2] – by a combination of mechanisms of deadlock, at first- and second-order levels. At the first-order a series of '*organic-constitutional statutes*' covered a vast range of areas of vital importance (education, police powers, the regulation of the mining industry, pensions, elections, etc., see Ansaldi and Vergara, 2020) which could only be passed, modified or abrogated if supported by a number of votes corresponding to 3/5 (later 4/7) of the deputies and senators in office. A second form of deadlock was introduced through the electoral laws that established *the binomial system* by which the members of both Houses of Congress were elected,[3] establishing two parliamentary seats per district allocated to the candidates of the parties that came first and second in votes, thus in effect creating a stalemate, *a continuous tie*, that made it practically impossible to reach the quora required to touch the organic laws. This handed a permanent veto to the Right, *whether it was in government or opposition*. Buttressing these mechanisms of deadlock was a third, enshrined in a system of *preventive constitutional review*, designed to take place before the legislative bills were enacted into valid statutes, and giving the Constitutional Court the power to pronounce on their constitutionality, significantly a power that the Court was able to exercise of its own accord, without the requirement that it be referred to the Court by the Legislature. These mechanisms were secured at the meta-level through *the rules for constitutional amendment*, stipulated, alongside the increased quora mentioned above, an aggravated procedure when it came to certain 'sensitive issues' (the reduction of the powers of the President of the Republic, the potential expansion of the powers of Congress, etc.) and 'crucial chapters' (Institutional Foundations, Constitutional Court, Armed Forces, and National Security Council), which additionally required the agreement of the President of the Republic.

Of course Chile is only one example and the '*pinochetista*' design of its constitutional situation cannot be generalised. What it exhibits in an alarming way is how the Right relied on a *strategy of formalism* to perpetuate a constitutional regime for the period when the barbarity of

---

[2] For a comprehensive account see Atria (2013b) and in the context of the recent upheaval, Ansaldi and Vergara (2020).

[3] As explained by Atria, this was the formula that the intellectual authors of the constitution implemented in order to 'mitigate the defects and evils of universal suffrage'. (These are their own words as registered in the proceedings of the Commission which prepared the Preliminary Draft.) (Atria, 2020)

its implementation could no longer rely on the military, for the period even when the government would pass to the Socialist party in 2006, and then again in 2014. There is clearly nothing that the self-corrective processes of the deliberative paradigm could achieve in this context of intransigence and against the deliberate deadlock of constitutional design. But is there a lesson here to be garnered for a formalist strategy for the Left? Not, as in Chile, in the sense of locking in a constitutional settlement, but in recruiting a militant formalism to exploit the formal achievements of the constitution (entrenchment, hierarchy) and its very particular level of the reduction of meaning as captured by homology (rationalisation).

Take, again, the case of Europe's social constitution. We have seen at some length how the distinction between *hard and soft law* has been increasingly used to navigate the paradoxical effects and externalities of the operation of markets on European societies. On any reasonable account of the unity of law, our practices are to be held up to scrutiny in terms of the principles they are meant to be instantiations for, and the constitutional function is to secure that continuity. To circumvent the constitutional function, the proponents of governance, as we saw at length earlier, import the soft/hard law distinction with a view to relegating constitutional aspiration into a separate realm of soft law, where the realm of 'soft' comes to encompass everything from constitutional preambles and general principles on the one hand, and recommendations, opinions, green papers, white papers, guidelines, etc., on the other. What holds these typologies together and allows the gathering under the generic 'soft', is the lack of direct applicability along with a broad reference to their 'orientation function'. This creeping constitutionalisation gradually spreads to the abstract constitutional values, and to the level of abstract principles expressing those values in social rights principles. But this conflation is a deliberate misreading of constitutional function, and we can turn to formalism to correct it. Because laws that are supposed instantiations of general principles and values and yet give the lie to those principles and values, are deficient laws to be righted as unconstitutional. Because in this case the rationality of law that depends on holding together principles and their instantiations is eroded, the dialectic is broken and with it any possibility of making sense of the law as a rational enterprise disappears.

The constitutional recourse to formalism delivers tangible correctives against this type of deliberate misreading. We looked earlier at how constitutional reflexivity organises the (legal) system's self-reference at the *formal* level. It achieves it through entrenching values as self-descriptions and generating a hierarchy of rules under the constitution. The system's capacity to control these processes, and create systemic 'order' out of societal 'noise', determines how the system operates its dual reference to itself and to its environment. Whatever the complexity that it faces, it must be able to organise the constitutional processes through formal criteria. This means not abandoning processes of norm-creation to evolutionary drift but controlling them by mapping them back onto the specific semantics of its self-descriptions (categories of capacity, representation, value). Constitutionality as the formal dimension of the *political* constitution is *not what happens to sediment as practice*, but the constitutional control of what variation is compatible with holding on to the unity of the legal system, so that constitutional practice might stand up to constitutional principle, intended, deliberate and planned! *Rationalisation* understood now as the gesture that collects instances of practice as instantiations of given principles and values, acquires a more productive strategic role. Against the abandonment to the shifting grounds of constitutionalisation and pluralism, it controls the criteria of constitutionality, the normativity of selections, with validity travelling down the *hierarchy* of norms. Reflexivity can be (strategically) mobilised here to control the evolutionary drift, and where necessary to stem the processes of shoring up market discipline that receive the *ex post* redemption of constitutionalisation. If further evidence is needed, a brief look back at the expansive reading of proportionality entertained by the CJEU would suffice. It was a reading of 'horizontal constitutional review'[4] that made a mockery of, and allowed for the judicial subversion of, the constitutional achievement of social democracy at state level. Formalism here stands for the democratic limitation, and proportionality as a 'corrective' to it, can only stand as complementary to democratic norm production, and not as a substitute to it.

'Societal Constitutionalism': Meta-Level Deployments

It is relatively uncontroversial to suggest that the financial crisis of 2008 provided the context for a re-thinking of the meaning of constitutionalism, that found itself marginalised and defeated in the surge of the

---

[4] I have benefited here from reading Johan van der Walt's meticulous constitutional analysis of 'horizontal effect' (van der Walt, 2014b).

economic crisis. But what does it take to re-think constitutionalism in the context of a crisis of capitalism, of a system that *renews itself through crisis*, both through its ordinary and, now, its exceptional manifestations? And what exactly does it mean to think the crisis from a 'constitutional perspective'? One of the most interesting suggestions here comes from Hauke Brunkhorst who combines Luhmann, Habermas and Marx to develop an erudite analysis of the 'return of crisis': 'The great illusion of nineteenth-century bourgeois ideology and twentieth-century neo-conservative thinking was, and still is, that there is no crisis' (2011: 134). Against the background of Marxism's forever renewed reminder that 'capitalism is an inherently catastrophic system', Brunkhorst suggests a concept of crisis that is structural. It is structural because it is the outcome of the functional differentiation of the economy, which 'if not regulated and institutionalized appropriately' leads to a 'new kind of class rule' (146). Conflict-positions proliferate: alongside capital-oriented conflicts he analyses state-oriented and belief-oriented conflicts, as well as the 'new' conflict between included and excluded populations. Despite Brunkhorst's occasional Habermassian moments of optimism ('there are at least some hopeful constellations of class conflict that could lead to further learning processes' (163)) the spectre of exclusion of vast swathes of the world's populations from meaningful participation in social life is one of the more devastating insights of his contribution. The one I want to stay with, however, is about how the confluence of conflicts leads to a point where functional differentiation can hold no longer and collapses into fragmentation and structural crisis.

Systems theory, with its nuanced architecture and heuristic, provides an enhanced perspective on the analysis of the crisis as a question of differentiation and fragmentation. Related to this enhancement comes an oft-repeated claim, by some of the theory's exponents, not only that systems theory has seen *a normative turn*, an argument explicitly discounted by Luhmann,[5] but that this normative turn has in its wake released a full-blown *critical* dimension. While the claim itself remains unconvincing, I would suggest that this most radical theory of formalism

---

[5] See Luhmann (1985/2018). For Fischer-Lescano, 'this allows for a normative turn of systems theory, whose theoretical complexity Luhmann appreciated but whose normative excess found no attention in the cold view of the Bielefeld observer. Luhmann found the concept of critical systems theory "burdened with the intention to create a synthesis of theories of 'critical-emancipatory' leaning with notions of 'responsive dogmatics' and sociological analyses of the 'legal system'"' (Fischer-Lescano, 2012: 4).

may offer some significant, if modest, suggestions for constitutional strategy at this juncture. Whether this qualifies systems theory as *critical theory* is a question that we will need to postpone.

'Critical systems theory', suggests Andreas Fischer-Lescano not without a degree of exaggeration, 'shares basic assumptions with the Critical theory of the first generation of the Frankfurt School'. Amongst these points of connection are 'the assumption that society is based on fundamental paradoxes, antagonisms, antinomies; the strategy to conceptualize justice as a contingent and transcendental formula; the form of immanent (and not morality-based, external) critique as an attitude of transcendence; [and] the aim of societal (and not only political) emancipation in an "association of free individuals" (Marx)' (2012: 3).

The last 'shared assumption' I think we can dispense with straight away. The idea of free *association*, entertained by systems theory as tied to functional differentiation, is 'free' in the thinnest sense. It is not just that Luhmann's individual freely associates to the extent that he freely moves amongst sub-systems, the 'flight' of his 'homo aviator'[6] as Luhmann puts it 'taking place above ... a rather thick cloud cover ... where only occasionally glimpses [are caught] of a larger stretch of landscape with the extinct volcanoes of Marxism',[7] but because it is doubtful that Teubner too, or for that matter any systems theorist, would fly any closer to them, and would find them any less 'extinct'. But what of the other suggestion, of 'the form of immanent critique as an attitude of transcendence'? 'For the project of critique,' says Fischer-Lescano, 'there is no fixed point outside of society; rather critique has to start with the transcendent reference overspill of immanence. Critique arises from the arcanum of society, critique is attitude, point of view and resistance' (2012: 12). It 'relates to one's own discrepancies' to 'thematize societal fundamental contradictions'; 'the critical legal (systems) theory integrates this normative demand, which in law turns against the law in paradox form and drives it to transcend itself into a permanent becoming of alterity justice' (12).

We will have the opportunity to look at immanent critique at length later (Chapter 4.4). And it is true that for systems theory everything is (and can only be) undertaken immanently, because there is no purchase point outside a system for either observation or critique. But it is also the case that there is a fundamental blockage from the point of view of systems

---

[6] See (Luhmann, 1986c) and Chapter 3.1 above.
[7] Quoted by Fischer-Lescano (2012: 4, fn. 2).

theory to that most crucial moment of immanent critique, which is the moment of transcendence. Immanent critique can be exercised of course but the leverage afforded to it by functional differentiation will only carry it so far, in the limited form of a recalibration of (sub)-systemic boundaries. To restore functional differentiation, typically against the expansionist logic of systems, is the limit of immanent critique, and this ties to system-specific semantics and function. From a systems perspective, to harness immanent critique to *a transcendence* in the direction of social emancipation, is what systems-theorists would invariably identify as some naïve sociological version, or other, of Marxism. But there is perhaps still something important here, in what Fischer-Lescano above called the 'reference overspill', and we must turn to Teubner's argument about 'self-subversive justice' (Teubner, 2009) for this. The main notion here that Fischer-Lescano takes from Teubner is a conception of 'justice as a contingent and transcendental formula', whereby if law indeed 'subjugate[s] itself to systemic constraints of alignment' it is only 'in order to get rid of them, and, like with Adorno, to 'break the spell' (2012: 13). But how convincing is this? And if it is not, is there still an insight to extract from it on the critical uses of sysyems theory?

We will need to take a few steps back to answer that. What characterises a systems-theoretical notion of *justice* is that, while its extension spans a number of systems (legal, political, economic justice), its semantic content is tied to each system of meaning in mutually incompatible ways. In this formulation we have both its opportunity and its limitation. We might say, with Luhmann, that 'justice' is *loosely* coupled in the overall system of society, and *strictly* coupled at the level of functional sub-systems. Which means that it allows these systems to communicate around it, and, in a crucial sense for Teubner, also to measure their adequacy by it. As far as the legal system is concerned, 'the idea of justice can be understood as *a formula for contingency* of the legal system' (Luhmann, 2004: 214) in a roughly equivalent way as 'scarcity' plays that role for the economic system. 'The system defines justice in such a way that makes it clear that justice must prevail' – at the risk of 'performative contradiction' as the discourse theorists would have it – 'and that the system identifies with it as an idea, principle or value' (ibid.). It gives the system of law orientation, it guides its reasons, it programmes its programmes: in a nutshell, it undergirds its function. In its *legal* specification, justice must achieve 'adequate complexity' to deal with an environment where justice claims abound: in the political system, in emancipatory struggle, in social movements, identity politics, economic justice claims, etc. For Teubner this move to internalise justice and contain it in the legal system creates a potentially 'subversive' situation in the way that justice strains at the containment. As he puts it very well, 'invoking justice makes explicit law's dependency on its ecologies, on its social, human and natural environment' (2009: 9). By re-directing law's attention to its adequacy to the outside world, it reveals to itself 'a strong contradiction' with that ecological orientation (2009: 10). Because of course all reference to the outside ecologies is, and can only be, ultimately a self-referential process. This creates the explosive situation, says Teubner, of 'a necessary but impossible self-transcendence of law's closure':

> Justice works as a subversive force with which the law protests against itself. ... it infuses into the legal order a tendency toward disorder, revolt, deviation, variation and change. It protests in the name of society, of human beings and of nature – but it does so from within the law. Subversive justice stirs up the law. The 'mutiny on the Bounty' is its message.
>
> (Teubner, 2009: 13)

Of course Teubner will rein the mutiny back in, because when law 'transcends itself' to enact its ecologies – 'society, people, nature' – the transcendence isn't really transcendence. There can be no transcendence because there is nowhere to go, no materiality to receive it; whatever 'spillover' there is will be routed back to the legal system, in a call to develop 'adequate legal concepts', an adequacy that, again, will receive a functional, not a normative, reading. And although much of the effort here is couched in the deconstructive idiom of Derrida, it is doubtful whether the legal system can endorse the 'transcendence formula' that Derrida offers without 'externalising its criteria, and put its hope in democracy or morality' that Teubner reminds us is exactly what it cannot do. That is why, despite him now, the 'irrational experience of self-transcendence' – irrational because what is transcended is precisely the systemic limit of rationality – will re-settle on either side of the clear demarcation between 'disorder and revolt' on the one side and 'variation and change' on the other *as its permissible and productive limit.*

For the reason that transcendence is an impossible concept for systems theory, systems theory does *not* avail itself as a form of immanent critique, or as critical theory in the tradition of the Frankfurt School. And yet systems theory offers us a heuristic of profound strategic importance. It is useful not in terms of its offer to transcend the 'contingency' formula of justice, but to defend it. It is as a *blocking* device that the sophisticated formalism of the theory can offer us its most emancipatory gift, against the transcendence tendencies that collapse its formula of contingency, reorient away from justice and towards efficiency, in the process of undoing the achievement that is law by externalising its criteria. Let us insist with Teubner that 'law's search for justice cannot put its hope in either democracy or justice, not to speak of rational choice', add economic efficiency to his list, but also incline the constitutional achievement to an ideal of political justice, or to its 'constituent' dimension as we have so far thematised it. This is not altogether unwarranted projection, as we will see, and Teubner offers us a fascinating route into meta-level reflexivity in *Constitutional Fragments* and other recent work on 'societal constitutionalism', which we will take with an eye always to strategic deployments.

We pick up the thread again from the question of what might be the proper constitutional response to crisis. For Teubner, 'a strengthened politics of reflection is required within the economy, and this has to be *supported* by constitutional norms'. 'Supported' because systems need to be allowed to channel societal responses to their expansion in the direction of their own self-limitation. This 'auto-limitative role' 'leads to the generation of powerful counter-structures: the limitation of power by power, money by money; in each case the system-specific medium turns against itself' (2012: 17, 21). The point about these instances is that they tap broader and vastly richer resources of social dynamism. The first thing that *the theory of societal constitutionalism* brings to the fore is the interconnectedness of systemic phenomena with the underlying social dynamics as expressed in 'constitutional arenas'. Social conflicts, social movements and social demands trigger at the sub-systemic level processes that cannot be ignored, and to which institutional 'solutions' offer nothing but temporary respite. They provide a continuous élan; and each sub-system re-acts to what initially are contradictory dynamics building up within them. It is in order to alleviate such contradictory developments that constitutional reflexivity develops, ultimately, Teubner will argue, with the support of the legal system. In that sense the 'medial reflexivity' described above ('the limitation of power by power, money by money [etc.]') is *not yet* constitutionalisation. It is in need of further '*support*'. It only becomes 'constitutional' in the form of a meta-coupling, as supported by the reflexivity of law. As Teubner puts it in his *Constitutional Fragments*:

> What is the reason, though, why secondary legal rules are supplementing social reflexivity? Law comes into the self- foundation processes of social systems when they cannot fully accomplish their autonomy. This happens either when the social system cannot be adequately closed by its own first-order and second- order operations, or when reflexive social processes are unable to stabilize themselves or, especially, when they are becoming paralyzed by their paradoxes. In such cases, additional closure mechanisms come in to support the self-foundation of social autonomy. The law is one of them—not the only one, but one among several.
>
> (2012: 107)

The idea of law as an 'additional closure mechanism' is vital here, and the suggestion that closure is achieved through law connects to the argument about a strategy of formalism. At no point, of course, is Teubner suggesting that the solution lies in applying the 'decision models' for politics or for law, to other social sectors, especially in the case of politics where such a transfer would install a 'politics-led integration of diverging rationalities by imposing on them an internal "political" constitution', and 'wrongly politicising them' (2012: 28, 29). Instead of such destructive transferrals – of the logic of one system onto another – Teubner will suggest a meta-level coupling of the systems in a highly innovative conception of constitutionality.

Constitutional processes, says Teubner, are an example of 'double closure' as suggested by von Foerster. 'They are triggered when systems develop a second order closure, in addition to their operative first-order closure, by applying their operations reflexively to their operations.' But this double closure depends crucially on a meta-level coupling with law. While the 'constitutional', second-order, closure finds expression in the system's reflexive structuring of its operations (for example, in politics, where power processes are organised via power processes: electoral procedures, competences, fundamental rights), that reflexive structuring of the political and economic systems is achieved in combination with the reflexivity of law. *Internally* that reflexivity is expressed as a coupling of first- and second-order operations; *externally* it is expressed as a coupling of the reflexive structures of the relevant system with the reflexive structure (the constitution) of law. 'Constitutions do not emerge until phenomena of double reflexivity appear: reflexivity of the self-constituting social system and reflexivity of the supportive legal system' (Teubner, 2012: 104). Constitutions emerge when a structural coupling of the reflexive mechanisms of law (i.e. secondary rules) with the reflexive mechanisms of the relevant social sector occurs. Teubner reserves the term *constitutional* only for the coupling of reflexive processes within both systems. Only this achieves the requisite density and permanence and ensures that we have constitutional co-evolution of the two social systems. The threshold of constitutionalisation is only reached once the 'hybrid binary meta-code' guides internal processes in both systems. How this is achieved is through the second-order coupling, with the help of 'hybrid meta-codes', that is 'codes' where the code-values constitutional/ unconstitutional function to enable the coupling of systems at the reflexive level (hence 'meta'), and 'hybrid' because in 'straddling' the two systems there is no direct transferral of meaning between the two orders of reflection, but in each system the coding releases opportunities for system-specific thematisation. Of what? Of what is constitutional or not, in relation to *the pursuit of the public interest*. In the idea of the public interest and 'public responsibility' as underlying the 'additional reflection' imported at the constitutional level, we find the normative pulse of the theory.

This is how Teubner puts it in *Constitutional Fragments*:

> The constitutional code of the social sphere concerned (constitutional/ unconstitutional) is given precedence over the legal code (legal/illegal). What is special about this meta- coding, though, is its *hybridity*, as it takes precedence not only over the legal code but also over the binary code of the function system concerned. Thus it exposes the binary-coded operations of the function system to an additional reflexion regarding whether or not they take account of the subsystem's public responsibility.
>
> (2012: 110)

The importance here of constitutionality is that, as a hybrid meta-structure, it achieves a heightened level of additional reflection. With regard to the 'auto-limitative' moment it protects against the blind reproduction of systems from crossing crucial thresholds between productive and catastrophic expansion. But this is only one of the effects of re-orienting and controlling the self-reproduction of systems in the direction of serving the common good. And it is here that a claim for the *politics of societal constitutionalism* is articulated and defended, 'outside institutionalised politics' but, Teubner insists, no less robust for that. 'Societal constitutionalism effectively calls for sites of political reflection to be firmly established in the spontaneous sphere and in the organized sphere of the economy' (2012: 119).

How to understand this form of politics? Certainly not, for Teubner, in the redundant forms of over-politicisation, the 'fetish of collectivization', 'the opium of the people', that Luhmann also ridiculed in the idea of having the 'world republicanised'.[8] '*La politique*' is reclaimed outwith the state form, to link constitutional reflexivity constitutively to its political dimension. We retain from this: (i) the notion of constitutionality as meta-level reflexivity with its emphasis on the deployment of hybrid couplings; (ii) the idea of 'public interest' (and of 'public responsibility') as foundational orientation value for constitutional reflexion; (iii) the constitutive role of law as providing in each case the pivot for reflection across the systems of law, politics and the economy. A coupling at the meta-level with the 'political' is what characterises political constitutionalism and what subtends its reflexivity. There is no transcendence here, no self-subversive justice. In all such operations the constituent political only ever appears alongside the law as accompanying self-reference. Which means, as we are always reminded, that all reference to its environment is mediated by the law's relation to itself. This is as close as it gets to extracting a theory of political constitutionalism from systems theory.

This is what Teubner confirms at the core of the theory of societal constitutionalism and if there is a normative turn here, it is not in the inflated terms of transcendence, but in the careful and painstaking effort to use the difficult heuristic of second-order observation in a critical direction. Second order observation is not critical per se. But it can be inclined in that direction if we take Teubner's distinctions as guiding distinctions and place the political ('la politique'), as he does, at the basis of the reflexivity of systems.

To preserve Teubner's prescription at this point, and to incline constitutional reflexion in a political direction (though that is not how he would put it), does not mean to tie it back to the *state*, but to *democracy* as the organising principle of the political, and *equality* as its horizon. While the connection of the political with the concept of the state as its principal expression is a contingent matter, a concept of the political that does not incorporate democracy and equality as constitutive of its meaning falls short definitionally, not merely normatively. If historically the operational requirements of the political system have short-circuited democracy to the state, only in terms of which the demos could be seen to act under systems of representation that were largely held as adequate (though against which other configurations of constituency, typically

---

[8] Fischer-Lescano (2012: 14), discussing Teubner (2019) and Luhmann (1986a).

class, levelled their challenge), democracy was of course never exhausted in its state form. Industrial democracy, radical forms of syndicalism or class struggle, to take some examples, were animated by and geared to the aspiration of democracy and equality, but never came under the sign of state politics. Cross-cutting and under-cutting identifications mark the history of democratic struggle, and these are the hallmarks of the political, not its pre-conditions. The political occurs as struggle over and against political ascriptions and given semantics. It is this intrinsic and irreducible reflexivity that is captured in the idea of the political (carried in the distinctions police/politics in Rancière, situation/event in Badiou, etc.).

In its various re-entries into the thematic and semantic discipline of sub-systems, the political impulse must adapt to the rationality of the particular system; but if it is to uphold the reflexivity, it must retain something of its constitutive orientation to democracy and equality. At least that is the aspiration that I read into societal constitutionalism. It is certainly the aspiration of a political constitutionalism as I have tried to defend it here. There is no question that the reflexivity meets extraordinary challenges at the point of re-entry.

Take the 're-entry' into the economic system, that concerns us centrally in the defence against market thinking: At the first order level of the operations of the economic system there can be little doubt that 'politicisation' is lost to what is operationalised as economically rational. If the political is constitutively oriented to democracy and equality, with any actual instantiation and programme measured against their promise, the economic, under conditions of functional differentiation and sub-systemic autonomy, has effectively removed the processes of the organisation of production, and therefore democracy, from its field of reference, and pared equality back to a simple premise of the exchange relation. The economically rational is measured in terms of how scarce means are allocated to competing ends against the background or in the context of 'substitutable choices'. This re-orientation of economic reason away from a logic of need, social labour and association, and towards 'the study of human behavior as a relationship between ends and scarce means which have mutually exclusive uses' (Becker, 1976: 1) has the effect of cutting it off from the problematic of participation in collective labour, let alone the aspirations of social justice and equality. This closure of economic reason around its own self-descriptions, these tautologies, will call for a reflexivity to take care of the blockages. But in the process it effects a displacement on the organising principles of the political economy. The very injunction that capitalism dispossesses the worker in substituting the value of the lived intelligibility and meaning of work with an exchange value for labour becomes unintelligible. *Economic reason makes redundant the notion of the political sphere itself as far as production is concerned.*

For us, concerned with reflexivity and the logic of couplings, what might we still insist *is* communicated at the level of (Teubner's) hybrid meta-couplings? From a systems-theoretical point of view we would never contemplate that common meanings might be transferred across systemic boundaries. But what might then be gained from the 'meta-coupling' of politics and economics, what survives entry into economic reason as the distinction between 'le politique/la politique', that is, as economically 'politicisable' in the direction of the 'common interest'? The obvious risk is that with the 're-entry' into the economic system's rationality the political ceases to impact, underdetermined to the point at which it is in all cases productive to the receiving system, and re-aligned to its functional imperatives. If we expect a limitative role from the constitutional, then 'public responsibility' – a moment of the political – must furnish an 'additional reflection' or independent criterion; it cannot fold seamlessly back into the logic of the reproduction of the system. The important lead that Teubner offers us is how *law and the economy pivot on the political to each sustain their own reflexivity*. Without that pivot and that reliance, no meta-level reflection can be sustained, and then also no possibility to think the 'limitative' exists.

My suggestion is to build on this insight and recruit constitutional reflexivity in a political role of guiding the selective withdrawal of certain areas of social action from the logic of price. The ambition at this level is to think the conditions of reversal of the 'generalisation of economic reason', the conditions of keeping market thinking within its proper boundaries. The key question and test for the reflexivity of 'societal constitutionalism' is whether it can put the market to question as appropriate register for a series of issues that any decent society with a fundamental commitment to the dignity of its members would not choose to commodify. Would a reflexive coupling allow some kind of return to thinking the *political* economy, such that incorporates democracy in production as irreducible value, irreducible, that is, to functional equivalents? Cutting through the logic of functional equivalence via political decisions is absolutely vital here. And the imperative is rendered vacuous if democracy is always-already aligned to market re-calibration through the logic of function and equivalence. The coupling at the reflexive level of the legal, political and economic systems, allows for first-order operations to be tested against the *truth values* of the second level [veridiction] that is produced via reflexive couplings.

The ambition of Teubner's theory of societal constitutionalism is to establish reflexive 'meta-couplings' not just between the legal and political systems, but also with the economic system. The question it asks is whether the *economy* too can pull itself on to the reflexive plane with the help of the political – and in the process also rein in its blind self-reproduction on the register of the *political* economy?[9] Only here can the limitative be fashioned as something capable of providing the independent criterion as that which *suspends*, in certain spheres, the self-reproduction of an economy that insatiably commodifies and feeds off its own aggressive expansion. In this suspension, reflexivity assumes the function of *blocking*: it withdraws certain issues, say the protection of collective agreements, from economic determination. Of course nothing guarantees the resilience of those political determinations that might sustain the 'constitutional' of economic constitutionalism. Here is the problem for the meta-level of the economy as I see it. The economic system hoists itself reflexively onto the meta-level, via the distinction 'in the public interest/not in the public interest' that, content-less, is too under-determined to sustain it on that plane. Either it seeks the criteria of what might fashion it as an independent, reflexive, move through political criteria; or it seeks them in the logic of price (CSR, activist shopping) which cannot sustain it at the meta-level, and collapses it back to the functional level. And what is significant about the difference is that in the latter case reflexivity is an *invitation* to the economy to think in the public

---

[9] In terms of meta-couplings, it is interesting to look at the limit placed by 'economic' reason on the political and legal systems. Foucault tells the story of the rise of the market system – a rise that he places as occurring at roughly the same time as Polanyi, between 1750 and 1830 – very much as the story of such a coupling of law with *the market as site of veridiction* (2004, lecture II). For public law, whose means of calibration and self-limitation had relied so far on what could be identified as an expansionist *eigen-dynamic*, the emergence of the market system plays the role of catalyst. The law is confronted with the 'truth' of natural equilibria. Against this truth it can measure the legitimacy of its intervention. The rationale of self-limitation acquires an external measure with the help of which a role proper for public law is fashioned. A coupling now ensures the proper self-limitation of power and crucially jurisdiction (the principle that 'one must not govern too much' is granted a means to rationalise 'excess'), it ensures the orientation of public law in terms of a guiding distinction of public/private that delimits proper spheres of application and a rationale for intervention, and connects the perennial quest for legitimacy to the veridiction of the market.

interest, whereas in the former it is an *injunction* against the commensurability of claims. It is a political injunction against the 'pooling' of freedoms of workers and entrepreneurs to strike and to reflag respectively, that through the flattening device of 'proportionality' allows 'balancings' of labour rights against economic rights. It is, therefore, an injunction against the submission of the dignity of labour to the economic reasoning of comparative advantage; an injunction, therefore, against the generalisation of economic reason.

Perhaps this returns us to thinking about societal constitutionalism with a clearer view of the stakes, and of the dilemma facing us. And perhaps we are also now in a position to raise otherwise the reflexive question over what is *societal* about societal constitutionalism. The double slippage that we began with now becomes clearer as the dilemma which confronts us: *the political* or *the market* as that which sustains constitutional reflection? Against the danger of market capture, where the market calls forth the '*societal*' by submitting it to functional imperatives, and, in the final instance, harnessing it to market allocations, we are invited to re-think it along the political dimension. I have warned against the logic of functional equivalence and have argued that a *critical* systems theory must embrace a political reflexivity if it is to claim back democratic self-understandings that have come increasingly to measure themselves against the market as site of veridiction. The promise of a constitutional perspective is a stubborn attempt to hold the line, and not forever slip into the partial rationalities of functional sub-systems that it is to enjoin or couple.

4.3

Constitution, Autogestion, Rupture

These Parisians storming Heaven

Marx

The Scandal of Democracy

Poland's Short Summer of Anarchy[1]

What unfolded in 1980/81 in Poland was one of the most striking experiments in industrial democracy in Europe, a leaf out of Rosa Luxemburg's *Mass Strike*. If the events are today largely forgotten, this is partly because of *Solidarity's* (Solidarność) later co-option and involvement as the party in government during the socially destructive programme of market implementation that took place in Poland after the fall of the Iron Curtain. But if it failed to impact on the democratic imagination of the West, it was for another reason too. What was distinctive about the Gdansk uprising was that it was an exercise both in *autogestionnaire* politics, and a re-assertion of the meaning of work buttressed by a collective commitment to its protection. *Solidarity* was an instance of a worker's movement rising against a workers' republic, unclassifiable in terms of the blunt binarisms that dominated the political imagination of both East and West. It was 'unclassifiable' because both the agent and the action defied locution in the constitutional space available to them at the time. This double negotiation (of agency and action) was only possible as an exercise of *constituent power* in the dynamic process of enactment of a *labour constitution*.

It is useful to recount the events of the extraordinary experiment that was the '*Polish summer*' of 1980. The first unconfirmed stoppages of work took place at Warsaw steelworks on 2 July 1980 as a result of a steep

---

[1] The reference is to Hans Magnus Enzensberger's 1972 book on the Spanish anarchist movement (1917–37), *Die kurze Sommer der Anarchie*.

rise in food prices. Strikers' demands were settled directly by management with the promise of a 5–10 per cent pay rise, the management's conciliatory attitude suggesting a pre-emptive gesture from above to satisfy workers' demands. A week later Party leader Edward Gierek announces in a speech to the Central Committee, broadcast on national television, that the increase in food prices would stay and any broader wage increases were out of the question. Almost immediately strike action is announced in over 20 factories in Lublin; the strikes then spread to Poznan, and the 'Roza Luksemburg' electricity plant in Warsaw. As the strikes in Lublin begin to affect the entire population of the city, there is a first official public admission that there have been 'stoppages'. On 18 July, a Politburo communiqué calls for a return to work, appealing to 'patriotic sentiments', and on the eve of the 'People's Poland' anniversary three days later, during muted celebrations and with walkouts, strikes and general unrest moving to the south of the country, Gierek appeals for civic discipline and responsibility. While he travels to the Crimea for a meeting with Brezhnev, news first reaches the west of strike-breaking attempts by the Polish security forces. At a surprise news conference for Western journalists on 8 August, the Politburo reinforces the message that the strikes are not political 'despite attempts by hostile forces to politicise them'. What is noteworthy is that the term 'strike' is first used officially to describe the action.

It is at the beginning of August that the strikes spread to the Gdansk shipyards. Here the action takes a definite political character, as the first all-out strike on 14 August demands, *inter alia*, the erection of a memorial for the fallen victims of the 1970 Baltic strikes, re-instatement of dismissed colleagues, and *free trade unions*. The government reacts with a communications blackout in Gdansk. As 50,000 workers join the strike, transport in the city comes to a standstill. On 16 August the Interfactory Strike Committee (MKS) is established in Gdansk to coordinate the strike and represent all strikers, those of the Lenin Shipyard and 20 other striking units. MKS draws up a list of 16 demands including freedom of speech, authentic syndicalist representation and freedom for the political prisoners.

Two days later, Gierek broadcasts over all radio and television channels that economic demands will be met with increases to family allowances and wage increases. While he admits that current trade union representation is unresponsive, he stops short of acknowledging union demands as political. He intimates that force will not be used against the strikers, but castigates the 'enemies of the people', warning that 'any challenge to the foundations of the socialist state will not be tolerated'. On 19 August, 25,000 workers in Szczecin, on the East German border, join the strikes, which have now spread across the entire Baltic coast, as the Soviet media TASS reports 'subversive antisocialist elements operating in Polish coastal region'. The Government's Pyka commission insists on dealing with each factory's representatives separately. The MKS makes it a condition of dialogue that they be recognised as sole bargaining partner, with Lech Walesa now emerging as strike leader, head of a 15-member presidium, representing 500 delegates from over nearly 400 factories. The first round of talks, on 23 August, is inconclusive. In the second round held on 26 August, the number of MKS delegates is estimated to have risen above 800.

On the last day of August 1980, the government and the strikers sign the *Gdansk Accord*, an agreement that meets all the workers' demands including the right to establish independent trade unions. With direct reference to ILO Convention 87, article 1 of the Accord 'acknowledges the necessity of creating new self-governing labor unions, genuinely representing the working class'; article 2 commits the unions to defending 'the social and material interests of the workers', 'based on the principle of the collective ownership of the means of production'; article 3 recognises the right to organise and conduct collective negotiations, according to ILO Convention 98; article 4 gives the Interfactory Strike Committee the form it will take as the 'constituent committee' of 'the new self-governing labor unions'; further articles commit to the release from prison of political prisoners pending review of their cases, offer radio broadcasts of Sunday mass, offer settlement of economic matters; etc. The Accord also specifies that the new law on labour unions will guarantee workers the right to strike.

The government agrees to make public the minutes of the negotiations and the text of the Accord. The strike is declared over. The Soviet TASS predictably accuses western media 'in many cases to be performing an openly instigative function', in its broadcast of 27 August finding it 'interesting to note that the bourgeois media, ignoring statements made by the Polish authorities, ... orient themselves around the statements of those oppositional elements that are trying to awaken an anti-state, anti-socialist feeling'. The Italian and French communist daily papers, *L Unità* and *L'Humanité*, give radically different accounts of the events.[2] To the

---

[2] *Poland 1981*, 241. All references from: 'Poland 1981: Solidarity, Programme Adopted by the First National Congress', in Raina Peter, ed., *Poland 1981: Towards Social Renewal*

non-orthodox Marxist Left the news was received with some trepidation. The 'Radio Free Europe Research' group had been publishing a daily account of the strikes, covering the broadcasts, as well as the daily strike bulletin put out by the Gdansk workers. In the document they publish in Munich two months after the accord was signed, the editor writes that there is no 'foreseeable ending' to what has occurred during those two extraordinary months since the beginning of the strike, and he speaks of the urgency to write what 'too often becomes lost in retrospect'. This is 'unchartered territory', writes the Director of the RFE Research Department Herbert Reed: 'the concept of independent trade unions which the party, however reluctantly, had to accept is an entirely unfamiliar one for Eastern Europe, and it is a precedent that Poland's allies must find unsettling' (1981: xiii).

Unsettling indeed, as we will see. And yet the months after the Accord, having garnered the momentum of the mass strike, *Solidarity*, by now numbering 9.5 million members, was able to assemble as *constituent assembly* to enact nothing short of a *Labour Constitution*. At a Congress that took place in two stages, in September 1981, 896 delegates representing 9.5 million members (well over half the working population of Poland) put forward the *'Programme for National Revival'*. 'The country's present situation', it reads, 'necessitates a two-sided program: immediate actions to see us through the difficult winter period; and, at the same time, a program of economic reform, which can no longer be postponed, of social politics and reconstruction of public life—a program which points toward a *self-governed republic.*' The recognition of status, the application of subsidiarity in democratic decision-making and the

(London 1981). Coverage in western Europe was contradictory in a most revealing way. *L Unità* in Italy had insisted throughout the summer that 'this was a crisis not just of the economy but of the socio-political system as such'. The editorial explains that 'an economy of a socialist type, especially one which has emerged from a period of emergency, isolation, or the heroic phase of take-off, cannot be directed only from above. It means that in order to get men involved in a productive and above all creative effort, there is need for a new development of democracy and participation ... This development cannot be confined to the party, a party which is making itself identical to the state' (306). On the other hand, the PCF's *L'Humanité*, with a permanent correspondent in Gdansk, reported only 'work stoppages', with economic, never political, demands. The PCF's weekly reported in July that 'the party of the working class [was] playing its role. The structures of self-government are very much developed. Problems are solved through discussion with the whole work force.' (Quoted in R. Schneider, 'PCF: The little echo of Warsaw', *L Express*, 6 Sept. 1980.) As late as 23 August, it reported that 'the major fact at present is the discussion going on within the party.' Other useful bibliography: MacDonald (1983); Laba (1991); Tittenbrun (1993); Glasman (1994).

establishment of enterprise democracy formed the basis of the proposed reforms, drawing from '"the workers" and democratic traditions of the labour world', it claimed. 'Society looks on us as the only guarantors of the agreements that have been signed. This is why the union considers that its main task is to take every possible short- and long-term action to save the country from bankruptcy, and society from poverty, despondency and self-destruction. The only way forward is to renew both state and economy through democratic social initiatives in every field. ... By implementing a comprehensive and profound reform, we shall be able to tap all those reserves of industriousness rooted in our society that have not been tapped so far' (367).

Among the first concerns was a commitment to social protection. Parts IV and V of the 'Solidarity Program' contain an extended discussion of labour protection and social service policy, identifying 'the trade union law [as] our most precious asset',[3] while Part VI establishes the foundations of the 'Self-Governed Republic'. Most notable amongst its theses, *thesis* 4 states that '[i]n its policy the Union will be governed by the principle that the terms of transition must guarantee the real income level of the less prosperous part of society. ... While acting with equal concern for each citizen we will accord particular solicitude to the poorest.' *Thesis 9* establishes that 'the right to work must be guaranteed, and the wage system overhauled'. *Thesis* 19 defends '[p]luralism of social, political and cultural ideas [as] the basis of democracy in the self-governed republic'. The emphasis is on re-invigorating civil society: 'For this reason, we shall struggle both for a change in state structures and for the development of independent, self-governing institutions in every field of social life. Only such a course can guarantee that the institutions of public life are in harmony with human needs.' *Thesis* 20 counters managerial prerogative: 'Genuine workers' self-management is the basis of the self-governing republic. The only solution is to create workers' self-management committees *which would make the workforce true masters of enterprises.* Our union demands that the self-management principle should be reintroduced into the cooperatives. It is essential to pass a new law protecting the cooperatives against interference by the

---

[3] 'The system which ties political to economic power, based on continual party interference in the functioning of enterprises, is the main reason for the present crisis of the Polish economy. The so-called nomenklatura principle rules out any rational cadre promotion policy, rendering the millions of workers who do not belong to any party second-class citizens.' (Part 4, para. 6)

state administration.' And concludes: 'The only way to change the situation is to create *genuine self-management* groups. The establishment of employees' councils was the means by which the responsibility of decision-making and the knowledge for successful enterprise adaptation were facilitated by access to information and the negotiation of strategic choices by all employees in the firm.' And in what reads like a direct passage from Karl Polanyi, '*work is for man, and what determines its sense is its closeness to man, to his real needs.* Our national and social rebirth must be based on the restored hierarchy of those goals.'

The *State Enterprise and Employee Self-Management Acts* were passed in October 1981. *Solidarity* made all other goals subordinate to co-determination, threatening a general strike if it were not implemented. This was the high mark of labour constitutionalism, its pure *autogestion-naire* expression, enacting an 'unfettered' economic democracy in a gesture of constituent power.

What followed is well known. A few months later, *Solidarity*'s leaders were arrested and the organisation was outlawed. 'In Poland in 1981, as in France in 1848, the army was sent in ... and democracy in the economy was decried as damaging to the national interest. The nomination of management by the state was restored.' And yet, Glasman continues, 'the imposition of martial law did not succeed in extirpating the ghost of *Solidarity*. Although ten thousand union activists were imprisoned, the decentralized structure of the union was flexible enough to mount rolling strikes which in May 1988 forced the party to share power' (Glasman, 1996: 96).

In the end it was not repression, but co-option, that 'extirpated the ghost of *Solidarity*'. The fall of the communist regime in 1989 ushered in a policy of State centralisation to create competition, and any notion of enterprise democracy was abandoned for good. The installation of market discipline took a massive toll on society and on working people. Alain Supiot (2010a) makes the important point, in *L'esprit de Philadelphie,* that in the discourse of 'enlargement', Europe significantly missed an opportunity to understand the process as one of *re-unification.* The difference is one of asymmetry. In exporting the market model eastwards, he says, no attempt was made to take account of the experience of these countries which did not share our political culture or anything like our material wealth. He argues that re-unification would have instead implied a kind of Marshall plan for the East with the condition attached that these countries would abstain from recourse to social dumping in order to compete with the western counterpart. What we saw instead was the opposite. The West made all aid conditional on pursuing a reform strategy 'the likes of which no modern western nation had ever considered imposing on itself for fear of the effects it would have on people's lives and livelihoods.'[4] One could add the following twist to Supiot's concern that Europe may have been 'won over to the communist market economy' (see the *Laval* and *Viking* decisions, earlier): that the annexation of the East followed the pattern of a *market Leninism*, led by market commissars on the basis of managerial prowess, technique and superior knowledge.[5]

Let us stay with *Solidarity*'s *constituent* achievement, because the Accord of 1980 and the Programme of 1981 offer us rare insight into the exercise of constituent power. The transferral of democratic categories from the sphere of citizenship to the sphere of work taps the rich, if under-theorised, resource of European constitutional thinking that enjoins democratic and collective categories. At stake here is the capacity to use political and democratic categories to conceptualise and regulate work, as is the question of recognition that concerns the constitutively political, collective and human activity that is labour. That this is more than a loose metaphor is borne out by how significant an opportunity was missed after the fall of the Iron Curtain to tap the resources of a civil society in a moment of genuine emergence, to understand the 'conjuncture', to promote the vital reserves of societies submitted to decades of devastation and undercutting. Granted, the promise of the market resonated with the form of the East's eagerness to negate the past. But Negri is surely right when he says that in those mobilisations of 1989 we 'saw the expression of a potential that was unknown to us in the West – a fully active civil society capable [in those moments at least] of expressing a collective political will in a way no longer found in the west' (Negri, 1990). These were indeed extraordinary accomplishments of working men and women, and they are sacrifices that the historiography of Europe as breathless pursuit of market integration has by and large misinterpreted or simply eliminated.

And yet in the Paris Commune, in the cooperative movement, in the Gdansk uprising, we encounter a novelty of political form that a different legacy of economic democracy has betrothed us. That the '*praxis that revolutionised reality*', to use an expression of one of the *new* Europe's

---

[4] Even Poland, by no means opposed to 'privatisation' saw warning strikes against the 'pauperisation' across the country in the wake of the Privatization Acts of 91–2.

[5] For the use of the term and for an incisive analysis, see Glasman (1996).

most famous sons,⁶ was received by the other side, first, in 1981, as an attack on socialism orchestrated by foreign forces, then, in 1989, as a call to be *annexed* to the market economy of maximising financial returns and at the cost of painful 'learning' processes of market discipline, misreads its message as it is programmed to do. In terms of the constitutional imaginary, on both registers of agency and action, Solidarity was a workers movement that sought representation where it was already represented; that sought a republic of work in what was nominally a workers' republic; that levelled a political demand where the demand could never have been more than an economic demand for wage or price adjustment. In every sense theirs was a *différend* in the precise way in which Jean-Francois Lyotard introduces the term where the means available to 'litigate' the conflict, here between workers and the government, *compounds the wrong* inflicted on the workers. The constituent strains against forms of the constituted that always-already lend it expression and before which it appears as theoretically naïve and politically dangerous; in other words, as nothing short of a scandal.

Democracy as Enactment: The Legacy of Athens

But then democracy first broke onto the scene as a *scandal*. This idea is articulated by Johann Bachofen as far back as 1861 in connection to tragedy and Dionysus, god of 'intoxication and the *antiform*'. For the deeply conservative, and profound 'mythologist' Bachofen, this 'sensualisation coincides with the dissolution of political organisation and with the decay of the life of the state. In place of the richly articulated hierarchy one finds the affirmation of the law of democracy, of the indistinct masses ... and which belong to the carnal aspect, the material side of human nature.'⁷ The latter refers to Dionysus' all-female *thiasoi*, integral to the otherness and ambiguity of what Richard Seaford memorably calls the 'cult of Dionysus'.⁸ We saw earlier, in Chapter 1.2, how Euripides ushers in this 'dissolution' with the *Bacchae*, with which the Apollonian moment of 'logos', which in *Helen* has come undone, is overflown by the 'last force of the old nature' and disappears into the

---

⁶ G. Lukacs, *Dialectique et Spontaneité* , unearthed only in 2001 in the ancient archives of the Lenin Institute in Moscow.
⁷ Bachofen, Preface to *Maternal* Law, 1861/1992, quoted in Bloch (1986: 107).
⁸ 'Dionysus is a god of the wild and the margins, who is also a stranger, a foreigner (ξένος). Rather than marking boundaries he crosses them' (Seaford, 1994: 250).

recesses of the Dionysian return to the ecstatic, to paroxysm ('*paralerema*') and the irrational (the α-λογον). In the *Bacchae* Euripides extols the supreme and final victory of Dionysus in a moment of high symbolism and radical undoing, literally a dismemberment, where Agaue with the help of the maenads of her all-female *thiasos* tear to pieces her own son Pentheus, King and representative of the polis of Thebes.[9] But the *Bacchae* is unusual in that respect. If tragedy is the dramatic enactment of myth before the citizens of the polis, it ordinarily carries a *containment of anomic phenomena*. Against this context, we might think of tragedy as the art-form that tracks the way that democracy erupted in the Athenian polis as a scandal, carrying the unruly sentiments of the populace onto the public sphere. It is a scandal because it turns on the antagonism that ruptures the logic of rule of monarchical city-states and the 'royal household',[10] and carries its necessary excess into publicness where the constitutive political surplus strains at the form of the 'politeia'.

Politeia of course means 'constitution' and Plato gives his treatise that title (translated as *Republic*) because *form* would discipline the political, as prior to it and accommodating of it. As Sheldon Wolin puts it,

> A form supplied a distinctive character, structure, order, and boundaries and a mode of ruling in which power was sublimated into presiding over and preserving the identity of that form. A constitutional form signified a structure to which politics should conform and become the kind of politics expressive of that constitution. Whatever did not conform was extra-constitutional, improper, illegal, and non- or anti-political.
>
> (Wolin, 1994: 49)

For Plato, that supreme champion of form, democracy was the scandal of an 'improper manifestation', a phenomenology off-kilter. Bernard Waldenfels reminds us that Plato opens the *Republic* with a discussion of an 'outrage' (2017). Athenian democracy had decided on the execution of Socrates, the man who in his very being exemplified it. For Plato, this is a wayward, inchoate politics, formless and unruly. Histories of

---

[9] Nietzsche offers a short and rather unconvincing dismissal of the tragedy. We do not need to dwell on this. What perhaps does need some dwelling on is a different trajectory, in Euripides' own oeuvre. If Nietzsche is right, and Euripides' early plays sacrifice the depth of, say, Aeschylus' theology, could it be that the *Bacchae* offer a culmination of sorts, as continuous to the rationalisation of the early plays but which now, contra Nietzsche, has nowhere to go except to implode on the unyielding limit of necessity? That is what I argued in Chapter 1.2.

[10] For Seaford, 'tragedy is the mythical representation of the self-destruction of the powerful (and often introverted) family' which is 'salutary to the polis' (1994: 342–3).

democracy that trace their origin to Ancient Greece ignore a crucial bifurcation that confronts such lineages. The constitutional form that Plato, and then Aristotle, celebrated, the agora and the free-flowing discourse of the paragons of Hellas, is not the democracy of Pericles, of the fifth century, of Sophocles and Euripides.[11] Athenian democracy – and Rancière again uses the same term 'scandal' to describe it, as did Bachofen, Waldenfels and Wood – involved the 'horde' of the poor, who lacked qualification as citizens, putting themselves on the scene in a way that upset 'the distribution of sense'. Ellen Meiksins Wood (1989) points out that democracy is scandalous because it involved an explosive radicalisation expressed in the function of drawing lots to determine the distribution of offices and the exercise of power. Importantly, she argues, the drawing of lots is democratic because the beneficiary is *not* a representative. Rancière says: 'Politics begins when those "who have no part in anything" protest, in the name of an overarching community, against the wrong inflicted by other parties.' Thus the supreme achievement of the Greek polis is the 'scandal' that the horde who have nothing, become *the people*, the political community of free Athenians. 'What they bring to the community strictly speaking is contention. The mass of men without qualities identify with the community in the name of the wrong done to them' (Rancière, 1999: 8). Democracy signals, to begin with, the rupture with form.

It is interesting that the later *aporiae* with which we have been engaging, between constituent democracy and constitutional form find here their earliest expression. On the one hand, 'the form was assigned a monopoly over the political and became the locus of legitimate politics. It reconstitutes politics as identity' (Wolin, 1994: 49). But it was confronted with the scandal of irrationality, of the aleatory institution of drawing lots to assign people to public office, and the demand 'to be counted' leveraged on a contentious commonality, a recognition that was forced by those who had no qualification to make the demand. Plato protests that democracy has no *archē* and no measure. Instead the 'singularity of the act of the demos – a κρατεῖν rather than ἄρχειν – is dependent on an originary disorder or miscount' (Rancière, 1992: 59). For both, *an outrage attends the democratic polis*. For Plato, the constitution must provide

---

[11] A closer, less schematic historical view, would need to include here at least the institutional changes by Solon, and later Cleisthenes, which gave Athenian democracy its very particular character. Without too much distortion however, we might identify the end of the fifth century as the transition between the 'radical democracy' of the fifth century and the 'constitutional democracy' of the fourth. (See Hignett, 1952: ch. 9.)

the form and *a priori* shape, the articulation prior to consent and defining of it;' (Wolin, 1994: 49). For the 'horde', any submission to form enacts another closure against democracy's *necessary* excess, another inadmission, its *constitutive* political surplus, constitutive because it must resist becoming locked within the logic of receiving form. The idea of a *constitutive surplus* is important in this description, as it has been in the history we have visited in Chapter 2.1 and throughout, as an expression of what makes for *constituent* power and what confronts it with the difficulty that its opportunity is thwarted by the very language in which it is summoned. And yet there is something about the 'scandal' of its originary moment, that imports a democratic demand for public reason to become reflexive of the terms in which it thinks. Let me explain this as a moment of critical phenomenology, with the help of Rancière, though it appears only fleetingly in *Disagreement* where it is introduced. He says of the forged 'contentious commonality' that claims its stage, that it 'speaks, is counted, and deliberates at the assembly, causing wordsmiths to write: εδοξε τω δημω' (1999: 9). This Rancière translates as 'it has pleased the people, the people have decided', but it better translates as 'it seemed to the people', or it 'appeared (right) to the people', and the difference is significant because it captures something of the phenomenological breakthrough that achieves 'the introduction of a visible into the field of experience, which then modifies the regime of the visible'. It achieves the appearance of 'something as something to the demos', and given that nothing in this formulation is settled, the reflexivity introduced receives no prior measure of warrant. Democracy is the animus that 'stirs up political philosophy because it is not a set of institutions or one kind of regime among others *but a way for politics to be*' (1999: 99).

There is much to admire here in Rancière's analysis, and much to unpack that is relevant to the discussion of 'autogestion and rupture', more generally. But note also how it connects back to *Solidarity*, especially as it concerns the moment of 'staging the collective' and the antagonistic form-giving practice. After all, *Solidarity*, too, broke on to the scene as a scandal. Its claim to speak on behalf of the working people of Poland defied the institutions that were instituted to represent the people and to carry its voice. *Solidarity*'s claim was to represent the demos of work, *its* action, *its* community, against the given distribution of sense. The scandal was first hushed, then displaced in the only terms that it could be accommodated, as an economic demand put to the Party leadership. But the demands of *Solidarity* for free unions, for the collective rights to association, for recognition of their fallen heroes, for the democratic control of workplaces and decisions over production and the conditions of work, were political demands that in the act of being presented also restored the integrity of their proper signification, and returned dignity to those terms: association, syndicalism, representation, economic democracy. Theirs was a claim to justice, not to better management, presented as a challenge to the ways in which meaning is ordered and policed, a disclosure that was brought about performatively.

Rancière offers the term 'dissensus' to make sense of the antagonism that is at the root of the phenomenology of the form-giving event. We might pursue it in three directions.

First, over appearance, 'doxa' and truth. If democracy is a 'scandal' for Plato it is because it pivots on the equivalence of two terms: *demos* and *doxa*. 'Doxa' for Plato means nothing more than that 'it has pleased [seemed right to] those who know only those illusions of more or less that are called pleasure and pain'. But appearance – what εδοξε τω δημω – is not an illusion that is opposed to the real. *Doxa* is *appearance* of something to the people. A regime of visibility is forged, something is made to appear. Rancière interjects that the formula 'simple doxa' carries a dual message, 'appearance *for* the people, appearance *of* the people'. Something profound has occurred in this simple equivalence. The political is identified with 'simple doxa' and claimed for the first time *its truth against* the proper distribution of sense. Which is why the doxa of the demos, public opinion, is subsequently identified by Plato as the form of untruth, the scandalous appearance of the people and their 'belief' that carries nothing of the sanction and warrant of truth. Plato can be granted his objection that the democratic doxa carries no warrant of truth, but this is because a new distribution of sense is also *a new distribution of criteria over what counts as a warrant*. The simultaneity of the 'for' and the 'of' in Rancière's formulation of equivalence, tied together in the emergence of democracy, reconfigures the field in which 'doxa' – the meaning of the people's opinion – appears and the stakes against which its truth will be measured. It is a constituent moment that binds the will to no measure external to its occurrence. Thus democracy, which *animates* politics, carries with it the possibility of a critical intervention such that reconfigures the space of appearance.

Secondly, the invocation of 'an overarching community'. Against the ordinary sequence, this is a community that comes about *through* the invocation, assuming the wager that the invocation may fail to call anything forth. What is certain is that at the time of its invocation it 'arches' over nothing. It is only 'over-arching' if the merger succeeds and the 'two worlds come into one' (in Rancière's oft-repeated formulation) in order that community might come to span them both. The merger is between the world that reproduces the given distribution of places and signs, and the world of those whose claim is disqualified by that distribution. The very creation of community in those circumstances is contentious, and that is why Rancière refers to '*the setting-up of a contentious commonality*'. It engages those 'who have no part' in a performative interpretation of community, 'performative' in that it transforms that which it interprets. It will be overarching if it succeeds, but its success depends on a reconfiguration of the political terrain such that the contestation may be seen in retrospect as having been a contestation about (an overarching) community all along.[12]

Thirdly, the objection to a wrong inflicted. Here is Rancière's formulation: 'Politics begins when those "who have no part in anything" protest, in the name of an overarching community, against the wrong inflicted by other parties.' A wrong is not just exclusion of those who have no part in anything, but the sealing over of that exclusion. The wrong inflicts invisibility. And that is why its redress cannot be simply an injunction against exclusion, because such an injunction is meaningless ('of course you are included': see above, Chapter 4.1) but can only take the form of *dissensus*, which is the modality in which politics occurs. Dissensus evokes a different distribution (of meaning) than that which is orchestrated in the field of the politics of consensus, rational discourse and the principle of *altera pars audiatur* ('listen to the other side') that animates it. Here the ambition is greater as it taps a *critical phenomenological move:* how is it that the political can be made to appear otherwise than as granted by institutional opportunity of the order of the police?

Key to Rancière's invitation to reconceptualise the field of politics is *the axiomatic sense of equality.* If equality provides the key, it is because it sustains the field of the political and acts against its closure around any given distribution of advantage. The axiomatic of equality is a forever accompanying reference or presupposition of the political, demanding to be verified. It is a point of departure, 'an axiom anterior to the

---

[12] In Rancière's formulation of the retroaction: 'The demos attributes to itself as its proper lot the equality that belongs to all citizens. In so doing, this party that is not one identifies its improper property with the exclusive principle of community and identifies its name – the name of the indistinct mass of men of no position – with the name of the community itself' (1999: 8–9). The new designation of subjects that upsets existing distributions of subject-positions and displaces social identification suggests a new unity, a new representation of the people.

constitution of a particular staging of politics and which makes such a staging possible', as Kristin Ross puts it (Ross, 2009: 26). Significantly the axiomatic of equality sustains an argument about inclusion as *irreducible*, the quality of democracy as reflexive, and politics as a forever renewed invitation to meet its demand. If the 'part that has no part' can claim its demand in the first place, it is because it can claim it as a demand to be treated as an equal partner and not as labour force whose 'recognition' would commit them à la Arendt to the domain of necessity. It is equality that holds up the possibility, however fleeting, that the logic of meeting social needs and the logic of political participation might articulate in a politics of economic democracy, and a politics of social citizenship, where the conjunction of terms is not seen or ignored as a category mistake (Arendt, renewed by Habermas) but where social and political categories operate *in tandem*. What forces the constitutive articulation is equality, whose claim can never be fully discharged and be done with. The distinction between the claim to equality (politics) and the distribution of political opportunity through existing institutions (police) is what constitutes, for Rancière, the space of emancipatory politics, and since the institutions of capitalist democracy are constitutively incapable of realising equality, the cleavage that sustains political action remains open.

It does not involve a large step to then see that in this dynamic contestation, *political subjectification* – the notion of becoming-subject – is constitutively linked to the logic of dissensus. With an eye also to what we said earlier about aesthetic acts, about what literature meant to the authors of the 'little narratives' of the *Nights of Labour*, a political subject is not a subject that 'finds its voice' within the existing opportunity structure of subject positions, but a capacity for enunciation not previously available. Because as subjects they begin, as they only can, from *misrecognition*. Recognition and representation are conflictual; they take place in a field of conflict and contestation. The conflict is not accommodated on a plane organised by consensus at any level or meta-level. It is important from the point of view of political phenomenology that what emerges is a new state of representation, not as a mere *assertion* of presence (of the 'we') but as an intervention that aims to reconfigure the political unity of the whole. The 'we' does not affirm any *given* intersubjectivity; instead – I borrow here Carrol Clarkson's beautiful formulation – 'the "we" announces the ephemeral and unstable limit of its reference' (Clarkson, 2014: 164).

The *event is form-giving*. What appears politically appears *as* interruption in the order of the police, which is, as we saw, Rancière's term for the institutional opportunity structure in place, opportunity spanning both what is actual and what is potential within it. This is not the pure act of the pure performative on a clean slate, as it were, it is not the general will that simply has to will to produce law, a position often ascribed to Rousseau and Robespierre. As Marx says in *The Civil War in France*, '[t]he working class did not expect miracles from the Commune. They have *no ready-made utopias to introduce par décret du peuple*. They know that in order to work out their own emancipation ... they will have to pass through long struggles, through a series of historic processes, transforming circumstances and men' (Marx: 1871/1972). The 'passage through' involves a field thick with content. This iconoclastic impetus, the moment of antagonism captures both the notion of rupture, but also that which, beyond the ruptured context, might leverage the moment of *autogestion*. We have looked at rupture and looked at how it informs the radical tradition on the registers of agency and action, in its original manifestation in Athenian democracy, in *Solidarity*'s radical experimentation at workers' self-government. Between the two, stands the supreme moment of *autogestionnaire* politics, of the workers of Paris 'storming heaven', as Marx memorably put it,[13] the Commune of 1871. We will now go on to look at the way it informed the ruptural principle par excellence, the *mass strike*.

The Mass Strike: Luxemburg, Sorel, Benjamin

Appearing within a couple of years from each other, the two key texts of the twentieth century on the mass strike were written in the long shadow of the expulsion of the Anarcho-syndicalists from the First International in 1872, a year after the defeat of the communards in Paris. Rosa Luxemburg's 1906 *The Mass Strike, the Political Party and the Trade Unions* and Georges Sorel's 1908 *Reflections on Violence* are the two final major theorisations of the *mass strike*, of its meaning and its tactical and strategic deployments. For both authors the expulsion from the International of Bakunin and his circle would have been formative, especially for the French unionists, the majority of whom were anarchists in the tradition of Proudhon. Key to the contestation was the role of the state. For Bakunin the Commune had been 'a bold, clearly formulated negation of the State'. For Marx, as we saw earlier, the unexpected event

---

[13] From Marx's letter to Kugelmann, 12 April 1871.

of the Commune had forced nothing short of a radical re-discovery of the 'political form ... under which to work out the economical emancipation of labor'. The economic emancipation of labour presupposes political forms that are themselves emancipatory. That is the 'lesson' that Marx takes from the Commune: '[t]he State form ... the political instrument of their enslavement cannot serve as the political instrument of their emancipation. ... The Commune was a revolution against the State itself ... a resumption by the people for the people of its own social life.' Had it been able to last, 'the Communal Constitution would have restored to the social body all the forces *hitherto absorbed by the state parasite feeding upon, and clogging the free movement of, society. By this one act, it would have initiated the regeneration of France.*' Far more important than any of the measures or laws the Commune managed to pass, says Marx in *The Civil War in France,* was simply 'its own working existence': the expansive, thoroughly democratic nature of its organisation. Its discovery of a 'thoroughly expansive political form', a 'completely new historical creation' was for Marx what made the Commune 'the greatest revolution of the century'. In that sense too the tradition of social republicanism and worker self-government that can be traced back to 1789 and 1848 finds its culmination in the Paris Commune, as the moment of constituent power in the political form most adequate to carry its exercise.

Marx writes this in 1871. Later in that year the Commune is liquidated in a bloodbath. '*Working, thinking, fighting, bleeding Paris*; almost forgetful, in its incubation of a new society, of the cannibals at its gates – radiant in the enthusiasm of its historic initiative' (Marx, 1871/1972). In 1872 the anarchists are expelled from the First International. A year later, at their Congress at Geneva they proclaim the general strike as a weapon for overthrowing the bourgeoisie by the mere cessation of work. This debate that remained alive at the end of the nineteenth century in the turbulent currents of European Leftist politics, set the background for Luxemburg's and Sorel's major theorisations of the *mass strike,* as did the more immediate tactics of the 1905 revolution in Russia, that 'dress rehearsal' as Lenin put it, with its extensive deployment of work stoppages. A third key text on the mass strike appears a decade later; Walter Benjamin's *Critique of Violence* is different both in focus and in range. But what we might say of all three texts is that they are marked by a belief in the pragmatics of strike action, certainly in the spontaneity of its eruption, and more importantly in its stakes. At the same time the texts have been sites of extraordinary polemics. Luxemburg is caught in the crossfire of two conflicts, with the reformist SPD on the one hand,[14] and the anarchists on the other.[15] The polemics with Bernstein in the context of the former, with the 'Bakuninists' on the other (and a decade later of course with Lenin, Trotsky and Lukács) are legendary. Sorel's work has been tainted by the adoption of its concepts 'myth' by the Italian fascists, for sure; and if that was, certainly, a reductive misreading, other misreadings of it abound. Certainly less worrying, and less reductive, has been Derrida's influential reading of Benjamin on the mass strike and on 'divine violence'. The double refraction of its reception and dissemination through his 'Force of Law' (Derrida's paper is a close reading of Walter Benjamin's *Critique of Violence*) has bestowed legal philosophy the dubious gift of an indirect reckoning: Derrida reading Benjamin reading Sorel.

We look at all three texts in turn. They can be seen as variations on the theme of the comprehensive withdrawal of work as catastrophic to capitalism, in line with Marx of *The Class Struggles in France*: 'The right to work is, in the bourgeois sense, an absurdity, a miserable, pious wish ... But behind the right to work stands the power over capital.'

*

Luxemburg begins her essay by drawing on the experience of the 1905 revolution in Russia, and the institution of the Petersburg Soviet. 'In order to carry out a direct political struggle as a mass the proletariat must be assembled as a mass', she writes in *The Mass Strike* as she extols the role that industrial action has played in the self-education and self-organisation of the Russian proletariat. In Russia she sees 'fermenting throughout the whole of the immense empire an uninterrupted economic strike of almost the entire proletariat against capital' (1906: 29) and then: 'a year of revolution has given the Russian proletariat the training which thirty years of parliamentary and trade union struggle cannot artificially give to the German proletariat' (1906: 64). When she attempts to generalise the experience ('the mass strike is shown not to be a specifically Russian product but *a universal form* of the proletarian class struggle'),

---

[14] A few months before the publication of *The Mass Strike*, the Socialist Party at its congress in Jena had adopted a resolution, moved by Bebel, to limit the use of the general strike.

[15] 'Anarchism has become in the Russian revolution [of 1905] not the theory of the struggling proletariat but the ideological sign-board of the counter-revolutionary lumpenproletariat, who like a school of sharks, swarm in the wake of the battleship of the revolution. And therewith the historical career of anarchism is well-nigh ended.' (Luxemburg, 1906/1925: 14)

numerous equivocations and tensions will gather in and around this acquisition of 'universal form'. Luxemburg struggles to sustain a refusal of any mediation of workers' constituent self-expression, and this infects her discussion of the 'form' of *the constituent*, which sustains itself imperfectly in mobilisation and withdrawal, impossible to contain or predict its course, until it becomes once again bound, caught in a series of antinomies of the 'in-between' – of socialism in Germany and in Russia, of economic and political struggle, of unionised and unionised workforces, and finally of spontaneity and the law-like phenomena that develop around it. Already in the introduction of the text, Luxemburg insists:

> If, therefore, the [1905] Russian Revolution teaches us anything, it teaches above all that the mass strike is not artificially 'made,' not 'decided' at random, not 'propagated,' but that it is a historical phenomenon which, at a given moment, results from social conditions with historical inevitability. It is not, therefore, by abstract speculations on the possibility or impossibility, the utility or the injuriousness of the mass strike, but only by an examination of those factors and social conditions out of which the mass strike grows in the present phase of the class struggle.

What does her invitation to immanence mean, to learn from the concrete situation in Russia, to draw conclusions about the mass strike 'as it has passed through a definite history in Russia?' If it is caught in its particular history, produced and defined through its history, how then to abstract from the concrete situation in order to generalise the phenomenon across the experience of the Russian and German proletariat? She will insist against any blueprint, abstract form or abstract *Sollen*, imposed on this concreteness. She does not always navigate the terrain convincingly, but what remains above all is the spirit of her text, its unwavering commitment to the 'reciprocal relation' that will allow both Germany and Russia to learn from 'the un-invented tactics of spontaneous struggle seeking its way forward'. In *The Broken Middle*, Gillian Rose calls 'diremptive' the 'and' that holds the antinomy of the mass strike together (economic *and* political, unionised *and* non-unionised, Germany *and* Russia); and she opposes it to the 'aporetic' (1992: 215). The joinings are not aporetic, she argues, because they do not prevent passage; 'diremption', or the 'broken middle', instead installs itself in the in-between of terms that are not, and could not be, tied in a dialectic relationship. Caught in the in-between of the terms of those many antinomies, the mass strike does not overcome or transcend them. Instead the notion of the mass strike *dwells in that antinomy*, and Luxemburg's is a metaphorical idiom that attests the antinomies in a language that carries the strike across many forms, in equivocation, transferral and displacement:

> The mass strike, as the Russian Revolution shows it to us, is such a changeable phenomenon that it reflects all the phases of the political and economic struggle, all stages and factors of the revolution. Its adaptability, its efficiency, the factors of its origin are constantly changing. It suddenly opens new and wide perspectives of the revolution when it appears to have already arrived in a narrow pass and where it is impossible for anyone to reckon upon it with any degree of certainty. It flows now like a broad billow over the whole kingdom, and now divides into a gigantic network of narrow streams; now it bubbles forth from under the ground like a fresh spring and now is completely lost under the earth. Political and economic strikes, mass strikes and partial strikes, demonstrative strikes and fighting strikes, general strikes of individual branches of industry and general strikes in individual towns, peaceful wage struggles and street massacres, barricade fighting – all these run through one another, run side by side, cross one another, flow in and over one another – it is a ceaselessly moving, changing sea of phenomena. And the law of motion of these phenomena is clear: it does not lie in the mass strike itself nor in its technical details, but in the political and social proportions of the forces of the revolution.
>
> (Luxemburg, 1906/1925: 43–4)

There is much to discuss and admire in this piece, actions that cross, flow into and over one another, overflow, mass action that divides and bubbles forth. There is nothing abstract that can be superimposed as blueprint to identify the mass strike, and nothing law-like contains it or lends it legibility, as the political and the economic, the organised and the non-unionised 'run side by side'. The labile form attests to the spontaneity of the strike action.

And while we note the productive antinomy in the way that it undergirds and 'overflows' its spontaneous expression, there is at the same time something highly determinate about Luxemburg's analysis, and instructive to political practice. Note that the extract ends on the term revolution, as the concept that ultimately gathers together the erratic and unsystematic developments, crossings and passages of the strike action. Writing in the wake of the 1905 events in St Petersburg, Luxemburg is keen to read the break-up of the general strike into partial and local actions as configurations, tactics and manoeuvres of a revolutionary movement. If she is tracing the 'transmission of struggle from one centre to another', it is because the transmission expresses a deeper continuity of struggle, rather than the episodes (the barricades, the wage struggles, the occupations) being definitive or exhaustive; the surface heterogeneity taps the ongoing maturation of class consciousness, and the fluctuations track in proportionate forms the deeper currents of revolutionary intent.

Historically, Luxemburg's stance is here at odds with other strands of industrial democracy that link it constitutionally to the State. The 'autogestionnaire' variant of industrial democracy that she develops, with its emphasis on strike action, is clearly separated from the state, and her gaze, in 1905 at least, is turned to the east and the theory, and latterly practice, of socialism under the Bolsheviks. And while it is anachronistic to make Luxemburg a full participant in the Weimar constitutional discussion, it is clear that *autogestion* stands in clear contrast to its State-organised other. The latter is a split tradition (both strands flourished in Germany) that comprises both that of 'economic constitutionalism' in the meaning that Sinzheimer and Neumann gave to it, and that of the associational social democracy principally associated with Gierke. In the first instance, the constitutional function (of the 'economic constitution') is that of 'announcing' the economic actors, of granting a speaking position to the workers, and in that sense constitutionally implicating them in dialogue as partners at the level of the state.[16] In the associational pluralist model, the emphasis is on giving constitutional protection to *intermediate associations*.

But there is more that Luxemburg's analysis offers to the theorisation of *autogestion* and rupture understood in tandem. There is rupture in Luxemburg's insistence that the available forms will not suffice; her exacerbation with the excessive and debilitating organisation of German trade unions, their overly cautious and complacently teleological approach to struggle.[17] Socialist democracy begins simultaneously with the beginnings of the destruction of class rule ('the mass strike is the rallying idea of the whole period of the class struggle'); in the moment of the mass strike everything is actual, and crucially the mass strike is *premature*: no historical logic delivers it and the conditions of the legibility of class action are not given in advance of its undertaking. Her insistence on what is 'fermented' and 'compounded' in the undertaking itself runs through the text. And there is *autogestion* in the 'spontaneity': constituted power and the rules of representation dissolve before the mass strike that 'alters its forms, its dimensions, its effects'. So much is clear. But there is a final thought that

---

[16] See Dukes (2008) and (2014).
[17] Rose, 1992: 213. See Luxemburg: 'Dame History from afar, smilingly hoaxes the bureaucratic lay figures who keep grim watch at the gate over the fate of German trade unions' (1906/1925: 35).

Luxemburg offers us, and it holds autogestion *and* rupture together in the way that Rose's term diremption intimates: the mass strike is not the exercise of constituent power *tout court*. It is the river, said Luxemburg, 'that overflows its banks, that divides into tributaries that join again': it is the power that upsets and reconfigures its path-dependencies as it is exercised, it is in the 'crossings' and 'transmissions' that it finds expression. In the deep equivocation between what is rationally gathered as the collective action of the emerging proletariat, that must remain spontaneous to the measure that nothing except its action collects it as an actor, and the lawlike conditions that might offer us a general description of the mass strike, sharpening its features, relating them across particular contexts, and abstracting from the particularity of place and industrial organisation, there lies the spectre of available form and the limit, caught up – we might say with Rose – in a restless affirmation *and* undermining of political form.[18]

In later exchanges, when the soviet that Luxemburg so admires in 1905, is given over to more sclerotic organisational form under the Bolsheviks,[19] Luxemburg will criticise the dispersal of the Constituent assembly by Lenin and Trotsky's 'rigid and schematic views', the role of Lenin's 'revolutionary political directorate' and the suppression of political freedoms. Lukács will in turn criticise her – 'the unsurpassed prophet of revolutionary Marxism' he calls her – for her 'spontaneous voluntarism'. 'For Luxemburg,' he says, 'experience demonstrates that ... the living fluid of the popular mood continuously flows around the representative bodies, penetrates, guides them', and this leads her 'to overestimate the spontaneous, elemental forces of the revolution, above all in the class summoned by history to lead it' (1923/1971: 277).[20]

*

If for Rosa Luxemburg *autogestion* must be guarded against the state form as the stake of a spontaneity that ultimately alone expresses the

---

[18] See Rose, 1992: 154–8. For Rose, this equivocation of the middle (the 'broken middle' of her title) *suspends* the ethical: it neither surrenders it nor posits it. It points to an 'aporetic universalism', a universalism that defies any easy passage, any commutability between universal and particular (law and love) and posits nothing.

[19] To whom she had given her support in 1907; in Stuttgart, in the Congress of the Second International, Luxemburg presented the anti-war resolution together with Lenin.

[20] For Lukács this formulation underplays how clearly the move – especially in the French experience – had been to purge recalcitrant elements from the parliamentary bodies, not to accommodate, flow around ... and guide them. The transformations that Rosa speaks of, for Lukács 'came devilishly close' to dispersing them (1923/1971: 279).

constituent 'we' of the workers' self-expression in emergent, reversible, re-negotiable institutional forms, Georges Sorel's analysis carries little of the fluidity of Luxemburg's. His major work is published two years later and shares with hers the central emphasis on the mass strike. There is less of the 'anxiety of authorship' in Sorel, and no 'broken middle' or 'diremption' upsets the rigidity of his dichotomy between the general proletarian strike as constituent action, in opposition to mere 'political strikes' with their incremental demands. In contrast to such partial instrumentalities, the proletarian general strike is the lever of the self-constitution of the proletariat. The general strike, he says unequivocally, is 'the myth in which Socialism is wholly comprised' (1908/1999: 145).[21] If it is the sole means of the overthrow of capitalism it is because the comprehensive withdrawal of labour, shorn of occupational demands and short-term ameliorations of the class position of workers, is *catastrophic* to capital.

Despite key common emphases, the works of Luxemburg and Sorel draw from radically different traditions. In the case of Sorel, the key three intellectual debts that converge in the *Reflections on Violence* are the philosophy of Henri Bergson, the Catholic radicalism of Charles Péguy, and the tradition of syndicalism as captured in the *Bourses*, the latter quite distinct from the guilds and more generally the associational tradition that in Germany was mainly linked to Gierke.

From Bergson, whose lectures at the Collège de France he reportedly attended without fail,[22] Sorel takes the key concept of the 'élan vital', what Bergson identified as an unreasoning life force turned inward, to map onto the dynamic and logic of mass mobilisation. He takes the notion of freedom as defined by Bergson to capture the measure to which self-awareness replaces any law-like causality as the reason for action. He borrows a concept of temporality in order to contrast an *activist* sociality to the long stretches of 'pure duration project[ing] into homogeneous space' (Bergson, 1889/2001: 231); 'there is no obstacle', Bergson will write, 'that cannot be broken down by wills sufficiently keyed up, if they deal with it in time' (Bergson, 1932/1977: 282). Several years later, and

---

[21] 'Certainly the conception—myth, in Sorel's terms—of the "historical mission of the proletariat" was in reality the burning flame of Marxism, and it is this flame that rises so high with the Russian Revolution.' (Victor Serge, *Carnets*, 5 January 1944 entry.)

[22] Bergson appreciated how Sorel's revolutionary morality could indirectly intersect with his own on the plane of action, but chafed at the anti-democratic content of Sorel's position (Horowitz, 1961/2009: 41–2).

breaking with any Marxist teleology on Bergsonian grounds, Sorel relies on these analyses to show that *contingency* is the mark of the creative workshop specifically, and historical events generally (Horowitz, 1961/ 2009: 50).

Charles Péguy was at the turn of the century the most significant voice in French social Christianity and inspired Sorel to see 'the restoration of work' as key 'to moral proletarian regeneration' (Péguy, 1958: 62–3). He offered Sorel the opportunity not only to pit the regeneration of the proletariat against the sterile and specious idealism of bourgeois self-satisfaction, but also to borrow from Catholicism the prototype of the 'organised myth' that becomes central to Sorel's work. Once the 'myth' is carried onto political terrain, argued Sorel, all that was radical in Catholicism is represented in socialism. If this representation is to operate politically, Sorel needed to identify the organisational form that would give it adequate carriage.[23] He finds it in the *'syndicats'*.

The radical tradition of political syndicalism we find in Sorel is heavily influenced by Fernand Pelloutier. But to understand the development in Sorel's thought in this respect, we need to place it in the historical context and the precarious political balance of France's *fin du siècle* Third Republic. The legislation of 1884 granting free association to the workers had allowed mass organisation of the workers' movement. Unlike Germany, reform socialism under Clemenceau had ushered in social legislation, including collective contracts and the enforcement of the eight-hour working day, and had encouraged unions to seek restitution against individual employers from the state. The creation of a Ministry for Labour expressed the willingness of the ruling class to find a 'partner' in labour, and Clemenceau's militant opposition to revolutionary socialism was echoed in the position of the great figures of the vanguard social democracy of the turn of the century, Jean Jaurès and Alexandre Millerand.

But 'if rationalism was the intellectual weapon of reform, then by the same token irrationalism had for Sorel become the virtù of revolutionary politics', as Horowitz puts it (1961/2009: 26). Sorel sought in Pelloutier's anarcho-syndicalism a way to counter the pledging of labour to the State. He found it in the principles of mutual assistance that since Blanc had stressed the horizontality of the bonds amongst workers against their vertical integration in the State, and were given institutional expression

---

[23] On the idea of Sorelian myth as the 'ideological point of condensation for proletarian identity', see the seminal work of Laclau and Mouffe (1985: 36ff.).

in the *Bourses*. For Pelloutier it was here that 'the beginnings of a mass political awakening' would be nurtured, because these unions beyond providing financial assistance to striking workers, had also taken over positive State functions such as the provision of education, and in all cases forged a superior system of values, to the point where party affiliation was seen as subsidiary to trade union association. Against the stifling organisation of the Party – there are clear affiliations with Luxemburg's autogestion here – for both Pelloutier and Sorel, the organic composition of the forces of resistance promises a different élan, harnessing authenticity and spontaneity, to the 'sense of struggle'. It is against this background that the Confederation Générale du Travail was formed in 1895, and it is testament to the split condition of its genesis that its history thereafter has been very much an attempt to hold together its dual nature as institution and movement, as interlocutor in State processes and as expression of revolutionary potential of the proletariat and orchestrator of its direct action.

There is a particular historical event that stands at the moment of breach: it is the last broad gathering of the *syndicats* in Paris in the international conference of 1907.[24] It is this event that catalyses the opposition between reformist socialism and its radical alternative, and sends Sorel's revolutionary socialism on its path. Sorel's *The Decomposition of Marxism,* his critique of Marxism as a 'deterministic system of science', and his major work *Reflections on Violence* are both published a year later. The *Decomposition* sets out to establish what *really* constitutes, in Sorel's words, 'the *Marxism of Marx'*. And what is most Marxist in Marx, in Sorel's eyes, is the radicalisation of the connection between the subject of politics and his or her action. Only such a re-orientation holds out the possibility of a maturation of radicalism in the new, twentieth century (Horowitz, 1961/2009: 204).

It is precisely this juncture – of collective subjectivity and collective action – that is developed in *Reflections*, and here the fusion of socialism and unionism is pronounced 'functionally complete' in the general proletarian strike. Remember that for Sorel the general strike is 'the myth in which Socialism is wholly comprised' (1908/1999: 145). Its essence is to invoke the deepest class allegiances. And in the comprehensive withdrawal of labour that it effects – not as *instrumental* to the satisfaction of workers' demands but *tout court* – it is catastrophic to capital. It is this

---

[24] Including the major European theorists of syndicalism, Arturo Labriola, Hubert Lagardelle and Victor Griffuelhes, founder and leader of the CGT.

rejection of any instrumentality to which strike action might be committed that, as we will see, so attracts Benjamin to Sorel. The theory of the mass strike, or at least Sorel's variation on the theme, does not involve violence as such[25] (though it does not preclude it in the form of sabotage etc.). It is 'violent' in the effect that it has, because the withdrawal of work is at the same time the catastrophic withdrawal from capital of the realisation of value through labour, and thus undoes the dialectical class entanglement at the root of production and social valorisation.

Having defined the general strike as 'diametrically opposed' (1908/1999: 175) to the political strike, Sorel says:

> The idea of the general strike has such power behind it that it drags into the revolutionary track everything it touches. In virtue of this idea, socialism remains ever young; ... the line of cleavage is never in danger of disappearing.
>
> (1908/1999: 152)

This *esse-in-actu* of politics that engages workers in the radicalising myth of their age, every age, is re-negotiable because it is caught up in the pragmatics of action. It is a moment of *anti-politique*, Sorel proclaims, a rupture with the order of politics, of the kind that many decades later Rancière will identify as a break with the order of the police.

A final note before we move to Sorel's profound influence on Walter Benjamin's thinking about violence, to link it back not to violence but to the constitutional *problématique* that runs through this book. Against the stifling rationalism of reformism, Sorel's constituent action introduces authenticity, a merger of radicalism with antagonism, the modality of being-against, the language of rupture and of *anti-politique*. If from Bergson, Sorel borrowed the notion of the élan vital, it is perhaps indicative of the influence of Sorel on his teacher, that Bergson much later, in 1932, offers his erstwhile student an argument from praxis philosophy to buttress Sorel's opposition to the instrumental logic he sees pervading the political strike. Bergson writes: '*action on the move creates its own route*, creates to a very great extent the conditions under which it is to be fulfilled, and thus baffles all calculation' (1932/1977: 285). If this insight

---

[25] If for Sorel the general strike was a catastrophic conception of socialism, the essence of the class struggle, nowhere does he endorse indiscriminate, brutal violence; only violence 'enlightened by the idea of the general strike' (1908: 278) is unconditionally defended, serving the 'immemorial interest of civilization' (113). He describes the Declaration of the Rights of Man as 'only a colorless collection of abstract and confused formulas, without any practical bearing' (235).

about praxis installing its own conditions of legibility comes later, on the heels of Lukács' hugely influential thinking of praxis, it is too late for Sorel, whose profound insight about the general proletarian strike will remain uneasily poised on the task of moulding a 'unique combination of radicalism and *irrationalism*' (Horowitz, 1961/2009: 13).

Sorel's 'irrationalism' then stands opposed to the rationalism of capitalism and that of dialectical Marxism; it invites interruption at every juncture. It stands opposed to capitalism identified as the rational economy, and its quantifiable outcomes. It stands opposed to the rationality of administrative action through which State objectives are directed and enforced, and against the search for organisation and the application of instrumental reason in the regulation of social policy. This would also apply to the rational organisation of the democratic parliamentary process which Sorel, unsurprisingly, took to be an irredeemably bourgeois phenomenon. But at the level of theoretical analysis too, Sorel's irrationalism stands opposed to the certainty of the historical future, Hegel's upward sweep of History that delivers the culmination of the pure rational order. Instead, for him, 'Le socialisme est nécessairement une chose très obscure' (Sorel, 1908/1999: 217). Against speculative metaphysics, and any notion of intersubjectivity emerging from 'rational' discourse, for Sorel what galvanises the collective into action is the unifying element of the 'myth' of the proletarian strike in which 'there is no longer any place for the reconciliation of contraries in the equivocations of the professors' (1908/1999: 140). That is the first stated dimension of the irrationalism that walks the path it alone opens; the second is the irreducible *wager* of socialism: no guarantees, historical or theoretical, deliver socialism.[26] Echoing Marx's *'whoever drafts programmes for the future is a reactionary'*,[27] for Sorel too 'every pre-established plan is utopian and reactionary'. The solution was left to the irrational impulse, to chance (in the Bergsonian sense of the 'vital impulse') and to 'spontaneity'.

*

---

[26] As Gramsci put it in *The Modern Prince and Other Writings* (1957: 136).
[27] Marx, letter to Edward S. Beesly, 1869. The letter was not included in the *Werke* of Marx and Engels, but is alluded to in Sorel (1908). Benjamin refers to it and writes, 'taking up occasional statement by Marx, Sorel rejects any idea of program, of utopia, in short, any kind of legal imposition, for the revolutionary movement.' (Quoted in Hamacher (2000: 130).)

Walter Benjamin writes his *Critique of Violence* just over a decade after Sorel's *Reflections*. What fascinates Benjamin in Sorel's analysis of the proletarian general strike is the concept of 'pure violence' that he deploys. Unlike the political strike, which is directed towards transformation and ultimately the seizing of the state apparatus, there is, says Benjamin, no positively discernable purpose in the general proletarian strike. There is no purpose *beyond* it. It is directed towards nothing. It is *pure suspension*. The withdrawal of work is simply non-action: nothing happens, nothing is done, nothing produced, nothing planned. And this location outside any means-ends relation (it is 'pure means' Benjamin will say) makes it tantamount to a severing of relation. That radical suspension is perhaps one way to get behind the fetish phenomenon. In any case, as Werner Hamacher – one of Benjamin's most profound readers – puts it, 'with the deposing of the rule of positive law, the imparting structure of language, the social itself would historically break through, and open up *another history*' (Hamacher, 2000: 119). What appears, therefore, what is 'manifested' as a result of the proletarian general strike, 'is the social *tout court*'. A fascinating use of phenomenological bracketing *in actu*, for sure; but what to make of this phenomenology of pure paring back?

The proletarian general strike, with the unconditional suspension of state power as its vis-à-vis, aims at neither coercion nor extortion, not the holding of power nor its transformation, but is instead the overthrow itself. Benjamin refers to it as 'an overthrow that this kind of strike not so much causes as accomplishes' (119). 'Not as a particular type of politics, but as a manifestation of the political as such', adds Hamacher. The accomplishment of this other manifestation is paradoxical because the 'pure violence' of the general proletarian strike signifies nothing: it is pure undoing. What it undoes – 'annihilates' in Benjamin's idiom – is all legal violence, state violence and with it the violence of the commodity form as it underlies the relation of work under capitalism. What an extraordinary rendition of constituent power inheres in this negative gesture! Constituent power here is neither 'thetic' nor performative; it does not assert presence but withdrawal. For Derrida it places an excessive demand; it is in excess of the situation that defines it. Excess is its only measure. Sorel calls it 'catastrophic' because it is expressed as the dissolution of the capitalist productive paradigm, and this includes the legal regulation of exchange relations, the performativity of the fetish phenomenon, the interpellation of the subject – the full complement of the performative function of 'legal violence'. The 'pure' violence of the general proletarian strike clears the space for the subject position of the proletariat. If the proletariat is the 'central void' of the capitalist system it is because it finds no locution in the capitalist 'situation' generally, and the constitutional 'situation' more particularly, with their total and totalising distribution of subject positions. (Lefort's 'empty space' was never a void but a fully functional location in that distribution.) The proletarian general strike is the 'event' that defies its anticipated locution, and placing in the distribution. And that is because, for both Sorel and Benjamin, the proletariat is *not* a sociological concept. It is also *not* the Hegelian-Marxist not-yet transcendent subject of the violated universal norm of its recognition. The proletariat is instead positively defined as the class that constitutes itself in and through the general strike. At least it is so for Benjamin's reading of Sorel, 'working with uncompromising notions of language and politics' (Hamacher, 2000: 131). No meta-position defines it, and no historical process delivers it dialectically, calling it to presence in the contradictory modality of the class-in-itself, only to offer it passage into the universal class (for-itself). It is the subject engaged in the ethico-political experience of the radical withdrawal, *offering neither demand nor justification*, immanent in the situation from which it takes leave, *pure negation*.

The Meaning of Negation

We return here to pick up the thread, again, from Marx's eleventh thesis. All theory, 'critical or traditional',[28] derives its statements about real relationships from basic universal concepts. But, unlike traditional theory, in critical theory these universal concepts do not install themselves on the one side of the distinction between diagnosis and cure, description and prescription, but on the boundary itself. Because if in traditional theory the object is not affected by the theory that describes it, critical theory casts its descriptions (its universal concepts) as relevant to its own emancipatory function vis-à-vis necessity. That is why Horkheimer says that 'a consciously critical attitude is part of the development of society'; because the diagnosis of the pathology is not independent of its overcoming. The judgement passed on the 'necessity' inherent in the previous course of events engages also a struggle to change it from 'a blind to a meaningful necessity'. Hence for Horkheimer, as we saw, 'necessity is a critical concept'; and that is why 'it contains a protest against the order of

---

[28] For this distinction, see Max Horkheimer's influential work (1932/1976).

things'. Where in traditional theory 'necessity means the independence of the event from the observer', critical theory as the 'tribunal of reason' theorises a world in which the necessity of an object becomes the necessity of a 'rationally mastered event'. (All quotes from Horkheimer, 1932/1976: 229–31.)

We return to critical theory to pick up the moment of negation in two directions: in terms, certainly, of how it carries the 'protest against the order of things' at the level of theory-construction; but first as it inscribes itself on an affective register. The affective register matters because what drives critical theory is not some *speculative* commitment to coherence, but a deficit that is *experienced* by social actors as alienation. It orients our thinking back to the question of suffering, and how we might draw the distinction between its necessary and unnecessary forms. The emphasis is on the experiential dimension, the lived experience, *and incomprehensibility*, of suffering. 'I do not know', Horkheimer wrote, 'how far metaphysicians are correct; ... But I do know that they are usually impressed only to the smallest degree by what men suffer.'[29] Is it incidental, then, that it is at this juncture that *bourgeois* theory most vocally rails against the connection of political action to suffering? The theoretical objection is raised with predictable anxiety whenever the solution is carried in the mode of engagement of those who have suffered the injustice on their skin, famously against the embarrassing presence – nothing short of a 'scandal' – of the 'sans-culottes' who forced their wretchedness on the streets of Paris during the French Revolution. Arendt warns repeatedly in *On Revolution* with palpable alarm that if you build a political theory on suffering, you end up with Robespierre and the Terror. And it is a measure of her influence in the Anglo-American academy that this argument has been taken up as credo by political theorists of the anti-dialectical bend.

Not for the theorists of the Frankfurt School this abstention and flight. In the *Negative Dialectics*, Adorno writes of the paramount significance of the 'concrete denunciation of the inhuman', and captures in the idea of the *negative* 'the reaction that cannot tolerate that the horror carries on' (Adorno, 1973: 216, 286). 'The transmission of theory is aroused by prevailing injustice', says Horkheimer, 'today, when the whole weight of the existing state of affairs is pushing mankind towards the surrender of all culture and relapse into darkest barbarism' (1932/1976: 241).

---

[29] Quoted in Jay (1973: 46).

The critical theorist finds himself *confronted* with the real experience of disharmony or alienation. For Horkheimer, the embeddedness in experience is crucial for immanent critique in this respect: it means that the representation of discrepancy and contradiction is not merely an expression of historical reality but a force of change within it. 'Immanence' always-already implicates the historically poised, necessarily unfinished nature of human engagement, which suggests that the engagement is not something subjects can stand back from, but one that comes upon them with the 'force of present distress' which they need to 'make rational' (1932/1976: 215).

We are interested here, as we continue to explore the logic of rupture, in the response that takes the form of *pure negation*: an injunction that '*this is unjust*'. We encountered it earlier in Paul Ricoeur's discussion of the injunction that crucially *precedes* the theories of justice that one might engage to justify it and lend it weight. 'The cry *"it is unfair"*,' he writes, 'often indeed expresses a clearer intuition regarding the true nature of society and the place that violence still holds within it, than any discourse over what justice rationally or reasonably requires' (1995: 190). This temporal 'anomaly' connotes something important about the critical function of *negation*, that can be illustrated with the help of an example.

In autumn 2005, the deaths of two young people in the Parisian suburb of Clichy-sous-Bois sparked rioting on an unprecedented scale. In a period of a few weeks the riots had spread to *banlieues* across France. In and around these suburban ghettos insurgent crowds burned cars, damaged buildings and clashed with police. The scale of the violence was such that it resulted in the decision by the French government to implement emergency laws dating from the Algerian war of independence. The reactions from both Government and the public intellectuals were characteristically damning. For the prominent Gaullist intellectual Alain Finkielkraut the riots sprung from a religiously motivated hate for the Republic, while Nicolas Sarkozy, at the time Interior Minister, adopted 'warlike semantics' and promised to clean the suburbs of the 'scum' inhabiting these areas.[30] If on the one side the *malaise des banlieues* was offered only mis-recognition ('religious hatred', 'thuggery'), if it was altogether denied the dignity of the signifier 'resistance' to the violence of systemic marginalisation that generated it, on the other

---

[30] See *Libération*, 31 October 2005.

side the normative dynamics of the uprisings were neither harnessed nor structured into meaningful political claim or strategy by the insurgents. Nor was there anything like collective agency.[31] As far as the *'banlieusards'* were concerned their action was played out on the field of negation that took the form of an objection: *'not this'* whose 'expression' was violence. What negation marks is a break with the *understandings* that have been offered to rationalise the situation, a break with the available 'distribution of the sensible' (Rancière) in which political discourse attributes meaning to actions and events. But negation does not yet equip the insurgency with a 'scheme of interpretation' or of 'intelligibility'; it does not equip it with an alternative signification. At the level of negation it is merely a marker of a normative gap between the normative language available and a social experience of the diminishment of life chances. At that level the insurgents' is an injunction against the ways in which the available categories of political rationality (democracy, rights, equality) *fail* to collect rationally, and to give expression to, *their* experience *as* French citizens. This falling-short of the categories available to signify the dispossession experienced, registers only as a suffering that *cannot find positive expression*. And the mobilisation, thematised from the point of view of political order (the 'order of the police' as per Rancière) as a meaningless lashing-out, has no language to dignify it as anything but that. This inadequacy walls in the suffering as necessary, written into the lives of the inhabitants of the ghettos, and immanent with the full weight of the impasse.

We will undertake a more extensive analysis of how critical theory's promise of recuperation articulates at this point with immanent critique as critical constitutional theory, in the final chapter. It is immanent in the sense described above, as carried in the experience of the dispossessed, and thus engaging them normatively. And it is immanent, too, to the language available to describe that experience, the language of rights, democracy and equality, the very categories, in other words, that the action attempts to place in doubt. Its challenge is to articulate and exploit *contradiction*: that which erupted as negation seeks a register in a language that might rationalise it as the political order's simultaneous *promise* and *denial* of speaking position (citizenship) and claim (rights, equality, justice). In all these cases the promise hits upon a constitutive

---

[31] In his work on the sociology of the uprisings, Michel Kokoreff states that the riots 'ont marqué une entrée en politique des jeunes non seulement animés par le désir de détruire mais par une volonté de confrontation' (Kokoreff, 2008: 528).

limitation, and, in this respect, critique distinguishes itself from criticism as simply directed to rectify inconsistencies. In contrast, critique is poised against the 'wrong' which attaches to the very 'recognition order' that organises the semiotic field, and also the meaning of resistance to it. At this point the circle closes and theory fastens on to transformative praxis. Because the solution *has to be* transcendent to the system that harboured it. But if constitutional strategy, in the modality of immanent critique, deploys contradiction in order to force constitutional solutions, the strategy of rupture that concerns us at present remains with the notion of negation, and the challenge it faces crucially is not how to transcend, but how to remain, to sustain itself in the modality of negation, to resist co-option, surrogation and substitution.[32] Here critique persists in the simple negativity of refusal.

*

One of the significant recent attempts to analyse the role of negation in a phenomenology of law is Hans Lindahl's theory of *a-legality*. In the concept of a-legality Lindahl seeks a point of resistance to the forms of closure and of internalisation that legal 'ordering' deploys as so many mechanisms of immunisation. These are junctures at which a-legality brings its normative, critical, impetus to *interrupt* – a favourite term – the mechanisms that seal over and remove from contestation what a collective calls *its* order. If this critical function matters, its significance increases with globalisation, and Lindahl sees his intervention primarily at that level: here a-legality, to the measure that it brings into relief the 'fault lines' that separate legal orders, prevents the homogenising logic of globalisation from claiming a smooth terrain for the operation of global law. Instead a thinking about globalisation cognisant of 'fault lines' points to an 'emergent intertwinement' that in turn grounds a plurality of significance around a diversity of 'home worlds', of '*nomoi*' as per Cover of normative embeddedness, that relate and contrast across the experience of familiarity and strangeness.

Let us stay with the key terms: 'strangeness' and 'fault lines'. They are the terms in which the negative is given expression in 'a-legality', and, we might venture, without doing injustice to Lindahl, that they furnish the phenomenology of law with its 'constituent' dimension. To see why, let

---

[32] I refer here to the ways in which the constituent folds back into the constituted in the mode of 'surrogation' and 'substitution' in Chapter 2.1.

us focus on what he tells us 'we need to ask: *what is the mode of appearance of a-legality?*' (2013: 159). And the reason that this is a question that needs to be asked before a-legality can do any work of its own, is because its appearance is, let's call it, *improbable*. To make its appearance, a-legality will pivot on the 'strange', a concept that Lindahl borrows from Husserl, and it will find its locution not across the *boundary* from legality, but across a *fault line*. Let us take this more gradually with Lindahl:

> [E]ach boundary drawn by a legal collective establishes what it deems to be important and relevant, partitioning it from what is unimportant and irrelevant. But because the unordered is a residual category, and as such *opaque* to joint action by a given legal collective, *the divide* between legal (dis)order and what is left unordered *functions* differently than boundaries within a legal order. On the one hand, boundaries join and separate elements *within a unity*. [But] the divide between a legal order and its unordered is a *limit*. A limit *marks* the discontinuity and asymmetry between legal (dis)order and its correlative domain of the unordered. *Limits are neither legal nor illegal* because the distinction between the legal and the illegal presupposes spatial, temporal, subjective, and material boundaries which join and separate dimensions of behaviour within the unity of a legal order.
>
> (2013: 95, my emphases)

There is significant phenomenological import in this formulation with its references to the 'opaque', the divide that must be 'drawn', what limits 'mark', on what registers they mark, all of them indices of visibility of actions that *make appear*. And if there is suggested here something of an active, critical, *intervention*, it is because the domain to be thematised, tapped and activated, is what 'ordinarily' lies 'beyond the pale of practical interest':

> The distinction between legality and illegality, as behaviour that is in and out of bounds, is a specification of this general feature of a home-world. On the other hand, the home-world has an external horizon which separates it from what Husserl calls an 'irrelevant outside' . . . As concerns law, this irrelevant outside, which lies beyond the pale of practical interest because it has been excluded from what is germane to joint action by a legal collective, is the domain of non-law.
>
> (93)

In the topology of fault lines, a-legality is 'out of bounds', 'external horizon', 'irrelevant outside'. And yet, Lindahl tells us that the a-legal runs alongside legality as its accompanying reference. In the way Lindahl puts it: 'In effect, this divide is not posited *separately* from the boundaries that determine who ought to do what, where, and when. To the contrary, the divide between legal (dis)order and the unordered runs along *each* of the boundaries whereby a collective establishes who ought to do what, where, and when' (2013: 95).

Now this 'alongside' is an odd trajectory to be on, and a-legality, as accompanying reference, must make some kind of intrusion[33] into the domain of the 'home world' of legality if it is going to bring into question legality's normal, quotidian distributions of entitlement and right. And that is why Lindahl asks the question: 'what is the mode of appearance of a-legality?' He borrows the term 'estrangement' from Husserl, for whom 'the strange is first of all the incomprehensible strange'. It is *incomprehensible* because its difference is *incompossible*, it operates asymmetrically to the differences that structure the home-world. And yet the strange must 'still have a core of what is known for otherwise it could not be experienced at all, not even as strange' (quoted in 2013: 160). A-legality's improbable demand is to provide some kind of '*accessibility in its genuine inaccessibility, in the mode of incomprehensibility*'. The a-legal marks presence *as* inaccessible, and imports it *as* strange. It is the mark of excess, the signifier of what is forgotten and beyond reach. Carried in the concept of the 'strange', a-legality is never imported as affirmation but remains the sign of persistent negativity.

As a question of a phenomenology *of law* I do not think that this suggestion works, because it stumbles on the nature of the legal system as a restricted economy (above). And yet it introduces something hugely instructive. Because Lindahl's concept of a-legality is the most ambitious attempt to thematise the negative, and if it cannot be entertained, as I think it cannot, in the domain of legal meaning, it tells us something important about rupture and the relation between legality and the political. And to the extent that it says something important about the limits of legality, it tells us something important about strategy too.

For this we must bring Lindahl into conversation with Luhmann, even if it will take us on a bumpy ride. Looking at a-legality through the phenomenological lens of systems theory,[34] suggests a difficult navigation

---

[33] A-legal behaviour carries 'irruptive force'. 'The term irruption – which means to break in or to break through – evokes the element of *force* in a-legality' (2013: 161).

[34] Luhmann's theory of meaning also draws explicitly from Husserl, for whom, Luhmann reminds us, a presentation is always surrounded by 'Appräsentationen' that stand before it as horizon. Meaning is the distinction between actuality and potentiality, and for

of the terrain of the ordinary operation of the law, and its *interruption*. Luhmann's phenomenology begins, as we know, with the operationalisation of the distinction between legality and illegality that reproduces the legal system by ascribing these values to acts in the world. The distinction between the positive and negative value opens up the *contingency space* for law that emplaces all possible states, acts and events within that space; not only is everything legal or illegal, *tertium non datur*, but something is legal in that it is not illegal: the negative value is the 'reflection value' in a system that vests meaning in events by closing off its domain self-referentially. It follows from this that 'illegality' is as internal, and as productive, to the legal system as is the ascription of legality to acts and events. *The illegal is not the index of any outside*: it is instead the negative value of the legal and thus a 'duplication value' that allows an act to register as meaningful because it could be otherwise, that is, it could be illegal (and vice versa). Of course the law needs to break its symmetry and relate to the world; but reach to the domain of the 'outside' is mediated by the founding distinction – the code – of legality. None of this is very far off from Lindahl's own analysis.

Now of course this closed 'duality' of the operation of coding needs to be both unfolded (it must refer to something *outside* it, events in the world, states of intention of actors, the pragmatics of social interchange, etc.) *and* interrupted. Interruption is the key term for Lindahl's a-legality too. But interruption needs to be staggered. Because the operation of legality is interrupted also when the normal reproduction of the system is 'surprised' in some way: either because classifications are challenged (e.g. indeterminacy) or because contradictions appear (e.g. conflict of laws, gaps) or because innovative interpretations are suggested and tested at the system's entry points – typically in court decisions. Legal interpretation here introduces a level of scrutiny over the proper distribution of legality and illegality to new events. But, as Lindahl says rightly, at *this* level the interruption occurs and is handled *within the referential unity* of the legal system, as a question of *legal interpretation*.[35]

Luhmann any actual selection mobilises potentiality alongside it as condition of its legibility. The selection is the 'marked side' of the distinction, the side that invites further linkages, the side where the action is as it were, and yet it is only because the other side holds up potentiality as horizon for what is ordered (through selections) and what is orderable (through future selections).

[35] 'The point of a legal practice becomes the object of explicit attention when the theoretical attitude sets in, when that which agents understand themselves and their fellow

It is not insignificant that at this point, and with reference to this normal, first-order, level of 'interruption', Luhmann will draw the most radical consequences in support, not of change, but of *immunisation*. For Luhmann, 'the system does not immunize itself against the "no" *but with the help of the "no"*'.[36] His thesis that systems function not by rejecting conflicts and contradictions, but by producing them as necessary to the activation of their own 'antibodies', places the entire Luhmannian discourse in the semantic orbit of immunity. We do not need to dwell on this, but we do need to ask: given immunisation, how much of this opportunity for systemic renewal draws from the 'strange'? On one reading, *none of it*. Novelty does indeed break into the legal system and interrupts the quotidian reproduction of legal meaning in the 'homeworld' of legality but that interruption occurs *within the limits* of the balance between variety and redundancy, experimentation and reaffirmation. There is nothing here yet about any meta-level disruption, as Lindahl would want it, of *this – our – *normative order with *its* distribution of entitlements, to invoke instead a just world that is, let us imagine, attentive to need. To be sure, legal interpretation, as opposed to mere legal understanding, might introduce another level of scrutiny over the proper distribution of legality and illegality to new events, that we might even reserve the term internal *critique* for. But where the mobilisation of legal-interpretative resources is thematised through the distinction between legal understanding and legal interpretation, the 'interruption' occurs and is still handled *within the referential unity* of the legal system. The 'ordering achievement of legal acts' (2013: 119) across the various axes (material, social, temporal) of legal meaning operate within the boundary of that unity, according to Lindahl's trenchant formulation as 'reiterative anticipations'. Edward Levi's 1948 article 'On legal reasoning' remains the supreme example of how the novelty of classifications as they are introduced into the legal system act to consolidate its unity *a posteriori*.[37] Never outwith the horizon of iteration, or outwith the 'iterability' of legal meanings, legal acts *re*-iterate

---

participants as doing together is *interrupted*. This is the moment at which *legal understanding yields to legal interpretation ...*' (Lindahl, 2013: 85, my emphases).

[36] He continues: 'to put this in terms of an older distinction, it protects through negation against annihilation, ... in order to assume the function of "society's specific immunitary system" as the legal system itself' (Luhmann, 2004: 372, 374).

[37] Levi (1948). See also Smith (1995) for an exceptional discussion linking Levi's theory of legal reasoning to Luhmann's; and for the notion of '*a posteriori* systematicity', see Bengoextea (1994).

and *re*-interpret 'disclosing 'something as something *anew*'. But of course renewal is not rupture, and the negative moment is re-integrated productively before it has time to carve out a space for itself, and sustain itself in the face of the stream of law's re-iterations.

In this context a-legality can only operate as a second-order interruption Here it must be understood as non-productive to the ordering because, to perform the function that Lindahl attributes to it, it must force a challenge to the very unity of reference of the system. This involves an 'incompossible' act because it stands incongruent to the act of interpretation that may have integrated it productively within that unity. A-legality taps a limit, and in this world of *intense liminality* that is thereby invoked, what is forced into appearance gets its traction from the impossibility of containment, however accommodating the order. But to remain incompossible, resistant and ruptural it needs to be insisted on and acted on *against* the order it challenges, and to remain unrepresentable within it. The a-legal evokes a different potentiality, asymmetrical to its conditions of appearance in legal interpretation (however imaginative). That I understand to be the meaning of the a-legal, at least in its 'robust sense'.[38] And arguably it is robust or not at all.

Throughout these processes of autopoietic meaning-creation and reproduction, meaning is only ever inner-systemic, and potentiality is mobilised alongside the application of the legal/illegal distinction as the inventory of new linkages. What makes the system of law *a restricted economy* is the fact that the 'excess' that the system re-orients itself to, is only ever productive to it. (The same does not apply to politics, which is not a restricted economy.[39]) But for law, the 'strange' as other-reference can only be source of connectivity. It can be internalised to introduce instability (instability, Luhmann was fond of saying, is law's source of stability, ceaseless renewal) or remain 'noise'. For Luhmann, potentiality – as accessibility to new linkages – only ever supports a restricted economy. In the law-world of meaning, the 'restricted economy' where potentiality *is* accessibility, the strange *per se* has no point of entry. The unity of reference cannot be thematised because it is the 'blindspot' of any operation of law;

---

[38] Lindahl draws a distinction between weak and robust a-legality (in 2013).
[39] The distinction between 'politics/police', 'le politique/la politique' etc. is the very source of political reflexivity, whereas the difference between the legal and the illegal cannot be put to question *legally*. (See Luhmann on the impossibility of the 'third question' (1988a).) For the distinction between restricted and general economy, see Chapter 4.1 above.

and no fault line can be meaningfully crossed because such crossing would undo the system as a reduction achievement and as locus of meaning.

By way of summary, maybe one way to put it, as Lindahl himself often reminds us, is that whatever boundary is in question can only be thematised from the inside. The a-legal only ever runs alongside legality, and it is legality that registers a-legality's intrusions as illegalities, always in its own lexicon and within the ambit of the referential unity that only legality (vis-à-vis illegality) can furnish. But a-legality's negation is not, cannot and should not be productive to the order of things: it professes a radical discontinuity, the emergence of something novel. But to mark a limit, to mark anything, its reception in the order can only be in terms that precede its newness. One might therefore put the question in this way: on what register is a-legality going to state its claim? How are we to understand its *semiosis*? Our insistence on the negative suggests, against Lindahl here, that its claim is in the field of being-against, that its demand is irreducibly political, irreducible, that is, to the semantic field of legality. Unless it is sustained *politically* as a refusal to yield to it (as legal signifier, interruption or surprise, or whatever), legality will only ever call 'the a-legal' forth (albeit it over a border or a 'fault line')[40] by calling it into line.

*

We have linked the notion of *rupture* to the *practice* of negation. What do they have in common, these various iconoclasms we have visited, that breach the 'picture that keeps them captive'?[41] What makes the rupture with the various economies of representation and with the order of the

---

[40] A fault line, Lindahl suggests, is not a '*Grenzbegriff*' or boundary-concept as Schmitt would describe sovereignty. ('Sovereignty is all about what ultimately counts as legal unity in the face of irreducible political plurality': 179–180.) A fault line must replace a concept such as envisaged by Schmitt as pivoting on the boundary, because it marks the end of legal ordering in a temporal and spatial way, and therefore marks the end of the unity of a legal order. An 'excessive normative claim' is one placed beyond what 'we, as a collective, have reached the end of our normative tether' (177). It defies rather than exploits the unity of reference of law, imports an incomprehensibility through the notion of the strange. We have asked about the meaning of this incomprehensibility in the restricted economy of the legal system, where negativity is either productive or not at all, because the idea of the meaningless cannot be carried in law at any level: for Luhmann, meaning comes neither in the form of a *fault line* or a *Grenzbegriff*; instead as *Letztbegriff* (1995a: 62), meaning is a fundamental concept of *closure*, for there is nothing outside meaning.

[41] The reference is to Wittgenstein: 'A picture kept us captive. And we could not get outside it, for it lay in our language and language seemed to repeat it to us inexorably.' (In *Philosophical Investigations* (trans. G. Anscombe) (1958: §115).)

constituted the 'republican principle of the first instance' if we might go back to pick up the radical moment in Rousseau? The answer that connects the various instances – the Athenian demos, the Commune, the mass strike, Solidarity – is a refusal on the part of the emergent collectivities to define themselves through the terms of reference available to them; a refusal of the representational space *afforded* to them and the extant distribution of speaking positions. With regard to the *subject* of constituent power, we are in the realm of what is 'most marxist in Marx', as Sorel put it, the radicalisation of the connection between the subject of politics and his action. As a question of *action*, their labours had to be read *against* the available registers that conferred value and meaning. Rupture places the emphasis on negation, on withdrawal, and, strategically, on what recuperation that withdrawal might allow.

The role of strategic thinking of rupture engages at *the second-order* level, because the *wrong* it confronts is of that order too. The question that is confronted at that level is what does it mean to redress a wrong where the wrong consists in the withdrawal of the language in which redress to injustice might be sought. Lyotard uses the term *différend* for this second-order silencing, and Rancière offers *dissensus* to address it. But it is perhaps Negri who gives us the more direct insight from the field of strategy. Take the frustration that marked his early work, the difficult injunction of the workerists of Operaismo and then of Autonomia to undertake political praxis 'dal punto di vista operaio'[42] both urgent and improbable because that 'point of view' forever slips back into the situation that labour inhabits, and makes alternatives visible only in terms of temporary dislocations it marks rather than any consistent programme of 'self-valorisation'. 'We find ourselves', Negri despairs, 'with a revolutionary tradition that has pulled the flags of the bourgeoisie out of the mud' (Negri, 2000: xx). Crucial to the thinking of redress is the refusal to accept the hegemonic representational order of Capitalism, a refusal to recognise class struggle in its idiom. Clearly 'recognition' is profoundly problematic a route if Marx's insight is to be preserved, because, to put it in the terms of the *Manifesto*, 'a class of labourers, live only so long as they find work, and find work only so long as their labour increases capital'. To resist the terms of capture, for Marx any recognition of the collective subject has to be *postponed*, to be achieved in the overcoming of the current structures that ascribe action to available

---

[42] See Beasley-Murray (1994) and Wright (2002) for fascinating histories of the workerist movements in post-War Italy.

subject positions and thereby short-circuit recognition to the operation of capital. That is why political action for the *Autonomia* was undertaken in terms of refusal to work, wildcat strikes, spontaneous slow downs, acts of sabotage, and the like. Negri can allude to this as a 'project of destruction' (Negri, 1988: 36) but in effect the recourse to the negative was spasmodic. It neither possessed the sweeping negation inherent in the mass strike, nor could it claim, as a second-order 'struggle for recognition', any leverage in terms of self-representation of the proletariat. What it did possess was the frustration that comes from a need to resist that can find no locution or leverage except in the categories it seeks to place in doubt, and that therefore carries the full weight of the *wrong*.

It was the *wrong* that confronted the striking workers in Gdansk, that denied them a collective speaking position and a political claim. Their demand for a free trade union to defend workers' rights and the self-determination of labour was incomprehensible as a claim addressed *against* a 'workers' republic'; the negative had no traction; and the Party commissars responded to the challenge as a challenge of subversion and sent in the army in 1981. For that other set of commissars that followed them a decade later, and whose task was to ensure market discipline, again nothing jarred the concentration on the task at hand. Any claim to the collective self-determination of labour collapsed into the ample accommodations of the market, and the workers were offered an economic constitution without economic democracy, of the EU variety. The demands for economic democracy and the labour constitution were pitted against the 'antithetical and complementary' choice (I will come back to this in Chapter 4.4) between the total State of 'really existing socialism' or the total Market of end-of-history neo-liberalism, and was defeated in the process. In these gestures of inclusion and accommodation a *différend* was exacted in the full sense of a silencing both effected and covered over.

It is against these gestures of inclusion and accommodation that any strategy of negation must measure itself. We can theorise the negative in two ways because it is delivered in two modalities: as the *transitory* step to a synthesis in the Hegelian sense of that which is *productive in its overcoming*; and in that which *persists* as negative. The first is typically the way in which the dialectic of constituent and constituted operates; the second is the logic that is (imperfectly) expressed in the logic of rupture. The first involves a restricted economy, in the sense that Derrida and Bataille describe it, restricted because the excess carried in the constituent is internalised productively in the constituted. We saw how the failure to draw that distinction marks the kind of elision that is rife in much 'poststructuralist' legal theory: the suggestion of 'excess' and the 'promise' that no determination will ever exhaust the meaning, say, of human rights, is *not yet*, not at all, a sign of empowerment and resistance to the order of capital. It is merely a suggestion that capital will renew itself by feeding off excess.[43] The stake of a theory of the negative as a theory of rupture must offer more by way of strategy than the vague invocation of excess. We explored a range of instances of this second, uncompromising, non-instrumental, sense of negation, and the difficulty confronted of sustaining it in that modality. In each case at stake was action that broke incongruently into given economies of representation, those expansive stretches of the 'constituted' imaginary, 'scandalously' as with Rancière above, and claiming the field of its enunciation. The question became how the collective action was to *sustain* itself in the field of 'mediacy' as 'spontaneity' with Luxemburg, as a 'withdrawal of labour' with Sorel (and Benjamin), that sought no amelioration and no instrumentality, *within* the field of its extraction.

I know of no work in which a statement of the constituent as an absolute *exteriority* has been put in such stark terms as in the 'Treatise on Nomadology' by Deleuze and Guattari (1988). In 'nomadology' the idea of the constituent stands irreducible to the constituted, and resistant to any dialectical articulation with it or expression through it. From Dumezil's work on Indo-European mythology and his account of how the exercise of sovereignty has always worked on a distinction between King and Jurist, 'binder and organiser', despot and legislator, they draw the insight that the functioning of the sets of pairings (the 'form of the distinctions') 'at once antithetical and complementary' involves a totalising gesture that lays out the *field of politics as 'a milieu of interiority'*. The use of the distinctions suspends between them the entire range of possibility, and domesticates them to the extant order since they both fall on the same ('constituted') side of the constituent/constituted distinction. Against this context-setting and comprehensive appropriation, the nomadic 'war-machine', as Deleuze and Guattari call it, fluid and – in itself – plural, claims for itself 'another justice, another movement, another space/time' (1988: 353), in other words *an absolute exteriority*. 'Nomadology' seeks this exteriority in the 'irruptive', in the transitory 'becoming',[44] in a 'pure and immeasurable

---

[43] I have argued this at length in other work (Christodoulidis, 2009) and already above (Chapter 2.1).

[44] Where 'becoming', they have argued earlier, 'lacks a subject distinct from it'; 'there is a reality specific to becoming' (238).

multiplicity, the pack' (1988: 352), in 'pure strategy' (1988: 353), in situational and not intrinsic properties, in the 'flow' of 'absolute war'. From all this, let us keep, first, the absence of any dialectic between inside and outside, and, secondly, the absence from the inside of terms of reference for the nomadic. For the representational order of the State the reality of the nomadic cannot be rationalised but only *confronted*. The encounter between inside and outside lacks a common idiom, and any possibility therefore of dialectical mediation. For each side the other is exterior and represents violence pure and simple, a sign of *the negative* that will yield to no over-arching commonality or hospitality. The *nomad* remains the archetype of the stranger, the political wild card, certainly *no possible guest*.[45] By remaining external, the nomad stands for a responsibility that is plainly not subsumable into an order of representation. Such resistance sustains the space for potentiality.[46] But if what is potential is to resist its circumscription and appropriation into a certain field of reference, if it is to remain meaningful in its own terms, it must define itself incongruently to the field of reference it refuses to fold into. This is where the discussion of *autogestionnaire* politics attaches to the theorisation of rupture.

In the mass strike, less so for Luxemburg, perhaps, more for Sorel, and definitely for Benjamin, the form of action involved cannot be thematised from the inside of the order it opposes because it is *pure withdrawal*. It is an event best understood not as positing a relation but as retracting from the set of relations and the field of reference within which it might be understood and co-opted. It does not define itself by reference to production or valorisation (which was Negri's anxiety, above, of a self-valorisation undercut *ab initio*) but through subverting the imperative to produce and valorise. As interruption it neither speaks nor posits, it simply abstains, and that is why the rupture it effects is at the meta-level, at the level of what grants expression, of what lends language. What

---

[45] The reference is to Derrida (2006). Drawing on the 'nomadology', Alberto Melucci's important book *Nomads of the Present* transfers its key insight to a theorisation of social movements, raising as central the question of whether there are forms of conflict that are *productively* being directed *against* the logic of complex systems. For Melucci, '[b]ecause collective action questions the system's structural logic it is destined to reproduce itself beyond the forms of mediation that can interpret it' (1989: 57). Negri, for his part, adopts the figure of the 'nomad' in *Empire* (2000: 212).

[46] 'Autogestionnaire' political action imports a different modality of agency and action and with it *an expanded sense of potentiality*. Aristotle's concise formulation of '*epidosis eis eauto*' – that which gives itself to itself – is at the heart of this constituent gesture, and was renewed in Spinoza's reflexive definition of self-constitution: *that which cannot be defined in relation to something else must be defined in relation to itself.*

attracts Benjamin to this concept of 'divine violence' is abstention from relation, which is also withdrawal from the economy of concepts, an undoing of the means of expression, a retraction from the impartability of meaning. This is what Benjamin reads into Sorel's theorisation of the general strike. It is a negation that it becomes impossible for capitalism to thematise productively, precisely because it is located at the meta-level of meaning construction. From the point of view of critical phenomenology we find ourselves at a limit point. It is the point at which the field of phenomenality – as a field of *positive* manifestation – withdraws. Something beyond the order of positing is obliquely indicated, in the ellipses and interruptions of the negative. Something that stands as 'other' to the system of mediation and therefore resistant to all possible recuperation. Maybe, suggests Werner Hamacher, the 'caesura' opened up by the strike offers 'the critical' in its purest form, which he calls 'afformative'.[47] It is a caesura, he says, intriguingly drawing this time on Benjamin's literary essay 'Elective Affinities', akin to Oedipus 'falling silent' at the end of the tragedy: a wordlessness that is pure withdrawal and – to the measure that *Oedipus at Colonus* is all about the polis and its authority to exile its citizens – pure subversion. On his part, Lyotard speaks of negation as a 'force that escapes the logic of the signifier' (1993: 64); that does not end up taking its place *within* the system of relations of the field of capitalism. There is much fascinating work on the negation, in Benjamin's 'caesura', in Badiou's event,[48] in Lyotard's *différend*, but I think enough has been said to make a more modest point about the strategic use of rupture.

It was Jacques Vergès who popularised the notion of the 'strategy of rupture' in the context of the criminal trial.[49] Much of his strategy drew on *contradiction* that we will identify in the next chapter as the hallmark of *immanent critique*: in his defence of Nazi criminal Klaus Barbie before the French Courts in 1987, Vergès' strategy consisted in the maximal use of the *'tu quoque'* in a way that would bring the French in direct confrontation with their hypocritical denunciation of a crime that Vergès claimed underpinned their own colonial legacy. But as far as

---

[47] 'Afformation' means 'not only deposition of what has been posited'. It 'means also exposing to the unposited, giving what cannot become a gift, an event of formation which is not exhaustible by any form' (Hamacher, 2000: 129).

[48] The general strike in the way we have analysed it belongs to the order of the 'event' as Badiou has theorised it, which breaks with the continuum of history as it does with the conditions of its cognition.

[49] Vergès, 1968. See also Christodoulidis, 2009.

the strategy of *rupture* is concerned, it had to do with a (selective) refusal to negotiate in terms of the criminal trial with *its* accommodations of discursive possibilities. Instead, Vergès deployed an antagonistic idiom aimed at confrontation and, with the denunciation of colonialism, at the opening of wounds. Our own analysis has suggested how rupture might be generalised in strategic deployment, predominantly by means of the strike, as means of redress in the constitutional situation, *as the gesture*, as it were, *of catching rationalising thought off guard.*

4.4

Constitutionalising Contradiction:
Towards an Open Constitutional Dialectic

On s'engage, et puis on voit[1]

Materialism and the 'Adventure' of the Dialectic

Written and revised over the course of twenty years, Louis Althusser's *Machiavelli and Us* remains perhaps his most unfinished work. Fragmentary, replete with corrections in turn revised, deleted and restored, this is an essay poised on what Althusser termed in the mid-1960s 'a theoretical conjuncture'. How unlikely the attraction of one of the most structuralist of Marxists to Machiavelli; Althusser was after all *par excellence* the theorist of totalities that arrogated questions of agency and action to themselves, describing the latter as mere epiphenomena of the tectonic movement of capitalist structures. What is it that attracts this theoretician of invariant structures to Machiavelli's singular conjunctures and the fleeting figurations of *virtù*? And yet, by the time Althusser comes latterly to write this treatise on *constituent power*, he finds Machiavelli's 'endeavour to think the conditions of an impossible task' as the one he too must confront. 'Machiavelli's question, the question how to begin from nothing, was my own.'[2]

In this section we will focus on Althusser's suggestion about how the key *encounter* between *fortuna* and *virtù* that he takes from Machiavelli, can be transferred to the *interface between structure and event*; and to hoist out of that encounter an *open dialectic*. The lead Althusser seeks

---

[1] Introduced by Napoleon as a military maxim, adopted by Lenin, and referred to by Althusser as the reversal that informs the notion of the 'theoretical conjuncture'.

[2] Althusser (1999). And it is tempting to read a parallel trajectory between the two theorists. The solitude that Machiavelli talks about in the *Discourses*, that 'every absolute beginning requires the absolute solitude of the reformer or founder', Althusser claimed as his own, in the demands that the 'conjuncture' placed on theoretical engagement, in the increasingly strained relationship with the PCF. (See his *Ce qui ne peut pas durer dans le Parti Communiste* (1978).

from Machiavelli is over how, in the face of the smooth reproduction of structures, the contingency associated with the encounter can bring into the world something incongruous to that reproduction. The 'event' of the encounter is unforeseen and unforeseeable from the point of view of the structures that set agency and action on their way: it names a *constituent* political praxis. The political actor – this is Machiavelli's key innovation – *does not yet exist*; it is brought about through an intervention which occurs at the juncture of *fortuna* and *virtù*. This is political agency that is neither pre-determined nor burdened by the ordering structures of the 'constituted'. It is precisely this, the question of what it means to invoke agency in the vein of the constituent, that Althusser, in the late writings, invites us to think with the help of Machiavelli. 'Machiavelli's central problem from a theoretical viewpoint could be summed up in the question of beginning, starting from nothing, an absolutely indispensable and necessary new state' (1999: xiv–xv). What fascinates Althusser is Machiavelli's *contradictory demand*, for a foundation 'at once indispensable and unrealisable'. In looking for that irruption of the new, of what does not seek its conditions in that which it resists, it 'is still Machiavelli we have to thank', he says. 'And if,' he adds, ' as indeed chance may have it, I overstep his field of thought, let us say that he opened up this space, among others, to us' (1999: 4). It is in the spirit of a similar debt to Althusser that the following thoughts are offered.

It is well known that *The Prince* was addressed by Machiavelli to the 'Magnificent' Lorenzo de Medici in the form of advice. Althusser endorses Gramsci's analysis of the *Prince* as a political *manifesto*, a manifesto in which 'Machiavelli *becomes the people*' (Gramsci, 1971: 126). For both theorists, to be truly political, that is to be a manifesto, the text must locate itself in the social field in which it is intervening and in which it thinks. Therefore, as manifesto the text is 'addressed to the masses in order to organise them into a revolutionary force' (Gramsci, 1971: 125). In this, like Marx and Engels' *Communist Manifesto*,[3] *The Prince* is addressed (to the Duke) 'from the viewpoint of the people' (Althusser, 1999: 24–5). Althusser adds this:

> I believe it is not hazardous to venture that Machiavelli is the first theorist *of* the conjuncture, or the first thinker consciously … – in an insistent,

---

[3] '*The Communist Manifesto* is likewise a written text that arranges social classes in the space of economic, political and ideological class struggle; a text that poses theoretically the problem posed socially and politically by the conjuncture, … and fixes the place of the force that must be constituted to resolve this problem. This place is the proletariat.' (1999: 25)

profound way – to think *in* the conjuncture: that is to say, in its concept of an aleatory, singular case.

(1999: 18, my emphases)

What to make of this 'venture'? While Machiavelli's theorisation of *virtù and fortuna* constitutes an exemplary instance of the 'encounter', hailing a political subject – a popular prince – that paradoxically does not [yet] exist, Machiavelli's broader theoretical contribution to theorising the conjuncture is twofold. First, is his ability to think *about* the conjuncture: to reflect on a political problem taking into account the concrete circumstances, their constituent elements, and their relations of force, or, as he famously put it, 'the concrete analysis of the concrete situation'. Second, is his perspicacity to think *in* the conjuncture: to grasp the 'contradictory system' of the elements of the situation and what that contradictory system dictates as a political problem, granting it with a corresponding solution and, hence, the contours of and content for political practice, that is, 'the forms, means and procedures' of (this political) practice (1999: 18–19). In the process Machiavelli 'treats his own text, in its turn and at the same time, as one of those means, making it serve as a means in the struggle he announces and engages. . . . [If] his writing is new it is [because it is] a political act' (1999: 23), the text itself a force within the forcefield it inscribes itself. Thinking *about* the conjuncture is a theoretical practice, but thinking *in* the conjuncture transforms elements of the conjuncture into 'real or potential forces in the struggle for the historical objective' (1999: 25). As a form of action, as political practice and intervention in the conjuncture, it brings out *the performative dimension* of aleatory materialism *material praxis* with real, political effects.

We need to take a few steps back to appreciate the Machiavellian 'turn' in Althusser's Marxism, because the idea of an open dialectic, which will become key to us in this final chapter, reflects that 'turn'. Much has been made of the 'epistemological break' between Althusser's early and late work, and there is some truth in the argument that the earlier 'plodding orthodoxy' of the 'ideological State apparatuses', with its at least implicit assumption of the separation between the order of knowledge and the order of the real, bears little connection to the 'philosophy of the encounter'.[4] I would, however, suggest that the discussion of a break is

---

[4] See Kyle McGee's excellent article (2012). On Althusser's own account of his debt to structuralism, see 'On Levi Strauss' in Althusser (2003). On the question of the epistemological break with Hegel, see Althusser's important essay 'Marx's relation to Hegel' (2004),

exaggerated, and that the insights on 'contradiction and over-determination' that Althusser offered in the early 1960s suggest links to the later work in the understanding of contingency that they introduce. The preoccupation that accounts for the continuity is around the question of how the 'new' might find expression *in and against* the semantic structures that in their reproduction establish the meaning available to 'renewal': one that already subsumes the new within the order of intelligibility of the extant. Arguably we discern this move in 'Contradiction and Overdetermination' (Althusser, 1962/1990), where Althusser confronts the problem of structuralism's notorious inability to produce the event as anything but the reflex of the structure. 'Overdetermination' is a gesture towards loosening the control of structures, marking a double movement of sorts: if on the one hand the contradiction is inseparable from the total structure of the social body in which it is found, inseparable from its formal conditions and the instances it governs, what it animates, and what results from that animation, does not have to submit to those structures, their order of rule and teleology. Althusser, as he often does, looks to Lenin to argue the point. Take Russia in 1917, he suggests, pregnant with two revolutions, overdue with its bourgeois revolution on the eve of the proletarian one. It could certainly not, says Althusser, withhold the second by delaying the first. And Lenin was absolutely right to *have forged* the conditions by means of a decisive *political* move. If the general contradiction, in other words, is sufficient to define the situation when revolution is 'the task of the day', that contradiction cannot of its own induce the revolution. If the contradiction is to become *active* as a 'ruptural principle', then the accumulation of circumstances need to 'fuse' into a 'unity'. The key point about 'overdetermination' is that the *accumulation* and layering of contradictions – often radically heterogeneous – *come into play in the same court*, as it were, to drive revolutionary action (Althusser, 1962/2005: 101, 115). The 'coming into play' is a key objective of political action, and of political-theoretical engagement, or to put it in Althusser's famous term, of the 'theoretical conjuncture'. In my reading of his theoretical trajectory, it is the same key that he later seeks in the notion of the *'encounter'*; the encounter that he now takes from Machiavelli to be that of *fortuna* with *virtù*.

Machiavelli is of course the theorist not of class struggle, but of national unity. What matters to Althusser is how that objective (which

---

and on Hegel's profound influence on the young Althusser, Vuillerod (2017) and Carlino (2015).

is not *his* objective) is read by Machiavelli at the level of *fortuna* as a question of historical 'need'. But how to understand the historical *need* that national unity captures, which is not yet legible *as such* since the conditions that would lead us to think it are not yet in place? Here is what makes the endeavour 'aleatory' as Althusser puts it: the *new form*, this instrument, is the national state and it must be assembled out of the elements of the situation. The new instrument, the national state, is committed to struggle against the terrain on which it stands, a terrain consisting of the many particularisms of the Italian city States, irredeemably marked by feudal relations, organically incapable of extending their market over the national territory, and incapable of resolving their political and economic differences with the rural constituencies. Feudal forms, political rivalries and meagre markets cannot 'furnish the political base from which Italian unity must be constructed'. Machiavelli looks to the material conditions that would allow the nascent bourgeoisie to conduct commercial activity in a process of expanded reproduction, allowing it to pit the new mode of production against the feudal forms. In the face of their wretchedness and destitution (55) 'the whole question becomes: In what form are all the positive forces currently available to be rallied in order to achieve the political objective (of national unity)? Machiavelli gives this form a name: the Prince' (19). As he is invoked he is not-yet sovereign, but as 'requisite historical form' for the constitution of the state, he 'stands before a task that history assigns to him: to re-assemble, and give shape to already existing material, *a matter aspiring to its form*' (13). Machiavelli's objective is not the *capture* of an *existing form* but the generation of a not-yet-existing form as dependent on a new arrangement of existing elements. 'Existing' because, for Althusser, dialectical materialism must still be extracted out of the existing material forms that confront the Prince-to-be as *fortuna*. Hic Rhodus, hic salta, if one is allowed to lend a Hegelian phrase to this deeply anti-Hegelian philosopher. An instrument is required here to forge the unity of praxis that has to negotiate the inhospitable terrain of *fortuna* (terrain, that is, un-accommodating of the new) with the insight and political forward-mindedness of *virtù*; and Machiavelli will urge the Prince: 'If it is impossible to construct the national state on the basis of feudal forms, that state must subordinate those forms to itself ... they are its raw material' (71). The fact is that everything is new, that the processes of becoming-the-principality and becoming-the-Prince are coincident. Because neither pre-exists the other 'they must begin together, and this beginning is what Machiavelli calls an "adventure" – that of passing from private citizen to ruler' (73). The *mutual constitution* assumes the form of a favourable 'encounter' between, 'on the one hand, the objective conditions of the conjuncture X of an unspecified region – *fortuna* – and on the other the subjective conditions of an equally indeterminate individual Y – *virtù*' (74). The form-giving moment of the encounter neither inheres nor is warranted by either set of preconditions, objective or subjective; it is instead the felicitous outcome of the event of their encounter.

But what to make of *this retroaction* that somehow inaugurates the conditions of its own emergence? To navigate this fundamental point, though we will inevitably forego some of the complexities of the discussion, we turn to the fascinating concept of the *clinamen*, that Althusser borrows from Epicurus (as did Deleuze, Negri, Nancy, Derrida, Serres and others). Epicurus' idea is that the *clinamen* is the 'swerve'[5] that makes visible the atoms that would otherwise be falling indistinctly through space. The atoms pre-exist the swerve, but it is the swerve that lends form and visibility to them. The question is over what it might mean to animate the elements of the structure *otherwise* so that retroaction might gather them, and in that 'swerve' allow it to found the new formation. It is this reconfiguration of elements, that in their materiality are given, but which are determinate only at the point at which they are caught up in the form-giving event. 'Machiavelli's whole theory, all its distinctive concepts', says Althusser in the *Écrits Philosophiques*, 'are only

---

[5] In the winter of 1417, writes Stephen Greenblatt in *The Swerve* (2011), the papal secretary Poggio Bracciolini made a great discovery. In an abbey in Germany he came across a manuscript of a long-lost classical poem, Lucretius' *De Rerum Natura* ('On the Nature of the Universe'). He sees it as the origin of the renaissance and, in effect, of modernity. According to Lucretius, who borrows the concept of the 'clinamen' from Epicurus, when atoms move straight down through the void by their own weight, they deflect a bit in space at a quite uncertain time and in uncertain places, just enough that you could say that their motion has changed. But if they were not in the habit of swerving, they would all fall straight down through the depths of the void, like drops of rain, and no collision would occur, nor would any blow be produced among the atoms. In that case, nature would never have produced anything. For Negri, 'Lucretius poses his clinamen on the tip of his tongue, *sotto voce*, almost hoping to cancel out the violence of the tear coming from this barely perceptible deviation that lets the world change, and lets it grasp the singular and along with it the meaning of freedom. A tiny yet enormous glow shines through the rainfall of atoms.' Negri (2000b) (The extract is taken from the English translation, published under the title 'Prolegomena to the Common (para. 11), available at www.generation-online.org/t/almavenus.htm.) In his excellent paper on 'aleatory materialism' Banu Bargu puts it like this: 'In this sense, the swerve has an ontological priority to the reality of the atoms, even if those atoms exist in abstract form before the swerve. It is the encounter of atoms due to a random swerve that grants these particles their reality' (Bargu, 2012: 86).

the impotent thought of this event, of the advent of this event'. The event is the encounter between *fortuna*, that which is given as material context, and *virtù*, the form-giving intervention. Note that *fortuna* is no longer the term for what – as structure – remains invariant, but instead holds up a context that can be reconfigured and recognised through the gesture that reconfigures it. The swerve is what in its retroaction signifies, because it recovers a meaning of what is gathered, what is re-assembled, through its gesture. This is retro*action* rather than retrospection because it *acts* on material conditions. It acts *if* and as long as the encounter persists, and this is an '*if*' open to the vagaries of history and the force of *virtù*. As Althusser explains it (1999: 197–203), once the encounter takes place and takes hold, the combination of disparate elements produces something irreducible to these elements. What lasts, what takes hold as accomplished fact, *gives itself* a foundation, a normative premise, but 'there is nothing which has become except as determined by the result of this becoming – the retroaction itself' (Althusser, 1982/2006: 193). The grounding reconfigures the ground, as we saw earlier. And no given combinatory secures it.

The encounter in effect *triangulates* the relationship between structure and event, and introduces potentiality of both action and agency. We will say something more about how this potentiality is poised on the theoretical conjuncture. It is the encounter that sends Althusser's dialectical materialism on its 'adventure', down a path that he calls 'aleatory'. 'Adventure' because it is a wager that receives no warrant, as it received none in Lucien Goldmann, earlier. Contingency is radicalised in the theory of 'aleatory materialism' as Althusser describes it, and this, against all the assumptions that usually accompany the term, is a materialism of chance, risk and openness, *aleatory* from the Latin term *alea* for the throwing of the dice. Althusser is introducing an open dialectic of the kind that turns Marx's theory to the future, and grants it the promise of the constituent. Its 'contradictory conjuncture' with all it entails, contains (sometimes *in nuce*) the argument for an open constitutional dialectic, while the overbearing *fortuna* instils what he calls, and Foucault later popularises, a *dispositif*. I will argue that the phenomenological method, as we have discussed it, gives us rare insight into the open dialectic in both dimensions, affective (i.e. how it attaches to the experience of actors) and hermeneutic (how it informs the construction of meaning). It is a phenomenology now poised on contradiction. It is Althusser that has brought us to this point: to have read him is to have read his reading of Machiavelli and Marx *in tandem*. We looked at the 'contradictory demand' that Althusser reads into Machiavelli, that forces open the dialectic of history, introduces the 'wager' of the aleatory and the production of the new in the encounter. And we looked at how the 'adventure' of the open dialectic is beholden neither to the contradiction from which it will ensue, nor to a telos. Althusser's renowned anti-Hegelianism puts a distance between that adventure and any 'teleological ballast'. And his use of the term 'adventure' is closer to the *Adventures of the Dialectic*, in which Maurice Merleau-Ponty had used the term 'adventure' to loosen the grip of the 'negative' in the dialectic of history, and the idea that history works to release a proletariat that exists as a 'suppression of itself'. Instead, 'one finds only proletarians who think and wish this or that, who see correctly or incorrectly, who are in any case always in the world', says Merleau-Ponty, closer to Marx of the *Grundrisse* and the analysis of 'friendly societies' one finds there. Most important for the current argument is Merleau-Ponty's insight that Marxism had underestimated the 'hold of positivity on the working class': 'in order to establish themselves on the terrain of history they must exist positively', he says (1955/1973: 89), and uses the term 'adventure' – with all the connotations of what is *waged* – to capture that positive undertaking. Similarly,[6] Althusser borrows the term *adventure* from Machiavelli to insist on the *generation* of a form, not a capture of an existing one, not the 'old wardrobe' of concepts that Marx berates in *The Eighteenth Brumaire*, but the forging of form he belatedly admires in the Communards in *The Civil War in France*. Finally, the theoretical conjuncture offers us a methodology that turns on *the performativity of knowledge production*, the critical insight of the eleventh thesis. And it thereby embraces the radical opening of philosophy in politics that is critical theory. The *phenomenological corrective* that carries across the spectrum of these Marxisms, that pivots on this term 'adventure', furnishes the agents of history with the knowledge of history in which, and on which, they can act. The emergence of this perspective carries its very own reflexivity that cuts an oblique path through praxis philosophy. Speaking of this other 'encounter' – between Marxism and Phenomenology – Bernard Waldenfels, summarises it beautifully for us: 'Were I to be asked about the point at which

---

[6] A loaded term to deploy, admittedly, in the context of the Marxisms of the late 1950s and 1960s in France. Althusser would have read Merleau-Ponty's *Adventures of the Dialectic* (1955/1973), which were written over a decade before he gave his own lectures on Machiavelli at the ENS, in which he cites Merleau-Ponty's 'Note on Machiavelli' (from the latter's *Eloge de la Philosophie*). For an intricate account, see Francois Matheron's 'editorial note' in Althusser (1999: vii–ix).

the genuine impulses of phenomenology and Marxism might encounter one another', he says, it would be around '*a vision that transforms the seen*' (Waldenfels, 1984: x).

Phenomenology, Contradiction and the Open Dialectic

In our earlier discussion of the phenomenological method, we saw that it is built around the key insight that the givenness of things in the world cannot be thought of independently of their givenness *to* structures of intentionality. The organising insight of *the phenomenological reduction* involves a bracketing of pure givenness (or self-existence), replaced by the *mediation* of the phenomena that appear by the subjective modes of access to them. The 'significative' (or 'significational') difference takes the form: 'what appears (meaningful) is what appears *as* something *to* someone'. The formulation is not further reducible as far as phenomenology is concerned: the significative difference lies at the point of recovery of meaning. Any attempt to dig deeper, any attempt to get *behind* it, already presupposes it.

All this has been discussed earlier. We return to it now to link the discussion of the 'significative difference' and the 'phenomenological reduction' to the *adventure* of the dialectic as we have followed its unfolding, with an emphasis on what it means to keep it 'open'. In this respect, how might phenomenology help us think about *potentiality*? But more troublingly perhaps, how does contradiction help us to navigate that terrain? How to make sense of what might install itself as contradictory at the level of the significative difference? It is argued that contradiction disturbs the ways in which meaning is settled, the ways it sediments and ossifies; it disturbs what is thus constituted as familiar, as natural and as given. Within that context something important emerges at the point where potentiality and contradiction articulate.

To think in a materialist way ('*en materialiste*' as per Althusser) is to depart from that which, as *fortuna*, constitutes the conditions of undertaking the 'adventure'. The field of the constituted, or 'institué', cannot be transcended, only bracketed. It is the field of mediations that as *lifeworld* informs our grasp of the world. The bonds that tie us to the world 'can only be slackened, not cut', says Merleau-Ponty.[7] In the stubborn navigation of the inert materiality of *fortuna* through subjective initiative, ability and intelligence – in other words, the subjective conditions of an

---

[7] For Merleau-Ponty's own 'adventure of the dialectic', see his *Phenomenology of Perception* (1945/1982: xv and passim).

undertaking for which Machiavelli reserved the term *virtù* – there emerges a phenomenological moment *in nuce* that Althusser gives expression to in the notion of the encounter, the form-giving event. It bears on the subjective dimension (the 'something to *someone*') of the phenomenological reduction, that positions the subject: the 'encounter' allows the Prince to emerge *as* Prince founding the principality in the very act of claiming it, establishing his speaking position in the act of speaking it. We explored the sense in which the processes of becoming-the-Prince and becoming-the-principality are coincident. What is striking in the analysis that Althusser offers of the mutual constitution, is that the Prince is uniquely and exclusively defined by the 'historical vacuum he must fill'. It is the same dilemma that Marx stands before when he identifies the proletariat as the *void* of early bourgeois society.[8] In both cases there is 'vacuum' or void because the significative difference that would have lent either situation legibility – the prince *as* representing national unity, the proletariat *as* a class *for*-itself – is not yet conceptually available, historically not yet in place. And if it is not yet available it is because the significative difference is indeterminate at both poles. The prince is summoned as a potential subject of a potential practice, and with potentiality at both poles the significative difference that would allow 'x as x' finds itself unhinged. The difference runs *alongside* the action, as it were, available only *a posteriori*, forged in the very act that offers signification. That was what the *'clinamen'* was about, the definitional swerve that gave form to the underdetermined material.[9] In the process, *fortuna* takes shape and is called forth as reconfigured through its encounter with *virtù*, and if Althusser's 'materialist' reading offers us a

---

[8] It is as 'void' that Alain Badiou defines it in *Being and Event*. In Badiou's earlier work that was centred on subjectivity, the notion of 'becoming-subject' involved a dialectical movement from 'working class' to 'proletariat', the former denoting the structural relations in place, the latter the agent of a historical *displacement*. This topology is qualified in *Being and Event* in terms of the distinction between situation/event. Here 'proletariat' is the name of the *evental site* in the capitalist *situation*, a site defined by the exploitation of waged labour. And yet it is from this particular labouring 'place' that a proletarian subject may rise to reconfigure the situation through an intervening event that demands fidelity to a project that can only claim its site in defiance of the given distribution of place. For a supportive reconstruction, see also Rancière (1989).

[9] It is the same swerve that that other important phenomenological endeavour, Luhmann's systems theory, captures through the difference between loose and strict coupling. For Luhmann, meaning is 'strictly coupled' in systems that lend coding and programming to what otherwise, as loosely coupled in the field of complexity (like Epicurus' loose atoms), does not yet yield meaning. The *medium* of language is there, but not yet (systemic) *form*.

bridge, it is because the 'phenomenological strain of Marxism'[10] that he is articulating, *strains* against the structural inertia of the materials out of which the event of 'the encounter' might be fashioned.

Where potentiality unsettled both poles of the significative distinction at once, *contradiction* comes to unsettle the 'as' on which they pivot. The clearest, and devastating, case where we encountered this is in what Marx called the fetish phenomenon. At the point at which the significative distinction operates to give meaning ('something as something to someone'), labour is summoned *as* a commodity *to* the proletariat. The self-understanding of labourers *as* owners of labour power is only available to them if labour power can be valorised by being put to use, but this realisability is contingent on the owners of capital. The contingency infects the significative difference and makes the *meaning* of what workers do and their agency as workers *provisional*. Meaninglessness at this point attaches to the very possibility of recognition, a pathology that Marx used the term 'alienation', and Lukács the term 'reification', to capture. Whether contradiction might be tapped, whether the contradictory conjuncture might be seen for what it is, requires us to look more closely at what contradiction *means, how it is experienced*, and how it operates vis-à-vis the significative difference. As the argument proceeds, I hope to show that a critical position might be fashioned out of these questions, and that contradiction might leverage a critical phenomenology in the direction of offering redress.

So, having now located potentiality and contradiction phenomenologically, let us look at how a critical phenomenology might see its task, a phenomenology that is critical in that it harbours *an open dialectic* of the type that can be derived from the phenomenological strain of Marxism that we have been discussing. The following features would qualify it as an *open* dialectic (I borrow Bernard Waldenfels' very useful categorisation from *Phenomenology and Marxism* (Waldenfels et al.: 1984)):

(i) The dialectic method involves a *unity* between the whole and the parts, a (vertical) relation that unfolds in time. For the dialectic to be open, the whole must be understood as an open horizon, one whose telos is not *already* envisaged as the *completion* of a form. The whole is not yet determined.

(ii) The dialectic involves a *succession* of stages, of affirmation, negation and supersession, and thus a directionality and a forward

---

[10] This is the term Habermas uses (1971: 28).

temporality. For the dialectic to be open in this respect, nothing guarantees either the 'synthesis' it must accomplish or any steady deployment of the temporal modality of the present-future. If the process inclines towards its goal, nothing warrants that it will reach it.

(iii) The dialectic involves a (horizontal) relation of *reciprocity* between subject and co-subject that stand towards each other in a relation of co-evolution and co-constitution, in which 'each simultaneously forms and transforms itself' (1984: 103). For the dialectic to be open in this respect, these dynamic processes of co-implication and recognition cannot be taken unambiguously as steps towards reconciliation. Reciprocity has not yet reached reconciliation.

Take each in turn. For *unity* to sustain – and be sustained – as an open dialectic, the relationship between the whole and the parts needs to remain 'alive' at both poles. Lukács was one of the first to draw attention to the way in which the reverse motion was underway under capitalism, with the severing, or 'autonomisation', of parts from the whole, that allowed them to appear as the reality of commodified exchange, as the *facts* of social life, raised to consciousness in the categories of the political economy and comprehended through formal rational laws.[11] Lukács calls them the 'static categories of bourgeois thought' because no transcendent reason can collect the fragments of exchange relationships in anything that might overcome the fragmentation and the meaninglessness it inflicts. It is a similar absence of any dialectical movement between whole and parts that underscores Hayek's one-way projection from the micro to the macro, that as we saw (in Chapter 3.1) comprehends the political economy as the generalisation of individual micro-economic behaviour upscaled. In his important but largely forgotten treatise, *Dialectics of the Concrete*, Karel Kosik explains the open dialectic in the following way: 'A dialectical conception of totality means that the parts not only internally interact and interconnect both among themselves and with the whole, but also that the whole cannot be petrified in an abstraction superior to the facts... because precisely in the interaction of its part does the whole *form* itself as a whole' (Kosik, 1967/2012: 23). Where everything is relation and movement, the historical present is a site of conflictual forces whose configuration is always unstable, and where the unity of the whole is exposed to both alignment and contradiction of the parts.

---

[11] See Andrew Feenberg, for a useful analysis (1981: 83).

'Without contradictions,' Kosik says, 'totality is empty and static; outside totality contradictions are formal and arbitrary' (30). It is arguably the same thought that drives Althusser to conceptualise 'unity as open horizon'. To understand what appears as unity as a matter of phenomenology, Althusser's 'adventure' introduced contingency into the heart of the materialist thinking of chance, where any *sense* of unity is waged on this contingency, and no totality can be fixed in advance as context of the distribution of parts. For Althusser, Machiavelli 'thinks and formulates' the 'theoretical disjuncture, this contradiction without wishing to propose any theoretical reduction or resolution of it. ... This thinking of the disjuncture stems from the fact that Machiavelli not only formulates, but thinks, his problem *politically* – that is to say, as a contradiction in reality that cannot be removed by thought, but only by reality', marking 'the presence of history and political practice in theory itself' (1999: 80).

When it comes to the temporal dimension, to *process* and the promise of *synthesis*, an open dialectic involves a to-and-fro, an oscillation between temporal modalities, progress, discontinuity, interruption and reversal. All of this with its full complement of false starts, impasses and aporiae, which the contradictory conjunction brings into the picture of historical unfolding. If for Hegel contradiction is the 'motor' of the dialectic of world History (its *Sprinquelle* as Marx puts it in *Capital*), Althusser's contrary concern was emphatically not with the unfolding of reason in history but with the inauguration of that which would not depend for its development on what was already in place. If the event was new it was because its conditions only gained legibility *post-factum*. To read the reversal involves something more than retrospection, it involves retroaction, as we said.

There is something very important about how we understand *genealogy* in this, in other words, about how we rethink the historical emergence of what we take for granted, and how we put that historical emergence to question. Foucault deployed the term in order to disrupt the conceptual operations that installed a narrative form of history with its enveloping logic that overdetermined 'discrepant' pasts. Link contradiction to genealogy, and it unsettles the narrative orderings of succession, of simultaneity, of futurity, of origin, releases them from sequence, paces and punctuates the past otherwise. Most importantly, it releases the thinking of the past from the points in time when certainties were installed that sent historical trajectories on their way. To think 'in the conjuncture', was Althusser's invitation, and that may indeed be a good way to think about the past from a point of view that, while embedded in historical narratives, is nevertheless invited to reflect – and insert critical distance between – 'it' and its embeddedness. If Althusser excavates in Machiavelli's work 'an exceptional form of thought' that 'ponders and preserves a theoretical disjuncture', it is to set thought before the historical challenge of 'the great adventure [that] begins apart from everything that actually exists, hence in an unknown place with an unknown man' (80). And if 'man' in this formulation denotes *anything* at all, the 'gathering' work that the concept performs relates first and foremost to contradiction rather than identity: *a signifier on the move*.

It has been argued that the notion of an open dialectic forces us to rethink the question of unity as a reciprocal relationship between whole and parts that resists completion, and to re-conceive historical processes as anything but inexorable. The role of contradiction was key in both cases in sustaining the openness. But to appreciate how much *is staked on contradiction* in turning the phenomenology critical, we must turn to the relations between subjects (Waldenfeld's third category, above) to look at the relations of reciprocity and recognition, the patterning of collectivity and association, the open processes of conflict and cooperation. Again, contradiction plays a crucial role in forestalling closure and preventing the *a priori* underwriting of consensus, even as regulative ideal: processes of co-implication and recognition cannot (and need not) be taken unambiguously as steps towards reconciliation. It is perhaps above all here, at the lifeworld sites of subject-formation and intersubjectivity, that contradiction offers phenomenology its most significant contribution. It involves both conceptual and affective registers. At the conceptual level it helps us to understand what it would mean to *achieve* hermeneutical traction – 'something as something' – with the help of contradiction. At the affective level, to explore the 'something as something to someone' as a question of the '*Dasein*' of the contradiction, as it were, in other words how it inscribes itself in the lifeworld of individuals as a crisis of articulation and expressibility. The achievement of the appearance of something as 'strange' lies in that it *appears at all*, rather than being experienced as meaningless compulsion.

At the level of conceptual analysis, the contradiction locates itself on the boundary of the significative difference, between the 'something' and the 'as something'. The difference itself marks the site of the phenomenological reduction; as a difference the significative difference separates and conjoins the two. The phenomenological reduction occurs in the crossing. To think of it as the site of contradiction is to think of a negativity that stands in the way of that crossing, that disturbs it, and with it disturbs the movement towards appearance or iteration. To put it in these terms is to pick up, with Marx, the self-undermining moment of thought hitting upon its limit *given* the categories available to it. While in Marx contradictions are indices of concrete historical situations, contrary to the cruder materialisms (of Engels and others) they (contradictions) are not to be understood as the reflections in thought of real material antagonisms. They need to be understood instead as *a shortfall of the categories available to us to make* sense of the processes of value production and social reproduction, *the mismatch between the categories of thought and the modes of social being*. Their emergence as contradictions marks the crisis-points of iteration, of expressibility and of intelligibility: of *meaninglessness* that is *experienced* as such. Something is thwarted. And alongside the thwarting appears, ever so obliquely, the opportunity to put a name to it. This is the potential moment of 'hermeneutical traction', and we will need recourse to strategy before we can mobilise it to identify a *claim* at this juncture. And yet already something has appeared here, as 'strange'. It is important to emphasise this experiential dimension, the lived incomprehensibility that emerges in particular experiential contexts and that carries its potential energies. It is the hallmark of *immanent* critique. The appearance of something new in the public sphere is not a normative but an existential event: what breaks into the economy of representation is not the abstract principle of a new set of subject positions but the lived reality of an existential deficit. It is the lived dimension that is the potential site of disruption of the economy of representation that would otherwise organise meaning, seal it over and, in this state of self-immunisation, place it out of reach. It is on the affective register that immanent critique achieves its inscription as an outrage against suffering, and offers an aperture for redress.

Thus, one of the most cherished insights that comes from Hegelian Marxism is that the categories at our disposal – the thwarted, historically poised, perpetually incomplete knowledge set that furnishes the reflexivity of the Age, any Age – do not quite give us the semantic reach that we strive for. They are instead caught up in a language – of labour valorisation, of right, of individual freedom – that already carries the deficit that they are meant to address. This applies most devastatingly to the language of the valorisation of labour, that inevitably does not carry Marx as far as his critical insight would have carried him. 'To change the world,' Merleau-Ponty argued, 'we need a truth which gives us a hold on adversity, not opaque and rigidified, but a world that is dense, and which moves' (1955/1973: 89). As the experience of deprivation reaches out for a language to express it, something in the dialectic of semantic and structure 'carr[ies] out *a displacement* ... makes *something move over (bouger)* in the internal disposition of the philosophical categories'. Earlier (Chapter 1.3) we saw that Althusser described it as a 'new *practice* of philosophy, a philosophical discourse that speaks *from somewhere else* than classical philosophical discourse did'. As Althusser puts the 'point' of the 'transformation', 'philosophical discourse changes its modality – speaks *otherwise (autrement)*, which creates the difference between interpreting the world and changing it' (174). It is a difference that critical phenomenology suggests may be *crossed*.

It is against this background that our discussion of contradiction proceeds. Critical thought located in the in-between (if this topological metaphor doesn't assume too much), the semantic reach of categories that carry that deficit, and what as antinomical, as contradictory, might disturb their 'fit'. At that interstice something emerges that might offer the experience of suffering the promise of hermeneutic traction with the categories under which it is administered. The cry 'this is unjust', that Ricoeur suggested earlier, is enigmatic because it precedes any theory of justice that might have grounded it, and Weil's 'cry' 'why am I being hurt?' that is 'infallible' because any attempt to answer it misses it, are revealing on the register on which the phenomenological concept of the 'strange' reveals.[12] They are revealing because they are expressed as interruptions to a necessity which otherwise asserts itself with the full weight of self-evidence and relentlessness. They are revealing not because something is already held as a counter-claim, but because the negative has disturbed the distribution of the sensible, as Rancière would call it. The 'strange' appears as the unsettling of given and programmed selections, an interruption in the stream of reassurances. In the field of living labour, time produces value but is recompensed as expenditure in the field of dead labour. On the affective register it appears strange, lacking sense, that the market situation forces everyone to make a living by creating value for the market in order that market distribute less employment, stagnant wages and more debt. The antinomy of the labour market situation *appears* as the contingency of the availability of work against the necessity of its performance (as was argued

---

[12] The concept of the 'strange' is developed by Husserl. See Lindahl's insightful deployment of the concept (2013), in Chapter 4.3 above.

earlier).[13] The antinomy between the superfluity and the necessity in the value-form of labour is radicalised where the crisis is intensified to the point where under conditions of the global organisation of production surplus populations, absolutely redundant to the needs of capital, are consolidated. The difference between necessary and unnecessary suffering is then the affective index of this antinomy.

If, in all this, the 'encounter' connotes a topology, a space of reception, it is a space that must be claimed. The space is forged, and the sovereign event, the moment of politics, finds its locution in the very act of inscribing itself. This is no meta-political topology, whether that involves Arendt's delimitations of the political and the social, or Lefort's empty space of sovereignty constituted and guarded to remain vacant. In Machiavelli, and in Althusser, there is no seat beckoning a Prince, as there is nothing empty about the site: it is replete with concrete practices. 'There is no lack of matter', says Machiavelli (1999: 28), though it is matter unaccommodating and unworthy of the advent of the event. Rancière's own use of contradiction as *dissensus*, is heavily resonant with this Althusserian message, despite the much-proclaimed break of Rancière from his former teacher. Rancière's critical phenomenological move is a move of contestation of political space as given, a strategic deployment of contradiction for which he reserves the term *dissensus*. His politics turns on claiming its stage, a conjuncture of sorts clearly at odds with any topology of political space, in other words, of any meta-political delineation. 'Metapolitics', he says, 'is the attempt to perform the task of politics by other means' (Rancière, 2009a: 122). We can leave the metaphor of political space and the full theoretical armoury of its delineation and evacuation to the Arendtians, as we move our discussion, finally, to *the material constitution*. Here we come up against the interplay between constitutional semantics and constitutional structures, and we will borrow from Foucault the concept of a *dispositif* to explore how critical thinking might inscribe itself in the constitutional dispositif to help navigate its contradictory terrain.

---

[13] Where Marx speaks of the production of a population which is superfluous to capital's average requirements for its own valorisation, and is therefore a surplus population. And in *Capital*: 'The working population ... produces both the accumulation of capital and the means by which it is itself made relatively superfluous; and it does this to an extent that is always increasing.' (Marx, 1867/1970: 625)

Semantics and Structures IV: The Constitutional 'Dispositif'

The relation between semantics and the structures that harbour them is perhaps the steepest challenges that present themselves to thinking the 'material constitution'. Althusser's invitation to think constitutional strategy *'en materialiste'* carries the organising distinction constituent/constituted power into the field of what he called the *dispositif*, a term that Michel Foucault later deployed to lend expression to the 'linkage' between 'discursive and non-discursive' elements. More specifically, for Foucault, the *dispositif* names

> [f]irst, an essentially heterogeneous ensemble, composed of discourses, institutions, architectural formations, regulatory decisions, laws, administrative measures, scientific statements, philosophical, moral, and philanthropic arguments; these are the elements of a dispositif – in short, what is said as much as what is unsaid [du dit aussi bien que du non-dit]. The dispositif itself is the network that might be established between these elements. Second, what I want to identify in a dispositif is precisely the nature of the linkage that exists between these heterogeneous elements ... These elements, whether they are discursive or non-discursive, are linked by something like a game, with changes of position or modifications of functions that can themselves be very different. Third, by dispositif I mean a kind of formation which has in a particular historical moment been given the important function of addressing some kind of urgent situation. Therefore, a dispositif has a predominantly strategic function, [which involves] a rational and concerted intervention in relations of force, either so as to develop them in a particular direction or so as to block them, stabilize them, or exploit them.[14]

Note the three elements in this account: first, the dispositif is defined as a network, or assemblage, of elements; secondly, what is salient is the nature of the linkage between discursive and material elements; and, thirdly, the dispositif is linked with time ('a particular historical moment', 'some kind of urgent situation') and strategic intervention ('rational and concerted'). Regarding the definition as *network*: to understand the dispositif as a set of relations or connections between elements is to understand how power can be concretely located and materialised. Connections and relations are forged through the organisation of space, the distribution of bodies, and

---

[14] Foucault, 'Le jeu de Michel Foucault', in *Dits et Ecrits*, Vol. iii (1994) 299, quoted by Alain Pottage (2012: 181) who provides an exceptional approximation of the work of Foucault and Luhmann.

the development of infrastructures (architectural forms and institutional locations, famously the 'panopticon', the barracks, the clinic, etc.), comprising both material structures (and infrastructures) and discursive forms. Regarding *'linkage'*: legal materiality heeds Foucault's call to examine precisely the nature of the linkage that exists between the heterogeneous elements in a dispositif. 'The potential of a legal materialist approach depends upon the ability of the scholarly interpreter to observe, distinguish, and reassemble the legal dispositif by attending to the specificities of material elements of legality engaged in the legal "game".'[15] If we think of the most celebrated of Foucault's 'dispositifs' – discipline, sexuality, governmentality – we are reminded that 'each of these incorporated or metabolized law, but they did so precisely by treating texts, practices, visibilities, and self-descriptions as elements that derived their sense and effect from their articulation in each given dispositif.[16] Elements are brought into relation and thereby *actualised* in the ordering. But finally and perhaps most importantly note how Foucault links *strategy* to the dispositif. Strategy, he tells us, is attentive to the particular historical context and intervenes in the opportune moment. *Time is nothing but intervention*, as Rancière puts it (1989). Foucault's analysis here presents us also with a theory of resistance as immanent to the social formation that mobilises a subjectivity that must negotiate a double bind, simultaneously bound to the process of subjectification, with all the disciplinary and biopolitical mechanisms that attend it, and as emergent subject present to itself, as it were (Foucault, 1982). It is the bind that the social anthropologist Tim Ingold alludes to when he describes 'converting the lines along which life is lived into boundaries in which it is contained' (Ingold, 2007: 2–3). Strategies of contesting such containment are tested at the junctures where the *constitutional dispositif* entrenches lines of force, and where institutional arrangements and systems of roles coalesce around that coherence. The notion moves constitutionalism beyond practices of interlocution and 'dialogue', beyond semantic and conceptual specification, and in the direction of systemic determinations that carry the weight (and inertia) of institutional and organisational determinants, hierarchical power relations and other *structural* givens that inform it and sustain it. To read *'en materialiste'*

---

[15] As Hyo Yoon Kang and Sara Kendall put it in 'Legal Materiality', in Del Mar et al. (2019).
[16] Pottage (2012: 181). Also: as in the case of Latour's actor-networks, dispositifs are 'assemblages [that] are made up of nothing other than what they assemble'; strategic or tactical modes of actualising and conjoining the elements of a dispositif are emergent articulations that are conditioned by the very elements that they purport to organise.

is to trace lines of demarcation within the dispositif, and to heighten and intensify those contradictions – discerning the lines of force that constitute it and the fault lines along which its weaknesses emerge.

Entrenchment on both structural and semantic registers discipline the constitutional imaginary strictly, at junctures that it becomes ever more difficult critically to negotiate let alone challenge. The constitutional situation thus emerges, with its own limited dynamism, its path-dependencies, its release of contingency – the possibility to think otherwise along these path dependencies. We discussed the constitutional situation earlier (Chapter 4.1) with an emphasis on the semantic and structural conditions imposed on constitutional discourse and the disciplining of its reach. With the 'dispositif' an organisational dimension is added to that disciplining, the opacities that are built into practices that the 'new materialisms' have done so much to reveal: everything from the deep structure of organisational and professional activity, to the minutiae of the ways files are kept and archived, topics discussed and minuted, etc. These are materialities understood as both facilitations and blockages of interpretative continuities that carry constitutive force into the field of semantics. Of course, forms of argumentation, rhetorical and narrative formations and condensations sometimes stretch the constitutional 'imaginary'. But there are lines of force, institutional arrangements, organisational elements that frame, and are neither reducible nor transparent to the field of interlocution and enunciation. They accompany the emergence of constitutional meaning in all its dimensions, the available thematisations in the material dimension, role relevant inflections in the social, the accelerations, delays and suspensions of discourse in the temporal, but as well as setting the context they are also its 'blind spots'. These materialities run alongside the processes of meaning formation, as apparatus, assemblage or 'network', alternately lending visibility and – in ANT's preferred idiom – 'black-boxing'. They are the forms that *fortuna* takes in the semiotic field of the constitution.

We will conclude with two materialist readings of the constitution that in both cases turn on the 'contradictory demand' that we are seeking theoretically to discern and exploit. The first is a text by Negri written in the 1960s but that could find no publication outlet for over a decade during the 'years of lead' in Italy, a text that centres the materialist reading explicitly on labour; the second is Rancière's argument about *dissensus* as the strategic staging of a contradictory dynamic.

*

Negri's 'Labor in the Constitution', his brief genealogy of leftist constitutionalism, is a treatise on the meaning of the *material constitution*. The Italian Constitution of 1948 famously proclaims in its first article: 'Italy is a democratic republic founded on labour', and backs this with the significant guarantees of articles 3 and 4.[17] What, asks Negri, is the meaning of this 'solemn proclamation' at the foundation of 'the fortified citadel of bourgeois economic and political power'? (1972/1994: 55) His analysis of the separation of a formal and material layer of constitutional formation drives him into the heart of the contradictory dynamics of the constitutional order between, on the one hand, the subsumption of the material, living, constitution, to the dead letter of the formal text, and on the other the promise of a 'laborist sublimation' of the constitutional order – for what else, he will insist, would the celebration of living labour at the heart of the new constitutional order *mean*? The separation between a formal level of constitutional iteration, and a material level of social valorisation, is key to the contradictory dynamic that concerns us, as it is key to any theory of the material constitution that tries to keep the two levels (of legal iteration and material valorisation) connected, dialectically or otherwise. We keep from this the promise of the *constitutional inscription of labour*, in all its ambivalence, as the antinomic foundation of the material constitution.

What does Negri make of the contradiction? There is no question for Negri that 'the normative character of these articles is recognised' even if they remain largely 'programmatic' absent the norms that would implement them at intermediate levels. But do they, he asks, form a 'coherent normative set'? He quotes Mortati for whom 'labor value contains the fundamental element of the informative political ideology of the entire state arrangement' (56). And he continues: 'In spite of all the ambiguities (and we will later see how they can be resolved) there is no doubt that the concept of the constitution that is principally acknowledged is that of productive labor ... It is a *polemical* concept then, both in the face of privileged social positions and in the face of capitalist exploitation aimed at private accumulation' (57, emphasis added).

---

[17] Article 3, s 2: It is the duty of the Republic to remove those obstacles of an economic and social nature which, really limiting the freedom and equality of citizens, impede the full development of the human person and the effective participation of all workers in the political, economic and social organization of the country. Article 4: The Republic recognizes the right of all citizens to work and promotes those conditions which will make this right effective.

A great deal hinges on this identification of the 'polemical concept' for constitutional strategy, that for Negri here is a formalist strategy that takes article 1 as the basis of its rationalising gesture. There can be no pluralistic solution to this constitutional antinomy for Negri. Such efforts 'are incorrect if intended to deny ... a unitary juridical norm that functions beyond the adversities embedded in its formulation. Scholarship and interpretation should grasp this unity and articulate it systematically' (57). Note the wager involved in this rationalising sweep over contradictory elements, this exercise of 'deviationist doctrine' *avant la lettre*, the insistence that 'the Constitution must be presented as a sufficiently unitary and coherent ordering' (57). This is a wager because the systematic reading that will import coherence might overcome the contradiction in either direction: socialist (if a rationalisation might achieve a coherent reading around the labour constitution) or capitalist (if the reformist reading prevails).

The latter is of course a very real danger, and Negri spends most of the time combating reformism. But crucially, once the social state has introduced the affirmation of social labour as its first, founding constitutional principle it cannot excise it, and the double movement becomes irreducibly present. To seize it as a question of strategy is the task he faces. To do this he will resort to a formalist theory of constitutional interpretation, in fact the most formalist of theories, where interpretation is all about coherence and systematicity. A constitutional order is an achievement of unity, and the most complete theory of such unity Negri finds in Kelsen, in *The General Theory of Law and State*. The problem is, of course, that in Kelsen the formal level eclipses the material in a gesture at once of abstention and unification.[18] The unity of the constitutional order finds its point of closure in an act of self-reference (the law hypothetically validates itself in the *Grundnorm*) that thereby severs any dependence on the material base on which it lies. 'All is foreseen, all is included in the constitutive process and the expansive rhythm of the ordering' (110). Here is a formalism that must close itself off ceaselessly from the material level which can only be its other-reference. *And yet* this is an other-reference it cannot retract from, cannot perpetually expel or excise, because it – social labour that is – is the source of its dynamism as a system, returning in new forms, necessitating a renewed gesture, in a process that

---

[18] '[F]or the first time the idea was posed that the entire social normation could derive from, be deduced from, and be validated by a fundamental norm that unified everything in itself' (Negri, 1972/1994: 109).

is ultimately contradictory and which, as the social constitutionalism compromise exhibits with clarity, depends on a disconnect that the constitution finds increasingly hard to maintain: 'the legal relationship is immediately social, and in this sociality the relationship is continually reconsidered and renovated, measuring itself against the concreteness of the cases to be solved making itself adequate to their plurality' (91).

So here are the elements of Negri's contradictory constitutionalism: its *motor is* 'the act of having assumed labor as its own constitutive category on a social level' (65). This means that the constitution has imported the source of antagonism as its own animating principle: as élan of its own development. Nothing that capitalism does (no 'principle of adequation': 70) will give it *adequate expression* despite its integration in the social state. But if social labour has been imported into the constitution as its motor, it also constitutes a limit to any principle of adequation, in other words, any notion that it can find adequate expression in constitutional terms. Let us expand on this. As *motor* of the constitution it animates constitutional development, it provides the élan of the production of value, the nucleus of constitutional development, and existential foundation of the formal edifice. As *limit*, articles 1, 3 and 4 of the labour constitution provide the threshold that cannot be crossed without giving the lie to the constitutive commitment to the dignity of labour. And if Negri here voices a widespread concern that the value of labour is expressed 'so generally as to be virtually innocuous' in these articles, the critical constitutional undertaking elevates them *as dogmatic resources* to form the foundations for what can be thematised as constitutional. This is not Negri's language, and yet an unlikely symmetry connects Negri's argument to the tradition of the dogmatic. What holds together the constitutional imaginary as *unity* will draw from dogma the non-negotiable origin of constitutional iteration. The commitment to labour inscribed in the Italian Constitution, for all the transmutations of its passage through the factory, the Fordist and post-Fordist figurations, remains something of a constitutional 'prerequisite' that is at once also – in its irreducible reference to cooperation, sociality and subjectivity – an irreducible trace that persists, in Negri, as a kind of latent communism within the real subsumption of society by capital. 'It is because the antagonism between concrete labor and abstract labor needed to be transformed into contradictions, and the entire path of contemporary juridical thought is oriented toward determining the specific mediations of these contradictions.' And finally: 'How is it possible at this point, once and for all, to abandon the conception of constituent power as necessarily negating itself in posing the constitution and recognize a constituent power that no longer produces constitutions separate from itself but is itself constitution?' (Negri, 1994: 309).

Let us stay with this antagonistic constitutional moment to link it back to an argument that that we made early on (Chapter 1.3) when we first addressed the question of how semantics and structures relate in a movement that affects both sides. We find the same *problématique* in Negri's account of the *semantics* of labour protection in the Italian Constitution and the organisational *structure* of its social state. There is something significant about how Negri struggles to explain that the 'double movement', as he put it, remains alive in the 'subsumption' of the material to the formal level that must pivot on an 'affirmation' but entertain with it a relation of being 'always within but always beyond' it, an *affirmation therefore that is contested even as it affirms*. We are again confronted with the conceptual categories that must provide the 'slack' in the very act of naming what they name. Negri says: 'the relationship between the working class and its organised movement is double and ambiguous' and the question of what is the 'relationship' – and therefore the 'movement' – in this formulation is begged in that term: *'its'*. What is the meaning of the distance (that might allow a relationship *between* terms) of the 'working class' from *its* 'organised movement', or of 'living labour' from *its* constitutional expression under the aegis of capital? A 'double movement' of belonging to it and negating it, since it is 'born' and 'expressed' (Negri tells us) antagonistically to a language that was developed to contain it. To understand the movement at the level of concepts, then, a movement that disturbs the smooth coincidence and containment, we need to hold on to the contradictory language that both gives expression to the containment while marking the limits of that containment.

What makes the double movement possible in Negri's constitutional analysis is that labour is a *polemical concept*. In the way that Marx put it in the *Grundrisse*, that 'there is not a single category of capital that can be taken out of this antagonism, out of this perpetually fissioning flux' (1857/2005: 131), for Negri, the affirmation that labour creates through its abstract form is confronted by the negation carried by the concrete form of labour. The disconnect 'between what is unified at the abstract level' and what is expressed 'in its real, living movement, is ferociously polemical' (1972/1994: 114). But the problem we face, in terms of the semiosis of the contradiction, its emergence in a critical phenomenology, is that the self-evidence of what is 'carried' at the concrete level is denied signification via the unitary affirmation. And on this point Negri remains silent, his solution carried (at least at the time) in a faith in the labour movement as its own 'autonomist' guarantee. Absent such a meta-guarantee, to navigate the impasse is difficult for the reason that we have seen all along: the contradiction must be *forced*, the event of the non-coincidence extracted out of materials that at the same time as the constitutional ordering *unfolds, folds* what is incongruous *back into* the constitutional *situation*. The conceptual difficulty is around what will break out as *event* from the comprehensive introversion where labour, the source of valorisation, is always-already invoked as a commodity, where 'living labour' is called forth as 'dead labour', and where the constitution orchestrates that invocation and that recall in the movement of formal and real subsumption. I have argued that a strategic resistance to these enfoldings can draw inspiration from the function of interdiction associated with the dogmatic function of the constitution. It is the same kind of interdiction that Negri begins with too; he will attach it to the wager of political action, and wage it on the terrain of the political constitution. Constitutional inscription thereby becomes a potential form-giving moment, a site where a contradiction might be forced against what the bourgeois reading of the constitution eclipses. 'Where there is unity we can see contradiction and where there is contradiction we can see antagonism', he concludes (1972/1994: 134). We remain with the 'we can see' as a visibility is forged on the antagonistic plane, such that what reaches impasse at the level juridical determination might open a perspective onto broader antagonisms, a political constitutionalism where these opportunities are not already displaced or substituted for; or at least have not yet given way to the smooth passage of market allocations.

*

No theorist has moved further away from Arendt and Lefort, it seems to me, while remaining within the 'aesthetic' register of the 'stage', than Rancière. His frequent use of spatial placeholders – the 'shores of politics', the 'scene', the 'stage' – belies Rancière's radical reversal of any *topology* understood as *the pre-political delineation* of political space as in Arendt and Lefort. Instead, Rancière's politics finds expression in the gesture of claiming its scene, not in positioning itself on one already given (positively as in Arendt's public *fora*, negatively as in Lefort's empty stage). Politics forever contests a space of figuration. We saw earlier how it comes about in disconnection, interruption and rupture. *And the event of politics,* that which lends it meaning, visibility, audibility, is captured in the eventhood of that disruption. Now we turn to contradiction. And Rancière offers us something significant and productive in the contradictory articulation of his two key conceptual categories: 'politics' and the 'police'. This is how Rancière contrasts the two orders:

> Politics is generally seen as the set of procedures whereby the aggregation and consent of collectivities is achieved, the organization of powers, the distribution of places and roles, and the systems for legitimizing this distribution. I propose to give this system of distribution and legitimization another name. I propose to call it the *police*. ... I now propose to reserve the term politics for an extremely determined activity antagonistic to policing: whatever breaks with the tangible configuration whereby parties and parts or lack of them are defined by a presupposition that, by definition, has no place in that configuration – that of the part of those who have no part. This break is manifest in a series of actions that reconfigure the space where parties, parts, or lack of parts have been defined. ... It makes visible what had no business being seen, and makes heard a discourse where once there was only place for noise; it makes understood as discourse what was once only heard as noise.
>
> (Rancière, 1999: 30)

The emphasis on making visible that which had 'no business being seen' and of making audible that which was 'only heard as noise', marks Rancière's phenomenological contribution. From the outset politics is confronted with contradiction, and the 'miscount' of politics. *Equality* is the concept that pivots the contradictory articulation, comprehensive and substantive. Where with the 'social question', Arendt attempted to excise the question of poverty from politics, Rancière brings it centre stage. 'Politics (that is the interruption of the simple effects of domination by the rich) causes the poor to exist as an entity' (1999: 11). As a collective identification that contrasts them to the rich, it carries them onto the political stage against the horizon of equality; poverty becomes here the political lever par excellence. And when Rancière says that 'politics has no object or issues of its own' (1999: 31), he is emphatically not making Arendt's point, that the political needs to be clearly distinguished from social issues. He is making the point that politics doesn't have an autonomous space because it is always bound up with the order of the police. The latter controls the 'distribution of the sensible' over the social – and what politics brings as its 'sole principle' to bear on that ordering is the principle of equality, that demands different allocations, antagonistic to the capitalist distribution of advantage. What 'politics' brings to the *contradictory* conjunction with the 'police' is the demand for equality.[19] And equality, as principle is not already laden with content but comes under-determined, to take shape in the political practices that will invoke it. In Rancière's own words:

> Nothing is political *in itself* for the political only happens by means of a principle that does not belong to it: equality. The status of this 'principle' needs to be specified. Equality is not a given that politics then presses into service, an essence embodied in the law or a goal politics sets itself the task of attaining. It is a mere assumption that needs to be discerned within the practices implementing it.
>
> (1999: 33)

Rancière argues in effect that when the logic of politics *encounters* the logic of the police, it unsettles it, because it imports a contradiction that cannot be circumvented. Politics occurs when the regular reproduction of the order of the police is stopped in its tracks. In that it inflicts 'a torsion or twist'. Contradiction is what gives political reflexivity its traction. No presence is afforded the constituent (politics) prior to its alignment to the constituted (police) across the axis of their difference, on which the political is played out. Appearance is tied to contradiction, not to the institutional modality of the political as in Arendt, or any co-originality of rights and democracy as in Habermas. None of this is to say that this placing-in-relation is not highly demanding of insight and loyalty. Politics is placed alongside the police, in a contradictory juxtaposition from which it gains its meaning and its leverage.[20] In other words, for political practice to be granted any duration and continuity, to resist being collapsed and absorbed back into the meaning-processing mechanisms of the order of the police, the staging of the political must hold on to the semiosis of its contradictory 'conjunction' with the order of the police.

*

We saw in discussing the *eleventh thesis* that against the reduction of reason to surface understandings that 'interpret the world', Marx argued that reason was properly deployed in thematising the 'existent' with the

---

[19] 'Politics occurs when the egalitarian contingency disrupts the natural pecking order ... The setting-up of politics is identical to the institution of the class struggle' (Rancière, 1999: 18).

[20] 'Politics is thus the name of nothing. It cannot be anything other than policing, that is, the denial of equality' (Rancière, 1999: 30).

view to forging social change. Against the irrationalities with which class society is fraught, irrationalities that emerge as contradictions, tautologies and impasses, against the irrationality of a system that promises justice as it relentlessly delivers injustice, the aim of the philosopher of the eleventh thesis is to restore a properly human rationality. Earlier (in Chapter 1.4) we spoke of the difficulty that Tom Nairn suggested was faced by those attempting to make sense of the 'revolutionary explosion' of May 1968. The events were heavy, he said, 'with a significance too great for our times to bear, a premonitory significance which the events of May could only sketch in outline' (Quattrocchi and Nairn, 1998: 86). Confronted with an event that broke with the theoretical models available to interpret it, the responsibility that befell theory was to lend praxis expression in terms that were *adequate to it*.

This theoretical intervention that carries the central impetus of praxis philosophy must locate itself in the forcefield of the interface between semantics and structures. The structure-semantics complex is crucial to a phenomenology of the field of constitutionalism attentive to meaning-construction. We have explored this in a succession of arguments interspersed through the text. Initially we looked at the improbable extraction of some semantic leeway from the overwhelming structural conditions that Marx (and Lukács) described as 'fetishisation' (and reification respectively). Later, with recourse to analytical approaches we looked at an irreducible normativity that attends the formation and deployment of concepts; and tied it more specifically to constitutional concepts whose normativity finds its most profound iteration in the 'dogmatic' resources of the *ratio juris*. Finally we looked at what it means to think in a materialist way about the constitution, which attaches constitutional semantics to the constitutional *dispositif*. Throughout the series of analyses of 'semantics and structures', crucial from the critical perspective remained the imperative to resist the phenomenological drift that 'constitutional' evolution entails, that finds expression in the mutations of pluralism and governance, and to forge out of these constellations the opportunity of meaningful resistance to semantic drift. For this, we remained with the notion of a *semantic strain, of a critical lagging-behind, to ask*: what is the meaning of the *strain* between the semantics of the constitution and the structural conditions brought about by the transnationalisation of capitalist activity that puts the constitution's *fit* to question? It is against this evolutionism, that views the strain as productive and as forever renewed opportunity of adjustment rather than as irreducible antinomy, that a *critical* project of constitutionalism measures itself. The book has been the effort to link the critical moment to the phenomenological one. The pertinent question that holds it together relates to how critical thought might *force appearance* in the constitutional sites that it must navigate, if it is to counter the inertias at semantic and structural levels. The account of antagonism that carries critique's *contradictory demand* completes the typology of constitutional strategic thinking that began in Chapter 4.2, took a 'ruptural' turn in Chapter 4.3, and insisted on constitutionalising contradiction in Chapter 4.4. At stake in each was to consider the possibilities of a critical phenomenology that enables the appearance of opportunities of redress.

With its threat of a comprehensive shift of the constitutional terrain, the question of holding on to the semantics of solidarity and dignity becomes both more urgent and more difficult. In our discussion of social rights (Chapter 2.3) we saw how the elevation of solidarity – as *dogmatic resource* – to constitutional value at the substantive level, and the constitutional entrenchment of its non-negotiability at formal level, expresses the political achievement of social rights constitutionalism, the *decision* to hold on to the aspiration of solidarity in the face of all that the market presents under the sign of necessity. 'Decision' and 'strategy' are key terms in resisting the shift and the reconfiguration of constitutional semantics, to pit political constitutionalism *against* its market varieties. Its *contradictory* articulation to market constitutional semantics became and remains crucial to the deployment of solidarity as a foundational constitutional value.

The contradictory dynamic at the level of semantics generates a *semantic surplus* and thereby a semantic *intervention* on strategic grounds, to think of dignity, equality, solidarity as carrying the integrity of the law on the register of the political constitution. In a seminal piece Rancière attaches the idea of such a *semantic surplus* to the question of political agency: *who is the Subject of the Rights of Man?* His question is over a structural drift – 'what lies behind the strange *shift* from Man to humanity and from Humanity to the Humanitarian?' (2004c: 298)[21] – and he asks it as a question of practice, of 'making something' of it:

> The rights of man are the rights of those who *make something* of that inscription. ... Man and Citizen do not designate collections of individuals. Man and Citizen are political subjects. Political subjects are not definite collectivities. They are *surplus names*, names that set out a

---

[21] This is the shift that also organises Samuel Moyn's (2012); see Chapter 2.4.

question or a dispute (*litige*) about who is included in their count. Correspondingly freedom and equality are not predicates belonging to definite subjects. Political predicates are open predicates: they open a dispute about what they exactly entail and whom they concern in which cases.

(Rancière, 2004c)

Rancière's example is the French revolutionary Olympe de Gouges who, standing before the guillotine, declared famously that if women were entitled to go to the scaffold, they were entitled to go to the assembly. For Rancière, in that statement she contests the border that separates the private sphere in which she 'properly' belongs as a woman, and the public sphere to which she does not, but within which her execution is mandated. Politics, he says, is about that border, politics occurs as crossing it. It is a border that for Arendt could not be crossed because the meaning of politics lay only on its one side. We might even venture that de Gouges' injunction is meaningless for Arendt because de Gouges misunderstood the world of politics and her place in the social sphere outside it, and, remember, to set something like the social/political distinction on a dialectical trajectory is the 'most heinous suggestion'. For Rancière the act is an act of dissensus because it does not respect the boundary of the order that organises the processes of reaching consensus within *given* demarcations of political space. The political subject is the subject that moves across the boundary that determines subject positions on either side of it. More than that, de Gouges' is a move that 'enacts' political subjectivity in defying those determinations.

Of course at one level Arendt is right: the subject position of the 'man' of the Rights of Man, is either already occupied (by the citizen) or is unavailable (to the refugee) (1951: 297). 'But there is no need for such a man', objects Rancière. 'The strength of those rights lies in the back and forth movement between the first inscription of the right and the dissensual stage in which it is put to test' (2004c: 305). This is where concepts move, and why their immobility, as Lukács insisted, is the hallmark of bourgeois thought. 'To change the world,' wrote Merleau-Ponty, 'we need a truth which gives us a hold on adversity – not opaque and rigidified, but a world which is dense and which moves' (1955/1973: 143). It is the immobility of the concepts that sends Arendt down the blind alleys of tautology and paradox. In contrast, *dissensus* introduces a negotiation – at the ground level of meaning construction – of the categories that call us forth as political actors to rethink right-holding, freedom and equality as 'open predicates' (2004c: 303), questions of relation and temporality, as well as the thematics of constitutional import, across all these categories of constitutional meaning in social, material and temporal dimensions. There is an irreducible wager in this 'litige'. Because it opens the use of concepts, imperfectly, straining, to normative dynamics, where what can be renegotiated can also be co-opted. This is perhaps an obvious point to make relating to the vicissitudes of strategic deployments. But it is still a significant one.

Political subject is thus a surplus name. It is 'a capacity for staging such scenes of dissensus' (2004c: 304). 'Political names', says Rancière, 'are litigious names', names whose extension and comprehension are uncertain and which open for that reason the space of a test or verification. This negotiation in the interval between two names, names something more than the appearance of contingency; it gives opportunity to negotiating the extension of the term of political subject, revisiting the normativity it calls forth, floating it across new stretches of equivalence, establishing new continuities in this passage, invoking different subject positions in the crossings.

We conclude, then, on a note about 'the people', that moving signifier par excellence, that in that very movement names the subject of constituent power. Not as the possessor of the 'general will' – that of Rousseau or Robespierre – which needs only to will in order to produce law in an act of pure affirmation; but neither as summoned under the names that submit collective subjectivity without remainder to the symbolic order of capital. 'The generic name of the subjects who stage such cases of verification is the name of *the people*', says Rancière, for whom the double inscription sets the stage of politics, and carries its necessary wager: a wager that puts a different spin on Pierre Rosanvallon's wonderful title *Le peuple introuvable*,[22] and that inhabits its profound enactments. I am reminded here of the account of an incident on the eve of Robespierre's execution in July 1794. He had been persuaded to sign a document as member of the committee of the Commune calling for the Sections to resist the Convention. From a number of sources we know that he dithered before signing, and that he asked the other members of the Committee '*in whose name?*' he was to sign it. When he finally came

---

[22] In Pierre Rosanvalon's political history of France, an absence haunts the history of democratic representation. Democracy, popular sovereignty, have represented for two centuries '*l'horizon évident du bien politique*'. And yet even in its lands of origin where it has been most affirmed and celebrated, democracies '*sont bien marquées par la déception, comme si elles incarnaient un idéal trahi et défiguré*' (Rosanvallon, 1998: 9).

round to it, the signature remained unfinished – a truncated *RO* – as the armed guards of the Convention burst in, and his jaw was blown away. And it was perhaps in that question, in the hesitant delay, and in that most precarious signature that – to adapt François Furet's phrase – 'the Revolution [spoke] through him its most tragic and purest discourse.'

Epilogue

'*If I could have made this enough of a book,*' wrote Ernest Hemingway in the Epilogue of *Death in the Afternoon*, a book that pulsates with nostalgia for his beloved Spain, '*if I could have made this enough of a book it would have had everything in it. The bare white mud hills looking across toward Casablanca; days on the train in August with the blinds pulled down on the side against the sun and the wind blowing them. . . . What else should it contain of a country you love so much? We never will ride back from Toledo in the dark, washing the dust out with Furdador, nor will there be that week of what happened in the night in that July in Madrid.*'

Extraordinary, beautiful, and undaunted is Hemingway's hold on the fleeting features of this Spain that he '*loved so much*'. He offers glimpses into memories that could be infinitely expanded, *fleeting and precise* in the way that Cezanne described art's responsiveness to life: 'a moment in the life of this world is going by: capture it as it is'. And *undaunted* is his account of the hard countenance of the age.

'*If you can get to see [the world] clear and as a whole, then any part you make will represent the whole if it is made truly. The thing to do is work and learn to make it. . . . The great thing is to last and to get your work done and see and hear and learn and understand; and write when there is something that you know; and not before; and not too damned much after either.*'

If I could have made this enough of a book it would have registered something of the acts of solidarity and sacrifice that dignify our societies of crisis; it would have registered our recognition for the generation of young people that austerity has sacrificed to unemployment and under-employment, a sacrifice exacted and not acknowledged; our recognition for the workers that were sacked en masse when *Cosco* bought the commercial quays of the Port of Piraeus and wiped out in one gesture the traditions that sustained and dignified the lives of labour of generations of dockworkers; it would have registered the attempts to make sense of precariousness, of the insecurity that attaches to the sense that one's work is expendable, returning to the same devastating questions: 'Who will employ us?' 'Are we too many?'

In his book *Portraits*, John Berger writes of the painter Gustave Courbet, that he refused the function of art as moderator of appearances, as that which ennobles the visible. Instead Courbet had painted life-size, on a 20-square-metre canvas, an assembly of figures at a graveside, which, Berger says, 'announces nothing except: *this is how we appear*'. I am reminded of that other reference in his novel *G*, where Berger is describing the popular movements in the Veneto during the *annus mirabilis* of 1848, with revolution spreading like bushfire across Europe. He says: 'the crowd is inexorably there. It has assembled to avenge the discrepancy. Its need is to overthrow the order that has defined and distinguished the possible from the impossible at its expense for generation after generation.' The narrative follows a teenage boy in the crowd, whose movements through the barricades Berger has traced for us with exactitude. And then comes an appeal, extraordinary in its humanity, which resonates so clearly with Simone Weil: '*Look at this head, this body, ill-taught, badly-fed, overworked. It deserves the best the world is able to offer.*'

If I could have made this enough of a book it would have offered a reading of redress in the startling form of *that* phenomenology, in the way that it is carried as a *counter-weighting*. Not in the foreclosures and enclosures of the economies of writing but in language's 'unexpected apprehensions' as Heaney spoke of them.

No. It is not enough of a book, but still there were a few things to be said. There were a few practical things to be said.

REFERENCES

Adorno, T. (1951/2005) *Minima Moralia: Reflections on a Damaged Life*. London and New York: Verso.
— (1973) *Negative Dialectics*. London: Routledge and Kegan Paul, 1990 reprint.
Adorno, T. and Horkheimer, M. (1944/2002) *Dialectic of Enlightenment*. Palo Alto, CA: Stanford University Press.
Agamben, G. (2008) *Signatura rerum. Sur la méthode*. Paris: Vrin.
Aleinikoff, T. A. (1987) 'Constitutional Law in the Age of Balancing' 96 *Yale Law Journal* 943.
Alexy, R. (1989) *A Theory of Legal Argumentation* (trans. R. Adler and D. N. MacCormick). Oxford: Clarendon Press.
— (2002) *A Theory of Constitutional Rights* (trans. J. Rivers). Oxford: Oxford University Press.
— (2003) 'Constitutional Rights, Balancing, and Nationality' 16(2) *Ratio Juris* 131.
Althusser, L. (1962/1990) 'Contradiction et surdetermination (Notes pour un recherche)' (trans. B. Brewster), in *For Marx*. London: Verso.
— (1968/2007) 'Sur le rapport de Marx à Hegel', trans. as 'Marx's Relation to Hegel' by Ben Brewster, in *Politics and History: Montesquieu, Rousseau, Marx*. London: NLB.
— (1969/2013) *On the Reproduction of Capitalism: Ideology and Ideological State Apparatuses* (trans. G. M. Goshgarian). London and New York: Verso.
— (1978) *Ce qui ne peut plus durer dans le Parti Communiste*. Paris: François Maspero.
— (1982/2006) 'The Underground Current of the Materialism of the Encounter' (trans. G. M. Goshgarian), in *Philosophy of the Encounter: Later Writings 1978–1987*. London: Verso.
— (1999) *Machiavelli and Us* (trans. G. Elliot). London: Verso.
— (2003) *The Humanist Controversy and Other Writings* (1966–67) (trans. G. M. Goshgarian). London: Verso.
— (2004) *Hegel and Contemporary Continental Philosophy*. Albany: SUNY Press.
Anderson, P. (1976) *Considerations of Western Marxism*. London: Verso.

Ansaldi, O. and Pardo-Vergara, M. (2020) 'What Constitution? On Chile's Constitutional Awakening' 31 *Law & Critique* 7.

Appleby, J. O. (2010) *The Relentless Revolution: A History of Capitalism*. New York: W. W. Norton & Co.

Arendt, H. (1951) *The Origins of Totalitarianism*. New York: Harcourt, Brace and Co.

(1958) *The Human Condition*. Chicago: Chicago University Press.

(1961) *Between Past and Future*. Harmondsworth: Penguin.

(1963) *On Revolution*. Harmondsworth: Penguin.

(1978) *The Life of the Mind*. Boston: Houghton Mifflin Harcourt.

(2011) *Essays in Understanding, 1930–1954: Formation, Exile, and Totalitarianism*. New York: Schocken.

Aristotle, T. A. Sinclair and T. J. Saunders (1992). *The Politics* (T. J. Saunders, ed.). Harmondsworth: Penguin.

Arrighi, G. (1994) *The Long Twentieth Century: Money, Power, and the Origins of our Times*. London and New York: Verso.

(2007) *Adam Smith in Beijing: Lineages of the Twenty-first Century*. London and New York: Verso.

Arrighi, G., T. Hopkins and I. M. Wallerstein (2012) *Antisystemic Movements*. London and New York: Verso.

Atria, F. (2013a) 'Living Under Dead Ideas: Law as the Will of the People', in M. Del Mar and C. Michelon, eds., *The Anxiety of the Jurist*. Farnham: Ashgate.

(2013b) *La constitución tramposa*. Santiago de Chile: LOM Ediciones.

(2015) 'Social Rights, Social Contract, Socialism' 24(4) *Social & Legal Studies* 598–613.

(2020) 'Constituent Moment, Constituted Powers in Chile' 31 *Law & Critique* 51.

Avineri, S. (1968) *The Social and Political Thought of Karl Marx*. Cambridge University Press.

Axelos, K. (1962) *Héraclite et la philosophie*. Paris: Les Éditions de Minuit.

Bachofen, J. (1861/1992) *Myth, Religion, and Mother Right: Selected Writings of JJ Bachofen*. Vol. 128. Princeton, NJ: Princeton University Press.

Badiou, A. (2007) *Being and Event*. London: A&C Black (Bloomsbury).

Bargu, B. (2012) 'In the Theater of Politics: Althusser's Aleatory Materialism and Aesthetics' 40(3) *Diacritics* 86.

Barnard, C. (2012a) 'A Proportionate Response to Proportionality in the Field of Collective Action' 37(2) *European Law Review* 124.

(2012b) *EU Employment Law*, 4th ed., Oxford University Press.

Baudrillard, J. (1973) *The Mirror of Production* (trans. Mark Poster). St Louis: Telos Press.

Baxi, U. (1985) 'Taking Suffering Seriously: Social Action Litigation in the Supreme Court of India' *Third World Legal Stud.* 107.

Beasley-Murray, J. (1994) 'Ethics as Post-political Politics' 7 *Research and Society* 5.
Beatty, D. (2004) *The Ultimate Rule of Law*. Oxford University Press.
Beck, U. (2006) *Cosmopolitan Vision*. Cambridge, UK and Malden, MA: Polity Press.
Becker, G. (1976) *The Economic Approach To Human Behavior*. Chicago and London: University of Chicago Press.
Beitz, C. (1999) *Political Theory and International Relations*. Princeton, NJ: Princeton University Press.
Benanav, A. and J. Clegg (2014) 'Misery and Debt: On the Logic and History of Surplus Populations and Surplus Capital' in A. Pendakis and J. Diamanti, eds. *Contemporary Marxist Theory: A Reader*. London: Bloomsbury.
Bengoextea, J. (1994) 'Legal System as a Regulative Ideal', *ARSP Beiheft* 53.
Benhabib, S. (1996) *The Reluctant Modernism of Hannah Arendt*. Thousand Oaks, CA: Sage.
Benjamin, W. (1921/1970) *Critique of Violence*. In *Reflections*. London: Jonathan Cape.
Bensaïd, D. (2007) 'The Return of Strategy' 113 *International Socialism*.
  (1997) *Le Pari mélancolique: Métamorphoses de la politique, politique des métamorphoses (Essais)*. Paris: Fayard.
Bercusson, B. (2007) 'The Trade Union Movement and the European Union: Judgment Day?' 13 *European Law Journal* 279.
Berger, J. (1996) *Photocopies*. London: Bloomsbury.
Bergson, H. (1889/2001) *Time and Free Will: An Essay on the Immediate Data of Consciousness (Essai sur les données immédiates de la conscience, 1889)*. Allen & Unwin 1910; Dover Publications 2001.
  (1932/1977) *The Two Sources of Morality and Religion (Les Deux Sources de la Morale et de la Religion, 1932)*. Paris: University of Notre Dame Press.
Berman, P. S. (2012) *Global Legal Pluralism: A Jurisprudence of Law Beyond Borders*. Cambridge University Press.
Bernstein, R. (1986) *Philosophical Profiles: Essays in a Pragmatic Mode*. Philadelphia: University of Pennsylvania Press.
Bevir, M. (2010) *Democratic Governance*. Princeton, NJ: Princeton University Press.
Black, J. (2013) 'Reconceiving Financial Markets – From the Economic to the Social' 13(2) *Journal of Corporate Law Studies* 401.
Blanchot, M. (1986) 'Marx's Three Voices' 7(1) *New Political Science* 17.
Bloch, E. (1986) *Natural Law and Human Dignity*. Cambridge, MA: MIT Press.
  (1986/2018) *On Karl Marx*. London: Verso.
Blum, L. and V. Seidler (1989) *A Truer Liberty: Simone Weil and Marxism*. London: Routledge.
Boltanski, L. and E. Chiapello (1999/2005) *The New Spirit of Capitalism* (trans. G. Elliott). London and New York: Verso.

Braithwaite, J. and P. Drahos (2000) *Global Business Regulation*. Cambridge University Press.
Breen, K. (2007) 'Work and Emancipatory Practice' 13 *Res Publica* 381.
Brunkhorst, H. (2000) 'Equality and Elitism in Arendt', in Villa, ed., *The Cambridge Companion to Hannah Arendt*. Cambridge University Press.
   (2011) 'The Return of Crisis', in P. Kjaer, G. Teubner and A. Febbrajo, eds., *The Financial Crisis in Constitutional Perspective*. Oxford: Hart.
   (2014) 'The European Crisis: Paradoxes of Constitutionalising Democratic Capitalism', in M. Fichera, S. Hanninen and K. Tuori, eds., *Polity and Crisis: Reflections on the European Odyssey*. Farnham: Ashgate.
   (2015) *Solidarity* (trans. J. Flynn). Cambridge, MA: MIT Press.
Calasso, R. (1994) *The Marriage of Cadmus and Harmony* (trans. Tim Parks). New York: Vintage.
Camatte, J. (1988) *Capital and Community* (trans. D. Brown). London: Unpopular Books.
Campbell, D. (2013) 'The Law of Contract and the Limits of the Welfare State', in M. del Mar and C. Michelon, eds., *The Anxiety of the Jurist*. Farnham: Ashgate.
Carlino, F. (2015) 'Lectures de Hegel «à la lumière du marxisme» et genèse de la «coupure épistémologique»' *Cahiers du GRM*, publiés par le Groupe de Recherches Matérialistes–Association 8.
Case C-370/12 *Pringle v Ireland*, judgment of 27 Nov 2012.
Castel, R. (2003) *From Manual Workers to Wage Labourers: Transformations of the Social Question*. New Brunswick: Transaction.
Castells, M. (2004) *The Network Society: A Cross-Cultural Perspective*. Cheltenham: Edward Elgar.
Castoriadis, C. (1975) *L'institution imaginaire de la société*. Paris: Seuil.
   (1990) 'Does the Idea of Revolution Still Make Sense' 26 *Thesis Eleven* 123.
Christodoulidis, E. (1996) *Law and Reflexive Politics*. Dordrecht: Kluwer.
   (2000) 'Truth and Reconciliation as Risks' 9(2) *Social & Legal Studies* 179–204.
   (2003) 'Constitutional Irresolution: Law and the Framing of Civil Society' 9(4) *European Law Journal* 401.
   (2004) 'The Objection that cannot be Heard: Communication and Legitimacy in the Courtroom', in Duff et al., *The Trial on Trial*. Oxford: Hart.
   (2007) 'Against Substitution: The Constitutional Thinking of Dissensus', in M. Loughlin and N. Walker, eds., *The Paradox of Constitutionalism: Constituent Power and Constitutional Form*. Oxford University Press.
   (2009) 'Strategies of Rupture' *Law & Critique* 1.
   (2017) 'Social Rights Constitutionalism: An Antagonistic Endorsement' 44(1) *Journal of Law and Society* 123.
   (2019) *Les « mots du Droit » et le monde vécu*, in A. Supiot ed., *Mondialisation v Globalisation: Les leçons de Simone Weil*. Paris: Ed Collège de France.

(2020) 'Simone Weil's Poem of Force and the Meaning of Courage', in S. Besson and S. Jube, eds., *Concerter les Civilisations. Melanges Alain Supiot.* Paris: Seuil.

Clarkson, C. (2007) 'The Time of Address', in S. Veitch, ed., *Law and the Politics of Reconciliation.* Aldershot: Ashgate.

(2014) *Drawing the Line: Toward an Aesthetics of Transitional Justice.* New York: Fordham.

Cohen, M. (1994) *The Wager of Lucien Goldmann.* Princeton, NJ: Princeton University Press.

Collective and A. Benanav (2010) 'Misery and Debt: On the Logic and History of Surplus Populations and Surplus Capital' *End Notes* 2.

Commons, J. (1924) *Legal Foundations of Capitalism.* New York: Macmillan.

Cordero, R. (2020) 'The Negative Dialectics of Law: Luhmann and the Sociology of Juridical Concepts' 29(1) *Social & Legal Studies* 3.

Coriat, B. (1994) *Penser à l'envers,* coll. Choix-essais. Paris: éd. Christian Bourgois.

Costamagna, F. (2018) 'National Social Spaces as Adjustment Variables in the EMU: A Critical Legal Appraisal' 24(2) *European Law Journal* 163.

Countouris, N. and S. Engblom (2014) 'Civilising the European Posted Workers Directive', in M. Freedland and J. Prassl, eds., *Viking, Laval and Beyond.* London: Hart.

Craig, P. P. (2013) '*Pringle*: Legal Reasoning, Text, Purpose and Teleology' 20 *Maastricht Journal of Law* 1.

Dannreuther, R. and K. Hutchings (1999) *Cosmopolitan Citizenship.* New York: St Martin's Press.

Davidov, G. and B. Langille, eds. (2011) *The Idea of Labour Law.* Oxford University Press.

Davies, A. (2005) 'Collective Labour Rights in the EU', in P. Alston, ed., *Labour Rights as Human Rights.* Oxford University Press.

(2008) 'One Step Forward, Two Steps Back? The Viking and Laval Cases in the ECJ' 37(2) *ILJ* 126-48.

Davis, D. (2008) 'Socioeconomic Rights: Do they Deliver the Goods?' 6 *I CON* 687.

Dawson, M. (2018) 'New Governance and the Displacement of Social Europe: The Case of the European Semester' 14(1) *European Constitutional Law Review* 191.

De Búrca, G. (2003) 'The Constitutional Challenge of New Governance in the European Union' 56(1) *Current Legal Problems* 403.

(2010) 'New Governance and Experimentalism: An Introduction' *Wis. L. Rev.* 227.

De Búrca, G., R. O. Keohane and C. Sabel (2014) 'Global Experimentalist Governance' 44(3) *British Journal of Political Science* 477-86.

De Sousa Santos, B. (2015) *Epistemologies of the South: Justice Against Epistemicide.* London: Routledge.

de Tocqueville, A. (1979). *The Recollections of Alexis de Tocqueville*. Westport, CT: Greenwood Press.
Deakin, S. (2007) 'A New Paradigm for Labour Law?' 31(3) *Melbourne University Law Review* 1161.
Deakin, S. and A. Supiot, eds. (2009) *Capacitas*. Oxford: Hart.
Deakin, S. and F. Wilkinson (2005) *The Law of the Labour Market: Industrialization, Employment, and Legal Evolution*. Oxford University Press.
Debray R. (1983) *Critique of Political Reason*. London: Verso.
Dejours, C. (1998) *Souffrance en France: la banalisation de l'injustice sociale*. Paris: Seuil.
  (2000) *Travail usure mentale (essai de psychopathologie du travail)*. Paris: Bayard.
Del Mar, M., B. Meyler and S. Stern, eds. (2019) *Oxford Handbook of Law and Humanities*. Oxford University Press.
Deleuze, G. and F. Guattari (1988) *A Thousand Plateaus*. London: Athlone.
Denning, M. (2010) 'Wageless Life' 66 *NLR* 79.
Deranty, J.-P. (2003) 'Rancière and Contemporary Political Ontology' 6(4) *Theory & Event*.
  (2005) 'Hegel's Social Theory of Value' 36(3) *The Philosophical Forum* 307.
  (2008) 'Work and the Precarisation of Existence' 11(4) *European Journal of Social Theory* 443.
Deranty, J.-P. and E. Renault (2009) 'Democratic Agon: Striving for Distinction or Struggle against Domination and Injustice?' in A. Schaap, ed., *Law and Agonistic Politics*. Farnham: Ashgate.
Derrida, J. (1976) 'From Restricted To General Economy – Hegelianism Without Reserves' 2(2) *Semiotexte* 25.
  (1992) 'Force of Law: The "Mystical Foundations of Authority"', in D. Cornell, M. Rosenfeld and D. G. Carson, eds., *Deconstruction and the Possibility of Justice*. New York: Routledge.
  (1994) *Specters of Marx* (trans. P. Kamuf). New York: Routledge.
  (2006) *Politics of Friendship*. London and New York: Verso.
Desrosières, A. (1998) *The Politics of Large Numbers: A History of Statistical Reasoning* (trans. C. Naish). Cambridge, MA: Harvard University Press. Orig.: (1993) *La politique des grands nombres: histoire de la raison statistique*. Paris: La Découverte.
  (2014) *Prouver et gouverner: une analyse politique des statistiques publiques*. Paris: La Découverte.
Dietz, M. (1994) '"The Slow Boring of Hard Boards": Methodical Thinking and the Work of Politics' 88 *American Political Science Review* 873.
Dobner, P. and M. Loughlin, eds. (2010) *The Twilight of Constitutionalism?* Oxford University Press.

Douzinas, C. (2000) *The End of Human Rights: Critical Thought at the Turn of the Century*. Oxford: Hart.

Dukes, R. (2008) 'Constitutionalising Employment Relations: Sinzheimer, Kahn-Freund and the Role of Labour Law' 25 *Journal of Law and Society* 341.

(2014) *The Labour Constitution: The Enduring Idea of Labour Law*. Oxford University Press.

Durkheim, E. (1925/1961) *Moral Education*. New York: Free Press.

Dworkin, R. (1986) *Law's Empire*. London: Fontana Press.

Dyzenhaus, D. (2012) 'Constitutionalism in an Old Key: Legality and Constituent Power' 1(2) *Global Constitutionalism* 229.

Eagleton, T., foreword in K. Ross (2008). *The Emergence of Social Space*. London: Verso.

(2020) 'Sign and Socius' 122 *NLR* 142.

Enzensberger, H. M. (1972) *Der kurze sommer der anarchie: Buenaventura durrutis leben und tod: Roman*. Frankfurt: Suhrkamp.

Euben, J. P. (2000) 'Weil's Hellenism' in D. Villa, ed., *The Cambridge Companion to Hannah Arendt*. Cambridge University Press.

Everson, M. (2015) 'An Exercise in Legal Honesty: Rewriting the Court of Justice and the Bundesverfassungsgericht' 21(4) *European Law Journal* 474.

Everson, M. and C. Joerges (2019) 'Facticity as Validity: The Misplaced Revolutionary Praxis of European Law', in E. Christodoulidis, R. Dukes and M. Goldoni, eds., *Research Handbook on Critical Legal Theory*. Cheltenham: Edward Elgar.

Ewing, K. (1995) 'Democratic Socialism and Labour Law' 24 *ILJ* 103.

Fabre-Magnan, M. (2007) 'La dignité en Droit: un axiome' 58(1) *Revue interdisciplinaire d'études juridiques* 1.

(2018) *L'institution de la liberté*. Paris: PUF.

Falk, R (1999) *Predatory Globalization: A Critique*. Cambridge: Polity.

Febbrajo, A. (2011) 'The failure of regulatory institutions – a conceptual framework', in P. Kjaer, G. Teubner and A. Febbrajo, eds., *The Financial Crisis in Constitutional Perspective: The Dark Side of Functional Differentiation*. Oxford: Hart.

Feenberg, A. (1981) *Lukács, Marx and the Sources of Critical Theory*. New Jersey: Rowman & Littlefield.

Finnis, J. (2011) *Natural Law and Natural Rights*. Oxford: Clarendon.

Fischer-Lescano, A. (2012) 'Critical Systems Theory' 38(1) *Philosophy & Social Criticism* 3.

Foucault, M. (1977) *Language, Counter-memory, Practice: Selected Essays and Interviews*. Ithaca, NY: Cornell University Press.

(1982) 'Afterword: The Subject and Power', in H. Dreyfus and P. Rabinow, *Michel Foucault: Beyond Structuralism and Hermeneutics*. Brighton: Harvester.

(1990) *The History of Sexuality: The Will to Knowledge*. London: Vintage.
(1991) 'Questions of Method', in C. Gordon, P. Miller and G. Burchell, eds., *The Foucault Effect: Studies in Governmentality*. Chicago: Chicago University Press.
(1994) 'Le jeu de Michel Foucault', in *Dits et écrits*, Vol. 3. Paris: Éditions Gallimard.
(2004) *The Birth of Biopolitics*. New York: Palgrave Macmillan.
Frank, J. A. (2010) *Constituent Moments: Enacting the People in Postrevolutionary America*. Durham, NC: Duke University Press.
Freedland, M. and J. Prassl (2014) '*Viking, Laval* and Beyond: An Introduction', in M. Freedland and J. Prassl, eds., *Viking, Laval and Beyond*. Oxford: Hart.
Freudenthal, G. (1997) 'Marx's Critique of Economic Reason' 10(1) *Science in Context* 171.
Fukuyama, F. (1996) *Trust: The Social Virtues and the Creation of Prosperity*. Harmondsworth: Penguin.
Fuller, L. (1964) *The Morality of Law*. New Haven: Yale University Press.
Gadamer, H. G. (1960/1989) *Truth and Method*. Oxford: Blackwell.
Gaita, R. (2013) *A Common Humanity: Thinking about Love and Truth and Justice*. London: Routledge.
Gallie, W. B. (1955) 'Essentially Contested Concepts', in *Proceedings of the Aristotelian Society* (Vol. 56, pp. 167–98). Aristotelian Society/Wiley.
Geissler, H. (2018) *Seasonal Associate*. South Pasadena, CA: Semiotexte(e).
Gill, S. (2003) *Power and Resistance in the New World Order*. Basingstoke: Palgrave Macmillan.
Giubboni, S. (2018) 'The Rise and Fall of EU Labour Law' 24(1) *European Law Journal* 7.
Glasman, M. (1994) 'The Great Deformation' 205 *New Left Review* 59.
(1996) *Unnecessary Suffering: Managing Market Utopia*. London and New York: Verso.
Golder, B. (2011) 'Foucault's Critical (Yet Ambivalent) Affirmation: Three Figures of Rights' 20(3) *Social & Legal Studies* 283.
(2015) *Foucault and the Politics of Rights*. Palo Alto: Stanford University Press.
Goldmann, L. (1955/2016) *The Hidden God: A Study of Tragic Vision in the Pensées of Pascal and the Tragedies of Racine*. London: Verso.
(1961) *Les sciences humaines et la philosophie*. Paris: PUF.
(1977) *Lukács and Heidegger: Towards a New Philosophy*. London: Routledge.
Goldoni, M. (2014) 'The Early Warning System and the Monti II Regulation: The Case for a Political Interpretation' 10(1) *European Constitutional Law Review* 90.
(2017) 'Rousseau's Radical Constitutionalism and Its Legacy', in *Constitutionalism Beyond Liberalism*. Cambridge University Press.

Goodrich, P. (2009) 'Law's Labour's Lost' 72(2) *Modern Law Review* 296.
Gorz, A. (1982) *Goodbye to the Working Class*. London: Pluto Press.
　(1989) *Critique of Economic Reason*. London: Verso.
　(1999) *Reclaiming Work: Beyond the Wage-based Society*. Cambridge: Polity.
Gramsci, A. (1957) *The Modern Prince and other Writings*. London: Lawrence & Wishart.
　(1971) *Selections from the Prison Notebooks* (trans. Q. Hoare). London: Lawrence & Wishart.
Granovetter, M. (1985) 'Economic Action and Social Structure: The Problem of Embeddedness' 91 *American Journal of Sociology* 481.
Gray, J. (1992) *The Moral Foundations of Market Institutions*. Institute of Economic Affairs.
Greenblatt, S. (2011). *The Swerve: How the World Became Modern*. New York: W. W. Norton & Co.
Greer, S. (2004) '"Balancing" and the European Court of Human Rights: A Contribution to the Habermas–Alexy Debate' 63 *CLJ* 412.
Grimm, D. (2007) 'Proportionality in Canadian and German Constitutional Jurisprudence' 57(2) *University of Toronto Law Journal* 383.
Günther, K. (1993) *The Sense of Appropriateness* (trans. John Farrell). Albany: SUNY Press.
　(1995) 'Legal Adjudication and Democracy' *European Journal of Philosophy*.
　(2011) 'The Criminal Law of "Guilt" as Subject of a Politics of Remembrance in Democracies', in E. Christodoulidis and S. Veitch, eds., *Lethe's Law*. Oxford: Hart.
Habermas, J. (1968/1987) *Knowledge and Human Interests*. Cambridge: Polity Press.
　(1973) 'Wahrheitstheorien', in H. Fahrenbach, ed., *Wirklichkeit und Reflexion: Walter Schulz zum 60. Geburtstag*. Pfullingen: Neske.
　(1974) 'Theorie der Gesellschaft oder Sozialtechnologie? Eine Auseinandersetzung mit Niklas Luhmann', in *Theorie der Gesellschaft oder Sozialtechnologie: Was leistet die Systemforschung?*, 2nd ed. Frankfurt: Suhrkamp.
　(1979) *Communication and the Evolution of Society*. Boston: Beacon Press.
　(1982) 'A Reply to my Critics', in J. Thompson and D. Held, *Habermas: Critical Debates*. London: Macmillan.
　(1983) *Moral Consciousness and Communicative Action*. Cambridge, MA: MIT Press.
　(1984) *The Theory of Communicative Action*. Cambridge: Polity Press.
　(1995) *Between Facts and Norms*, Cambridge: Polity Press.
　(1999) 'Reconciliation through the Public Use of Reason', in C. Cronin, ed., *The Inclusion of the Other*. Cambridge: Polity.
　(2001) 'Constitutional Democracy: A Paradoxical Union of Contradictory Principles?' 29 *Political Theory* 766.

(2005) *Truth and Justification* (trans. Barbara Fultner). Cambridge, MA: MIT Press.

(2008) *Between Naturalism and Religion*. Cambridge: Polity.

Hall, S. and M. Jacques, eds. (1983) *The Politics of Thatcherism*. London: Lawrence & Wishart.

Hamacher, W. (2000) 'Afformative, Strike: Benjamin's' Critique of Violence', in A. Benjamin and P. Osborne, eds., *Walter Benjamin's Philosophy*. Manchester: Clinamen.

Hardin, G. (1968) 'The Tragedy of the Commons' 162 *Science* 1243.

Hardt, M. and A. Negri (2000) *Empire*. Cambridge, MA: Harvard University Press.

Harris, R. (2016) *Introduction*, in F. Saussure, ed., *Course in General Linguistics*. London: Bloomsbury.

Hart, H. L. A. (1961). *The Concept of Law*. Oxford: Clarendon.

Hayek, F. A. (1935) *Socialist Calculation I: The Nature and History of the Problem. Individualism and Economic Order*. Chicago University Press.

(1944/2014) *The Road to Serfdom*. London: Routledge.

(1960/2013) *The Constitution of Liberty*. London: Routledge.

(1964) *The Theory of Complex Phenomena. The Critical Approach to Science and Philosophy*. London: Collier McMillan.

(1973/2002) *Law, Legislation and Liberty, Volume 1: Rules and Order*. Chicago University Press.

(1974/2002) 'Competition as a Discovery Procedure' 5(3) *The Quarterly Journal of Austrian Economics* 9.

(1976/2002) *Law, Legislation and Liberty, Volume 2: The Mirage of Social Justice*. Chicago University Press.

(1979/2002) *Law, Legislation and Liberty, Volume 3: The Political Order of a Free People*. Chicago University Press.

(1988/2013) *The Fatal Conceit: The Errors of Socialism*. London: Routledge.

Heaney, S. (1995) *The Redress of Poetry*. London: Faber & Faber.

Hegel, G. W. F. (1807/1976) *The Phenomenology of Spirit* (trans. A. V. Miller). Witham, Essex: Galaxy Books.

(1820/2002) *The Philosophy of Right* (trans. A. White). Cambridge, MA: Hackett.

(1828/1980) *Lectures on the Philosophy of World History*. Cambridge University Press.

Heidegger, M. (1996) *Being and Time*. Albany, NY: SUNY Press.

Heller, A. (1982) 'Habermas and Marxism', in J. Thompson and D. Held, *Habermas: Critical Debates*. London: Macmillan.

Hignett, C. (1952) *A History of the Athenian Constitution to the End of the Fifth Century B.C.* Oxford: Clarendon.

Hill, M., ed. (1979) *Hannah Arendt: The Recovery of the Public World*. New York: St Martin's Press.

Hirschl, R. (2007) *Towards Juristocracy*. Cambridge, MA: Harvard University Press.

Holman, C. (2011) 'Dialectics and Distinction: Reconsidering Hannah Arendt's Critique of Marx' 10 *Contemporary Political Theory* 332.

Holmes, S. and C. Sunstein (1999) *The Cost of Rights: Why Liberty Depends on Taxes*. New York: W. W. Norton & Co.

Honneth, A. (1982) 'Work and Instrumental Action' 26 *New German Critique* 31.

(1997) *The Critique of Power: Reflective Stages in a Critical Social Theory*. Cambridge, MA: MIT Press.

(2008) *Reification: A New Look at an Old Idea*. Oxford University Press.

Horkheimer, M. (1932/1976) 'Traditional and Critical Theory', in *Critical Theory: Selected Essays* (trans. M. O'Connell). New York: Continuum.

Horowitz, I. L. (1961/2009) *Radicalism and the Revolt Against Reason: The Social Theories of Georges Sorel* with a Translation of his Essay on the Decomposition of Marxism. London: Routledge.

Hunnicutt, B. (1988) *Work Without End: Abandoning Shorter Hours for the Right to Work*. Philadelphia: Temple University Press.

Husserl, E. (1900/1970) *Logical Investigations* (trans. J. N. Findlay). London: Routledge and Kegan Paul.

(1902/2013) *The Idea of Phenomenology: A Translation of Die Idee Der Phänomenologie. Husserliana II* (Vol. 8). Berlin and New York: Springer.

(1913/2012) *General Introduction to a Pure Phenomenology*. London: Routledge.

(1931/1993) *Cartesian Meditations*. Dordrecht: Kluwer.

(1936/1970) *The Crisis of European Sciences and Transcendental Phenomenology*. Evanston: Northwestern University Press.

(1939/1973) *Experience and Judgment: Investigations in a Genealogy of Logic*, Ludwig Landgrebe, ed. (trans. J. Churchill and K. Ameriks). London: Routledge and Kegan Paul.

Hyman, R. (2006) 'Flexible Rigidities: A Model for Social Europe?' in L. E. Alonso and M. Martínez Lucio, eds., *Employment Relations in a Changing Society: Assessing the Post-Fordist Paradigm*. London: Palgrave Macmillan.

Ingold, T. (2007) *Lines: A Brief History*. London: Routledge.

Jaume, L. (1989) *Le Discours Jacobin et la Democratie*. Paris: Fayard.

(2007) 'Constituent Power in France: The Revolution and its Consequences', in M. Loughlin and N. Walker, eds., *The Paradox of Constitutionalism: Constituent Power and Constitutional Form*. Oxford University Press.

Jay, M. (1973) *The Dialectical Imagination: A History of the Frankfurt School and the Institute of Social Research, 1923–1950*. Berkeley: University of California Press.

Joerges, C. (2005) 'What is Left of the European Economic Constitution? A Melancholic Eulogy' 30 *European Law Review* 461.

(2011) 'Will the Welfare State Survive European Integration?' 1 *European Journal of Social Law* 4.

Joerges, C. and J. Falke, eds. (2011) *Karl Polanyi, Globalisation and the Potential of Law in Transnational Markets.* Oxford: Hart.

Joerges, C. and F. Rödl (2004) '"Social Market Economy" as Europe's Social Model?' in L. Magnusson and B. Ståth, eds., *A European Social Citizenship?* Brussels: P. Lang.

Jubé, S. (2009) *La normativité comptable: un angle mort du droit social.* Paris: Editions Dalloz.

Julius, A. J. (2006) 'Nagel's Atlas' 34(2) *Philosophy and Public Affairs* 176.

Karatani, K. (2005) *Transcritique: On Kant and Marx.* Cambridge, MA: MIT Press.

Kerruish, V. (2007) 'Commodity Fetishism: Marx's Dialectic of Content and Form' 2 *Dilemmata: Jahrbuch der ASFPG* 19–55.

Kilpatrick, C. (2009) 'Laval's Regulatory Conundrum: Collective Standard-setting and the Court's New Approach to Posted Workers' 34 *EurLR* 844.

(2018) 'The Displacement of Social Europe: A Productive Lens of Inquiry' 14(1) *European Constitutional Law Review* 62.

Kingsbury, B. (2009) 'The Concept of "Law" in Global Administrative Law' 20 *EJIL* 23.

Kjaer, P., G. Teubner and A. Febbrajo, eds. (2011) *The Financial Crisis in Constitutional Perspective.* Oxford: Hart.

Klaes, M. and E. M. Sent (2005) 'A Conceptual History of the Emergence of Bounded Rationality' 37(1) *History of Political Economy* 27.

Klare, K. (1998) 'Legal Culture and Transformative Constitutionalism' 14 *South African Journal on Human Rights* 146.

Knight, F. H. (1921) *Risk, Uncertainty and Profit.* New York: Harper & Row.

Kochi, T. (2019) *Global Justice and Social Conflict: The Foundations of Liberal Order and International Law.* London: Routledge.

Kojève, A. (1943/1981) *Esquisse d'une phenomenologie du Droit.* Paris: Gallimard.

Kokoreff, M. (2008) *Sociologie des émeutes.* Paris: Payot.

Koselleck, R. (1989/2004) 'The Historical-Political Semantics of Asymmetric Counterconcepts', in Koselleck, *Futures Past: On the Semantics of Historical Time.* New York: Columbia University Press.

Kosik, K. (1967/2012) *Dialectics of the Concrete: A Study on Problems of Man and World.* Berlin and New York: Springer.

Koskenniemi, M. (2001) *The Gentle Civilizer of Nations: The Rise and Fall of International Law.* Cambridge and New York: Cambridge University Press.

(2007) 'The Fate of Public International Law: Between Technique and Politics' 70(1) *MLR* 1.

Koukiadaki, A. and L. Kretsos (2012) 'Opening Pandora's box: The Sovereign Debt Crisis and Labour Market Regulation in Greece' 41(3) *Industrial Law Journal* 276.

Krahl, H.-J. (1971) *Institution und Klassenkampf.* Frankfurt: Suhrkamp.
Kukovec, D. (2015) 'Law and the Periphery' 21(3) *ELJ* 406.
Kuo, M.-S. (2009) 'From Myth to Fiction' 29(3) *OJLS* 579.
La Hovary, C. (2013) 'Showdown at the ILO? A Historical Perspective on the Employers' Group's 2012 Challenge to the Right to Strike' 42(4) *Industrial Law Journal* 338.
Laba, R. (1991) *The Roots of Solidarity.* Princeton, NJ: Princeton.
Laclau, E. (1996) *Emancipation(s).* London: Verso.
Laclau, E. and C. Mouffe (1985) *Hegemony and Socialist Strategy.* London: Verso.
Ladeur, K.-H. (1999) 'Der "Eigenwert" des Rechts', in C. J. Meier-Schatz, ed., *Die Zukunft Des Rechts.* Basel: Helbing & Lichtenhahn.
  (2004) 'Globalization and the Conversion of Democracy to Polycentric Networks: Can Democracy Survive the End of the Nation-State?' in *Public Governance in the Age of Globalization.* London: Routledge.
  (2011) 'The Financial Market Crisis – a Case of Network Failure?' in P. Kjaer, G. Teubner and A. Febbrajo, eds., *The Financial Crisis in Constitutional Perspective: The Dark Side of Functional Differentiation.* London: Bloomsbury.
Latour, B. (1988) 'Irreductions', in Latour, *The Pasteurization of France* (Part 2, pp. 153–238). Cambridge, MA: Harvard University Press.
  (2012). *We Have Never Been Modern.* Cambridge, MA: Harvard University Press.
Lattimore, R. A. (1957) 'Preface', in *Euripides: The Cyclops.* University of Chicago Press.
Lazzarato, M. (2012) *The Making of the Indebted Man: An Essay on the Neoliberal Condition.* Cambridge, MA: MIT Press.
Lear, J. (1998) *Open Minded: Working Out the Logic of the Soul.* Cambridge, MA: Harvard University Press.
Leczykiewicz, D. (2014) 'Conceptualising Conflict between the Economic and the Social in EU Law after *Viking* and *Laval*', in M. Freedland and J. Prassl, eds., *Viking, Laval and Beyond.* Oxford: Hart.
Lefort, C. (1986) *The Political Forms of Modern Society.* Cambridge: Polity.
  (1987) 'L'oeuvre de Clastres', in M. Abensour, ed., *L'esprit des lois sauvages.* Paris: Seuil.
  (1988) *Democracy and Political Theory.* [1986] Minneapolis: University of Minnesota Press.
Levi, E. H. (1948) 'An Introduction to Legal Reasoning' 15(3) *University of Chicago Law Review* 501.
Lindahl, H. (2007) 'Constituent Power and Reflexive Identity: Towards an Ontology of Collective Selfhood', in *The Paradox of Constitutionalism.* Oxford University Press.
  (2013) *Fault Lines of Globalization: Legal Order and the Politics of A-legality.* Oxford University Press.

Loughlin, M. (2010) 'What is Constitutionalisation?' in P. Dobner and M. Loughlin, eds., *The Twilight of Constitutionalism.* Oxford University Press.

Löwy, M. (1997) 'Lucien Goldmann or the Communitarian Wager' 11(1) *Socialism and Democracy* 25.

Luhmann, N. (1957) *Grundrechte als Institution.* Berlin: Duncker & Humblot.

(1962) 'Funktion und Kausalität' 14 *Kolner Zeitschrift fur Soziologie und Sozialpsychologie* 618.

(1971) 'Die Weltgesellschaft' 57 *ARSP* 1.

(1972/1985). *Rechtssoziologie.* Hamburg: Rowohlt. (English trans. by E. King-Utz and M. Albrow, *A Sociological Theory of Law.* London: Routledge and Kegan Paul, 1985.)

(1977) *The Differentiation of Society.* New York: Columbia University Press.

(1980) *Gesellschaftstruktur und Semantik,* Vol. 1. Frankfurt: Suhrkamp.

(1981) 'Die Funktion des Rechts: Erwartungssicherung oder Verhaltenssteuerung', in N. Luhmann, *Ausdifferenzierung des Rechts.* Frankfurt: Suhrkamp.

(1986a) *Ecological Communication* (trans. J. Bednarz). Cambridge: Polity Press.

(1986b) 'Distinctions Directrices: Uber Codierung von Semantiken und systems', in Neidhardt, Lepsius and Weiss, eds., 'Kultur und Gesellschaft' (special issue), 27 *Kolner Zeitschrift fur Soziologie und Sozialpsychologie* 145.

(1986c) 'The Individuality of the Individual: Historical Meanings and Contemporary Problems', in T. C. Heller, M. Sosna and D. E. Wellbery, eds., *Reconstructing Individualism: Autonomy, Individuality, and the Self in Western Thought.* Palo Alto, CA: Stanford University Press.

(1988) 'The Third Question: The Creative Use of Paradoxes in Law and Legal History' 15 *JL & Society* 153.

(1990a) *Essays on Self Reference.* New York: Columbia University Press.

(1990b) 'Verfassung als evolutionäre Errungenschaft' 9 *Rechtshistorisches Journal* 176.

(1992) 'The Concept of Society' 31 *Thesis Eleven* 67.

(1993) *Risk: A Sociological Theory.* New Brunswick: Transaction Publishers.

(1995a) *Social Systems* (trans. John Bednarz Jr with Dirk Baecker). Palo Alto, CA: Stanford University Press.

(1995b) 'Legal Argumentation: An Analysis of Its Form' 58 *Modern Law Review* 285.

(1997) 'Globalisation or World Society: How to Conceive of Modern Society?' 7(1) *International Review of Sociology* 67.

(2002) 'What is Communication?' in W. Rasch, ed., *Theories of Distinction: Redescribing the Descriptions of Modernity.* Palo Alto, CA: Stanford University Press.

(2004) *Law as a Social System* (trans. K. Ziegert). Oxford University Press.

Lukács, G. (1914/1971) *The Theory of the Novel* (trans. A Bostock). Cambridge, MA: MIT Press.

(1923/1971) *History and Class Consciousness: Studies in Marxist Dialectics* (trans. R. Livingstone). London: Merlin.

(1925/2001) *Dialectique et spontanéité. En défense de l'Histoire et conscience de classe*. Paris: Éditions de la Passion.

Luxemburg, R. (1904/1971) 'Organisational Questions of Russian Social Democracy', in D. Howard, ed., *Selected Political Writings of Rosa Luxemburg*. New York: Monthly Review.

(1906/1925) *The Mass Strike, the Political Party and the Trade Unions* (trans. P. Lavin). Marxist Educational Society of Detroit. London: Merlin Press.

Lyotard, J.-F. (1988): *The Differend* (trans. G van den Abbeele). Manchester University Press.

(1993) 'March 23', in *Political Writings* (trans. B. Readings and K. P. Geiman). Minneapolis: University of Minnesota Press.

MacCormick, D. N. (1981) *H L A Hart*. Oxford: Clarendon.

(1989) 'Spontaneous Order and the Rule of Law: Some Problems' 2(1) *Ratio Juris* 41.

(1993) 'Beyond the Sovereign State' 56 *Modern LR* 1.

(1999) *Questioning Sovereignty: Law, State, and Nation in the European Commonwealth*. Oxford University Press.

MacDonald, O. (1983) 'The Polish Vortex: Solidarity and Socialism' 139 *NLR* 5.

MacIntyre, A. (1977) 'Epistemological Crises, Dramatic Narrative and the Philosophy of Science' 60 *The Monist* 453.

(1981) *After Virtue*. London: Duckworth.

(1998) 'Theses on Feuerbach: A Road Not Taken', in K. Knight, *The MacIntyre Reader*. Notre Dame, IN: University of Notre Dame Press.

Magri, L. (2008) 'Tailor of Ulm' 51 *New Left Review* 47.

Marcuse, H. (1989) 'Philosophy and Critical Theory' 6(1) *Negations* 147.

Marder, M. (2014) *Phenomena-Critique-Logos*. London and Lanham, MD: Rowman & Littlefield.

Marion, J.-L. (1998) *Reduction and Givenness*. Evanston, IL: Northwestern University Press.

(2012) *Being Given: Toward a Phenomenology of Givenness*. Palo Alto, CA: Stanford University Press.

Marshall, T. H. (1950/1992) 'Citizenship and Social Class', in T. Bottomore, ed., *Sociology at the Crossroads and Other Essays*. London: Heinemann.

Marx, K. (1843/1977) 'A Contribution to the Critique of Hegel's Philosophy of Right', in *Collected Works (MECW)*, Vol. 3. London: Lawrence & Wishart.

(1843/2000) 'On the Jewish Question', in *Karl Marx: Selected Writings*. USA: Oxford University Press.

(1844/1975) *The Holy Family*. Moscow: Progress Publishing.

(1845/1936) *The Poverty of Philosophy*. London: Lawrence & Wishart.

(1846/1970) *The German Ideology*. Geneva: International Publishers.
(1852/1979) 'The Eighteenth Brumaire of Louis Bonaparte', in *Collected Works (MECW)*, Vol. 11. London: Lawrence & Wishart.
(1857/2005) *Grundrisse* (trans. M. Nicolaus). London: Penguin.
(1867/1970) *Capital*. London: Lawrence & Wishart.
(1871/1972) *The Civil War in France*. Moscow: Progress Publishers.
(1875/2008) *Critique of the Gotha Programme*. Maryland: Wildside Press.
Marx, K. and F. Engels (1848/2002) *The Communist Manifesto*. Harmondsworth: Penguin.
(1979) *Collected Works (MECW)*, Vols. 1–49. London: Lawrence & Wishart.
Marzal, T. (2017) 'From Hercules to Pareto: Of Bathos, Proportionality, and EU Law' 15(3) *International Journal of Constitutional Law* 621.
Maupain, F. (2005) 'Is the ILO Effective in Upholding Workers' Rights?' in P. Alston, ed., *Labour Rights as Human Rights*. Oxford University Press.
McDonald, J. (2013) *Rousseau and the French Revolution 1762–1791*. London: Bloomsbury.
McGee, K. (2012) 'Aleatory Materialism and Speculative Jurisprudence (I): From Anti-humanism to Non-humanism' 23(2) *Law & Critique* 141.
(2014) *The Normativity of Networks*. London: Routledge.
(2016) 'On the Grounds Quietly Opening Beneath Our Feet', in B. Latour, ed., *Reset Modernity*. Cambridge, MA: MIT Press.
McLellan, D. (1989) *Simone Weil: Utopian Pessimist*. London: Macmillan.
McNay, L. (2014) *The Misguided Search for the Political*. New York: John Wiley & Sons.
Mead, G. H. (1899) 'The Working Hypothesis in Social Reform' 5(3) *American Journal of Sociology* 367.
Melucci, A. (1989) *Nomads of the Present*. London: Hutchinson Radius.
Menendez, A. (2017) 'The Crisis of Law and the European Crises' 44(1) *Journal of Law and Society* 56.
Merleau-Ponty, M. (1945/1982) *Phenomenology of Perception* (trans. D. Landes). London: Routledge.
(1947/1969) *Humanism and Terror* (trans. J. O'Neill). Boston: Beacon Press.
(1955/1973) *Adventures of the Dialectic* (trans. J. Bien). Evaston, IL: Northwestern.
Merry, S. E. (2016) *The Seductions of Quantification: Measuring Human Rights, Gender Violence, and Sex Trafficking*. Chicago University Press.
Mezzadra, S. and B. Neilson (2013) *Border as Method, or, the Multiplication of Labor*. Durham, NC: Duke University Press.
Michelman, F. (1988) 'Law's Republic' 97 *Yale LJ* 1493.
Micklitz, H.-W. (2018) *The Politics of Justice in European Private Law: Social Justice, Access Justice, Societal Justice*. Cambridge University Press.
Miller, D. (2020) 'The Nature and Limits of the Duty of Rescue' 1 *Journal of Moral Philosophy* 1.

Mocnik, R.(1999) 'After the Fall: Through the Fogs of the 18th Brumaire of the Eastern Springs', in J. Derrida et al., *Ghostly Demarcations*. London: Verso.

Möllers, C. (2004) 'Transnational Governance without a Public Law?' in C. Joerges I.-J. Sand and G. Teubner, eds., *Transnational Governance and Constitutionalism*. Oxford: Hart.

Moncrieff, L. (2016) 'Law, Scale, Anti-zooming, and Corporate Short-termism' 16(1) *Law, Culture and the Humanities* 1.

Moyn, S. (2010) *The Last Utopia: Human Rights in History*. Cambridge, MA: Harvard University Press.

(2012) 'Substance, Scale and Salience' 8 *Annual Review of Law and Social Science* 123.

Mulhall, S. (2001) *Inheritance and Originality*. Oxford University Press.

Müller, J.-W. (2010) 'The Promise of Demoi-cracy: Diversity and Domination in the European Public Order' in J. Neyer and A. Wiener, *The Political Theory of the European Union*. Oxford University Press.

(2011) *Contesting Democracy: Political Ideas in Twentieth-Century Europe*. New Haven, CT: Yale University Press.

Nagel, T. (2005) 'The Problem of Global Justice' 33(2) *Philosophy & Public Affairs*.

Negri, A. (1972/1994) 'Labor in the Constitution', in M. Hardt and A. Negri, *Labor of Dionysus*. Minneapololis: University of Minnesota Press.

(1988) *Revolution Retrieved*. London: Red Notes.

(1989) *The Politics of Subversion: A Manifesto for the Twenty-first Century*. Oxford: Polity/Blackwell.

(1994) 'The Physiology of Counter-power: When Socialism is Impossible and Communism so Near' (trans. M. Hardt), in M. Ryan and A. Gordon, eds., *Body Politics: Disease, Desire, and the Family*. Boulder, CO: Westview Press.

(1999a) *Insurgencies: Constituent Power and the Modern State*. Minneapolis: University of Minnesota Press.

(1999b) 'The Specter's Smile', in J. Derrida et al., *Ghostly Demarcations*. London: Verso.

(2000) *The Savage Anomaly: The Power of Spinoza's Metaphysics and Politics*. Minneapolis: University of Minnesota Press.

Negri, A. and F. Guatari (1990) *Communists Like Us*. New York: Semiotext(e).

Neves, M. (1992) *Verfassung und Positivitaet des Rechts in der peripheren Moderne*. Berlin: Duncker & Humblot.

(2001) 'From the Autopoiesis to the Allopoiesis of Law' 28(2) *Journal of Law and Society* 242.

(2013) *Transconstitutionalism*. London: Bloomsbury.

Nicolaïdis, K. (2003) 'Our European Demoï-cracy: Is this Constitution a Third Way for Europe?' in K. Nicolaïdis and S. Weatherill, *Whose Europe? National Models and the Constitution of the European Union*. Oxford University Press.

Nietzsche, F. (1872/1990). *The Birth of Tragedy* (trans. C. Fadiman). New York: Dover Publications.
Nonet, P. and P. Selznick (1978) *Law and Society in Transition: Toward Responsive Law*. New York: Octagon Books.
Novitz, T. (2003) *International and European Protection of the Right to Strike*. Oxford University Press.
  (2005) 'The European Union and International Labour Standards', in P. Alston, ed., *Labour Rights as Human Rights*. Oxford University Press.
Offe, C. (2003) 'The European Model of "Social" Capitalism: Can it Survive European Integration?' 11(4) *Journal of Political Philosophy* 437.
  (2009) 'Governance: An "Empty Signifier"?' 16(4) *Constellations*.
  (2013) 'Europe Entrapped: Does the EU have the Political Capacity to Overcome its Current Crisis?' 19(5) *European Law Journal* 595.
O'Neill, O. (1986) *Faces of Hunger: An Essay on Poverty, Justice and Development*. London: Allen & Unwin.
Owen, R. (1849/1973) *The Revolution in the Mind and Practice of the Human Race*. New York: A. M. Kelley.
Parekh, B. (1981) *Hannah Arendt and the Search for a New Political Philosophy*. Berlin and New York: Springer.
Parents, A. (2014) 'The Life of a Death Foretold: The Proposal for a Monti II Regulation', in M. Freedland and J. Prassl, eds., *Viking, Laval and Beyond*. Oxford: Hart.
Parsons, T. (1951) *The Social System*. London: Routledge and Kegan Paul.
Parsons, T. and E. Shils (1951) *Toward a General Theory of Action*. Cambridge, MA: Harvard University Press.
Paul, A. (2001) 'Organizing Husserl: On the Phenomenological Foundations of Luhmann's Systems Theory' 1(3) *Journal of Classical Sociology* 371.
Pavlakos, G. (2007a) *Our Knowledge of the Law*. Oxford: Hart.
  ed. (2007b) *Law, Rights and Discourse: The Legal Philosophy of Robert Alexy*. London: Bloomsbury.
  (2011) 'Constitutional Rights, Balancing and the Structure of Autonomy' 24(1) *Canadian Journal of Law & Jurisprudence* 129.
Peacock, A. and H. Willgerodt, eds. (1989) *Germany's Social Market Economy. Origins and Evolution*. New York: St Martin's Press.
Peters, A. (2006) 'Compensatory Constitutionalism: The Function and Potential of Fundamental International Norms and Structures' 19 *LJIL* 579.
Pétrement, S. (1988) *Simone Weil: A Life*. New York: Schocken.
Picciotto, S. (2011) *Regulating Global Corporate Capitalism*. Cambridge University Press.
Pitkin, H. (1981) 'Justice: On Relating Public and Private' 9(3) *Political Theory* 327.
  (1998) *The Attack of the Blob: Hannah Arendt's Concept of the Social*. Chicago University Press.

Pogge, T. (1989) *Realizing Rawls*. Ithaca, NY: Cornell University Press.
Polanyi, K. (1944) *The Great Transformation*. Boston: Beacon Press.
Pottage, A. (2012) 'The Materiality of What?' 39(1) *Journal of Law and Society* 167.
Poulantzas, N. (1976) *State, Power, Socialism*. London: Verso.
Quattrocchi, A. and T. Nairn (1998) *The Beginning of the End: France, May 1968*. London: Verso.
Raina, P. (1985) *Poland 1981: Towards Social Renewal*. London: G. Allen & Unwin.
Rancière J. (1976) *La parole ouvrière*. Paris: Union générale d'éditions.
  (1983) *Le philosophe plébéien* Paris: La Découverte.
  (1989) *The Nights of Labor: The Workers' Dream in Nineteenth-century France*. Philadelphia: Temple University Press.
  (1989) '"Time is Nothing More than Intervention"' 8 *Le Cahier du Collège international de philosophie*, Paris: Éditions Osiris.
  (1992) 'Politics, Identification and Subjectivisation' 61 *October* 58.
  (1994) *The Names of History: on the Poetics of Knowledge*. Minneapolis: University of Minnesota Press.
  (1998) 'Le concept de critique et la critique de l'économie politique des "manuscripts de 1844" au "Capital"', in *Lire le Capital*, Paris: PUF.
  (1999) *Disagreement: Politics and Philosophy* (trans. Julie Rose). Minneapolis: University of Minnesota Press.
  (2004a) *The Flesh of Words: The Politics of Writing* (trans. C. Mandell). Palo Alto, CA: Stanford University Press.
  (2004b) *The Philosopher and His Poor*. Durham, NC: Duke University Press.
  (2004c) 'Who is the Subject of the Rights of Man?' 103 *South Atlantic Quarterly* 297.
  (2009a) 'A Few Remarks on the Method of Jacques Rancière' 15(3) *Parallax* 114.
  (2009b) 'The Method of Equality', in G. Rockhill and P. Watts, eds., *Jacques Rancière: History, Politics, Aesthetics*. Durham, NC: Duke University Press.
Rastko, M. (1999) 'After the Fall: Through the Fogs of the 18th Brumaire of the Eastern Springs', in Derrida et al., *Ghostly Demarcations*. London: Verso.
Raz, J. (1990) Practical *Reason* and Norms. Princeton, NJ: Princeton University Press.
Renault, E. (2007) 'Reconnaisance et travail' 18(2) *Travailler* 119.
  (2010) 'L'invisibilisation Du Travail Comme Défi Philosophique' 33(1) *Cahiers Simone Weil* 61.
Renner, M. (2011) 'Death by Complexity' in Poul F. Kjaer, G. Teubner and A. Febbrajo, eds., *The Financial Crisis in Constitutional Perspective: The Dark Side of Functional Differentiation*. London: Bloomsbury Publishing.
Ricoeur, P. (1992) 'L'acte de juger' 183(7) *Esprit (1940–)* 20.
  (2003) *The Just* (orig. *Le Juste*. Paris: *Esprit*, 1995). University of Chicago Press.
  (2008) *From Text to Action. Essays in Hermeneutics*. London: Continuum.

Ripley, P. (1986) *The General Will before Rousseau: The Transformation of the Divine into the Civic.* Princeton, NJ: Princeton University Press.

(2001) 'Rousseau's General Will', in *The Cambridge Companion to Rousseau.* Cambridge University Press.

Rittel, H. W. J. and M. Webber (1973) 'Dilemmas in a General Theory of Planning' 4(2) *Policy Sciences* 155.

Ritter, J. (1984) *Hegel and the French Revolution.* Cambridge, MA: MIT Press.

Rittich, K. (2008) 'Social Rights and Social Policy', in D. Barak-Erez and A. M. Gross, eds., *Exploring Social Rights: Between Theory and Practice.* Oxford: Hart.

Robespierre, M. (2007) *Virtue and Terror.* Speeches selected by J. Ducange (trans. John Howe). New York: Verso.

Roedl, F. (2009) 'Arbeitsverfassung', in A. von Bogdany and J. Bast, eds., *Europaeisches Verfassungsrecht.* Berlin and New York: Springer.

Rogers, B. (2017) 'Basic Income in a Just Society' 15 *The Boston Review*, http://bostonreview.net/forum/brishen-rogers-basic-income-just-society.

Röpke, W. (1937/1951). *Die Lehre von der Wirtschaft, Wien–Berlin 1937*, 6. Erlenbach-Zurich: Aufl.

Rosa, H. (2005) 'The Speed of Global Flows and the Pace of Democratic Politics' 27(4) *New Political Science.*

Rosanvallon, P. (1998) *Le Peuple Introuvable.* Paris: Gallimard.

(2009) 'Democratic Universalism as a Historical Problem' 16(4) *Constellations* 539.

Rose, G. (1992) *The Broken Middle.* Oxford: Blackwell.

Ross, K. (1988) *The Emergence of Social Space.* London: Verso.

(2009) 'Historicising Untimeliness', in G. Rockhill and P. Watts, eds., *Jacques Rancière: History, Politics, Aesthetics.* Durham and London: Duke University Press.

Rousseau, J.-J. (1775/1992) *Discourse on the Origin of Inequality* (trans. D. A. Cress). Indianapolis: Hackett Pub. Co.

Rubin, I. I. (1973) *Essays on Marx's Theory of Value.* Montreal: Black Rose Books.

Russell, M. and A. Montin (2015) 'The Rationality of Political Disagreement: Rancière's Critique of Habermas' 22(4) *Constellations* 543.

Sabel, C. (1994) 'Learning by Monitoring: The Institutions of Economic Development', in N. Smelser and R. Swedberg, eds., *The Handbook of Economic Sociology.* Princeton, NJ: Princeton University Press.

(2001) 'A Quiet Revolution of Democratic Governance', in *Governance in the 21st Century.* Paris: OECD Publishing.

Sabel, C. F. and J. Zeitlin (2012) 'Experimentalism in the EU: Common Ground and Persistent Differences' 6 *Regulation and Governance* 410.

Salais, R. and M. Storper (1993) *Les mondes de production: Enquête sur l'identité économique de la France.* Paris: Editions de l'Ecole des hautes études en sciences sociales.

Salais, R. (2004) 'La politique des indicateurs', in B. Zimmerman, ed., *Les Sciences Sociales à l'épreuve de l'action*. Nantes: éditions MSH.
  (2006) 'On the Correct and Incorrect Use of Indicators in Public Action' 27 *Comp. Labor Law & Pol'y Journal* 101.
  (2011) 'Employment and the Social Dimension of Europe: What Constitutive Conventions of the Market?' in R. Rogowski, R. Salais and N. Whiteside, eds., *Transforming European Employment Policy: Labour Market Transitions and the Promotion of Capability*. Aldershot: Edward Elgar.
  (2013) *Le Viol d'Europe*. Paris: PUF.
Sassen, S. (1990) *The Mobility of Labor and Capital: A Study in International Investment and Labour Flow*. New York: Cambridge University Press.
Saussure de, F. (1973) *Cours de Linguistique Générale*. Paris: Payot (trans. and intro by Roy Harris, *Course in General Linguistics* (La Salle, IL: Open Court, 1983).
Scharpf, F. (2002) 'The European Social Model: Coping with the Challenges of Diversity' 40 *Journal of Common Market Studies* 645.
  (2016) 'Forced Structural Convergence in the Eurozone: Or a Differentiated European Monetary Community'. No. 16/15. MPIfG Discussion Paper.
Schmitt, C. (1922/1985) *Political Theology: Four Chapters on the Concept of Sovereignty* (trans. G. Schwab). Cambridge, MA: MIT Press.
Scott, J. and D. Trubek (2002) 'Mind the Gap: Law and New Approaches to Governance in the European Union' 8(1) *European Law Journal* 1.
Seaford, R. (1994) *Reciprocity and Ritual: Homer and Tragedy in the Developing City-state*. Oxford: Clarendon Press.
Segal, C. (1971) 'The Two Worlds of Euripides' Helen' in *Transactions and Proceedings of the American Philological Association* (Vol. 102, pp. 553–614). Johns Hopkins University Press, American Philological Association.
Sen, A. (2009) *The Idea of Justice*. Oxford University Press.
Sennett, R. (2006) *The Culture of the New Capitalism*. New Haven: Yale University Press.
Serge, V. (1985) *Carnets*. Arles: Actes Sud.
Shklar, J. (1976) *Freedom and Independence*. Cambridge University Press.
Simmonds, N. (1993) 'Judgment and Mercy' 13 *Oxford J. Legal Studies* 52.
Simon, H. (1957) *Models of Man; Social and Rational*. New York: Wiley.
  (1991) 'Bounded Rationality and Organizational Learning' 2(1) *Organization Science* 125.
Simon, W. (2015) 'Critical Theory and Institutional Design', in De Búrca et al., eds., *Critical Legal Perspectives on Global Governance*. London: Bloomsbury.
Slaughter, A.-M. (2005) *A New World Order*. Princeton, NJ: Princeton University Press.

Smith, S. C. (1995) 'The Redundancy of Reasoning', in Bankowski, White and Hahn, eds., *Informatics and the Foundations of Legal Reasoning*. Dordrecht: Kluwer.
Sorel, G. (1908/1999) *Reflections on Violence*. Cambridge University Press.
Srnicek, N. (2017) *Platform Capitalism*. New Jersey: John Wiley & Sons.
Srnicek, N. and A. Williams (2015) *Inventing the Future: Postcapitalism and a World without Work*. London and New York: Verso.
Stäheli, U. (1997) 'Exorcising the "Popular" Seriously: Luhmann's Concept of Semantics' 7(1) *International Review of Sociology* 127.
Stavropoulos, N. (1996) *Objectivity in Law*. Oxford University Press.
Streeck, W. (1995) 'Neo-Voluntarism: A New European Social Policy Regime?' 1(1) *European Law Journal* 31.
   (2015) 'Why the Euro Divides Europe' 95 *New Left Review* 5.
Streit, M. E. (1993) 'Cognition, Competition, and Catallaxy in Memory of Friedrich August von Hayek' 4(2) *Constitutional Political Economy* 223.
Streit, M. E. and W. Mussler (1995) 'The Economic Constitution of the European Community: From Rome to Maastricht' 1(1) *European Law Journal* 5.
Strengers, I. (2011) *Thinking with Whitehead: A Free and Wild Creation of Concepts*. Cambridge, MA: Harvard University Press.
Supiot, A. (1990) 'Pourquoi un droit du travail?' *Droit Social* 491.
   (1999) 'The Transformation of Work and the Future of Labour Law in Europe: A Multidisciplinary Perspective' 138 *International Labour Review* 31.
   (2000) 'The Dogmatic Foundations of the Market' 29(4) *Industrial Law Journal* 321.
   (2007) *Homo Juridicus: On the Anthropological Function of the Law* (original Seuil, 2005) (trans. Saskia Brown). London: Verso.
   (2009) 'En guise de conclusion: la capacité, une notion à haut potentiel', in S. Deakin and A. Supiot, eds., *Capacitas*. Oxford: Hart.
   (2010a) *L'esprit de la Philadelphie: la justice social face au marché total*. Paris: Seuil.
   (2010b) 'Simone Weil, juriste du travail' 33(1) *Cahiers Simone Weil* 3.
   (2011) 'La pensée juridique de Simone Weil', in I. Schömann, ed., *Mélanges à la mémoire de Yota Kravaritou*. Brussels: European Trade Union Institute (ETUI).
   (2012) 'Under Eastern Eyes' 73 *New Left Review* 29.
   (2013) 'Grandeur and Misery of the Social State' 82 *New Left Review* 99.
   (2017) *Governance by Numbers: The Making of a Legal Model of Allegiance*. Oxford: Hart.
Supiot, A., P. Meadows and M. E. Casas (2001) *Beyond Employment: Changes in Work and the Future of Labour Law in Europe*. Oxford University Press.

Susskind, D. (2020) *A World Without Work*. Harmondsworth: Penguin.
Syrpis, P. (2011) 'Reconciling Economic Freedoms and Social Rights – The Potential of Commission v Germany' 40 *ILJ* 222.
Taylor, F. W. (1911) *The Principles of Scientific Management*. New York: Harper.
Teubner, G. (1983) 'Substantive and Reflexive Elements in Modern Law' 17 *Law & Society Review* 239.
  (1989) 'How the Law Thinks: Towards a Constructivist Epistemology of Law' 23 *Law & Society Review* 727. Reprinted in Teubner, G., *Legal Theory and the Social Sciences*. London: Routledge, 2017.
  (1992) 'The Two Faces of Janus: Rethinking Legal Pluralism' 13 *Cardozo LR* 1419.
  (1993) *Law as an Autopoietic System*. Oxford: Blackwell.
  (2009) 'Self-Subversive Justice: Contingency or Transcendence Formula of Law?' 72 *Modern Law Review* 1.
  (2012) *Constitutional Fragments: Societal Constitutionalism and Globalization*. Oxford University Press.
  (2019) 'Global Bukowina: Legal Pluralism in the World Society', in *Critical Theory and Legal Autopoiesis*. Manchester University Press.
Thompson, E. P. (1963/2016) *The Making of the English Working Class*. London: Vintage.
Thornhill, C. (2001) 'Politics and Metaphysics: A Problem in German Philosophy' 5 *Social and Political Thought* 48.
  (2007) 'Niklas Luhmann, Carl Schmitt and the Modern Form of the Political' 10(4) *European Journal of Social Theory* 499.
  (2010a) *German Political Philosophy: The Metaphysics of Law*. London: Routledge.
  (2010b) 'Carl Schmitt and Early Western Marxism', in D. Ingram, ed., *Critical Theory to Structuralism: Philosophy, Politics, and the Human Sciences*. Slough, Buckinghamshire: Acumen.
  (2011) *A Sociology of Constitutions: Constitutions and State Legitimacy in Historical-Sociological Perspective*. Cambridge University Press.
  (2012a) 'Contemporary Constitutionalism and the Dialectic of Constituent Power' 1(3) *Global Constitutionalism* 369.
  (2012b) 'Legal Pluralism: The Many Books on Europe's Many Constitutions' 22 *Social & Legal Studies* 413.
  (2012c) 'Sociological Enlightenments and the Sociology of Political Philosophy' 1 *Revue internationale de philosophie* 55.
  (2014) 'Rights and Constituent Power in the Global Constitution' 10(3) *International Journal of Law in Context* 357.
  (2016) *A Sociology of Transnational Constitutions: Social Foundations of the Post-National Legal Structure*. Cambridge University Press.

Tittenbrun, J. (1993) *The Collapse of Real Socialism in Poland*. London: Janus Publishing.

Tribe, K. (1995) *Strategies of Economic Order: German Economic Discourse 1750–1950*. Cambridge University Press.

Trubek, D. (1979) 'Public Advocacy – Administrative Government and the Representation of Diffuse Interests', in M. Cappelletti and B. Garth, eds., *Access To Justice*, Vol. 3. Milan: Giuffrè Editore.

Trubek, D. and J. Mosher (2001) New Governance, EU Employment Policy, and the European Social Model. No. 15. Jean Monnet Chair.

Trubek, D. and L. G. Trubek (2004) 'Hard Law and Soft Law in the Construction of Social Europe' 2004 *ELJ* 343.

Tuori, K. (2010) 'The Many Constitutions of Europe', in K. Tuori and S. Sankari, eds., *The Many Constitutions of Europe*. Farnham: Ashgate.

Tuori, K. and K. Tuori (2014) *The Eurozone Crisis: A Constitutional Analysis*. Cambridge University Press.

Uchitelle, L. (2006) *The Disposable American: Layoffs and their Consequences*. New York: Vintage.

Unger, R. M. (1996) 'Legal Analysis as Institutional Imagination' 59 *MLR* 1.

Van der Walt, J. (2012) 'Law and the Space of Appearence in Arendt's Thought', in M. Goldoni and C. McCorkindale, *Hannah Arendt and the Law*. Oxford: Hart.

(2014a) 'Law, Utopia, Event: A Constellation of Two Trajectories', in A. Sarat et al., *Law and the Utopian Imagination*. Palo Alto, CA: Stanford University Press.

(2014b) *The Horizontal Effect Revolution and the Question of Sovereignty*. Berlin: Walter de Gruyter.

Veitch, S. (1998) 'Doing Justice to Particulars', in E. Christodoulidis, ed., *Communitarianism and Citizenship*. Farnham: Ashgate.

Vergès, J. (1968) *De la Stratégie Judiciare*. Paris: Minuit.

Vernant, J.-P. (1962) *Les origins de la pensée grecque*. Paris: PUF.

Villa, D., ed. (2000) *The Cambridge Companion to Hannah Arendt*. Cambridge University Press.

Volk, C. (2015) *Arendtian Constitutionalism: Law, Politics and the Order of Freedom*. London: Bloomsbury.

Vuillerod, J.-B. (2017) 'La dialectique en héritage: Althusser jeune hégélien' *Implications philosophiques*.

Wagner, G. (2012) 'Function and Causality' *Revue Internationale de philosophie* 35.

Waldenfels, B. (2017) *Platon: Zwischen Logos und Pathos*. Frankfurt: Suhrkamp.

Waldenfels, B., J. Broekman and A. Pažanin, eds. (1984) *Phenomenology and Marxism*. London: Routledge and Kegan Paul.

Walker, N. (2002) 'The Idea of Constitutional Pluralism' 65 *MLR* 317.

(2010) 'Multi-level Constitutionalism: Looking Beyond the German Debate', in K. Tuori and S. Sankari, eds., *The Many Constitutions of Europe*. Farnham: Ashgate.

(2015) *Intimations of Global Law*. Cambridge University Press.

Wallerstein, I. M. (2004) *World-Systems Analysis: An Introduction*. Durham, NC: Duke University Press.

Webster, T. B. L. (1967) *The Tragedies of Euripides*. London: Methuen.

Wedderburn, Lord (1989) 'Freedom of Association and Philosophies of Labour Law' 18 *LJ* 1.

Wegman, M. (2010) 'European Competition Law: Catalyst of Integration and Convergence', in K. Tuori and S. Sankari, eds., *The Many Constitutions of Europe*. Farnham: Ashgate.

Weil, D. (2014) *The Fissured Workplace*. Cambridge, MA: Harvard University Press.

Weil, S. (1940) *L'Iliade ou le Poème de la Force*. Marseille: Les Cahiers du Sud (available at http://teuwissen.ch/imlift/wp-content/uploads/2013/07/Weil-L_Iliade_ou_le_poeme_de_la_force.pdf).

(1951/2009) *Waiting on God*. London: Routledge.

(1955) *Oppression et Liberté*. Paris: Gallimard.

(1963). *Gravity and Grace:* London: Routledge and Kegan Paul.

(1966) *Sur la science*. Paris: Gallimard.

(1978) *Lectures on Philosophy* (trans. H. Price). Cambridge University Press.

(1987) *Formative Writings: 1929–1941* (ed. and trans. D. Tuck McFarland and W. Van Ness). Amherst, MA: University of Massachusetts Press.

(1989) 'On Human Personality' (orig. 1957), in D. McLellan, *Simone Weil: Utopian Pessimist*. London: Macmillan.

(2002) *The Need for Roots*. London: Routledge. [Original (L'Enracinement), Paris: Gallimard.]

Weiler, J. (1999) *A Constitution for Europe*. Cambridge University Press.

Wellmer, A. (1974) *Critical Theory of Society*. New York: Seabury Press.

Williams, B. (1979) 'Internal and External Reasons', in R. Harrison, ed., *Rational Action*. Cambridge University Press.

Wittgenstein, L. (1953) *Philosophical Investigations* (trans. G. Anscombe). Oxford: Blackwell.

Wokler, R. (1998) 'Contextualizing Hegel's Phenomenology of the French Revolution and the Terror' 26(1) *Political Theory* 48.

Wolf, C. (2000). *Cassandra*. New York: Farrar, Straus and Giroux.

Wolin, S. (1994) 'Norm and Form: The Constitutionalizing of Democracy', in J. P. Euben, J. R. Wallach and J. Ober, eds., *Athenian Political Thought and the Reconstruction of American Democracy*. Ithaca, NY: Cornell University Press.

Wood, E. M. (1989) *Peasant-Citizen and Slave: The Foundations of Athenian Democracy*. London: Verso.

Woolfson, C. (2010) 'The Swedish Model and the Future of Labour Standards after Laval' 41 *Industrial Relations Journal* 333.
Wright, S. (2002) *Storming Heaven*. London: Pluto Press.
Wypijewski, J. (2006) 'Workless Blues' 42 *New Left Review* 141.
Young, I. M. (2004) 'Responsibility and Global Labor Justice' 12(4) *Journal of Political Philosophy* 365.
Zumbansen, P. (2015) 'Knowledge in Development, Law and Regulation, or How are We to Distinguish between the Economic and the Non-Economic?' in De Búrca et al., eds., *Critical Legal Perspectives on Global Governance*. London: Bloomsbury.

INDEX

Ackerman, Bruce, 166
Action
 Communicative/strategic, 23, 41, **443–55**
 Labour/work/action distinction, 17–29, 31
Actor-Network Theory (ANT), 325, 363–4, 442, 543
Adorno, Theodor, 27, 77, 98, 161, 238, 290, 429, 470, 508, 558
Aeschylus, 55–60, 419, 488
Agamben, Giorgio, 280, 457
Agonism, 30, 35, 40–1, 51, 64, 70, 102, 342, 354
 and antagonism, 30, 37, **40–2**, 85, 118, 156, 170, 172, 257, 342, 434, 452, 469, 488, 491, 504, 538, 546, 548, 552
A-legality, 511–17
Aleinikoff, Alexander, 409
Alexy, Robert, 409–13, 418, 448
Althusser, Louis
 Aleatory materialism, 526, 529–30
 Conjuncture, 129, 463, 524, 526–7, 536
 Coupure epistemologique, 115
 on Machiavelli, 524–41
Anarchosyndicalism, 44, 494, 502
Antinomy, 114, 140, 192, 232, 246, 498, 545
Apel, Otto-Karl, 446
Appleby, Joyce, 441
Arendt, Hannah
 Action, 18, 21–30, 34, 37–8, 41
 Compassion, 37–9, 161
 Natality, 23, 33, 35, 70, 102
 Phenomenology, 17–29

 Plurality, 19, 21–7, 35–7, 41, 48, 70
 Praxis/poiesis, 96–7
 Recognition, 31, 40
 Social question, 25, 30, 41, 161, 166, 221
 Social/political distinction, 5, 17–42, 161, 163, 168
 Vita activa/contemplativa, 31, 37, 96
 Worldliness, 29–40
Aristophanes, 419
Aristotle, 6, 96, 122, 160–1, 412, 489
Athenian democracy, 62, 488, 494
Atria, Fernando, 152, 464
Autogestion, 46, 177, 480–523
Automation, 79–96
Autopoiesis, 202–8, 227, 285, 304, 462
Axiomatic, 122, 232–42, 492

Babeuf, Gracchus, 164
Bachofen, Johann, 62, 487, 489
Badiou, Alain, 70, 128, 450, 454, 476, 522
Bakhtin, Mikhail, 259
Bakunin, Mikhail, 494
Barnard, Catharine, 400, 421–2
Bataille, Georges, 439, 519
Baudrillard, Jean, 109
Baxi, Upendra, 461
Benjamin, Walter, 406, 496, 504, 506, 522
Bensaïd, Daniel, 69, 456
Berger, John, 65, 557
Bergson, Henri, 51, 501, 504
Biaggini, Giovanni, 277
Blanc, Louis, 502
Bloch, Ernst, 8, 140, 144, 151, 159, 164, 179, 191, 238, 301, 456

INDEX 585

Böckenförde, Ernst-Wolfgang, 409
Bolsheviks, 499–500
Bourdieu, Pierre, 126
Brandom, Robert, 257
Brunkhorst, Hauke, 242, 290, 382, 468

Camatte, Jacques, 117
Capabilities theory, 424, 426–8
Castel, Robert, 93
Castoriadis, Cornelius, 17, 189, 221
Catallaxy, 9, 309–15, 320, 360, 439
Cezanne, Paul, 556
Clarkson, Carrol, 493
Clinamen, 529, 533
Clunie, Gregor, 323
Collective
  Action, 67–8, 143, 146, 335–43
  Agency/subject position, 146, 510
Commodity
  Cipher of, 116
  Commodification, 9, 49, 103, 126
  Exchange, 87, 104, 111, 114, 117, 147, 242, 246
  Labour as a, 108, 112–13, 395–430
  Logic of, 78, 105, 109, 318, 443
Common good, 9, 142, 161, 268, 272, 275, 280, 291, 324, 335–6, 339, 341, 354, 359, 387, 435, 450, 456, 474
Commons, John, 325, 438
Communication, 5, 74, 78, 199, 210, 446
  and interaction, 94–6
  and lifeworld. *See* Lifeworld
  and strategy, 13, 36, 448
  Communicative action, 23, 100–2, 443–8
  Legal communication, 202–7, 218
  Uncoerced, 94–101, 447
Competition, 80, 263, 390, 404, 406, 429
Condorcet, Nicholas, 30, 165
Conflict, 12, 468, 472
  Class, 41, 72, 297, 300, 399
Consensus, 217, 269, 337, 359, 445, 447
  'Well-grounded', 449–51
  Consent/dissent, 217–19

Dissensus, 119, 253, 454, 491–2, 518, 540, 543, 553. *See also* Rancière, Jacques
  Uncoerced, 449
Constituent power/constituted power, 3, 18, 33, 35, 147, **151–92**, 194, 207, 219–21, 433–4, 452, 458, 463, 518–20
Constitutional
  'Moments', 14, 166, 290, 367, 376, 395, 399, 547
  Deficit, 374
  Dispositif, 540, 542, 551
  Entrenchment, 205–11, 229, 283, 289, 369, 424, 466, 552
  Function, 9, 200–2, 267, 285, 291, 312, 314–15, 355, 361, 462–7
  Hierarchisation, 193–216
  Paradox, 8, 152–3, 157, 162, 166, 185, 197
  pluralism, 8, 216, 259–78, 283, 435
  Rationalisation, 467, 478
  Situation, 433–60
Constitutionalisation, 8, 216, 259–66, 278, 291–2, 304, 404, 407, 436, 457, 474
  Hard/soft law, 192, 254, 373, 386, 388, 404, 466
  of EU Law, 370, 373, 384, 390, 405
Constitutionalism
  'From below', 264
  Formal/substantive, 193–258
  Legal/political, 193–200, 271, 304
  Multi-level, 263–7
  Social rights constitutionalism, 229, 239, 242, 247–55, 290, 461, 552
  Societal, 263, 304, 467–79
Contingency, 22–3, 34, 60, 63, 129, 151, 180, 210, 217, 220, 297, 443, 502, 514, 530
  and frailty, 40
  and necessity, 4, 53, 70, 253, 310, 324
  and uncertainty, 363
  Formula, 305, 439–40, 472
Contradiction
  Constitutionalising Contradiction, 524–55

Contradiction (cont.)
  Contradictory demand, 525, 531, 543, 552
Conventions of equivalence, 343, 350, 392, 394
Critical theory, 3, 12, 14, 29, 76, 86, 100, 109, 181, 424, 456–7, 469, 471, 507, 531
  and traditional theory, 139–41
  of the constitution, 286
Critical Theory
  Deviationist doctrine, 249, 545
  Immanent critique. See Immanent critique
  Marx's eleventh thesis, 42, 110, 116, 129, 138–47, 162, 183, 433, 507, 531, 551

Davies, Anne, 377, 400
De Búrca, Gráinne, 339, 343
De Saussure, Ferdinand, 277
Debray, Regis, 179
Dejours, Christophe, 91–3, 100
Deleuze, Gilles, 520, 529
Democracy
  Associational, 329, 499
  Athenian. See Athenian Democracy
  Double inscription of, 151, 184
  Experimentalist/democratic experimentalism, 9, 283, 285, 331, 336–43, 377, 435
  Industrial, 281, 329, 476, 480, 499
  Political, 405
  Scandal of, 480–7
Demos, 385, 475, 489, 491
  Concept of, 152
  European, 260
  the fear of the, 151, 179
Derrida, Jacques, 106–7, 110, 114, 124, 167, 173–5, 178, 471, 496, 506, 519, 529
Descartes, René, 43, 66, 131
Desrosières, Alain, 343–4, 352, 391–4
Determinatio, 241, 412
Dialectic
  and negation, 141, 507–11
  As process-thinking, 24, 27
  Open, 524, 530, 532–40

Dieu caché, 66, 70
Différend, 487, 518–19, 522
Dignity, 6, 8, 45, 48, 50, 89, 102, 121, 125, 232–42, 245, 256, 276, 388, 416, 418, 456, 459, 552
Dimensions of meaning, 209–28
Discourse. See Communication
Discrimination, 302, 422
Dispositif, 530, 541–4
Distinction
  Distinction directrice, 154
  Signicative difference, 532–7
Dogma, 8, 125, 232–47, 289, 337, 412, 418, 546, 551–2
  Question dogmatique, 232
Double movement, 76
  Negri, Antonio, 547
  Polanyi, Karl, 246
Douzinas, Costas, 191
Dukes, Ruth, 368, 395, 401, 499
Dumézil, Georges, 520
Durkheim, Emile
  Anomie, 299
  Differentiation, 298
  Solidarity, 300

Economic
  Freedoms, 301, 376, 383, 385, 400, 403, 419
  Reason, 147, 232, 306, 308–27, 361, 370, 376, 436, 474, 479
Enzensberger, Hans-Magnus, 13, 480
Epicurus, 529
Equilibrium, 88, 297, 425
Eucken, Walter, 377–82
Euripides
  Bacchae, 61–3
  Helen, 58–63
  Iphigenia in Aulis, 56–8
  Medea, 57
European Union
  Democratic deficit, 8, 259, 436
  ECJ (CJEU), 369, 375, 384, 395
  EU labour law, 366, 368, 395
  European Semester, 373, 404
  Lisbon Treaty, 265, 349, 366, 372–3
  Maastricht Treaty, 366, 370, 395

Memoranda of Understanding, 374, 405
Monti II, 402, 419
New functionalism, 367, 403–7
Open method of coordination, 263, 385, 387
Posted Workers Directive, 396, 397
Rome Treaty, 365, 368
Subsidiarity. *See Subsidiarity*
Exclusionary reasons, 347–8
Expectations
 Normative/cognitive, 11, 225, 279, 282, 356, 358, 433, 437
Exploitation, 26, 37, 50, 75, 86, 94, 129, 144, 192, 426, 457, 544

Fabre-Magnan, Muriel, 233, 275, 388
Febbrajo, Alberto, 269–71
Feuerbach, Ludwig, 74, 138
Finkielkraut, Alain, 509
Finnis, John, 241, 412
First International, 494
Fischer-Lescano, Andreas, 469–70
Fordism, 45, 78–86
Formalism, 11, 206, 255, 262, 381, 384, 406, 458, 461–79, 545
Foucault, Michel, 6, 12, 334, 542
 Biopower, 78
 Dispositive. *See Dispositif*
 Rights (politics of), 192
Frankfurt School, 29, 78, 139, 190, 448, 451, 469, 508
Freiburg School, 377
French Revolution
 and Hegel. *See Hegel, Georg Wilhelm Friedrich*
 and Marx. *See Marx, Karl*
 and the Thermidor, 165, 171
 De Gouges, Olympe, 553
 Declarations, 30, 164–5, 504
 National Assembly, 163, 165, 173
 Sans-culottes, 26, 32, 37, 165
French Revolution
 and Rousseau. *See Rousseau, Jean-Jacques*
 Jacobinism, 19, 25, 30, 159–60, 163–8, 173–9
Fukuyama, Francis, 80

Fuller, Lon, 237–9, 241, 415, 446
Functional
 Differentiation, 196–7, 271, 297–308, 327, 376, 468–9
 Equivalence, 268–77, 328, 477, 479
 Method, 328, 347
Furet, François, 554

Gadamer, Hans-Georg, 136, 301
Gaita, Rai, 120, 124
Galton, Francis, 392
Gauny, Louis Gabriel, 127–9
Geissler, Heike, 85
Genealogical method, 4, 155, 168, 178, 333, 352, 376, 391, 457
Genealogical Method. *See also Foucault, Michel*
Glasman, Maurice, 246, 382, 436, 485
Globalisation, 219, 245
 Definition of, 303
Goffman, Erving, 124
Golder, Ben, 192
Goldmann, Lucien, 66–71, 94, 145, 530
Gorz, André, 6, 47, 67, 80, 82, 95, 147, 300
Governance
 Constitutional, 335, 355–62, 438
 Democratic, 328, 342, 385
 Experimental, 264, 437
 Joined-up, 331
 New, 329–43, 351, 356, 376, 385, 442
Gramsci, Antonio, 525
Gray, John, 317
Guattari, Félix, 364, 520
Günther, Klaus, 160, 445

Habermas, Jürgen, 5, 36, 41, 74, 78, 94–102, 109, 190, 223, 409–12, 435, 443–55, 493, 550
Hamacher, Werner, 506, 522
Hart, H. L. A., 200–1, 237–8, 255–7
Hayek, Friederich von, 9, 226, 308–26, 329–32, 359–64, 390, 415, 430, 439, 442, 535
Heaney, Seamus, 1, 5, 556
Hegel, Georg Wilhelm Friedrich, 13, 79, 111, 113–17, 138–42, 163, 167, 171, 176, 252, 505, 536

Hegel, Georg Wilhelm Friedrich (cont.)
  Dialectic, 27, 178, 240, 519
  Hegelian Marxist heritage, 72–8
  on the French Revolution, 168–71
  Rational/Real, 181–3
  Verstand/Vernunft, 66, 73, 115, 323, 433
Heidegger, Martin, 24, 66, 136, 537
Heine, Heinrich, 37
Hellenism, 51–5
Heller, Agnes, 448
Hemingway, Ernest, 556
Hermeneutic, 136–8, 180, 231–42, 244, 247, 280, 433, 538
  Double. *See Weber, Max*
  Phenomenology, 530
  Traction, 13, 253, 255, 280, 537, 539
Heterarchy, 360
Holmes, Stephen, 249
Homology, 111, 458, 463–4
Honneth, Axel, 93, 99
Horkheimer, Max, 139, 507–9
Husserl, Edmund, 6, 129–38, 141, 512

Iliad, 51–4, 63, 69
Immanent critique, 2, 12, 144, 192, 240, 290, 458–60, 469–70, 509–10, 522, 538
Immunity, 63, 181
Inclusion, 85, 144, 204, 292, 306, 328, 335, 338, 359, 376, 402, 423, 452, 493, 519
  Rights as a mechanism of, 301–3
Indicators
  and quantification, 345
  Bench-marking, 292, 348, 353–4, 373, 385, 390, 393
  Best practice, 349–54
  Critical theory of, 345–7
  Hidden normativity of, 348–54
Ingold, Tim, 542
Interdiction, 234–6, 238–43, 247, 548
International Labour Organisation (ILO), 245, 254, 396, 482
Intersubjectivity, 33, 98, 100, 124, 131–8, 451, 493, 505, 537

Jameson, Frederic, 257
Jubé, Samuel, 429

Julius, A. J., 274
Jurisgenesis, 190, 192
Justice
  Global, 272
  Political, 122, 274, 472
  Transcendence formula, 471

Kant, Immanuel, 98, 114, 168, 174, 184, 320
Kelsen, Hans, 153, 178, 183–7, 201, 458, 462, 545
Kerruish, Valerie, 104
Keynes, John Maynard, 84
Kilpatrick, Claire, 373
Kingsbury, Benedict, 354, 439
Knight, Frank, 441–2
Kojève, Alexandre, 218
Koselleck, Reinhart, 277, 289, 291
Kosik, Karel, 108, 535
Koskenniemi, Martii, 415, 461
Krahl, Hans-Jurgen, 75, 109
Kripke, Saul, 255, 257
Kukovec, Damien, 421

Labour
  Aristocracy, 419, 423
  Commodification. *See Commodity*
  Constitution, 8–9, 11, 368, 394, 401, 482–3, 485, 545–6
  Dignity. *See Dignity*
  Exchange value, 104–9, 114, 117, 477
  Flexibility/flexicurity, 81, 83, 426
  Fragmentation, 80, 83, 95, 99, 457, 535
  Insecurity, 90, 93, 125, 144, 252, 331, 557
  Market thinking, 422, 425. *See also Market thinking*
  Mutations, 78–86
  Power, 104, 112–18, 425–6, 534
  Precarious, 306, 425
  Social (promise of), 72–86, 94–5, 98–102, 107, 109, 111, 114, 319, 434, 476, 545–6
  Solidarity, 229–58. *See also Solidarity*
  Suffering, 47, 86–93, 100, 280
  Underemployment, 86, 144, 289
  Unemployment, 84, 117, 332, 349, 373, 393, 459, 557

Workplace control, 50, 79, 81, 85, 90, 99
Workplace democracy, 99, 491
Ladeur, Karl-Heinz, 358–64, 439
Lafayette, Marquis de, 164
Latour, Bruno, 310, 322, 443
Law and Economics, 239, 383–4
Lefort, Claude, 156, 221–2, 507, 540, 548
Legendre, Pierre, 43, 233–4
Lenin, Vladimir Ilyich, 40, 45, 246, 419, 495, 500, 527
Levi, Edward, 515
Lifeworld, 50, 99, 131, 145, 263, 317, 532, 537
Lindahl, Hans, 135, 454, 511–17
Linklater, Andrew, 273
Loughlin, Martin, 262
Lucretius, 529
Luhmann, Niklas
  Constitution (as evolutionary), 7, 187, 196, 284, 436
  Constitutionality, 193–228
  Equivalence domain, 333
  Function, performance, reflection, 198–200, 205
  Functional differentiation. *See Functional differentiation*
  Normative/cognitive expectations, 224–8. *See also Expectations*
  Phenomenology, 209–28
  Positivisation of Law, 196
  Reduction achievement, 194, 202, 211, 228, 231, 257, 285–6, 298, 517
  Roles, programmes, values, 211–16
  System (definition), 194
Lukács, Georg, 76, 86–8, 94, 104, 114, 141, 144, 146, 178, 181
  Augenblick, 67, 76
  Reification. *See Reification*
Luxemburg, Rosa, 45, 178, 181, 459
  Autogestion. *See Autogestion*
  Mass strike, 480, 494–503, *See also Strike*
Lyotard, Jean-François, 93, 487, 518, 522

MacCormick, Neil, 201, 262
Machiavelli, Niccolò. *See Althusser, Louis on Machiavelli*
MacIntyre, Alasdair, xiii, 142, 337, 352
Magri, Lucio, 13
Malthus, Thomas, 30
Managerialism, 415
Marcuse, Herbert, 73, 94, 139, 141, 323
Marion, Jean-Luc, 132–5
Market thinking, 2, 8, 10, 244, 252, 272, 308, 323, 327–64, 370, 377, 415, 423, 425–30, 436, 454, 462, 477
  Efficiency assumption, 427
  Equilibrium assumption, 425
  Value assumption, 426
Marquant, David, 329
Marshall, Thomas, 247–55
Marx, Karl
  Alienation, 74, 79, 87, 95, 101, 106, 534
  and Hegel, 72–8
  Commodification of Labour. *See Commodity*
  Dialectic. *See Dialectic*
  Eleventh thesis on Feuerbach. *See Critical Theory*
  Fetish phenomenon, 73, 103–4, 108, 111, 117, 145, 183, 506, 534, 551
  Ideology, 5, 25, 27, 44, 74, 126, 172, 178, 313, 460
  Mystery, 107
  Paris Commune, 176–8
  Subsumption, 116
Marzal, Toni, 415
Materialism, 524–32, 538, 543
  Aleatory. *See Althusser, Louis*
  and Weil. *See Weil, Simone*
McDowell, John, 255
McGee, Kyle, 438
Menendez, Agustin, 390
Merleau-Ponty, Maurice, 531, 538, 553
Merry, Sally Engle, 346–7, 352, 389
Metapolitics, 540
Migration, 81, 86, 263
Miller, David, 273
Möllers, Christoph, 355, 361, 439
Mortati, Constantino, 544
Moyn, Samuel, 279–81, 552
Muller-Armack, Alfred, 379

Nagel, Thomas, 272–6, 453
Nancy, Jean-Luc, 529

Negation. *See Dialectic and negation*
Negri, Antonio, 18, 33, 41, 151–8, 162–7, 173, 178, 364, 452, 486, 518, 521, 529, 543
Network, 274, 285, 328, 331, 335–6, 338, 357–64, 393, 437, 456, 541
Neumann, Franz, 377, 499
Neves, Marcelo, 271, 277, 304
New Deal, 392, 394
New Right, 308, 328–9, 436
Nietzsche, Friedrich, 55–7, 62

O'Neill, Onora, 273
Oakeshott, Michael, 317
Offe, Claus, 338–9, 371
Ohlin Report, 367
Operaismo, 178
Ordoliberalism, 365–84

Paris Commune, 459, 486, 495. *See Marx, Karl, Paris commune*
in May 1968, 143
Mob. *See French Revolution*
riots, 509
Parsons, Talcott, 217, 297, 306, 327
Pascal, Blaise, 44, 66–8
Pashukanis, Evgeny, 185
Pavlakos, George, 411
Péguy, Charles, 501
Pelloutier, Fernand, 502
Pernice, Ingolf, 265
Phenomenology
 'Bracketing', 19, 130, 137, 290
 'Strange' (concept of), 512–13, 515–16, 537–40
 Arendt, 17–29
 Critical, 119–47
 Givenness, 23, 31, 73, 129–36, 141
 Habermas, 217
 Husserl. *See Husserl, Edmund*
 Lindahl. *See Lindahl, Hans*
 Marion. *See Marion, Jean-Luc*
 Marxism, 2, 77, 146, 178, 531, 534
 Noema and Noesis, 131, 134
 Phenomenological blockage, 102–11
 Phenomenological fold, 107

Phenomenological reduction, 22, 130, 134, 211, 288, 532, 537
Ricoeur. *See Ricouer, Paul*
Socially weighted, 134, 136
Subjectivity. *See Intersubjectivity*
Waldenfels. *See Waldenfels, Bernhard*
Philadelphia Declaration, 8, 244
Pinochet, 464
Plato, 63, 488–91
Pogge, Thomas, 273
Polanyi, Karl, 6, 9, 118, 245, 325, 403, 485
 Fictitious commodity, 108, 245
Polis, 28, 58, 97, 488–9, 522
Posner, Richard, 310
Potentiality, 7, 42, 74, 155, 179, 208, 216, 423, 516, 521, 532–4
Poulantzas, Nicos, 223
Praxis
 and Poiesis. *See Arendt, Hannah*
 Philosophy, 2, 41, 76–7, 94, 102, 504, 531
Price mechanism, 12, 103, 106, 117, 222, 270, 311, 316, 331, 379, 424, 429, 443
Productivity
 Ohno system, 81
 Toyotisation, 80–1
Proportionality, 10, 216, 251, 375–6, 389, 407–19, 467, 479
Proudhon, Pierre-Joseph, 46, 494
Public interest, 337, 401, 408, 419, 474, 478
 Litigation, 462
Publicness, 160, 488

Quetelet, Adolphe, 391

Rancière, Jacques, 6, 119, 125–9, 146, 253, 453–5, 476, 489–94, 504, 510, 518, 520, 539–40, 542–3, 548–50
 Dissensus. *See Consensus and Dissensus*
 Equality, 6, 549–50, 553
 Labour enthnography, 5
 Politics/Police, 550

INDEX

Rationality
  Economic, 12, 370, 476
  Instrumental, 21, 95–6, 353
  Ratio Juris, 8, 145, 232, 310, 418, 433, 551
Rawls, John, 223, 272–3
Raz, Joseph, 348
Recognition, 49–50, 74, 79, 90, 93, 141, 200, 230, 244, 253, 447, 453, 486, 493, 519, 535, 537
  Arendt. *See Arendt, Hannah*
Reification, 49, 73, 78, 86–8, 104, 141, 147, 245, 534, 551
Representation, 28, 216–24, 238, 336, 342, 347, 391
  and presence, 21, 41
Restricted and general economies, 439
Ricardo, David, 112, 115
Ricoeur, Paul, 122–4, 137, 509, 539
  Distantiation, 137
  Unjust, 122
Rights
  'Rights of Man', 26, 166, 314, 552–3
  Categories of, 246–9
  Individual and collective, 245, 249, 254, 490
  Language of, 119, 121, 125, 232, 240, 242, 510
  Politics of, 192
Rimbaud, Arthur, 177
Ripley, Patrick, 160, 170
Risk and uncertainty, 441
Ritter, Joachim, 168–70
Robespierre, Maximilien, 25, 30, 37, 162, 165, 167, 171, 494, 508, 554
Röpke, Wilhelm, 378–82
Rosa, Hartmut, 219
Rosanvallon, Pierre, 157, 220, 224, 554
Rose, Gillian, 170, 497, 500
Ross, Kristin, 126, 493
Rousseau, Jean-Jacques, 19, 37, 166, 171, 452, 518, 554
  Emile, 160
  General will, 19, 36, 158–63
  on the French Revolution, 159, 165, 167–8, 170, 178, 494

Rustow, Alexander, 382
Ryle, Gilbert, 317

Sartre, Jean-Paul, 66–7, 94
Scarcity
  Institutionalisation of, 116, 313, 318, 425
Schiller, Friedrich, 56
Schmitt, Carl, 153, 178, 219, 241, 416, 457
Schumpeter, Joseph, 117, 394, 426
Seaford, Richard, 487–8
Self-reference, 200–9
  Self-observation, 194, 205, 285, 290, 360
  Eigenvalues, 286
Semantic drift, 116, 289, 551
Sennett, Richard, 92
Serge, Victor, 77
Sieyès, Emmanuel Joseph, 165, 222
Signifier
  Empty, 343, 390
  Floating, 259, 277, 354, 375
Sinzheimer, Hugo, 368, 377, 499
Smith, Adam, 112, 315, 360
Social
  Protection, 2, 93, 166, 243, 252, 256, 260, 281, 307, 366, 375, 384–5, 389, 399, 417, 436, 443, 461, 484
Social dialogue, 340, 366, 371–2, 385
Social dumping, 419–30
Social insurance, 243, 379, 392, 442
Social market, 10, 251, 365–94, 422, 424, 427
Solidarity
  Mechanical/organic. *See Durkheim, Emil*
Solidarność (Solidarity), 480–7
  Gdansk Accord, 482
Sophocles
  Antigone, 61, 96
  Oedipus at Colonus, 522
Sorel, Georges, 459, 495, 500–7, 518, 520, 522
Sovereignty, 170, 210, 216, 220, 222, 224, 251, 265, 359, 520, 540
Statistical reason, 316, 321, 323, 343–4, 353, 391–2

Streeck, Wolfgang, 83, 369, 375, 462
Strengers, Isabelle, 333
Strike
  General strike, 485, 495, 498, 501, 503–7, 522
  in Poland. *See Solidarność*
  Mass strike, 46, 110, 480, 494–503, 518, 521
  Right to strike, 253, 289, 397–401, 408, 482
Subsidiarity, 349, 371, 384–5, 399, 402, 407, 483
Sunstein, Cass, 249
Supiot, Alain, 43, 48, 82, 92, 229, 232–42, 244–7, 340, 344, 427, 442, 485
Syndicalism, 491
Syndicalism/syndicats, 44, 476, 501–3
Systems (theory)
  Autopoiesis, 7, 193, 201–5, 227, 304, 462, 516
  Coding/programming, 202, 211–13, 227, 285, 300, 414, 474, 514
  Coupling (meta-level), 12, 472–8
  Coupling (structural), 197–200, 262–4, 304–5, 434, 438
  Function/Performance. *See Luhmann, Niklas*
  Redundancy/variety, 94, 213–16, 257, 284–5, 357, 463–5, 515
  Re-entry, 154, 184, 204, 206–8, 353, 476–7
  Reference, 200–9
  Reflexivity/reflexion, 199, 201–5, 208, 210, 211, 225, 228, 230, 261, 284, 298, 357, 376, 463. *See also Luhmann, Niklas*
  Values, 211–16

Taylorism, 45, 78–83, 86, 95, 97, 99
Terror, 167, 170, 176, 508
Teubner, Gunther, 193, 211, 257, 269, 271, 275, 303–5, 356, 358, 361, 469–79
Thornhill, Chris, 163, 186–9, 199, 220, 262, 289–90, 303, 435
Trade unionism, 81, 254, 308–10, 329

Tragedy
  Greek, 4, 51, 54, 65–6, 70, 487–8, 522
  Hubris, 54, 57–61, 63, 248
Tragedy of the commons, 248, 453
Tronti, Mario, 85, 178
Trotsky, Leon, 45, 496, 500

USSR, 24, 45, 377, 420, 482, 496, 500
Uchitelle, Louis, 91
Unger, Roberto Mangabeira, 462
Universal pragmatics, 444–6, 449, 453

Vergès, Jacques, 522
von Foerster, 473
von Gierke, Otto, 499, 501
von Mises, Ludwig, 275, 278, 315–16

Waldenfels, Bernhard, 2, 488, 531, 534
Walker, Neil, 263, 265–9
Wallerstein, Immanuel, 85
Weber, Max, 125, 183
  Double hermeneutic, 180
  Ideal types, 180–3
Weil, Simone, 1–2, 5–6, 13
  Attention, 5–6, 49, 53–5, 63, 71, 119, 121–4, 240
  Epic/Iliad, 51–63, 69
  Factory work, 43, 45, 75, 88–90, 127
  Fragility, 123–5, 240
  Necessity, 5, 44, 69–71
  Personality, 89, 121, 124
  Responsibility, 59, 71, 122–5
  Rights (middle language of). *See Rights, language of*
Weimar Republic, 178, 183, 499
Wellmer, Albrecht, 29, 98
Wicked problem, 332, 349, 356
Wittgenstein, Ludwig, 255, 421
Wolin, Sheldon, 488
Wood, Ellen Meiksins, 489
Workerism, 110, 518
Worldliness, 5, 32, 51, 63–5, 69–70, 102, 125, 221

Young, Iris Marion, 273

Zweckrational, 48

CPSIA information can be obtained
at www.ICGtesting.com
Printed in the USA
BVHW041750080421
604549BV00012B/280